FIFTH EDITION

Public Speaking

An Audience-Centered Approach

Steven A. Beebe   *Southwest Texas State University*

Susan J. Beebe   *Southwest Texas State University*

Boston • New York • San Francisco
Mexico City • Montreal • Toronto • London • Madrid • Munich • Paris
Hong Kong • Singapore • Tokyo • Cape Town • Sydney

Senior Editor: Karon Bowers
Editor-in-Chief: Karen Hanson
Development Editor: Carol Alper
Editorial Assistant: Jennifer Trebby
Associate Development Editor: Alyssa Pratt
Marketing Manager: Mandee Eckersley
Composition and Prepress Buyer: Linda Cox
Manufacturing Manager: Megan Cochran
Editorial-Production Coordinator: Mary Beth Finch
Editorial-Production Service: Thomas E. Dorsaneo
Electronic Composition: Seventeenth Street Studios
Photo Researcher: Helane Manditch-Prottas
Cover Administrator: Linda Knowles
Text Designer: Deborah Schneck

For related titles and support materials, visit our online catalog at www.ablongman.com

Between the time Website information is gathered and then published, it is not unusual for some sites to have closed. Also, the transcription of URLs can result in unintended typographical errors. The publisher would appreciate notification where these errors occur so that they may be corrected in subsequent editions.

Library of Congress Cataloging-in-Publication Data
Beebe, Steven A.
    Public speaking: an audience-centered approach / Steven A. Beebe, Susan J. Beebe.—
5th ed.
        p. cm.
    Includes bibliographical references and index.
    ISBN 0-205-35863-2
        1. Public speaking. 2. Oral communication. I. Beebe, Susan J. II. Title

PN4121 .B385 2003
808.5'1—do21   2001055989

Printed in the United States of America
10 9 8 7 6 5 4 3   VHP 07 06 05 04 03

Dedicated to our parents,
Russell and Muriel Beebe
Herb and Jane Dye

And to our sons,
Mark and Matthew Beebe

Brief Contents

Contents

CHAPTER 3

Ethics and Free Speech   43

CHAPTER 4

Listening   59

CHAPTER 9   Organizing Your Speech 191

CHAPTER 18 Special-Occasion Speaking 415

CHAPTER 19 Speaking in Small Groups 431

Preface

The audience writes the speech. Although developed and delivered by the speaker, a good speech is centered on the needs, values, and hopes of the audience. We believe the audience should be first and foremost in a speaker's mind during every step of the speech development and delivery process, thus helping to "write" the speech.

The fifth edition of *Public Speaking: An Audience-Centered Approach* continues its decade-and-a-half tradition of emphasizing that it is the listener who ultimately determines whether a speech is effective. So it should be that listeners remain foremost in mind during every step of the speech crafting and delivery process. We didn't invent the audience-centered approach to public speaking. Over 2300 years ago, Aristotle said, "For of the three elements in speechmaking—speaker, subject, and person addressed—it is the last one, the hearer, that determines the speaker's end and object." We think Aristotle was right. Our goal is to provide a book that serves as a practical and friendly guide to help students of public speaking express their hearts and minds to communicate with their listeners.

The fifth edition of *Public Speaking: An Audience-Centered Approach* is written to be the primary text for a college-level public speaking course. We offer strategies that are anchored in ethical principles to assist speakers in articulating a message that connects with their audience. We emphasize that an effective speaker is an ethical speaker. Being audience-centered does not mean that a speaker tells an audience only what they want to hear; if you are not true to your own values and sense of right and wrong, you will have become a manipulative, unethical communicator rather than an audience-centered one. Audience-centered speakers articulate truthful messages that give audience members free choice in responding to a message, while also using effective means of ensuring message clarity and credibility.

True to our own audience-centered principles, we have listened to students and instructors to make the fifth edition an even more effective tool to help students enhance their public speaking abilities. We've made the connection between being an audience-centered speaker and speaking to culturally diverse audiences more explicit. Expanded discussion in every chapter emphasizes the ever-important task of understanding, appreciating, and adapting to listeners who have cultural traditions that are different from the speaker's. We've updated our discussion of the role of technology in enhancing a speaker's message; we've revised our popular *Speaker's Homepage* feature with new Websites offering a wealth of additional tips and strategies for being an audience-centered speaker. We have also updated our discussion of using the latest technological tools to plan and present a speech. New strategies to help students overcome the apprehension and anxiety they often experience when facing their audience have been included in Chapter 2. New material to enhance students' rhetorical criticism and evaluative listening skills will help students be not only better speakers, but also better consumers of rhetorical messages. We have also updated examples. These include excerpts from important speeches and discussion of free-speech issues prompted by the terrorist attacks of September 11, 2001. Other new speech examples illustrate how to be audience-centered at each step in the process of making and delivering a speech.

A Focus On the Audience

As we have in the previous four editions, we continue to emphasize the importance of analyzing listeners and then adapting to them as the quintessential element of effective communication. It is not unusual for a public speaking book to discuss audience analysis. What is unique about our audience-centered approach is that our discussion of audience analysis and adaptation is not contained in a single chapter; rather, we emphasize the importance of considering the audience throughout our entire discussion of the speech preparation and delivery process.

Preparing and delivering a speech involves a sequence of steps. Our audience-centered model integrates the step-by-step process of speech preparation and delivery with the ongoing process of considering the audience.

Our audience-centered model of public speaking, shown here, and introduced in Chapter 2, reappears throughout the text to remind students of the steps involved in speech preparation and delivery, while simultaneously emphasizing the importance of considering the audience. Viewing the model as a clock, the speaker begins the process at the "12 o'clock" position with "Select and Narrow Topic" and moves around the model clock-wise to "Deliver Speech." Each step of the speech construction process touches the center portion of the model labeled "Consider the Audience." Arrows connect the center with each step of the process to emphasize that the audience influences each of the steps involved in designing and presenting a speech. Arrows point in both directions around the central process of "Consider the Audience" to remind us that a speaker may sometimes revise a previous step because of further information or additional thoughts about the audience. You may, for example, decide after you have gathered supporting materials for the speech that you need to go back and revise your speech purpose. Visual learners will especially appreciate the panoramic overview of the entire public speaking process presented in the model.

The diagram is a circular clock-style model. The center reads "Consider the Audience." Around the circle clockwise from the top: Select and Narrow Topic, Determine Purpose, Develop Central Idea, Generate Main Ideas, Gather Supporting Material, Organize Speech, Rehearse Speech, Deliver Speech.

The colorful, easy-to-understand synopsis of how to design and deliver a speech will also be appreciated by people who learn best by having an overview of the entire process before beginning the first step of speech preparation.

After introducing the model in Chapter 2, we emphasize the centrality of considering the audience by providing a visual reminder in the form of a miniature version of the model, like the icon shown here in the margin. When you see this icon, it will remind you that the material presented has special significance for considering your audience.

A Focus On Diversity

An important addition to the text is an additional emphasis on how being audience-centered is inherently tied to understanding and appreciating the diverse background of an audience. To be audience-centered is to acknowledge the different ethnic and cultural backgrounds, attitudes, beliefs, values, and a host of other differences present when people congregate to hear a speech. It is rare that you speak to an audience of like-minded people with cultural, ethnic, age, and gender backgrounds similar to your own. Like the topic of audience analysis, diversity is covered in most current public speaking textbooks, sometimes in a separate chapter or in "diversity boxes" sprinkled throughout the book. But the concept of being audience-centered means that as a speaker you are constantly aware of and striving to adapt to the cultural, co-cultural, gender, and experiential diversity of the audience members to whom you are speaking. Adapting to diverse audiences is an integral part of the audience-centered process. Our audience-centered model has a built-in emphasis on diversity.

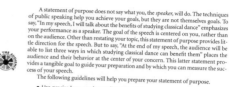

Features Retained From Previous Editions

Much of the praise we have received for our previous four editions, we owe to our collaboration with public speaking teachers, many of whom have used our audience-centered approach for a decade and a half. We have retained those features of previous editions that have been applauded by both teachers and students. Readers have especially valued our clear, concise style, lively voice, and interesting examples—both classic and contemporary—that are drawn from both student speakers and famous orators. We've received high praise for our overview of the public speaking process in Chapter 2 and our discussion of speech ethics in Chapter 3. Our two chapters on persuasion (Chapters 16 and 17) and our discussion of informative speaking (Chapter 15) have also received high marks for both their clarity and their comprehensive treatment of rhetorical issues and principles. We've retained the built-in pedagogical features of previous editions, including ReCap boxes (periodic summaries of important material), chapter outlines, learning objectives, narrative summaries, and chapter-end questions that stimulate critical thinking and spark discussions about ethical issues in public speaking. We've added new suggested activities and continued our inclusion of questions and activities that draw upon both technology and media.

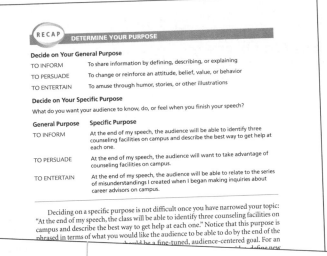

RECAP · DETERMINE YOUR PURPOSE

Decide on Your General Purpose

TO INFORM	To share information by defining, describing, or explaining
TO PERSUADE	To change or reinforce an attitude, belief, value, or behavior
TO ENTERTAIN	To amuse through humor, stories, or other illustrations

Decide on Your Specific Purpose

What do you want your audience to know, do, or feel when you finish your speech?

General Purpose	Specific Purpose
TO INFORM	At the end of my speech, the audience will be able to identify three counseling facilities on campus and describe the best way to get help at each one.
TO PERSUADE	At the end of my speech, the audience will want to take advantage of counseling facilities on campus.
TO ENTERTAIN	At the end of my speech, the audience will be able to relate to the series of misunderstandings I created when I began making inquiries about career advisors on campus.

Deciding on a specific purpose is not difficult once you have narrowed your topic: "At the end of my speech, the class will be able to identify three counseling facilities on campus and describe the best way to get help at each one." Notice that this purpose is phrased in terms of what you would like the audience to be able to do by the end of the ... should be a fine-tuned, audience-centered goal. For an ... define new

F or of the three elements in speechmaking—speaker, subject, and person addressed—it is the last one, the hearer, that determines the speech's end and object.

ARISTOTLE

Lift Up Thy Voice and Sing, 1942–1944. Oil on paperboard, 64.9 × 54.0 cm. Smithsonian American Art Museum, Washington, D.C./Art Resource, New York

CHAPTER **5**

Analyzing Your Audience

objectives

After studying this chapter you should be able to do the following:

1. Describe informal and formal methods of analyzing your audience.

2. Discuss the importance of audience analysis.

3. Explain how to gather demographic, psychological, and situational information about your audience and the speaking occasion.

4. Identify methods of assessing your audience's reactions to your speech while it is in progress.

5. Identify methods of assessing audience reactions after you have concluded your speech.

being audience-centered

A Sharper Focus

CONSIDERING YOUR AUDIENCE

▶ Being audience-centered means considering the background and interests of your listeners at each step in developing and presenting your speech.

▶ Adapt your language and choice of words to the education level of your listeners; depending on your listener's background, don't speak "over their heads" or use such simplistic words and phrases that you insult their intelligence.

CONSIDERING AUDIENCE DIVERSITY

▶ The cultural background of your audience will have a major effect on your listeners' expectations as to how you should organize, support, and present your speech.

▶ Because of the wide cultural variety in most communities and on most college campuses in the United States, you need not travel to an international destination to speak to people with differing cultural backgrounds.

CRITICAL THINKING QUESTIONS

1. Mike Roberts, president of his fraternity, is preparing to address the university academic council to persuade them to support establishment of a Greek housing zone on campus. This is his first major task as president, and he is understandably nervous about his responsibility. What advice would you give to help him manage his nervousness?

2. Jason Reed has just received his assignment for his first speech in his public-speaking class. What key skills does he need to master to become a competent public speaker?

3. Shara Yobonski is preparing to address the city council in an effort to tell them about the Food for Friendship program she has organized in her neighborhood. What steps should she follow to prepare and deliver an effective speech?

ETHICAL QUESTIONS

1. A friend of yours took public speaking last year and still has a file of speech outlines. Even though you will give the speech yourself, is it ethical to use one of her outlines as a basis for your speech? Explain.

2. Your first assignment is to give a speech about something interesting that has happened to you. You have decided to talk about the joys and hassles of a train trip you took last year. Your sister recently returned from a cross-country train trip and had several interesting tales to tell. Would it be ethical to tell one of her experiences as if it had happened to you? Why or why not?

3. You read an article in *Reader's Digest* that could serve as the basis for a great speech about the ravages of AIDS. Would it be ethical to paraphrase the article, using most of the same examples and the overall outline as the basis for your speech if you *tell* your listeners that your speech is based on the article?

SUGGESTED ACTIVITIES

1. Describe one informative purpose and one persuasive purpose for each of the following topics:

Nuclear power plants

Caffeine

Public speaking

Political parties

Your school

Terrorism

2. For the following central idea sentences, identify possible major divisions in the speech according to one of these questions: Does the central idea have logical *divisions*? Can you think of several *reasons* the central idea is true? Can you support the central idea with a series of *steps*?

The conflict in the Middle East has a long history.

The method of choosing a president in the United States is flawed.

Any one of several diets could help you lose weight.

The 70-mile-per-hour speed limit is a bad idea.

Our national parks need more resources to maintain their beauty.

The Internet has an interesting history.

IQ can be measured in several ways.

There are several ways to ensure a stress-free lifestyle.

3. Identify at least three tips for helping you become a confident speaker. Write a brief paragraph explaining why you think those techniques will be helpful to you.

4. Imagine that your instructor has assigned your first speech, a five-minute speech to inform, and it's due in two weeks. Develop a sample schedule describing deadlines for developing your ideas, researching your topic, writing an outline, and rehearsing your speech.

5. Write a paragraph in which you describe the diverse backgrounds of your classmates in your public-speaking class based on initial impressions and information that has been shared. Although you may not yet have had the opportunity to conduct a more formal analysis of your audience, based on conversations you've had with your colleagues, or comments they've made if they have more formally introduced themselves in a short speech to the class, note similarities and differences among your audience members.

Features New to the Fifth Edition

In addition to retaining what readers like best, we've worked hard to polish and update the book you are holding in your hands, striving to create a powerful and contemporary resource to help speakers connect to their audience. Specifically, we have significantly expanded our discussion of diversity, especially as it relates to being audience-centered. We've updated references to the latest information about public speaking that can be mined from the vast and ever-growing resources available on the Internet; we've added new information about the role of technology in communicating with others. To help students manage their fear about speaking in public, we've included several new, research-based suggestions. Drawing upon the work of rhetorical theorists, we've added new material about the power of myth and narrative to help speakers, regardless of whether their goal is to inform or to persuade. New material in Chapter 4 helps students enhance their rhetorical criticism and critical listening. Our revised discussion of persuasion helps provide practical advice during the speech-preparation process; we've more closely linked our discussion of persuasive speech preparation to our audience-centered model of communication. And as in previous editions, we've added new examples, illustrations, and speeches to bring our principles of audience-centered speaking to life. Students learn best when they have not only sound principles, but also models of communication excellence.

Expanded Discussion of Diversity

Although each edition of *Public Speaking: An Audience-Centered Approach* has included information about audience diversity, with this edition we've more explicitly clarified the link between being audience-centered and speaking to diverse audiences. We have added a new feature at the end of each chapter called "Being Audience-Centered: A Sharper Focus," where we summarize chapter content from two perspectives. First, in a sub-section called "Considering Your Audience," we summarize all general references to principles and strategies of analyzing and adapting to listeners. In a second sub-category called "Considering Audience Diversity," we cull specific references to strategies that help speakers adapt to diverse listeners. This new two-part chapter summary feature helps speakers see that considerations of adapting to diverse audiences should not be an afterthought, but woven into the fabric of the entire speech process. From topic selection to delivering the speech, diversity should be considered as a seminal speech design element.

We've also added references to the latest communication research and practical suggestions for adapting to diverse listeners in every chapter. Our expanded discussion of audience diversity in Chapter 5 offers several perspectives for speaking to audiences who are culturally diverse.

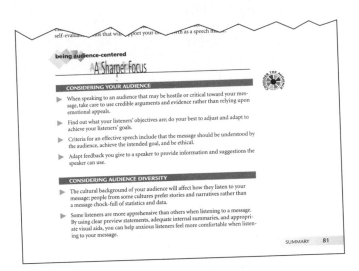

New Information About Technology and Public Speaking

In our technological age, public speakers need to know how the latest technological tools can help them in both the preparation and delivery of a speech. To help students more efficiently use the Internet, we've polished our well-received *Speaker's Homepage* feature to include accurate and contemporary sources. All of the Web links we've included in the book also can be easily found on our Companion Website by clicking on www.ablongman.com/beebe. We've revised our coverage of electronic searches and databases in Chapter 7 to keep current with the latest methods and resources. To help students use technology while presenting a speech we've added information about using PowerPoint (previously in a separate appendix) into Chapter 14. We've also added a discussion of using additional technological tools as preparation and presentation aids.

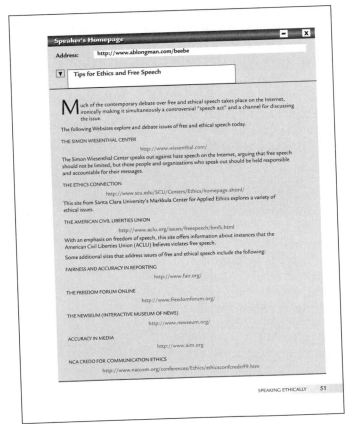

New Strategies to Help Manage
Communication Listener Apprehension

One of the biggest obstacles to success for many students is the anxiety they experience, even when merely entertaining the thought of speaking in front of an audience. To help them manage their fear, we've expanded our discussion of communication apprehension. We've added new information supported with the latest research findings to help students understand why they may feel nervous about speaking in public. We have also added descriptions of new techniques, such as how to look for positive listener support when delivering a message, to help manage speaker apprehension. In addition, we've referenced new research to encourage students not to prolong their preparation for a speech; procrastination only adds to the problem of nervousness, in addition to decreasing speech effectiveness. New research about the power of positive visualization also provides a strategy to bolster students' communication confidence.

In addition to new material about speaker apprehension, we've added a new section in Chapter 4 about receiver apprehension. Some listeners suffer from a fear of *listening* to information. To help them overcome this anxiety, we offer research-based suggestions to help manage the concern they have for misunderstanding or misinterpreting spoken messages.

New Information About the Power of Narrative and Myth

Effective speakers know how to tell stories. In this new edition we've strengthened our discussion of the power of stories and narratives to help students connect with their listeners. In Chapter 8 we offer strategies for using effective illustrations to make ideas come alive. In Chapter 12 we offer new examples and illustrations of how narrative language can polish dusty ideas. In our discussion of informative speaking (Chapter 15) we emphasize the power of stories both to clarify and to gain and maintain listener interest. Drawing upon rhetorical theory, in Chapter 18 we describe how the power of myths can provide additional pathos, which can be a useful strategy to change or reinforce attitudes, beliefs, values, and opinions. Since the dawn of time speakers have told stories. We help today's students understand how the centuries-old practice of story telling can provide contemporary sparkle to their messages.

New Discussion of Critical Listening Skills and Rhetorical Criticism

Besides learning how to speak in public, one of the most valued benefits of studying public speaking is becoming a more discriminating listener. In an expanded section on listening and critical thinking (Chapter 4) and analyzing and evaluating speeches, we help students better understand their role as rhetorical critic. We stress that rhetorical criticism is much more than just pointing out speaker errors or faultfinding; rather, it is the process of using a method or standards to evaluate the effectiveness and appropriateness of messages; rhetorical criticism helps illuminate a message. In material new to Chapter 4, we foreshadow the discussion of evidence and reasoning that appears in Chapter 17 to help students discern the qualities of well-supported ideas and arguments. We have also expanded our discussion of the three criteria for evaluating messages: The message should be understood, and should achieve its intended effect, while also being ethical.

New Application of the Audience-Centered Model to Persuasive Speaking

In a revision of Chapter 16, we walk students through the audience-centered speaking process step by step. In a new section called "Consider the Audience," we remind students of the importance of focusing on listeners, especially when the purpose is to persuade. We provide new information about cultural diversity and persuasion. We also offer additional tips for selecting and narrowing a persuasive speech topic; we consider how to frame a persuasive speech purpose; and we link our discussion of propositions of fact, value, and policy to the task of developing central and main ideas. By seeing clearer connections between our discussion of persuasive speaking and our audience-centered model, students are better able to build upon their knowledge and skills of public speaking when constructing persuasive messages. New material in Chapter 17 makes explicit suggestions for how use evidence, make appeals to action, and structure a persuasive message when speaking to a culturally diverse audience.

New Student Speeches

We've added a number of new student speeches at the ends of several chapters, as well as in Appendix C, to provide positive models of effective speeches. These student-authored speeches inspire beginning students of public speaking—not only can famous people or experienced politicians develop effective messages; students can successfully follow the lead of their peers. Reading these student speeches, annotated to point out

successful applications of speaking principles and practices, offers implicit encouragement and good examples that beginning speakers can emulate.

New Examples and Illustration

Students learn by example. Our new illustrations and examples help students master the art of public speaking. As in previous additions, we draw upon both student speeches and speeches delivered by well-known people.

Our Partnership With Instructors and Students

Students rarely learn public speaking from reading a book. Students learn best in partnership with an experienced instructor who can offer encouragement as well as advice about being an audience-centered speaker.

Instructors' Supplements

To support the instructor's skill and experience in teaching public speaking, we offer a rich abundance of resources to supplement their advice and guidance.

Print Materials

- *Instructors' Resource Manual,* by Melinda Villagrin, Southwest Texas State University, (with contributions from Charles Wise and Diana Ivy). This manual provides resources for both new and experienced instructors, including a chapter-at-a-glance guide to the teaching package, chapter outlines, activities, and assignments.

- *Test Bank,* by Anne Fox, College of Charleston. The test bank contains more than 1,000 questions, including multiple choice, true/false, short answer, and in-depth essay questions.

- *VideoWorkshop for Public Speaking Instructor's Guide,* by Tasha Van Horn, Citrus College, and Marilyn Reineck, Concordia University-St. Paul. This guide provides answers to the Student Guide questions and teaching suggestions that will help instructors use the *VideoWorkshop for Public Speaking CD-ROM* in class. A correlation guide helps instructors relate the materials to this text. The Instructor's Guide also contains the CD-ROM and the complete Student Guide.

- *A Guide for New Public Speaking Teachers: Building Toward Success, Second Edition* by Calvin L. Troup, Duquesne University. This guide helps new instructors learn to manage, organize, and teach the public speaking course effectively.

- *Allyn & Bacon Public Speaking Transparency Package.* Contains 100 full-color transparencies to provide visual support for classroom lectures and discussion.

- *Great Ideas for Teaching Speech (GIFTS)* by Raymond Zeuschner, California Polytechnic State University. This book provides descriptions of and guidelines for assignments successfully used by experienced public speaking instructors in their classrooms.

- *ESL Guide for Public Speaking* by Debra Grodher Vinik, Bronx Community College of the City University of New York. This guide provides strategies and resources for instructors teaching in a bilingual or multi-lingual classroom. It also includes suggestions for further reading and a list of related websites.

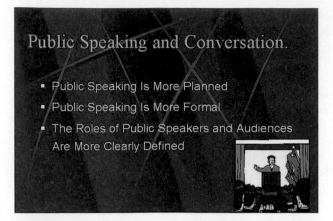

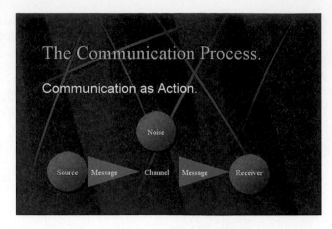

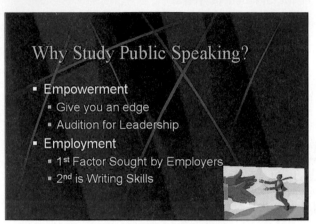

Electronic Materials

- *Computerized Testing Program.* This computerized version of the test bank is available with Tamarack's easy-to-use TestGen software, which lets you prepare tests for printing as well as for network and online testing. It provides full editing capability for Windows and Macintosh.

- *PowerPoint Presentation Package,* by Dan Cavanaugh. Available at www.ablongman.com/ppt, this package includes text-specific lecture outlines for every chapter.

- *Allyn & Bacon PowerPoint Presentation Package for Public Speaking.* Available at www.ablongman.com/ppt, this package includes 125 slides and a brief user's guide.

- *The Allyn & Bacon Digital Media Archive for Communication, Version 2.0.* This CD-ROM contains still images, video excerpts, helpful Web links, and assorted lecture resources that can be incorporated into multimedia presentations.

- *CourseCompass.* Powered by Blackboard, CourseCompass is the most flexible online course management system on the market today. By using this powerful suite of online tools, you can create an online presence for your course in under thirty minutes. Log on at www.coursecompass.com, and find out how you can get the most out of this dynamic teaching resource.

Video Materials

- *Allyn & Bacon Student Speeches Video Library.* Instructors can choose one video from the Allyn & Bacon Student Speeches Library with speeches covering a wide range of informative and persuasive speaking topics. The library includes a new video prepared by Lori Charron, Concordia University-St. Paul; Tasha Van Horn, Citrus College; and Michael Charron, Concordia University-St. Paul, that features persuasive, informative, and special occasion speeches given by a diverse group of student speakers.

- *Allyn & Bacon Communication Video Library.* This collection of videos, produced by Films for the Humanities and Sciences, is available to qualified adopters. Some restrictions apply. Ask your local Allyn & Bacon representative for details.

- *Allyn & Bacon Public Speaking Key Topics Video Library.* This library contains three videos that address core topics covered in the classroom: Critiquing Student Speeches, Speaker Apprehension, and Addressing Your Audience. Some restrictions apply. Contact your local Allyn & Bacon representative for details.

- *Allyn & Bacon Public Speaking Video.* This video includes excerpts of classic and contemporary speeches as well as student speeches to illustrate aspects of the public speaking process.

Students' Supplements

To support student learning, we provide a selection of study and enrichment materials.

Print Materials

- *VideoWorkshop for Public Speaking Student Guide,* by Tasha Van Horn, Citrus College and Marilyn Reineck, Concordia University-St. Paul. This combination *VideoWorkshop Student Guide* and CD-ROM package contains all the materials students need to get started: a CD-ROM containing specially selected video clips of student speeches and a tear-out-page workbook with Learning Objectives, Web Links, Observation Questions, Next Step Questions, and multiple choice quizzes.

- *ContentSelect: A Student's Guide for Speech Communication.* This guidebook includes information on how to access and use ContentSelect, a free research database, as well as tips for conducting searches and citing research materials in a paper.

- *iSearch for Speech Communication.* This resource guide for the Internet covers the basics of using the Internet, conducting web searches, and critically evaluating and documenting Internet sources. It also contains Internet activities and URLs specific to the discipline of speech communication.

- *Preparing Visual Aids for Presentations, Third Edition,* by Dan Cavanaugh. This 32-page booklet provides ideas to improve presentations, including suggestions for planning a presentation, designing visual aids, and storyboarding, and a PowerPoint preparation walk-through.

- *Speech Preparation Workbook,* by Jennifer Dreyer and Gregory Patton, San Diego State University. This helpful workbook takes students through the various stages of speech creation and provides guidelines, tips, and fill-in pages.

- *Public Speaking in the Multicultural Environment, Second Edition,* by Devorah A. Lieberman, Portland State University. This booklet helps students analyze the cultural diversities within their audience(s) and provides them with specific tools to adapt their presentations.

- *Outlining Workbook,* by Reeze L. Hanson and Sharon Condon, Haskell Indian Nations University. This workbook includes activities, exercises, and answers to help students develop and master the critical skill of outlining.

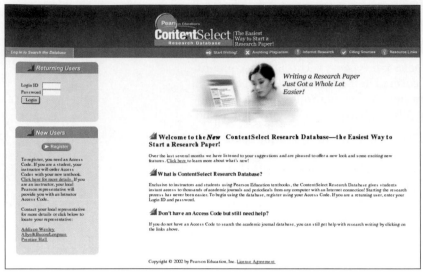

- *VideoWorkshop for Public Speaking CD-ROM,* by Tasha Van Horn, Citrus College and Marilyn Reineck, Concordia University-St. Paul. This CD-ROM, available only in the student workbook or the Instructor's Guide for this VideoWorkshop, contains video clips from student speeches that have been specifically chosen to illustrate the various steps in the public speaking process.

- *Companion Website with Online Practice Tests,* by Kristi Schaller, University of Hawaii at Manoa. This Website, available at www.ablongman.com/beebe, expands on the text's "Speaker's Homepage" feature and includes additional Web activities as well as an online study guide.

- *ContentSelect.* This free research database, searchable by keyword, offers immediate access to hundreds of scholarly journals and other popular quality publications via a PIN code in available packages with the text. See your Allyn & Bacon representative for details.

- *Allyn & Bacon Public Speaking Website,* at www.ablongman.com/pubspeak, by Terrence Doyle, Northern Virginia Community College. This Website contains five modules that students can use along with the text to learn about the process of public speaking and help prepare for speeches.

- *Interactive Speechwriter Software, Version 1.1, by Martin R. Cox.* This interactive software (available in Windows and Macintosh formats) provides supplemental material and enhances students' understanding of key concepts discussed in the text.

- *The Speech Writer's Workshop CD-ROM, Version 2.* This interactive CD-ROM assists students with speech preparation and enables them to write better speeches. The software includes four separate features: 1) a speech handbook with tips for researching and preparing speeches plus information about grammar, usage, and syntax, 2) a speech workshop which guides students through the speech-writing process and includes a series of questions at each stage, 3) a topics dictionary containing hundreds of speech ideas—all divided into sub-categories to help students with outlining and organization, and 4) a citation database that formats bibliographic entries in MLA or APA style.

Acknowledgements

Writing a book is a partnership not only with each other as co-authors, but with many people who have offered us the benefit of their experience and advice about how to make this the best possible teaching and learning resource. We appreciate all of the authors and speakers we have quoted or referenced; their words and wisdom have added resonance to our knowledge and richness to our advice. We are grateful for our students, colleagues, adopters, friends, and the editorial team at Allyn and Bacon.

Many talented reviewers have helped us shape the content and features of this edition. These talented public speaking teachers have supplemented our experience to help us make decisions about how to present and organize the content of this book. We express our sincere appreciation to the following reviewers who have shared their advice, wisdom, and expertise.

Reviewers of the 5th edition: Judy H. Carter, Amarillo College; Mark Chase, Slippery Rock University; Larry Haapanen, Lewis-Clark State College; Dayle C. Hardy-Short, Northern Arizona University; Elaine B. Jenks, West Chester University; Richard L. Quianthy, Broward Community College; Rebecca Roberts, University of Wyoming; Kristi Schaller, University of Hawaii at Manoa; Tasha Van Horn, Citrus College.

Reviewers of previous editions: Melanie Anson of Citrus College; Richard Armstrong of Wichita State University; Nancy Arnett, Brevard Community College; David E. Axon, Johnson County Community College; Ernest W. Bartow, Bucks County Community College; John Bee, University of Akron; Jaima L. Bennett, Golden West College; Donald S. Birns, SUNY-Albany; Tim Borchers, Moorhead State University; Barry Brummett, University of Wisconsin, Milwaukee; John Buckley, University of Tennessee; Thomas R. Burkholder, University of Nevada-Las Vegas; Marilyn J. Cristiano, Paradise Valley Community College; Dan B. Curtis, Central Missouri State University; Ann L. Darling, University of Illinois, Urbana-Champaign; Conrad E. Davidson, Minot State University; Terrence Doyle, Northern Virginia Community College; Gary W. Eckles, Thomas Nelson Community College; Thomas G. Endres, University of St. Thomas; Darla Germeroth, University of Scranton; Myra G. Gutin, Rider University; Phyllis Heberling, Tidewater Community College; James L. Heflin, Cameron University; Susan A. Hellweg, San Diego State University; Wayne E. Hensley, Virginia Polytechnic Institute and State University; Judith S. Hoeffler, Ohio State University; Stephen K. Hunt, Illinois State University; Paul A. Hutchins, Cooke County College; Nanette Johnson-Curiskis, Gustavus Adolphus College; Cecil V. Kramer, Jr., Liberty University; Michael W. Kramer, University of Missouri; Ed Lamoureux, Bradley University; David Lawless, Tulsa Junior College; Robert S. Littlefield, North Dakota State University; Jeré W. Littlejohn, Mississippi State University; Harold L. Make, Millersville University of Pennsylvania; Jim Mancuso, Mesa Community College; Deborah F. Meltsner, Old Dominion University; Rebecca Mikesell, University of Scranton; Maxine Minson, Tulsa Junior College; Rhonda Parker, University of San Francisco; Roxanne Parrott, University of Georgia; Carol L. Radetsky, Metropolitan State College; Mary Helen Richer, University of North Dakota; K. David Roach, Texas Tech University; Kellie W. Roberts, University of Florida; Val Safron, Washington University; Shane Simon, Central Texas College; Cheri J. Simonds, Illinois State University; Glenn D. Smith, University of Central

Arkansas; David R. Sprague, Liberty University; Jessica Stowell, Tulsa Junior College; Edward J. Streb, Rowan College; Aileen Sundstrom, Henry Ford Community College; Susan L. Sutton, Cloud County Community College; Jim Vickrey, Troy State University; Denise Vrchota, Iowa State University; Beth M. Waggenspack, Virginia Polytechnic Institute and State University; David E. Walker, Middle Tennessee State University; Lynn Wells, Saddleback College; Nancy R. Wernm, Glenville State College; Charles N. Wise, El Paso Community College; and Merle Ziegler, Liberty University.

We are again grateful to our friend and colleague Tom Burkholder from the University of Nevada-Las Vegas, who wrote the excellent essay in Appendix A. It is the best distillation of the history of classical rhetoric that we have read. We thank Melinda Villagrin for sharing the wealth of teaching ideas and strategies in the revised *Instructor's Resource Manual.* We thank Kristi Schaller for the excellent Website which accompanies this book. We thank Lori Charron, Tasha Van Horn, and Michael Charron for their work on the new video; and Marilyn Reineck and Tasha Van Horn for their work on the *VideoWorkshop for Public Speaking.* Kosta Tovstiadi provided help in checking the Websites and assistance in securing permission for selected material in the book. Our editorial support team at Allyn and Bacon, Senior Editor Karon Bowers, Development Editor Carol Alper, and Associate Development Editor Alyssa Pratt, have done another outstanding job of offering skilled advice to make this a better book.

We have enjoyed strong support and mentorship from a number of teachers, friends, and colleagues who have influenced our work over the years. Our colleagues at Southwest Texas State University continue to be supportive of our efforts. Tom Willett, retired professor from William Jewell College; Dan Curtis emeritus professor at Central Missouri State University; John Masterson at Texas Lutheran University, and Thompson Biggers are long-time friends and exemplary teachers who continue to influence our work and lives. Sue Hall, Department of Speech Communication administrative assistant at Southwest Texas State University, again provides exceptional support and assistance to keep our work on schedule.

We view our work as authors of a textbook as primarily a teaching process. Both of us have been blessed with gifted teachers whose dedication and mentorship continues to inspire and encourage us. Mary Harper, former speech, English, and drama teacher at Steve's high school alma mater, Grain Valley High School, Grain Valley, Missouri, and Sue's speech teacher, Margaret Dent, now retired from Hannibal High School, Hannibal, Missouri, provided initial instruction in public speaking that remains with us today. We also value the life lessons and friendship we receive from Erma Doty, also a former teacher at Grain Valley High, who continues to offer us encouragement and support not only with what she says but by how she lives her life in service for others. We appreciate the patience and encouragement we received from Robert Brewer, our first debate coach at Central Missouri State University, where we met each other more than thirty years ago and the ideas for this book were first discussed. We both served as student teachers under the unforgettable energetic guidance of the late Louis Banker at Fort Osage High School, near Buckner, Missouri. Likewise, we have both benefited from the skilled instruction of Mary Jeanette Smythe of the University of Missouri, Columbia. We wish to express our appreciation to Loren Reid, Emeritus Professor, also from the University of Missouri-Columbia; to us, he is the quintessential speech teacher.

Finally, we value the patience, encouragement, proud support, and love of our sons, Mark and Matthew Beebe. They offer many lessons in rhetorical criticism, listening, persuasion, ethos, logos, and pathos, and continue to be our most important audience.

Stephen A. Beebe and Susan J. Beebe,
San Marcos, Texas

Public Speaking

An Audience-Centered Approach

A journey of a thousand miles
begins with a single step.

OLD CHINESE PROVERB

1

Introduction to Public Speaking

objectives

After studying this chapter you should be able to do the following:

1. Explain why it is important to study public speaking.

2. Describe how public speaking differs from casual conversation.

3. Sketch and explain a model that illustrates the components and process of communication.

4. Discuss in brief the history of public speaking.

5. Explain how becoming an audience-centered public speaker can help you speak effectively to diverse audiences.

Perhaps you think you have heard this speaker—or even taken a class from him. *"His eyes were buried in his script. His words in monotone emerged haltingly from behind his mustache, losing volume as they were sifted through hair. Audiences rushed to see and hear him, and after they had satisfied their eyes, they closed their ears. Ultimately, they turned to small talk among themselves while the great man droned on."* [1]

But the speaker described here in such an unflattering way is none other than Albert Einstein. Sadly, although the great physicist could attract an audience with his reputation, he could not sustain their attention and interest because he lacked public-speaking skills.

Although you may not be blessed with his intellect, you have at least one distinct advantage over Einstein: the opportunity afforded by this course and this text to study and practice public speaking. Right now, however, the experience may seem less like an opportunity and more like a daunting task. Why undertake it?

Why Study Public Speaking?

As you study public speaking, you will learn and practice strategies for effective delivery and critical listening. You will discover new applications for skills you may already have, such as focusing and organizing ideas and gathering information from print and electronic sources. In addition to learning and applying these fundamental skills, you will gain long-term advantages related to *empowerment* and *employment*.

Empowerment

You will undoubtedly be called on to speak in public at various times in your life: as a student participating in a classroom seminar; as a businessperson convincing your boss to let you undertake a new project; as a concerned citizen addressing the city council's zoning board. In each of these situations, the ability to speak with competence and confidence will provide **empowerment**. It will give you an edge that other, less skilled communicators lack—even those who may have superior ideas, training, or experience. It will position you for greater things. Former presidential speechwriter James Humes, who labels public speaking "the language of leadership," says, "Every time you have to speak—whether it's in an auditorium, in a company conference room, or even at your own desk—you are auditioning for leadership." [2]

Employment

John H. McConnell, CEO of Worthington Industries, suggests a second and perhaps even more compelling reason to study public speaking: The skills you develop in this class may someday help you get a job. McConnell notes,

Many students who work summers at our plants, then go back to school in the fall, ask me what courses they should take to be best prepared for business. I always say,

empowerment
Influence and potential leadership, gained in part by speaking with competence and confidence

"Take all the speech courses and communication courses you can because the world turns on communication."[3]

McConnell's advice is supported by research as well as personal observation. In a 1999 nationwide survey, prospective employers of college graduates said they seek candidates with "public speaking and presentation ability."[4] Other surveys of personnel managers, both in the United States and internationally, have confirmed that they consider communication skills the top factor in helping graduating college students obtain employment.[5] (See Table 1.1.)

Public Speaking and Conversation

As you begin to study and practice public speaking, you will discover that it has much in common with conversation, a form of communication in which you engage every day. Like conversation, public speaking requires you to focus and verbalize your thoughts:

"Alicia, do you ever feel that people here are giving you trouble because you're Hispanic?" asks her roommate Sharon.

Alicia wrinkles her brow in thought, then replies, "I guess once in a while, but not for the reasons you'd expect. Like I notice the Anglos getting all nervous when I stand close to them when we talk. And they don't like to look me in the eye for a long time."

TABLE 1.1

Top Factors in Helping Graduating College Students Obtain Employment

Rank/Order	Factors/Skills Evaluated
1	Oral (speaking) communication
2	Written communication skills
3	Listening ability
4	Enthusiasm
5	Technical competence
6	Work experience
7	Appearance
8	Poise
9	Résumé
10	Part-time or summer employment
11	Specific degree held
12	Leadership in campus/community activity
13	Recommendations
14	Accreditation of program
15	Participation in campus/community activity
16	Grade point average
17	School attended

Source: Jerry L. Winsor, Dan B. Curtis, and Ronald D. Stephens, "National Preferences in Business and Communication Education: A Survey Update," *Journal of the Association for Communication Administration* 3 Sept. 1997: 174.

Alicia could easily build a speech about differences between Hispanic and Anglo nonverbal behavior on these same two points.

When you have a conversation, you have to make decisions "on your feet." If your friends look puzzled or interrupt with questions, you re-explain the idea you have been talking about. If they look bored, you insert a funny story or talk more animatedly. As a public speaker, you will learn to make similar adaptations based on your knowledge of who your listeners are, their expectations for your speech, and their reactions to what you are saying. In fact, because we believe that the ability to adapt to your audience is so vital, this book focuses on public speaking as an audience-centered activity.

But if public speaking were exactly like conversation, Albert Einstein's lectures would have been more riveting, there would be no reason to take a public-speaking class, and there would be no need for this book. Let's take a look at some of the ways in which public speaking differs from conversation.

Public Speaking Is More Planned

First, public speaking is more planned than conversation. A public speaker may spend hours or even days planning and practicing his or her speech. Having already worked on his inaugural address for several weeks, President-elect John F. Kennedy rose before 8 A.M. on January 20, 1961, to review the speech and make final corrections. He practiced aloud while he took a bath, dressed, walked from room to room, and even while he ate breakfast.[6]

Nearly forty years later, then–vice president Al Gore worked with speechwriters through 17 drafts of his August 2000 acceptance of the Democratic nomination for president. A few hours before he delivered the speech, an aide quipped, "It's in draft 625."[7]

Both Kennedy's painstaking rehearsing and Gore's relentless revising reflect the forethought and planning typical of public speaking.

Public Speaking Is More Formal

Public speaking is also more formal than conversation. The slang or casual language we often use in conversation is not appropriate for most public speaking. Audiences expect speakers to use standard English grammar and vocabulary. The nonverbal communication of public speakers is also more formal. People engaged in conversation often sit or stand close together, gesture spontaneously, and move about restlessly. The physical distance between public speakers and their audiences is usually greater. And although public speakers may certainly use extemporaneous gestures while speaking, they also plan and rehearse some gestures and movement to emphasize especially important parts of their speeches.

The Roles of Public Speakers and Audiences Are More Clearly Defined

Finally, public speaking is less fluid and interactive than conversation. People in conversation may alternately talk and listen, and perhaps even interrupt one another, but in public speaking the roles of speaker and audience are more clearly defined and remain stable. Rarely do audience members interrupt or even talk to speakers, although some cultures and contexts invite more speaker–audience interaction than do others. Even under these circumstances, however, the roles of speaker and audience are still clearly defined and stable.

Of course, occasionally a speaker is interrupted by applause or a heckler's shout. *The New York Times* reported that when President George W. Bush spoke at Yale University's 2001 commencement, "The boos from graduating students were as loud as the cheers, and he gazed ... at hundreds of yellow paper signs with messages that protested his policies and positions."[8]

RECAP

PUBLIC SPEAKING AND CONVERSATION

Similarities
- Focus and vocalize thoughts
- Adapt to listeners

Differences

PUBLIC SPEAKING	CONVERSATION
• Planned	• Spontaneous
• Formal language and nonverbal communication	• Casual language and nonverbal communication
• Roles of speaker and listener are clearly defined and stable	• Roles of speaker and listener are fluid and interactive

Speaking in public, then, requires you to sharpen existing communication skills and to learn and apply new ones. To better understand what is involved, let's look now at several models of communication that illustrate the public-speaking process and its components.

The Communication Process

Even the earliest theorists recognized that communication is a process. The models they formulated were linear, suggesting a simple transfer of meaning from a sender to a receiver, as shown in Figure 1.1. More recently, theorists have tried to create models that better demonstrate the complexity of the communication process. Let's explore what some of those models can teach us about what happens when we communicate.

FIGURE **1.1**

A model of communication as action

Communication as Action

Although they were simplistic, the earliest linear models of communication as action identified most of the elements of the communication process. We will explain each element as it relates to public speaking.

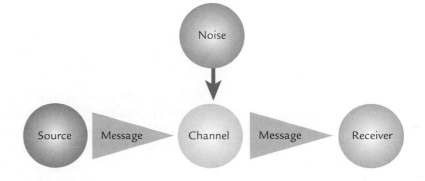

SOURCE A public speaker is a **source** of information and ideas for an audience. The job of the source or speaker is to **encode** or translate the ideas and images in his or her mind into verbal or nonverbal symbols (a **code**) that an audience can recognize. The speaker may encode into words (for example, "The fabric should be 2 inches square") or into gestures (showing the size with his or her hands).

MESSAGE The **message** in public speaking is the speech itself—both what is said and how it is said. If a speaker has trouble finding words to convey his or her ideas, or sends contradictory nonverbal symbols, listeners may not be able to **decode** the speaker's verbal and nonverbal symbols back into a message.

CHANNELS A message is usually transmitted from sender to receiver via two **channels:** *visual* and *auditory.* Audience members see the speaker and decode his or her nonverbal symbols—eye contact (or lack of it), facial expressions, posture, gestures, and dress. If the speaker uses any visual aids, such as graphs or models, these too are transmitted along the visual channel. The auditory channel opens as the speaker speaks. Then the audience members hear words and such vocal cues as inflection, rate, and voice quality.

RECEIVER The **receiver** of the message is the individual audience member, whose decoding of the message will depend on his or her own particular blend of past experiences, attitudes, beliefs, and values. As already emphasized, an effective public speaker should be receiver- or audience-centered.

NOISE When something interferes with the communication of a message, we call it *noise.* Noise may be physical, **external noise.** If your 8 A.M. public-speaking class is frequently interrupted by the roar of a lawn mower running back and forth under the window, it may be difficult to concentrate on what your instructor is saying. A noisy air-conditioner, a crying baby, or incessant coughing may also make it difficult for audience members to hear or concentrate on a speech.

Noise may also be **internal.** It may stem from either *physiological* or *psychological* causes and may directly affect either the source or the receiver. A bad cold (physiological noise) may cloud a speaker's memory or subdue his or her delivery. An audience member who is worried about an upcoming exam (psychological noise) is unlikely to remember much of what the speaker says. Regardless of whether it is internal or external, physiological or psychological, or whether it originates with the sender or the receiver, noise interferes with the transmission of a message.

Communication as Interaction

Realizing that linear models were overly simplistic, later communication theorists designed models that depicted communication as a more complex process (see Figure 1.2). These models were circular, or interactive, and added two important new elements: feedback and context.

FEEDBACK As noted earlier, one way in which public speaking differs from casual conversation is that the public speaker does most or all of the talking. But public speaking is still interactive. Without an audience to hear and provide **feedback,** public speaking serves little purpose. Skillful public speakers are audience-centered. They

source
The public speaker

encode
Translate ideas and images into verbal or nonverbal symbols

code
A verbal or nonverbal symbol for an idea or image

message
Both the content and the delivery of a speech

decode
Translate verbal or nonverbal symbols into ideas and images

channel
The visual and auditory means by which a message is transmitted from sender to receiver

receiver
A listener or an audience member

external noise
Physical sounds that interfere with communication

internal noise
Physiological or psychological interference with communication

feedback
Verbal and nonverbal responses provided by an audience to a speaker

depend on the nods, facial expressions, and murmurings of the audience to adjust their rate of speaking, volume, vocabulary, type and amount of supporting material, and other variables to communicate their message successfully.

CONTEXT The **context** of a public-speaking experience is the environment or situation in which the speech occurs. It includes such elements as the time, the place, and the speaker's and audience's cultural traditions and expectations. To paraphrase John Donne, no *speech* is an island. No speech occurs in a vacuum. Rather, each speech is a blend of circumstances that can never be replicated exactly again.

The person whose job it is to deliver an identical message to a number of different audiences at different times and in different places can attest to the uniqueness of each speaking context. If the room is hot, crowded, or poorly lit, these conditions affect both speaker and audience. The audience who hears a speaker at 10 A.M. is likely to be fresher and more receptive than a 4:30 P.M. audience. A speaker who fought rush-hour traffic for 90 minutes to arrive at his or her destination may find it difficult to muster much enthusiasm for delivering the speech.

Many of the skills that you will learn from this book relate not only to the preparation of effective speeches (messages), but also to the elements of feedback and context in the communication process. Our audience-centered approach focuses on "reading" your listeners' responses and adjusting to them as you speak.

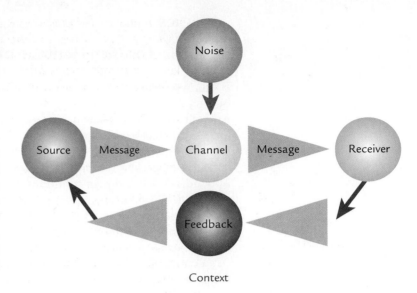

Context

FIGURE 1.2

An interactive model of communication

Communication as Transaction

The most recent communication models do not label individual components. Transactive models focus instead on communication as a simultaneous process. As the model in Figure 1.3 suggests, we send and receive messages concurrently, adapting to the context and interpreting the verbal and nonverbal feedback of others as we speak.

Although communication models have been developed only recently, the elements of these models have long been recognized as the keys to successful public speaking. As you study public speaking, you will continue a tradition that goes back to the very beginnings of Western civilization.

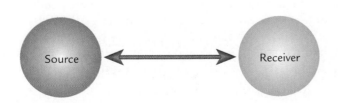

FIGURE 1.3

A transactive model of communication

context
The environment or situation in which a speech occurs

The Rich Heritage of Public Speaking

Long before many people could read, they listened to public speakers. The fourth century B.C. was a golden age for rhetoric in the Greek Republic, where the philosopher Aristotle formulated guidelines for speakers that we still follow today. As politicians and poets attracted large followings in ancient Rome, Cicero and Quintilian sought to define the qualities of the "true" orator. On a lighter note, it is said that Roman orators invented the necktie. Fearing laryngitis, they wore "chin cloths" to protect their throats.[9] Appendix A details the contributions of early rhetoricians.

In medieval Europe, the clergy were the most polished public speakers. People gathered eagerly to hear Martin Luther expound his Articles of Faith. In the eighteenth century, citizens of the New World listened to the town criers and impassioned patriots of colonial America.

Vast nineteenth-century audiences heard speakers such as Henry Clay and Daniel Webster debate states' rights; they listened to Frederick Douglass, Angelina Grimke, and Sojourner Truth argue for the abolition of slavery, and to Lucretia Mott plead for women's suffrage; they gathered for an evening's entertainment as Mark Twain traveled the lecture circuits of the frontier.

Students of nineteenth-century public speaking spent very little time developing their own speeches. Instead they practiced the art of **declamation**—the delivery of an already-famous address. Favorite subjects for declamation included speeches by such Americans as Patrick Henry and William Jennings Bryan, and by the British orator Edmund Burke. Collections of speeches, such as Bryan's own ten-volume set of *The World's Famous Orations,* published in 1906, were extremely popular.

Hand in hand with declamation went the study and practice of **elocution,** the expression of emotion through posture, movement, gestures, facial expression, and voice. From the mid-nineteenth to early twentieth centuries, elocution manuals, providing elaborate and specific prescriptions for effective delivery, were standard references not only in schools, but also in nearly every middle-class home in America.[10] Mark Twain was undoubtedly thinking back to the practitioners of declamation and elocution he had heard in his youth when he described the Reverend Mr. Sprague in *The Adventures of Tom Sawyer:*

> *He was regarded as a wonderful reader. At church "sociables" he was always called upon to read poetry; and when he was through, the ladies would lift up their hands and let them fall helplessly in their laps, and "wall" their eyes, and shake their heads, as much as to say, "Words cannot express it; it is too beautiful, too beautiful for this mortal earth."* [11]

declamation
The delivery of an already famous speech

elocution
The expression of emotion through posture, movement, gestures, facial expression, and voice

In the first half of the twentieth century, radio made it possible for people around the world to hear Franklin Delano Roosevelt decry December 7, 1941, as "a date which will live in infamy." In the last half of the century, television provided the medium through which audiences saw and heard the most stirring speeches: Martin Luther King, Jr., declaring, "I have a dream"; Gerald Ford assuring a nation reeling from Watergate that "Our long national nightmare is over"; George Bush affirming the American sense of community as "a thousand points of light"; and Charles Spencer of Britain eulogizing his sister, Princess Diana, as "the unique, the complex, the extraordinary and irreplaceable Diana."

With the twenty-first century dawned a new era of speechmaking. It was to be an era that would draw on historical public-speaking traditions—an era in which the Declaration of Independence would be declaimed on July 4, 2001, at Philadelphia's Independence Hall by actors Michael Douglas, Morgan Freeman, Mel Gibson, Whoopi Goldberg, Kevin Spacey, and others. But it was also to be an era that would expand the parameters of public speaking—an era in which legal assistant Erin Brockovich would address the 2001 graduates of Jones International University in Englewood, Colorado, via streaming video over the Internet.

And it was to be an era that would summon public speakers to meet some of the most difficult challenges in history—an era in which a U.S. President would face a nation badly shaken by the events of September 11, 2001, and assure them that "Terrorist attacks can shake the foundations of our biggest buildings, but they cannot touch the foundation of America. These acts shattered steel, but they cannot dent the steel of American resolve."[12] Speakers of the future will continue to draw on a long and rich heritage, in addition to forging new frontiers in public speaking.

The fame Erin Brokovich gained from the popular movie about her life may well have played a part in her ability to book speaking engagements. But she had carefully honed her speaking skills even before the movie made her famous.

[Photo: Dennis Cook/AP/Wide World Photos]

RECAP — THE RICH HERITAGE OF PUBLIC SPEAKING

Time Period	Event
Fourth Century B.C.	Greek rhetoric flourishes—Age of Aristotle (see Appendix A).
Fifteenth Century	European clergy are the primary practitioners of public speaking.
Eighteenth Century	American patriots make impassioned public pleas for independence.
Nineteenth Century	Abolitionists and suffragists speak out for change; frontier lecture circuits flourish.
Twentieth Century	Electronic media make possible vast audiences.
Twenty-First Century	A new era of speechmaking, using changing technology and media, but drawing on a rich heritage of providing information, influencing thought and action, entertaining, and paying tribute via the spoken word.

Public Speaking and Diversity

Although the history of public speaking is as old as the history of civilization, only during the last half of the twentieth century has attention focused on the rhetoric of diversity. People are just beginning to understand that such factors as the gender, ethnicity, and culture of both speaker and audience are crucial components of the context of a speaking event.

Diverse audiences have different expectations for appropriate and effective speech topics, argument structure, language style, and delivery. For example, a speech that may be quite persuasive to Native Americans may not have the same effect on Anglos who do not share the beliefs and values underlying the message.

Similarly, a presentation that seems perfectly sensible and acceptable to a U.S. businessperson who is accustomed to straightforward, problem-oriented logic, may seem shockingly rude to a Chinese business counterpart who expects more circuitous, less overtly purposeful rhetoric. And some African-American audiences "come to participate in a speech event,"[13] expecting the speaker to generate audience response through rhythmic "call response formulas"[14] from the African-American oral tradition.

To be effective, then, public speakers need to understand, affirm, and adapt to diverse audiences. And it is with this acknowledgment of the critical role of the audience that we come full circle. Aristotle was right. The audience is the most important component in the communication process. It was true in the fifth century B.C., when

Speaker's Homepage

Address: http://www.ablongman.com/beebe

▼ **The Power of the Internet**

Unlike countless speakers of previous generations, you have an amazing array of Internet resources available to help you design and deliver a speech. Throughout this book, in a feature we call "Speaker's Homepage," we describe some of these resources to help you prepare your speeches. We identify specific Internet sites that provide practical tips to help you identify speech topics, research your speech, find useful stories and illustrations, develop dazzling visual images (and even retrieve sound and video clips), as well as provide strategies to help you polish your delivery. We encourage you to explore these sites to help you with the speaking assignments for your course, as well as with speeches that you'll prepare for audiences other than your public-speaking class. All the Web addresses from our "Speaker's Homepage" featured throughout the book, including the updates if some Websites change, can be found at

http://www.ablongman.com/beebepub

One rich Website that we refer to in several "Speaker's Homepage" features is Allyn & Bacon's Website on public speaking. This site provides a wealth of ideas and Internet links to help you assess, analyze, research, organize, and deliver your speech. It can be found on the Web at

http://www.ablongman.com/pubspeak/

Culture and ethnicity are strong factors in determining an audience's response to both the content of a speech and the speaker's delivery style. These Korean-Americans are displaying their enthusiasm in a manner that might seem restrained to members of other ethnic groups.

[Photo: Starr '92/Stock Boston]

students listened to the Greek rhetorician Gorgias. It was true in the nineteenth century, when parents of elocution students attended a school recital. And it was still true on September 20, 2001, when George W. Bush declared to the citizens of the United States, "My fellow citizens, for the last nine days, the entire world has seen for itself the state of the union, and it is strong."[15]

It is the focus on audience that provides a coherent framework for the history of public speaking, from classical rhetoric to the contemporary rhetoric of diversity.

Adapting to diverse audiences also provides the unifying principle of this text. In Chapter 2 we present a model of speech preparation that emphasizes the importance of the audience. Then, throughout the text, we illustrate how this focus on and consideration of audience can guide a speaker effectively through each stage of speech preparation and delivery. In addition, at the end of each chapter we offer a feature entitled "Being Audience-Centered: A Sharper Focus." This feature, which follows the conventional chapter summary, synthesizes the chapter content related specifically to the concepts of audience and audience diversity.

SUMMARY

As you are called on to speak in public at various times throughout your life, skill in public speaking can empower you. It can also help you secure employment or advance your career.

Although similar in some ways to conversation, public speaking is more planned and formal, and the roles of speaker and audience more clearly defined. Like other forms of communication, public speaking is a process. As you develop the skills you need to participate effectively in that process, your study will be guided by experience and knowledge gained over centuries of making and studying speeches. Throughout history, speechmakers have acknowledged that the audience is the most important element in the communication process. Focus on and consideration of the audience help a speaker understand, affirm, and adapt to even those audiences whose expectations for appropriate and effective speech topics, argument structure, language style, and delivery may differ from those of the speaker.

being audience-centered

A Sharper Focus

CONSIDERING YOUR AUDIENCE

▶ As a public speaker, you will learn to adapt to your audience based on who your listeners are, their expectations for your speech, and their reactions to what you are saying.

▶ Audiences expect speakers to use standard English grammar and vocabulary.

▶ The decoding of a speaker's message will depend on the receiver's, or listener's, particular blend of past experiences, attitudes, beliefs, and values.

▶ An audience member experiencing either external or internal noise is unlikely to hear or remember much of what the speaker says.

▶ Without an audience to hear and provide feedback, public speaking serves little purpose.

▶ Skilled speakers depend on the nods, facial expressions, and murmurings of the audience to adjust their rate of speaking, volume, vocabulary, type and amount of supporting material, and other variables in order to communicate their message successfully.

▶ The audience is the most important component in the communication process.

CONSIDERING AUDIENCE DIVERSITY

▶ Although audience members rarely interrupt or talk to speakers, some cultures and contexts invite more speaker-audience interaction than do others.

▶ The audience's cultural traditions and expectations are part of the context of a public-speaking experience.

▶ Diverse audiences have diverse expectations for appropriate and effective speech topics, argument structure, language style, and delivery.

CRITICAL THINKING QUESTIONS

1. How do you think this course in public speaking can help you with your career goals? With your personal life?

2. Give an example of internal noise that is affecting you as you read this question.

3. Explain how you think your culture influences your expectations of a public speaker.

ETHICAL QUESTIONS

Declamation is defined in this chapter as "the delivery of an already-famous address." Is it ethical to deliver a speech written and/or delivered by someone else? Explain your answer.

SUGGESTED ACTIVITIES

1. Listen to an entire public speech, either on TV or in person. In what ways does this speech seem more intentional, structured, and formal than would a conversation with this same speaker?

2. Write a brief analysis of the speech you listened to for Activity 1, identifying each of the elements of the communication process discussed in this chapter: source, receiver, message, channel, noise, feedback, and context.

USING TECHNOLOGY AND MEDIA

Rent videos of Shakespeare's *Hamlet,* starring first Laurence Olivier (1948) and later Mel Gibson (1991) and Kenneth Branaugh (1996). Compare Hamlet's "To be, or not to be" soliloquy from each film.

If all my talents and powers were to be taken from me by some inscrutable Providence, and I had my choice of keeping but one, I would unhesitatingly ask to be allowed to keep the Power of Speaking, for through it, I would quickly recover all the rest.

DANIEL WEBSTER

2

Overview of the Speechmaking Process

objectives

After studying this chapter you should be able to do the following:

1. Describe why speakers sometimes feel nervous about speaking in public.

2. Use several techniques to become a confident speaker.

3. List and describe the key steps in preparing and presenting a speech.

Unless you have some prior experience in higher mathematics, you may not have the foggiest notion of what calculus is when you first take a class in that subject. But when you tell people that you are taking a public-speaking class, most at least have some idea what a public speaker does. A public speaker talks while others listen. You hear speeches almost every day. Each evening, when you turn on the news, you get a "sound bite" of some politician delivering a speech. Each day when you attend class, an instructor lectures. But even after hearing countless speeches, you may still have questions about how a speaker prepares and presents a speech.

In Chapter 1, we discussed the importance of learning to speak publicly and described the components of effective communication. In this chapter, we will preview the preparation and presentation skills that you will learn in this course. But before we address the nuts and bolts of developing and presenting a speech, we'll discuss a major obstacle for many speakers: nervousness. Following this discussion, we'll take a comprehensive look at the public-speaking process. Undoubtedly you will have a speech assignment early in your public-speaking course. Although it would be ideal to read *Public Speaking: An Audience-Centered Approach* from cover to cover before tackling your first speech, that would be impractical. To help you begin, we present this chapter, a step-by-step overview designed to serve as the scaffolding on which to build your skill in public speaking.

Improving Your Confidence as a Speaker

Let's address this problem right at the beginning: Many people are nervous about giving a speech. As one anonymous sage once said, "The mind is a wonderful thing. It starts working the minute you're born and never stops . . . until you get up to speak in public." Perhaps public speaking is a required class for you, but, because of the anxiety you feel when you deliver a speech, you've put it off as long as possible. The first bit of comfort we offer is this: *It's normal to be nervous.* In a survey seeking to identify people's phobias, public speaking ranked as the most anxiety-producing experience most people face. Forty-one percent of all respondents reported public speaking as their most significant fear; fear of death ranked only sixth![1] Based on these statistics, comedian Jerry Seinfeld suggests, "Given a choice, at a funeral most of us would rather be the one in the coffin than the one giving the eulogy." Another study found that more than 80 percent of the population feel anxious when they speak to an audience.[2] You may find comfort in knowing you are not alone in experiencing speech anxiety. Some people find that speaking is quite frightening; studies suggest that about 20 percent of all college students are highly apprehensive about speaking with others.[3]

Even if your anxiety is not overwhelming, you can benefit from learning some positive approaches that allow your nervousness to work *for* you. First, we will help you understand why you become nervous. Knowledge is power. Then we will offer specific strategies to help you speak with greater comfort and less anxiety.

Understanding Your Nervousness

What makes you feel nervous about speaking in public? Why do your hands sometimes shake, your knees quiver, your stomach flutter, and your voice seem to go up an octave? What is happening to you? Believe it or not, your brain is signaling your body to help you with a difficult task. Sometimes, however, because your brain offers more "help" than you need, this assistance is not useful.

Your view of the speaking assignment, your perception of your speaking skill, and your self-esteem interact to create anxiety.[4] You want to do well, but you're not sure you can or will. Presented with this conflict, your body responds by increasing your breathing rate, pumping more adrenaline, and causing more blood to rush through your veins. In short, you have more energy to deal with the conflict you are facing. Your brain switches to its default fight-or-flight mode: You either fight to respond to the challenge or avoid the cause of the anxiety. To put it more technically, you are experiencing physiological changes because of your psychological state. Increased energy and other physical changes explain why you may have a more rapid heartbeat, shaking knees and hands, a quivering voice, and increased perspiration. You may experience butterflies in your stomach because of changes in your digestive system. Due to your discomfort, you may also make less eye contact with your audience, use more vocalized pauses ("Um," "Ah," "You know"), and speak too rapidly. Although you see these events as hindrances, your body is simply trying to help you with the task at hand.

A study by two communication researchers found that people offer many reasons they feel nervous when they speak in public.[5] Reasons include fear of humiliation, concern about not being prepared, worry about how they look, pressure to perform, personal insecurity, concern that the audience won't be interested in them or the speech, inexperience, making mistakes, and an overall fear of failure. As you look at this list, you'll probably find a reason that resonates with you; as we've mentioned, most people feel some nervousness when they speak before others. You're not alone if you are apprehensive about giving a speech.

When are you most likely to feel nervous about giving a speech in your communication class? Research suggests you'll probably feel most nervous right before you give your speech.[6] The second-highest level of anxiety you'll feel, if you're typical, is when your instructor explains the speech assignment. You'll feel the *least* anxiety when you're preparing your speech. One practical application of this research is to understand when you'll need the most help managing your anxiety—right before you speak. Realize that as you begin speaking, anxiety begins to decrease—often dramatically. Another application of the research is to realize that you'll feel less anxious about your speech when you're doing something positive to prepare for it. Don't put off working on your speech; you'll not only have a better speech, you'll also feel less anxious about presenting it.

What else can you do to understand and manage your fear and anxiety? Consider the following observations.

YOU ARE GOING TO FEEL MORE NERVOUS THAN YOU LOOK   When she finished her speech, Carmen sank into her seat and muttered, "Ugh, was I shaky up there! Did you see how nervous I was?"

"Nervous? You were nervous?" asked Kosta, surprised. "You looked pretty calm to me."

Realize that your audience cannot see everything you feel. If you worry that you are going to appear nervous to others, you may, in fact, increase your anxiety. Your body will exhibit more physical changes to deal with your self-induced state of anxiety.

ALMOST EVERY SPEAKER EXPERIENCES SOME DEGREE OF NERVOUSNESS   President Kennedy was noted for his superb public-speaking skills. When he spoke, he seemed perfectly at ease. Former British prime minister Winston Churchill was also hailed as one of the twentieth century's great orators. Amazingly, both Kennedy and Churchill were extremely fearful of speaking in public. The list of famous people who admit to feeling nervous before they speak may surprise you: Katie Couric, Conan O'Brien, Jay Leno, Carly Simon, and Oprah Winfrey have all reported feeling anxious and jittery before they speak in public.[7] Almost everyone experiences some anxiety when speaking. It is unrealistic to try to eliminate speech anxiety. Instead, your goal should be to manage your nervousness so that it does not create so much internal noise that it keeps you from speaking effectively.

ANXIETY CAN BE USEFUL   Extra adrenaline, increased blood flow, pupil dilation, increased endorphins to block pain, increased heart rate, and other physical changes caused by anxiety improve your energy level and help you function better than you might otherwise. Your heightened state of readiness can actually help you speak better, especially if you view the public-speaking event positively instead of negatively. Speakers who self-label the increased feelings of physiological arousal as "nervousness" are more likely to feel anxious and fearful; but the same physiological feelings are interpreted as enthusiasm or excitement in speakers who don't label the increased arousal as fear, anxiety, or nervousness. You are more likely to gain the benefits of the extra help your brain is trying to give you if you think positively rather than negatively about speaking in public. Don't let your initial anxiety convince you that you cannot speak effectively.

When you first choose your career, you might not realize that delivering speeches could become an important part of your job. The skills you learn in your public-speaking course in college can help you learn to communicate effectively and confidently throughout your career.

[Photo: Mark Richards/PhotoEdit]

Building Your Confidence

"Is there anything to help manage my nervousness and anxiety when I give a speech?" you may wonder. Both contemporary research and centuries of experience from seasoned public speakers suggest some practical advice.

KNOW YOUR AUDIENCE   Know to whom you are speaking, and learn as much about your audience as you can. The more you can anticipate the kind of reaction your listeners will have to your speech, the more comfortable you will be in delivering your message. As you are preparing your speech, periodically visualize your listeners as you are delivering your message. Consider their needs, goals, and hopes as you prepare your message. Be audience-centered rather than speaker-centered. A speaker-centered presenter focuses on his or her nervousness; don't keep telling yourself how nervous you are going to be.[8] An audience-centered speaker focuses on connecting to listeners rather than focusing on fear. Chapter 5 provides a detailed approach to analyzing and adapting to your audience.

BE PREPARED   The following formula will apply to most speaking situations you experience: The better prepared you are, the less anxiety you will experience. Being prepared means that you have researched your topic and practiced your speech several times before you deliver it. Being prepared also means that you have developed a logically coherent outline rather than one that is disorganized and difficult to follow. Transitional phrases and summaries can help you present a well-structured, easy-to-understand message.

SELECT AN APPROPRIATE TOPIC   You will feel less nervous if you talk about something with which you are familiar or have some personal experience. Your comfort with the subject of your speech will be reflected in your delivery. In the chapters ahead, we offer more detailed guidance about how to select a topic.

RE-CREATE THE SPEECH ENVIRONMENT WHEN YOU PRACTICE   When you practice your speech, imagine that you are giving the speech to the audience you will actually address. Stand up. Imagine what the room looks like, or consider rehearsing in the room in which you will deliver your speech. What will you be wearing? Practice rising from your seat, walking to the front of the room, and beginning your speech. Practice aloud, rather than just saying the speech to yourself. A realistic rehearsal will increase your confidence when your moment to speak arrives.

KNOW YOUR INTRODUCTION AND YOUR CONCLUSION   You are likely to feel the most anxious during the opening moments of your speech. Therefore, it is a good idea to have a clear plan for how you will start your speech. We aren't suggesting memorizing your introduction word for word, but you should have it well in mind. Being familiar with your introduction will help you feel more comfortable about the entire speech.

If you know how you will end your speech, you will have a safe harbor in case you lose your place. If you need to end your speech prematurely, a well-delivered conclusion can permit you to make a graceful exit.

VISUALIZE YOUR SUCCESS   Studies suggest that one of the best ways to control anxiety is to imagine a scene in which you exhibit skill and comfort as a public speaker.[9] As you imagine giving your speech, picture yourself walking confidently to the front and delivering your well-prepared opening remarks. Visualize yourself giving the entire speech as a controlled, confident speaker. Imagine yourself calm and in command. Positive visualization is effective because it boosts your confidence by helping you see yourself as a more confident, accomplished speaker.[10]

USE DEEP-BREATHING TECHNIQUES   One of the symptoms of nervousness is a change in your breathing and heart rates. Nervous speakers tend to take short, shallow breaths. To help break the anxiety-induced breathing pattern, consider taking a few slow deep breaths before you rise to speak. No one will be able to detect that you are taking deep breaths if you just slowly inhale and exhale from your seat before your speech begins. Besides breathing deeply, try to relax your entire body. Combine deep breathing with the visualization just mentioned, to help you relax.

One of the best ways to reduce speaker anxiety is to experience what it's like to deliver a speech successfully. Seek out opportunities, perhaps at student events on your college campus, where the audiences are likely to be receptive to your message.
[Photo: Robert E. Daemmrich/ Stone]

FOCUS ON YOUR MESSAGE RATHER THAN YOUR FEAR   The more you think that you are anxious about speaking, the more you will increase your level of anxiety. Instead, think about what you are going to say. In the few minutes before you address your listeners, mentally review your major ideas, your introduction, and your conclusion. Focus on your ideas rather than on your fear.

GIVE YOURSELF A MENTAL PEP TALK   You may think that people who talk to themselves are slightly loony. But silently giving yourself a pep talk can give you confidence and take your mind off your nervousness. Here's a sample mental speech you could deliver to yourself right before you speak: "I know this stuff better than anyone else. I've practiced it. My message is well organized. I know I can do it. I'll do a good job." When you feel yourself getting nervous, use positive messages to replace negative thoughts that may creep into your consciousness. Examples include the following:

NEGATIVE THOUGHT	POSITIVE SELF-TALK
I'm going to forget what I'm supposed to say.	I've practiced this speech many times. I've got notes to prompt me. If I lose my place, no one will know I'm not following my outline.
So many people are looking at me.	I can do this! My listeners want me to do a good job. I'll seek out friendly faces when I feel nervous.
People will think I'm dull and boring.	I've got some good examples. I can talk to people one-on-one, and people seem to like me.
I just can't go through with this.	I have talked to people all my life. I've given presentations in classes for years. I can get through this because I've rehearsed and I'm prepared.

CHANNEL YOUR NERVOUS ENERGY   One common symptom of being nervous is shaking hands and wobbly knees. As we noted earlier, what triggers this jiggling is the extra boost of adrenaline and resulting energy that has to go somewhere. Your muscles may move whether you've asked them to move or not. Take control by channeling that energy. While you are seated waiting to speak, grab the edge of your chair (without calling attention to what you are doing) and gently squeeze the chair to release tension; no one needs to know you're doing this. Unobtrusively, squeeze and relax, squeeze and relax. Another way to release tension is to take a leisurely walk before you arrive at class to speak. Taking a slow, relaxing walk can help calm you down and use up some of your excess energy. You can also purposely tense and then release your muscles in your legs and arms while you're seated in your classroom. Don't look like you're going into convulsions, just imperceptibly tense and relax your muscles to burn energy. One more tip: You may want to keep both feet on the floor and gently wiggle your toes rather than sitting with your legs crossed. Crossing your legs can sometimes result in one leg or foot going to sleep. Keeping your feet on the floor and slightly moving your toes can ensure that all of you will be wide awake and ready to go when it's your turn to speak.

As you are waiting to be introduced, focus on remaining calm. Act calm to feel calm. As you are waiting for your turn to speak. Give yourself a pep talk; tense and release your muscles to help you relax. Then, when your name is called, walk to the front of the room in a calm and collected manner. Before you present your opening, attention-catching sentence, take a moment to look for a friendly, supportive face. Think calm and act calm to feel calm.

SEEK SPEAKING OPPORTUNITIES   The more experience you gain as a public speaker, the less nervous you will feel. Researchers have found that those speakers who were the most nervous at the beginning of a public-speaking class experienced the most decreases in nervousness by the end of the class.[11] Consider joining organizations and clubs that provide opportunities for you to hold an office and participate in public presentations. Consider joining a local chapter of Toastmasters, an organization dedicated to improving public-speaking skills by providing a supportive group of people to help you polish your speaking and overcome your anxiety. As you develop a track record of successfully delivering speeches, you will have more confidence. This course in public speaking will give you opportunities to enhance both your confidence and your skill through frequent practice.

Speaker's Homepage   ▬ **X**

Address: http://www.ablongman.com/beebe

▼   **Tips for Managing Your Communication Apprehension**

As we have emphasized in this chapter, it is not unusual for public speakers to feel anxious about delivering a speech. Many speakers feel they need some extra help to manage their nervousness. To supplement the ideas and strategies provided in this chapter, many useful Websites can give you new ways to manage your nervousness.

http://www.school-for-champions.com/speaking/fear.htm

This site provides advice from a person who developed ways of overcoming his nervousness when he delivers speeches.

ASSESSING YOUR LEVEL OF NERVOUSNESS WHEN YOU SPEAK

http://www.newsorlando.com/apprehension.htm

http://www.bodary.com/cm211/prcaform.html

Both these sites present the Personal Report of Communication Apprehension test designed by James McCroskey and Virginia Richmond.

A GUIDE TO PHYSICAL RELAXATION

http://www.health-center.com

http://ourworld.compuserve.com/hompages/har/test.htm

These two Websites offer simple ideas to help you relax.

LOOK FOR POSITIVE LISTENER SUPPORT OF YOUR MESSAGE   Evidence suggests that if you think you see audience members who are critical of you or your message, you may feel more apprehensive and nervous when you speak.[12] Stated more positively, when you are aware of positive audience support you will feel more confident and less nervous. Building on our previous advice, it is important to be audience-centered. Although you may face some audiences that won't respond positively to you or your message, the overwhelming majority of listeners will be responsive to your message. Looking for positive, reinforcing feedback and finding it can help you feel more confident as a speaker. This research finding has implications for you as a listener: When you're listening to speakers in your communication class, help your colleagues by being a positive, supportive listener: Provide eye contact, and offer additional appropriate positive nonverbal support, such as nodding in agreement and providing a positive but sincere facial expression. You can help your fellow students feel more comfortable as speakers, and they can do the same for you; watch for their support.

DON'T PROCRASTINATE IN PREPARING YOUR SPEECH   One research study confirmed what you probably already knew: Speakers who are more apprehensive about speaking put off working on their speeches, in contrast to speakers who are less anxious about public speaking.[13] The fear of speaking often means that speakers don't do their best, because they delay preparing their speeches until the last minute. The lack of thorough preparation often results in a poorer speech performance, reinforcing the speaker's perception that public speaking is difficult. Realize that if you become nervous when speaking, you'll tend to put off working on your speech. Take charge by tackling the speech assignment early, giving yourself every chance to be successful. Don't let your fear freeze you into inaction. Prepare early.

RECAP   **TIPS FOR BUILDING CONFIDENCE**

Things to Do

Learn as much as possible about your audience.

Be prepared and well organized.

Select a topic you are interested in or know something about.

Rehearse aloud.

Be familiar with how you will begin and end the speech.

Visualize being successful.

Take deep breaths to relax.

Focus on the message.

Give yourself a pep talk.

Channel your nervous energy.

Seek other speaking opportunities to gain experience and confidence.

Look for positive listener support of you and your message.

Don't procrastinate.

Preparing Your First Speech: An Overview of the Speechmaking Process

Now that we've discussed some principles and strategies for managing your nervousness, let's look at the key elements of preparing and presenting a speech. You've been speaking to others since you were 2 years old. Talking to people has seemed such a natural part of your life that you may never have stopped to analyze the process. But as you think about preparing your first speech for your speech class, you may wonder, "What do I do first?" Your assignment may be to introduce yourself to the class. Or your first assignment may be a brief informative talk—to describe something to your audience. Regardless of the specific assignment, however, you need some idea of how to begin.

As we noted earlier, you don't need to read this book cover to cover before you give your first speech. But it is useful to see an overview of the various steps and skills involved in giving a speech. To help you see this overview, Figure 2.1 diagrams the various tasks involved in the speech-making process, emphasizing audience as the central concern at every step of the process. We'll refer to this audience-centered model of public speaking throughout the text. *To emphasize the importance of being audience-centered, we have placed a smaller version of this model in the margins throughout the text to draw your attention to information that discusses the importance of always being mindful of your audience. (See icon in the margin.) When you see the icon, it means we're discussing the central theme of this book: Always make choices in designing and delivering your speech with your audience in mind.*

We will begin our discussion of the speech-making process with the central element: considering your audience. We will then discuss each step of the process, starting with selecting and narrowing a topic, and moving clockwise around the model, examining each interrelated step.

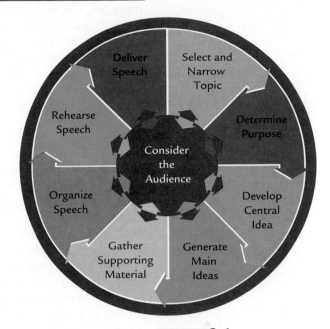

FIGURE 2.1

This model of the speech-making process emphasizes the importance of considering your audience as you work on each task involved in designing and presenting a speech. As we discuss each task in depth throughout the book, we also use a smaller image of this model to flag information and advice that remind you to consider your audience.

Consider Your Audience

Why should the central focus of public speaking be the audience? Why is it not topic selection, outlining, or research? The simple truth is, your audience influences the topic you choose and every later step of the speechmaking process. Your selection of topic, purpose, and even major ideas should be based on a thorough understanding of your listeners. In a very real sense, your audience "writes" the speech.[14]

As Figure 2.1 shows, considering your audience is an ongoing activity. The needs, attitudes, beliefs, values, and other characteristics of your audience should play a leading role at every step. After you select your topic, you need to consider how the audience will respond to your examples, organization, and delivery. That's why, in the model, arrows connect the center of the diagram with each step of the process. At any point during the process, you may need to revise your thinking or your material if you learn new information about your audience. So the model also has arrows pointing both ways across the boundaries of each step in the process. Chapter 5 contains a comprehensive discussion of the principles and strategies involved in analyzing and considering your audience.

Being audience-centered involves making decisions about the content and style of your speech *before* you speak, based on knowledge of your audience's values and beliefs. It also means being sensitive to your audience's responses *during* the speech so that you can make appropriate adjustments.

Different cultures have radically different conventions for public speaking. In Russia, for example, speakers have a "no frills" approach that emphasizes content over delivery. When one of your authors taught public speaking for several semesters in the Bahamas, however, he shocked students by suggesting that they try to achieve a conversational, informal manner. Bahamian audiences, the author quickly discovered, expect formal oratory from their speakers, very much as U.S. audiences in the nineteenth century preferred the grandiloquence of Stephen A. Douglas to the quieter, homespun style of Abraham Lincoln. So your author had to embellish his own style when he taught the class.

You need not teach or give speeches in foreign countries to recognize the importance of adapting to the cultural expectations of different audiences. The population of the United States is highly diverse in terms of culture, age, ethnicity, sexual orientation, and religious tradition. Consider the backgrounds of your classmates. How many different cultural and ethnic traditions do they represent? Several years ago, the typical college student was a newly minted high-school graduate between the ages of 18 and 21. Today your classmates probably reflect a wide range of ages, backgrounds, and experiences. You will want to adjust not only your delivery style but also your topic, pattern of organization, and even your dress, according to who they are and what subject or subjects they are interested in. If you learn to analyze your audience and adapt to their expectations, you can apply these skills in numerous settings: a job interview, a business presentation, a city council campaign—even a marriage proposal.

Select and Narrow Your Topic

While keeping your audience foremost in mind, your next task is to determine what you will talk about and to limit your topic to fit the constraints of your speaking assignment. Pay special attention to the guidelines your instructor gives you for your assignment.

If your first speech assignment is to introduce yourself to the class, your **speech topic** has been selected for you—*you* are the topic. It is not uncommon to be asked to speak on a specific subject. But often you will be asked to speak and not be given a topic. The task of selecting and narrowing a topic will be yours. Choosing or finding a topic on which to speak can be frustrating. "What should I talk about?" can become a haunting question.

Although there is no definitive answer to what you should talk about, you may discover a topic by asking three standard questions: "Who is the audience?" "What is the occasion?" and "What are my interests, talents, and experiences?"

WHO IS THE AUDIENCE?   Your topic may grow from basic knowledge about your audience. For example, if you know that your audience members are primarily between the ages of 25 and 40, this information should help you select a topic of interest to people who are probably working and either seeking partners or raising families. An older audience may lead you to other concerns or issues: "Will Social Security be there when I need it?" or "The advantages of belonging to the American Association of Retired Persons."

speech topic
The key focus of the content of a speech

WHAT IS THE OCCASION?   Besides your audience, you should consider the type of occasion when choosing a topic. A commencement address calls for a different topic, for example, from a speech to a model railroad club.

WHAT ARE MY INTERESTS, TALENTS, AND EXPERIENCES?   Rather than racking your brain for exotic topics and far-flung ideas, examine your own background. Your choice of major in college, your hobbies, and your ancestry are sources for topic ideas. What issues do you feel strongly about? Reflect on jobs you've held, news stories that catch your interest, events in your hometown, your career goals, or interesting people that you have met. Chapter 6 contains a discussion of specific strategies for finding topics, and Appendix B provides topic ideas that you can modify to suit your audience and the occasion.

Once you have chosen your topic, narrow it to fit the time limits for your talk. If you've been asked to deliver a ten-minute speech, the topic "how to find counseling help on campus" would be more manageable than the topic "how to make the most of your college experience." As our model suggests, your audience should be foremost in your mind when you work on your topic.

Determine Your Purpose

You might think that once you have your topic, you are ready to start the research process. Before you do that, however, you need to decide on both a general and a specific purpose. Chapter 6 describes three types of **general purposes** for giving a speech: to *inform,* to *persuade,* and to *entertain.* Even though we identify each purpose separately, they often overlap. For example, you may want to inform and entertain your audience while suggesting creative ways to avoid long lines during registration. In speech classes, your main purpose will most often be set by your instructor.

Speaking to inform is the primary objective of class lectures, seminars, and workshops. When you inform, you teach, define, illustrate, clarify, or elaborate on a topic. Chapter 15 will show you how to construct an effective speech with an informative purpose.

Ads on TV and radio, sermons, political speeches, and sales presentations are examples of speeches designed to persuade. They seek to change or reinforce attitudes, beliefs, values, or behavior. To be persuasive, you need to be sensitive to your audience's attitudes toward you and your topic. Chapters 16 and 17 will discuss the principles and strategies for persuasive speeches.

The third general purpose for giving a speech is to entertain your audience. After-dinner speeches and comic monologues are mainly intended for entertainment. Often the key to an effective entertaining speech lies in your choice of stories, examples, and illustrations, as well as in your delivery. Appendix C has examples of informative, persuasive, and entertaining speeches.

After making sure you understand your general purpose, you need to formulate a **specific purpose:** a concise statement indicating what you want your listeners to be able to know, do, or feel when you finish your speech: *It identifies the audience response you desire.* Here again, we emphasize the importance of focusing on the audience as you develop your specific speech purpose. Perhaps you have had the experience of listening to a speaker and wondered, "What's the point? I know he's talking about education, but I'm not sure where he's going with this subject." You may have understood the speaker's general purpose, but the specific one wasn't clear. If you can't figure out what the specific purpose is, it is probably because the speaker does not know either.

general purpose
The overarching goal of a speech—to inform, persuade, or entertain

specific purpose
A concise statement of the desired audience response indicating what you want your listeners to be able to know, feel, or do when you finish speaking

Decide on Your General Purpose

TO INFORM	To share information by defining, describing, or explaining
TO PERSUADE	To change or reinforce an attitude, belief, value, or behavior
TO ENTERTAIN	To amuse through humor, stories, or other illustrations

Decide on Your Specific Purpose

What do you want your audience to know, do, or feel when you finish your speech?

General Purpose	Specific Purpose
TO INFORM	At the end of my speech, the audience will be able to identify three counseling facilities on campus and describe the best way to get help at each one.
TO PERSUADE	At the end of my speech, the audience will want to take advantage of counseling facilities on campus.
TO ENTERTAIN	At the end of my speech, the audience will be able to relate to the series of misunderstandings I created when I began making inquiries about career advisors on campus.

Deciding on a specific purpose is not difficult once you have narrowed your topic: "At the end of my speech, the class will be able to identify three counseling facilities on campus and describe the best way to get help at each one." Notice that this purpose is phrased in terms of what you would like the audience to be able to do by the end of the speech. Your specific purpose should be a fine-tuned, audience-centered goal. For an informative speech, you may simply want your audience to restate an idea, define new words, or identify, describe, or illustrate something. In a persuasive speech, you may try to rouse your listeners to take a class, buy something, or vote for someone.

Once you have formulated your specific purpose, write it down on a piece of paper or note card and keep it before you as you read and gather ideas for your talk. Your specific purpose should guide your research and help you choose supporting materials that are related to your audience. As you continue to work on your speech, you may even decide to modify your purpose. But if you have an objective in mind at all times as you move through the preparation stage, you will stay on track.

 ## Develop Your Central Idea

You should now be able to write the **central idea** of your speech. Whereas your statement of a specific purpose indicates what you want your audience to do when you have finished your speech, your central idea identifies the essence of your message. Think of it as a one-sentence summary of your speech. Here are two examples:

TOPIC:	DVD players
GENERAL PURPOSE:	To inform.
SPECIFIC PURPOSE:	At the end of my speech, the audience will be able to identify the key reason digital video disk (DVD) players offer greater sound and picture fidelity than do videotape players.

central idea
A one-sentence summary of
the speech content

CENTRAL IDEA:	DVD players have greater sound and picture quality because they "read" the music and video information digitally, rather than analogically.
TOPIC:	Kachina dolls
GENERAL PURPOSE:	To inform
SPECIFIC PURPOSE:	At the end of my speech, the audience will be able to describe the significance of kachina dolls to the Hopi Indians.
CENTRAL IDEA:	Kachina dolls, carved wooden figures used in Hopi Indian ceremonies, are believed to represent spirits of the dead that will help produce a good harvest.

Generate the Main Ideas

"A good many people can make a speech," said columnist H. V. Prochnow, "but saying something is more difficult." Effective speakers are good thinkers; they say something. They know how to play with words and thoughts to develop their **main ideas.** The ancient Romans called this skill **invention**—the ability to develop or discover ideas that result in new insights or new approaches to old problems. The Roman orator Cicero called this aspect of speaking the process of "finding out what [a speaker] should say."

With an appropriate topic, a specific purpose, and a well-worded central idea on paper, the next task is to identify the major divisions of your speech, or key points that you wish to develop. To determine how to subdivide your central idea into key points, ask these three questions:

1. Does the central idea have logical divisions?

2. Can you think of several reasons why the central idea is true?

3. Can you support the central idea with a series of steps?

Let's look at each of these questions along with examples of how to apply them.

DOES THE CENTRAL IDEA HAVE LOGICAL DIVISIONS?   If the central idea is "There are three ways to interpret the stock-market page of your local newspaper," your speech could be organized into three parts. You will simply identify the three ways to interpret the stock-market page and use each as a major point. A speech about the art of applying theatrical makeup could also be organized into three parts: eye makeup, face makeup, and hair makeup. Looking for logical divisions in your speech topic is the simplest way to determine key points.

CAN YOU THINK OF SEVERAL REASONS THE CENTRAL IDEA IS TRUE?   If your central idea is "Medicare should be expanded to include additional coverage for individuals of all ages," each major point of your speech could be a reason you think Medicare should be extended. For example, Medicare should be expanded because (1) not enough people are being served by the present system, (2) the people currently being served receive inadequate medical attention, and (3) the elderly cannot afford to pay what Medicare does not now cover. If your central idea is a statement that suggests that whatever you are talking about is good or bad, you should focus on the reasons your central idea is true. Use these reasons as the main ideas of the speech.

main idea
The key points of a speech

invention
The development or discovery of ideas and insights

CAN YOU SUPPORT THE CENTRAL IDEA WITH A SERIES OF STEPS? Suppose your central idea is "Running for a campus office is easy to do." Your speech could be developed around a series of steps, telling your listeners what to do first, second, and third to get elected. Speeches describing a personal experience or explaining how to build or make something can usually be organized in a step-by-step progression.

Your time limit, topic, and information gleaned from your research will determine how many major ideas will be in your speech. A three- to five-minute speech might have only two major ideas. In a very short speech, you may develop only one major idea with examples, illustrations, and other forms of support. Don't spend time trying to divide a topic that does not need dividing. In Chapters 6 and 9, we will discuss how to generate major ideas and organize them.

Gather Verbal and Visual Supporting Material

With your main idea or ideas in mind, your next job is to gather material to support them—facts, examples, definitions, and quotations from others that illustrate, amplify, clarify, and provide evidence. Here, as elsewhere in preparing your speech, the importance of being an audience-centered speaker cannot be overemphasized. An old saying has it that an ounce of illustration is worth a ton of talk. If a speech is boring, it is usually because the speaker has not chosen supporting material that is relevant or interesting to the audience. Don't just give people data; connect facts to their lives. As one sage quipped, "Data is not information any more than 50 tons of cement is a skyscraper."[15]

Supporting material should be personal and concrete, and it should appeal to your listeners' senses. Tell stories based on your own experiences and provide vivid descriptions of things that are tangible so that your audience can visualize what you are talking about. Besides sight, supporting material can appeal to touch, hearing, smell, and taste. The more senses you trigger with words, the more interesting your talk will be. Descriptions such as "rough, splintery surface of weather-beaten wood" or "the sweet, cool, refreshing flavor of cherry Jell-O" evoke sensory images. In addition, relating abstract statistics to something tangible can help communicate your ideas more clearly. For example, if you say Frito-Lay sells 2.6 billion pounds of snack food each year your listeners will have a hazy idea that 2.6 billion pounds is a lot of Fritos and potato chips; but if you add that 2.6 billion pounds is triple the weight of the Empire State Building you've made your point more memorably.[16] We will discuss in Chapter 8 the variety of supporting material available to you.

How does a public speaker find interesting and relevant supporting material? By developing good research skills. President Woodrow Wilson once admitted, "I use not only all the brains I have, but all that I can borrow." Although it is important to have good ideas, it is equally important to know how to build on existing knowledge. You can probably think of a topic or two about which you consider yourself an expert. Chances are that if you gave a short speech about a sport that you had practiced for years or about a recent trip that you took, you would not need to gather much additional information. But sooner or later, you will need to do some research on a topic in order to speak on it intelligently to an audience. If your college classes up to this point have required only brief forays into the library, that experience is about to change shortly. By the time you have given several speeches in

Giving your first speech will be a positive experience if you prepare yourself well and consider your audience at each step of the speech-making process.

[Photo: B. Daemmrich/The Image Works]

this course, you will have learned to use a number of the following resources: your library's computerized card catalog, the *Social Sciences Index,* the *Directory of American Scholars, Bartlett's Familiar Quotations,* government document holdings, your library's periodical indexes, and an assortment of CD-ROM indexes. You would also be wise to spend some time learning to use electronic databases such as LEXIS-NEXIS. To navigate the World Wide Web, learn to use browsers such as Netscape or Internet Explorer, and directories and search engines such as Excite, Google, and Yahoo! Throughout this book we identify useful Websites in our Speaker's Homepage feature. These Websites will help you both design and deliver your speeches.

In addition to becoming a skilled user of library and electronic resources, you will also learn to be on the lookout as you read, watch TV, and listen to the radio for ideas, examples, illustrations, and quotations that could be used in a speech. Finally, you will learn how to gather information through interviews and written requests for information on various topics. Chapter 7 will explain more thoroughly how to use all these resources.

Besides searching for verbal forms of supporting material, you can also seek visual supporting material. For many people, seeing is believing. Almost any presentation can be enhanced by reinforcing key ideas with visual aids. Often the most effective visual aids are the simplest: an object, a chart, a graph, a poster, a model, a map, or a person—perhaps yourself—to demonstrate a process or skill. The sample speech "Can You Read My Mind?" later in this chapter incorporates simple, yet effective, visual aids. Today there are many technologies for displaying visual aids. One of the most basic is an overhead projector that displays 8½- by 11-inch acetate transparencies. Most classrooms now have video players, so you can show brief video segments to introduce or reinforce a point. The latest graphics packages for personal computers can help you generate colorful graphs, charts, signs, and banners. And with today's technology you can project stunning video images with the proper equipment. Of course, using this high-tech equipment requires new skills and often extra rehearsal time.

In Chapter 14 we discuss some basic advice about using presentation aids: Make your visual images large enough to be seen and allow plenty of time to prepare them; look at your audience, not your presentation aid; control your audience's attention by timing your visual displays; and keep your presentation aids simple. Always concentrate on communicating effectively with your audience, not on dazzling your listeners with glitzy presentation displays.

The simplest visual aids are often the most effective. For an informal presentation, flip charts can be an effective way for you to communicate your message to the audience.

[Photo: Bob Daemmrich/ Stock Boston]

Organize Your Speech

A wise person once said, "If effort is organized, accomplishment follows." A clearly and logically structured speech helps your audience remember what you say. It also helps you feel more in control of your speech, and greater control helps you feel more comfortable while delivering your message.

Ideas, information, examples, illustrations, stories, and statistics need to be presented in a logical order. Classical rhetoricians—early students of speech—called the process of developing an orderly speech **disposition.** Speakers need to present ideas and illustrations in an orderly sequence so that listeners can easily follow what they are saying.

Every well-prepared speech has three major divisions: the introduction, the body, and the conclusion. The introduction helps capture attention, serves as an overview of the speech, and provides your audience with reasons to listen to you. The body presents the main content of your speech. The conclusion summarizes your key ideas. You may

disposition
The organization and arrangement of ideas and illustrations

have heard this advice on how to organize your speech: "Tell them what you're going to tell them (the introduction), tell them (the body of the speech), and tell them what you told them (the conclusion)."

As a student of public speaking, you will study and learn to apply variations of this basic pattern of organization (chronological, topical, cause–effect, problem–solution) that will help your audience understand your meaning. You will learn about previewing and summarizing—methods of oral organization that will help your audience retain your main ideas. In the following sample speech, notice how the introduction catches the listener's attention, the body of the speech identifies the main ideas, and the conclusion summarizes the key ideas.

Because your introduction previews your speech and your conclusion summarizes it, most public-speaking teachers recommend that you prepare your introduction and conclusion *after* you have carefully organized the body of your talk. If you have already generated your major ideas by divisions, reasons, or steps, you are well on your way to developing an outline. Indicate your major ideas by Roman numerals. Use capital letters for your supporting points. Use Arabic numerals if you need to subdivide your ideas further. Do *not* write your speech word for word. If you do, your speech will sound stilted and unnatural. It may be useful, however, for you to use brief notes—written cues on note cards—instead of a complete manuscript.

You may want to look in Chapters 9 and 11 for approaches to organizing a message and sample outlines. Chapter 10 provides more detailed suggestions for beginning and ending your speech. Some public-speaking teachers may require a slightly different outline format. For example, your teacher may want you to outline your speech introduction using a Roman numeral I for the introduction, a II for the body, and a III for your conclusion. Make sure you follow the precise guidelines your instructor provides for outlining your speech. For your first speech, you may want to adapt the following simple outline format to your talks.[17] Your instructor may want you to add more detailed information about your supporting material in outlines you submit in class.

Description:

TOPIC:

Could be assigned by your instructor, or selected by you

GENERAL PURPOSE:

To inform, persuade, or entertain—your instructor will probably assign your general purpose

SPECIFIC PURPOSE:

A clear statement indicating what your audience should be able to do after hearing your speech

CENTRAL IDEA:

A one-sentence summary of your talk

Example:

TOPIC:

How to invest money

GENERAL PURPOSE:

To inform

SPECIFIC PURPOSE:

At the end of my speech, the audience should be able to identify two principles that will help them better invest their money.

CENTRAL IDEA:

Knowing the source of money, how to invest it, and how money grows can lead to increased income from wise investments.

Description:	Example:
INTRODUCTION:	**INTRODUCTION:**
Attention-catching opening line	Imagine for a moment that it is the year 2050. You are 65 years old. You've just picked up your mail and opened an envelope that contains a check for $100,000! No, you didn't win the lottery. You smile as you realize your own modest investment strategy over the last forty years has paid off handsomely.
PREVIEW MAJOR IDEAS	Today I'd like to answer three questions that can help you become a better money manager: First, where does money come from? Second, where do you invest it? And third, how does a little money grow into a lot of money?
TELL YOUR AUDIENCE WHY THEY SHOULD LISTEN TO YOU	Knowing the answers to these three questions can literally pay big dividends for you. With only modest investments and a well-disciplined attitude, you could easily have an annual income of $100,000 or more.
BODY:	**BODY:**
I. Major Idea	I. There are two sources of money.
A. Supporting idea	A. You already have some money.
B. Supporting idea	B. You will earn money in the future.
II. Major Idea	II. You can do three things with a dollar.
A. Supporting idea	A. You can spend your money.
B. Supporting idea	B. You can lend your money to others.
C. Supporting idea	C. You can invest your money.
III. Major Idea	III. Two principles can help make you rich.
A. Supporting idea	A. The "magic" of compound interest can transform pennies into millions.
B. Supporting idea	B. Finding the best rate of return on your money can pay big dividends.
CONCLUSION:	**CONCLUSION:**
Summarize main ideas and restate central idea.	Today I've identified three key aspects of effective money management: (1) sources of money, (2) what you can do with money, and (3) money-management principles that can make you rich. Now, let's go "back to the future"! Remember the good feeling you had when you received your check for $100,000? Recall that feeling again when you are depositing your first paycheck. Remember this simple secret for accumulating wealth: Part of all I earn is mine to keep. You truly have it within your power to "go for the gold."

In addition to developing a written outline for your use, consider using presentation aids to add structure and clarity to your major ideas. Developing simple visual reinforcers of your key ideas can help your audience retain essential points.

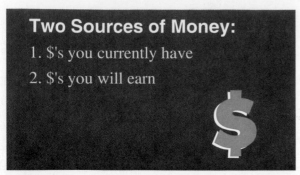

Two Sources of Money:

1. $'s you currently have
2. $'s you will earn

FIGURE 2.2

Presentation graphic for the first major idea in your speech

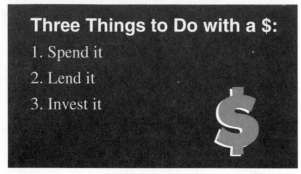

Three Things to Do with a $:

1. Spend it
2. Lend it
3. Invest it

FIGURE 2.3

Presentation graphic for the second major idea in your speech

How to Get Rich:

1. Use the "magic" of compound interest
2. Search for the best rate of return

FIGURE 2.4

Presentation graphic for the third major idea in your speech

In Chapter 14 we offer tips for designing computer graphics using such popular software as PowerPoint. For example, in the outline we just presented, the first major idea could be summarized on a visual aid such as Figure 2.2.

The second major idea in our speech example could look like Figure 2.3.

The third major idea could be reinforced with a visual such as Figure 2.4.

For all the steps we have discussed so far, your success as a speaker will ultimately be determined by your audience. That is why throughout the text we refer you to the audience-centered speechmaking model presented in this chapter.

Once you are comfortable with the structure of your talk and you have developed your visual aids, you are ready to rehearse.

Rehearse Your Speech

Remember this joke? One man asks another, "How do you get to Carnegie Hall?" The answer: "Practice, man, practice." The joke may be older than Carnegie Hall itself, but it is still good advice to all beginners, including novice speakers. A speech is a performance. As with any stage presentation, be it music, dance, or theater, you need to rehearse. A sage once said, "The best rule for talking is the one carpenters use: Measure twice, saw once." Rehearsing your speech is a way to measure your message so that you get it right when you present it to your audience.

The best way to practice is to rehearse your speech aloud, standing just as you will when you deliver it to your audience. As you rehearse, try to be comfortable with the way you phrase your ideas, but don't try to memorize your talk. In fact, if you have rehearsed your speech so many times that you are using exactly the same words every time, you have rehearsed long enough. Rehearse just enough so that you can discuss your ideas and supporting material without leaving out major parts of your speech. It is all right to use notes, but most public-speaking instructors limit the number of notes you may use.

As you practice, seek as much eye contact with your audience as you can. Also be certain to speak loudly enough for all in the room to hear. If you are not sure what to do with your hands when you rehearse, just keep them at your side. Focus on your message, rather than worrying about how to gesture. Avoid jingling change with your hand in your pocket or using other gestures that could distract your audience. If you practice your speech as if you were actually delivering it, you will be a more effective speaker when you talk to the audience.

Besides rehearsing your physical delivery, you also will make decisions about the style of your speech. "Style," said novelist Jonathan Swift, "is proper words in proper places." The words you choose and your arrangement of those words make up the style of your speech. As we have said, some audiences respond to a style that is simple and informal. Others prefer a grand and highly poetic style. To be a good speaker, you must become familiar with the language your listeners are used to hearing and must know how to select the right word or phrase to communicate an idea. Work to develop an ear for how words will sound to your audience.

Deliver Your Speech

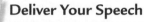

The time has come, and you're ready to present your speech to your audience. Delivery is the final step in the preparation process. Before you walk to the front of the room, look at your listeners to see if the audience assembled is what you were expecting. Are the people out there the same age, race, and gender that you had predicted? Or do you need to make any last-minute changes in your message to adjust to a different distribution?

When you are introduced, walk calmly and confidently to the front of the room, establish eye contact with your audience, smile naturally, and deliver your attention-catching opening sentence. Concentrate on your message and your audience. Deliver your speech in a conversational style, and try to establish rapport with your listeners. Deliver your speech just as you rehearsed it before your imaginary audience: Maintain eye contact, speak loudly enough to be heard, and use some natural variation in pitch. Finally, remember the advice of columnist Ann Landers: "Be sincere, be brief, and be seated."

RECAP

THE BASIC STEPS IN THE SPEECHMAKING PROCESS

1. Consider your audience.

2. Select and narrow your topic.

3. Determine your purpose.

4. Develop your central idea.

5. Generate main ideas.

6. Gather verbal and visual supporting material.

7. Organize your speech.

8. Rehearse your speech.

9. Deliver your speech.

Now that we've seen what effective speakers must be able to do, let's look at a speech that illustrates these capabilities. The following speech by public-speaking student Christopher Therit models many of the attributes of a well-crafted message that we have discussed.[18]

"CAN YOU READ MY MIND?"

Christopher Therit, Millersville University

The dog ran into the barn.

Let me tell you something about myself. ("The dog ran into the barn" is written on the chalkboard.) What's the matter? You look a bit confused. You know nothing more about me now than before I wrote on the board, right? There is something behind those letters other than the chalkboard. Can you see it? Graphology, the study of a person's handwriting.

Did you know that over 1500 firms use graphology in order to hire new employees? I'm going to be telling you things today that will better help you understand yourself, as well as others. If you don't know that you can analyze your own handwriting, you may not know the real you.

I'm going to be answering three specific questions for you today: (1) What is graphology? (2) How does it work? (3) How is it used today?

According to an article entitled "Graphoanalysis—Choosing the 'Write' Person" by Marion Chesney, graphology is defined as "the scientific study of the individual strokes of handwriting to determine the character and personality of the writer." The terms graphoanalysis and graphology are synonymous. "Graphology takes into account over 400 factors, including height and width of letters, the degree the writer has simplified or ornamented those letters, the space between the letters, the slant and slope of the letters, and how connected or disconnected the letters are," says Diane Cole, author of an article called "What Your Handwriting Says about You." Just like your fingerprints, your handwriting is uniquely yours.

So how does graphology work? As I stated before, over 400 factors go into determining a person's personality. Today I will be showing you just a few of those factors.

The first one is slanting . . . the way that our writing slants reveals certain characteristics about us. This is a graphometer. If your writing slants less than 5° to the right or left of the center, you are said to be self-reliant. If your handwriting slants to the left more than 5° of this line, you are said to be defiant, or resistant to an opposing authority or force . . . . Finally, if your writing slants more than 5° right of the center line, you are said to be compliant or cooperative. The farther that your writing slants to the (left or) right of the line, the more (self-reliant or) compliant or cooperative you (are).

Christopher uses the blackboard to catch the attention of his listeners.

He tells his audience why his speech may be of interest to them. This helps establish a motivation for his audience to listen to him.

These three questions are an excellent way to provide a preview of the three key ideas he presents in his speech, and they will help the audience follow the flow of his speech.

Using a definition, especially as quoted from an expert, adds clarity and credibility to his message.

He returns to the second rhetorical question to introduce his second major point, and then tells the audience how this question will be answered.

He uses a visual aid to help make his first subpoint.

SUMMARY

Beginning public speakers sometimes feel nervous just thinking about giving a speech. Don't be surprised if you feel more nervous than you look to others. Remember that almost every speaker experiences some nervousness, and that some anxiety can actually be useful. Specific suggestions to help you manage your apprehension include following the advice for effective speaking; imagining the speech environment when you rehearse; and using relaxation techniques such as visualization, deep breathing, and focusing thoughts away from your fears.

The second is T crosses . . . This is a T-chart. The first *T* indicates enthusiasm, follow-through, and a person who will get the job done. This second one is ambition, but a lot of times the ambition is above potential in this T-cross because it's high above the stem. The next one is procrastination. This is indicated when the cross is to the left of the stem. . . . This next one indicates high goals but (lack) of enthusiasm. This is indicated when the cross is very short and still above the stem. The cup on the cross indicates a shallow purpose. The bent-like stem indicates a short-tempered or tight person or someone who is trying to keep something under control. Finally, the tent-like stem of this *T* indicates a person who is stubborn.

Florence Anthony, a teacher at the New York School for Social Research states, "You can never pin down one trait and say it means the same thing in every handwriting, 100% of the time." Ruby Allen, a handwriting expert, says, "Handwriting reveals the inner workings of man, because the hand is guided by the brain. And when you write, that's the way it is. First you think, then you react. You put on the surface of paper an impression of your conscious and your subconscious. We see you, how you feel, what you think, and what you are. Your handwriting forms a tapestry of your personality."

So how is graphology used today? As I mentioned earlier, over 1500 firms use it to hire their new employees. Imagine going for a job interview and being asked to write an essay to be turned in with your résumé, only to have that essay turned over to a graphologist to be read and analyzed. Your acceptance to the position would hinge on your handwriting instead of your résumé. A dermatologist in Hawaii has found graphoanalysis to be beneficial to his practice. He found that emotions are responsible for more than 50% of skin ailments.

As you can see, many professional people use graphology to help people with their jobs and personal problems. The more you know about yourself, the more self-confident you may be in life. Self-confidence brings the world to you, puts it in your hands, and allows you to mold it in any way you wish.

Being the intelligent audience that you are, I'm sure you now know what graphology is . . . how it works, and how [we use it] today. I want to challenge each and every one of you to focus on your own handwriting and see if you notice some of the elements that I talked about today. Do you see anything about yourself that you've never seen before? Do you?

Here he uses another visual aid to make his second subpoint.

Christopher uses quotations from experts to add credibility and help clarify the point he is making.

He introduces his final point by returning to his third rhetorical question, as well as to the information in the introduction. This helps the audience keep track of the information being presented (because it is so clearly organized) and ties the speech together.

To help draw the audience in, he makes a direct reference to his listeners.

In concluding his speech, he summarizes the three key points he has developed.

To help you prepare for your first speaking assignment, you can follow the steps involved in preparing and presenting a speech, showing how the audience is the central focus at each step. Our audience-centered model of public speaking suggests that throughout the speech crafting and delivery process, the choices you make about designing and presenting your message should be guided by your knowledge of your audience. Based on information about your listeners, you then select and narrow your topic, determine your purpose, develop your central idea, and generate the main ideas. These speech-preparation steps are followed by gathering and organizing your supporting material, including visual aids. With a draft of your speech outline in hand, you are then ready to rehearse and deliver your speech.

A Sharper Focus

CONSIDERING YOUR AUDIENCE

▶ Being audience-centered means considering the background and interests of your listeners at each step in developing and presenting your speech.

▶ Adapt your language and choice of words to the education level of your listeners; depending on your listener's background, don't speak "over their heads" or use such simplistic words and phrases that you insult their intelligence.

CONSIDERING AUDIENCE DIVERSITY

▶ The cultural background of your audience will have a major effect on your listeners' expectations as to how you should organize, support, and present your speech.

▶ Because of the wide cultural variety in most communities and on most college campuses in the United States, you need not travel to an international destination to speak to people with differing cultural backgrounds.

CRITICAL THINKING QUESTIONS

1. Mike Roberts, president of his fraternity, is preparing to address the university academic council to persuade them to support establishment of a Greek housing zone on campus. This is his first major task as president, and he is understandably nervous about his responsibility. What advice would you give to help him manage his nervousness?

2. Jason Reed has just received his assignment for his first speech in his public-speaking class. What key skills does he need to master to become a competent public speaker?

3. Shara Yobonski is preparing to address the city council in an effort to tell them about the Food for Friendship program she has organized in her neighborhood. What steps should she follow to prepare and deliver an effective speech?

ETHICAL QUESTIONS

1. A friend of yours took public speaking last year and still has a file of speech outlines. Even though you will give the speech yourself, is it ethical to use one of her outlines as a basis for your speech? Explain.

2. Your first assignment is to give a speech about something interesting that has happened to you. You have decided to talk about the joys and hassles of a train trip you took last year. Your sister recently returned from a cross-country train trip and had several interesting tales to tell. Would it be ethical to tell one of her experiences as if it had happened to you? Why or why not?

3. You read an article in *Reader's Digest* that could serve as the basis for a great speech about the ravages of AIDS. Would it be ethical to paraphrase the article, using most of the same examples and the overall outline as the basis for your speech if you *tell* your listeners that your speech is based on the article?

SUGGESTED ACTIVITIES

1. Describe one informative purpose and one persuasive purpose for each of the following topics:

   Nuclear power plants

   Caffeine

   Public speaking

   Political parties

   Your school

   Terrorism

2. For the following central idea sentences, identify possible major divisions in the speech according to one of these questions: Does the central idea have logical *divisions*? Can you think of several *reasons* the central idea is true? Can you support the central idea with a series of *steps*?

   The conflict in the Middle East has a long history.

   The method of choosing a president in the United States is flawed.

   Any one of several diets could help you lose weight.

   The 70-mile-per-hour speed limit is a bad idea.

   Our national parks need more resources to maintain their beauty.

   The Internet has an interesting history.

   IQ can be measured in several ways.

   There are several ways to ensure a stress-free lifestyle.

3. Identify at least three tips for helping you become a confident speaker. Write a brief paragraph explaining why you think those techniques will be helpful to you.

4. Imagine that your instructor has assigned your first speech, a five-minute speech to inform, and it's due in two weeks. Develop a sample schedule describing deadlines for developing your ideas, researching your topic, writing an outline, and rehearsing your speech.

5. Write a paragraph in which you describe the diverse backgrounds of your classmates in your public-speaking class based on initial impressions and information that has been shared. Although you may not yet have had the opportunity to conduct a more formal analysis of your audience, based on conversations you've had with your colleagues, or comments they've made if they have more formally introduced themselves in a short speech to the class, note similarities and differences among your audience members.

6. As you begin your public-speaking class, note holidays or other dates or celebrations that may be of interest to your audience. Will you be speaking on or near the Mexican holiday Cinco de Mayo, May 5, or the French holiday July 14, Bastille Day? Noting special days on the calendar may give you ideas for speech topics or specific strategies for adapting your message to your listeners.

7. Complete the Personal Report of Public Speaking Anxiety (PRPSA) to assess your level of communication apprehension.

DIRECTIONS: This instrument is composed of thirty-four statements concerning feelings about communicating with other people. Indicate the degree to which the statements apply to you by marking whether you (1) strongly agree, (2) agree, (3) are undecided, (4) disagree, or (5) strongly disagree with each statement. Work quickly; record your first impression.

_____ 1. While preparing for giving a speech, I feel tense and nervous.

_____ 2. I feel tense when I see the words "speech" and "public speech" on a course outline when studying.

_____ 3. My thoughts become confused and jumbled when I am giving a speech.

_____ 4. Right after giving a speech I feel that I have had a pleasant experience.

_____ 5. I get anxious when I think about a speech coming up.

_____ 6. I have no fear of giving a speech.

_____ 7. Although I am nervous just before starting a speech, I soon settle down after starting and feel calm and comfortable.

_____ 8. I look forward to giving a speech.

_____ 9. When the instructor announces a speaking assignment in class, I can feel myself getting tense.

_____ 10. My hands tremble when I am giving a speech.

_____ 11. I feel relaxed while giving a speech.

_____ 12. I enjoy preparing for a speech.

_____ 13. I am in constant fear of forgetting what I prepared to say.

_____ 14. I get anxious if someone asks me something about my topic that I do not know.

_____ 15. I face the prospect of giving a speech with confidence.

_____ 16. I feel that I am in complete possession of myself while giving a speech.

_____ 17. My mind is clear when giving a speech.

_____ 18. I do not dread giving a speech.

_____ 19. I perspire just before starting a speech.

_____ 20. My heart beats very fast just as I start a speech.

_____ 21. I experience considerable anxiety while sitting in the room just before my speech starts.

_____ 22. Certain parts of my body feel very tense and rigid while giving a speech.

_____ 23. Realizing that only a little time remains in a speech makes me very tense and anxious.

_____ 24. While giving a speech, I know I can control my feelings of tension and stress.

_____ 25. I breathe faster just before starting a speech.

_____ 26. I feel comfortable and relaxed in the hour or so just before giving a speech.

_____ 27. I do poorer on speeches because I am anxious.

_____ 28. I feel anxious when the teacher announces the date of a speaking assignment.

_____ 29. When I make a mistake while giving a speech, I find it hard to concentrate on the parts that follow.

_____ 30. During an important speech I experience a feeling of helplessness building up inside me.

	31.	I have trouble falling asleep the night before a speech.
____	32.	My heart beats very fast while I present a speech.
____	33.	I feel anxious while waiting to give my speech.
____	34.	While giving a speech, I get so nervous I forget facts I really know.

SCORING: To determine your score on the PRPSA, complete the following steps:

Step 1: Add the scores for items 1, 2, 3, 5, 9, 10, 13, 14, 19, 20, 21, 22, 23, 25, 27, 28, 29, 30, 31, 32, 33, and 34.

Step 2: Add the scores for items 4, 6, 7, 8, 11, 12, 15, 16, 17, 18, 24, and 26.

Step 3: Complete the following formula:
PRPSA = 132 – Total from Step 1 + Total from Step 2.

Your score should range between 34 and 170. If your score is below 34 or above 170, you have made a mistake in computing the score.

Interpreting the Personal Report of Public-Speaking Anxiety

For people with scores between 34 and 84 on the PRPSA, very few public-speaking situations would produce anxiety.

Scores between 85 and 92 indicate a moderately low level of anxiety about public speaking. While some public-speaking situations would be likely to arouse anxiety in people with such scores, most situations would not be anxiety arousing.

Scores between 93 and 110 indicate moderate anxiety in most public-speaking situations, but the level of anxiety is not likely to be so severe that the individual won't be able to cope with it and eventually become a successful speaker.

Scores that range between 111 and 119 suggest a moderately high level of anxiety about public speaking. People with such scores will tend to avoid public speaking because it usually arouses a fairly high level of anxiety. While some public-speaking situations may not cause too much of a problem, most will be problematic.

Scores between 120 and 170 indicate a very high level of anxiety about public speaking. People with scores in this range have very high anxiety in most, if not all, public-speaking situations and are likely to go to considerable lengths to avoid them. It is unlikely that they can become successful public speakers unless they overcome or significantly reduce their anxiety.

Source: From *Communication: Apprehension, Avoidance, and Effectiveness,* 5th ed., by Virginia P. Richmond and James C. McCroskey. Copyright © 1998 by Allyn and Bacon. Reprinted by permission.

USING TECHNOLOGY AND MEDIA

If you are not familiar with the electronic databases in your school library, such as LEXIS-NEXIS, make an appointment with a librarian early in the course to begin learning what electronic resources are available to you for doing research. Learning how to use these databases now will help you in developing speeches throughout this course.

Free speech not only lives, it rocks!

OPRAH WINFREY

Ethics and Free Speech

objectives

After studying this chapter you should be able to do the following:

1. Define ethics.

2. Explain the relationship between ethics and free speech.

3. List and explain five criteria for ethical public speaking.

4. Define and discuss how best to avoid plagiarism.

5. List and explain three criteria for ethical listening.

nly a few days after the September 11, 2001, terrorist attacks on the United States, Bill Maher, host of the late-night, intentionally controversial television talk show "Politically Incorrect," declared on the air that the terrorists were not cowards, but that it was cowardly for the U.S. military to launch retaliatory cruise missiles from thousands of miles away. Maher's remarks were sharply and publicly criticized by White House Press Secretary Ari Fleischer, who noted that at times like these, people should "watch what they say and watch what they do."[1] Fleischer was not questioning Maher's *right* to **free speech,** but his *ethics*.

Ethics are the beliefs, values, and moral principles by which we determine what is right or wrong. Ethics serve as criteria for many of the decisions we make in our personal and professional lives, and also for our judgments of others' behavior. The student who refuses to cheat on a test, the employee who will not call in sick to gain an extra day of vacation, and the property owner who does not claim more storm damage than was actually inflicted, have all made choices based on ethics. We read and hear about ethical issues every day in the media. Cloning, surrogate pregnancies, and drug testing have engendered heated ethical debates among medical professionals. Advertising by some attorneys has incensed others, who believe that the current increase in frivolous litigation is tarnishing the profession. And in the political arena, debates about social program reform, fiscal responsibility, and the regulation of business and industry all hinge on ethical issues.

Although you are undoubtedly familiar with many of these issues, you may have given less thought to ethical issues that affect public speaking. These issues center around one main concern: In a country in which free speech is protected by law, the right to speak freely must be balanced by the responsibility to speak ethically. In 1999 the National Communication Association developed a Credo for Communication Ethics, which emphasizes the fundamental nature and far-reaching impact of ethical communication:

> *Ethical communication is fundamental to responsible thinking, decision making, and the development of relationships and communities within and across contexts, cultures, channels, and media. Moreover, ethical communication enhances human worth and dignity by fostering truthfulness, fairness, responsibility, personal integrity, and respect for self and others.* [2]

Ethical considerations should guide every step of the public-speaking process we discussed in Chapter 2. As you determine the goal of your speech, outline your arguments, and select your evidence, think about the beliefs, values, and morals of your audience, as well as your own. Ethical public speaking is inherently audience-centered, always taking into account the needs and rights of the listeners.

Any discussion of ethical public speaking is complicated by the fact that ethics are not hard-and-fast objective rules. Each person's ethical decisions reflect his or her individual values and religious beliefs, as well as cultural norms. Although we cannot, therefore, offer a universal definition of ethical public speaking, we can offer principles and guidelines that reflect the ethics of contemporary North American society and the legal guarantees granted under the U.S. Constitution, including the right to free speech. And as we offer guidelines for ethical speaking and listening, we will include suggestions for acknowledging and encouraging diversity.

free speech
Legally protected speech or speech acts

ethics
The beliefs, values, and moral principles by which people determine what is right or wrong

We will turn first to a discussion of free speech and both its protection and restriction by law and public policy. Then we will discuss the ethical practice of free speech by speakers and listeners, providing guidelines to help you balance your right to free speech with your responsibilities as an audience-centered speaker and as a critical listener. Within this framework, we will define and discuss plagiarism, one of the most troublesome violations of public-speaking ethics. ■

Speaking Freely

In 1791 the **First Amendment** to the U.S. Constitution was written to guarantee that "Congress shall make no law . . . abridging the freedom of speech." In the more than 200 years since then, entities as varied as state legislatures, college and university campuses, the American Civil Liberties Union, and the federal courts have sought to define through both law and public policy the phrase "freedom of speech."

Occasionally, the government has tried to restrict free speech, but these efforts have been countered by strong protests from both elected officials and private citizens. Only a few years after the ratification of the First Amendment, Congress passed the Sedition Act, providing punishment for those who spoke out against the government. When both Jefferson and Madison declared this act unconstitutional, however, it was allowed to lapse. More than 100 years later, during World War I, the U.S. Supreme Court again tried to restrict speech that presented "a clear and present danger" to the nation. This led to the founding, in 1920, of the American Civil Liberties Union, the first organization formed to protect free speech. In 1940 Congress declared it illegal to urge the violent overthrow of the federal government. However, even as they heard the hate speech employed by Hitler and the Nazis, U.S. courts and lawmakers argued that only by *protecting* free speech could the United States protect the rights of minorities and the disenfranchised. For most of the last half of the twentieth century, the U.S. Supreme Court continued to protect rather than limit free speech, upholding it as "the core aspect of democracy."[3]

In 1964 the Supreme Court narrowed the definition of slander, or false speech that harms someone. The Court ruled that before a public official can recover damages for slander, he or she must prove that the slanderous statement was made with "actual malice."[4] Another 1964 boost for free speech occurred not in the courts, but on a university campus. In December of that year, more than 1,000 students at the University of California in Berkeley took over three floors of Sproul Hall to protest the recent arrest of outspoken student activists. The Berkeley Free Speech Movement, as the incident came to be known, permanently changed the political climate of U.S. college campuses. In a written statement on the thirty-year anniversary of the protest, Berkeley's vice chancellor Carol Christ wrote, "Today it is difficult to imagine life in a university where there are serious restrictions on the rights of political advocacy."[5]

The First Amendment protects the rights of protest speakers, such as Patricia Ireland at this abortion rights rally in San Francisco, to speak out about controversial issues.

[Photo: Gary Wagner/Stock Boston]

First Amendment
The amendment to the U.S. Constitution that guarantees free speech; the first one of the ten amendments to the U.S. Constitution known collectively as the Bill of Rights

Emerging from the courtroom after the verdict in her favor in the freedom of speech case against the Texas cattlemen, Winfrey shouted, "Free speech not only lives, it rocks!"

[Photo: L. M. Otero/AP/Wide World Photos]

Further strengthening of free speech protection has occurred in the last two decades, during which the Supreme Court has found "virtually all attempts to restrain speech in advance . . . unconstitutional," regardless of how hateful or disgusting the speech may seem to some.[6] In 1989 the Supreme Court defended the burning of the U.S. flag as a **"speech act"** protected by the First Amendment. In 1997 the Court struck down the highly controversial federal Communications Decency Act of 1996, which had imposed penalties for creating, transmitting, or receiving obscene material on the Internet. The Court ruled that "the interest in encouraging freedom of expression in a democratic society outweighs any theoretical but unproven benefit of censorship."[7]

Perhaps no recent test of free speech has received more publicity than the sensational 1998 lawsuit of four Texas cattlemen against popular talk-show host Oprah Winfrey. In a 1996 televised show on mad cow disease, Winfrey had declared that she would never eat another hamburger. Charging that her statement caused cattle prices to plummet, the cattlemen sued for damages; however, Winfrey's attorneys successfully argued that the case was an important test of free speech. Emerging from the courtroom after the verdict in her favor, Winfrey shouted, "My reaction is that free speech not only lives, it rocks!"[8]

RECAP

HISTORY OF FREE SPEECH IN THE UNITED STATES

1791	First Amendment guarantees that "Congress shall make no law . . . abridging the freedom of speech"
1798	Sedition Act passes
1919	U.S. Supreme Court suggests that speech presenting a "clear and present danger" may be restricted
1920	American Civil Liberties Union is formed
1940	Congress declares it illegal to urge the violent overthrow of the federal government
1964	U.S. Supreme Court restricts definition of slander; Berkeley Free Speech Movement takes place
1989	U.S. Supreme Court defends the burning of the U.S. flag as a "speech act"
1997	U.S. Supreme Court strikes down Communications Decency Act of 1996, in defense of free speech on the Internet
1998	Oprah Winfrey successfully defends her right to speak freely on television
2001	September 11 terrorist attacks spark new debate over the balance between national security and free speech

speech act
A behavior, such as flag burning, that is viewed by law as nonverbal communication and is subject to the same protections and limitations as verbal speech

In the months and years following the terrorist attacks on September 11, 2001, free speech will face new challenges as the United States engages in what has been called "a new, more difficult debate over the balance among national security, free speech, and patriotism."[9]

Speaking Ethically

As the boundaries of free speech expand, the importance of **ethical speech** increases. As we have said, there is no definitive ethical creed for a public speaker. But teachers and practitioners of public speaking generally agree that an ethical speaker is one who has a clear, responsible goal; uses sound evidence and reasoning; is sensitive to and tolerant of differences; is honest; and avoids plagiarism. In the discussion that follows, we offer suggestions for observing these ethical guidelines.

Have a Clear, Responsible Goal

The goal of a public speech should be clear to the audience. For example, if you are trying to convince the audience that your beliefs on abortion are more correct than others', you should say so at some point in your speech. If you keep your true agenda hidden, you violate your listeners' rights. In addition, an ethical goal should be socially responsible. A socially responsible goal is one that gives the listener choices, whereas an irresponsible, unethical goal is either physically or psychologically coercive. The brainwashing and physical torture of POWs during the Vietnam War and of captured U.S. fliers during Operation Desert Storm are examples of unethical coercion. Adolf Hitler's speeches, which incited the German people to hatred and genocide, were also coercive, and so were those of Chinese leader Deng Xiaoping, who tried to intimidate Chinese citizens into revealing the whereabouts of leaders of the unsuccessful 1989 student uprising in Tiananmen Square.

If your overall objective is to inform or persuade, it is probably ethical; if your goal is to coerce or corrupt, it is unethical. But law and ethics do not always agree on this distinction. As we have pointed out, Congress and the U.S. Supreme Court have at times limited speech that incites sedition, violence, and riot, but they have also protected free speech rights "for both the ideas that people cherish and the thoughts they hate."[10] Even those who defend a broad legal right to free speech recognize that they are protecting unethical, as well as ethical, speech. The controversy regarding the public broadcasts of extremist hate groups exemplifies this dilemma. So, too, does the proliferation of hate speech and pornography on the Internet.

Use Sound Evidence and Reasoning

Ethical speakers use critical-thinking skills such as analysis and evaluation to draw conclusions and formulate arguments. Unethical speakers substitute false claims and manipulation of emotion for evidence and logical arguments.

In the early 1950s, Wisconsin senator Joseph McCarthy incited national panic by charging that Communists were infiltrating every avenue of American life. Thousands of people came under suspicion, many losing jobs and careers because of the false

ethical speech
Speech that is responsible, honest, and tolerant

accusations. Never able to substantiate his claims, McCarthy nevertheless succeeded in his witch-hunt by exaggerating and distorting the truth. One United Press reporter noted, "The man just talked in circles. Everything was by inference, allusion, never a concrete statement of fact. Most of it didn't make sense."[11] Although today we recognize the flimsiness of McCarthy's accusations, in his time the man wielded incredible power. Like Hitler, McCarthy knew how to manipulate emotions and fears to produce the results he wanted. It is sometimes tempting to resort to false claims to gain power over others, but it is always unethical to do so.

It can also be tempting simply to bypass sound evidence and reasoning. In our current political environment, both media "sound bites" and presidential debates have come under fire as shallow forums. Former CBS anchor Walter Cronkite has called the presidential debates "part of the unconscionable fraud that our political campaigns have become," because "substance is to be avoided if possible. Image is to be maximized."[12] Although using clever phrases and emphasizing positive images are not in themselves unethical, if they substitute for sound evidence and reasoning, then these tactics can become unethical practices.

One last, but important, requirement for the ethical use of evidence and reasoning is to share with an audience all information that might help them reach a sound decision, including information that may be potentially damaging to your case. Even if you proceed to refute the opposing evidence and arguments, you have fulfilled your ethical responsibility by presenting the perspective of the other side. And you can actually make your own arguments more convincing by anticipating and answering counter-arguments and evidence.

 ## Be Sensitive to and Tolerant of Differences

As we noted in Chapter 2, being audience-centered requires that you become as aware as possible of others' feelings, needs, interests, and backgrounds. Former New Jersey Senator Bill Bradley has described this ethical dimension as "tolerance, curiosity, civility—precisely the qualities we need to allow us to live side by side in mutual respect."[13] Sometimes called **accommodation,** sensitivity to differences does not mean that speakers must abandon their own convictions for those of their audience members. It does mean that speakers should demonstrate a willingness to listen to opposing viewpoints and learn about different beliefs and values. Such willingness not only communicates respect; it can also help a speaker to select a topic, formulate a purpose, and design strategies to motivate an audience.

Your authors are currently involved in an informal educational exchange with a professor from the St. Petersburg Cultural Institute in Russia and recently had a chance to visit the professor and her family in St. Petersburg. In talking with the professor's talented teenage daughter, we inquired as to her plans after she finished her university education. Smiling at us in both amusement and amazement, she replied, "Americans are always planning what they are going to do several years in the future. In Russia, we do not plan beyond two or three weeks. Life is too uncertain here." Having gained this insight into Russian life, we know now that it would raise false hopes to attempt to motivate Russian audiences with promises of benefits far in the future. Our new understanding helps us see that speaking of immediate, deliverable rewards is a more realistic and ethical approach.

A speaker who is sensitive to differences also avoids language that might be interpreted as in any way biased or offensive. Although it may seem fairly simple and com-

accommodation
Sensitivity to the feelings, needs, interests, and backgrounds of other people

monsense to avoid overtly abusive language, it is not so easy to avoid language that discriminates more subtly. In Chapter 12, we will look at some specific words and phrases that can be unintentionally offensive and that ethical speakers should avoid.

Be Honest

Knowingly offering false or misleading information to an audience is an ethical violation. In 2000, Democratic presidential candidate Al Gore was criticized for embroidering his experiences, falsely claiming, among other things, that he and wife Tipper were the model for the couple in the 1970s best-selling novel *Love Story*.[14] In 1999, Toronto Blue Jays manager Tim Johnson was fired after it was revealed that the stories he told to his team about his combat experiences in Vietnam were false. During the war, it turned out, he actually played ball while serving with the Reserves in California.[15] Perhaps most famously, in January 1998, then-President Bill Clinton's finger-wagging declaration that "I did not have sexual relations with that woman—Miss Lewinsky" was a serious breach of ethics that came back to haunt him. Many of the American people were willing to forgive the inappropriate relationship; fewer could forgive the dishonesty.

A seeming exception to the dictum to avoid false information is the use of hypothetical illustrations—illustrations that never actually occurred but that might happen. Many speakers rely on such illustrations to clarify or enhance their speeches. As long as the speaker makes clear to the audience that the illustration is indeed hypothetical—for example, prefacing the illustration with a phrase such as "Imagine that . . ."—such use is ethical.

Honesty also requires that speakers give credit for ideas and information that is not their own. The *Publication Manual of the American Psychological Association* states that "an author does not present the work of another as if it were his or her own work. This can extend to ideas as well as written words."[16] Presenting the words and ideas of others without crediting them is called *plagiarism*. This ethical violation is both serious enough and widespread enough to warrant a separate discussion.

Avoid Plagiarism

Most people are taught from earliest childhood that it is wrong to steal. Yet even those who would never think of stealing money or shoplifting may be tempted to **plagiarize**—to steal ideas. Perhaps you can remember copying a grade-school report directly from the encyclopedia, or maybe you've even purchased or "borrowed" a paper to submit for an assignment in high school or college. These are obvious forms of plagiarism. A less obvious form is **patchwork plagiarism**—lacing a speech with compelling phrases you find in a source that you do not credit. Whether your lapse is intentional or due merely to careless or hasty note taking, the offense is equally serious.

Most colleges impose stiff penalties on students who plagiarize. Plagiarists almost always fail the assignment in question, frequently fail the course, and are sometimes put on academic probation or even expelled. Penalties for plagiarism outside the classroom are severe as well, costing one U.S. senator his bid for the Democratic nomination for president. In August 1987, Delaware Senator Joseph Biden plagiarized the words of former British Labor Party Leader Neil Kinnock, in a speech in Des Moines, Iowa. When the plagiarism was exposed, along with evidence of a previous plagiarism from a speech

plagiarize
Present someone else's words or ideas as though they were one's own

patchwork plagiarism
Failure to give credit for compelling phrases taken from another source

by Robert Kennedy, Biden was forced to withdraw from the presidential race. Publicized evidence of plagiarism also haunted Boston University Dean H. Joachim Maitre, who in 1991 used phrases from a movie critic's essay in a commencement speech without crediting the critic. And more recently, Hastings College (Nebraska) President Richard Hoover announced his retirement amid allegations that he had plagiarized part of a speech from an email forward he had received. Biden, Maitre, and Hoover violated their ethical responsibilities and paid the price for that violation with their reputations and careers.

DO YOUR OWN WORK   The most flagrant cases of plagiarism result from not doing your own work. For example, while you are poking around the library for ideas to use in a speech assignment, you may discover an entire speech or perhaps an article that could easily be made into a speech. However tempting it may be to use this material, and however certain you are that no audience member could possibly have seen it, resist the urge to plagiarize. First, you will be doing yourself a disservice if you do not learn how to compose a speech on your own. After all, you are in college to acquire new skills. In addition, the risk may be much greater than you suspect.

A few years ago one of your authors heard an excellent student speech on the importance of detecting cancer early. The only problem was, she heard the same speech again in the following class period! On finding the "speech"—actually a *Reader's Digest* article that was several years old—both students were certain that they had discovered a surefire shortcut to an *A*. Instead, they failed the assignment, ruined their course grades, and lost your author's trust. The consequences of academic plagiarism can be even more dire, including expulsion in many schools.

Another way speakers sometimes attempt to shortcut the speech preparation task is to ask another person to edit a speech so extensively that it becomes more that other person's work than their own. This is another form of plagiarism, as well as another way of cheating themselves out of the skills they need to develop.

ACKNOWLEDGE YOUR SOURCES   Our admonition to do your own work in no way suggests that you should not research your speeches and then share the results with audience members. In fact, as we have said, an ethical speaker is responsible for doing just that. Furthermore, some information is so widely known that you do not have to acknowledge a source for it. For example, you need not credit a source if you say that the HIV virus must be present for a person to develop full-blown AIDS, or that the Treaty of Versailles was signed on June 28, 1919. This information is widely available in a variety of reference sources. However, if you decide to use any of the following in your speech, then you must give credit to the source:

- Direct quotations, even if they are only brief phrases

- Opinions, assertions, or ideas of others, even if you paraphrase them rather than quote them verbatim

- Statistics

- Any nonoriginal visual materials, including graphs, tables, and pictures

oral citation
The oral presentation of such information about a source as the author, title, and year of publication

To be able to acknowledge your sources, you must first practice careful and systematic note taking. Indicate with quotation marks any phrases or sentences that you photocopy or copy by hand verbatim from a source, and be sure to record the author, title, publisher or Website, publication date, and page numbers for all sources from

Address: http://www.ablongman.com/beebe

▼   Tips for Ethics and Free Speech

Much of the contemporary debate over free and ethical speech takes place on the Internet, ironically making it simultaneously a controversial "speech act" and a channel for discussing the issue.

The following Websites explore and debate issues of free and ethical speech today.

THE SIMON WIESENTHAL CENTER

http://www.wiesenthal.com/

The Simon Wiesenthal Center speaks out against hate speech on the Internet, arguing that free speech should not be limited, but those people and organizations who speak out should be held responsible and accountable for their messages.

THE ETHICS CONNECTION

http://www.scu.edu/SCU/Centers/Ethics/homepage.shtml/

This site from Santa Clara University's Markkula Center for Applied Ethics explores a variety of ethical issues.

THE AMERICAN CIVIL LIBERTIES UNION

http://www.aclu.org/issues/freespeech/hmfs.html

With an emphasis on freedom of speech, this site offers information about instances that the American Civil Liberties Union (ACLU) believes violates free speech.

Some additional sites that address issues of free and ethical speech include the following:

FAIRNESS AND ACCURACY IN REPORTING

http://www.fair.org/

THE FREEDOM FORUM ONLINE

http://www.freedomforum.org/

THE NEWSEUM (INTERACTIVE MUSEUM OF NEWS)

http://www.newseum.org/

ACCURACY IN MEDIA

http://www.aim.org

NCA CREDO FOR COMMUNICATION ETHICS

http://www.natcom.org/conferences/Ethics/ethicsconfcredo99.htm

which you take quotations, ideas, statistics, or visual materials. Additional suggestions for systematic note taking are offered in Chapter 7.

In addition to keeping careful records of your sources, you must also know how to cite your sources for your audience, both orally and in writing. Perhaps you have heard a speaker say, "Quote," while holding up both hands with index and middle fingers curved to indicate quotation marks. This is an artificial and distracting way to cite a source; an **oral citation** can be integrated more smoothly into the speech. For example, you might say, "In a March 2001 online fact sheet entitled 'Facts About Mold,' the New York City Health Department describes *Stachybotrys chartarum* as"—then pause briefly to signal that you are about to begin quoting—"a greenish-black mold that can grow on materials with a high cellulose content—such as dry-wall sheetrock, dropped ceiling tiles, and wood—that become chronically moist or water-damaged."[17] Notice that this example provides the author, title, year, and the fact that the information is available online, sufficient for oral documentation of an online source.

You can also provide a **written citation** for a source. In fact, your public-speaking instructor may ask you to provide a bibliography of sources along with the outline or other written materials he or she requires for each speech. Instructors who require a bibliography will usually specify the format in which they want the citations; if they do not, you can use a style guide such as those published by the MLA (Modern Language Association) or the APA (American Psychological Association), both of which guides are now available online as well as in traditional print format. Here is an example of a written citation in MLA format for the source we cited orally in the preceding paragraph. Notice that the citation provides two dates: first, the date the material was posted online; and second, the date it was accessed by the researcher.

New York City Department of Health. "Facts About Mold." March 2001. 27 June 2001 http://www.ci.nyc.ny.us/html/doh/html/ei/eimold.html.

Additional information about citing sources and preparing a bibliography can be found in Chapter 7.

Perhaps now you are thinking, What about those "gray areas," those times when I am not certain whether information or ideas I am presenting are "common knowledge"? A good rule is this: *When in doubt, document.* You will never be guilty of plagiarism if you document something you didn't need to, but you could be committing plagiarism if you do not document something you really should have.

SPEAKER ETHICS

THE ETHICAL PUBLIC SPEAKER . . .

Has a clear, responsible goal

Uses sound evidence and reasoning

Is sensitive to and tolerant of differences

Is honest

Avoids plagiarism

written citation
The written presentation of such information about a source as the author, title, and year of publication, usually formatted according to a conventional style guide

Listening Ethically

Until now, we have been focusing primarily on the ethical exercise of free speech by the speaker. But audience members also share responsibility for ethical communication. In the fourth century B.C., Aristotle warned, "Let men be on their guard against those who flatter and mislead the multitude...." And contemporary rhetorician Harold Barrett has said that the audience is the "necessary source of correction" for the behavior of a speaker.[18] The following guidelines for ethical listening incorporate what Barrett calls "attributes of the good audience."

Communicate Your Expectations and Feedback

As an audience member, you have the right—even the responsibility—to enter a communication situation with expectations about both the message and how the speaker will deliver it. Know what information and ideas you want to get out of the communication transaction. Expect a coherent, organized, and competently delivered presentation. Communicate your objectives and react to the speaker's message and delivery through appropriate nonverbal and verbal feedback. For example, maintain eye contact with the speaker. Nod in agreement when you support something the speaker says; look puzzled if you do not understand the speaker's point. Turn your head to one side and tilt it slightly forward to communicate that you are having trouble hearing. If a question-and-answer period follows the speech, ask questions you may still have about the speaker's topic or point of view.

Perhaps no public-speaking situation better illustrates the effectiveness of audience feedback than the traditional African-American sermon, during which the congregation's willingness to "finish the preacher's sentence, shout encouragement or warn the preacher that he's wandered off the point...lets a preacher know whether he is misfiring or connecting from the pulpit."[19] Although such outspokenness is not appropriate to many public-speaking settings, the African-American congregation's enthusiastic involvement is a good example of how listener feedback can affect the communication process.

Listeners share responsibility with speakers in maintaining high ethical standards for public speech. If a speaker is spewing messages filled with hatred and bias—or simply hiding or distorting information—don't hesitate to communicate your disapproval by frowning, looking away, or even walking out.

[Photo: John Ficara/Woodfin Camp & Associates]

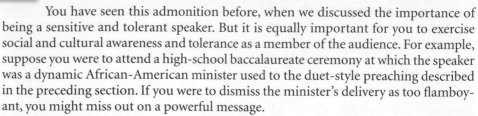

Be Sensitive to and Tolerant of Differences

You have seen this admonition before, when we discussed the importance of being a sensitive and tolerant speaker. But it is equally important for you to exercise social and cultural awareness and tolerance as a member of the audience. For example, suppose you were to attend a high-school baccalaureate ceremony at which the speaker was a dynamic African-American minister used to the duet-style preaching described in the preceding section. If you were to dismiss the minister's delivery as too flamboyant, you might miss out on a powerful message.

Understanding diverse cultural norms can sometimes pose quite a complex ethical-listening challenge. For example, Jesse Jackson has in the past been accused of making dishonest claims in some of his speeches about his background and behavior. He has said that he left the University of Illinois because of racism on the football team, yet former teammates insist that he did not become starting quarterback simply because he was not the strongest player. Jackson has also overstated the poverty he experienced as a child, when in fact he grew up in a fairly comfortable middle-class home. Although many have criticized such exaggeration, at least one communication researcher has defended Jackson, arguing that although his "tall tales" are not necessarily "the truth" in a strictly objective sense, they are part of a valid African-American oral tradition that focuses on the "symbolic import of the story" and in which speakers traditionally exaggerate to enhance the impact of their illustrations.[20]

Be attentive and courteous. Consider diverse cultural norms and audience expectations as part of the context within which you listen to and evaluate the speaker. Making an effort to understand the needs, goals, and interests of both the speaker and other audience members can help you judge how to react appropriately and ethically as a listener.

Listen Critically

Courtesy and tolerance are not the same as approval or agreement. In fact, the necessary check on free speech is the listener who recognizes and refuses to license abusive or dangerous ideas or plans. As University of Chicago professor and ethicist Richard M. Weaver explains, "It is the principle of our society that we can listen to propaganda from all the special interests . . . and do a pretty fair job of sifting the true claims from the false."[21] In other words, it is our job to listen critically.

To listen critically is to hold the speaker to his or her ethical responsibilities. Is the speaker presenting both sides of the issue? Is the speaker disclosing all the information to which he or she has access, or is the speaker trying to hide something? Is the speaker being honest about the purpose of the speech? As already noted, you can communicate to the speaker through nonverbal feedback during a speech. Frowning, shaking your head, or looking away can signal to the speaker that you do not approve of his or her message. If there is a chance that you may have misunderstood the speaker, take advantage of opportunities after the speech to question him or her. Read more about the topic for yourself, to check the speaker's facts. And if you conclude that the speaker's message or motives are indeed unethical, discuss your opinion with others, and seek out or create a forum through which you can express your dissent. Although you can and should refuse to sanction unethical messages and tactics, seek ways to question and refute ideas and arguments without being discourteous or resorting to unethical tactics yourself. In Chapter 4 we will provide further discussion of strategies for skillful listening.

THE ETHICAL LISTENER . . .

Communicates expectations and feedback

Is sensitive to and tolerant of differences

Listens critically

SUMMARY

Ethical speaking and listening are very important in a society that protects free speech. Although Congress and the courts have occasionally limited free speech by law and policy, more often they have protected and broadened its application. The right to free speech has also been upheld in this country by such organizations as the American Civil Liberties Union and by colleges and universities.

Speakers who exercise their right to free speech are responsible for tempering what they say by applying ethics, or moral principles and values. Although there is no definitive standard of ethics, most people agree that public speakers must be responsible, honest, and tolerant in order to be ethical.

Plagiarism is one of the most common violations of speech ethics. You can usually avoid plagiarism by understanding what it is, doing your own work, and acknowledging the sources for any quotations, ideas, statistics, or visual materials you use in a speech.

Ethical listening is guided by the following: Ethical listeners should provide feedback; be sensitive to and tolerant of differences; and listen critically, refusing to sanction unethical messages and tactics.

being audience-centered

A Sharper Focus

CONSIDERING YOUR AUDIENCE

▶ As you determine the goal of your speech, outline your arguments, and select your evidence, think about the beliefs, values, and morals of your audience, as well as your own.

▶ Ethical public speaking is inherently audience-centered, always taking into account the needs and rights of the listeners.

▶ The goal of a speech should be clear to the audience. If you keep your true agenda hidden, you violate your listeners' rights.

▶ A socially responsible goal for a speech is one that gives the listener choices, whereas an irresponsible, unethical goal is either physically or psychologically coercive.

▶ An important requirement for the ethical use of evidence and reasoning is to share with an audience all information that might help them reach a sound decision, including information that may be potentially damaging to your case.

▶ Cite your sources for your audience, both orally and in writing.

CONSIDERING AUDIENCE DIVERSITY

▶ Accommodation, or sensitivity to differences, means that speakers should demonstrate a willingness to listen to opposing viewpoints and learn about different beliefs and values.

▶ A speaker who is sensitive to differences avoids language that might be interpreted as in any way biased or offensive.

▶ The African-American congregation's enthusiastic involvement in a sermon is a good example of how listener feedback can affect the communication process.

CRITICAL THINKING QUESTIONS

1. Explain how ethics serve as a balance to free speech.

2. Why do you think the U.S. Supreme Court has historically considered flag burning and pornography to be "free speech acts"?

3. The following passage comes from a book entitled *Abraham Lincoln, Public Speaker,* by Waldo W. Braden:

   The Second Inaugural Address, sometimes called Lincoln's Sermon on the Mount, was a concise, tightly constructed composition that did not waste words on ceremonial niceties or superficial sentiment. The shortest Presidential inaugural address up to that time, it was only 700 words long, compared to 3,700 words for the First, and required from 5 to 7 minutes to deliver.[22]

   Now determine which of the following statements should be credited to Braden if you were to use them in a speech:

   Lincoln's second inaugural is sometimes called Lincoln's Sermon on the Mount.

   Because he was elected and sworn in for two terms as president, Abraham Lincoln prepared and delivered two inaugural addresses.

   Lincoln's second inaugural was 700 words and 5 to 7 minutes long.

ETHICAL QUESTIONS

1. There is evidence that Franklin D. Roosevelt's long-time aide Louis Howe actually wrote the famous line from Roosevelt's first inaugural address: "The only thing we have to fear is fear itself." More recently, it has been openly acknowledged that George Bush's widely praised speech to Congress and the nation on Thursday, September 20, 2001, "was a collaboration by administration wordsmiths."[23]

2. An aide assigned to work with speakers and speeches during both the 1996 and 2000 Republican National Conventions compared the relative freedom allowed speakers at the 2000 convention with the censorship of the 1996 convention speeches. Speeches at the 1996 convention "were diligently reviewed and monitored by convention organizers, who insisted that speakers promise to stick to their script before allowing them to go on."[24] Is such censorship a violation of the speakers' freedom of speech?

SUGGESTED ACTIVITIES

Photocopy or clip any articles you discover during your public speaking that discuss and/or censure the ethics of public speakers. Determine in each case which of the ethical principles discussed in this chapter were violated.

USING TECHNOLOGY AND MEDIA

Watch and take notes on at least five prime-time television commercials. Do you think these commercials are ethical? Why or why not? If not, what are your rights and responsibilities as an ethical listener/consumer?

Learn how to listen and you will prosper—
even from those who talk badly.

PLUTARCH

Listening

objectives

After studying this chapter you should be able to do the following:

1. Identify the stages in the listening process.

2. List and describe five barriers to effective listening.

3. Discuss strategies to become a better listener.

4. Identify strategies for improving your note-taking skills.

5. Discuss the relationship between listening and critical thinking.

6. Use criteria for evaluating speeches.

Are you a good listener? Considerable evidence suggests that your listening skills could be improved. Within twenty-four hours after listening to a lecture or speech, you will recall only about 50 percent of the message. Forty-eight hours later, you are above average if you remember more than 25 percent of the message. (And in a recent survey of adult listeners, only 15 percent reported that they were above-average listeners.)

A psychology professor had dedicated his life to teaching and worked hard to prepare interesting lectures, yet he found his students sitting through his talks with glassy-eyed expressions.[1] To learn what was wrong, and also find out what was on his students' minds if they were not focusing on psychology, he would, without warning, fire a blank from a gun and then ask his students to record their thoughts at the instant they heard the shot. Here is what he found:

20 percent were pursuing erotic thoughts or sexual fantasies.

20 percent were reminiscing about something (they weren't sure what they were thinking about).

20 percent were worrying about something or thinking about lunch.

8 percent were pursuing religious thoughts.

20 percent were reportedly listening.

12 percent were able to recall what the professor was talking about when the gun fired.

You hear more than 1 billion words each year. Yet how much information do you retain? In this chapter, we are going to focus on improving your listening skills. If you apply the principles and suggestions we offer, we believe you will become not only a better listener but also a better public speaker. In addition, improving your listening skills will strengthen your ability to think critically and evaluate what you hear, and also enhance your one-on-one interpersonal listening. In this chapter, we will discuss how people listen and identify barriers and pitfalls that keep both speakers and audiences from listening effectively. We will also make some suggestions for improving your listening and note-taking skills. Finally, we will discuss how you can enhance your ability to listen critically and evaluate speeches.

Barriers to Effective Listening

Listening barriers are created when we fail to select, attend to, understand a message, or remember what was said. To **select** a sound is to single out a message from several competing messages. A listener has many competing messages to sort through, including personal thoughts. Your job as a public speaker is to develop a message that motivates your listeners for focus on *your* message.

The sequel to selecting is attending. To **attend** to a sound is to focus on it. For most people, the average attention span while listening to someone talk is about 8 seconds.[2] One of your key challenges as a public speaker is to capture and hold the attention of your audience. Your choice of supporting material is often the key to gaining and maintaining attention; we'll talk much more about strategies for gathering and using supporting material in the chapters ahead.

select
Single out a message from several competing messages

attend
Select incoming information for further processing

Boiled down to its essence, communication is the process of making sense out of the world and sharing that sense with others.[3] Understanding is the process of making sense out of our experiences. To **understand** something, people assign meaning to the stimuli that come their way. Although no single theory explains how people make sense of words, we do know that you understand what you hear by relating it to something you have already seen or heard. As a speaker, your job is to facilitate listener understanding by making sure you clearly explain your ideas in terms and images to which your listeners can relate. Again, the challenge of being understood comes back to a focus on the audience.

The speaker and the audience need to work together to overcome listening distractions like the noise of a large crowd. The listener can force himself or herself to focus on the speaker's message. The speaker can provide occasional wake-up messages to keep the listeners' attention.

[Photo: Najlah Feany/Stock Boston].

The final stage in the listening process is remembering. To **remember** is to recall ideas and information. Most listening experts believe that the main way to determine if listening has occurred is to determine what listeners remember. Your geography professor determines how well you understand geography by testing you on the content of his or her lecture. But intentionally or not, the professor is testing your listening skill as well as your knowledge of geography.

Your goal as a public speaker is to develop and deliver a speech that audience members will listen and respond to. The more you know about potential obstacles that keep your listeners from listening, the better able you will be to develop messages that hold their interest. Let's look at specific barriers that keep listeners from selecting, attending to, understanding, and remembering a message; we'll also suggest ways in which you, as both speaker and audience member, can overcome these barriers.

Information Overload

We all spend a large part of each day listening. That's good news and bad news. The good news is that because we listen a lot, we have the potential to become very effective listeners. The bad news is that instead of getting better at it, we often get tired of listening because we hear so much information that we "tune out."

As a public speaker, you can keep your audience from tuning out by delivering a message that is clear and easy to understand. Using interesting and vivid supporting material is another key to keeping your listeners listening. Finally, as mentioned earlier, you must build redundancy into your message so that if listeners miss an idea the first time you present it, perhaps they will catch it during your concluding remarks. Remember that listening is hard work. Decide what is important in a speech and focus on that.

Personal Concerns

You are sitting in your African history class on a Friday afternoon. It's a beautiful day. You slump into your seat, open your notebook, and prepare to take notes on the lecture. As the professor talks about an upcoming assignment, you begin to think

understand
Assign meaning to the stimuli to which you attend

remember
Recall ideas and information

about how you are going to spend your Saturday. One thought leads to another as you mentally plan your weekend. Suddenly you hear your professor say, "For Monday's test, you will be expected to know the principles I've just reviewed." What principles? What test? Because you were present in class, you heard the professor's lecture, but you're not sure what was said.

Your own thoughts are among the biggest competitors for your attention when you are a member of an audience. Most of us would rather listen to our own inner speech than to the message of a public speaker. As the psychology professor with the gun found, sex, lunch, worries, and daydreams are major distractions for the majority of listeners.

To counteract this problem, as a speaker, you can focus on maintaining your audience's attention, using occasional "wake-up" messages such as "Now listen carefully, because this will affect your future grade (or family or employment)." As a listener, you can learn to recognize when your own agenda is keeping you from listening, then force yourself to focus on the speaker's message. Later in this chapter, we will offer specific suggestions for what to do when you find your attention flagging.

Outside Distractions

While sitting in class, you notice that a fluorescent light is flickering overhead. Two classmates behind you are swapping stories about their favorite soap opera plots. Out the window you see a varsity hero struggling to break into his car to retrieve the keys he left in the ignition. As your history professor drones on about the Bay of Pigs invasion, you find it difficult to focus on his lecture. Most of us don't listen well when physical distractions are competing with the speaker.

When you are the speaker, try to control the physical arrangements of the speaking situation before you begin your speech. Do the best you can to reduce or eliminate distractions (close windows and window shades to limit sight and sound in the room in which you are speaking; turn off blinking fluorescent lights if you can; try to discourage whispering in the audience). Try to empathize with your listeners. Check out the room ahead of time, sit where your audience will be seated, and look for possible distractions.

As a listener, you also need to do your best to control the listening situation. If you must, move to another seat. If the speaker has failed to monitor the listening environment, you may need to close the blinds, turn up the heat, turn off the lights, close the door, or do whatever is necessary to minimize distractions.

Prejudice

Your buddy is a staunch Democrat. He rarely credits a Republican with any useful ideas. So it's not surprising that when the Republican governor from your state makes a major televised speech outlining suggestions for improving the state's sagging economy, your friend finds the presentation ludicrous. As the speech is broadcast, your buddy constantly argues against each suggestion, mumbling something about Republicans, business interests, and robbing the poor. The next day he is surprised to see editorials in the press praising the governor's speech. "Did they hear the same speech I did?" your friend wonders. Yes, they heard the same speech, but they listened differently. When you prejudge a message, your ability to understand it decreases.

Another way to prejudge a speech is to decide that the topic has little value for you before you even hear the message. Most of us at one time or another have not given our full attention to a speech because we decided beforehand that it was going to bore us.

Sometimes we make snap judgments about a speaker based on his or her appearance, and then fail to listen because we dismissed his or her ideas in advance as inconsequential or irrelevant. Female speakers often complain that males in the audience do not listen as attentively as they would to another male; members of ethnic and racial minorities may feel slighted in a similar way.

On the flip side, some people too readily accept what someone says just because they like the way the person looks, sounds, or dresses. For example, Tex believes that anyone with a Texas drawl must be an honest person. Such positive prejudices can also inhibit your ability to listen accurately to a message.

What can you do as a public speaker to counteract this sort of **prejudice?** The most effective strategy is to use your opening statements to grab the audience's attention. Focus on your particular listeners' interests, needs, hopes, and wishes. When addressing an audience that may be critical or hostile toward your message, use arguments and evidence that your listeners will find credible. If you think audience members are likely to disagree with you, strong emotional appeals will be less successful than careful language, sound reasoning, and convincing evidence. As a listener, you need to guard against becoming so critical of a message that you don't listen to it or so impressed that you decide *too quickly* that the speaker is trustworthy.

Wasting Speech Rate and Thought Rate Differences

Ralph Nichols, a pioneer in listening research and training, has identified a listening problem that centers on the way you process the words you hear.[4] Most people talk at a rate of 125 words a minute. But you have the ability to listen to up to 700 words a minute. Some studies suggest that you may be able to listen to 1,200 words a minute. Regardless of the exact numbers, you have the ability to process words much faster than you generally need to. The problem is that the difference gives you time to ignore a speaker periodically. Eventually, you stop listening. Your "extra" time allows you to daydream and drift from the message.

Nichols suggests that the different rates of speech and thought need not be a listening liability. Instead of drifting away from the speech, you can enhance your listening effectiveness by mentally summarizing what the speaker is saying from time to time.

As a speaker, you need to be aware of your listeners' tendency to stop paying attention. If they can process your message much faster than you can say it, you need to build in message redundancy, be well organized, and make your major ideas clear. Just talking faster won't do much good. Even if you could speak as fast as 200 words a minute, your listeners would still want to go about four times faster than that. We offer several additional suggestions for developing a clear message in Chapter 15, where we discuss approaches to informative speaking.

Receiver Apprehension

You already know about speaker apprehension or the fear of *speaking* to others, but did you know that some people may be fearful of *listening* to information?

prejudice
Prejudging a message; the process of forming preconceived opinions, attitudes, and beliefs about a person, place, or thing.

Barrier	Listener's Tasks	Speaker's Tasks
Information overload	• Concentrate harder on the message; identify the most important parts of the message.	• Develop a message that is clear and easy to understand. Use interesting supporting material. Build in redundancy.
Personal concerns	• Focus on the speaker's message rather than on your own self-talk.	• Use attention-holding strategies and "wake-up" messages.
Outside distractions	• Aggressively attempt to control the listening environment.	• Monitor the physical arrangements before you begin your speech. Take action by doing such things as closing the shades if there are distractions outside, or turning up the air-conditioner if it's too warm.
Prejudice	• Focus on the message, not the messenger.	• Use strong opening statements that focus on listeners' interests.
Wasting speech rate and thought rate differences	• Mentally summarize the speaker's message while you listen.	• Build in redundancy. Be well organized and use strategies to maintain your listeners' attention throughout your speech.
Receiver apprehension	• Make an audio recording of the speaker, mentally summarize the message, and take well-organized notes.	• Provide a clear preview statement of your major ideas, use appropriate internal summaries, summarize major ideas at the end of your message, and use appropriate reinforcing presentation aids during your talk.

Researchers have discovered a listening barrier called receiver apprehension. **Receiver apprehension** is fear of misunderstanding or misinterpreting, or not being able to adjust psychologically to, messages spoken by others.[5] Some people are just uncomfortable or nervous about hearing new information; their major worry is that they won't be able to understand the message. In some cases, their worry about not being able to understand a message is the primary barrier that keeps them from comprehending accurately. If you are one of those people who are nervous about being in a listening situation, you may have difficulty understanding all you hear. Your anxiety about listening creates "noise" that may interfere with how much information you comprehend. To find out if this listening barrier applies to you, take the short Receiver Anxiety Scale included at the end of this chapter.

If you experience receiver apprehension, you will have to work harder to comprehend the information presented by others. Using a tape recorder to record a lecture may help you feel more comfortable and less anxious about trying to remember each point made by the speaker.[6] Another strategy to overcome this barrier is to summarize mentally what you hear a speaker saying during a speech. Taking accurate notes can also be an active strategy that helps you feel more comfortable about being a listener.

As a speaker, be mindful that some listeners may be anxious about understanding your message. You can help people with receiver apprehension by being more redundant. Offer clear preview statements that give an overview of your main ideas. Include appropriate internal summaries while you're making a transition from one point to the next. Summarize major ideas at the end of your talk. Using presentation aids to summarize key ideas—such as listing major ideas on an overhead transparency, PowerPoint slide, chalkboard, or flipchart—can also help increase comprehension and decrease receiver apprehension.

Receiver apprehension
The fear of misunderstanding or misinterpreting the spoken messages of others

Becoming a Better Listener

Now that we have examined barriers to effective listening, we will offer some additional suggestions for improving your listening skill.

Adapt to the Speaker's Delivery

Good listeners focus on a speaker's message, not on his or her delivery style. To be a good listener, you must adapt to the particular idiosyncrasies some speakers have. You may have to ignore or overlook a speaker's tendency to mumble, speak in a monotone, or fail to make eye contact. Perhaps more difficult still, you may even have to forgive a speaker's lack of clarity or coherence. Rather than mentally criticizing an unpolished speaker, you may need to be sympathetic and try harder to concentrate on the message. Good listeners focus on the message, not the messenger.

Poor speakers are not the only challenge to good listening. You also need to guard against glib, well-polished speakers. Just because a speaker may have an attractive style of delivery does not necessarily mean that his or her message is credible. Don't let a smooth-talking salesperson convince you to buy something without carefully considering the content of his or her message.

Listen with Your Eyes as Well as Your Ears

Even though we have cautioned you against letting a speaker's style of delivery distract you, don't totally ignore a speaker's body language. Nonverbal clues play a major role in communicating a message. One expert has estimated that as much as 93 percent of the emotional content of a speech is conveyed by nonverbal clues.[7] Even though this statistic does not apply in every situation, emotion is primarily communicated by unspoken messages. For example, facial expressions help identify the emotions being communicated; a speaker's posture and gestures can reinforce the intensity of the emotion.[8] If you have trouble understanding a speaker, either because he or she speaks too softly or because he or she speaks in an unfamiliar dialect, get close enough so that you can see the speaker's mouth. A good view can increase your level of attention and improve your understanding.

Monitor Your Emotional Reaction to a Message

Heightened emotions can affect your ability to understand a message. If you become angered at a word or phrase a speaker uses, your listening comprehension decreases. Because of differing cultural backgrounds, religious convictions, and political views, listeners may become emotionally aroused by certain words. Words that connote negative opinions about a person's ethnic origin, nationality, or religious views can trigger strong emotions. Cursing and obscene language are red flags for some listeners.

Yin Ping is an Asian American who has distinguished himself as a champion debater on the college debate team. One sly opposing team member sought to distract him by quoting a bigoted statement that disparaged Asian Americans for "taking over the country." It was tempting for Yin Ping to respond emotionally to the insult, but he kept his wits, refuted the argument, and went on to win the debate. When someone uses a word or phrase you find offensive, you need to overcome your repugnance and continue to listen. Don't let a speaker's language close down your mind.

How can you keep your emotions in check when you hear something that sets you off? First, recognize when your emotional state is affecting your rational thoughts. Second, use the skill of self-talk to calm yourself down. Say to yourself, "I'm not going to let this anger get in the way of listening and understanding." You can also focus on your breathing for a moment to calm down.

Avoid Jumping to Conclusions

"Not another speech about religion," you groan to yourself as your classmate, Frank Fuller, a divinity student, gets up to speak. "He's always preaching to us." As Fuller begins his slide lecture, you slump down in your seat, prepared to be bored and bothered. Sure enough, his opening line is "The Bible: It's not what you think!" But about halfway through the speech, you start listening to Fuller and realize that he is presenting some fascinating historical evidence connected with Noah's Ark. He's not trying to convert you; he's just describing some of the archaeological evidence related to the Bible. At the end of the speech, your classmates give him a hearty round of applause. Now you're sorry you missed the first part of the speech.

Don't jump to conclusions prematurely. Give a speaker time to develop and support his or her main point before you decide whether you agree or disagree or think the message has any value. As we've already noted, if you mentally criticize a speaker's style or message, your listening efficiency will decline.

Be a Selfish Listener

Although this suggestion may sound crass, being a selfish listener can help you maintain your powers of concentration. If you find your attention waning, ask yourself questions such as "What's in it for me?" and "How can I use information from this talk?" Granted, you will find more useful information in some presentations than others, but be alert to the possibility in all speeches. Find ways to benefit from the information you are listening to, and try to connect it with your own experiences and needs.

Listen for Major Ideas

In a classic study, Ralph Nichols asked both good and poor listeners what their listening strategies were.[9] The poor listeners indicated that they listened for facts, such as names and dates. The good listeners reported that they listened for major ideas and principles. Facts are useful only when you can connect them to a principle or concept. In speeches, facts as well as examples are used primarily to support major ideas. Try to summarize mentally the major idea that the specific facts support.

If you had been present on that brisk March morning in 1933 to hear Franklin Delano Roosevelt deliver his first inaugural address, you would have heard him introduce his key idea in the fourth sentence of the speech: "This great Nation will endure as it has endured, will revive and will prosper. So, first of all, let me assert my firm belief that the only thing we have to fear is fear itself." A good listener would recognize this immediately as the core of the speech.

How can you tell what the major ideas in a speech are? A speaker who is well organized or familiar with good speaking techniques will offer a preview of the major ideas early in the speech. If no preview is provided, listen for the speaker to enumerate major points: "My first point is to talk about the history of Jackson County." Transitional phrases and a speaker's internal summaries are other clues that can help you identify the major points. If your speaker provides few overt indicators, you may have to discover them on your own. In that event, mentally summarize the ideas that are most useful to you. As suggested earlier, be a selfish listener. Treat a disorganized speech as a river with gold in the sands. Take your mental mining pan and search for the meaningful nuggets.

Identify Your Listening Goal

If you are a typical student, you spend over 80 percent of your day involved in communication-related activities.[10] You spend about 9 percent of your communication time writing, 16 percent reading, 30 percent speaking, and at least 45 percent listening (see Figure 4.1). You listen a lot. Your challenge is to stay on course and keep your listening focused.

One way to stay focused is to determine your listening purpose. There are at least four major listening goals: listening for pleasure, empathy, evaluation, and information. Being conscious of your listening goal can help you listen more effectively. If, for example, your listening goal is simply to enjoy what you hear, you need not listen at the same intensity as when you are trying to remember what you are hearing.

LISTENING FOR PLEASURE   You listen to some things just for the fun of it. You might watch TV, listen to music, go to a movie, or chitchat with a friend. You won't be tested on *Seinfeld* reruns. Nor will you be asked to remember every joke in David Letterman's comedy monologue. So, when listening for pleasure, just enjoy what you hear. You can, however, observe how effective speakers or entertainers gain and maintain attention to keep you interested in their messages.

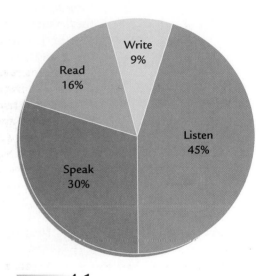

FIGURE 4.1

What You Do With Your Communication Time

LISTENING TO EMPATHIZE   To have empathy means you attempt to feel what the speaker is feeling. Usually, empathic listening occurs in one-on-one listening situations with a good friend. Sometimes, in your job, you may need to listen empathically to a client, customer, or co-worker. Listening to empathize requires these essential skills:

1. *Stop.* Stop what you are doing and give your complete attention to the speaker.

2. *Look.* Have eye contact and pay attention to nonverbal cues that reveal emotions.

3. *Listen.* Pay attention to both the details of the message and the major ideas.

4. *Imagine.* Visualize how you would feel if you had experienced what your listening partner had experienced.

5. *Check.* Check your understanding of the message by asking questions to clarify what you heard and by summarizing what you think you heard.

LISTENING TO EVALUATE When you evaluate a message, you are making a judgment about its content. You are interested in whether the information is reliable, true, or useful. When evaluating what you hear, the challenge is to not become so critical of the message that you miss a key point the speaker is making. In such instances, you must be able to juggle two very difficult tasks: You must make judgments as well as understand and recall the information you are hearing. Our point is this: When you are listening to a message and also evaluating it, you have to work harder than at other times to understand the speaker's message. Your biases and judgments act as noise, sometimes causing you to misunderstand the intended meaning of the message.

LISTENING FOR INFORMATION Since elementary school, you have been in listening situations in which someone wanted you to learn something. Keys to listening for information are to listen for the details of a message and to make certain you link the details to major ideas. Poor listeners either listen only for facts and pieces of a message, or they are only interested in the bottom line. By concentrating on both facts and major ideas, while also mentally summarizing the information you hear, you can dramatically increase your ability to remember messages. Also, remember to compare unfamiliar information to ideas and concepts with which you are familiar.

Knowing your listening goal can help you develop an appropriate listening strategy. Be conscious of what you are seeking from a message.

As a speaker, it is also important for you to know your audience's objectives. If you planned to deliver an educational lecture, but it turns out your listeners are there only for pleasure, you will have to make some quick adjustments to meet your audience's needs. Audience-centered speakers consider the listening goals of their audiences.

Practice Listening

Because we've noted that you spend at least 45 percent of your time listening each day, you may wonder why we suggest that you practice listening. Listening skills do not develop automatically. You learn to swim by getting proper instruction; you don't develop your aquatic skills by just jumping in the water and flailing around. Similarly, you learn to listen by practicing the methods we recommend. Researchers believe that poor listeners avoid challenge. For example, they listen to and watch TV situation comedies rather than documentaries or other informative programs. Skill develops as you practice listening to speeches, music, and programs with demanding content.

Become an Active Listener

An active listener is one who remains alert and mentally re-sorts, rephrases, and repeats key information when listening to a speech. As we noted, you can listen to words much faster than a speaker can speak them. Therefore, it's natural that your mind may wander. But you can use the extra time instead to focus on interpreting what the speaker says.

First, use your listening time to *re-sort* disorganized or disjointed ideas. If the speaker is rambling off strings of disorganized ideas, seek ways to rearrange them into a new, more logical pattern. You can also *rephrase* or summarize what the speaker is saying. This mental activity will help you stay alert so you can follow the speaker's flow of ideas. Listen for main ideas, and then put them into your own words. You are more likely to remember your mental paraphrase than the speaker's exact words.

An additional active listening strategy is to look for *"information handles"* provided by the speaker. In the opening few minutes of the speech, an effective speaker should give an overview of the message; listen for this preview. During the speech, listen for the speaker to identify major ideas by using transition phrases or sign posts; sign posts occur when the speaker says, "My first point is . . . . Now, here's my second point" and so on. Finally, concentrate on the conclusion of the speech. Does the speaker clearly summarize the major ideas? Listening for the overall structure of the message as evidenced through preview, transitions, signposts, and summary statements can help you remain actively involved as a listener.

Finally, do more than just rephrase the information as you listen to it. Periodically, *repeat* key points you want to remember. Go back to essential ideas and restate them to yourself. If you follow these steps for active listening, you will find yourself feeling stimulated and engaged instead of tired and bored as you listen to even the dullest of speakers.

RECAP ACTIVE LISTENING

Steps	Definition	Example
Re-sort	Reorganize jumbled or disorganized information.	What the speaker said: "There are several key dates to remember: 1776, 1492, and 1861."
		You re-sort: 1492, 1776, 1861.
Rephrase	Paraphrase the speaker's ideas, rather than trying to remember his or her exact words.	What the speaker said: "If we don't stop the destructive overspending of the defense budget, our nation will very quickly find itself much deeper in debt and unable to meet the many needs of its citizens."
		You rephrase: "We should spend less on defense, or we will have more problems."
Repeat	Periodically, mentally restate key ideas you want to remember.	Repeat your paraphrase five minutes further into the speech.
Look for information hurdles	Pay attention to the speaker's preview, transition phrases, and summary.	What the speaker said: "I'll focus on three areas in my speech. First, what were voting trends in the past? Second, what are voting trends today? And third, what are projections for voting trends in the next national election?"
		You mentally summarize: "What are voting trends in the past, present, and future?"

RECAP THE RICH HERITAGE OF PUBLIC SPEAKING

The Good Listener . . .	The Poor Listener . . .
Adapts to the speaker's delivery	Is easily distracted by the delivery of the speech
Looks for nonverbal clues to aid understanding	Focuses only on the words
Controls emotions	Erupts emotionally when listening
Listens before making a judgment about the value of the content	Jumps to conclusions about the value of the message
Mentally asks, "What's in it for me?"	Does not attempt to relate to the information personally
Listens for major ideas	Listens for isolated facts
Remains focused	Does not mentally summarize
Seeks opportunities to practice listening skills	Avoids listening to difficult information

Improving Your Note-Taking Skills

"What's everyone taking notes for?" wondered Carolyne, scanning the lecture hall during her U.S. history class. "Can't they remember the key points without trying to scribble them in their notebooks?" At the end of the lecture, however, Carolyne found that she was getting confused about the dates and events her professor had mentioned, so she tried to borrow some notes from one of her fellow listeners.

So far in this chapter, we have suggested ways to improve your listening skills. But we also recognize that you will not remember everything you listen to. It is difficult to recall the details of a lengthy speech unless you have taken notes. Coupling improved listening skills with increased skills in taking notes can greatly enhance your ability to retrieve information. Try the following suggestions to improve your note-taking skills.

PREPARE   Come prepared to take notes, even if you're not sure you need to. Bring a pencil or pen and paper to every class, lecture, or meeting.

DETERMINE WHETHER YOU NEED TO TAKE NOTES   After the presentation has started, decide whether you need to take notes. If you receive a handout that summarizes the content of the message, it may be best to pay attention, concentrate on the message, and take very few notes.

MAKE A DECISION ABOUT THE TYPE OF NOTES YOU NEED TO TAKE   If notes seem necessary, decide whether you need to outline the speech, identify facts and principles, jot down key words, or just record major ideas. Some speakers do not follow organized outline patterns, in which case it is tricky to outline the message. If you are going to take an objective test on the material, you may need to note only facts and principles. Noting key words may be enough to help you recall what was said if you are going to prepare a report for someone else to read. Or you may want to write down just major ideas. The type of notes you take will depend on how you intend to use the information you get from the speech.

MAKE YOUR NOTES MEANINGFUL   Beware of taking too many notes; the goal is to remember the message, not to transcribe it. Instead, use the re-sorting and rephrasing techniques we discussed earlier and write down only what will be meaningful to you later.

Leave a blank area in your notes to use as a recall column.[11] A recall column is a blank margin about 2 or 3 inches wide that you leave on either the right- or left-hand side of your notes. Don't fill this column in while you are taking notes. Use it when reviewing your notes to sift through the ideas you have written down and pull out the key material you want to remember. After you have heard the entire message, you may have a better idea of the most significant content you want to recall later.

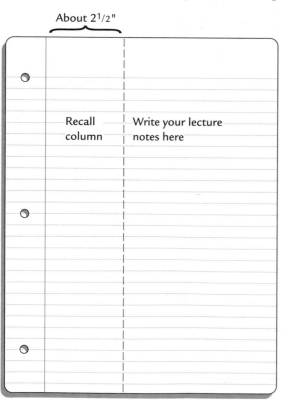

About 2¹/₂"

Recall column | Write your lecture notes here

FIGURE **4.2**

Sample page for note taking

IMPROVING YOUR NOTE-TAKING SKILLS

1. Prepare.

2. Determine whether you need to take notes.

3. Make a decision about the type of notes you need to take.

4. Make your notes meaningful.

Listening and Critical Thinking

Effective listening also requires the ability to listen critically. To listen as well as to think critically involves a variety of skills we return to throughout this text. **Critical listening** is the process of listening to evaluate the quality, appropriateness, value, or importance of the information you hear. A skill related to being a critical listener is being a critical thinker. **Critical thinking** is a mental process of making judgments about the conclusions presented by what you see, hear, and read. The goal of a critical listener or critical thinker is to evaluate information to make a choice. Whether you are listening to a political candidate giving a persuasive presentation to get your vote, a radio announcer extolling the virtues of a new herbal weight-loss pill, or someone asking you to invest in a new dot.com technology company, the goal of a critical listener is to assess the quality of the information and validity of the conclusions presented.

Effective critical listeners use not just one skill but also a set of skills that helps them evaluate messages. In your public-speaking class you may well listen to more than 100 speeches during your semester or term. Rather than merely listen to your classmates' speeches as just something you're supposed to do, make an effort to practice being a critical listener. We should emphasize that being a critical listener does not mean you're only looking for what the speaker says that is wrong; we're not suggesting that you listen to a speaker only to rhetorically pounce on the message and messenger at the conclusion of the speech. Listen to identify what the speaker does that is effective, as well as to identify which conclusions don't hold up. Specifically, what does a critical listener do? Consider the following sets of skills.

Separate Facts from Inferences

The ability to separate facts from inferences is one of the most basic critical-thinking and listening skills. **Facts** are based on something that has been proven true by direct observation. For example, it has been directly observed that water boils at 212 degrees Fahrenheit, that the direction of the magnetic north pole can be found by consulting a compass, and that U.S. presidents have been inaugurated on January 20 every four years for several decades. An **inference** is a conclusion based on partial information, or an evaluation that has not been directly observed. You infer that your favorite sports team will win the championship or that it will rain tomorrow. You can also infer, if more Republicans than Democrats are elected to Congress, that the next president might be a Republican. But you can only know this for a *fact* after the presidential election. Facts are in the realm of certainty; inferences are in the realm of probability and

critical listening
The ability to evaluate the reasoning, logic, and quality of information, ideas, and arguments that a person hears.

critical thinking
The mental process of making judgments about the conclusions presented by what you see, hear, and read

facts
Information based on something that has proven to be true by direct observation

inference
A conclusion based on partial information, or an evaluation that has not been directly observed

opinion—where most arguments advanced by public speakers reside. A critical listener knows that when a politician running for office claims, "It's a fact that my opponent is not qualified to be elected," this statement is *not* a fact, but an inference.

evidence
The facts, examples, opinions, and statistics that a speaker uses to support a conclusion.

 ## Evaluate the Quality of Evidence

Evidence consists of the facts, examples, opinions, and statistics that a speaker uses to support a conclusion. Researchers have documented that the key element in swaying a jury is the quality and quantity of the evidence presented to support a case.[12]

Without credible supporting evidence, it would not be wise to agree with the conclusion reached by a speaker.

What should you listen for when trying to decide if the evidence is credible? If, for example, a speaker says, "It's a fact that this herbal weight-loss pill helps people lose weight," as a listener your job is to determine if that statement is, in fact, a fact. As we've just discussed, a fact is something that has been proven with direct observation to be true. The speaker has an obligation to provide evidence to support the statement asserted.

Some speakers support a conclusion with examples. But if the examples aren't typical, or only one or two examples are offered, or other known examples differ from the one the speaker is using, then you should question the conclusion.

Another form of evidence used to convince you is an opinion. Simply stated, an opinion is a quoted comment from someone. The best opinions come from reliable, credible sources. What makes a source credible? A credible source is someone who has the credentials, experience, and skill to make an observation about the topic at hand. Listen for whom a speaker cites when quoting an expert on a subject.

A fourth kind of evidence often used, especially with a skeptical listener, is statistics. A statistic is a number that summarizes other examples. Some of the same kinds of questions that should be raised about other forms of evidence should be raised about statistics: Are the statistics reliable, unbiased, recent, representative, and valid? Here we've introduced you to the importance of *listening* for good evidence. Because evidence is an important element of public speaking, we'll provide more detailed information about (1) how to *use* evidence, when we discuss using supporting material in Chapter 8 and (2) using evidence to persuade, in Chapter 17.

Evaluate the Underlying Logic and Reasoning

An effective critical listener not only listens for the evidence, but also listens for the overall structure of the logic or argument the speaker uses to reach a conclusion. **Logic** is a formal system of rules applied to reach a conclusion. A speaker is logical if he or she offers appropriate evidence to reach a valid, well-reasoned conclusion. For example, when Angela was trying to convince her listeners to take Xetalean as a weight-loss herb because many stores sell this diet product; she did not provide a strong logical framework for her conclusion. Just because Xetalean is readily available does not mean that it's effective and safe.

Reasoning is the process of drawing a conclusion from evidence within the logical framework of the arguments. Can we reasonably conclude that everyone will lose weight by taking the diet simply because it's available in many stores? The evidence does not reasonably support this conclusion. When a speaker is seeking to change your behavior, listen especially carefully to the logic or structure of the arguments presented. Is the speaker trying to convince you to do something because one or two specific examples are offered? Or is the speaker reaching a conclusion based on a fundamental principle such as "All herbal diet medicine will cause you to lose weight?" The critical listener appropriately reviews the logic and reasoning used to reach a conclusion. When we discuss reasoning fallacies in Chapter 17, we will elaborate on different types of reasoning as well as identify several ways speakers misuse logic, reasoning, and evidence.

You might reasonably suspect that a primary goal of a public-speaking class would be to enhance your speaking skill, and you'd be right. But in addition to becoming a better speaker, a study of communication principles and skills should also help you become a better *consumer* of messages. Being a critical listener is an important benefit you will enjoy by learning about how messages are constructed. But is there evidence

logic
A formal system of rules used to reach a conclusion

reasoning
The process of drawing a conclusion from evidence

that learning about critical listening and thinking will be beneficial? A key benefit of taking a public-speaking course is that it improves your critical listening and thinking skills. In fact, researchers found that a student who has completed any communication course such as debate, argumentation, or public speaking, is likely to show improved critical-thinking ability. The introduction to critical-listening and thinking skills presented here is reinforced throughout by discussions of how to become an audience-centered public speaker.

Analyzing and Evaluating Speeches

Your critical-thinking and listening skills will help you evaluate not only the speeches of others but also your own speeches. When you evaluate something, you judge its value and appropriateness. To make a judgment about the value of something, it's important to use criteria for what is and is not effective or appropriate. **Rhetorical criticism** is the process of using a method or standards to evaluate the effectiveness and appropriateness of messages. Rhetorical critics often point to educator and philosopher John Dewey's description of criticism: "Criticism . . . is not fault-finding. It is not pointing out evils to be reformed. It is judgment engaged in discriminating among values. It is talking through as to what is better and worse . . . with some consciousness of why the worse is worse."[13] A critic not only evaluates a message but also helps *illuminate* it.[14] To illuminate is to metaphorically shine a light on the message to help others better interpret it. We'll first suggest criteria for evaluating messages and then offer specific strategies for sharing your evaluations with others.

Criteria for Evaluating Speeches

What makes a speech good? For more than 2000 years, rhetorical scholars have been debating this question. Our purpose here is not to take you through the centuries of dialogue and debate about this issue but to offer some practical ways to help you evaluate your own messages as well as the messages of others. Your public-speaking teacher will probably have an evaluation form that includes many of the same criteria we've included on pages 78 and 79. Underlying the lengthy list of what a good speaker should do are three overarching goals: To be effective, a speaker's message should be understandable to listeners, achieve its intended purpose, and be ethical.[15] These three requirements can translate into criteria for evaluating a speech.

THE MESSAGE SHOULD BE UNDERSTOOD BY THE AUDIENCE   Public speaking is also sometimes called *public communication*. A goal of any communication effort is to develop a common understanding of the message from both the sender's and receiver's perspectives. The words *common* and *communication* resemble one another. If listeners fail to comprehend the speaker's ideas, the speech fails. "A good many people can make a speech," quipped H. V. Prochnow, "but saying something is more difficult." Even more difficult than saying something is saying something a listener understands. In this course you'll learn an array of principles and strategies to help you develop a common understanding between you and your audience. The process of communicating to be understood is anchored first and foremost in considering the needs of your listeners. As you listen to speeches, a fundamental criterion when considering whether the message

rhetorical criticism
The process of using a method or standards to evaluate the effectiveness and appropriateness of messages

is a good one or not, is to determine whether the message was understood by the listener.

THE MESSAGE SHOULD ACHIEVE ITS INTENDED PURPOSE Another way to evaluate a message is to assess whether it achieved its intended goal. When you communicate intentionally with someone, it is for a specific purpose: to achieve a goal or accomplish something. Typical general goals of public speaking are to inform, to persuade, and to entertain. The challenge in using this criterion in evaluating speeches of others is that you may not always know what the true intent of the speaker was. Often the best you can do is try to determine the purpose by being a careful listener.

An effective listener knows how to determine whether or not a speech is effective: It must be understandable, achieve its purpose, and be ethical.

[Photo: Charles Gupton/Stock Boston]

In speeches you develop, it's important to carefully consider your speech goal. As you learned in Chapter 2, we suggest you not only have a general purpose in mind, but also a specific purpose that is audience-centered: it spells out what you want the audience members to be able to do at the end of your speech. If *you* don't know what the purpose of your message is, it's unlikely your listeners will know the goal. Your organization of your message, the examples and illustrations you use, and the words you use, as well as your delivery, are key methods you can employ to gain and maintain attention as well as sometimes motivate listeners to take action.

THE MESSAGE SHOULD BE ETHICAL As we discussed in Chapter 3, a good speaker is an ethical speaker. Ethics are the beliefs, values, and moral principles by which people determine what is right or wrong. An ethical public speaker tells the truth, gives credit for ideas and words where credit is due, and doesn't plagiarize. If a speaker's message is clearly understood by the audience and also gets the reaction the speaker desired, but uses unethical means to achieve the goal, it may be an *effective* message, but not an *appropriate* message.

You will probably speak to audiences with a wide array of cultural backgrounds. Regardless of the cultural tradition of your listeners, your listeners hold an underlying ethical code. Although not every culture has the same precise ethical rules, some generalizations about ethics seem to transcend culture. All religions of the world, for example, have a moral code that provides a framework for how to respect the rights of others. Christians and Jews share the values described in the Ten Commandments. Christians rely on the "Golden Rule," "Do unto others what you would have others do unto you." Buddhists value the admonition, "One should seek for others the happiness one desires for one's self." Hindus, "Do nothing to others that would cause pain if done to you" and Muslims, "No one of you is a believer until he desires for his brother that which he desires for himself" express a similar perspective on considering the needs of others. In essence, these precepts state the value of being audience-centered by considering how others would like to be treated. An ethical public speaker focuses not only on achieving the goal of the message but on doing so while being sensitive and responsive to listeners.

Giving Feedback to Others

With these three criteria in mind—that a message should be understood, achieve its intended purpose, and be ethical—we turn now to the issues of evaluating speeches, providing feedback to others, and responding to others' feedback to improve your own speeches. The Speech Evaluation Form in Figure 4.3 at the end of this discussion reflects our audience-centered model of the speechmaking process. You can fill it in while you listen to a speech or immediately afterward. Focusing on the criteria listed in the form will help you listen critically and effectively. Most likely, your public speaking teacher will invite you and your classmates to provide comments about one another's speeches. You can use this form as a starting point.

When you're invited to critique your classmates, your feedback will be more effective if you keep some general principles in mind. The word *criticism* comes from a Greek word meaning "to judge or discuss." Therefore, as noted earlier, to criticize a speech is to discuss the speech—identifying both strengths and aspects that could be improved. Effective criticism stems from developing a genuine interest in the speaker rather than from seeking to find fault. When given the opportunity to critique your classmates, supplement the evaluations you provide on the form with the following kinds of feedback.

1. BE DESCRIPTIVE.   In a neutral way, describe what you saw the speaker doing. Act as a mirror for the speaker to help him or her become aware of gestures and other nonverbal signals of which he or she may not be aware. (If you are watching a videotape of the speech together, you can help point out behaviors.) Avoid providing a list of only your likes and dislikes; provide descriptive information instead.

EFFECTIVE:	Stan, I noticed that about 50 percent of the time you had direct eye contact with your listeners.
LESS EFFECTIVE:	Your eye contact was lousy.

2. BE SPECIFIC.   When you describe what you see a speaker doing, make sure your descriptions are precise enough to give the speaker a clear image of your perceptions. Saying that the speaker had "poor delivery" doesn't give him or her much information—it's only a general evaluative comment. Be as specific and thoughtful as you can.

EFFECTIVE:	Dawn, your use of color on your overhead transparency helped to keep my attention.
LESS EFFECTIVE:	I liked your visuals.

3. BE POSITIVE.   Begin and end your feedback with positive comments. Some teachers call this approach the "feedback sandwich." First, tell the speaker something he or she did well. This will let the speaker know you're not an enemy who's trying to shoot holes in his or her performance. Then share a suggestion or two that may help the speaker improve the presentation. End your evaluation with another positive comment or restate what you liked best about the presentation. Beginning with negative comments immediately puts the speaker on the defensive and can create so much internal "noise" that he or she stops listening. Starting and ending with positive comments engender less defensiveness.

EFFECTIVE:	Gabe, I thought your opening statistic was very effective in catching my attention. You also maintained direct eye contact when you delivered it. Your overall organizational pattern would have been clearer to me if you had used more signposts and transition statements. Or perhaps you could use a visual aid to summarize the main points. You did a good job of summarizing your three points in your conclusion. I also liked the way you ended your speech by making a reference to your opening statistics.
LESS EFFECTIVE:	I got lost when you were in the body of your speech. I couldn't figure out what your major ideas were. I also didn't know when you made the transition between the introduction and the body of your speech. Your intro and conclusion were good, but the organization of the speech was weak.

4. BE CONSTRUCTIVE.   Give the speaker some suggestions or alternatives for improvement. It's not especially helpful to rattle off a list of things you don't like, without providing some suggestions for improvement. As a student of public speaking, your comments should reflect your growing skill and sophistication in the speech-making process.

EFFECTIVE:	Jerry, I thought your speech had several good statistics and examples that suggest you spent a lot of time in the library researching your speech. I think you could add credibility to your message if you shared your sources with the listener. Your vocal quality was effective, and you had considerable variation in your pitch and tone. At times the speech rate was a little fast for me. A slower rate would help me catch some of the details of your message.
LESS EFFECTIVE:	You spoke too fast. I had no idea whom you were quoting.

5. BE SENSITIVE.   "Own" your feedback by using I-statements rather than you-statements. An I-statement is a way of phrasing your feedback so that it is clear that your comments reflect your personal point of view. "I found my attention drifting during the body of your speech" is an example of an I-statement. A you-statement is a less sensitive way of describing someone's behavior by implying that the other person did something wrong. "You didn't summarize very well in your conclusion" is an example of a you-statement. A better way to make the same point is "I wasn't sure I understood the key ideas you mentioned in your conclusion." Here's another example:

EFFECTIVE:	Mark, I found myself so distracted by your gestures that I had trouble focusing on the message.
LESS EFFECTIVE:	Your gestures were distracting and awkward.

6. BE REALISTIC. Provide usable information. Provide feedback about areas in which the speaker can improve rather than about aspects of the presentation that he or she cannot control. Maybe you have heard this advice: "Never try to teach a pig to sing.

FIGURE 4.3

Speech Evaluation Form

Speaker _____

Evaluator _____

Use the following scale to evaluate elements of the speech:

Outstanding	Good	Average	Fair	Poor
5	4	3	2	1

In addition to entering a number on each blank line, provide written comments to identify strengths and suggest ways to improve the speech.

Audience Orientation

The speaker was audience-centered. _____

The speaker adapted to the listeners. _____

Comments:

Introduction

The introduction caught my attention. _____

The introduction provided an overview of the main ideas. _____

The introduction established the speaker's credibility. _____

The introduction established a motivation to listen. _____

Comments:

Topic Selection

The topic was appropriate for the audience. _____

The topic was appropriate for the occasion. _____

The topic was appropriate for the speaker. _____

The topic was appropriate for the time limits. _____

Comments:

Purpose

The purpose was clear. _____

The purpose was appropriate for the audience. _____

The purpose was achieved. _____

Comments:

continued next page

Speech Evaluation Form   continued

Organization

The speech had an introduction, body, and conclusion. _____

The speaker used transitions and signposts to clarify

the organization. _____

The main ideas were clear to the audience. _____

Comments:

Supporting Material

The supporting material was credible. _____

The supporting information was varied and interesting. _____

The speaker used evidence to support conclusions. _____

The speaker appropriately used stories and illustrations. _____

Comments:

Visual Aids

The visual aids were large enough to be seen clearly. _____

The visual aids were attractive and understandable. _____

The visual aids were introduced at appropriate points

in the speech. _____

Comments:

Delivery

The speaker made appropriate eye contact with the audience. _____

The speaker appropriately varied his or her voice and tone. _____

The speaker used appropriate gestures. _____

The speaker used good posture and effective movement. _____

Comments:

Conclusion

The speaker summarized the key points. _____

The speaker ended the speech in a memorable,

effective way. _____

Comments:

Ethics

The speaker cited sources for information and ideas

appropriately. _____

The speaker presented viewpoints other than his or her own. _____

The speaker clearly stated the true purpose of the speech. _____

Comments:

It wastes your time. It doesn't sound pretty. And it annoys the pig." Saying things such as "You're too short to be seen over the lectern," "Your lisp doesn't lend itself to public speaking," or "You looked nervous" is not constructive. Concentrate on behaviors over which the speaker has control.

EFFECTIVE: Taka, I thought your closing quote was effective in summarizing your key ideas, but it didn't end your speech on an uplifting note. Another quote from Khalil Gibran that I'll share with you after class would also summarize your key points and provide a positive affirmation of your message. You may want to try it if you give this speech again.

LESS EFFECTIVE: Your voice isn't well suited to public speaking.

As you provide feedback, whether in your public speaking class or to a friend who asks you for a reaction to his or her speech, remember that the goal of feedback is to offer descriptive and specific information that helps a speaker build confidence and skill.

Giving Feedback to Yourself

While you are collecting feedback from your instructor, classmates, family, and friends, keep in mind that the most important critic of your speeches is *you*. The ultimate goal of public-speaking instruction is to learn principles and skills that enable you to be your own best critic. As you rehearse your speech, use self-talk to comment about the choices you make as a speaker. After your speech, take time to reflect on both the virtues and areas for improvement in your speechmaking skill. As an audience-centered speaker, you must learn to recognize when to make changes on your feet, in the middle of a speech. For example, if you notice that your audience just isn't interested in the facts and statistics you are sharing, you may decide to support your points with a couple of stories instead. We encourage you to consider the following principles to enhance your own self-critiquing skills.

1. *Look for and reinforce your skills and speaking abilities.* Try to recognize your strengths and skills as a public speaker. Take mental note of how your audience analysis, organization, and delivery were effective in achieving your objectives. Such positive reflection can reinforce the many skills you are learning in this course. Resist the temptation to be too harsh or critical of your speaking skill. After each speaking opportunity, identify what you did right, and add a suggestion or two for ways to improve.

2. *Evaluate your effectiveness based on your specific speaking situation and audience.* Throughout the book we offer many suggestions and tips for improving your speaking skill. We also stress, however, that these prescriptions should be considered in light of your specific audience. Don't be a slave to rules. If you are giving a pep talk to the Little League team you are coaching, you might not have to construct an attention-getting opening statement. Be flexible. Speaking is an art as well as a science. Give yourself permission to adapt principles and practices to specific speech situations.

3. *Identify one or two areas for improvement.* You may be tempted to overwhelm yourself with a long list of things you need to do as a speaker. Rather than trying to work on a dozen goals, concentrate on two or three, or maybe even just one key skill you would like to develop. To help you make your decision, use the audience-centered model of public speaking we introduced in Chapter 2.

Ultimately, the goal of this course is to teach you how to listen to your own commentary and become your own expert in shaping and polishing your speaking style.

SUMMARY

Listening is a process that involves selecting, attending, understanding, and remembering. Some of the barriers that keep people from listening at peak efficiency include information overload, personal concerns, outside distractions, and prejudice. Several suggestions to overcome these barriers and improve your listening skill are as follows:

Adapt to the speaker's delivery.	Listen for major ideas.
Listen with your eyes as well as your ears.	Identify your listening goal.
Monitor your emotional reaction.	Practice listening.
Avoid jumping to conclusions.	Become an active listener.
Be a selfish listener.	

Effective notes can help you retain information that you hear. Learn the criteria for good speech, and learn to give and receive evaluative feedback on speeches and exchanges with your peers and instructors. The goal of this text is to help you develop self-evaluation skills that will support your own growth as a speech maker.

being audience-centered
A Sharper Focus

CONSIDERING YOUR AUDIENCE

▶ When speaking to an audience that may be hostile or critical toward your message, take care to use credible arguments and evidence rather than relying upon emotional appeals.

▶ Find out what your listeners' objectives are; do your best to adjust and adapt to achieve your listeners' goals.

▶ Criteria for an effective speech include that the message should be understood by the audience, achieve the intended goal, and be ethical.

▶ Adapt feedback you give to a speaker to provide information and suggestions the speaker can use.

CONSIDERING AUDIENCE DIVERSITY

▶ The cultural background of your audience will affect how they listen to your message; people from some cultures prefer stories and narratives rather than a message chock-full of statistics and data.

▶ Some listeners are more apprehensive than others when listening to a message. By using clear preview statements, adequate internal summaries, and appropriate visual aids, you can help anxious listeners feel more comfortable when listening to your message.

CRITICAL THINKING QUESTIONS

1. You are heading for your least favorite class: British Literature of the 1800s. You know you are in for another boring lecture delivered by a professor who does nothing but read in a monotone from yellowed notes. What are some strategies you can use to increase your listening effectiveness in this challenging situation?

2. For some reason, when Alberto hears the president speak, he just tunes out. What are some of the barriers that may keep Alberto from focusing on the message he is hearing?

3. Jackie aspires to be a broadcast journalist, following in the footsteps of well-known announcers such as Jane Pauley and Diane Sawyer. Although she is a pretty good listener, she often has difficulty taking accurate notes on what she hears. What strategies do effective note takers use to capture messages accurately?

ETHICAL QUESTIONS

1. Margo discovered that one of her classmates who had taken world history the previous semester was selling the lecture notes. Margo studied the notes and found she could pass the exams without attending class. Is this kind of "listening" behavior ethical? Why or why not?

2. Chester was going to hear a congressional candidate speak at a benefit. Chester decided he would bring a book to read during the speech because the speaker was from a political party different from Chester's. Was Chester being fair to the speaker?

3. Janice was assigned the task of critiquing one of her classmate's speeches. Although she thought the speech was pretty good, she gave the speaker low marks because she strongly disagreed with what the speaker was saying. Was this an appropriate evaluation? Why or why not?

SUGGESTED ACTIVITIES

1. Rank from most significant to least significant the barriers to effective listening discussed in this chapter, as they apply to your own listening habits.

Information overload	Prejudice
Personal concerns	Speech-rate/thought-rate differences
Outside distractions	Receiver apprehension

Describe your plan to help manage your three most troublesome listening barriers.

2. While you are listening to a speech by one of your classmates, listen for major ideas and construct a rough outline of the speech. If your classmate worked from an outline, compare your notes with that outline. If your outline is markedly different from your classmate's, try to analyze why.

3. Watch a documentary on TV. Every four or five minutes, mentally summarize key ideas presented in the program. When the program is over, write down the key ideas and summarize as much information as you can. The next day, without looking at what you wrote, again summarize the program's content. Note differences

between your immediate recall and your twenty-four-hour recall. Two weeks after viewing the program, write another summary and note the differences among your immediate response, your twenty-four-hour recall, and your two-week memory.

4. Receiver apprehension is the anxiety some people feel when they listen to others; this anxiety stems from a fear of misunderstanding messages or concern about psychologically adjusting to the information someone presents. Take the following test to assess your level of receiver apprehension. Scores range from 50 to 10. The higher your score, the more you're likely to experience some anxiety when you listen to others and the harder you'll have to work at developing strategies to improve your listening comprehension.

RECEIVER ANXIETY SCALE

Respond to each of these questions about how much this *describes you,* using a five-point scale.

5 = Strongly Agree; 4 = Agree; 3 = Uncertain or Sometimes;
2 = Disagree; 1 = Strongly Disagree

_____ 1. When I am listening, I feel nervous about missing information.

_____ 2. I worry about being able to keep up with the material presented in lecture classes.

_____ 3. Sometimes I miss information in class because I am writing down the notes.

_____ 4. I feel tense and anxious when listening to important information.

_____ 5. I am concerned that I won't be able to remember information I've heard in lectures or discussions.

_____ 6. Although I try to concentrate, my thoughts sometimes become confused when I'm listening.

_____ 7. I worry that my listening skill isn't very good.

_____ 8. I regularly can't remember things that I have just been told.

_____ 9. I feel anxious and nervous when I am listening in class.

_____10. I prefer reading class material rather than listening to it, so I don't have to be stressed about catching all the information the first time.

Source: L. Wheeless, "An Investigation of Receiver Apprehension and Social Context Dimensions of Communication Apprehension," *The Speech Teacher* 24 (1975): 261–268.

USING TECHNOLOGY AND MEDIA

1. Tape record one of your professor's lectures while you also take notes. Replay the lecture as you reexamine your notes, to determine whether they captured the important points of the lecture.

2. Listen to a speech on the Internet. Practice your note-taking skills as you listen to the speech. Then listen to the speech again to assess your skill in taking effective, comprehensive notes.

F or of the three elements in speechmaking—speaker, subject, and person addressed—it is the last one, the hearer, that determines the speech's end and object.

ARISTOTLE

Analyzing Your Audience

objectives

After studying this chapter you should be able to do the following:

1. Describe informal and formal methods of analyzing your audience.

2. Discuss the importance of audience analysis.

3. Explain how to gather demographic, psychological, and situational information about your audience and the speaking occasion.

4. Identify methods of assessing your audience's reactions to your speech while it is in progress.

5. Identify methods of assessing audience reactions after you have concluded your speech.

t seemed harmless enough. Charles Williams was asked to speak to the Cub Scout pack about his experience as a young cowboy in Texas. The boys were learning to tie knots, and Williams, a retired rancher, could tell them how to make a lariat and how to make and use other knots.

His speech started out well. He seemed to be adapting to his young audience. However, for some reason, Williams thought the boys might also enjoy learning how to exterminate the screw worm, a pesky parasite of cattle. In the middle of his talk about roping cattle, he launched into a presentation about the techniques for sterilizing male screw worms. The parents in the audience fidgeted in their seats. The 7- and 8-year-olds didn't have the foggiest idea what a screw worm was, what sterilization was, or how male and female screw worms mate.

It got worse; his audience analysis skills deteriorated even more. Williams next talked about castrating cattle. Twenty-five minutes later he finally finished the screw-worm–castration speech. The parents were relieved. Fortunately, the boys hadn't understood it.

Williams' downfall resulted from his failure to analyze his audience. He may have had a clear objective in mind, but he hadn't considered the background or knowledge of his listeners. Audience analysis is essential for any successful speech.

Becoming an Audience-Centered Speaker

Chapter 1 identified the key elements in communication: source, receiver, message, channel. All four elements are important, but perhaps the most important is the receiver. In public speaking, the receiver is the audience, and the audience is the reason for a speech event.

In Chapter 2, we presented a model that provides an overview of the entire process of speech preparation and delivery (see Figure 5.1). We stressed there and reemphasize here the concept of public speaking as an audience-centered activity. At each stage in crafting your speech, you must be mindful of your audience. The audience-analysis skills and techniques that we present in this chapter will help you throughout the public-speaking process. Consciousness of your audience will be important as you select a topic, determine the purpose of your speech, develop your central idea, generate main ideas, gather supporting material, firm up your organization, rehearse, and deliver your speech.

When you think of your audience, don't think of some undifferentiated mass of people waiting to hear your message. Instead, think of individuals. Public speaking is the process of speaking to a group of individuals, each with a unique point of view. Your challenge as an audience-centered public speaker is to find out as much as you can about these individuals. From your knowledge of the individuals, you can then develop a general profile of your listeners.

How do you become an audience-centered speaker? There are two steps. First, analyze your audience to assess who your listeners are; identify their psychological profile, as well as consider the occasion at which you are speaking. Second, once you have analyzed your audience, you'll use the information you've gathered to adapt to them in an ethical way. As our audience-centered model illustrates, each decision you make when designing and delivering your message should consider the needs and backgrounds of your audience. We'll talk about these two steps in more detail.

Analyze Your Audience

Audience analysis is the process of examining information about the listeners whom you expect to hear your speech. That analysis helps you adapt your message so that your listeners will respond as you wish. You analyze audiences every day as you speak to others or join in group conversations. Most of us do not deliberately make offensive comments to our family and friends. Rather, we adapt our message to the individuals with whom we are speaking.

Adapt to Your Audience

Audience adaptation is the process of ethically using information you've gathered when analyzing your audience to help your message be clearly understood and to achieve your speaking objective. If you only analyze your audience but don't use the information to help you customize your message, the information you've gathered will be of little value. Using your skill both to learn about your listeners and then to adapt to them can help you maintain your listeners' attention and make them more receptive to your ideas.

Here's an example of how analyzing and adapting to others works: Mike spent a glorious spring break at Daytona Beach. He and three close friends piled in a car and headed for a week of adventure. When he returned from the beach, sunburned and fatigued from merrymaking, people asked how his holiday went. He described his escapades to his best friend, his mother, and his communication professor.

To his best friend, he bragged, "We partied all night and slept on the beach all day. It was great!" He informed his mother, "It was good to relax after the hectic pace of college." And he told his professor, "It was mentally invigorating to have time to think things out." It was the same vacation—but how different the messages were! Mike adapted his message to the people he addressed; he had analyzed his audiences.

When you are speaking in public, you should use the same process. The principle is simple, yet powerful: An effective public speaker is audience-centered. Several key questions can help you formulate an effective approach to your audience:

To whom am I speaking?

What does my audience expect from me?

What topic would be most suitable to my audience?

What is my objective?

What kind of information should I share with my audience?

How should I present the information to them?

How can I gain and hold their attention?

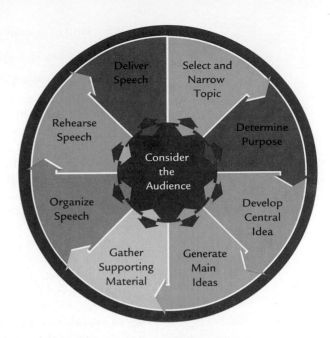

FIGURE 5.1

Audience analysis is central to the speechmaking process.

audience adaptation
The process of ethically using information to analyze an audience so the message will be clear and achieve the speaking objective

audience analysis
The process of examining information about the expected listeners to a speech

What kind of examples would work best?

What language or linguistic differences exist among audience members?

What method of organizing information will be most effective?

Being audience-centered does not mean you should tell your listeners only what they want to hear, or that you should fabricate information simply to please your audience or achieve your goal. If you adapt to your audience by abandoning your own values and sense of truth, then you will become an unethical speaker rather than an audience-centered one. It was President Truman who pondered, "I wonder how far Moses would have gone if he'd taken a poll in Egypt?" The audience-centered speaker adjusts his or her topic, purpose, central idea, main ideas, supporting materials, organization, and even delivery of the speech in such a way that encourages the audience to listen to his or her ideas. The goal is to make the audience come away from the speaking situation, if not persuaded, then at least feeling thoughtful rather than offended or hostile.

In this chapter, you will learn both formal and informal strategies for gathering information about your audience. You will examine ways to analyze and adapt to your audience before, during, and after your speech. You will also learn to use the information you gather to achieve your purpose.

Analyzing Your Audience Before You Speak

It is unlikely that audience members for the speeches you give in class will have similar backgrounds. In most colleges and universities, the range of students' cultural backgrounds, ethnic ties, and religious traditions is rapidly expanding. Learning about your audience members' backgrounds and attitudes can help you in selecting a topic, defining a purpose, and developing an outline, and in other speech-related activities. It is important to analyze your audience before doing anything else. We will discuss three basic dimensions you can use for prespeech analysis:

1. Demographic audience analysis

2. Psychological audience analysis

3. Situational audience analysis

Demographic Audience Analysis

demographics
Information about the age, sexual orientation, race, gender, educational level, and religious views of an audience

demographic audience analysis
Analyzing an audience by examining demographic information to help a speaker develop a clear and effective message

A basic approach to analyzing an audience is to identify its demographic makeup. **Demographics** involve population data, including such characteristics as age, race, gender, educational level, and religious views. In essence, demographic information provides clues to help you determine how to adapt to your listeners. Let's consider how demographic information, or **demographic audience analysis,** can help you better understand your audience.

AGE Knowing the age of your audience can be very helpful in choosing your topic and approach. Although you must use caution in generalizing from only one factor such as age, that information can suggest the kinds of examples, humor, illustrations, and other types of supporting material to use in your speech.

For example, many students in your public-speaking class will probably be in their late teens or early twenties. Some, however, may be older. The younger students may know the latest rap performers or musicians, for example, but the older ones may not be familiar with Ludicrous, UGK, or OutKast. If you are going to give a talk on rap music, you will have to explain who the performers are and describe or demonstrate their style if you wish to have all the members of your class understand what you are talking about.

Contrary to early findings on gender differences in listening, current research indicates that women are just as critical as men in evaluating persuasive messages.

[Photo: Najilah Feeney/Stock Boston]

GENDER   Josh began his speech by thanking his predominantly female audience for taking time from their busy schedules to attend his presentation on managing personal finances. Not a bad way to begin a talk. He continued, however, by noting that their job of raising children, keeping their homes clean and feeding their families was among the most important tasks in America. Josh thought he was paying his audience a compliment. He did not consider that today, most women work outside the home as well as in it. Many of his listeners were insulted. Many of his listeners stopped being listeners.

A key question to ask when considering your audience is "What is the ratio of males to females?" No matter what the mix, avoid making sweeping judgments based on gender stereotypes. A person's **sex** is determined by biology as reflected in his or her anatomy and reproductive systems; someone is born either male or female. **Gender** is the culturally constructed and psychologically based perception of one's self as feminine or masculine. Gender-role identity, on the continuum of masculine and feminine, is learned or socially reinforced by others as well as by one's own personality and life experiences; genetics also plays a part in shaping gender identity.

Although you can certainly make some legitimate assumptions about topics that might interest each sex, it would be as inappropriate to assume that all males are sports fanatics as to conclude that all females enjoy an evening at the ballet. Instead, try to ensure that your remarks reflect sensitivity to diversity in your listeners' points of view.

One goal of an audience-centered speaker is to avoid sexist language or remarks. A sexist perspective stereotypes or prejudges how someone will react based on his or her sex. Take time to educate yourself about what words, phrases, or perspectives are likely to offend or create psychological noise for your listeners. Think carefully about the implications of words or phrases you take for granted. For example, many people still use the words *ladies* or *matrons* without thinking about their connotations in U.S. culture. Be especially wary about jokes. Many are derogatory to one sex or the other. Avoid stereotypes in your stories and examples as well.

In addition, make your language, and your message, as inclusive as possible. If you are speaking to a mixed-sex audience, make sure your speech relates to all your listeners, not just to one gender. If, for example, you decided to discuss breast cancer, you could note how this disease affects the lives of husbands, fathers, and brothers as well as those of women.

Finally, be cautious about assuming that men and women will respond differently to your message. Early social science research found some evidence that females were more susceptible to efforts to persuade them than were males.[1] For many years textbooks and communication teachers presented this conclusion to students. More contemporary research, however, suggests there may be no major differences between how susceptible men and women are to persuasive messages.[2]

Sex
A person's sex is determined by biology as reflected in his or her anatomy and reproductive system

Gender
The culturally constructed and psychologically based perception of one's self as feminine or masculine

Moreover, although some research suggests women are socialized to be more emotional and empathic than men, additional evidence suggests men can be equally sensitive.[3] Although it is clear there are learned sex differences in language usage and nonverbal behavior, we caution against making sweeping gender-based assumptions about your audience.

SEXUAL ORIENTATION   Another demographic factor to consider about your audience is sexual orientation. Whether you approve or disapprove of a person's sexual orientation, your attitudes and beliefs should not interfere with your goal of being an effective, audience-centered public speaker. An audience-centered speaker is sensitive to issues and attitudes about sexual orientation in contemporary society.

What strategies can help you walk the fine line between being inclusive and being aware of the range of attitudes about gays and lesbians that members of your audience may hold? We encourage you to be mindful of the examples and language that you use so that you do not disenfranchise a significant part of your audience from focusing on your message. The audience-centered speaker's goal is to enhance understanding rather than create "noise" that may distract your audience from becoming listeners, regardless of the attitudes or beliefs audience members may hold about sexual orientation. Specifically, monitor the way in which you talk about sexual orientation when delivering a public presentation. You already know that it is inappropriate to use racially charged terms that demean a person's race or ethnicity; it is equally important not to use terms that degrade a person's sexual orientation. Similarly, stories, illustrations, and humor that have a point or punch line at the expense of a person because of his or her sexual orientation may result not only in lowered perceptions of your credibility from gay and lesbian members of your audience, but also from audience members who disdain bias against gays and lesbians.

People evaluate credibility by behavior, not just intentions. Sometimes we unintentionally offend someone through more subtle misuse of language. For example, gays and lesbians typically prefer to be referred to as "gay" and "lesbian" rather than "homosexuals." Further, it is not appropriate to single out gays and lesbians as a separate category of people "from another planet" who are assumed to hold political, ideological, or religious views consistently different from those of non gays and lesbians.

However, don't ignore the existence of gays and lesbians. Don't assume that everyone in your audience is heterosexual; a person's sexual orientation is invisible, in the sense that you can't typically identify whether someone is gay or lesbian just by looking at him or her. We are not suggesting that in every speech you present you should address this issue by using examples of gay or lesbian people. But neither should all examples of couples assume that the two people are of the opposite sex. Monitor your language choice and use of illustrations and humor so you don't disenfranchise members of your audience.[4] No matter what your personal views on the issue of sexual orientation are, the goal is to be an effective communicator. Be sensitive in your language use; in your approach to the speech topic; and in the examples, illustrations, and humor you use.[5] Make your points so that you competently communicate effectively and appropriately to each audience member.

CULTURE, ETHNICITY, AND RACE   **Culture** is a learned system of knowledge, behavior, attitudes, beliefs, values, and norms shared by a group of people. **Ethnicity** is that portion of a person's cultural background that relates to a national or religious heritage. A person's **race** is his or her biological heritage, such as Caucasian or Hispanic. The cultural, ethnic, or racial background of your audience influences the way they perceive your message. An effective speaker adapts to differences in culture, race, and ethnicity.

culture
A learned system of knowledge, behavior, attitudes, beliefs, values, and norms that is shared by a group of people

ethnicity
That portion of a person's cultural background that relates to a national or religious heritage

race
A person's biological heritage

As you approach any public-speaking situation, avoid an ethnocentric mind-set. **Ethnocentrism** is an attitude that your own cultural approaches are superior to those from other cultures. If your audience catches even a whiff that you think you and your cultural traditions are better than their cultural traditions, you have built walls between you and your listeners. Most of us would become defensive if a speaker visited our community and suggested that our ways of doing things were backward, ineffective, and inferior. The audience-centered speaker is sensitive to cultural differences and avoids saying things that would disparage the cultural background of the audience.

You need not have international students in your class to have a culturally diverse audience. Special ethnic and cultural traditions thrive among people who have lived in the United States all their lives. Students from a Polish family in Chicago, a German family in Texas, or a Haitian family in Brooklyn may be native U.S. citizens with cultural traditions different from your own. Effective public speakers seek to learn as much as possible about the special cultural values and knowledge of their audience so that they can understand the best way to deliver their message.

Researchers classify or describe cultural differences along several lines.[6] Understanding these classifications may provide clues to help you adapt your message when you speak before diverse audiences.

- **Individualistic and Collectivistic Cultures**   Some cultures place greater emphasis on individual achievement, whereas others place more value on group or collective achievement. Among the countries that tend to value individual accomplishment are Australia, Great Britain, the United States, Canada, Belgium, and Denmark. Japan, Thailand, Colombia, Taiwan, and Venezuela are among those that have more collectivist cultures. Audience members from individualistic cultures tend to value and respond to appeals that encourage personal accomplishment and single out individual achievement. Audience members from collectivistic cultures may be more likely to value group or team rewards and achievement.

- **High-Context and Low-Context Cultures**   The terms *high* and *low* refer to the importance of unspoken or nonverbal messages. In high-context cultures, people place considerable importance on such contextual factors as tone of voice, gestures, facial expression, movement, and other implied aspects of communication. People from low-context traditions are just the opposite. They place greater emphasis on the words themselves; the surrounding context has a relatively low impact on the meaning of the message. The Arab culture is a high-context culture, as are those of Japan, Asia, and southern Europe. Low-context cultures, which place a high value on words, include those of Switzerland, Germany, the United States, and Australia. Listeners from low-context cultures will need and expect more detailed and explicit information from you as a speaker. Subtle and indirect messages are less likely to be effective. People from high-context cultures will pay particular attention to your delivery and to the communication environment when they try to interpret your meaning. These people will be less impressed by a speaker who boasts about his or her own accomplishments; such an audience will expect and value more indirect ways of establishing credibility.

- **Tolerance of Uncertainty and Need for Certainty**   Some cultures are more comfortable with ambiguity and uncertainty than others. Those cultures in which people need to have details "nailed down" tend to develop very specific regulations and rules. People from cultures with a greater tolerance of uncertainty are more comfortable with vagueness and are not upset when all the details aren't spelled out.

ethnocentrism
An attitude that your own cultural perspectives and methods are superior to those of other cultures

Cultures with a high need for certainty include those of Russia, Japan, France, and Costa Rica. Cultures that have a higher tolerance for uncertainty include those of Great Britain and Indonesia. If you are speaking to an audience with many people who have a high need for certainty, make sure you provide concrete details when you present ideas.

● **High-Power and Low-Power Cultures**   Power is the ability to influence or control others. Some cultures prefer clearly defined lines of authority and responsibility; these are said to be high-power cultures. Low-power cultures are more comfortable with blurred lines of authority and less formal titles. Austria, Israel, Denmark, Norway, Switzerland, and Great Britain typically have an equitable approach to power distribution. Cultures that are high on the power dimension include those of the Philippines, Mexico, Venezuela, India, Brazil, and France; when you speak, people from these cultural traditions tend to respond positively to clearly defined power roles and structures. Those from low-power cultures often favor more shared approaches to leadership and governance.

RECAP

DESCRIBING CULTURAL DIFFERENCES

INDIVIDUALISTIC CULTURES	Individual achievement is emphasized more than group achievement.
COLLECTIVISTIC CULTURES	Group or team achievement is emphasized more than individual achievement.
HIGH-CONTEXT CULTURES	The context of a message—including nonverbal cues, tone of voice, posture, and facial expression—is often emphasized more than the words.
LOW-CONTEXT CULTURES	The words in a message are emphasized more than the surrounding context.
TOLERANCE OF UNCERTAINTY	People can accept ambiguity and are not bothered if they do not know all the details.
NEED FOR CERTAINTY	People dislike ambiguous messages and want to know what their future holds.
HIGH-POWER CULTURES	Status and power differences are emphasized; roles and chains of command are clearly defined.
LOW-POWER CULTURES	Status and power differences receive less emphasis; people strive for equality rather than exalting those in positions of leadership.

RELIGION   Marsha is a follower of Scientology, and she believes that *Dianetics* is as important as the Bible. Planning to speak before a Bible-belt college audience, many of whose members view Scientology as a cult, Marsha would be wise to consider how her listeners will respond to her message. This is not to suggest that she should refuse the speaking invitation. She should, however, be aware of her audience's religious beliefs as she prepares and presents her speech.

When touching on religious beliefs or an audience's values, use great care in what you say and how you say it. Again, remind yourself that some members of your audience will undoubtedly not share your own beliefs, and that few beliefs are held with the same intensity as religious ones. If you do not wish to offend your listeners, plan and deliver your speech with much thought and sensitivity.

GROUP MEMBERSHIP   It's said we are each members of a gang—it's just that some gangs are more socially acceptable than others. We are social creatures; we congregate in groups to gain an identity, to help accomplish projects we support, and to have fun. So it's reasonable to assume that many of your listeners belong to groups, clubs, or organizations. Knowing what groups your listeners belong to can help you make inferences about their likes, dislikes, beliefs, and values. For example, if you are speaking to a service group such as the Lions Club or Kiwanis Club, you can reasonably assume that your listeners value community service and will be interested in how to make their community a better place to live.

You're likely to find that most audiences have listeners who may belong to several different types of organizations. Find out which organizations your audience members have joined. Are they members of the Parent and Teachers Association, fraternities, sororities, musical groups, academic organizations, or other clubs? Being able to make specific references to the activities that your audience members may participate in can also help to tailor your speech to your specific audience. One way to develop common ground with an audience is to offer sincere support for the groups and causes that audience members support or to mention that you are also a member of similar organizations. Politicians know that a sure-fire way to get applause when delivering their "stump speeches" is to mention how they support the local sports team; this reference to sports is a method of establishing a positive, common bond with their listeners. We don't encourage you to offer phony flattery or fake allegiance to groups and club memberships just to get applause. But a heart-felt reference to a group or organization that both you and your audience support can help establish a link with your listeners.

SOCIOECONOMIC STATUS   **Socioeconomic status** is a person's perceived importance and influence based on such factors as income, occupation, and education level. North Americans often don't like to talk about or acknowledge status differences in society. The beliefs "All people are created equal," "Equal justice under the law," and "All persons are of equal worth" permeate the democratic approach to government and decision making. In Europe, Asia, the Middle East, and other parts of the world, however, centuries-old traditions of acknowledging status differences still exist today. Status differences nonetheless exist in the United States but are often more subtle. Having an idea about audience members' incomes, occupations, and education levels can be helpful as you develop a message that connects with listeners.

• **Income.**   It's considered rude to ask people how much money they make, yet having some general idea of the income level of your listeners can be of great value to you as a speaker. The amount of disposable income of your listeners can influence your topic and your approach to the topic. For example, if you know that most audience members are struggling to meet weekly expenses, it is unwise to talk about how to see the cultural riches of Europe by traveling first class. But talking about how to get your way paid to Europe by serving as a courier may hold considerable interest.

• **Occupation.**   What people do for a living also has socioeconomic status implications. Although there is often a link between income and occupation, the two do not necessarily go hand in hand in assessing status. Knowing what people do for a living can give you useful information about how to adapt your message to them. Speaking to teachers gives you an opportunity to use different examples and illustrations than if you were speaking to lawyers, ministers, or automobile assembly workers. Many college-age students may hold jobs, but don't yet hold the jobs they aspire to after they graduate from college. Knowing their future career plans can help you adjust your topic and supporting material to your listeners' professional goals.

socioeconomic status
A person's perceived importance and influence based on income, occupation, and education level

● **Education.**   About one-third of U.S. high-school graduates obtain a college diploma. Fewer than 10 percent of the population earn graduate degrees. Knowing the educational background of your listeners is yet another component of socioeconomic status that can help you plan your message. In your college-level public-speaking class, you have a good idea that your classmates and audience members value education, because they are striving, often at great sacrifice, for an advanced education. Knowing the educational background of your audience can also help you make decisions about your choice of vocabulary, your language style, and your use of examples and illustrations. For example, Mary White Eagle, a Native American from Roswell, New Mexico, was invited to speak to her daughter's grade-school class. Although she could have talked about the oppression of her ancestors by whites, she instead selected a topic more appropriate to her listeners: She spoke about the houses that Native Americans had to build and rebuild to follow the herds of buffalo that roamed the Southwest. As an audience-centered speaker, she used her knowledge of the education level of her listeners to guide her in her topic selection.

ADAPTING TO DIVERSE LISTENERS   The most recent U.S. census figures document what you already know from your own life experiences: We all live in an age of diversity. For example,

● The U.S. foreign-born population recently topped 28 million people.[7]

● Immigrants among all U.S. citizens have more than doubled in the past thirty years; an increase from just under 5 percent of the population in 1970, to over 10 percent in 2001.[8]

● Whites are the minority ethnic group in nearly half of the largest cities in the United States.[9]

● For the first time in modern U.S. history, non-Hispanic whites are in the minority in California.[10]

● New Jersey experienced a 77 percent increase in its Asian population between 1990 and 2000.[11]

Virtually every state in the United States has experienced a dramatic increase in foreign-born residents. If trends continue as they have during the past quarter-century, cultural and ethnic diversity will continue to grow during your lifetime. This swell of immigrants translates to increased diversity in all aspects of society, including the people in most audiences you'll face, whether in business, people attending school-board meetings, or listeners in your college or university class.

Audience diversity, however, involves more factors than just ethnic and cultural differences. Central to our point about considering your audience is examining the full spectrum of audience diversity, not just cultural differences. Each topic we've reviewed when discussing demographic and psychological aspects of an audience contributes to overall audience diversity. Diversity simply means differences. Audience members are diverse. Differences in age, gender, religion, education, group membership, and psychological makeup all suggest that each audience you face will consist of people with a variety of backgrounds and experiences. In your public-speaking class, you'll likely find a mix of Democrats, Republicans, and a variety of other political views. Contemporary student audiences also reflect increasing diversity in age and in religious views. The question and challenge for a public speaker is "How do I adapt to listeners with such different backgrounds and experiences?" We offer several general strategies. You could decide to focus on a target audience, consciously use a variety of methods of adapting to listeners, seek to find common ground, or consider using powerful visual images to present your key points.

• **Focus on a Target Audience.** A **target audience** is a specific segment of your audience that you most want to address or influence. Just as an archer shoots an arrow with a specific spot on the target in mind, as a speaker you may want to customize your message to influence a certain portion of your audience, especially if your audience is diverse. You've undoubtedly been a target of skilled communicators and may not have been aware that messages had been tailored just for you. For example, most colleges and universities spend a considerable amount of time and money encouraging students to apply to them for admission. You probably received some of this recruitment literature in the mail during your high school years. But not every student in the United States receives the same brochures from every college. College admissions officers have sophisticated ways of finding students they think would be a good fit for their institution. Colleges and universities targeted you based on your test scores, your interests, where you live, and your involvement in co-curricular or extracurricular activities. Just as college admissions officers targeted you, as a public speaker, you may want to think about the portion of your audience you most want to understand your message or convince.

The challenge when consciously focusing on a target audience is not to lose or alienate the rest of your listeners. Keep the entire audience in mind while making a specific attempt to hit your target segment. For example, Sasha was trying to convince his listeners to invest in the stock market instead of relying on the Social Security system. He wisely decided to focus on the younger listeners; those approaching retirement age have already made their major investment decisions. Although he focused on the younger members of his audience, however, he didn't forget the mature listeners. He suggested, that older listeners encourage their children or grandchildren to consider his proposal. He focused on a target audience, but didn't ignore others.

• **Use Diverse Strategies for a Diverse Audience.** Another approach you can adopt, either separately or in combination with a target audience focus, is to use a variety of strategies to reflect the diversity of your audience. Based on your efforts to gather information about your audience, you should know the various constituencies that will likely be present for your talk. Consider using several methods of reaching the different listeners in your audience. Using a variety of supporting materials can appeal to people with different backgrounds. For example, some Asian and Middle Eastern cultures prefer and are more comfortable with stories and parables to make a point or support an argument. Many people from the predominant North American culture may expect more logical, statistical evidence to support an argument. Rather than relying on one or the other, when faced with audience members with different preferences and expectations, consider using both strategies—stories *and* logical support—to make your point.

• **Use Common Audience Perspectives.** People have debated for a long, long time as to whether universal human values, common to all cultures, exist. The debate continues. Several scholars have made strong arguments that common human values do exist. Communication researcher David Kale suggests that all humans should seek to protect the dignity and worth of other people.[12] Thus, he argues, all people can identify with the struggle to enhance their own dignity and worth, although different cultures express that in different ways. A second common value is the search for a world at peace. Underlying such quests in a civilized society is a fundamental desire

target audience
A specific segment of an audience that you most want to influence

Technology can help you transcend language differences. This speaker has provided a simultaneous translation device so that even audience members who do not understand the language can participate as listeners.

[Photo: Larry Mangino/ The Image Works]

for equilibrium, balance, stability, and peace. Although there appears to be a small but corrosive minority of people whose actions do not support the universal value of peace, the prevailing human values in most cultures ultimately support peace. As a public speaker, you could link the underlying values of personal dignity and peace values to the information you share or positions you advocate.

Intercultural-communication scholars Larry Samovar and Richard Porter suggest other commonalities that people from all cultures share. They propose that all humans seek physical pleasure and avoid personal harm as well as emotional and psychological pleasure and confirmation.[13] Although each culture defines what constitutes pleasure and pain, it may be useful to interpret human behavior with these general assumptions in mind. Most people also realize that their biological life will end; to some degree each person is isolated from all other human beings; we each make choices; and each person seeks to give life meaning. Although Samovar and Porter further explain how each of us is also different from one another, the similarities offer some basis for developing common messages with universal meaning. The search for a truly comprehensive human communication theory continues. Cultural differences exist. However, noting major principles that help motivate human behavior may help you, in your role as a public speaker, to develop a message that can speak to a variety of cultural and ethnic traditions and also can transcend differences in age and gender.

● **Rely on Visual Materials That Transcend Language Differences.**   Pictures and images can communicate universal messages—especially emotional ones. Although there is no universal language, most listeners, regardless of culture and language, can comprehend visual expressions of pain, joy, sorrow, and happiness. Showing a picture of a war-ravaged Serbian village can clearly and dramatically illustrate the devastation of armed conflict, regardless of audience members' cultural backgrounds. Words alone do not have as powerful an impact. An image of a mother holding the thin, frail, malnourished body of her dying child communicates the ravages of famine without elaborate verbal explanations. The more varied your listeners' cultural experiences, the more effective it can be to use visual materials to illustrate your ideas.

BEFORE YOU SPEAK . . .	Assess your listeners' cultural backgrounds and expectations about the speaking process.
	Assess your own cultural background, expectations, and biases about the speaking process.
	Assess the level of formality your listeners expect.
	Assess whether your listeners will respond to a linear, step-by-step structure.
DURING YOUR SPEECH . . .	Beware of developing a message that would be effective only with people just like you; be audience-centered.
	Avoid making sweeping generalizations about your audience's culture or ethnicity.
	Use a mix of supporting materials to make your points clear and memorable.
	Use visual aids that have universal appeal.
	Present stories, illustrations, and narratives with messages that span cultural backgrounds.
	Tailor your speech to a set of target or primary listeners in your audience.
	Identify common values and assumptions held by your listeners.

Psychological Audience Analysis

Demographic information lets you make some useful inferences about your audience and to predict likely responses. Learning how the members of your audience feel about your topic and purpose may provide specific clues about possible reactions. A **psychological audience analysis** explores an audience's attitudes toward a topic, purpose, and speaker, while probing the underlying beliefs and values that might affect these attitudes.

It is important for a speaker to distinguish among *attitudes, beliefs,* and *values.* The attitudes, beliefs, and values of an audience may greatly influence a speaker's selection of a topic and specific purpose, as well as various other aspects of speech preparation and delivery.

An **attitude** reflects likes or dislikes. Do you like health food? Are you for or against capital punishment? Do you think it is important to learn cardiopulmonary resuscitation (CPR)? Should movies be censored? What are your views on nuclear energy? Your answers to these widely varied questions reflect your attitudes.

A **belief** is what you hold to be true or false. Beliefs underlie attitudes. Why do you like health food? You may *believe* natural products are better for your health. That belief explains your positive attitude. Why are you against capital punishment? You may *believe* it is wrong to kill people for any reason. Again, your belief explains your attitude. It is useful for a speaker to probe audience beliefs. If the speaker can understand why audience members feel as they do about a topic, he or she may be able to address that underlying belief, whether trying to change an attitude or reinforce one.

psychological audience analysis
Analyzing the attitudes, beliefs, values, and other psychological information about an audience to help a speaker develop a clear and effective message

attitude
An individual's likes or dislikes

belief
An individual's perception of what is true or false

A **value** is an enduring concept of good and bad, right and wrong. More deeply ingrained than either attitudes or beliefs, they are therefore more resistant to change. Values support both attitudes and beliefs. For example, you like health food because you believe that natural products are more healthful. And you *value* good health. You are against capital punishment because you believe that it is wrong to kill people. You *value* human life. As with beliefs, a speaker who has some understanding of an audience's values is better able to adapt a speech to them.

ANALYZING ATTITUDES TOWARD THE TOPIC   The topic of a speech provides one focus for an audience's attitudes, beliefs, and values. It is useful to know how members of an audience feel about your topic. Are they interested or apathetic? How much do they already know about the topic? If the topic is controversial, are they for or against it? Knowing the answers to these questions from the outset lets you adjust your message accordingly. For example, if you plan to talk about increasing taxes to improve education in your state, you may want to know how your listeners feel about taxes and education.

When you are analyzing your audience, it may help to categorize the group along three dimensions: interested–uninterested, favorable–unfavorable, and captive–voluntary. With an *interested* audience, your task is simply to hold and amplify interest throughout the speech. If your audience is *uninterested,* you need to find ways to "hook" the members. In Chapter 16 we describe ways to motivate an audience by addressing issues related to their needs and interests. Given our visually oriented culture, consider using visual aids to gain and maintain the attention of apathetic listeners

You may also want to gauge how *favorable* or *unfavorable* your audience may feel toward you and your message before you begin to speak. Some audiences, of course, are neutral, apathetic, or simply uninformed about what you plan to say. We provide explicit suggestions for approaching favorable, neutral, and unfavorable audiences in Chapter 17 when we discuss persuasive speaking. But even if your objective is simply to inform, it is useful to know whether your audience is predisposed to respond positively or negatively toward you or your message. Giving an informative talk about classical music would be quite challenging, for example, if you were addressing an audience full of die-hard punk-rock fans. You might decide to show the connections between classical music and punk, to arouse their interest.

YOUR SPEECH CLASS AS AUDIENCE   You may think that your public-speaking class is not a typical audience because class members are required to attend. Your speech class is a *captive* audience rather than a *voluntary* one. A captive audience has external requirements for existing (such as a requirement to attend class). Because class members must show up to earn credit for class, you need not worry that they will get up and leave during your speech. However, your classroom speeches are still *real* speeches. Your class members are certainly real people with likes, dislikes, beliefs, and values. And even though audience members may not physically leave the class, you must still keep them from leaving mentally.

You will undoubtedly give other speeches to other captive audiences. Audiences in professional settings at work or at professional meetings are often captive in the sense they may be required to attend lectures or presentations to receive continuing-education credit or be required to attend a presentation as part of their job duties. Your goal with a captive audience is the same as with other types of audiences. You should make your speech just as interesting and effective as one designed for a voluntary audience. You still have an obligation to address your listeners' needs and interests and to keep them

value
Enduring concept of good
and bad, right and wrong

engaged in what you have to say. A captive audience gives you an opportunity to polish your speaking skills. An effective speech designed for a captive audience should not seem as if you are presenting it only because you must. Your classroom speeches should connect with your listeners so they forget they are required to be in the audience. They should listen because your message has given them new, useful information; touched them emotionally; or persuaded them to change their opinion or behavior in support of your position.

RECAP ADAPTING YOUR MESSAGE TO DIFFERENT TYPES OF AUDIENCES

Type of Audience	Example	How to Be Audience-Centered
Captive	Students in a public-speaking class	Find out who will be in your audience, and use this knowledge to adapt your message to them.
Voluntary	Parents attending a lecture by the new principal at their children's school	Anticipate why they are coming to hear you, and speak about the issues they want you to address.
Interested	Mayors who attend a talk by the governor about increasing security and reducing the threat of terrorism	Acknowledge audience interest early in your speech; use the interest they have in you and your topic to gain and maintain their attention.
Uninterested	Junior high students attending a lecture about retirement benefits	Make it a high priority to tell your listeners why your message should be of interest to them. Remind your listeners throughout your speech how your message relates to their lives.
Favorable	A religious group that meets to hear a group leader talk about the importance of their beliefs	Use audience interest to move them closer to your speaking goal; you may be more explicit in telling them what you would like them to do in your speech conclusion.
Neutral	Members of a school-cafeteria staff who attend a lecture about the new school-bus schedule	Increase interest in your message by noting how your ideas relate to their life and the lives of their family and friends.
Undecided	Members of the community who have heard both candidates running for school-board president, yet can't decide how they will vote	Help clarify issues by describing advantages and disadvantages of a proposal; provide new information that will help them be more responsive to your speaking goal.
Unfavorable	Students who attend a lecture by the university president explaining why tuition and fees will increase 15 percent next year	Be realistic in what you expect to accomplish; acknowledge their opposing point of view; consider using facts to refute misperceptions they may hold.

ANALYZING ATTITUDES TOWARD YOU, THE SPEAKER   The audience's attitude toward you in your role as speaker is another factor that can influence their reaction to your speech. Regardless of how they feel about your topic or purpose, if members of an audience regard you as credible, they will be much more likely to be interested in, and supportive of, what you have to say.

Credibility—being perceived as trustworthy, knowledgeable, and interesting—is one of the main factors that will shape your audience's attitude toward you. If you establish your credibility before you begin to discuss your topic, your listeners will be more likely to believe what you say, and to think that you are knowledgeable, interesting, and dynamic.

When a high-school health teacher asks a former drug addict to speak to a class about the dangers of cocaine addiction, the teacher recognizes that the speaker's experiences make him credible and that his message will be far more convincing than if the teacher just lectured on the perils of cocaine use.

An audience's positive attitude toward you as a speaker can overcome negative or apathetic attitudes they may have toward your topic or purpose. If your analysis reveals that your audience does not recognize you as an authority on your subject, you will need to build your credibility into the speech. If you have had personal experience with your topic, be sure to let the audience know. You will gain credibility instantly. We will provide additional strategies for enhancing your credibility in Chapter 17.

Situational Audience Analysis

So far we have concentrated on the people who will be your listeners, as the primary focus of being an audience-centered speaker. You should also consider your speaking situation. **Situational audience analysis** includes examining the time and place of your speech, size of your audience, and speaking occasion. Although these elements are not technically an element of audience analysis, they can have a major effect on how your listeners may respond to you.

TIME. You may have no control over when you will be speaking, but when designing and delivering a talk, a skilled public speaker considers the time of day as well as audience expectations about the speech length. If you are speaking to a group of exhausted parents during a midweek evening meeting of the band-boosters club, you can bet they will appreciate a direct, to-the-point presentation more than a long oration. If you are on a program with other speakers, speaking first or last on the program carries a slight edge, because people tend to remember what comes first or last. Speaking early in the morning when people may not be quite awake, after lunch when they may feel a bit drowsy, or late in the afternoon when they are tired may mean you'll have to strive consciously for a more energetic delivery to keep your listeners' attention. Another aspect of time: Be mindful of your time limits. If your audience expects you to speak for 20 minutes, it is usually better to end either right at 20 minutes or even a little earlier; most North Americans don't appreciate being kept overtime for a speech. In your public-speaking class you will be given a speaking time limit, and you may wonder whether such strict time-limit expectations occur outside of public-speaking class. The answer is a most definite yes. Whether it's a business presentation or a speech to the city council or school board, time limits are often strictly enforced.

SIZE. The size of your audience directly affects speaking style and audience expectations about delivery. As a general rule, the larger the audience, the more likely they will expect a more formal style. In an audience of ten or fewer, you can punctuate a very conversational style by taking questions from your listeners. If you and your listeners are so few that you can be seated around a table, they may expect you to stay seated for your presentation. Many business "speeches" are given around a conference table.

A group of between 20 to 30 people—the size of most public-speaking classes—will expect more formality than the dozen-or-less audience. Your speaking style should still be conversational in quality but should include appropriate, well-structured organization, and your delivery may include more expansive gestures than you display during a one-on-one chat with a friend or colleague.

situational audience analysis
An examination and adaptation to the time and place of your speech, the audience size, and the speaking occasion

Audiences that fill a lecture hall will still appreciate a direct, conversational style, but your gestures may increase in size, and, if unamplified, you will be expected to speak with enough volume and intensity so that people in the last row can hear you.

LOCATION.   In your speech class, you have the advantage of knowing what the room looks like, but in a new speaking situation, you may not have that advantage. If at all possible, visit the place in which you will speak to examine the physical setting and find out, for example, how far the audience will be from the lectern. Physical conditions can affect your performance, audience response, and the overall success of the speech.

Room arrangement and decor may affect the way an audience responds. Be aware of the arrangement and appearance of the room in which you will speak. If your speaking environment is less than ideal, you may need to work especially hard to hold your audience's attention. Although you probably would not be able to make major changes in the speaking environment, it is ultimately up to you to obtain the best speaking environment you can. The arrangement of chairs, placement of audiovisual materials, and opening or closing of drapes should all be in your control.

OCCASION.   Another important clue about your listeners is to consider the reason this audience is here. What occasion brings this audience together? The mind-set of people gathered for a funeral will obviously be different from that of people who've asked you to say a few words after a banquet. Knowing the occasion helps you predict both demographic characteristics of the audience as well as the members' psychological state of mind.

If you're presenting a speech at an annual or monthly meeting, you have the advantage of being able to ask those who've attended previous presentations what kind of audience typically gathers for the occasion. Your best source of information may be either the person who invited you to speak or someone who has attended similar events. Knowing when you will speak on the program or whether a meal will be served before or after you talk will help you gauge what your audience expects from you.

In preparing for a speaking assignment, ask the following questions, and keep the answers in mind:

1. How many people are expected to attend the speech?

2. How will the audience seating be arranged?

3. How close will I be to the audience?

4. Will I speak from a lectern?

5. Will I be expected to use a microphone?

6. Will I be on a stage or a raised platform?

7. What is the room lighting like? Will the audience seating area be darkened beyond a lighted stage?

8. Will I have adequate equipment for my visual aids?

9. Where will I appear on the program?

10. Will there be noise or distractions outside the room?

Try to avoid running into last-minute surprises about the speaking environment and the physical arrangements for your speech. A well-prepared speaker adapts his or her message not only to the audience but also to the speaking environment.

Also keep in mind that when you arrive to give your speech, you can make changes in the previous speaker's room arrangements. The purpose of the speaker who spoke immediately before Yue Hong was to generate interest in a memorial for Asian Americans who fought in Vietnam. Because he wanted to make sure the audience felt free to ask questions, he asked to have the chairs arranged in a semicircle and made sure the lights were turned on. But Yue Hong was giving a more formal presentation on the future of the Vietnamese population in his talk, which included a brief slide show. So when the preceding speaker had finished, he rearranged the chairs and darkened the room.

ELEMENTS OF AUDIENCE ANALYSIS

DEMOGRAPHIC CHARACTERISTICS	Age
	Gender
	Sexual orientation
	Cultural, ethnic, or racial background
	Religion
	Group membership
PSYCHOLOGICAL CHARACTERISTICS	Socioeconomic status
	Attitudes
	Beliefs
	Values
SITUATIONAL CHARACTERISTICS	Time
	Audience size
	Location
	Occasion

ANALYZING AND ADAPTING TO THE SPEAKING SITUATION

Questions to Ask

Adaptation Strategies

Time

What time of the day will I be speaking?

If your audience may be tired or not yet awake, consider increasing your delivery energy level.

Where will I appear on the program?

Audiences are more likely to get the strongest impressions from those who speak first or last.

What are the time limits for the speech?

Unless you are a spell-binding speaker, most listeners do not appreciate speakers who exceed their time limit. Don't speak longer than your listeners expect you to.

Size

How many people will be in the audience?

Smaller audiences usually expect a more conversational, informal delivery quality; larger audiences usually expect a more formal presentation.

Will the audience be so large I'll need a microphone?

Make sure you understand the mechanics of the microphone system before you rise to speak.

Location

How will the room be arranged?

If you want to project a more informal speaking atmosphere, consider arranging the chairs in a circle. If necessary, in a large room consider inviting people in the back of the room to move closer to the front.

What is the room lighting like?

If the audience will be in the dark, it's more difficult to gauge their nonverbal responses. If you need to use presentation aids, make sure the room lighting is easy to adjust so people can see your images clearly.

Will there be noise or distractions outside the room?

Before the speech begins, consider strategies to minimize outside noise such as closing windows and doors, adjusting window blinds or shades, or politely asking that people in other nearby rooms be mindful of your presentation.

Questions to Ask

Adaptation Strategies

Occasion

What occasion brings the audience together?

Make sure you understand what your listeners expect, and strive to meet those expectations.

Is your speech an annual or monthly event? Has a similar speaking occasion occurred with this audience before?

Learn how other speakers have adapted to the audience. Ask for examples of what successful speakers have done to succeed with this audience. Or ask if certain issues or topics may offend your audience.

Gathering Information About Your Audience

Now that we have discussed *why* you should do a demographic, attitudinal, and environmental analysis of your audience, you may wonder, "*How* do I go about researching all this information about my audience?" As an audience-centered speaker, you should try to find out as much as you can about the audience *before* planning the speech. There are two approaches you can take: informal and formal. Let's look at these two approaches in detail.

To analyze your audience informally, you can simply observe them and ask questions before you speak. Informal observations can be especially important in helping you assess obvious demographic characteristics. For example, you can observe how many members of your audience are male or female, and you can also make some inferences from their appearance about their educational level, ethnic or cultural traits, and approximate age.

If, for example, you were going to address your local PTA meeting about a new store you were opening to help students and parents develop science projects, you could attend a meeting before your speaking date. Note the general percentage of men and women in the audience. Note the ages of the parents who attend. You could also ask whether most parents who show up for PTA meetings are parents of elementary, middle-school, or high-school students. Knowing these key pieces of information will help you tailor your speech to address your listeners' interests.

Also talk with people who know something about the audience you will be addressing. If you are invited to speak to a group you have not seen before, ask the person who invited you some general questions about the audience members: What is their average age? What are their political affiliations? What are their religious beliefs? What are their attitudes toward your topic? Try to get as much information as possible about your audience before you give your speech.

Rather than relying only on inferences drawn from such conversations, if time and resources permit, you may want to conduct a more formal survey of your listeners to gather both demographic data and information about their attitudes, beliefs, and values. How do you develop a formal survey? First, decide what you want to know about your audience that you don't already know. Let your topic and the speaking occasion help you determine the kinds of questions you should pose. Once you have an idea of what you would like to know, you can ask your potential audience straightforward questions about such demographic information as age, sex, occupation, and memberships in professional organizations. There is a sample questionnaire in Figure 5.2.

You can modify this questionnaire according to your audience and topic. If your topic concerns the best approach to finding a rental apartment and you are speaking in a suburban area, find out how many members of your audience own a home and how many are presently living in an apartment. You may also want to ask how they found

FIGURE 5.2

Demographic Audience-
Analysis Questionnaire

Demographic Audience-Analysis Questionnaire

1. Name (optional):_____

2. Sex: Male ❏ Female ❏

3. Occupation:_____

4. Religious affiliation:_____

5. Marital status: Married ❏ Single ❏ Divorced ❏

6. Major in school:_____

7. Years of schooling beyond high school:_____

8. Annual income: _____

9. Age:_____

10. Ethnic background:_____

11. Hometown and state: _____

12. Political affiliation: Republican ❏ Democrat ❏ Other ❏ None ❏

13. Membership in professional or fraternal organizations:_____

their current apartment, how many are now searching for an apartment, and how many anticipate searching for one. Answers to these questions can give you useful information about your audience and may also provide examples to use in your presentation.

Although knowing your audience's demographics can be helpful, again we caution you that inferences based on generalized information may lead to faulty conclusions. For example, it might seem reasonable to infer that if your audience consists mainly of 18- to 22-year-olds, they will not be deeply interested in retirement programs. But unless you have talked to them specifically about these topics, your inference may be incorrect. Whenever possible, ask specific questions about audience members' attitudes.

To gather useful information about audience members' attitudes, beliefs, and values, you can ask two basic types of questions. **Open-ended questions** allow for unrestricted answers, without limiting answers to choices or alternatives. Use open-ended questions when you want more detailed information from your audience. Essay questions, for example, are open-ended. **Closed-ended questions** offer several alternatives from which to choose. Multiple-choice, true–false, and agree–disagree questions are examples of closed-ended questions.

After you develop the questions, it is wise to test them on a small group of people to make sure they are clear and will encourage meaningful answers. Suppose you plan to address an audience about school-based health clinics that dispense birth-control pills in high schools. The sample questions in Figure 5.3 illustrate various open and closed formats.

open-ended questions
Questions that allow for unrestricted answers, without limiting answers to choices or alternatives

closed-ended questions
Questions that offer an alternative for answers, such as true–false, agree–disagree, or multiple-choice questions

Adapting to Your Audience as You Speak

So far, we have focused on discovering as much as possible about an audience before the speaking event. Prespeech analyses help with each step of the public-speaking process: selecting a topic, formulating a specific purpose, gathering supporting material, identifying major ideas, organizing the speech, and planning its delivery. Each of these components depends on understanding your audience. But audience analysis and adaptation do not end when you have crafted your speech. They continue as you deliver your speech.

FIGURE **5.3**

Sample Questions

Sample Questions

Open-Ended Questions

1. What are your feelings about having high-school health clinics that dispense birth-control pills?

2. What are your reactions to the current rate of teenage pregnancy?

3. What would you do if you discovered your child was receiving birth control pills from your high-school health clinic?

Closed-Ended Questions

1. Are you in favor of dispensing birth-control pills to high-school students in school-based health clinics?

   Yes ❏ No ❏

2. Birth-control pills should be given to high-school students who ask for them in school-based health clinics. (Circle the statement that best describes your feeling.)

   Agree strongly   Agree   Undecided   Disagree   Disagree strongly

3. Check the statement that most closely reflects your feelings about school-based health clinics and birth-control pills.

   ❏ Students should receive birth-control pills in school-based health clinics whenever they want them, without their parents' knowledge.

   ❏ Students should receive birth-control pills in school-based health clinics whenever they want them, as long as they have their parents' permission.

   ❏ I am not certain whether students should receive birth-control pills in school-based health clinics.

   ❏ Students should not receive birth-control pills in school-based health clinics.

4. Rank the following statements about school-based health clinics and birth-control pills, from most desirable (1) to least desirable (5).

   ❏ Birth-control pills should be available to all high-school students in school-based health clinics, whenever students want them, and even if their parents are not aware that they are taking the pills.

   ❏ Birth-control pills should be available to all high-school students in school-based health clinics, but only if their parents have given their permission.

   ❏ Birth-control pills should be available to high-school students without their parents' knowledge, but not in school-based health clinics.

   ❏ Birth-control pills should be available to high-school students, but not in school-based health clinics, and only with their parents' permission.

   ❏ Birth-control pills should not be available to high-school students.

Address: http://www.ablongwood.com/beebe

▼   **Gathering Information About Your Audience**

The following Websites provide information that may help you better understand your listeners' backgrounds and interests. As you surf these sites, consider the following questions:

1. How does the demographic and attitudinal information of the population described in the site translate to my audience?
2. How recent are the results of opinion polls and surveys?
3. How can I use this information to develop my message?

U.S. BUREAU OF LABOR STATISTICS

This is a great source for socioeconomic data.

http://stats.bls.gov/datahome.htm/

THE WORLD-WIDE WEB VIRTUAL LIBRARY DEMOGRAPHY AND POPULATION STUDIES

This site provides a link to a wealth of other sites about various aspects of demography.

http://www.cdi.anu.edu.au

GALLUP POLL

Provides selected results from the vast resources of the Gallup polling organization.

http://www.gallup.com

U.S. BUREAU OF THE CENSUS

This is a valuable source that includes reports on demographics.

http://www.census.gov/

Go here for recent census data, as well as a page of tools to help you access other demographic data.

http://www.census.gov/cgi-bin/gazetteer/

THE INSTITUTE FOR RESEARCH IN SOCIAL SCIENCES

This page has a great database for polls:

http://www.irss.unc.edu/data_archive/pollsearch.html/

Demographic Data from Your Zip Code

http://www.infods.com/freedata/

Generally, a public speaker does not have an exchange with the audience unless the event is set in a question-and-answer or discussion format. Once the speech is in progress, the speaker must rely on nonverbal clues from the audience to judge how people are responding to the message.

Once, when speaking in India, Mark Twain was denied eye contact with his listeners by a curtain separating him from his audience. Mark Twain's daughter, Clara, recalled this experience of her famous father: "One of Father's first lectures was before a Purdah audience; in other words, the women all sat behind a curtain through which they could peek at Mark Twain without being seen by him . . . a deadly affair for the poor humorist, who had not even the pleasure of scanning the faces of his mute audience."[14] Mark Twain missed learning how well his speech was being received as he was speaking. You could experience the same disadvantage if you fail to look at your listeners while you're speaking and adapt to them as you speak.

Many beginning public speakers may find it challenging at first not only to have the responsibility of presenting a speech they have rehearsed but also to have to change or modify the speech on the spot. We assure you that with experience you can develop the sensitivity to adapt to your listeners, much as a jazz musician adapts to the other musicians in the ensemble, but it will take practice. Although it's not possible to read your listeners' minds, it is important to analyze and adapt to cues that can enhance the effectiveness of your message. The first step in developing this skill is to be aware of the often unspoken clues that your audience either is hanging on every word or is bored. After learning to "read" your audience, you then need to consider developing a repertoire of behaviors to help you connect with your listeners.

Identifying Nonverbal Audience Cues

EYE CONTACT   Perhaps the best way to determine whether your listeners are maintaining interest in your speech is to note the amount of eye contact they have with you. The more contact they have, the more likely it is that they are listening to your message. If you find them looking down at the program (or, worse yet, closing their eyes), you can reasonably guess that they have lost interest in what you're talking about.

FACIAL EXPRESSION   Another clue as to whether an audience is "with you" is facial expression. An attentive audience not only makes direct eye contact but also wears an attentive facial expression. Beware of a frozen, unresponsive face. This sort of expression we call the "in a stupor" look. The classic in a stupor expression consists of a slightly tilted head, a faint, frozen smile, and often a hand holding up the chin. This expression may have the appearance of interest, but it more often means that the person is daydreaming or thinking of something other than your topic.

RESTLESS MOVEMENT   An attentive audience doesn't move much. An early sign of inattentiveness is fidgeting fingers, which may escalate to pencil wagging, leg jiggling, and arm wiggling. Seat squirming, feet shuffling, and general body movement often indicate that members of the audience have lost interest in your message.

NONVERBAL RESPONSIVENESS   An interested audience is one in which members verbally and nonverbally respond when encouraged or invited by the speaker. When you ask for a show of hands and audience members sheepishly look at one another and eventually raise a finger or two, you can reasonably infer lack of interest and enthusiasm. Frequent applause and head nods of agreement with your message are indicators of interest and support.

VERBAL RESPONSIVENESS Not only will some audiences indicate agreement nonverbally, but some will also indicate their interests verbally. Audience members may shout out a response or more quietly express agreement or disagreement to people seated next to them. A sensitive public speaker is constantly listening for verbal reinforcement or disagreement.

Responding to Nonverbal Cues

The value in recognizing nonverbal clues from your listeners is that you can respond to them appropriately. If your audience seems interested, supportive, and attentive, your prespeech analysis has clearly guided you to make proper choices in preparing and delivering your speech.

If your audience becomes inattentive, however, you may need to make some changes while delivering your message. If you think audience members are drifting off into their own thoughts or disagreeing with what you say, or if you suspect that they don't understand what you are saying, then a few spontaneous changes may help. It takes experience and skill to make on-the-spot changes in your speech. Consider the following tips for adapting to your listeners that seasoned public speakers use.[15]

If Your Audience Seems Inattentive or Bored:

- Tell a story.
- Use an example to which the audience can relate.
- Use a personal example.
- Remind your listeners why your message should be of interest to them.
- Eliminate some abstract facts and statistics.

- Use appropriate humor.
- Make direct references to the audience, using members' names or mentioning something about them.
- Ask the audience to participate by asking questions or asking them for an example.

- Ask for a direct response, such as a show of hands, to see whether they agree or disagree with you.
- Pick up the pace of your delivery.
- Pause for dramatic effect.

If Your Audience Seems Confused and Doesn't Understand Your Point:

- Be more redundant.
- Try phrasing your information in another way, or think of an example you can use to illustrate your point.
- Use a handy visual aid such as a chalkboard or flip chart to clarify your point.

- If you have been speaking rapidly, slow your speaking rate.
- Clarify the overall organization of your message to your listeners.
- Ask for feedback from an audience member to help you discover what is unclear.

- Ask someone in the audience to summarize the key point you are making.

If Your Audience Seems to Be Disagreeing With Your Message:

- Provide additional data and evidence to support your point.
- Remind your listeners of your credibility, credentials, or background.

- Rely less on anecdotes and more on facts to present your case.
- Write facts and data on a chalkboard, overhead transparency, or flip chart if one is handy.

- If you don't have the answers and data you need, tell listeners you will provide more information by mail, telephone, or e-mail (and make sure you get back in touch with them).

Remember, it is not enough to note your listeners' characteristics and attitudes. You must also *respond* to the information you gather by adapting your speech to retain their interest and attention. Moreover, you have a responsibility to ensure that your audience understands your message. If your approach to the content of your speech is not working, alter it and note whether your audience's responses change. If all else fails, you may need to abandon a formal speaker–listener relationship with your audience and open up your topic for discussion. Of course, in your speech class, your instructor may expect you to keep going, to fulfill the requirements for your assignment. With other audiences, however, you may want to consider switching to a more interactive question-and-answer session to ensure that you are communicating clearly to your listeners. Later chapters on supporting material, speech organization, and speech delivery will discuss other techniques for adjusting your style while delivering your message.

RECAP   ANALYZING AND ADAPTING TO YOUR AUDIENCE AS YOU SPEAK

Signs You Are Connecting to Your Audience	Signs You Are Not Connecting to Your Audience	Strategies for Adapting to an Unsupportive Audience
Audience members make eye contact; most audience members look you in the eye while you are speaking.	Audience members don't make eye contact with you.	• Tell a story. • Use more personal examples or illustrations. • Consider making direct references to your listeners by mentioning some people by name.
Listeners have sincere smiles or pleasant facial expressions.	Listeners frown or display blank or unresponsive facial expressions.	• Ask the audience members if they understand your message. • Increase your speaking energy. • Remind your listeners why your message is important to them. • Consider clarifying your message by using a chalkboard or other handy visual aid.
Audience members are quiet.	Audience members are talking to other audience members.	• Pause to gain listeners' attention. • Ask the audience a question—either rhetorical (one you don't expect them to literally answer) or a question to which you do expect a response.
Audience members aren't shuffling their hands and feet; there is little audience movement.	Audience members are restless; their hands and feet are nervously moving or twitching.	• Pick up the pace of your delivery. Use appropriate humor. • Use more concrete examples.
Audience members respond to your requests for information, respond to questions, or appropriately raise their hands when you ask a question.	Audience members do not respond to your questions or do not show interest in your message.	• Ask audience members if they understand the question you've asked. • Repeat your question, and make it clear that you'd like their response and participation.
Audience members make appropriate verbal responses; they laugh when you use humor.	Audience members don't respond to your questions; they don't laugh at your use of humor.	• If listeners are not responsive to your humor, rely less on jokes and use more stories or personal illustrations.

Analyzing Your Audience After You Speak

After you have given your speech, you're not finished analyzing your audience. It is important to evaluate your audience's positive or negative response to your message. Why? Because it can help you prepare your next speech. Postspeech analysis helps you polish your speaking skill, regardless of whether you will face the same audience again. From that analysis you can learn whether your examples were clear and your message was accepted by your listeners. Let's look at some specific methods for assessing your audience's response to your speech.

Nonverbal Responses

The most obvious nonverbal response is applause. Is the audience simply clapping politely, or is the applause robust and enthusiastic, indicating pleasure and acceptance? Responsive facial expressions, smiles, and nods are other nonverbal signs that the speech has been well received.

Realize, however, that audience members from different cultures respond to speeches in different ways. Japanese audience members, for example, are likely to be restrained in their response to a speech and show little expression. Some Eastern European listeners may not maintain eye contact with you; they may look down at the floor when listening. In some contexts, African-American listeners may enthusiastically voice their agreement or disagreement with something you say during your presentation.[16]

Nonverbal responses at the end of the speech may express some general feeling of the audience, but they are not much help in identifying which strategies were the most effective. Also consider what the members of the audience say, both to you and to others, after your speech.

Verbal Responses

What might members of the audience say to you about your speech? General comments, such as "I enjoyed your talk" or "Great speech," are good for the ego—which is important—but are not of much analytic help. Specific comments can indicate where you succeeded and where you failed. If you have the chance, try to ask audience members how they responded to the speech in general as well as to specific points in which you have a particular interest.

Survey Responses

You are already aware of the value of conducting audience surveys before speaking publicly. You may also want to survey your audience after you speak. You can then assess how well you accomplished your objective. Use the same survey techniques discussed earlier. Develop survey questions that will help you determine the general reactions to you and your speech, as well as specific responses to your ideas and supporting materials. Professional speakers and public officials often conduct such surveys. Postspeech surveys are especially useful when you are trying to persuade an audience. Comparing prespeech and postspeech attitudes can give you a clear idea of your effectiveness. A significant portion of most political-campaign budgets goes toward evaluating how a candidate is received by his or her constituents. Politicians want to know what portions of their messages are acceptable to their audiences so they can use this information in the future.

If your objective was to teach your audience about some new idea, a posttest can assess whether you expressed your ideas clearly. Actually, classroom exams are posttests that determine whether your instructor presented information clearly.

Behavioral Responses

If the purpose of your speech was to persuade your listeners to do something, you will want to learn whether they ultimately behave as you intended. If you wanted them to vote in an upcoming election, you might survey your listeners to find out how many did vote. If you wanted to win support for a particular cause or organization, you might ask them to sign a petition after your speech. The number of signatures would be a clear measure of your speech's success. Some religious speakers judge the success of their ministry by the amount of contributions they receive. Your listeners' actions are the best indicators of your speaking success.

SUMMARY

It is important to become an audience-centered speaker. To be an effective speaker, learn as much as you can about your listeners before, during, and after your speech. Before your speech, you can perform three kinds of analysis: demographic, attitudinal, and situational. You can use informal and formal approaches to gather information about your listeners for your analyses.

While speaking, look for feedback from your listeners. Audience eye contact, facial expression, movement, and general verbal and nonverbal responsiveness provide clues as to how well you are doing. Finally, evaluate audience reaction after your speech. Again, nonverbal clues as well as verbal ones will help you judge your speaking skill. The best indicator of your speaking success is whether your audience is actually able or willing to follow your advice or remembers what you have told them.

being audience-centered
A Sharper Focus

CONSIDERING YOUR AUDIENCE

▶ Becoming an audience-centered speaker involves two steps. First, analyze your audience to assess who your listeners are. Second, ethically adapt your message to meet their needs and achieve your speaking goals.

▶ Gather such demographic information about your listeners as their age, race, gender, socioeconomic status, and religious views.

▶ Psychological audience analysis helps you gauge the interests, attitudes, beliefs, and values of listeners.

▶ Determine whether your audience is captive or voluntary, interested or uninterested, favorable or unfavorable toward you and your message.

▶ Situational audience analysis includes examining the time and place of your speech, and size of your audience, as well as the speaking occasion.

▶ Observe the nonverbal cues of your listeners to determine whether you need to change or adapt your message to maintain interest and achieve your speaking objective.

CONSIDERING AUDIENCE DIVERSITY

▶ Consider the proportion of males and females in your audience, to help you appropriately adapt your message to them; avoid sexist language and make sure your message addresses the needs and interests of both men and women in your audience.

▶ Individualistic cultures place greater emphasis on individual achievement; people from Australia, Great Britain, the United States, and Canada tend to reflect more individualistic values.

▶ Collectivistic cultures tend to emphasize community, group, and team accomplishment more than individual achievement; people from Japan, Thailand, Colombia, Taiwan, and Venezuela are among those that have more collectivist cultures.

▶ High-context cultures place considerable emphasis on such contextual cues as nonverbal messages and the environment when interpreting messages of others.

▶ Low-context cultures emphasize the words and explicit statements of others when interpreting messages.

▶ People from some cultures such as Russia, Japan, France, and Costa Rica have a high need for certainty; they want to know what will happen in the future more than do people with a low need for certainty (such as people from Austria, Israel, Denmark, Switzerland, and Norway).

▶ High-power cultures differentiate between high-status and low-status people; low-power cultures strive for greater equality than do people from high-power cultures.

▶ Strategies for adapting to a diverse audience include the following: Focus on a target audience, use diverse strategies for a diverse audience, use common audience perspectives, and rely on visual materials that transcend language differences.

CRITICAL THINKING QUESTIONS

1. Dr. Cassandra Ruiz has been invited to speak on birth control to a women's group. She thought her audience would be women of child-bearing age. After writing her speech, however, she found out that all the women to whom she will be speaking are at least twenty years older than she expected. What changes, if any, should she make?

2. Phil Owens is running for a seat on the school board. He has agreed to speak to the chamber of commerce about his views, but he wants to know what his audience believes about a number of issues. How can he gather this information?

3. You are in the middle of your presentation, trying to persuade a group of investors to build a new shopping mall in your community. You notice a few of the audience members are losing eye contact with you, shifting in their seats, and looking at their watches. What do you do to regain their attention?

ETHICAL QUESTIONS

1. Maria strongly believes the drinking age should be increased to 22 years of age in her state. Yet when she surveyed her classmates, the overwhelming majority thought the drinking age should be lowered to 18. Should Maria change her speech topic and her purpose to avoid facing a hostile audience? Why or why not?

2. Dan knows that most of the women in his audience will be startled and probably offended if he begins his speech by saying, "Most of you broads in this audience are too sensitive about sexist language." This is how Dan really feels. Should he alter his language just to appease his audience? Explain.

3. Do most politicians place too much emphasis on the results of political-opinion polls to shape their stand on political issues? Explain your position.

4. Has political correctness gotten out of hand on college campuses today? Are we becoming too sensitive to cultural, ethnic, and gender issues in our public dialogue? Or are we not sensitive enough? Explain.

SUGGESTED ACTIVITIES

1. Conduct a demographic analysis of your speech class. Identify as much information as you can by observing (informal method). Then, using a formal method, construct a survey to assess other demographic characteristics of your audience. Compare the formal and informal methods of gathering information for accuracy and completeness.

2. Conduct a formal attitudinal analysis of your speech class, assessing the students' attitudes about one of the following topics:

Availability of Social Security

Children of divorce

Abortion and birth control

Financing a college education

Criteria for choosing a career

Nursing-home care

Character and credibility of elected officials

Impeachment of U.S. presidents

Preventing minority-student dropouts

Student politics

Opening student credit-card accounts

3. Give each class member a white card, a red card, and a green card. While a student is rehearsing a speech, class members should hold up the green card if they agree with what the speaker is saying, the red card if they disagree, and the white card if they are neutral or indifferent about the speech content. The speaker should seek to adapt to the audience feedback.

4. List the nonverbal clues that let you know that your audience is enjoying your speech or agreeing with your message. Make a second list identifying the nonverbal clues that communicate audience disagreement or boredom.

5. Ask people from a variety of different cultural and ethnic backgrounds (such as students in your public-speaking class, family, or friends) what characteristics they like best as well as those traits they find most annoying in a public speaker. Compare differences between the two lists, noting any cultural trends.

6. To assess your comfort level in communicating with people who have a different cultural background from your own, complete the following Personal Report of Intercultural-Communication Apprehension.

7. Personal Report of Intercultural Communication Apprehension

Neuliep and McCroskey designed the following self-report scale to measure your intercultural communication apprehension. This instrument is composed of fourteen statements concerning your feelings about communication with people from other cultures. Please indicate in the space provided the degree to which each statement applies to you by marking whether you (1) strongly agree, (2) agree, (3) are undecided, (4) disagree, or (5) strongly disagree with each statement. There are no right or wrong answers, and many of the statements are designed to be similar to other statements. Do not be concerned about this. Work quickly and record your first impressions. Respond to these statements as honestly as possible or else your score will not be valid.

_____ 1. Generally, I am comfortable interacting with a group of people from different cultures.

_____ 2. I am tense and nervous while interacting in group discussions with people from different cultures.

_____ 3. I like to get involved in group discussions with others who are from different cultures.

_____ 4. Engaging in a group discussion with people from different cultures makes me tense and nervous.

_____ 5. I am calm and relaxed when interacting with a group of people who are from different cultures.

_____ 6. While participating in a conversation with a person from a different culture, I feel very nervous.

_____ 7. I have no fear of speaking up in a conversation with a person from a different culture.

_____ **8.** Ordinarily I am very tense and nervous in conversations with a person from a different culture.

_____ **9.** Ordinarily I am very calm and relaxed in conversations with a person from a different culture.

_____ **10.** While conversing with a person from a different culture, I feel very relaxed.

_____ **11.** I'm afraid to speak up in conversations with a person from a different culture.

_____ **12.** I face the prospect of interacting with people from different cultures with confidence.

_____ **13.** My thoughts become confused and jumbled when interacting with people from different cultures.

_____ **14.** Communicating with people from different cultures makes me feel uncomfortable.

To score the instrument, reverse your original response for items 2, 4, 6, 8, 11, 13, and 14 (1 = 5, 2 = 4, 3 = 3, 4 = 2, and 5 = 1). For example, if your original score for item 2 was 1, change it to a 5. If your original score for item 4 was a 2, change it to a 4, and so forth. After reversing the score for these seven items sum all fourteen items. Scores cannot be higher than 70 or lower than 14. Higher scores (50–70) indicate high intercultural communication apprehension. Low scores (14–28) indicate low intercultural communication apprehension. To the degree to which you answered the items honestly, your score is a fairly reliable and valid assessment of your motivation to approach or avoid intercultural communication.

Source: J. W. Neuliep and J. C. McCroskey, "The Development of Intercultural and Interethnic Communication Apprehension Scales," _Communication Research Reports_ 14 (1997), 145–56.

USING TECHNOLOGY AND MEDIA

1. Conduct a survey for your next speech via e-mail or the Internet. Either send your audience-analysis survey on the Internet, or give each class member a hard copy of the survey and invite those with Internet access to respond to your survey via e-mail.

2. Watch a televised presidential address and compare your own reaction to the speech with the instant postspeech audience analysis available through e-mail or phone surveys immediately following the speech.

3. Videotape your audience while you are giving a speech. When you watch the video later, note whether you adapted or adjusted to your audience's nonverbal cues.

In all matters, before beginning,
a diligent preparation should be made.

CICERO

Developing Your Speech

objectives

After studying this chapter you should be able to do the following:

1. Select a topic for a classroom speech that is appropriate to the audience, the occasion, and yourself.

2. Narrow a topic so that it can be thoroughly discussed within the time limits allotted for a specific assignment.

3. Write an audience-centered, specific-purpose statement for an assigned topic.

4. Explain three ways of generating main ideas from a central idea.

5. Develop a blueprint for a speech by combining the central idea and a preview of the main ideas.

6. Apply to a speaking assignment the four steps for getting from a blank sheet of paper to a plan for the speech.

E d Garcia has arranged the books and papers on his desk into neat, even piles. He has sharpened his pencils and laid them out parallel to one another. He has even dusted his desktop and cleaned the computer monitor's screen. Ed can think of no other task to delay writing his speech. He loads his word-processing program, carefully centers the words *Informative Speech,* and then slouches in his chair, staring glumly at the blank expanse that threatens his well-being. Finally, he types the words *College Football* under the *Informative Speech* heading. Another long pause. Hesitantly, he begins his first sentence: "Today I want to talk to you about college football." Rereading his first ten words, Ed decides that they sound moronic. He deletes the sentence and tries again. This time the screen looks even blanker than before. He writes—deletes—writes—deletes. Half an hour later, Ed is exhausted and still mocked by a blank screen. And he is frantic—this speech *has* to be ready by 9 in the morning.

Getting from a blank screen or sheet of paper to a speech outline is often the biggest hurdle you will face as a public speaker. Fortunately, however, it is one that you can learn to clear. If your earlier efforts at speech writing have been like Ed Garcia's, take heart. Just as you learned to read, do long division, drive a car, and get through college registration, so too can you learn to prepare a speech.

The first steps in preparing a speech are as follows:

1. Select and narrow your topic.

2. Determine your purpose.

3. Develop your central idea.

4. Generate your main ideas.

At the end of step 4, you will have a plan for the speech and will be ready to develop and polish your main ideas further.

As we observed in Chapter 5, audience-centered speakers consider the needs, interests, and expectations of their audience during the entire speech-preparation process—needs, interests, and expectations that will be as diverse as audiences themselves. As you move from topic selection to speech plan, remember that you are preparing a message for your listeners. Always keep the audience as your central focus.

Select and Narrow Your Topic

Y our first task, illustrated by Figure 6.1, is to choose a topic on which to speak. You will need to narrow this topic to fit your time limits. Sometimes you can eliminate one or both of these steps because the topic has been chosen and properly defined for you. For example, because you visited England's Lake District on your tour of Great Britain last summer, your English-literature teacher asks you to speak about the mountains and lakes of that region before your class studies the poetry of Wordsworth and Coleridge. Or imagine a future day in which the Lions Club asks you to speak at its weekly gathering about the goals of the local drug-abuse task force, which you chair. In both cases, your topic and its scope have been decided for you.

In other instances, the choice of topic may be left entirely to you. In your public-speaking class, your instructor may provide such guidelines as time limits and type of speech (informative, persuasive, or entertaining) but allow you to choose your topic freely. In this event, you should realize that the success of your speech may rest on this decision. But how do you go about choosing an appropriate, interesting topic?

Guidelines for Selecting a Topic

Davy Crockett was scheduled to speak first on a platform with a political opponent known always to deliver the same standard speech. So Davy memorized that speech, gave it, and left the opponent speechless.[1]

CONSIDER THE AUDIENCE   The downfall of Crockett's literally speechless opponent was that he relied on a standard spiel, rather than tailoring his speeches to each specific audience. In Chapter 5 we discussed the reasons and methods for finding out about your audience. "What interests and needs do the members of this audience have in common?" and "Why did they ask me to speak?" are important questions to ask yourself as you search for potential speech topics. Keeping in mind each audience's interests and expectations; for example, a university president invited to speak to a civic organization should talk about some new university program or recent accomplishment; a police officer speaking to an elementary school's PTA should address the audience's concern for the safety of young children.

FIGURE **6.1**

Selecting and narrowing the topic and determining the general and specific purpose of the speech are early speechmaking tasks.

Not only should a speaker's choice of topic be relevant to the *interests* and *expectations* of his or her listeners, it should also take into account the *knowledge* listeners already have about the subject. For example, the need for a campuswide office of disability services would not be a good topic for a group of students with disabilities, who would already be well aware of such a need. The speech would offer them no new information.

Finally, speakers should choose topics that are *important*—that matter to their listeners, as well as to themselves. It was a poignant moment when Al Gore delivered his televised concession of the 2000 presidential election.

In your public-speaking class, too, you should offer speeches on topics of real or potential importance to your audience. In November 1994 Bruce Gronbeck, then-president of the Speech Communication Association (now the National Communication Association), reminded an audience of communication instructors that the kinds of speeches students need to give "have nothing to do with macramé, perfect fudge every time, or how to set up a functional study area in a dorm room."[2] At least by the end of the semester, Gronbeck maintained, students should be giving "the important kinds of . . . speeches that show . . . people how to confront the issues that divide them . . . ." Table 6.1 offers examples of topics appropriate for the interests, expectations, knowledge, and concerns of given audiences.

TABLE 6.1

Sample Audience-Centered Topics

Audience	Topic
Retirees	Preserving Social Security benefits
Civic organization	The Special Olympics
Church members	Starting a community food bank
First graders	What to do in case of a fire at home
Teachers	Building children's self-concepts
College fraternity	Campus service opportunities

CONSIDER THE OCCASION   On December 17, 1877, Mark Twain was invited to be one of the after-dinner speakers for American poet John Greenleaf Whittier's seventieth-birthday celebration.[3] The guest list included such dignitaries as Oliver Wendell Holmes, Ralph Waldo Emerson, William Dean Howells, and Henry Wadsworth Longfellow.

When it was Twain's turn to speak, he began with a burlesque in the style of today's "Saturday Night Live," featuring Longfellow, Emerson, and Holmes as drunken card-playing travelers in Nevada. Used to laughter and applause from his audiences, Twain was stunned by the silence that descended and seemed to grow as he continued.

What had gone wrong? Was Mark Twain's topic of *interest* to his listeners? Undoubtedly. Did they *expect* to hear someone talk about the distinguished guests? Yes. Could Twain *add to their knowledge* of the subject? Probably. Was his topic *appropriate to the occasion*? Definitely not!

Although after-dinner speeches are usually humorous, Twain's irreverence was inappropriate to the dignity of the birthday observance. Even though he had considered his audience, he had not considered carefully enough the demands of the occasion. Twain's irreverent talk aroused quite a commotion at the time and is said to have embarrassed him for years afterward. To be successful, a topic must be appropriate to both audience and occasion.

CONSIDER YOURSELF   What do you talk about with good friends? You probably discuss school, mutual friends, political or social issues, hobbies or leisure activities, or other topics of interest and importance to you. As with most people, your liveliest, most animated conversations revolve around topics of personal concern and conviction.

The best public-speaking topics are also ones that reflect your personal experience or especially interest you. Where have you lived? Where have you traveled? Describe your family or your ancestors. Have you held any part-time jobs? Describe your first days at college. What are your favorite classes? What are your hobbies or interests? What is your favorite sport? What social issues especially concern you? Here is one list of topics that was generated by such questions:

Blues music

"Yankee, go home": the American tourist in France

Why most diets fail

Behind the counter at McDonald's

My first day at college

Maintaining family ties while living a long distance from home

Getting involved in political campaigns

An alternative to selecting a topic with which you are already familiar is to select one you would like to know more about. Your interest will motivate both your research and your eventual delivery of the speech.

Strategies for Selecting a Topic

All successful topics reflect audience, occasion, and speaker. But just contemplating those guidelines does not automatically produce a good topic. Sooner or later, we all face a speech for which we cannot think of a good topic, whether it is the first speech of the semester, that all-important final speech, or a speaking engagement long after your school years are over. Nothing is so frustrating to a public speaker as floundering for something to talk about!

Fortunately, there are several strategies that can help generate speech topics. They are somewhat more artificial than considering audience, occasion, and self to produce a "natural" topic choice. Nevertheless, they can yield good topics.

BRAINSTORMING　A problem-solving technique widely used in such diverse fields as business, advertising, writing, and science, **brainstorming** can easily generate ideas for speech topics as well.[4] To brainstorm a list of potential topics, get a sheet of paper and a pencil or pen. Set a minimum time limit of, say, three to five minutes. Write down the first topic that comes to mind. Do not allow yourself to evaluate it. Just write it down, as a simple word or a phrase, a vague idea or a well-focused one. Now jot down a second idea—again, anything that comes to mind. The first topic may remind you of a second possibility. Such "piggybacking" of ideas is perfectly OK. Continue without any restraints until your time is up. At this stage, anything goes. Your goal is quantity—as long a list as you can think up in the time you have.

The following list of twenty-one possible topics came from a brainstorming session of about three minutes:

Music

Reggae

Bob Marley

Sound-recording technology

Retro music

Buddy Holly

The Beatles

John Lennon

Alternative music

Popular rock bands

MTV

Censorship of music

Movie themes

Oscar-winning movies of the 1990s

brainstorming
A creative problem-solving technique used to generate many ideas

Great epic movies

Titanic (the movie)

Salvaging the *Titanic* (the ship)

Treasure hunting

Key West, Florida

Ernest Hemingway

Cats

If your brainstorming yields several good topics, so much the better. Set aside a page or two in your class notebook for topic ideas, and list the extra topics there. You can then consider them when you get your next assignment.

RECAP HOW TO BRAINSTORM FOR A TOPIC

1. Get a blank sheet of paper.

2. Set a time limit for brainstorming.

3. Begin writing as many possible topics for a speech as you can.

4. Do not stop to evaluate your topics; just write them down.

5. Let one idea lead to another—free-associate; piggyback off your own ideas.

6. Keep writing until your time is up.

LISTENING AND READING FOR TOPIC IDEAS   Very often something you see, hear, or read triggers an idea for a speech. A current story on the evening TV news or in your local paper may suggest a topic. The following list of topics was brought to mind by recent headline stories in a large daily newspaper:

How to read and interpret stock-market indicators

Prison overcrowding

Health codes and restaurants

The Nobel Prizes

How record prices for art and artifacts are affecting museum acquisitions

Television evangelism

Deteriorating interstate highways

Mothers Against Drunk Driving

In addition to discovering topics in news stories, you might find them in an interesting segment of *60 Minutes, 20/20, Dateline,* or *Oprah.* Chances are that a topic covered in one medium has been covered in another as well, allowing extended research on the topic. For example, Oprah's interview of the parents of a child suffering from a genetic disease may be paralleled by *Newsweek*'s report on stem-cell research.

You may also find speech topics in one of your other classes. A lecture in an economics or political-science class may arouse your interest and provide a good topic for your next speech. The instructor of that class could probably suggest additional references on the subject.

Sometimes even a subject you discuss casually with friends can be developed into a good speech topic. You have probably talked with classmates about such campus issues as dormitory regulations, inadequate parking, or frustrations with registration and advisers. Campuswide concerns would be relevant to the student audience in your speech class, as would such matters as how to find a good summer job or the pros and cons of living on or off campus.

Just as you jotted down possible topics generated by brainstorming sessions, remember to write down topic ideas you get from media, class lectures, or informal conversations. If you rely on memory alone, what seems like a great topic today may be only a frustrating blank tomorrow.

SCANNING WEB DIRECTORIES By now, you probably have a list of topics from which to choose. But if all your efforts have failed to produce any ideas that satisfy you, try the following strategy.

Access a **Web directory** such as *Yahoo!* (www.yahoo.com). Select a category at random. Click on it, and look through the subcategories that come up. Click on one of them. Continue to follow the chain of categories until you see a topic that piques your interest—or until you reach a dead end, in which case you can return to the *Yahoo!* homepage and try again.

A recent random directory search yielded the following categories, listed from general to specific:

Social Science

Migration and Ethnic Relations

Refugees

Refuge! (a Website of Amnesty International)

How is a refugee made?

Conflict

Bosnian refugees

This search, which took only a few minutes, yielded at least two possible topics: the work of Amnesty International and the plight of Bosnian refugees. An additional advantage of this strategy is that you begin to develop your preliminary bibliography while you are searching for a topic. In Chapter 7, we will talk about Web directories and about gathering supporting materials in greater detail.

A final word of caution before moving forward in the speech-preparation process. For most brief classroom speeches (under ten minutes), you should allow at least one week from topic selection to speech delivery. A week gives you enough time to develop and research your speech. Many habitual procrastinators (like Ed Garcia, at the opening of this chapter) who grudgingly agree to begin an assignment a week in advance, learn to their surprise that the whole process is far easier than when they delay work until the night before they are supposed to deliver their speech.

RECAP

SELECTING A TOPIC

Guidelines: Consider the audience.

Consider the occasion.

Consider yourself.

Strategies: Brainstorm.

Listen and read.

Scan Web directories.

Web directory
Website that allows access to the World Wide Web through categories that are then broken down into ever-more-specific categories

Narrowing the Topic

After brainstorming, reading the newspaper, surfing the Web, and talking to friends, you have come up with a topic. For some students, the toughest part of the assignment is over at this point. But others soon experience additional frustration because their topic is so broad that they find themselves overwhelmed with information. How can you cover all aspects of a topic as large as "television" in three to five minutes? Even if you trained yourself to speak as rapidly as an auctioneer, it would take days to get it all in!

The solution is to narrow your topic so that it fits within the time limits set by your assignment. The challenge lies in *how* to do this.

If you have a broad, unmanageable topic, you might first try narrowing it by constructing categories similar to those created by Web directories. Write your general topic at the top of a list, with each succeeding word a more specific or concrete topic.

Megan uses categories to help her narrow her general topic, music. She writes "Music" at the top of a sheet of paper, and constructs a categorical hierarchy:

Music

Folk music

Irish folk music

The popularity of Irish folk music in the United States

Megan later discovers her topic is still a bit too broad. She simply cannot cover all the forms of Irish folk music popular in the United States in a talk of no more than five minutes. So she chooses one form of music—dance—and decides to talk about the kind of Irish hard-shoe dance music featured in *Riverdance*.

Be careful not to narrow your topic so much that you cannot find enough information for even a three-minute talk. If you do, just go back a step. In our example, Megan could return to the popularity of Irish folk music in the United States.

Determine Your Purpose

Now that you have selected and narrowed your topic, you need to decide on a purpose (as shown in Figure 6.1). If you do not know what you want your speech to achieve, chances are your audience won't either. Ask yourself, "What is really important for the audience to hear?" and "How do I want the audience to respond?" Clarifying your objectives at this stage will ensure a more interesting speech and a more successful outcome.

General Purpose

The **general purpose** of virtually any speech is either to inform, to persuade, or to entertain. The speeches you give in class will generally be either informative or persuasive. It is important that you fully understand what constitutes each type of speech so you do not confuse them and fail to fulfill an assignment. You certainly do not want to deliver a first-rate persuasive speech when an informative one was assigned! Although Chapters 15 through 18 will discuss the three general purposes at length, we summarize them here so that you can understand the basic principles of each:

SPEAKING TO INFORM　An informative speaker is a teacher. Informative speakers give listeners information. They define, describe, or explain a thing, person, place, concept, process, or function. In this excerpt from a student's informative speech on anorexia nervosa, the student describes the disorder for her audience:

Anorexia nervosa is an eating disorder that affects 1 out of every 200 American women. It is a self-induced starvation that can waste its victims to the point that they resemble victims of Nazi concentration camps.

Who gets anorexia nervosa? Ninety-five percent of its victims are females between the ages of 12 and 18. Men are only rarely afflicted with the disease. Anorexia nervosa patients are usually profiled as "good" or "model" children who have not caused their parents any undue concern or grief over other behavior problems. Anorexia nervosa is perhaps a desperate bid for attention by these young women.[5]

general purpose
Statement of whether a speech is intended primarily to inform, to persuade, or to entertain

To construct a speech about a visit to Yellowstone National Park, you would probably begin with a broad conception of your topic, like the panoramic image on the left. Then, using either a ladder or a tabular diagram, you would begin to pinpoint what interested you most during the visit. Finally, you might recall the day your car was stuck behind a wandering herd of bison. A ranger told you that this was an increasingly perplexing park management problem. Voila! This specific aspect of your visit would be a perfect topic to research and transform into a speech.

[Photo: left, A & L Siniboldi/Stone/Getty Images; right, John Warden/Stone/Getty Images]

Most lectures you hear in college are informative. The university president's annual "state of the university" speech is also informative, as is the colonial Williamsburg tour guide's talk. Such speakers are all trying to increase the knowledge of their listeners. Although they may use an occasional bit of humor in their presentations, their main objective is not to entertain but to inform. Although they may provoke an audience's interest in the topic, their main objective is not to persuade but to inform. Chapter 15 provides specific suggestions for preparing an informative speech.

SPEAKING TO PERSUADE   Persuasive speakers may offer information, but they use the information to try to change or reinforce an audience's convictions and often to urge some sort of action. For example, Brian offered compelling statistics to help persuade his audience to take steps to prevent and alleviate chronic pain:

A hundred million Americans, nearly a third of the population, [suffer] from chronic pain due to everything from accidents to the simple daily stresses on our bodies.[6]

The representative from Mothers Against Drunk Driving (MADD) who spoke at your high-school assembly urged you not to drink and drive and urged you to help others realize the inherent dangers of the practice. The fraternity president talking to your group of rushees tried to convince you to join his fraternity. Appearing on television during the last election, the candidates for president of the United States asked for your vote. All these speakers gave you information, but they used that information to try to get you to believe or do something. Chapters 16 and 17 focus in more detail on persuasive speaking.

SPEAKING TO ENTERTAIN   The entertaining speaker tries to get the members of an audience to relax, smile, perhaps laugh, and generally enjoy themselves. Storyteller Garrison Keillor spins tales of the town and residents of Lake Wobegon, Minnesota, to amuse his listeners. Comedian Whoopi Goldberg delivers a comic patter to make her audience laugh. Most after-dinner speakers talk to entertain their banquet guests. Like persuasive speakers, entertaining speakers may inform their listeners, but providing knowledge is not their main goal. Rather, their objective is to produce a smile at least and a belly laugh at best. Appendix C includes the speech "Schadenfreude," which is an example of a speech to entertain.

You need to decide at the beginning which of the three general purposes your speech is to have. This decision keeps you on track throughout the development of your speech. The way you organize, support, and deliver your speech depends, in part, on your general purpose.

GENERAL PURPOSES FOR SPEECHES

To inform   To share information with listeners by defining, describing, or explaining a thing, person, place, concept, process, or function

To persuade   To change or reinforce a listener's attitude, belief, value, or behavior

To entertain To help listeners have a good time by getting them to relax, smile, and laugh

Specific Purpose

Now that you have a topic and you know generally whether your speech should inform, persuade, or entertain, it is time you decided on its **specific purpose.** Unlike the general purpose, which can be assigned by your instructor, the specific purpose of your speech must be decided by you alone, because it depends directly on the topic you choose.

To arrive at a specific purpose for your speech, you must think in precise terms of what you want your audience to be able to *do* at the end of your speech. This kind of goal or purpose is called a **behavioral objective,** because you specify the behavior you seek from the audience. For a speech on how television comedy represents the modern family, you might write, "At the end of my speech, the audience will be able to explain how comedy portrays American family life today." The specific-purpose statement for a how-to speech using visual aids might read, "At the end of my speech, the audience will be able to use an online periodical index." For a persuasive speech on universal health care, your specific-purpose statement could say, "At the end of my speech, the audience will be able to explain why the United States should adopt a plan of national health insurance." A speech to entertain has a specific purpose, too. A stand-up comic may have a simple specific purpose: "At the end of my speech, the audience will laugh and applaud." An after-dinner speaker whose entertaining message has more informative value than that of the stand-up comic may say, "At the end of my speech, the audience will list four characteristics that distinguish journalists from the rest of the human species."

FORMULATING THE SPECIFIC PURPOSE   Note that all our sample specific-purpose statements begin with the same twelve words: "At the end of my speech, the audience will be able to . . ." The next word should call for an observable, measurable action that the audience should be able to take by the end of the speech. Use verbs such as *list, explain, describe,* or *write*. Do not use vague words such as *know, understand,* or *believe*. You can discover what your listeners know, understand, or believe only by having them show their increased capability in some measurable way.

specific purpose
What you want your audience to be able to do after listening to your speech; depends on topic and general purpose

behavioral objective
Wording of a specific purpose in terms of desired audience behavior

A statement of purpose does not say what you, the *speaker*, will do. The techniques of public speaking help you achieve your goals, but they are not themselves goals. To say, "In my speech, I will talk about the benefits of studying classical dance" emphasizes your performance as a speaker. The goal of the speech is centered on you, rather than on the audience. Other than restating your topic, this statement of purpose provides little direction for the speech. But to say, "At the end of my speech, the audience will be able to list three ways in which studying classical dance can benefit them" places the audience and their behavior at the center of your concern. This latter statement provides a tangible goal to guide your preparation and by which you can measure the success of your speech.

The following guidelines will help you prepare your statement of purpose.

- Use precise language in wording the specific purpose.

IMPRECISE: At the end of my speech, the audience will know some things about Hannibal, Missouri.

PRECISE: At the end of my speech, the audience will be able to list five points of interest in the town of Hannibal, Missouri.

- Limit the specific purpose to a single idea.   If your statement of purpose has more than one idea, you will have trouble covering the extra ideas in your speech. You will also run the risk of having your speech "come apart at the seams." Both unity of ideas and coherence of expression will suffer.

TWO IDEAS: At the end of my speech, the audience will be able to write a simple computer program in BASIC and play the CD-ROM game *Half-Life*.

ONE IDEA: At the end of my speech, the audience will be able to write a simple computer program in BASIC.

- Make sure your specific purpose meets the interests, expectations, and knowledge level of your audience.   Also be sure that your specific purpose is important. Earlier in this chapter, we discussed these criteria as guidelines for selecting a speech topic. Consider them again as you word your purpose statement.

Behavioral statements of purpose help remind you that the aim of public speaking is to win a response from the audience. In addition, using a specific purpose to guide the development of your speech helps you focus on the audience during the entire preparation process.

RECAP

GENERAL PURPOSES FOR SPEECHES

Your Specific Purpose Should . . .

Be written in precise language

Be limited to a single idea

Meet the needs, interests, expectations, and level of knowledge of your audience

USING THE SPECIFIC PURPOSE   Everything you do while preparing and delivering the speech should contribute to your specific purpose. The specific purpose can help you assess the information you are gathering for your speech. For example, you may find that an interesting statistic, although related to your topic, does not help achieve your specific purpose. In that case, you can substitute material that directly advances your purpose.

As soon as you have decided on it, write the specific purpose on a 3-by-5-inch note card. That way you can refer to it as often as necessary while developing your speech.

Develop Your Central Idea

Having stated the specific purpose of your speech, you are ready to develop your **central idea,** the first step highlighted in Figure 6.2. The central idea is a one-sentence summary of the speech. The central idea (sometimes called the *thesis*), like the purpose statement, restates the speech topic. But whereas a purpose statement focuses on audience behavior, the central idea focuses on the content of the speech.

Professional speech coach Judith Humphrey explains the importance of a central idea:

> *Ask yourself before writing a speech . . . . "What's my point?" Be able to state that message in a single clear sentence. Everything else you say will support that single argument.*[7]

The following guidelines can help you put your central idea into words.

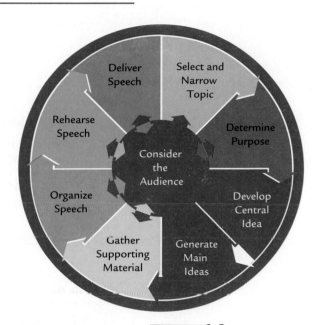

A Complete Declarative Sentence

The central idea should be a complete declarative sentence—not a phrase or clause, and not a question.

PHRASE:	Car maintenance
QUESTION:	Is regular car maintenance important?
COMPLETE DECLARATIVE SENTENCE	Maintaining your car regularly can ensure that it provides reliable transportation.

The phrase "car maintenance" is really not a central idea, but a topic. It does not say anything about car maintenance. The question "Is regular car maintenance important?" is more complete but does not reveal whether the speaker is going to support the affirmative or the negative answer. By the time you word your central idea, you should be ready to summarize your stand on your topic in a complete declarative sentence.

FIGURE 6.2

State your central idea as a one-sentence summary of your speech, and then generate main ideas by looking for natural divisions, reasons, or steps to support your central idea.

central idea
A one-sentence summary of the speech

Direct, Specific Language

The central idea should use direct, specific language rather than qualifiers and vague generalities.

QUALIFIER:	In my opinion, censorship of school textbooks threatens the rights of schoolchildren.
DIRECT LANGUAGE:	Censorship of school textbooks threatens the rights of schoolchildren.
VAGUE:	Tropical Storm Allison affected Houston, Texas.
SPECIFIC:	Killing 22 people and inflicting more than $5 billion in damage, Tropical Storm Allison changed forever the lives of the citizens of Houston, Texas.

A Single Idea

The central idea should be a single idea.

TWO IDEAS:	Deforestation by lumber interests and toxic-waste dumping are major environmental problems in the United States today.
ONE IDEA:	Toxic-waste dumping is a major environmental problem in the United States today.

More than one central idea, like more than one idea in a purpose statement, only leads to confusion and lack of coherence in a speech.

An Audience-Centered Idea

The central idea should reflect consideration of the audience. You considered your audience when selecting and narrowing your topic, and when composing your purpose statement. In the same way, you should consider your audience's needs, interests, expectations, and knowledge when stating your central idea. If you do not consider your listeners, you run the risk of losing their attention before you even begin developing the speech. If your audience consists mainly of college juniors and seniors, the second of the following central ideas would be better suited to your listeners than the first.

INAPPROPRIATE:	Scholarships from a variety of sources are readily available to incoming first-year college students.
APPROPRIATE:	Although you may think of scholarships as a source of money for freshmen, a number of scholarships are available only to students beyond their first year.

PURPOSE STATEMENT VERSUS CENTRAL IDEA

The purpose statement	**The central idea**
Indicates what the audience should know or be able to do by the end of the speech	Summarizes the speech
Guides the speaker's choices throughout the preparation of the speech	Guides the audience in their understanding of the speech

CRITERIA FOR A CENTRAL IDEA

THE CENTRAL IDEA SHOULD . . .

Be a complete declarative sentence

Use direct, specific language

Be a single idea

Be an audience-centered idea

Generate and Preview Your Main Ideas

Next to selecting a topic, probably the most common stumbling block in developing speeches is coming up with a speech plan. Trying to decide how to subdivide your central idea into two, three, or four **main ideas** can make you chew your pencil, scratch your head, and end up as you began, with a blank sheet of paper. The task will be much easier if you use the following strategy.

Generating Your Main Ideas

Write the central idea at the top of a clean sheet of paper. Then ask these three questions:

- Does the central idea have *logical divisions?* (These may be indicated by such phrases as "three types" or "four means.")

- Can you think of several *reasons* the central idea is true?

- Can you support your central idea with a series of *steps* or a chronological progression?

You should be able to answer yes to one or more of these questions. With your answer in mind, write down the divisions, reasons, or steps you thought of. Let's see this technique at work with several central idea statements.

FINDING LOGICAL DIVISIONS   Suppose your central idea is "A liberal-arts education benefits the student in three ways." You now turn to the three questions. But for this example, you needn't go beyond the first one. Does the central idea have logical divisions? The phrase "three ways" indicates that it does. You can logically divide your speech into ways in which the student benefits. A brief brainstorming session then helps you come up with three ways in which a liberal-arts education benefits students:

main ideas
Subdivisions of the central idea

1. Job opportunities

2. Appreciation of culture

3. Concern for humankind

At this stage, you needn't worry about Roman numerals, parallel form, or even the order in which the main ideas are listed. We will discuss these and the other features of outlining in Chapter 11. Your goal now is simply to generate ideas. Moreover, just because you write them down, don't think that the ideas you come up with now are engraved in stone. They can—and probably will—change. After all, this is a *preliminary* plan. It may undergo many revisions before you actually deliver your speech. In our example, three points may well prove to be too many to develop in the brief time allowed for most classroom speeches. But because it is much easier to eliminate ideas than to invent them, list them all for now.

ESTABLISHING REASONS   Suppose your central idea is "Upholstered-furniture fires are a life-threatening hazard."[8] Asking whether there are logical divisions of this idea is no help at all. There are no key phrases indicating logical divisions—no "ways," "means," "types," or "methods" appear in the wording. The second question, however, is more productive: Having done some initial reading on the topic, you can think of *reasons* this central idea is true. Asking yourself, "Why?" after the statement yields three answers:

1. Standards to reduce fires caused by smoldering cigarettes has lulled furniture makers into a false sense of security.

2. Government officials refuse to force the furniture industry to reexamine its standards.

3. Consumers are largely ignorant of the risks.

Notice that these main ideas are expressed in complete sentences, whereas the ones in the preceding example were in phrases. At this stage, it doesn't matter. What does matter is getting your ideas down on paper. You can rewrite and reorganize them later.

TRACING SPECIFIC STEPS   "U.S.–Israeli relations underwent great upheaval from 1990 to 2001." You stare glumly at the central idea you so carefully formulated yesterday. Now what? You know a lot about the subject; your international-relations professor has covered it thoroughly this semester. But how can you organize all the information you have? Again, you turn to the three-question method.

Does the main idea have logical divisions? You scan the sentence hopefully, but you can find no key phrases suggesting logical divisions.

Can you think of several reasons the thesis is true? You read the central idea again and ask, "Why?" at the end of it. Answering that question may indeed produce a plan for a speech, one in which you would talk about the reasons for the upheaval. But your purpose statement reads, "At the end of my speech, the audience will be able to trace the upheaval in U.S.–Israeli relations from 1990 to 2001." Giving reasons for the upheaval would not directly contribute to your purpose. So you turn to the third question.

Can you support your central idea with a series of steps? Almost any historical topic, or any topic requiring a chronological progression (for example, topics of how-to speeches), can be subdivided by answering the third question. You therefore decide that your main ideas will be a chronology of U.S.–Israeli relations from 1990 to 2001:

1. Early 1990: Decreased Soviet threat weakens need for strategic alliance between United States and Israel.

2. Late 1990:   Israel lacks clear role in Persian Gulf crisis.

3. 1992:   Rabin government elected; relations improve.

4. 1993:   Clinton inaugurated; relations continue to improve with support for Israeli–PLO Declaration of Principles and the peace process.

5. 1997:   Israel linked up to the U.S. missile-warning satellite system, which will provide Israel with real-time warning if a missile is launched against it.

6. 2001:   Despite continuing peace efforts by both the Clinton and Bush Administrations, more than 1,000 Israelis and Palestinians die in a year of conflict.

You know that you can add to, eliminate, or reorganize these ideas later. But you have a start.

Notice that you consulted your purpose statement as you generated your main ideas in that last example. If these main ideas do not help achieve your purpose, you need to rethink your speech. You may finally change either your purpose or your main ideas; but whichever you do, you need to synchronize them. Remember, it is much easier to make changes at this point than after you have done your research and produced a detailed outline.

RECAP

GENERATING MAIN IDEAS

Ask Whether Your Central Idea . . .

Has *logical divisions*

Is true for a number of *reasons*

Can be supported with *steps*

Previewing Your Main Ideas

Once you have generated your main ideas, you can add a preview of those main ideas to your central idea to produce a **blueprint** for your speech. Preview the ideas in the same order you plan to discuss them in the speech. In Chapter 9, we discuss in greater detail how to organize your speech.

Some speakers, like Nicole, integrate their central idea and preview into one blueprint sentence:

Obsolete computers are straining landfills because they contain hazardous materials and take a distinctively long time to decay.[9]

In this example, Nicole started with a central idea: "*Obsolete computers are straining landfills.*" Asking herself "Why?" yielded two reasons, which became her two main points: "*They contain hazardous materials*" and "*They take a distinctively long time to decay.*" Combining these reasons with her central idea produced a blueprint.

Other speakers, like Erin, state their blueprints in several sentences:

Today I would like to expose the myth that owning a gun guarantees your personal safety. First, I will discuss the fact that guns are rarely reached in time of need. Then I will address the risk of accidental shootings and how this is greatly increased by people's failure to receive proper gun-handling training. And finally, I will propose an alternative solution, self-defense.[10]

Erin also started with a central idea: *Owning a gun does not guarantee your personal safety.* Like Nicole, she generated reasons for her central idea, which in this case were that *guns are rarely reached in time of need* and that *the risk of accidental shootings is increased.* She decided also to discuss martial-arts *self-defense* as a solution to the problem. Thinking that a single sentence might become unwieldy, Erin decided to use four shorter sentences for her blueprint.

blueprint
The central idea plus a preview of main ideas

Meanwhile, Back at the Computer . . .

It's a long time since we abandoned Ed Garcia, the student in the opening paragraphs of this chapter who was struggling to write a speech on college football. Even though he has procrastinated, if he follows the steps we have discussed he still should be able to plan a successful informative speech.

Ed has already chosen his topic. His audience is likely to be interested in his subject. Because he is a varsity defensive tackle, they probably expect him to talk about college football. And he himself is passionately interested in and knowledgeable about the subject. It meets all the requirements of a successful topic.

But "college football" is too broad for a three- to five-minute talk. Ed needs to narrow his topic to a manageable size. He goes online to *Yahoo!* and clicks on the category *Sports*. This search yields a fairly long list of subcategories. He is just about to select *College and University* when another category catches his eye: *Medicine*. Sports medicine. Hmmmm. Ed has suffered several injuries and feels qualified to talk about this aspect of football. Ed doesn't need to go further. He has his topic: "injuries in college football."

Now that he has narrowed the topic, Ed needs a purpose statement. He decides that his audience may know something about how players are injured, but they probably do not know how these injuries are treated. He types, "The audience will be able to explain how the three most common injuries suffered by college football players are treated."

A few minutes later, Ed derives his central idea from his purpose: "Sports medicine specialists have developed specific courses of treatment for the three most common kinds of injuries suffered by college football players."

Generating main ideas is also fairly easy now. Because his central idea mentions three kinds of injuries, he can plan his speech around those three ideas (logical divisions). Under the central idea Ed lists three injuries:

1. Bruises

2. Broken bones

3. Ligament and cartilage damage

Now Ed has a plan and is well on his way to developing a successful three- to five-minute informative speech.

SUMMARY

Four main steps are involved in getting from a blank piece of paper to a speech plan:

1. Select and narrow your topic.

2. Determine your purpose.

3. Develop your central idea.

4. Generate your main ideas.

The difficulty of selecting a topic varies greatly from speech to speech. Sometimes speakers are asked to address a specific topic. At other times they may be given only such broad guidelines as time limits and occasion. As speakers consider possible topics, they must consider the interests, expectations, and knowledge levels of their audiences. They should select topics of importance, and consider the special demands of the occasion. Finally, speakers must take into account their own interests, abilities, and experiences. Usually these "boundaries" help them select appropriate topics. If still undecided, they may try such strategies as brainstorming, consulting the media, or scanning Web directories for potential topics.

After choosing a broad topic area, a speaker may need to narrow the topic so that it fits within the time limits that have been set.

The next task a speaker faces is deciding on general and specific purposes. He or she must consider first whether a speech is going to be informative, persuasive, or entertaining. With a general purpose in mind, the speaker can write a specific-purpose statement. A specific purpose should be worded behaviorally, in terms of what the speaker wants the audience to be able to do at the end of the speech. The specific purpose serves as a yardstick by which the speaker can measure the relevance of ideas and supporting materials while developing the speech.

Specific-purpose statements indicate what speakers hope to accomplish; central ideas, by contrast, summarize what they will say. The central idea should be a complete declarative sentence. From the central idea, the speaker can generate main ideas.

One strategy for generating main ideas is to determine whether the central idea has logical divisions, can be supported by several reasons, or can be traced through a series of steps. These divisions, reasons, or steps become the speech plan, which the speaker will probably preview in the introduction and summarize in the conclusion. Now the speaker is ready to move on to gathering supporting material for the speech.

being audience-centered
A Sharper Focus

CONSIDERING YOUR AUDIENCE

▷ "What interests and needs do the members of this audience have in common?" and "Why did they ask me to speak?" are important questions as you search for potential speech topics.

▷ As you determine your purpose for speaking, ask yourself, "What is really important for the audience to hear?" and "How do I want the audience to respond?"

▷ Informative speakers give listeners information, defining, describing, or explaining a thing, person, place, concept, process, or function.

▷ Persuasive speakers may offer information, but they use the information to try to change or reinforce an audience's convictions and often to urge some sort of action.

▷ The entertaining speaker tries to get the members of an audience to relax, smile, perhaps laugh, and generally enjoy themselves.

▷ To arrive at a specific purpose for your speech, think in precise terms of what you want your audience to be able to *do* at the end of your speech.

▷ Using a specific purpose to guide the development of your speech helps you focus on the audience during the entire preparation process.

▶ Audience-centered public speakers consider the needs, interests, and expectations of their audience during the entire speech-preparation process—needs, interests, and expectations that are as diverse as audiences themselves.

▶ Not only should a speaker's choice of topic be relevant to the *interests* and *expectations* of his or her listeners, it should also take into account the *knowledge* listeners already have about the subject.

▶ You can discover what your listeners know, understand, or believe only by having them show their increased capability in some measurable way.

▶ Be sure your specific purpose meets the interests, expectations, and level of knowledge of your audience.

▶ When stating your central idea, consider your audience's needs, interests, expectations, and knowledge.

CRITICAL THINKING QUESTIONS

1. Your public-speaking class invites a gubernatorial candidate to address the class. The candidate accepts the invitation and speaks for thirty minutes on the topic "Why the state should increase funding of public transportation." Analyze the candidate's choice of topic according to the guidelines presented in this chapter.

2. Several specific-purpose statements appear next. Analyze each according to the criteria presented in this chapter for formulating a specific purpose. Rewrite the statements to correct any problems.

   At the end of my speech, the audience will know more about the Mexican Free-Tailed Bat.

   I will explain some differences in nonverbal communication between Asian and Western cultures.

   At the end of my speech, the audience will be able to list some reasons for xeriscaping one's yard.

   To describe the reasons I enjoy spelunking as a hobby.

   At the end of my speech, the audience will be able to prepare a realistic monthly budget.

   The advantages and disadvantages of living in a college dormitory.

3. Below are the topic, general purpose, and specific purpose Marylin has chosen for her persuasive speech. Write an appropriate central idea and main ideas for the speech. Be prepared to explain how you derived the main points from the central idea.

TOPIC:	National presidential primary
GENERAL PURPOSE:	To persuade
SPECIFIC PURPOSE:	At the end of my speech, the audience will be able to list and explain three reasons the United States should adopt a national presidential primary.

CENTRAL IDEA:

MAIN IDEAS:

ETHICAL QUESTIONS

1. Like Davy Crockett's crestfallen opponent described early in this chapter, many speakers prepare a stock speech and proceed to deliver it to a variety of audiences and on a variety of occasions. Is this practice ethical? Explain your answer.

2. While eating lunch in the student-center cafeteria, you overhear a stranger at the next table describing a paper she is writing for her political-science class. She mentions a book she used to support her argument that the death sentence should not be abolished. Would it be ethical for you to "borrow" her topic and consult the book she mentioned, to prepare a speech for a public-speaking course assignment?

SUGGESTED ACTIVITIES

1. Brainstorm a list of at least fifteen potential topics for an informative classroom speech. Applying the criteria discussed in this chapter, select the topics best suited to your audience, the occasion, and yourself. If you wish, use one of these topics for an assigned informative speech.

2. Browse through a current newspaper, news magazine, or *TV Guide*. See how many potential speech topics you can discover in the stories your source contains. Write them down. File or copy your list into your speech notebook or computer file.

3. Narrow each of the following general categories into a workable topic for a three- to five-minute informative speech:

   The ocean

   Technology

   Money

USING TECHNOLOGY AND MEDIA

1. Watch a television news magazine such as *60 Minutes, 20/20,* or *Dateline.* Keep a scratch pad and pen at hand, and jot down potential speech topics as they come to mind during the program. Don't forget the commercials—they often raise questions or issues that would make good topics.

2. Access a few online chat rooms and special-interest-group exchanges. Jot down any speech topic ideas that come to mind; then transfer them to your speech notebook or computer file. When you decide on a topic, you may want to return to one of the chat rooms to discuss your idea or gather more information.

Learn, compare, collect the facts! . . .
Always have the courage to say to yourself—
I am ignorant.

IVAN PETROVICH PAVLOV

7

Gathering Supporting Material

objectives

After studying this chapter you should be able to do the following:

1. List five potential sources of supporting material for a speech.

2. Discuss the variety of resources available on the World Wide Web.

3. Explain six criteria for evaluating Websites.

4. List seven types of library resources.

5. Plan and conduct an effective interview.

6. Explain what items of information a researcher should record to document resources.

Apple pie is your specialty. Your family and friends relish your flaky crust, spicy filling, and crunchy crumb topping. Fortunately, not only do you have a never-fail recipe and technique, but you also know where to go for the best ingredients. Fette's Orchard has the tangiest pie apples in town. For your crust, you use only Premier shortening, which you buy at Meyer's Specialty Market. Your crumb topping requires both stone-ground whole-wheat flour and fresh creamery butter, available on Tuesdays at the farmer's market on the courthouse square.

Just as making your apple pie requires that you know where to find specific ingredients, a successful speech requires knowledge of both sources and types of supporting material that speechmakers typically use. Chapters 7 and 8 together cover the speech-development step illustrated by Figure 7.1: Gather Supporting Material. In this chapter we will identify various sources of information and discuss ways to access them. In Chapter 8 we will focus on recognizing and effectively using various types of supporting material.

Personal Knowledge and Experience

Because you will probably give speeches on topics in which you have a special interest, you may find that *you* are your own best source. Your speech may be on a skill or hobby in which you are expert, such as tropical fish, stenciling, or stamp collecting. Or you may talk on a subject with which you have had some personal experience, such as buying a used car, deciding whether to join a club, or seeking assisted living for an elderly relative. Don't automatically run to your computer or the library to find every piece of supporting material for every topic on which you speak. It is true that most well-researched speeches include some objective material gathered from outside sources. But you may also be able to provide an effective illustration, explanation, definition, or other type of support from your own knowledge and experience. As an audience-centered speaker, you should realize, too, that personal knowledge often has the additional advantage of heightening your credibility in the minds of your listeners. They will accord you more respect as an authority when they realize that you have firsthand knowledge of a topic.

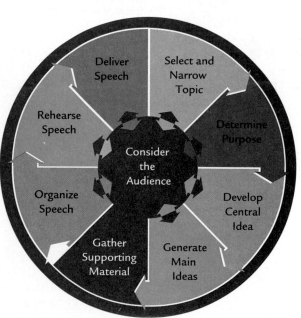

FIGURE **7.1**

Finding, identifying, and effectively using supporting material are activities that comprise an essential step of the speech-preparation process.

The Internet

Science-fiction author William Gibson first used the term *cyberspace* to describe an environment in which computers and people coexisted in virtual reality. Today, cyberspace describes a real phenomenon, which is called the **Internet.**[1] Originating as a modest network of four computers in 1969, the Internet today is a vast collection of computers accessible to millions of people all over the world.

In just a few short years, the Internet has gone from a novel, last-resort resource to the first place most people turn when faced with a research task. More specifically, it is the **World Wide Web,** the most popular information-delivery system of the Internet, that is of primary interest when you are searching for supporting materials for a speech. Understanding the World Wide Web, the tools for accessing it, and some of the amazing types of information available can help make research easier, more productive, and even more fun.

The World Wide Web

The World Wide Web delivers Internet information to your computer as text, graphics, and audio and moving visual images. **Websites** and **Web pages** may include personal and company pages, periodicals, newspapers, reference material, and government documents, as well as indexes and catalogs of these resources. Each Website and Web page has its own address or uniform resource locator (**URL**), the line of characters that will access the site when typed into the designated space on your **browser** software. Netscape Navigator and Microsoft Internet Explorer are the most commonly used browsers.

As well as being accessible by address, Web pages are hyperlinked: Each one is linked to other, related pages, to form a web of information. **Hyperlinks** are usually indicated by colored and underlined words in text, or they may be images. Clicking with your mouse on a hyperlink automatically calls up the linked page, without your having to know its address. Your browser lets you set an electronic **bookmark** on any interesting page so that you can return directly to it in the future without beginning a new search or going through other links.

Directories and Search Engines

When you are just beginning to research a topic, you may not know an address for a relevant Website. Even if you do, you may find the hyperlinks not particularly useful for continuing your research. You need a **directory** or **search engine** such as those provided by *Yahoo!, Google, Alta Vista,* or another of the sites listed in Figure 7.2. Regardless of whether you have spent countless hours surfing the Web or are a relative newcomer to its remarkable array of resources, today's directories and search engines make the Web easy to use.

At times, you might want to browse broad categories of information on the Web, just as you would browse a section of library shelves for books all on the same subject. Directories work by setting up broad categories that are subdivided into ever-more-specific categories. When you call up a directory, you see a list of broad categories that include such areas as education, entertainment, government, reference, and science.

Internet
A vast collection of hundreds of thousands of computers accessible to millions of people all over the world

World Wide Web
The most popular information-delivery system of the Internet

Website
A location on the World Wide Web that includes a number of related Web pages

Web page
An individual file or screen that is part of a larger Website

URL
Uniform resource locator; the address of a Website or Web page

browser
Software that accesses Websites and Web pages

hyperlink
Colored and underlined words or icons on a Web page that connect the user with another Web page or Website

bookmark
A browser feature that allows a user to save a URL for future reference

directory
A site that works by offering the user ever-more-specific categories of information from which to select

search engine
A site that works much like a traditional card catalog or index, by allowing the user to perform a subject or key-word search

Alta Vista	http://www.altavista.com
Argus Clearinghouse	http://www.clearinghouse.net
Google	http://www.google.com
Lycos	http://www.lycos.com
Yahoo!	http://www.yahoo.com

FIGURE 7.2

Popular World Wide Web Directories and Search Engines

Simply click on the category that seems most appropriate to your needs. You will likely be taken to a second level of categories; again, click on the most likely subcategory. Eventually, you will get a list of **hits**, or Websites and Web pages that deal with the category you have selected.

At other times, you might prefer to access Websites and Web pages by key words or subjects, much as you would search a traditional library card catalog. Search engines index the World Wide Web in this manner. At one time, most Websites specializing in Internet searches were *either* directories *or* search engines; most now offer both functions.

Only a few years ago, students struggled to find enough information for speeches and papers. One of the ways in which the World Wide Web has changed research is that today students often find themselves overwhelmed by *too much* material. One strategy that can help you narrow your search is called an advanced or **Boolean search**. Boolean searches let you enclose phrases in quotation marks or parentheses so that a search yields only those sites on which all words of the phrase appear in that order, rather than sites that contain the words at random. Boolean searches also permit you to insert "AND" or "+" between words and phrases to indicate that you wish to see results that contain both phrases. Conversely, they let you exclude certain words and phrases from your search. And they let you restrict the dates of your hits—see only documents posted within a specified time frame. These relatively simple strategies can help you narrow a list of hits from, in some cases, millions of sites, to a more workable number.

Here is an example of how the advanced search capabilities of *Yahoo!* can help you limit a search for information for your speech on the Volkswagen Beetle:

1. Type the key word *beetle* in the search box, and click on *Search.*

2. *Yahoo!* finds 130 sites.

3. Click on the *Advanced Search* option. Now type in *beetle – insect* to communicate that you are interested only in sites on beetles that are *not* about the insect known as a beetle. *Yahoo!* yields 106 sites.

4. Clarify that you only want sites about the Volkswagen Beetle. Type in *beetle – insect + Volkswagen. Yahoo!* now finds 57 sites.

5. Restrict your search to sites posted in the last three months. Now you have only 28 sites—a more reasonable number of sources with which to begin.

Different search engines use slightly different syntaxes for advanced searches. Most provide search tips that can help you format searches and interpret results.

Evaluating Web Resources

In Chapter 3, we discussed the Web as an unparalleled experiment in free speech. Never before have so many people and organizations been so readily able to publish their ideas, opinions, and information as on the World Wide Web. Although the Web is a great victory for those who support free speech, the lack of legal, financial, or editorial restriction on what is published presents both a logistical and an ethical challenge to researchers.

Earlier in this chapter, we talked about how to narrow a Web search so that the sheer quantity of resources is not so overwhelming. However, no search strategy can ensure the quality of the sites you discover. As you begin to explore those sites, you need to evaluate them according to a consistent standard. The following six criteria can serve as such a standard:[2]

ACCOUNTABILITY   Find out what individual or organization is responsible for the Website. First, look to see whether the page is signed. If you find the name of the author, but not his or her qualifications, to be able to assess the author's expertise and authority you need to seek further information. You may be able to get such information by following hyperlinks from this page to other documents. Another way to get information is to enter the author's name, enclosed in quotation marks, in a search engine.[3] You may find either information about, or other pages by, this author.

Many organizations, like Allyn & Bacon, the publisher of this textbook, maintain complex Websites with vast amounts of information. When you encounter a potentially useful Website, use the criteria listed here to determine how valuable the site may in fact be for you.

If the Website is unsigned, you may still be able to find out what organization sponsors it. Look for a header or footer that indicates affiliation. Or you may be able to follow a hyperlink at the top or bottom of the page to the homepage of which this document is a part. If you can identify an organization, but still do not know anything about its reputation, the **domain**, indicated by the last three letters of a site's URL, can give you additional information. The following domains are used by the types of organizations indicated:[4]

.com or **.net**—commercial sites

.org—nonprofit groups

.edu—educational institutions

.gov—government agencies

.mil—military groups

You can also try entering the name of the organization, enclosed in quotation marks, in a search engine.

If you have tried these strategies and still cannot identify or verify the author or sponsor of a Website, be extremely wary of the site. If no one is willing to be accountable for the information it contains, you cannot be accountable to your audience for using the information in a speech. Continue your search elsewhere.

ACCURACY   Unless you are an expert in the area your Website addresses, it may be difficult to determine whether the information it contains is accurate. However, two considerations can help you assess accuracy.

First, realize that accuracy is closely related to accountability. If the author or sponsoring organization of a Website is a credible authority on the subject, the information posted on the site is more likely to be accurate than is information on an anonymous or less thoroughly documented site.

Second, assess the care with which the Website has been written. References or hyperlinks should be provided for any information that comes from a secondary source. The site should also be relatively free of common errors in usage and mechanics. A site laden with such errors may contain errors in content, as well.

If you find yourself still feeling somewhat uncertain about the accuracy of information you find on a Website, conduct further research. You may be able to verify or refute the information on another site or in a print resource.

OBJECTIVITY   Like accuracy, objectivity is related to accountability. Once you know who is accountable for a site, consider the interests, philosophical or political biases, and source of financial support of that individual or organization. Are these interests or biases likely to slant the information presented? The more objective the author, the more credible the facts and information presented.

DATE   Look for evidence that the site was recently posted or is kept current. At the bottom of many sites you will find a statement of when the site was posted and when it was last updated. If you do not find a date there, click on the "View" menu at the top of your Netscape screen, and go down to "Page Info." When you click on "Page Info," you will open a screen that includes a "Last Modified" date. Still another strategy is to search for the title of the Website on a search engine. The information that comes up should include a date. In most cases, when you are concerned with factual data, the more recent, the better.

USABILITY   The layout and design of the site should facilitate its use. Frames, graphics, and multimedia resources can enhance a site, but may also slow down the speed with which you can load it, or cause your computer to freeze. Some sites offer a "text-only" or "non-tables" option. Also consider whether there is a fee for access to any of the information on the site. Balance the graphics features and any possible cost against practical efficiency.

DIVERSITY[5]   A diversity-sensitive Website will be free of material that communicates bias against any ethnic, racial, gender, or sexual-preference subgroup, or against people with disabilities. Such a site may also offer divergent perspectives through hyperlinks or invite divergent perspectives through interactive forums. A site friendly to people with disabilities may offer a large-print option or an audio alternative to printed text.

As of June 2001, U.S. federal government Websites must comply with a set of standards that include such requirements as making sure hyperlinks can be detected by color-blind users and supplying captions to audio and video clips for people with hearing impairment.[6]

RECAP

FINDING SUPPORTING MATERIAL ON THE WORLD WIDE WEB

1. Use a directory or search engine to find relevant sites.

2. Expect to discover a wide variety of sites: books, periodicals, newspapers, wire services, reference resources, and government documents.

3. Evaluate Websites according to these six criteria: accountability, accuracy, objectivity, date, usability, and diversity.

The first four of the criteria just listed can serve as a guide to evaluating any resource, regardless of whether it is a Website, a print document, or even information you obtain in an interview. In Chapter 8, we will provide additional criteria to help you make your final selection of supporting material from both electronic and print resources.

▬ **X**

Address: http://www.ablongman.com/beebe

▼ | **Evaluating Websites**

The following site provides multicultural criteria for evaluating Websites.

MULTICULTURAL CHECKLIST

http://curry.edschool.virginia.edu/go/multicultural/net/comps/model.html

Widener University has developed checklists to help you evaluate different kinds of Websites. Here's a list of addresses for those checklists to help you evaluate the quality of the information you find on the Web.

CHECKLIST FOR AN ADVOCACY WEBSITE

http://www2.widener.edu/Wolfgram-Memorial-Library/webevaluation/advoc.htm

CHECKLIST FOR A BUSINESS/MARKETING WEBSITE

http://www2.widener.edu/Wolfgram-Memorial-Library/webevaluation/busmark.htm

CHECKLIST FOR AN INFORMATION WEBSITE

http://www2.widener.edu/Wolfgram-Memorial-Library/webevaluation/inform.htm

CHECKLIST FOR A NEWS WEBSITE

http://www2.widener.edu/Wolfgram-Memorial-Library/webevaluation/news.htm

CHECKLIST FOR A PERSONAL HOMEPAGE

http://www2.widener.edu/Wolfgram-Memorial-Library/webevaluation/perspg.htm

These next two sites provide additional information about how to check the validity and reliability of information that you find on the Web.

EVALUATING INFORMATION ON THE INTERNET

http://thorplus.lib.purdue.edu/~techman/eval.html

http://milton.mse.jhu.edu:8001/research/education/net.html

Library Resources

Despite the rapid development of the World Wide Web, you should not rely solely on Internet resources to support your speech. The more traditional holdings of libraries remain rich sources of supporting material. Although your college or university library may seem a forbidding maze, all libraries, from the smallest village library to the huge Library of Congress, house the same sorts of material and are organized in a similar way.

Unless you have already done so, spend some time becoming familiar with your library's layout and services. Some libraries offer staff-guided tours; most others will at least have floor plans and location guides available. Before you have to do research under pressure, explore the library at a leisurely pace. Find out what electronic resources are available and where they are located. In addition, find where and how to access the following resources and services:

Books

Periodicals

Full-text databases

Newspapers

Reference resources

Government documents

Special services

Books

When you think of libraries, you generally think of books. And with good reason: Most of the floor space of a library is devoted to books.

STACKS   Libraries' collections of books are called the **stacks.** Stacks may be either open or closed, depending on library policy. In an open-stack library, collections are on open shelves and available to anyone who wishes to browse through them. Open stacks give researchers the chance to make lucky finds, because books on a particular subject are shelved next to one another. For example, if you are looking for a specific book on play therapy, you may, on the same shelf, find two or three other books on the same subject. The main drawback to open stacks is that they are vulnerable to both loss of materials and misplacement of books by careless users.

The closed-stack library is one in which only people granted certain privileges are allowed in the stacks—most generally, librarians, library aides, faculty, and graduate students. Undergraduates and others must consult the card catalog and copy onto a retrieval card or call slip the title, author, and call number of the book they want. This card or slip is then given to a librarian at the circulation desk, who sends it to the appropriate area of the stacks. A library worker there will find the desired book and send it to circulation, where the borrower can either check it out or use it in the study area of the library.

The advantages of the closed-stack library are that users are saved some legwork and that stacks generally stay more orderly than in an open-stack system. The chief dis-

stacks
The collection of books in a library

Title:	Deliberation, democracy, and the media / edited by Simone Chambers and Anne Costain.
Call Number:	JC591.D45 2000
Publisher:	Lanham, Md. : Rowman & Littlefield Publishers, c2000.
Subject Heading(s):	Freedom of Speech.
	Freedom of the press.
	Liberty of conscience.
	Democracy.
	Mass media—Political aspects.
	Display Related Subjects
Description:	xiv, 243 p. : ill. ; 23 cm.
Notes:	Includes bibliographic references (pp. 209–225) and index.
Series Title:	Critical media studies
Other Name:	Chambers, Simone.
	Costain, Anne N.,
ISBN:	0847698106 (alk. paper)
DBCN:	AEN-0317
Holdings:	**Item Holdings**

Title

Author/Editor

Subject

FIGURE 7.3

An entry from a computerized card catalog. The same entry appears on the screen regardless of whether the book is accessed through title, author, or subject.

advantages are the length of time it can sometimes take to get materials and the impossibility of making a lucky find. Whatever the setup, you will have to adapt to the particular method your library uses.

CARD CATALOG Just how do you find what you want from among those several floors in your college library? You probably have used a **card catalog** in a smaller public or school library. College libraries are no different. Even though their holdings are much larger than those of the average public library, college libraries also contain card catalogs. Today even very small community and school libraries are likely to have computerized card catalogs. Instead of running around a huge number of filing cabinets, trying to find the drawers you need, you go to a screen or monitor, turn it on, and follow the directions given. Often you do not even have to go to the library to access the card catalog. Many libraries' card catalogs are available online, allowing researchers to build preliminary bibliographies of books and call numbers before they ever come to the library building. Figure 7.3 illustrates a sample entry from a computerized card catalog.

The books you find in your library will be important sources as you prepare your speeches. Books can provide in-depth coverage of topics, which is simply not possible in shorter publications. However, books are inherently outdated. Most books are written two or three years before they are published. If your speech addresses a current topic or if you want to use current examples, you will probably not find these in books. For up-to-date information, turn to periodicals and newspapers.

Periodicals

The term *periodicals* refers to both general-interest magazines, such as *Newsweek*, *Consumer Reports*, and *Sports Illustrated*, and trade and professional journals, such as *Communication Monographs*, the *Quarterly Journal of Economics*, and *American Psychologist*. Both types of periodicals are useful to researchers. As we just

card catalog
A file of information about the books in a library; may be an index-card filing system or a computerized system

FIGURE 7.4

A typical subject entry from the *Reader's Guide*. A key to abbreviations can be found in each volume.

EDUCATIONAL TESTS AND MEASUREMENTS
   See also
      Performance assessment (Education)
   Accountability for what? R. Knowles and T. Knowles. *Phi Delta Kappan* v82 no5 p390-2 Ja 2001
   The authentic standards movement and its evil twin.
      S. Thompson. bibl f *Phi Delta Kappan* v82 no5 p358-62 Ja 2001
   Fighting the tests: a practical guide to rescuing our schools. A. Kohn.
      bibl f *Phi Delta Kappan* v82 no5 p348-57 Ja 2001
   News from the test resistance trail. S. Ohanian. *Phi Delta Kappan* v82 no5 p363-6 Ja 2001

observed, periodicals are more timely than books. Current periodicals may be only a few days old. These days, many periodicals are available online, as well as in the library.

Just as you need a card catalog to help you find books, you need help to decide what periodicals might be useful. A large number of **periodical indexes** are published, covering a large number of subject areas and listing most of the thousands of periodicals published on a regular basis. Many of these indexes are available online or on CD-ROM. If your library subscribes to the electronic formats, you may be able to access the indexes from remote locations via the library's Website. Some of the best-known indexes include the following:

- *The Reader's Guide to Periodical Literature* is the oldest and most frequently consulted periodical index. It lists both popular magazines and a few trade and professional journals. Articles are alphabetized according to both subject and author. The most convenient way to use the *Reader's Guide* is to search for subjects or key words, much as you would when using a World Wide Web search engine or a card catalog.

Figure 7.4 illustrates a typical subject entry in the *Reader's Guide*. The *Reader's Guide* is a cumulative index, published every two weeks. The volumes are combined into quarterly and annual volumes. Its cumulative structure allows the *Reader's Guide* to be available for very current material, as well as for information from past years. Some libraries now subscribe to the *Reader's Guide* electronic databases available.

- *InfoTrac* is not a single periodical index, but a collection of indexes available through a single company. Examples of specific InfoTrac indexes include the *Health Reference Center, Expanded Academic Index, General BusinessFile,* and *Business Index Backfile.*

- The *Social Sciences Index* and the *Humanities Index* list professional, trade, and specialty publications dealing with the social sciences and the humanities. Originally published as the *Reader's Guide Supplement,* the *Social Sciences Index* and the *Humanities Index* are organized and cumulated like the *Reader's Guide.* Like the *Reader's Guide,* these indexes are now available on CD-ROM. In addition, some libraries subscribe to Web-based versions that include full-text articles dating from the early 1980s to the present. These versions are called *Social Sciences Full Text* and *Humanities Full Text.* Other full-text databases are discussed next.

periodical index
A listing of bibliographical data for articles published in a group of magazines and/or journals during a given time period

- The *Education Index* lists articles not only about education but also on various subjects that are taught (think about the wide range of departments within a university, and you will have some idea of the scope). Its format is similar to that of the other periodical indexes.

- The *Public Affairs Information Service Bulletin* (P.A.I.S.) indexes both periodicals and books in such fields as sociology, political science, and economics. Entries are listed alphabetically by subject, in much the same format as the other indexes. An electronic P.A.I.S. is also available.

Other specialized indexes may also prove valuable, depending on your topic and purpose. The *Business Periodicals Index,* the *Psychology Index,* the *Music Index,* the *Art Index,* and the *Applied Science and Technology Index* are a few of these specialized publications that you may wish to explore at one time or another.

Full-Text Databases

Another contribution made by the electronic age to the world of research is the **full-text database.** Periodicals are the most common type of resource available in this format, although newspapers and government documents may also be included. Full-text databases combine both index and text, allowing you to locate not only bibliographic information, but the resources themselves, through a keyword or subject search.

- LEXIS-NEXIS is an extensive full-text database that includes periodicals, newspapers, government documents, and law journals. If your college library subscribes to LEXIS-NEXIS, you can probably access it from any computer on campus, or by dialing into campus, or perhaps from other remote locations by using an assigned code.

- *CARL UnCover* is a multidisciplinary full-text database, including articles from more than 15,000 journals. The index function of *CARL UnCover* is free. Full texts may be ordered with a charge card and faxed to a local fax machine for a charge of about $10.

A number of other databases provide some combination of index, abstracts, and full-text documents. Popular resources in this category include *ERIC,* which focuses on education; *ABI/Inform,* which indexes more than 1,000 business and trade periodicals; and *Periodical Abstracts,* which covers more than 600 general and academic periodicals.

Newspapers

Just as periodicals are more up-to-date than books, so newspapers are more current than periodicals. By reading the latest edition of a daily newspaper, you may be able to find information that is only hours old. Newspapers also offer more detailed coverage of events and special stories than do periodicals, simply because they are published more often. Finally, newspapers usually cover stories of local significance that most often would not appear in national news magazines.

Generally, libraries have only the latest newspapers in their racks. Back issues are quickly transferred to microfilm for more efficient and permanent storage. Don't let microfilm intimidate you. Microfilm readers are easy to use, and most librarians or aides working in the newspaper section will be glad to show you how to set up the reader with the film you need. In recent years, newspapers ranging in size and circulation from major national newspapers to local and college newspapers have also become available online.

full-text database
A World Wide Web or CD-ROM indexing system that provides not only bibliographic data but also full texts of entries

As with any research, before you can consult a newspaper, you have to know where to look. To find relevant information on your subject, you need to consult a **newspaper index.** In addition to the electronic *National Newspaper Index* and *NewsBank,* a number of medium-to-large newspapers publish their own indexes. Your library may carry several of these; most online newspapers include an index function.

When doing newspaper research, keep this tip in mind: If you need information about a specific event and you know the date on which it occurred, you can simply locate a newspaper from that or the following day and probably find a news story on the event.

Reference Resources

All major libraries contain reference resources. Reference resources are indexed in the card catalog with a *ref* prefix or suffix to their call numbers, to show that they are housed in the reference section of the library. Like periodicals, newspapers, and microfilms, they are usually available only for in-house research and cannot be checked out.

Reference resources include encyclopedias, dictionaries, directories, atlases, almanacs, yearbooks, books of quotations, and biographical dictionaries. All may, at one time or another, prove useful to the speaker. Let's examine a few of the most frequently consulted reference works, many of which today have online or CD-ROM versions.

- *Encyclopedias.* The standard general encyclopedia has for many years been the *Encyclopaedia Britannica.* Nearly every library will have a fairly recent set of *Britannica,* as well as several other general encyclopedias, such as the *Encyclopedia Americana.* An online version of the *Encyclopedia Britannica* is now available at http://www.brittannica.com/. Your library may provide access to other online or CD-ROM encyclopedias, as well as bound sets.

  In addition, there are a number of specialized encyclopedias. Art, philosophy, psychology, and music are just a few of the fields covered by specialty encyclopedias.

- *Dictionaries.* The foremost dictionary of the English language is the *Oxford English Dictionary,* or *OED.* Published in twelve large volumes or available on CD-ROM or the Web at <http://www.oed.com/> *OED* provides definitions, pronunciations, etymologies, and usage histories for every word in the dictionary. No other dictionary is this comprehensive. Realistically, however, you will rarely need as much information about a word as the *OED* provides. A good desktop dictionary, such as *Webster's Collegiate Dictionary,* will serve most purposes.

  Specialty dictionaries also exist. *Black's Law Dictionary,* which provides legal definitions, is one example. Such diverse fields as geography, music, and economics also have their own special dictionaries.

- *Directories.* The *Encyclopedia of Associations,* the *Directory of Nonprofit Organizations,* and other directories, including telephone directories, are usually available in the reference section.

- *Atlases.* An atlas is a geographical tool that provides maps, tables, pictures, and facts about the people and resources of various regions. Frequently used atlases include *Goode's World Atlas,* the *Rand McNally College World Atlas,* and the *Township Atlas of the United States.* There are also specialized atlases of history and politics.

- *Almanacs and yearbooks.* Almanacs and yearbooks are compilations of facts. The *Statistical Abstract of the United States* is published annually by the Census

newspaper index
A listing of bibliographical data for articles published in a newspaper (or group of newspapers) during a given time period

Bureau and contains statistics on nearly every facet of life in the United States, including birth and mortality rates, income, education, and religion. An abridged version is available online at <http://www.census.gov/statab/www/>. The *World Almanac* contains factual information about almost every subject imaginable. Its content ranges from facts about ruling monarchs of the eighteenth century to a list of every winner of the Kentucky Derby.

- *Books of quotations.* These are compilations of quotes on almost every conceivable subject. Most of these books are arranged alphabetically by subject; a few are arranged according to author, with the subject entered in an index. The *Oxford Dictionary of Quotations* and *Bartlett's Familiar Quotations* are two widely consulted works. An early edition of *Bartlett's* is now available online at <http://www.bartleby.com/100/>.

- *Biographical dictionaries.* These are reference works that contain biographical articles—some short, others not—on people who have achieved some recognition. Biographical dictionaries are usually organized alphabetically. Probably the best-known general works in this area are the *Who's Who* series, which include brief biographies of international, national, and regional figures of note. The *Dictionary of National Biography* provides biographies of famous British subjects who are no longer living; the *Dictionary of American Biography* does the same for deceased Americans of note. The *Directory of American Scholars* provides information about American academicians (you can probably find profiles of some of your current professors in this work). And if none of those just mentioned has the biography you are seeking, you might try the *Biography Index,* a quarterly publication that lists current articles and books containing biographical sketches. One of these directories or indexes might be especially useful to the speaker who wants to quote a reputed expert but does not know anything about the expert's credentials.

Reference librarians are specialists in the field of library science. They are often able to suggest additional print or electronic resources that you might otherwise overlook. A suggestion here: If you plan to use the reference section, visit the library during daytime working hours. A full-time reference librarian is more likely to be on hand and available to help you at that time than in the evenings or on weekends.

Government Documents

Government documents can be a rich source of materials. The federal government researches and publishes information on almost every conceivable subject, as well as keeping exhaustive records of almost all official federal proceedings. Documents published by the government are usually housed together in a special area of the library called the government-document section.

The most important index of government documents is the *Catalog of U.S. Government Publications,* available online at <http://www.access.gpo.gov/su_docs/locators/cgp/index.html>. Also useful to speakers is the *American Statistics Index,* which indexes government statistical publications exclusively and is also available through some libraries online.

The huge number and wide variety of formats of government pamphlets, reports, and other publications have long presented a challenge to both library archivists and to researchers. The World Wide Web has made these resources much more easily accessible.

Special Services

In addition to the resources just described, most libraries offer a number of special services. These include interlibrary loan and reciprocal borrowing privileges with other area libraries.

Interlibrary loan is one way to obtain resources that you have found indexed, but that are not owned by your library. You might, for example, discover in an article you are reading, a reference to a book that you might also want to read. But your library does not have the book in its collection. Interlibrary loan can locate the book at another library and get it to you, usually within a few days. Some libraries charge a small fee for this service.

Many libraries also have reciprocal borrowing arrangements with libraries of neighboring colleges and universities. You may find that in addition to your own college library, two or three others within a fairly convenient radius are available for your use.

RECAP

GATHERING SUPPORTING MATERIALS IN THE LIBRARY

Library Resources May Include

- Books
- Periodicals
- Full-text databases
- Newspapers
- Reference resources
- Government documents
- Special services

Interviews

If you don't know the answers to some of the important questions raised by your speech topic, but you can think of someone who might, consider interviewing that person to get material for your speech. For example, if you are preparing a speech on the quality of food in the dining hall, who better to ask about the subject than the director of food services? If you want to discuss the pros and cons of building a new prison in an urban area, you might interview an official of the correctional services, a representative of the city administration, and a resident of the area. Or if you want to explain why Al Gore lost the 2000 presidential election even though he won the popular vote, you might consult your professor of political science or American history.

A word of caution, however, before you decide that an interview is necessary: Be sure that your questions cannot be answered easily by looking at a Website or reading a newspaper article or book. Do some preliminary reading on your subject before you decide to take up someone's valuable time in an interview. If you decide that only an interview can give you the material you need, you should prepare for it in advance.

Determining the Purpose of the Interview

The first step in preparing for an interview is to establish a purpose or objective for it. Specifically, what do you need to find out? Do you need hard facts that you cannot obtain from other sources? Do you need the interviewee's expert testimony on your subject? Does the person you are going to interview have a particularly significant personal experience that you wish to hear described firsthand? Or do you need an explanation of some of the information you have found in print sources? Before you begin preparing for the interview, decide just what you want to have or know when the interview is over.

Setting Up the Interview

Once you have a specific purpose for the interview and have decided with whom you are going to talk, arrange a meeting. It is unwise to arrive unannounced at the office of a businessperson, public official, educator, or other professional and expect an on-the-spot interview. Even veteran journalist Mike Wallace has been refused under such circumstances! Instead, several days in advance, telephone the office of the person you hope to interview, explain briefly who you are and why you are calling, and ask for an appointment. Most people are flattered to have their authority and knowledge recognized and willingly grant interviews to serious students if schedules permit.

If you are considering recording the interview on audio- or videotape, ask for the interviewee's OK during this initial contact. If permission is refused, you will need to be prepared to gather your information without electronic assistance.

Planning the Interview

Now that you know what you need to find out, whom you will see, and when the meeting will take place, your next step is to prepare for the interview itself. Do not try to "wing it" and let the interviewee ramble at will. To ensure the results you want, you need to plan your questions.

GATHER BACKGROUND INFORMATION   Experienced interviewers are successful largely because they prepare so thoroughly for their interviews. Likewise, before you interview someone, find out as much as you can about both your subject and the person you are interviewing. Prepare questions that take full advantage of the interviewee's specific knowledge of your subject. You can do this only if *you* already know a good deal about your subject. Build your line of questioning on facts, statements the interviewee has made, or positions he or she has taken publicly.

PLAN SPECIFIC QUESTIONS   In addition to learning something about your subject and the person you are going to interview, it is helpful to think about how you should combine the two basic types of interview questions: closed-ended and open-ended.

As we discussed in Chapter 5, closed-ended questions call for a yes or no answer or some brief statement of fact. "How many years have you served in the job?" and "Do you think that next month's tax referendum will pass?" are examples of closed-ended questions.

If you ask only closed-ended questions, however, you will limit and possibly frustrate your interviewee. You may also frustrate yourself. Open-ended questions allow the

interviewee to express a personal point of view more fully. They may also give you more of the kind of information you probably want: expert testimony and personal experience. "Why do you think the asbestos should not be removed?" and "What, in your opinion, are the most serious potential consequences if it is removed?" are examples of open-ended questions. Open-ended questions often follow closed-ended questions. If the person you are interviewing answers a closed-ended question with a simple yes or no, you may wish to follow up by asking, "Why?"

If both parties are comfortable with it, the use of a tape recorder can free the interviewer and the interviewee from the need to concentrate on careful note taking.

[Photo: Frank Siteman/PhotoEdit]

PLAN A SEQUENCE OF QUESTIONS   Once you have designed your questions to yield the information you want, you need to consider the order in which to ask them. You may want to organize questions according to subject categories, with three or four questions on one topic followed by three or four on another. You may want to arrange them according to complexity of information, with the easiest questions first, in part to ensure that you understand the subject. Or you may want to order them by content sensitivity, building some rapport with your interviewee and ensuring that you get at least some information, should he or she decline to answer the more sensitive or difficult questions.

PLAN A RECORDING STRATEGY   Audio and video recorders can free you from having to take copious notes. You can concentrate instead on processing and analyzing the ideas and information being presented. Another advantage is that your record of the interview is complete. You will not have to decipher hastily scribbled notes a day or two after the interview.

The main disadvantage of using an electronic recorder is that it makes some people more self-conscious and nervous than if you were scribbling notes. You want the person being interviewed to concentrate on your questions, not on vocal inflection. Ask in advance whether the person you are interviewing will allow you to tape the session. Even if he or she gives permission, be prepared to turn off the device and switch to manual note taking if you sense at any time that the interviewee is distracted by it.

When taping an interview, there are a number of questions that you should ask yourself. What kind of recorder should you use? Would a simple tape recorder with a built-in mike be less intimidating than a video camera on a tripod? Although the person you are interviewing is aware that you are taping the interview, would he or she be more comfortable if the machine were out of sight? Ask the interviewee. You might also want to ask some casual questions before turning on the recorder so that both of you can ease into the interview proper.

RECAP

HOW TO PLAN AN INTERVIEW

1. Obtain background information about the person you wish to interview.

2. Design the questions you will ask.

3. Plan a questioning sequence—what you will ask first, second, and so on.

4. Determine how you will record the responses of the person you interview: Will you use a tape recorder or video camera, or will you take notes?

Conducting the Interview

ON YOUR MARK ...   Dress for the interview. For most interviews, conservative, businesslike clothes show that you are serious about the interview and that you respect the norms of your interviewee's world.

Take a pad and pen or pencil for note taking. Even if you are planning to use a tape recorder, you may want to turn it off at some point during the interview. Or Murphy's Law may snarl your tape or break your recorder. Ensure that the interview can continue, in spite of any mishaps.

GET SET ...   Arrive for the interview a few minutes ahead of the scheduled hour. Be prepared, however, to wait patiently, if necessary. Although the interview may be a high priority for you, the person you will interview has granted it as a courtesy and may need to complete something before speaking with you.

Once you are settled with the person you will interview, remind him or her of your purpose. If you are familiar with and admire the work the interviewee has done or published, don't hesitate to say so. Sincere flattery can help set a positive tone for the exchange. If you have decided to use a recorder, set it up. You may keep it out of sight once the interviewee has seen it, but never try to hide a recorder at the outset—such a ploy is unethical. If you are going to take written notes, get out your paper and pen. Now you are ready to begin asking your prepared questions.

GO!   As you conduct the interview, use the questions you have prepared as a guide but not a rigid schedule. If the person you are interviewing mentions an interesting angle you did not think of, don't be afraid to pursue the point. Listen carefully to the person's answers, and ask for clarification of any ideas you don't understand.

Do not prolong the interview beyond the time limits of your appointment. The person you are interviewing is probably very busy and has been courteous enough to fit you into a tight schedule. Ending the interview on time is simply returning the courtesy. Thank your interviewee for his or her contribution, and leave.

Following Up the Interview

As soon as possible after the interview, read through your notes carefully and rewrite any portion that may be illegible. If you recorded the interview, label the tape with the date and the interviewee's name. You will soon want to transfer any significant facts, opinions, or anecdotes from either notes or tape to 4- by 6-inch index cards or to a word processing file. You will find a format for transcribing notes later in this chapter.

Resources from Special-Interest Groups and Organizations

Business and industrial groups, nonprofit organizations, and professional societies produce pamphlets, books, fact sheets, and other information about an extraordinarily wide variety of subjects. How do you find out about such resources? Those available online may be discovered through Web searches. Others may be found through consulting some of the reference works we have already discussed, such as the *Encyclopedia of Associations* and the *Directory of Nonprofit Organizations*. Although these reference works do not indicate specific publications, they provide the names, addresses, and telephone numbers of businesses and organizations that may have a special interest in, and produce resources related to, your topic. Such resources may be available online or by mail at little or no cost.

Remember that private companies and organizations set up Websites and produce printed resources because they have a vested interest in the topic. You can expect oil companies, for example, to minimize the harm oil spills can do to an environment. The criteria offered earlier in this chapter for evaluating Websites should be applied to all kinds of resources obtained from special-interest groups and organizations.

Research Strategies

You have access to a computer with an Internet connection and Web browser software. You know the kinds of materials and services your library offers and how to use them. In short, you're ready to begin researching your speech. But unless you approach this next phase of speech preparation systematically, you may find yourself wasting a good deal of time and energy retracing steps to find bits of information you remember seeing but forgot to bookmark, print out, or write down the first time.

Well-organized research strategies can make your efforts easier and more efficient. You need to develop a preliminary bibliography; locate and evaluate materials; take notes; and identify possible visual aids.

Develop a Preliminary Bibliography

A **preliminary bibliography,** or list of promising resources, should be your first research goal. The preliminary bibliography should include electronic resources, as well as print materials. You will probably discover more resources than you actually look at or refer to in your speech; at this stage, the bibliography simply serves as a menu of possibilities.

You will need to develop a system for keeping track of your resources. As we mentioned earlier in this chapter, Web browsers let you bookmark pages for future reference and ready access. Your bookmarks can serve as one part of your preliminary bibliography. If you are using a CD-ROM index connected to a printer, you may be able to print out the references you discover there. These printouts can be a second part of your preliminary bibliography. If you are using more traditional catalogs and indexes, you will need to copy down the necessary bibliographical information, a process we will discuss in more detail shortly. Using 3- by 5-inch note cards will give you the greatest flexibility. Later you can omit some of the cards, add others, write comments on them, or alphabetize them much more easily than if you had made a list on a sheet of paper.

The key to developing a useful bibliography is to establish a consistent format so that you can easily find and cite the page number, title, publisher, or some other vital fact about a publication. As noted in Chapter 3, the two most common formats or documentation styles are the MLA (Modern Language Association) and the APA (American Psychological Association). MLA style is usually used in the humanities; APA style in the natural and social sciences. Although we describe and use the MLA format here, check with your instructor about which format he or she prefers.

preliminary bibliography
A list of potential resources to be used in the preparation of a speech

For a book, you should record the author's name, title of the book, publisher and date of publication, and the library's call number. Figure 7.5 illustrates how to transfer information from an electronic catalog entry to a bibliography card. For an article in a periodical or newspaper, you should document the author, title of the article, title of the periodical, date of publication, and inclusive page numbers of the article. Figure 7.6 illustrates a bibliography entry in MLA style for an article in *Newsweek*.

For government publications, pamphlets, newsletters, fact sheets, or other specialized information formats, as long as you record the title, author, publisher, date, and page number, you will probably have at hand the information you need to locate any print material. For a government document, you will also need to record the Superintendent of Documents classification number, available in the *Catalog of U.S. Government Publications*.

Documentation formats for Web pages and other electronic resources are still evolving, although they are similar to the formats for other kinds of material.

The basic MLA format is this:

Author's name (last name first). **Title of article** (if any—enclosed in quotation marks). **Title of Website** (underlined) or **a description such as Homepage** (not underlined). **Date of Internet publication. Date of access** <URL>. (The URL should be enclosed in angle brackets, as illustrated here. Break a URL between lines only after a slash, period, or hyphen.)

If you cannot find an item of this information (such as author, or date of Internet publication), simply skip it and go directly to the next item.

The most distinctive features of Web documentation are, of course, the address of the Web page and the date you accessed the page. Figure 7.7 illustrates an MLA bibliography entry for an article in *The New York Times on the Web*.

If you have additional questions about how to format electronic resources, the Web itself can be your best ally. A number of sites provide instructions on how to cite

MATERIAL: Book
CALL NUMBER: KF4772 .H343 1993

AUTHOR: Haiman, Franklyn Saul.

TITLE: "Speech acts" and the First Amendment / Franklyn S. Haiman; with a foreword by Abner J. Mikva.

PUBLICATION: Carbondale : Southern Illinois University Press, c1993.
DESCRIPTION: x, 103 p. ; 23 cm.

NOTES: Includes bibliographical references (pp. 89–97) and index.

SUBJECT: Freedom of speech—United States.
SUBJECT: Hate speech—United States.

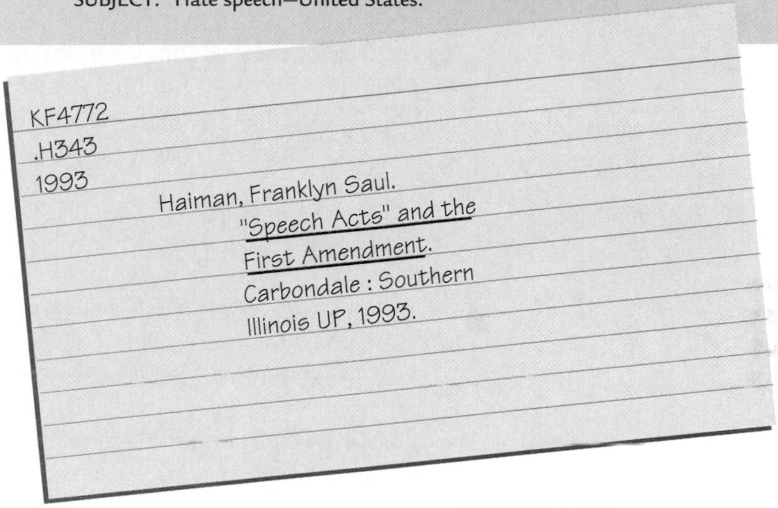

KF4772
.H343
1993

Haiman, Franklyn Saul.
   "Speech Acts" and the First Amendment.
   Carbondale : Southern Illinois UP, 1993.

FIGURE 7.5

Transferring information from an electronic catalog entry to a bibliography card.

Sloan, Allan. "Profiting From the Darkness." *Newsweek.* 14 May 2001, 23.

FIGURE 7.6

A bibliography entry in MLA style for an article in *Newsweek*.

FIGURE 7.7

A bibliography entry in MLA style for an article in *The New York Times on the Web.*

Bradshear, Keith. "Ford Intends to Replace 13 Million Firestone Wilderness Tires." *The New York Times on the Web.* 23 May 2001. 23 May 2001 <http://www.nytimes.com/2001/05/23/business/23TIRE.html>.

electronic resources according to various style guides. For example, **Purdue University's On-Line Writing Lab (OWL)** can be found at <http://owl.english.purdue.edu/handouts/research/r_docElectric.html/>. This resource provides links to both MLA and APA documentation formats for electronic resources.

How many resources should you list in a preliminary bibliography for, say, a ten-minute speech? A reasonable number might be ten or twelve that look promising. If you have many more than that, you may feel overwhelmed. If you have fewer, you may have too little information. Out of a list of three books, three articles, three Web pages, and a pamphlet, you might find that two of the Web pages are not really very useful, your library does not have a couple of the articles, and one of the books is checked out. If you are left with three or four good resources, you are doing well.

Locate Resources

The World Wide Web and CD-ROM full-text servers will provide you with the actual texts of resources. But for all the other items in your preliminary bibliography, you will need to locate the resources yourself.

BOOKS Let's suppose that you decide to look first for the books you want. In a closed-stack library, you fill out a request card to get the books you're interested in. Take the card to the circulation desk and wait nearby for your books to arrive.

In an open-stack library, you look for books yourself. To find them, remember that books are shelved according to call numbers. The first letter or number of a call number indicates the general type of book—literature, social science, religion, and so on. Letters or numbers following the initial designation indicate a subcategory. A location guide can tell you the floor or section of the stacks that houses books carrying the call numbers in which you are interested.

Once you know where to find a book you want, go to that area and check the call-number guides on the ends of the bookcases to find exactly where on the shelves your book should be. Like dictionary guide words, the call-number guides indicate the call numbers of the first and last book in each bookcase. All books with call numbers between the two guide numbers are located in that bookcase.

If the title you want is not where it should be and you think it will be an important resource for your speech, you can go to the circulation desk and ask to place a hold on the book. Then when the book is returned by its current borrower, it will be reserved for you.

PERIODICALS Before searching for an article in a periodical, you need to determine whether your library does in fact subscribe to the periodical you need. You can find out by consulting a periodicals list or checking with a librarian. Once you know what periodicals are available, your library's location guide will tell you where they are housed. Some libraries devote a floor or section just to periodicals. All the bound periodicals will be arranged on shelves there, in alphabetical order. Current issues may be displayed on magazine racks, or they may be located in a reading room or other special area of the library.

Other libraries shelve their periodicals in the stacks. You look up the title of the periodical in the card catalog, copy the call number, and proceed as if you were looking for a book. As a rule, periodicals cannot be checked out, so you need to take notes at the library or photocopy the articles you want for further reference.

Microfilm or microfiche periodicals are probably stored in large filing cabinets with labeled drawers. Microfilm and microfiche readers are usually located nearby. Don't hesitate to ask for help from a librarian if you are inexperienced with microfilm and microfiche.

NEWSPAPERS Newspapers are usually housed together in their own section of the library, although current newspapers, like current magazines, may be in a separate reading room. As mentioned earlier, older issues of newspapers are usually on microfilm, and many are now on the Web.

GOVERNMENT DOCUMENTS The government documents section usually arranges material according to the Superintendent of Documents classification number, which, as noted earlier, can be found in the *Monthly Catalog of U.S. Government Publications.* Government document sections may have other ways of organizing their information as well, including vertical files of material. If you do not have much experience using government documents, the librarian in that section can be very helpful.

REFERENCE MATERIAL Reference material is usually housed in the reference section of the library and cannot be removed from that area. You must either take notes or make photocopies of the information you want.

Consider the Potential Usefulness of Resources

It makes sense to gauge the potential usefulness of your resources before you begin to read more closely and take notes. Think critically about how the various resources you have found are likely to help you achieve your purpose and about how effective they are likely to be with your audience. Glance over the tables of contents of books, and flip quickly through the texts to note any charts, graphs, or other visual materials that might be used as visual aids. Skim a key chapter or two. Skim shorter articles, pamphlets, and fact sheets as well.

You may wish to devise a number or letter system to rank your resources according to their potential. You can write this code on your bibliography card or printout. If none of the resources looks particularly good, you may need to return to the bibliography-building stage to try to locate more potential resources.

Take Notes

Once you have located, previewed, and ranked your resources, you are ready to begin more careful reading and note taking. Start with the resources that you thought had the greatest potential. If you are looking at a Web page, an article, a pamphlet, an encyclopedia entry, or another kind of short document, you can read the whole text fairly quickly. But you probably do not have time to read entire books, so read only those chapters or sections that seem particularly relevant and potentially useful to your speech.

We discuss specific types of supporting material in Chapter 8. For now, it is sufficient to say that when you find an example, a statistic, an opinion, or other material that might be useful to your speech, write it down, photocopy it, download it into a computer file, or print it. Be sure to identify the source.

Don't create extra work for yourself by scribbling notes on scratch paper, the inside of a book cover, a checkbook, or a printout of the latest e-mail from Mom. Instead, have on hand a notebook, floppy disk (if computers are available where you will be working), or note cards. Even if you plan to photocopy or enter most of your notes into a word-processing file, it is a good idea to carry a few 4- by 6-inch note cards with you whenever you are working on a speech. You can use one to jot down an idea that comes to mind while you are sipping coffee or to record a fact you discover in a magazine article you read in a doctor's office or at a friend's house. Another advantage of using note cards is that you can later arrange them in the order of your speech outline, simplifying the integration of your ideas and supporting material into the speech.

What should you include in your notes? First, put only one item of supporting material or one idea on each card or each page of your speech notebook or word-processing file. If you are photocopying your sources or printing out Web pages, and you find a single page with several pieces of supporting material, you may want to "cut and paste"—literally cut the page apart and paste the separate items onto separate note cards. There is no rule as to how many note cards or pages you will have for each source. You may write only one note card or page from one article you read, five from another, and twenty from a third. The amount of useful supporting material you find will vary widely from source to source.

If you copy a phrase, sentence, or paragraph verbatim from a source, be sure to put quotation marks around it when you write it down or enter it. You may need to know later in the preparation process whether it was a direct quote or a paraphrase. This information will be obvious, of course, on printouts or photocopies.

In addition to copying the information itself, you need to indicate the source from which it came. In Chapter 3, we discussed the ethical importance of crediting sources of ideas and information. If you consistently record your sources when you take notes, you will avoid the possibility of committing unintentional plagiarism later. You may wish to number the entries in your bibliography and then place the source number at the top of each note card or page of information or quotes from that source. Then you will need to add only the page number of each note. A somewhat more extended option is to use only the author's last name, title, and page number or Web address on the note card. Or you may wish to write a complete bibliographic reference on each card or page. This procedure takes more time but ensures that you will have vital reference information immediately at hand as you work on your speech later.

Finally, leave enough space at the top of each note card or page to summarize the idea expressed in the note. Such headings make it easier to find a particular bit of material quickly when you are ready to assemble the speech. Figure 7.8 illustrates two note cards—one with a paraphrased note and one with a direct quotation.

Identify Possible Presentation Aids

As we noted earlier in this chapter, in addition to discovering verbal supporting material in your sources, you may also find charts, graphs, photographs, or other potentially valuable visual material. You may think you will later be able to remember what visuals were in which sources. But many speakers have experienced frustrating

FIGURE **7.8**

Sample note cards.

Paraphrased Note

Influence of Audience on Invention

Barrett, Harold. <u>Rhetoric and Civility</u>:
 <u>Human Development, Narcissism, and</u>
 <u>The Good Audience</u>. Albany: SUNY P,
 1991. 40.

Audience = most important influence
in invention

Direct Quotation

Hate Speech Protected

Walker, Samuel. <u>Hate Speech: The History</u>
 <u>of an American Controversy</u>. Lincoln:
 U of Nebraska, 1994. 3.

"As a matter of law and national
policy, hate speech is protected by the
First Amendment."

searches for the "perfect" presentation aid they remember seeing somewhere while they were taking notes for their speech. Even if you are not certain at this point that you will even use presentation aids in the speech, print out, photocopy, or sketch any good possibilities on note cards, recording sources of information just as you did for your written materials. Then, when the time comes to consider if and where presentation aids might enhance the speech, you will have some readily at hand. In Chapter 14, we will discuss types of presentation aids and provide guidelines for their use.

RECAP

RESEARCH STRATEGIES

1. Develop a preliminary bibliography.

2. Locate sources.

3. Consider the potential usefulness of sources.

4. Take notes.

5. Identify possible visual aids.

SUMMARY

Public speakers need to know where and how to find supporting material to use in their speeches. Five sources of supporting material are personal knowledge and experience; the Internet; library resources; interviews; and resources from government agencies, special-interest groups, and organizations.

Most speakers can provide some illustrations, explanations, definitions, or other supporting material from their own knowledge and experience. Such material has the advantage of increasing the audience's respect for the speaker's authority.

The Internet provides a vast collection of resources, easily accessible on the World Wide Web through directories and search engines. Because Websites are not subject to any quality control or censorship, the speaker needs to evaluate whether they are accountable, accurate, objective, current, usable, and sensitive to diversity.

Even with access to the World Wide Web, most speakers still use library resources—books, periodicals, full-text databases, newspapers, reference resources, and government documents—as sources of supporting material. This chapter discussed how these resources are indexed and the general kinds of supporting material a speaker might expect to find in each. Libraries may also offer such special services as interlibrary loan and reciprocal borrowing privileges with area libraries.

Interviewing someone who is an expert on the subject of the speech or who has a unique point of view about the subject is a fourth way to gather supporting material. Interviewers may take written notes or tape their interviews; later, they can transcribe the information they have gathered onto note cards.

Finally, information about many topics is available from various special-interest groups and organizations. Because many such entities produce printed resources primarily to support their vested interests, a speaker should consider how accountable, accurate, objective, and current such resources are.

Once a speaker discovers possible resources, he or she should develop a preliminary bibliography of those resources, locate them, consider their potential usefulness, take notes, and identify possible presentation aids.

A Sharper Focus

CONSIDERING YOUR AUDIENCE

▶ Your audience will accord you more respect as an authority when they realize that you have firsthand knowledge of a topic.

▶ If no one is willing to be accountable for the content of a Website, you cannot be accountable to your audience for using the information from that Website in a speech.

▶ Think critically about whether the various resources you discover are likely to be effective with your audience.

CONSIDER AUDIENCE DIVERSITY

▶ A diversity-sensitive Website is free of material that communicates bias against any divergent subgroup. Such a site may also offer or invite divergent perspectives and/or offer print, graphic, or audio alternatives for users with disabilities.

CRITICAL THINKING QUESTIONS

1. Imagine that you are preparing an informative speech on buying a new computer. Specifically, you want your audience to be able to make informed choices about platform, power, speed, and various available options. Explain how you might use each of the five key sources of supporting material in developing this speech.

2. For each of the following topics, list at least two library resources likely to yield relevant information:

   The Battle of San Jacinto

   The charter-school movement

   The Devil's Triangle

   Election reform

   El Niño

   How HMOs operate

   The trial of Julius and Ethel Rosenberg

3. In what reference works would you look first for the following information?

   All the vice presidents of the United States

Biographic information on Anne Brontë

The history of opera

The origin of the term *spoonerism*

The ten most popular names for newborn boys in America in 2002

The name of the person who said, "Democracy becomes a government of bullies tempered by editors."

ETHICAL QUESTIONS

1. As the Internet has become increasingly accessible, questions regarding copyright and fair use have become increasingly complex. A speaker can find graphs, pictures, and other potentially valuable visual aids as easily as clicking a mouse. Under what conditions, if any, is it ethical to use such material in a speech?

2. While in the library gathering material for a speech on endangered species in your region, you find a wonderful, quotable magazine article from which you take copious notes. However, in your excitement, you neglect to record bibliographic information for this source on your note cards. You discover your omission as you begin composing your speech the night before you must deliver it; you have no time to return to the library. How can you solve your problem in an ethical way?

3. Both electronic and print indexes and databases sometimes include abstracts of books and articles, rather than full texts. If you have read only the abstract of a source, is it ethical to include that source on your speech bibliography?

SUGGESTED ACTIVITIES

1. Use library resources to discover the answers to the following questions.

   a. Does your library have the following periodicals? Indicate whether each is available in bound volumes or on microfilm.

   American Art Journal

   Consumers Research Magazine

   Ecological Monographs

   Physics Teacher

   Western Political Quarterly

   b. The front page of the *New York Times,* November 20, 1952, had a story about the financial condition of U.S. colleges. What was the headline of that story? Who wrote the story?

   c. Who won the Academy Award for Best Actor in 1962? For what film? Where did you find the information?

   d. What is the call number for Herman Melville's *Moby Dick*?

2. Use one of the World Wide Web search engines listed in Chapter 7 to find the answers to the following questions.[7] (They're not as obvious as you may think!)

   a. How long did the Hundred Years War last?

   b. Which country makes Panama hats?

   c. From which animal do we get catgut?

   d. What is a camel's-hair brush made of?

   e. The Canary Islands in the Pacific are named after what animal?

   f. What was King George VI's first name?

   g. What color is a purple finch?

   h. Where are Chinese gooseberries from?

USING TECHNOLOGY AND MEDIA

1. Which of the following services does your library offer?

Interlibrary loan

LEXIS-NEXIS

Newsbank

Reciprocal borrowing privileges

2. Obtain or create as comprehensive a list as possible of the online and CD-ROM databases and indexes to which your library provides access.

I use not only all the brains I have,
but all I can borrow.

WOODROW WILSON

Supporting Your Speech

objectives

After studying this chapter you should be able to do the following:

1. Explain the importance of supporting material to a speech.

2. List the six main types of supporting material.

3. Explain at least one guideline for using each of the six types of supporting material.

4. List and explain six criteria for determining which supporting material to use in a speech.

obacco heir Patrick Reynolds speaks frequently at universities, youth assemblies, and corporate seminars around the country.[1] He has appeared on most of the major network and cable news and talk shows, including "Good Morning, America" and "Oprah." Reynolds's objective is not, as one might suppose, to defend the tobacco industry, but to campaign aggressively *against* it.

Citing information from the American Cancer Society, the American Lung Association, and the federal government, Reynolds points out that one out of every five deaths in the United States is caused by smoking, making it the leading killer in this country. He tells his audiences that 60 percent of all smokers start by age 14, with 90 percent becoming addicted by the age of 19. And then Reynolds adds his own personal, tragic, and ironic illustrations: His father, mother, aunt, and half-brother have all died of smoking-related causes.

Patrick Reynolds has been described as a "compelling" speaker. Why? At least in part, because of the skill with which he combines explanations, illustrations, and statistics to capture and maintain the attention of his audiences. Without effective supporting material, a speaker such as Reynolds would find his plea dismissed as only so much hot air.

As you saw in the previous chapter, gathering appropriate supporting material is an essential step in the speech-preparation process. And once you have gathered a variety of material, you will need to make decisions about how to use your information to best advantage. You will need to look at your speech from your audience's perspective and decide where an explanation might help them understand a point, where statistics might convince them of the significance of a problem, and where an illustration might stir their emotions. In this chapter, we will discuss these and other types of supporting material, and present guidelines for using them effectively. ▬

Illustrations

When Hugh Stuart-Buttle was preparing to introduce to the news media the products made by his company, Ciba Specialty Chemicals, for protection against the sun's ultraviolet rays, he remembered how, when he was a little boy, his mother insisted that he cover up before he went out into the sun. He decided to draw on this memory in his presentation. His coach, communication consultant Karen Berg, approved. "Anything that engages the mind's eye is more memorable than just getting up and spouting off data," she says. "[The audience] will remember the visual images."[2]

Stuart-Buttle's use of a personal anecdote is hardly a revolutionary public-speaking strategy. Political and after-dinner speakers have always told stories to help make their points and keep their listeners' attention. Until recently, however, business speakers rarely did so. Now they are beginning to discover what speakers in other contexts have always known: *Everybody likes to hear a story*. If you remember nothing else from this chapter, remember that one principle. An **illustration**—a story or anecdote that provides an example of an idea, issue, or problem the speaker is discussing—almost always ensures audience interest. We also discuss the use of stories, in Chapter 15.

With an understanding of the value of illustrations, let's look more closely at different kinds of illustrations and examine some guidelines for using them.

illustration
A story or anecdote that provides an example of an idea, issue, or problem the speaker is discussing

Brief Illustrations

Brief illustrations are often no longer than a sentence or two. To drive home a point about how diversity and inclusion can lead to business success, one speaker offered the following two brief illustrations:

Quaker Oats sponsors free blood pressure tests at African-American churches because African Americans suffer from a high incidence of high blood pressure. The Food and Drug Administration has designated oats as a food that lowers blood pressure. Good strategy for capturing that part of the market.

Macy's in San Francisco increased its inventory and selection in petite sizes. Why? Asians are typically smaller than their European and African counterparts. That simple move increased sales at Macy's 175 percent over the previous two years. Asian Americans today make up a significant percentage of their customer base.[3]

Communication consultant Karen Berg coaches her clients to think about the audience when they speak. The use of personal stories can help listeners focus on the speaker's message.

[Richard L. Harbus/The New York Times]

Why use multiple brief illustrations? Sometimes a series of brief illustrations can have more impact than either a single brief illustration or a more detailed extended illustration. In addition, although an audience could dismiss a single illustration as an exception, two or more strongly suggest a trend or norm. Consider George W. Bush's series of brief illustrations of how the Taliban government oppressed the people of Afghanistan:

Women are not allowed to attend school. You can be jailed for owning a television. Religion can be practiced only as their leaders dictate. A man can be jailed in Afghanistan if his beard is not long enough.[4]

Extended Illustrations

Longer and more detailed than the brief illustration is the **extended illustration.** It resembles a story. It is more vividly descriptive than a brief illustration, and it has a plot—which includes an opening, complications, a climax, and a resolution.

Glen offered this extended personal illustration in his speech on what he called the "Tragic Trilogy"—gangs, drugs, and guns:

I, like most of us, had become desensitized to the violence, the shootings, the mindless, motiveless drive-bys with which we are bombarded every day. At least, I was until that fumble rolled to my feet. It happened when Jason died. He was my friend.

We grew up together, played high school football together. He pursued his only dream, which was to play in the NFL. He was a prize recruit, receiving a full scholarship to the University of Houston to play middle linebacker. Halfway through his freshman year, he was playing. He was living his dream.

His dream came to an end as he walked down a Houston street wearing a red Kansas City Chief's hat. He was in the wrong part of town, wearing the wrong color, and he was shot and killed from the window of a moving car.[5]

brief illustration
An unelaborated example, often only a sentence or two long

extended illustration
A detailed example

To use an extended illustration takes more time than to cite a brief example, but longer stories can be more dramatic and emotionally compelling. As we will discuss in Chapter 10, extended illustrations can work well as speech introductions. And Chapter 15 will discuss further the use of extended illustrations in informative speeches.

Hypothetical Illustrations

Hypothetical illustrations may be either brief or extended. They are different from the illustrations we have discussed so far, because they have not actually occurred. Rather, they are scenarios that *might* happen. Plausible hypothetical illustrations may serve your purpose better than any real examples by enabling your audience to put themselves in a particular situation. The following hypothetical illustration introduced a speech on how universities profit from sweatshop labor:

> *Imagine one day walking into class, only to find children chained to desks, sewing T-shirts, jackets, and other products representing your school.*[6]

Notice the word *imagine* in this illustration. The purpose of a hypothetical illustration is not to trick your listeners into believing a bogus story. They should be aware from the beginning that the illustration is hypothetical. In his January 8, 1992, "state of the state" address, California Governor Pete Wilson related several encounters with citizens hard hit by the recession. Unfortunately, because he did not make clear that these illustrations were hypothetical, his own press office spent four days trying to track down the fictitious citizens.

Using Illustrations Effectively

Illustrations are almost guaranteed attention getters, as well as a way to support your statements. But even this excellent form of support can be ineffective if not used to its best advantage. The following suggestions can help you use illustrations more effectively in your speeches.

BE CERTAIN THAT YOUR ILLUSTRATIONS ARE DIRECTLY RELEVANT TO THE IDEA OR POINT THEY ARE SUPPOSED TO SUPPORT. As obvious as this principle seems, many student speakers, learning of the value of illustrations, go to great lengths to use as many of them as they can in their speeches. They are so eager, in fact, that some of their illustrations have little bearing on the specific point they are trying to make. Their listeners become confused. Never leave your audience in doubt as to why you used a certain illustration. Be sure that illustrations are obviously related to the idea they support.

THE ILLUSTRATIONS YOU CHOOSE SHOULD REPRESENT A TREND. It is not ethical to find one or two isolated illustrations and use them as though they were typical. If your illustrations are rare instances, you owe it to your listeners to tell them so.

MAKE YOUR ILLUSTRATIONS VIVID AND SPECIFIC. You probably know people who cannot tell a joke. They just can't relate a story or deliver a punch line. Or they lack the sense of timing needed to make a joke funny. Unfortunately, some speakers bumble their best illustrations in a similar way. Some years ago, a speech professor was fascinated to discover that one of his students had been on the last voyage of the ill-

hypothetical illustration
An example that might happen, but has not actually occurred

fated Italian ship, *Andrea Doria.* Early in the semester, he urged the young man to relate his experience as part of an informative speech on how humans respond to danger. The professor expected a speech with great dramatic impact. Instead, much to his surprise, the student's narrative went something like this: "Well, there was a loud noise and then the sirens went off and we all got in lifeboats and the ship sank."[7] Hardly the stuff great drama is made of! If you have chosen to tell a poignant story, give it enough detail to make it come alive in the minds of your listeners. Paint a mental picture of the people, places, and things involved.

USE ILLUSTRATIONS WITH WHICH YOUR LISTENERS CAN IDENTIFY. Just as you should use illustrations that are typical, so too should you use audience-centered illustrations—ones with which the members of your audience can relate. If, on hearing your illustration, your listeners mentally shrug and think, "That could never happen to me," the power of your story is considerably lessened. The best illustrations are the ones that your listeners can imagine happening to themselves. Other compelling stories, like the sinking of the *Andrea Doria,* can illustrate such great human drama that everyone listening will be immediately interested and attentive. If you cannot find a plausible example, you may want to invent a hypothetical one, which you can gear specifically to your audience. You can then be sure of its pertinence to your listeners.

REMEMBER THAT THE BEST ILLUSTRATIONS ARE PERSONAL ONES. Speakers gain conviction and enthusiasm when they talk about personal experiences. Patrick Reynolds, for example, with whom we opened this chapter, is a compelling speaker in large part because he shares his own tragic personal experiences that resulted from smoking. Of course, you will not have had personal experience with every topic on which you may speak. In a speech on the conflict between the legislative and executive branches of government, a good illustration might be the working relationship between the president and the speaker of the house. The best illustrations for a speech on American military strategy during the Revolutionary War might come from the letters of George Washington. But if you *have* had personal experience with the subject on which you are speaking, be sure to describe that experience to the audience.

Descriptions and Explanations

Probably the most commonly used forms of support are **descriptions** and **explanations.** A description tells you *what* something is like. Descriptions provide the details that allow audience members to develop mental pictures of what their speakers are talking about. An explanation is a statement that makes clear *how* something is done or *why* it exists in its present form or existed in its past form.

Describing

To describe is to produce word pictures—detailed sensory information that allows an audience mentally to see, hear, smell, touch, or taste the object of your description. The more senses you appeal to with your word pictures, the better. Good descriptions are vivid, accurate, and specific; they make people, places, and events come alive for the audience. More specific instructions for constructing word pictures are given in Chapter 15.

description
A statement that provides a word picture of something

explanation
A statement that makes clear how something is done or why it exists in its present or past form

Words can paint pictures that allow your listeners to envision and even experience vicariously your encounters with objects, people, and settings. What sensory details would you use to describe for an audience this colorful scene on a Colombian river?

[Photo: Jeremy Horner/Stone/Getty Images]

Description may be used in a brief example, an extended illustration, or a hypothetical instance, or by itself. In a speech on noise pollution, a student described everyday sounds:

Imagine the sounds you hear every day—the wake-up call of your alarm clock, the crunch of leaves underfoot, voices of family and friends, or the laughter and giggling of children playing in the park.[8]

Explaining How

Tammy had already pointed out that some seven out of ten American adults suffer from gum disease. Her next step was to explain how gum disease puts a person at greater risk for heart disease:

. . . when we brush or occasionally floss diseased gums and cause any type of bleeding, gum disease bacteria are then released into our bloodstream, and gum disease bacteria, unlike other types of bacteria, have the distinct ability to make blood clot. These blood clots help clog arteries. Gum bacteria have been found inside artery-plugging plaque.[9]

Speakers who discuss or demonstrate processes of any kind rely at least in part on explanations of *how* those processes work.

Explaining Why

Explaining *why* involves giving causes or reasons for a policy, principle, or event. In his speech on the negative impact of televised professional wrestling on children, Nathaniel explained why wrestling is inappropriate for children:

Psychologically, children of all ages are not mature enough to handle this programming. Newsweek of February 7, 2000, explains that for our youngest elementary-aged children, wrestling is inappropriate because they can't "differentiate between fantasy and reality" while watching wrestling programs.[10]

Often, once having explained the causes or reasons, the speaker can then tailor a solution to those specific causes. A student seeking to reverse a university policy against freshmen having cars on campus can first explain *why* that policy was adopted and then point out *why* it is no longer needed. In short, explaining *why* some condition or event exists provides an analysis that often leads to better solutions.

Using Descriptions and Explanations Effectively

Perhaps because they are the most commonly used forms of support, descriptions and explanations are also among the most frequently abused. When large sections of a speech contain long, nonspecific explanations, audience eyelids are apt to fall. The following suggestions can help you use descriptions and explanations effectively in your speeches.

KEEP YOUR DESCRIPTIONS AND EXPLANATIONS BRIEF. Length alone is often the reason for boredom with many descriptions and explanations. An explanation should supply only enough details for an audience to understand how or why something works or exists. Too many details may make your listeners say your speech was "everything I *never* wanted to know about the subject."

USE LANGUAGE THAT IS AS SPECIFIC AND CONCRETE AS POSSIBLE. Explanations tend to be general and thereby somewhat deadly. Vivid and specific language brings your explanations alive. Liveliness helps you hold the audience's attention and paint in your listeners' minds the image you are trying to communicate. Chapter 12 will provide more tips on making your language specific.

AVOID TOO MUCH DESCRIPTION AND EXPLANATION. Even brief, specific explanations are boring if used alone, without other kinds of support. You can hold your audience's attention more effectively if you alternate explanations and descriptions with other types of supporting material, such as brief examples or statistics.

Definitions

Steve thought and thought but couldn't come up with a good opening for his speech. In desperation, he turned to the dictionary. To introduce his speech on modern legal training in the United States, he decided to define *lawyer*. Much to Steve's disappointment, his introduction only succeeded in putting his 8 A.M. class soundly back to sleep. Steve's problem? He had misused a perfectly legitimate form of support. He did not need to define *lawyer* for a college class—or for any class beyond elementary school, for that matter. Steve had resorted to an unnecessary definition as a crutch, and it didn't hold up.

Definitions have two justifiable uses in speeches. First, a speaker should be sure to define any and all specialized, technical, or little-known terms in his or her speech. If

definition
A statement about what something means

Steve had discussed "tort reform," he would have needed to define that phrase early in his speech. Such definitions are usually achieved by *classification,* the kind of definition you would find in a dictionary. Second, a speaker may define a term by showing how it works or how it is applied in a specific instance—what we call an *operational definition.* Let's look at examples of both types of definitions.

Definitions by Classification

If you have to explain the meaning of a term, you may use a **definition by classification** from the *Oxford English Dictionary,* a desktop *Webster's,* or another reputable general dictionary, or you may turn to a specialized dictionary, such as *Black's Law Dictionary.* Any of these references defines words by classification—that is, by first placing a term in the general class, group, or family to which it belongs and then differentiating it from all the other members of that class. A dictionary definition also has authority. This can be an important advantage, especially when you are discussing a controversial subject. If you quote a reputable dictionary, the audience usually accepts without question the definition you are using.

In simpler or less controversial instances, it is also possible to define by classification in your own words, as Shannon did in her speech on the dangers of vaccines: "A vaccine is basically a dead viral cell that is injected into the patient's body."[11] Note how this definition fits our explanation of how to define by classification: generally speaking, a vaccine is a "dead viral cell," but it differs from other dead viruses by being "injected into the patient's body."

Operational Definitions

As noted earlier, sometimes a word or phrase may not be totally unfamiliar to an audience, but you as a speaker may be applying it in a unique or specific way that needs to be clarified. At other times, defining a word by classification may result only in an abstract notion that does not particularly clarify the word's meaning. In such cases, you would be better off to provide a more concrete **operational definition,** explaining how a word or phrase works or what it does. The phrase "child abuse" is defined operationally in the following example:

> *When we hear of child abuse, we think of children physically battered. Yet there is a kind of abuse just as crippling, just as horrifying: emotional abuse. It leaves no scars on the body, but breaks a child's heart and spirit.*[12]

Operational definitions are usually original; they are not found in dictionaries. Although they may lack the credibility of dictionary definitions by classification, they can be specifically tailored to a speech.

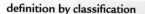

Using Definitions Effectively

The following suggestions can help you use definitions more effectively in your speeches.

USE A DEFINITION ONLY WHEN NEEDED. As we mentioned, novice speakers too often use a definition as an easy introduction or a time filler. Resist the temptation to

definition by classification
A "dictionary definition," constructed by first placing a term in the general class to which it belongs and then differentiating it from all other members of that class

operational definition
A statement that shows how a word or phrase works or what it does

provide a definition unless you are using a relatively obscure term or one with several definitions. Unnecessary definitions are boring and, more serious still, insulting to the listeners' intelligence.

BE CERTAIN THAT YOUR DEFINITION IS UNDERSTANDABLE. You probably have had the frustrating experience of looking up a word in the dictionary, only to find that the full definition is as confusing as the word itself. The word *dogmatic,* for example, may be defined as "characterized by or given to the use of dogmatism." To find a more satisfactory definition, look down the column until you find *dogmatism.* Your listeners do not have that capability, so make certain you give them definitions that are immediately and easily understandable—or you will have wasted your time and perhaps even lost your audience.

BE CERTAIN THAT YOUR DEFINITION AND YOUR USE OF THE TERM THROUGH-OUT A SPEECH ARE THE SAME. Even seemingly simple words can create confusion if not defined and used consistently. For example, Roy opened his speech on the potential hazards of abusing nonprescription painkillers by defining *drugs* as nonprescription painkillers. A few minutes later, he confused his audience by using the word *drug* to refer to cocaine. Once he had defined the term, he should have used it only in that context throughout the speech.

Analogies

An **analogy** is a comparison. Like a definition, it increases understanding; unlike a definition, it deals with relationships and comparisons—the new to the old, the unknown to the known. In her speech to the 1990 graduating class of Wellesley College, Barbara Bush found the concept of color a unifying analogy for the speaker, the occasion, and school tradition:

> *Now I know your first choice for today was Alice Walker, known for* The Color Purple. *Instead you got me—known for the color of my hair! Of course, Alice Walker's book has a special resonance here. At Wellesley, each class is known by a special color, and for four years the class of '90 has worn the color purple. Today you meet on Severance Green to say goodbye to all that, to begin a new and very personal journey, a search for your own true colors.*[13]

Analogies can help your listeners understand unfamiliar ideas, things, and situations by showing how these matters are similar to something they already know.

There are two types of analogies. A *literal* analogy compares things that are actually similar (two sports, two cities, two events). A *figurative* analogy may take the form of a literary simile or metaphor. It compares things that at first seem to have little in common (the West Wind and revolution)[14] but share some vital feature (a fierce impetus for change).

Literal Analogies

Sonya opened her speech on the dangers of lead poisoning by describing how ancient Rome was ultimately conquered not by invading armies, but by lead contamination. She then proceeded to compare Rome's fate to the lead poisoning that threatens the United States today:

analogy
A comparison between two things

From an historical perspective, we can easily understand how the Romans made such a costly mistake. What is far more difficult to understand, is why today, when the devastating effects of lead poisoning are common knowledge, our nation is threatened much the way the Romans were.[15]

Sonya's comparison of the effects of lead on two powerful civilizations is a **literal analogy**—a comparison between two similar things. If your listeners are from a culture or group other than your own, or other than the one from which the speech derives, literal analogies that draw on the listeners' culture or group may help them understand more readily the less-familiar places, things, and situations you are discussing. In addition, literal analogies are often employed by people who want to influence public policy. For example, proponents of trade restrictions argue that because Japan maintains its trade balance through stringent import controls, so should the United States. If Columbia, Missouri, solved both ecological and financial woes by successfully instituting an aluminum can tax, why not try the same approach in Lawrence, Kansas? The more similarities a policymaker can show between the items being compared, the better his or her chances of being persuasive.

Figurative Analogies

On a warm July afternoon in 1848, feminist Elizabeth Cady Stanton delivered the keynote address to the first women's-rights convention in Seneca Falls, New York. Near the end of her speech, she offered this impassioned analogy:

Voices were the visitors and advisers of Joan of Arc. Do not "voices" come to us daily from the haunts of poverty, sorrow, degradation, and despair, already too long unheeded? Now is the time for the women of this country, if they would save our free institutions, to defend the right, to buckle on the armor that can best resist the keenest weapons of the enemy—contempt and ridicule.[16]

A literal analogy might have compared the status of women in medieval France to that of women in nineteenth-century America. But the **figurative analogy** Stanton employed compared the voices that moved Joan of Arc to the social causes motivating nineteenth-century women.

Because it relies not on facts or statistics, but rather on imaginative insights, the figurative analogy is not considered "hard" evidence. But because it is creative, it is inherently interesting and should help grab an audience's attention. Speakers often employ figurative analogies in their introductions and conclusions. Eric opened his speech on the National Flood Insurance Program with this figurative analogy between gambling on horse races and gambling with nature:

If someone were to lose thousands of dollars gambling on horse races, would you want your tax dollars to bail them out? Probably not. What if they lost those thousands of dollars without having any knowledge they were even gambling? What if I told you sooner or later you might find yourself or someone you know in a similar predicament? Currently in the United States there are millions of people gambling not on horse races, but on Mother Nature by living on flood plains or coasts. When these people lose, they lose big: beach houses, farm houses, and apartment houses go out to sea, down the river, or simply soak up catastrophic damages.[17]

literal analogy
A comparison between two similar things

figurative analogy
A comparison between two essentially dissimilar things that share some common feature on which the comparison depends

Using Analogies Effectively

These suggestions can help you to use literal and figurative analogies more effectively.

BE SURE THAT THE TWO THINGS YOU COMPARE IN A LITERAL ANALOGY ARE VERY SIMILAR. If you base your speech on a literal analogy, it is vital that the two things you compare be very much alike. In an informative speech, a literal analogy that doesn't quite work may hamper rather than help an audience's understanding of the thing or idea you are trying to explain. In a persuasive speech, few things give your adversaries as much joy as being able to point up a major dissimilarity in a literal analogy. For example, the two cities being compared are in actuality more different than alike, the opponent may argue. One is relatively poor; the other is wealthy. One has an elected mayor and a city council; the other has an elected board of commissioners and an appointed city manager. What worked in one will not work in the other. One reason socialized medicine has not been adopted in the United States is that critics of the idea have pointed out how dissimilar the United States is to most of the countries that have adopted such programs. What works in those nations would not work here, they argue. The more alike the two things being compared are, the more likely it is that the analogy will stand up under attack.

THE ESSENTIAL SIMILARITY BETWEEN THE TWO OBJECTS OF A FIGURATIVE ANALOGY SHOULD BE READILY APPARENT. When you use a figurative analogy, it is crucial to make clear the similarity on which the analogy is based. If you do not, your audience will end up wondering what in the world you are talking about. And you will only confuse your listeners further if you try to draw on that same analogy later in your speech. It may be a good idea to try out a figurative analogy on an honest friend before using it during a speech. Then you can be certain that your point is clear.

Statistics

Many of us live in awe of numbers, or **statistics**. Perhaps nowhere is our respect for statistics so evident—and so exploited—as in advertising. If three out of four doctors surveyed recommend Pain Away aspirin, it must be the best. If Sudsy Soap is 99.9 percent pure (whatever that means), surely it will help our complexions. And if nine out of ten people like Sloppy Catsup in the taste test, we will certainly buy some for this weekend's barbecue. How can the statistics be wrong?

The truth about statistics lies somewhere between such unconditional faith in numbers and the wry observation that "There are three kinds of lies: lies, damned lies, and statistics."

Using Statistics as Support

Just as three or four brief examples may be more effective than just one, a statistic that represents hundreds or thousands of individuals may be more persuasive still.

statistics
Numeric data that summarize examples

Statistics can help a speaker express the magnitude or seriousness of a situation:

The National Center for Health Statistics estimates that by the end of this year 50,000 teenagers, in the U.S. alone, will attempt suicide; at least 5,000 will succeed.[18]

Or statistics can express the relationship of a part to the whole:

The National Highway and Traffic Safety Administration reports that a whopping 40% of car repair costs last year were either fraudulent or unnecessary.[19]

Whatever their purpose, statistics are considered by most people to be the ultimate "hard" evidence—firm, convincing fact.

Using Statistics Effectively

The following discussion can help you analyze and use statistics effectively and correctly.

USE RELIABLE SOURCES.   It has been said that figures don't lie, but liars figure! And indeed, statistics can be produced to support almost any conclusion desired. Your goal is to cite *reputable, authoritative,* and *unbiased* sources.

The most reputable sources of statistics are usually government agencies, independent survey organizations, scholarly research reports, and such statistical reference works as the *World Almanac* and the *Statistical Abstract of the United States.* Private businesses may also be reputable, but view their statistics with a bit more caution. These organizations may use questionable data collection methods, or their data may be biased by special interests.

Statistical sources should also be authoritative. No source is an authority on everything and thus cannot be credible on all subjects. For example, we expect the U.S. surgeon general's office to gather and release statistics on smokers' risks of developing lung cancer. But we would look askance at statistics from that same office that dealt with the numbers of hurricanes that have hit the coastal United States in the last 100 years. The most authoritative source is the **primary source**—the original collector and interpreter of the data. If you find an interesting statistic in a newspaper or magazine article, look closely to see whether a source is cited. If it is, try to find that source and the original reporting of the statistic. Do not just assume that the secondhand account, or **secondary source**, has reported the statistic accurately and fairly. As often as possible, go to the primary source.

As well as being reputable and authoritative, sources should be as unbiased as possible. We usually extend to government research and various independent sources of statistics the courtesy of thinking them unbiased. Because they are, for the most part, supposed to be unaffiliated with any special interest, their statistics are presumed to be less biased than those coming from such organizations as the American Tobacco Institute, the AFL-CIO, or the Burger King Corporation. All three organizations have some special interest at stake and are more likely to reflect their biases when gathering and reporting data.

As you evaluate your sources, try to find out how the statistics were gathered. For example, if a statistic relies on a sample, how was the sample taken? A Thursday after-

primary source
The individual or organization that collects information or data

Secondary source
An individual, organization, or publication that reports information or data gathered by another entity

noon telephone poll of 20 registered voters in Brooklyn is not an adequate sample of New York City voters. The sample is too small and too geographically limited. In addition, it excludes anyone without a telephone or anyone unlikely to be at home when the survey was conducted. Sample sizes and survey methods do vary widely, but most well-known polls involve samples of 500 to 2,000 people, selected at random from a larger population.

Of course, finding out about the statistical methodology may be more difficult than discovering the source of the statistic, but if you can find it, the information will help you to analyze the value of the statistic.

INTERPRET STATISTICS ACCURATELY.   People are often swayed by statistics that sound good but have in fact been wrongly calculated or misinterpreted. In an interview for *The New York Times*, Joel Best, author of *Damned Lies and Statistics: Untangling Numbers from the Media, Politicians, and Activists*, offered his favorite "bad statistic":

> *A student of mine quoted an article that contained the sentence, "Every year since 1950, the number of American children gunned down has doubled." This is [a] mutant statistic. If one child were gunned down in 1950, and two in 1951, then by 1995, the year that the article was written, there would have been 35 trillion children gunned down, more than the total number of people who ever lived.*[20]

A misinterpretation of day-care statistics was the focus of a student speaker's criticism:

> *Newsweek estimates that 2 million children receive formalized day care in the United States today. Unfortunately, this still leaves out the 5½ million children left alone, along with countless others under the care of unreliable relatives or neighbors. . . . And even if these children were in licensed day care, the facilities for most centers are wholly inadequate.*[21]

The large number of children in formalized day care—2 million—would seem to indicate that the problem of child care is under control. However, as the student speaker pointed out, that figure is not a measure of success at all. If anything, it is an indicator of the huge size of the problem.

In each of these cases, the speaker's skillful analysis helped listeners understand the true situation. Unfortunately, in other cases, the speaker may be the culprit in misinterpreting the statistics. Both as a user of statistics in your own speeches and as a consumer of statistics in articles, books, and speeches, be constantly alert to what the statistics actually mean.

MAKE YOUR STATISTICS UNDERSTANDABLE AND MEMORABLE.   You can make your statistics easier to understand and more memorable in several ways. First, you can *compact* a statistic, or express it in limits that are more meaningful or more easily understandable to your audience. When he outlined his first budget to a joint session of Congress on February 27, 2001, President George W. Bush compacted a statistic to help his listeners understand what a $1,600 tax savings could mean to an average American family:

> *Now $1,600 may not sound like a lot to some, but it means a lot to many families: $1,600 buys gas for two cars for an entire year. It pays tuition for a year at a community college. It pays the average family grocery bill for three months. That's real money.*[22]

Country of Origin	Preferred Family Size	
	0–2	3 or more
Iceland	26%	69%
United States	50%	41%
Mexico	56%	42%
Thailand	69%	30%
Germany	77%	17%
India	87%	12%

Note: "No opinion" omitted.

FIGURE **8.1**

Family-size preference and country of origin.

You might also make your statistics more memorable by *exploding* them. Exploded statistics are created by adding or multiplying related numbers—for example, cost per unit times number of units. Because it is larger, the exploded statistic seems more significant than the original figures from which it was derived. Sandra Mims Rowe, editor of *The Oregonian,* a Portland newspaper, used an exploded statistic to good advantage in a speech to the annual convention of the American Society of Newspaper Editors:

> *High-tech firms average more than $900 per employee a year on training, and the average of all companies is $500. If newspaper spending on training equaled that of high-tech firms, a newspaper staff of 100 would invest $90,000 annually in training.*[23]

Finally, you can *compare* your statistic with another that heightens its impact. Talking about decaying school buildings, one student speaker pointed out that the 1994 School Facilities Infrastructure Bill provided $100 million for school repairs. However, she went on to say,

> *Contrast this to the $1.3 billion which will go to state and local prisons each year for the next 6 years as part of the recently passed crime bill, and it starts to look as if we don't care about our kids.*[24]

ROUND OFF NUMBERS WHENEVER YOU CAN DO SO WITHOUT DISTORTING OR FALSIFYING THE STATISTIC. It is much easier to grasp and remember "2 million" than 2,223,147. Percentages, too, are more easily remembered if they are rounded off. And most people seem to remember percentages even better if they are expressed as fractions. "About 30 percent" is a better way to express "31.69 percent," and "about one third" is even easier to understand and remember.

USE VISUAL AIDS TO PRESENT YOUR STATISTICS. Most audience members have difficulty remembering a barrage of numbers thrown at them during a speech. But if the numbers are placed on a table or graph in front of your listeners, they can more easily grasp the statistics. Figure 8.1 illustrates how a speaker could lay out a table of statistics regarding what people from various countries perceive to be an ideal number of children for a family to have. Using such a table, you would still need to explain what the numbers mean, but you wouldn't have to recite them. We will discuss visual aids in Chapter 14.

Opinions

Three types of **opinions** may be used as supporting material in speeches: the testimonies of expert authorities, the testimonies of ordinary (lay) people with firsthand or eyewitness experience, and quotations from literary works. If the person you quote is a recognized authority in the area of your topic, citing his or her opinion may add credibility to your own arguments. Or the person you quote may have "said it in a nutshell"—phrased an argument or observation clearly, succinctly, and memorably. Let's look at the specific purposes and advantages of both expert testimonies and literary quotations.

Expert Testimony

Having already offered statistics on the number of cigars Americans consume annually, Dena emphasized the danger to both smoker and secondhand recipient by providing **expert testimony** from a National Cancer Institute adviser:

James Repace, an adviser to the National Cancer Institute, states, "If you have to breathe secondhand smoke, cigar smoke is a lot worse than cigarette smoke."[25]

Regardless of whether your topic is controversial or not currently the object of widespread concern, the testimony of a recognized authority can add a great deal of weight to your arguments. Or if your topic requires that you make predictions—thought processes that can be supported only in a marginal way by statistics or examples—the statements of expert authorities may prove to be your most convincing support. You may quote experts directly or paraphrase, as long as you are careful not to alter the intent of their remarks.

Lay Testimony

You are watching the nightly news. Newscasters, reporting on the forest fires that continue to rage in Florida, explain how these fires started. They provide statistics on how many thousands of acres have burned and how many hundreds of homes have been destroyed. They describe the intense heat and smoke at the scene of one of the fires, and ask an expert—a veteran firefighter—to predict the likelihood that the fires will be brought under control soon. But the most poignant moment of this news story is an interview with a woman who has just been allowed to return to her home and has found it in smoldering ashes. She is a layperson—not a firefighter or an expert on forest fires, but someone who has experienced the tragedy firsthand.

Like illustrations, **lay testimony** can stir an audience's emotions. And, although neither as authoritative or as unbiased as expert testimony, lay testimony is often more memorable.

opinion
A statement made by an individual

expert testimony
An opinion offered by someone who is an authority on the subject

lay testimony
An opinion offered by a nonexpert who has firsthand experience

Literary Quotations

Another way to make a point memorable is to include a **literary quotation** in your speech. A student speaking on historical heresies quoted George Orwell to explain why distortion of historical fact is a problem:

> *In his infamous novel 1984, George Orwell asserts, "Who controls the past controls the future; who controls the present controls the past."*[26]

Orwell's words express the speaker's point in a poetic and memorable way. Note too that the quotation is short. Brief, pointed quotations usually have greater audience impact than longer, more rambling ones. As Shakespeare said, "Brevity is the soul of wit" (*Hamlet*, II:2).

Literary quotations have the additional advantage of being easily accessible. As noted in Chapter 7, a number of quotation dictionaries exist on the Web and in the reference sections of most libraries. Arranged alphabetically by subject, these compilations are easy to use.

Using Opinions Effectively

Here are a few suggestions for using opinions effectively in your speeches.

BE CERTAIN THAT ANY AUTHORITY YOU CITE AS AN EXPERT IS AN EXPERT ON THE SUBJECT YOU ARE DISCUSSING. Unless the authority you are calling on has expertise in the subject on which he or she is expressing an opinion, your quote will have little value. Quoting the opinions of an atomic scientist about works of art, for example, is to do little more than accept the opinions of the average person. Be sure, then, that the sources you quote are not merely recognized authorities but recognized in the particular subject area they are talking about. Advertisements, especially, ignore this rule when they use sports figures to endorse such items as flashlight batteries, breakfast cereals, and cars. Sports figures may indeed be experts on athletic shoes, tennis rackets, or stopwatches, but they lack any specific qualifications to talk about most of the products they endorse.

IDENTIFY YOUR SOURCES. Perhaps you chose an eminently qualified authority on your subject. Unless the audience, too, is aware of the qualifications of your authority, they may not grant him or her any credibility. If a student who quotes the director of the Literacy Services of Wisconsin identifies that person only as Vyvyan Harding, no one will recognize the name, let alone acknowledge her authority.

In Chapter 3, we discussed the importance of citing your sources orally. In the course of doing so, you can provide additional information about the qualifications of those sources. Note how the student speakers in the following examples use a variety of phrases and sentence structures to help them identify their sources for their audiences in a fluent way:

> *Dr. Jane Henney, commissioner of the FDA, argues in her congressional testimony on March 21, 2000, that many sites "advertise products that make fraudulent health claims, drugs for recreational use, or unapproved drug products."*[27]

> *According to Barry Scheck of Cordoza Law School, in the September 22, 1999, Dallas Morning News, [failure to use DNA technology] is a manpower and money*

literary quotation
An opinion from a writer who speaks in a memorable and often poetic way

issue. Scheck asserts, "Frankly, we have a national scandal in the failure of government to fund crime labs to take advantage of DNA technology as an investigative tool."[28]

"The media is doing a disservice," explain Judith Martin and Thomas Nakayama in Intercultural Communication in Context, *published in 2000. "Most individuals rely on the mass media for perceptions of others with which they don't have regular interpersonal contact."*[29]

CITE UNBIASED AUTHORITIES.   Just as the most reliable sources of statistics are unbiased, so too are the most reliable sources of opinion. The chairman of General Motors may offer an expert opinion that the Chevrolet Lumina is the best midsized car on the market today. His expertise is unquestionable, but his bias is obvious and makes him a less than trustworthy source of opinion on the subject. A better source would be the *Consumer Reports* analyses of the reliability and repair records of midsized cars.

CITE OPINIONS THAT ARE REPRESENTATIVE OF PREVAILING OPINION.   Perhaps you have found a bona fide expert who supports your conclusions. Unless most of the experts in the field share his or her opinion, its value is limited. Citing such opinion only leaves your conclusions open to easy rebuttal.

QUOTE YOUR SOURCES ACCURATELY.   If you quote or paraphrase either an expert or a layperson, be certain that your quote or paraphrase is accurate and within the context in which the remarks were originally made. Major misunderstandings may result from someone's being quoted inaccurately. "Letters to the Editor" columns in major news publications often include letters from irate readers who have found themselves misquoted in recent articles.

USE LITERARY QUOTATIONS SPARINGLY.   Even though a relevant literary quote may be just right for a speech, use it with caution. Overuse of such quotations often bores an audience and causes them to doubt your creativity and research ability and to view you as somewhat pretentious. It is sometimes better not to use any quotation than to use literary quotations out of desperation, just because you can't find anything better. Be sure that you have a valid reason for citing a literary quotation, and then use only one or two at most in a speech.

RECAP

TYPES OF SUPPORTING MATERIAL FOR A SPEECH

ILLUSTRATIONS	Relevant stories
EXPLANATIONS	Statements that make clear how something is done or why it exists in its present or past form
DESCRIPTIONS	Word pictures
DEFINITIONS	Concise explications of a word or concept
ANALOGIES	Comparisons of one thing to another
STATISTICS	Numbers that summarize data or examples
OPINIONS	Testimony or quotations from someone else

Address: http://www.ablongman.com/beebe

▼ | **Using the Internet to Find
Interesting Supporting Material**

The Internet can be a useful tool to help you find that perfect story, riveting illustration, recent statistic, or well-worded definition. We offer several sites to help you plumb cyberspace for supporting material. For your next speech, go to one or more of the following sites to find relevant and interesting support for your speech.

VIRTUAL REFERENCE DESK OF PURDUE UNIVERSITY

http://thorplus.lib.purdue.edu/reference/index.html

This powerful site provides links to some of the most common reference material found in most libraries.

BIOGRAPHY FIND

http://www.biography.com

Use the "biosearch" feature of this site to find information on more than 20,000 famous people. Anecdotes about them can serve as illustrations for a speech.

FEDERAL GOVERNMENT STATISTICS

http://www.census.gov/dmd/www/2khome.htm

This U.S. Bureau of the Census site may provide just the statistic you need from the 2000 U.S. census.

http://www.info.gov/

This is a good clearinghouse for government documents from several U.S. federal agencies.

http://www.fedstats.gov

This is another good and easy-to-search source of statistics from various U.S. government agencies.

Selecting the Best Supporting Material

In Chapter 7, we discussed six criteria for evaluating Websites: accountability, accuracy, objectivity, date, usability, and diversity. Throughout this chapter, we have presented guidelines for using each of the six types of supporting material effectively. However, even after you have applied these criteria and guidelines, you may still have more supporting material than you can possibly use for a short speech. How do you decide what to use and what to eliminate? The following considerations can help you make that final cut.

- *Magnitude* Bigger is better. The larger the numbers, the more convincing your statistics. The more experts who support your point of view, the more your expert testimony will command your audience's attention.

- *Proximity* The best supporting material is that which is the most relevant to your listeners, or "closest to home." If you can demonstrate how an incident could affect audience members themselves, that illustration will have far greater impact than a more remote one.

- *Concreteness* By themselves abstract assertions and explanations bore an audience. If you need to discuss principles and theories, explain them with concrete examples and specific statistics.

- *Variety* Even if your supporting material meets the first four requirements, if it is all of the same type, your audience may lose interest or question your research. A mix of illustrations, opinions, definitions, and statistics is much more interesting and convincing than the exclusive use of any one type of supporting material.

- *Humor* Audiences usually appreciate a touch of humor in an example or opinion. Only if your audience is unlikely to understand the humor or your speech is on a *very* somber and serious topic is humor not appropriate.

- *Suitability* Your final decision about whether to use a certain piece of supporting material will depend on its suitability to you, your speech, the occasion, and—as we continue to stress throughout the book—your audience. For example, you would probably use more statistics in a speech to a group of scientists than in an after-luncheon talk to the local Rotary Club.

SUMMARY

Interesting, convincing supporting material is essential to a successful speech. You can choose from various types of supporting material, including illustrations, descriptions and explanations, definitions, analogies, statistics, and opinions.

Once you find material to support your ideas, follow the suggestions presented in this chapter to gauge the validity and reliability of your evidence. Six additional criteria—magnitude, proximity, concreteness, variety, humor, and suitability—can help you choose the most effective support for your speech.

being audience-centered

A Sharper Focus

CONSIDERING YOUR AUDIENCE

▶ An illustration almost always ensures audience interest.

▶ An audience could dismiss a single illustration as an exception, but two or more strongly suggest a trend or norm.

▶ Plausible hypothetical illustrations may serve your purpose better than any real examples by enabling your audience to put themselves in a particular situation.

▶ Make listeners aware from the beginning of a hypothetical illustration that the illustration is hypothetical.

▶ Be certain that your illustrations are clearly relevant; never leave an audience in doubt as to why you have used a certain illustration.

▶ If your illustrations are rare instances, you owe it to your listeners to tell them so.

▶ If you have chosen to tell a poignant story, give it enough detail to make it come alive in the minds of your listeners. Paint a mental picture of the people, places, and things involved.

▶ Good descriptions are vivid, accurate, and specific; they make people, places, and events come alive for the audience.

▶ An explanation should supply only enough details for an audience to understand how or why something works or exists.

▶ Vivid and specific language in an explanation helps you hold the audience's attention and paint in your listeners' minds the image you are trying to communicate.

▶ You will hold your audience's attention more effectively if you alternate explanations and descriptions with other types of supporting material, such as brief examples or statistics.

▶ Even if your subject is controversial, if you quote a reputable dictionary, listeners usually accept without question the definition you are using.

▶ Unnecessary definitions are boring, and more serious still, insulting to the listeners' intelligence.

▶ Make certain that you provide definitions that are immediately and easily understandable, or you will have wasted your time and perhaps even lost your audience.

▶ Analogies can help your listeners understand unfamiliar ideas, things, and situations by showing how these matters resemble something they already know.

▶ A literal analogy that doesn't quite work may hamper rather than help an audience's understanding of the thing or idea you are trying to explain.

▶ When you use a figurative analogy, it is crucial to make clear the similarity on which it is based. If you do not, your audience will end up wondering what in the world you are talking about.

▶ Most listeners consider statistics to be the ultimate "hard" evidence—firm, convincing fact.

▶ Most listeners can remember rounded numbers and fractions more easily than exact numbers and percentages.

▶ If you display numbers in a table or graph, listeners can more easily grasp the statistics.

▶ Lay testimony can stir an audience's emotions and is likely to remain in its memory.

▶ Unless the audience members are aware of the qualifications of a quoted authority, they may not grant him or her any credibility.

▶ The more experts who support your point of view, the more your expert testimony will command your audience's attention.

▶ The best supporting material is that which is the most relevant to your listeners, or "closest to home."

▶ Abstract assertions and explanations by themselves bore an audience. Use concrete examples and specific statistics.

▶ A mix of illustrations, opinions, definitions, and statistics is much more interesting and convincing than the exclusive use of any one type of supporting material.

CONSIDERING AUDIENCE DIVERSITY

▶ Once you have gathered a variety of supporting material, look at your speech from your audience's perspective and decide where an explanation might help listeners understand a point, where statistics might convince them of the significance of a problem, and where an illustration might stir their emotions.

▶ Use audience-centered illustrations—ones to which the members of your audience can relate.

▶ If your listeners are from a culture or group other than your own, or other than the one from which the speech derives, literal analogies that draw on the listeners' culture or group may help them understand more readily the less familiar places, things, and situations you are discussing.

▶ Humor is inappropriate if your audience is unlikely to understand it.

▶ Your final decision about whether or not to use a certain piece of supporting material will depend on its suitability to your audience.

CRITICAL-THINKING QUESTIONS

The following excerpts from student speeches contain various types of supporting material discussed in this chapter. Read each excerpt and then identify the type of supporting material it contains. (Some may contain more than one type. In that case, identify the *primary* type of supporting material contained in the excerpt.)

_____ 1. It was another beautiful day at the amusement park. Warm sunshine, the smell of cotton candy, the kids, and the rides. The roller coaster's whooshing 60-miles-per-hour speed was accompanied by the familiar screams of delight from kids of all ages. Another ride, the comet, was flying gracefully through the heavens when suddenly a chain broke, flinging one of the gondolas 75 feet into the air before it crashed, killing a man and seriously injuring his son.[30]

_____ 2. A report released on April 15, 1999, by the California Health and Human Services Agency revealed a 273 percent increase in children diagnosed with autism in the past decade in California alone.[31]

_____ 3. "The bottom line," says former CPSC Chairperson Nancy Steorts, "is that the American consumer has no way of knowing the level of safety on a particular ride at a particular location. In effect, we are forcing the consumer to play amusement ride roulette with his or her family's safety."[32]

_____ 4. Maryland has one of the best [amusement-park] safety records in the country, and it is essential that all states adopt and consistently enforce the same thorough regulations.[33]

_____ 5. Do you remember what the weather was like a few months ago? Recall when it was cold; when you would shiver getting out of bed, getting out of the shower, walking outside; when it was most wise to stay inside, wrap yourself in a warm blanket, and turn up the heat.[34]

_____ 6. Imagine you are poor, according to a wide variety of government standards. It is nearly impossible for you to pay your heating bills. So you would be eligible for a portion of the . . . [money] allocated for this program. . . .[35]

_____ 7. [Solar] storms cause the sun to throw off electrically charged ions that, combined with charged particles, enter the Earth's atmosphere from outer space.[36]

ETHICAL QUESTIONS

1. Go back through the chapter and reread each of the "Using _____ Effectively" guidelines for each type of supporting material. Which of these guidelines for *effective* use of supporting material might also be considered a guideline for *ethical* use of supporting material? Explain your choices.

2. Is it ever ethical to invent supporting material if you have been unable to find what you need for your speech? Explain.

SUGGESTED ACTIVITIES

1. Read an investigative story in a newspaper or a national news magazine. See how many different types of supporting materials you can identify in the story.

2. From the same story you used for Activity 1, select three different types of supporting materials. Apply to each one the relevant "Using _____ Effectively" suggestions found in this chapter. Determine whether you think the author used each piece of supporting material effectively. If not, which suggestion(s) did he or she *not* follow?

USING TECHNOLOGY AND MEDIA

1. Videotape a minimum of five 60-second television commercials aired during evening prime time. Create a log such as the following, in which you briefly identify each commercial and the types of supporting material it incorporates. Mark the appropriate box every time each type of supporting material is used. What was the most frequently used type of supporting material in these five television commercials?

Brief Description of Commercial	Illustrations	Explanations/ Descriptions	Definitions	Analogies	Statistics	Opinions
Type(s) of Supporting Material Used						
1.						
2.						
3.						
4.						
5.						

2. Was your sample size for Question 1 large enough to allow you to generalize your findings (that is, to say that _____ is the most frequently used type of supporting material in *all* television advertising)? Explain your answer.

Organized thought is the basis
of organized action.

ALFRED NORTH WHITEHEAD

Organizing Your Speech

objectives

After studying this chapter you should be able to do the following:

1. List and describe five patterns for organizing the main ideas of a speech.

2. Explain how organizational strategies can vary according to culture.

3. List five patterns of organization applicable to subpoints.

4. Describe how to integrate supporting material into a speech.

5. List and explain four organizational strategies specifically adapted to supporting material.

6. List and define three types of verbal and nonverbal speech signposts.

7. Explain how visual aids can supplement signposts.

Maria went into the lecture hall feeling exhilarated. After all, Dr. Anderson was a Nobel laureate in literature. He would be teaching and lecturing on campus for at least a year. What an opportunity!

Maria took a seat in the middle of the fourth row, where she had a clear view of the podium. She opened the notebook she had bought just for this lecture series, took out one of the three pens she had brought with her, and waited impatiently for Dr. Anderson's appearance. She didn't have to wait long. Dr. Anderson was greeted by thunderous applause when he walked out onto the stage. Maria was aware of an almost electric sense of expectation among the audience members. Pen poised, she awaited his first words.

Five minutes later, Maria still had her pen poised. He had gotten off to a slow start. Ten minutes later, she laid her pen down and decided to concentrate just on listening. Twenty minutes later, she still had no idea what point Dr. Anderson was trying to make. And by the time the lecture was over, Maria was practically asleep. Disappointed, she gathered her pens and her notebook (which now contained one page of lazy doodles) and promised herself she would skip the remaining lectures in the series.

Dr. Anderson was not a dynamic speaker. But his motivated audience of young would-be authors and admirers might have forgiven that shortcoming. What they were unable to do was to unravel his hour's worth of seemingly pointless rambling—to get some sense of direction or some pattern of ideas from his talk. Dr. Anderson had simply failed to organize his thoughts.

This scenario actually happened. Dr. Anderson (not his real name) disappointed many who had looked forward to his lectures. His inability to organize his ideas made him an ineffectual speaker. You, too, may have had an experience with a teacher who possessed awesome knowledge and ability in his or her field but could not organize his or her thoughts well enough to lecture effectively. No matter how knowledgeable speakers may be, they must organize their ideas in logical patterns to ensure that their audience can follow, understand, and remember what is said. Our model of audience-centered communication emphasizes that speeches are organized *for* audiences, with decisions about organization being based in large part on an analysis of the audience.

In the first eight chapters of this book, you learned how to plan and research a speech based on audience needs, interests, and expectations. The planning and research process has taken you through five stages of speech preparation:

- Select and narrow a topic.

- Determine your purpose.

- Develop your central idea.

- Generate main ideas.

- Gather supporting material.

As the arrows on the model in Figure 9.1 suggest, you may have moved *recursively* through these first five stages, returning at times to earlier stages to make changes and revisions based on your consideration of the audience. Now, with the results of your audience-centered planning and researching in hand, it is time to begin to put the speech together—in other words, to organize your ideas and information. The next stage in the audience-centered public-speaking process is simply that:

- Organize your speech.

In this chapter, we will discuss the patterns of organization commonly used to arrange the main ideas of a speech. Then we will discuss how to organize subpoints and supporting materials. Finally, we will talk about transitions, previews, and summaries. Chapter 10 will discuss introductions and conclusions, and Chapter 11 will deal with outlining, the final two components of the organizational stage of the preparation process.

Organizing Your Main Ideas

In Chapter 6, we discussed how to generate a preliminary plan for your speech by determining whether your central idea had logical divisions, could be supported by several reasons, or could be explained by identifying specific steps. These divisions, reasons, or steps became the main ideas of the body of your speech and the basis for the organization task highlighted in Figure 9.1.

Now you are ready to decide which of your main ideas to discuss first, which one second, and so on. You can choose from among five organizational patterns: (1) chronological, (2) topical, (3) spatial, (4) causal, and (5) problem–solution. Or you can combine several of these patterns. One additional variation of the problem–solution pattern is the motivated sequence. Because it is used almost exclusively in persuasive speeches, the motivated sequence will be discussed in Chapter 17.

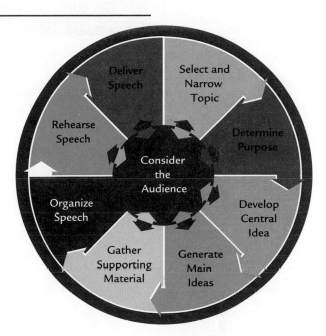

FIGURE 9.1

Organize your speech to help your audience remember your key ideas and to give your speech clarity and structure.

Ordering Ideas Chronologically

If you decide that your central idea could be explained best by a number of steps, you will probably organize those steps chronologically. **Chronological organization** is organization by time; that is, your steps are ordered according to when each step occurred or should occur. Historical speeches and how-to speeches are the two kinds of speeches usually organized chronologically.

Examples of topics for historical speeches might include the history of the women's movement in the United States, the sequence of events that led to the 1974 resignation of President Richard Nixon, or the development of the modern Olympic Games. You may wish to organize your main points either from earliest to most recent (forward in time) or from recent events back into history (backward in time). The progression you choose depends on your personal preference and on whether you want to emphasize the beginning or the end of the sequence. According to the principle of **recency,** the event discussed *last* is usually the one the audience will remember best.

chronological organization
Organization by time or sequence

recency
Arranging ideas from the least to the most important

In the following speech on the nation's 911 system, the speaker moves forward in time, making his last point the one that remains fresh in the minds of his audience at the end of his speech.

PURPOSE STATEMENT: At the end of my speech, the audience will be able to trace the decline in the effectiveness of the 911 emergency system in the United States.

CENTRAL IDEA: The 911 system has decreased in effectiveness since its inception in 1967.

MAIN IDEAS:

I. In 1967, Lyndon Johnson signed legislation creating the 911 system.

II. In 1987, the average 911 response time was 6 minutes.

III. By 1998, the average 911 response time was 12 minutes.

IV. By 2001, 911 was struggling to handle the booming mobile-phone industry.[1]

Note that in this example, the central idea and main ideas together form the kind of blueprint we introduced in Chapter 6 and will discuss in more detail later in this chapter.

In another historical speech, this one discussing the factors that led to the literary Renaissance in England, the speaker believes the introduction of the printing press to be the most important influence and organizes the speech backward in time in order to discuss the printing press last.

PURPOSE STATEMENT: At the end of my speech, the audience will be able to list and explain the two forces that prompted the English literary Renaissance.

CENTRAL IDEA: Two powerful forces for change led to the English literary Renaissance, which began late in the fifteenth century.

MAIN IDEAS:	I.	1485—Henry VII defeated Richard III at the Battle of Bosworth Field, ascended the throne, and began the Tudor dynasty.
	II.	1476—William Caxton brought the printing press to England.

Using the principle of recency, the speaker gives the printing press the greater emphasis in the speech.

Chronological organization, then, involves either forward or backward progression, depending on which end of a set of events the speaker intends to emphasize. The element common to both movements is that dates and events are discussed in sequence rather than in random order.

How-to explanations usually follow a sequence or series of steps arranged from beginning to end, from the first step to the last—forward in time. A speech explaining how to strip painted furniture might be organized as follows:

PURPOSE STATEMENT:		At the end of my speech, the audience will be able to list the four steps involved in stripping old paint from furniture.
CENTRAL IDEA:		Stripping old paint from furniture requires four steps.
MAIN IDEAS:	I.	Prepare work area and gather materials.
	II.	Apply chemical stripper.
	III.	Remove stripper with scrapers and steel wool.
	IV.	Clean and sand stripped surfaces.

Organizing Ideas Topically

If your central idea has natural divisions, you can often organize your speech topically. Speeches on such diverse topics as factors to consider when selecting a mountain bike, types of infertility treatments, and the various classes of ham-radio licenses all could reflect **topical organization.**

Natural divisions are often fairly equal in importance. It may not matter which point you discuss first, second, or third. You can simply arrange your main points as a matter of personal preference. At other times, you may wish to emphasize one point more than the others. If so, you will again need to consider the principle of *recency*. As we observed earlier, audiences tend to remember best what they hear last. For example, if your speech is on the various living arrangements available to college students, you may decide to discuss living at home, rooming in a dorm, joining a fraternity or sorority, and renting an apartment. If you want your audience of fellow students to consider living at home because of the savings involved, you would probably discuss that possibility as the fourth and last option. Your speech might have the following structure:

PURPOSE STATEMENT:	At the end of my speech, the audience will be able to discuss the pros and cons of the four lifestyle options for college students.
CENTRAL IDEA:	College students have at least four living arrangements available to them.

topical organization
Organization according to the speaker's discretion, recency, primacy, or complexity

MAIN IDEAS:	I. Living in a dormitory
	II. Renting an apartment
	III. Joining a fraternity or sorority
	IV. Living at home

By contrast, if your topic is controversial and you know or suspect that your audience will be skeptical or hostile toward your ideas, you may want to organize your main ideas according to the principle of **primacy,** or putting the most important or convincing idea first. This way you do not risk losing or alienating your audience before you can reach your most significant idea. Further, your strongest idea may so influence your listeners' attitudes that they will be more receptive to the rest of your speech.

PURPOSE STATEMENT:	At the end of my speech, the audience will be able to explain the applications of stem cell research.
CENTRAL IDEA:	Stem cell research has three important applications.
MAIN IDEAS:	I. At the most fundamental level, understanding stem cells can help us to understand better the process of human development.
	II. Stem cell research could streamline the way we develop and test drugs.
	III. Stem cell research can generate cells and tissue that could be used for "cell therapies."[2]

In this example, the speaker realizes the controversial nature of stem-cell research. The three main points of the speech are therefore arranged according to primacy, advancing the most persuasive argument first.

One other set of circumstances may dictate a particular order of the main points in your speech. If your main points range from simple to complicated, it makes sense to arrange them in order of **complexity,** progressing from the simple to the more complex. If, for example, you were to explain to your audience how to compile a family health profile and history, you might begin with the most easily accessible source and proceed to the more involved.

PURPOSE STATEMENT:	At the end of my speech, the audience will be able to compile a family health profile and history.
CENTRAL IDEA:	Compiling a family health profile and history can be accomplished with the help of three sources.
MAIN IDEAS:	I. Elderly relatives
	II. Old hospital records and death certificates
	III. National health registries[3]

primacy
Arranging ideas from the most to the least important

complexity
Arranging ideas from the simple to the more complex

Teachers from the very early elementary grades on, use order of complexity to organize their courses and lessons. The kindergartner is taught to trace circles before learning to print a lowercase *a.* The young piano student practices scales and arpeggios before playing Beethoven sonatas. The college freshman practices writing 500-word essays before attempting a major research paper. You have learned most of your skills by order of complexity.

Arranging Ideas Spatially

When you say, "As you enter the room, the table is to your right, the easy chair to your left, and the kitchen door straight ahead," you are organizing your ideas spatially. **Spatial organization** arranges items according to their location and direction. It does not usually matter whether the speaker chooses to progress up or down, east or west, forward or back, as long as ideas are developed in a logical order. If the speaker skips up, down, over, and back, he or she will only confuse the audience rather than paint a distinct word picture for it.

Speeches on such diverse subjects as the Heard Museum in Phoenix, the travels of Robert Louis Stevenson, and the makeup of an atom, can all be organized spatially. Here is a sample outline for the first of those topics:

PURPOSE STATEMENT: At the end of my speech, the audience will be able to list and describe the four permanent exhibits of the Heard Museum.

CENTRAL IDEA: The Heard Museum in Phoenix has four large permanent exhibits on Native American anthropology and culture.

MAIN IDEAS:

I. Ethnological and historical materials of southwestern Native Americans

II. Basketry

III. Jewelry and pottery

IV. Kachina dolls

The organization of this outline is spatial, progressing from the front entrance through the Heard Museum.

Organizing Ideas to Show Cause and Effect

A speech organized to show **cause and effect** may first identify a situation and then discuss the effects that result from it (cause→effect). Or the speech may present a situation and then seek its causes (effect→cause). As the recency principle would suggest, the cause→effect pattern emphasizes the effects; the effect→cause pattern emphasizes the causes.

In the following example, Vonda organizes her speech according to cause→effect, discussing the cause (widespread adult illiteracy) as her first main idea, and its effects (poverty and social costs) as her second and third main ideas:

PURPOSE STATEMENT: At the end of my speech, the audience will be able to identify two effects of adult illiteracy.

CENTRAL IDEA: Adult illiteracy affects everyone.

MAIN IDEAS:

I. (*Cause*): Adult illiteracy is widespread in America today.

II. (*Effect*): Adult illiterates often live in poverty.

III. (*Effect*): Adult illiteracy is costly to society.[4]

spatial organization
Organization according to location or position

cause-and-effect organization
Organization by discussing a situation and its causes, or a situation and its effects

In contrast, Laurel organizes her speech on writing wills according to an effect→cause pattern, discussing the effect (people not writing wills) as her first main idea, and its causes (having to face mortality and being ignorant of how to prepare a will) as her second and third main ideas:

PURPOSE STATEMENT:	At the end of my speech, the audience will be able to explain and counter the reasons people don't write wills.
CENTRAL IDEA:	People fail to prepare wills for several reasons.
MAIN IDEAS:	I. (*Effect*): People are hesitant to write wills.
	II. (*Cause*): Writing a will brings people face to face with their own mortality.
	III. (*Cause*): Many people don't know how to prepare a will.[5]

In both of the preceding examples, the speakers may decide in what order they will discuss their points II and III by considering the principles of recency, primacy, or complexity that we discussed earlier in this chapter.

Organizing Ideas by Problem and Solution

If you want to discuss why a problem exists or what its effects are, you will probably organize your speech according to cause and effect, as discussed in the previous section. However, if you want to emphasize how best to *solve* the problem, you will probably use a **problem-and-solution** pattern of organization.

Like causes and effects, problems and solutions can be discussed in either order. If you speak to an audience that is already fairly aware of a problem but uncertain how to solve it, you will probably discuss the problem first and then the solution(s), as in this example:

PURPOSE STATEMENT:	At the end of my speech, the audience will be able to list and explain three ways in which crime on university campuses can be reduced.
CENTRAL IDEA:	Crimes on university campuses can be reduced by implementing three safety measures.
MAIN IDEAS:	I. (*Problem*): Crimes against both persons and property have increased dramatically on college campuses over the last few years.
	II. (*Solution*): Crimes could be reduced by stricter enforcement of the Student Right to Know and Campus Security Acts.
	III. (*Solution*): Crimes could be reduced by assigning student identification numbers that are different from students' Social Security numbers.
	IV. (*Solution*): Crimes could be reduced by converting campus buildings to an integrated security system requiring key cards for admittance.[6]

problem-and-solution
Organization by discussing a problem and then various solutions, or a solution and then the problems it would solve

However, if your audience knows about an action or program that has been implemented, but does not know the reasons for its implementation, you might select instead a solution–problem pattern of organization. In the following example, the speaker knows that her listeners are already aware of a new business–school partnership program in their community, but that they may be unclear as to exactly why it has been established:

PURPOSE STATEMENT: At the end of my speech, the audience will be able to explain how business–school partnership programs can help solve two of the major problems facing our public schools today.

CENTRAL IDEA: Business–school partnership programs can help alleviate at least two of the problems faced by public schools today.

MAIN IDEAS: I. (*Solution*): In a business–school partnership, local businesses provide volunteers, financial support, and in-kind contributions to public schools.

                      II. (*Problem*): Many public schools can no longer afford special programs and fine-arts programs.

                     III. (*Problem*): Many public schools have no resources to fund enrichment materials and opportunities.

Acknowledging Cultural Differences in Organization

Although the five patterns just discussed are typical of the way in which speakers in the United States are expected to organize and process information, they are not necessarily typical of all cultures.[7] In fact, each culture teaches its members patterns of thought and organization that are considered appropriate for various occasions and audiences. On the whole, U.S. speakers tend to be more linear and direct than Semitic, Asian, Romance, or Russian speakers are. Semitic speakers support their main points by pursuing tangents that might seem "off topic" to many U.S. speakers. Asians may only allude to a main point through a circuitous route of illustration and parable. And speakers from Romance and Russian cultures tend to begin with a basic principle and then move to facts and illustrations that only gradually are related to a main point. The models in Figure 9.2 illustrate these culturally diverse patterns of organization.

Of course, these are very broad generalizations. But as an audience member, when you are listening to a speech, recognizing the existence of cultural differences can help

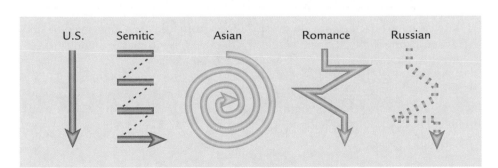

FIGURE **9.2**

Organizational patterns by culture

(Source: D. A. Lieberman, *Public Speaking in the Multicultural Environment.* Copyright © 2000. All rights reserved. Reprinted by permission of Allyn and Bacon.)

you appreciate and understand the organization of a speaker from a culture other than your own. He or she may not be disorganized, but simply using organizational strategies different from the ones presented earlier in this chapter.

RECAP

ORGANIZING YOUR MAIN POINTS

Pattern	Description
Chronological	Organization by time or sequence
Topical	Organization according to the speaker's discretion, recency, primacy, or complexity
Spatial	Organization according to location or position
Cause-and-effect	Organization by discussing a situation and its causes, or a situation and its effects
Problem-and-solution	Organization by discussing a problem and then various solutions, or a solution and then the problems it would solve

Subdividing Your Main Ideas

After you have decided how to organize your main ideas, you may need to subdivide at least some of them.[6] For example, if you give a how-to speech on dog grooming, your first main idea may be

I. Gather your supplies.

"Supplies" indicates that you need more than one piece of equipment, so you add subpoints that describe the specific supplies needed:

I. Gather your supplies.

   A. Soft brush

B. Firm brush

C. Wide-toothed comb

D. Fine-toothed comb

E. Scissors

F. Spray-on detangler

The organization of the main ideas of this speech on dog grooming is chronological, but the subpoints of the first main idea are arranged topically. Any of the five organizational patterns that apply to main ideas can apply to subpoints as well. As in this example, you can arrange your main ideas according to one pattern and your subpoints according to another.

Right now, don't worry about such outlining details as Roman numerals, letters, and margins. We cover them in Chapter 11. Your goal at this point is to get your ideas and information on paper. Keep in mind, too, that until you've delivered your speech, none of your decisions is etched in stone. You may add, regroup, or eliminate main ideas or subpoints at any stage in the preparation process, as you consider the needs, interests, and expectations of your audience. The Nobel Prize–winning author Isaac Bashevis Singer has observed, "The wastebasket is a writer's best friend." He could just as accurately have said "speaker" instead of "writer." Multiple drafts indicate that you are working and reworking ideas to improve your product and make it the best you can. They do *not* mean that you are a poor writer or speaker.

Integrating Your Supporting Material

Once you have organized your main ideas and subpoints, you are ready to flesh out the speech with your supporting material. If you have entered your supporting material into a word-processing file, you may want to print out a hard copy of this file so that you can have it in front of you while you work on your speech plan. When you determine where in the speech you need supporting material, find what you need on the hard copy and then go back into the word-processing file to cut and paste that supporting material electronically into your speech plan.

If you have written or pasted supporting material on note cards, write each main idea and subpoint on a separate note card of the same size as the ones on which you recorded your supporting material. Arrange these note cards in the order in which you have organized your speech. Then go through your supporting-material note cards, one by one, and decide where in the speech you will use each one. The headings you wrote at the top of each card should help in this process. Place each supporting-material card behind the appropriate main-idea or subpoint card. You now have a complete plan for your speech on note cards.

If most of your supporting material is photocopied, search these copies for what you need and then write or type this supporting material into your speech plan. Regardless of which strategy you use to integrate your supporting material, take care to maintain the source of the supporting material.

Once your supporting material is logically placed into your plan, your next goal is to incorporate it smoothly into your speech so as not to interrupt the flow of ideas. Notice how skillfully this goal is met by a speaker delivering a speech on media literacy:

While schools provide our children with a formal education, the media is one of the most predominant informal ways that children learn about the world around them.

In fact, according to Stephen Kline's 1993 book Out of the Garden, *by high school graduation, the average child will spend about 11,000 hours in the classroom. Yet nearly double that time, more than 20,000 hours, will be spent in front of the television. The key, then, is that the media is a teacher that kids find extremely attractive.*[8]

In this example, the speaker has followed four steps to integrate the supporting material into the speech:

1. *State the point.* This statement should be concise and clear so that the audience can grasp it immediately. In our example, the speaker's point is "While schools provide our children with a formal education, the media is one of the most predominant informal ways that children learn about the world around them."

2. *Cite the source of the supporting material.* This does not mean that you have to give complete bibliographic information. It is unlikely that your listeners will either remember or copy down a Website address. But as we discussed in Chapter 3 when we talked about using oral citations to prevent suspicion of plagiarism, provide the author's name (if available) and the title and date of the publication. The speaker in our example mentions all three. He might also have offered an additional bit of information: the qualifications of the author. Chances are that none of his audience will recognize as an authority the name Stephen Kline.

3. *Present the supporting material.* State the statistic, opinion, illustration, or other form of supporting material you have chosen to substantiate your idea. In the example, the speaker uses the statistic from Kline's book to make his point.

4. *Explain how the supporting material substantiates or develops the point.* Do not assume that audience members will automatically understand the connection. The speaker in our example draws the conclusion that "the media is a teacher that kids find extremely attractive."

Your listeners may not remember too many specific facts and statistics after a speech, but they should remember the important points. Connecting ideas and supporting material make it more likely that they will.

Organizing Your Supporting Material

Suppose you have decided what supporting material to use and identified the ideas in your speech that require support. Now you realize that in support of your second main idea you have an illustration, two statistics, and an opinion. In what order should you present these items?

You can sometimes use the five standard organizational patterns to arrange your supporting material, as well as your main ideas and subpoints. Illustrations, for instance, may be organized chronologically. In the following excerpt from a speech on Boy Scouting, a student arranges several brief examples in a chronological sequence:

Since the days of Teddy Roosevelt [every one] of our nation's Presidents has been involved in Boy Scouting. President John F. Kennedy expressed his sincere belief in Boy Scouting when he said, "In a very real sense, the principles learned and practiced as Boy Scouts add to the strength of America and her ideals." President Gerald Ford shared with the American public, "I am the first Eagle Scout to become Presi-

dent, and I thank scouting for the three great principles: Self-Discipline, Teamwork, and Moral Values, which are the basic building blocks of great leadership."[9]

At other times, however, none of the five patterns may seem suited to the supporting materials you have. In those instances, you may need to turn to an organizational strategy more specifically adapted to your supporting materials. These strategies include (1) primacy or recency, (2) specificity, (3) complexity, and (4) "soft" to "hard" evidence.

Primacy or Recency

We have already discussed how the principles of primacy and recency can determine whether you put material at the beginning or end of your speech. These patterns are used so frequently to arrange supporting materials that we mention them again here. Suppose that you have several statistics to support a main point. All are relevant and significant, but one is especially gripping. In her speech on the impact of periodontal disease on overall health, Mindy opts to sequence three statistics according to recency: The most dramatic one is saved for last.

Up to 18% of early births may be attributed to gum disease. That number represents 45,000 babies a year. Advanced Periodontics of Texas, in 1999, reported that such babies are forty times more likely than full-term babies to die.[10]

Although Mindy applies recency to three statistics, the principles of primacy and recency can also apply to groups of examples, opinions, or any combination of supporting material.

Specificity

Sometimes your supporting material will range from very specific examples to more general overviews of a situation. You may either offer your specific information first and end with your general statement, or make the general statement first and support it with specific evidence.

In her speech on how universities contribute to the exploitation of sweatshop labor, Carrie begins with a general statement of the problem and then moves to four specific illustrations:

The selling of university goods is big business. Collegiate administrations have long engaged in partnerships with multinational corporations in sale of T-shirts, sweatshirts, jackets, and other products in agreement to use the school's official names, colors, and insignias. The Boston Globe of April 18, 1999, explains that "Manufacturers pay a lucrative licensing fee, which the school can use as revenue for their general fund, scholarships, or athletic budget." For example, Harvard University made at least $500,000 in 1998 from licensing fees. UCLA, $1.2 million. Boston College, $2.6 million. And the University of Michigan, $5.7 million.[11]

Complexity

We have already discussed moving from the simple to the complex as a way to organize subtopics. The same method of organization may also determine how you order your supporting material. In many situations, it makes sense to start with the simplest ideas that are easy to understand and work up to more complex ones. In her speech on solar radiation, Nichole first explains the most obvious effects of solar peaks—electrical blackouts and disruptions in radio broadcasts—and then goes on to the more complex effect, cosmic radiation:

> *The sun produces storms on its surface in 11-year cycles. During solar maximum, these storms will make their presence known to the land-bound public through electrical blackouts and disruptions in radio broadcasts. These storms cause the sun to throw off electrically charged ions that, combined with charged particles, enter the Earth's atmosphere from outer space. This is known collectively as cosmic radiation.*[12]

 ## "Soft" to "Hard" Evidence

Supporting material can also be arranged from "soft" to "hard." **Soft evidence** rests on opinion or inference. Hypothetical illustrations, descriptions, explanations, definitions, analogies, and opinions are usually considered soft. **Hard evidence** includes factual examples and statistics. Actually, it is more accurate to think of soft and hard as two ends of a continuum, with various supporting material falling somewhere between. The U.S. surgeon general's analysis of the AIDS crisis, for example, would be placed nearer the hard end of the continuum than would someone's experience of seeing the NAMES Project AIDS Memorial Quilt, even though both would be classified as opinions. The surgeon general is a more credible speaker whose analysis is the result of his or her extensive knowledge of and research into the subject.

Soft-to-hard organization of supporting material relies chiefly on the principle of recency—that the last statement is remembered best. Notice how Rebecca moves from an opinion to a statistic, in her speech on the dangers of personal watercraft:

> *The August 1997* BC Cycle *noted Kathryn Burke, Director for the Centers for Disease Control and Prevention in Atlanta, when she said, "The major cause of injury last summer was jet skiers hitting swimmers." The U.S. Coast Guard Boating Statistics, cited in the August 1997* Journal of the American Medical Association, *support the fact that jet ski accidents have increased 400% since 1990.*[13]

The speaker has arranged her supporting material from soft to hard.

RECAP

ORGANIZING YOUR SUPPORTING MATERIAL

Strategy	Description
Primacy	Most important material first
Recency	Most important material last
Specificity	From specific information to general overview or from general overview to specific information
Complexity	From simple to more complex material
Soft to hard evidence	From opinion or hypothetical illustration to fact or statistic

soft evidence
Supporting material based mainly on opinion or inference. Includes hypothetical illustrations, descriptions, explanations, definitions, analogies, and opinions

hard evidence
Factual examples and statistics

Developing Signposts

Once you have organized your note cards, you have a logically ordered, fairly complete plan for your speech. But if you tried to deliver the speech at this point, you would find yourself frequently groping for some way to get from one point to the next. Your audience might become frustrated or even confused by your hesitations and awkwardness. Your next organizational task is to develop **signposts**—words and gestures that allow you to move smoothly from one idea to the next throughout your speech, showing relationships between ideas and emphasizing important points. Three types of signposts can serve as glue to hold your speech together: transitions, previews, and summaries.

Transitions

Transitions indicate that a speaker has finished discussing one idea and is moving to another. Transitions may be either verbal or nonverbal. Let's consider some examples of each type.

VERBAL TRANSITIONS   A speaker can sometimes make a verbal transition simply by repeating a key word from an earlier statement or by using a synonym or a pronoun that refers to an earlier key word or idea. This type of transition is often used to make one sentence flow smoothly into the next. This sentence itself is an example: "This type of transition" refers to the sentence that precedes it. Other verbal transitions are words or phrases that show relationships between ideas. Note the italicized transitional phrases in the following examples:

- *In addition to* transitions, previews and summaries are *also* considered to be signposts.

- *Not only* does plastic packaging use up our scarce resources, it contaminates them *as well.*

- *In other words,* as women's roles have changed, they have *also* contributed to this effect.

- *In summary,* Fanny Brice is probably the best remembered star of Ziegfeld's Follies.

- *Therefore,* I recommend that you sign the grievance petition.

Simple enumeration (*first, second, third*) can also point up relationships between ideas and provide transitions.

One type of transitional signpost that can occasionally backfire and do more harm than good is one that signals the end of a speech. *Finally* and *in conclusion* give the audience implicit permission to stop listening, and they often do. If the speech has been too long or has otherwise not gone well, the audience may even audibly express relief. Better strategies for moving into a conclusion include repeating a key word or phrase, using a synonym or pronoun that refers to a previous idea, offering a final summary, or referring to the introduction of the speech. We will discuss the final summary in more detail later in this chapter. Both of the last two strategies will also be covered in Chapter 10.

signpost
A verbal or nonverbal signal that a speaker is moving from one idea to the next

Internal previews and summaries, which we will discuss shortly, are yet another way to provide a verbal transition from one point to the next in your speech. They have the additional advantage of repeating your main ideas, thereby enabling audience members to understand and remember them.

Repetition of key words or ideas, the use of transitional words or phrases, enumeration, and internal previews and summaries all provide verbal transitions from one idea to the next. You may need to experiment with several alternatives before you find the smooth transition you seek in a given instance. If none of these alternatives seems to work well, consider a nonverbal transition.

RECAP   **VERBAL TRANSITIONS**

Strategy	Example
Repeating a key word, or using a synonym or pronoun that refers to a key word	*"These problems* cannot be allowed to continue."
Using a transitional word or phrase	*"In addition* to the facts that I've mentioned, we need to consider one additional problem."
Enumerating	*"Second,* there has been a rapid increase in the number of accidents reported."
Using internal summaries and previews	*"Now that we have discussed the problems* caused by illiteracy, *let's look at some of the possible solutions."*

NONVERBAL TRANSITIONS   Nonverbal transitions can occur in several ways, sometimes alone and sometimes in combination with verbal transitions. A change in facial expression, a pause, an altered vocal pitch or speaking rate, or a movement all may indicate a transition.

For example, a speaker talking about the value of cardiopulmonary resuscitation began his speech with a powerful anecdote of a man suffering a heart attack at a party. No one knew how to help, and the man died. The speaker then looked up from his notes and paused, while maintaining eye contact with his audience. His next words were "The real tragedy of Bill Jorgen's death was that it should not have happened." His pause, as well as the words that followed, indicated a transition into the body of the speech.

Like this speaker, most good speakers use a combination of verbal and nonverbal transitions to move from one point to another through their speeches. You will study more about nonverbal communication in Chapter 13.

Previews

In Chapter 12, we will discuss the differences between writing and speaking styles. One significant difference is that public speaking is more repetitive. Audience-centered speakers need to remember that the members of their audiences, unlike readers, cannot go back to review a missed point. As its name indicates, a preview is a statement of what is to come. Previews help to ensure that audience members will first anticipate and later remember the important points of a speech. Like transitions, previews also help to provide coherence.

Two types of previews are usually used in speeches: the preview statement or initial preview, and the internal preview. We discussed the preview statement in Chapter 6. It is a statement of what the main ideas of the speech will be and is usually presented in conjunction with the central idea as a blueprint for the speech at or near the end of the introduction. Speaking on illiteracy among athletes, Melody offers the following blueprint at the end of her introduction:

Illiteracy among athletes must be stopped. In order to fully grasp the significance of this problem, we will look at the root of it, and then move to [its] effects, and finally, we will look at the solution.[14]

In this blueprint, Melody clearly previews her main ideas and introduces them in the order in which she will discuss them in the body of the speech.

Sometimes speakers enumerate their main ideas to identify them even more clearly:

To solve this issue, we must first examine the problem itself. Second, we'll analyze the causes of the problem, and finally we'll turn to a number of solutions on the problem of children in the diet culture.[15]

Notice that both of the preceding examples consist of two sentences. As we noted in Chapter 6, the term *preview statement* does not necessarily mean one long, rambling sentence.

In addition to using previews near the beginning of their speeches, speakers also use them at various points throughout. These internal previews introduce and outline ideas that will be developed as the speech progresses. As noted, internal previews also serve as transitions. The following speaker, for example, has just discussed the dangers associated with organic farming. She then provides this transitional preview into her next point:

Having seen the dangers of our anti-pesticide attitude, we can now look to some solutions to stop the trend toward organic foods.[16]

Having heard this preview, her listeners expect her next to discuss solutions to the problems associated with organic farming. Their anticipation increases the likelihood that they will later remember the information.

Sometimes speakers couch internal previews in the form of questions they plan to answer. Note how the question in this example provides an internal preview:

Now that we know about the problem of hotel security and some of its causes and impacts, the question remains, what can we do, as potential travelers and potential victims, to protect ourselves?[17]

Just as anticipating an idea helps audience members remember it, so mentally answering a question helps them plant the answer firmly in their minds.

 Summaries

Like previews, summaries provide additional exposure to a speaker's ideas and can help ensure that audience members will grasp and remember them. Most speakers use two types of summaries: the final summary and the internal summary.

A final summary occurs in or just before the end of a speech, often doing double duty as a transition between the body and the conclusion.

The final summary is the opposite of the preview statement. The preview statement

Pat phrases at the end of your speech may set your audience to daydreaming. Instead, refer back to an important idea or summarize key points to sustain their attention.
[Photo: Bob Daemmerich/Stock Boston]

gives an audience their first exposure to a speaker's main ideas; the final summary gives them their *last* exposure to those ideas. Here is an example of a final summary from a speech on U.S. Customs:

> *Today, we have focused on the failing U.S. Customs Service. We have asked several important questions, such as "Why is Customs having such a hard time doing its job?" and "What can we do to remedy this situation?" When the cause of a serious problem is unknown, the continuation of the dilemma is understandable. However, the cause for the failure of the U.S. Customs Service is known: a lack of personnel. Given that fact and our understanding that Customs is vital to America's interests, it would be foolish not to rectify this situation.[18]*

This final summary leaves no doubt as to the important points of the speech. We will discuss the use of final summaries in more detail in Chapter 10.

Internal summaries, as their name suggests, occur within and throughout a speech. They are often used after two or three points have been discussed, to keep those points fresh in the minds of the audience as the speech progresses. Susan uses this internal summary in her speech on the teacher shortage:

> *So let's review for just a moment. One, we are endeavoring to implement educational reforms; but two, we are in the first years of a dramatic increase in enrollment; and three, fewer quality students are opting for education; while four, many good teachers want out of teaching; plus five, large numbers will soon be retiring.[19]*

Like internal previews, internal summaries can help provide transitions. In fact, internal summaries are often used in combination with internal previews to form transitions between major points and ideas. Each of the following examples makes clear what has just been discussed in the speech as well as what will be discussed next:

> *Now that we've seen how radon can get into our homes, let's take a look at some of the effects that it can have on our health once it begins to build.[20]*

We have looked at the great need. Americans are dying now. You and I can help.[20]

So now we are aware of the severity of the disease and unique reasons for college students to be concerned, we will look at some steps we need to take to combat bacterial meningitis.[21]

It seems as though everyone is saying that something should be done about NutraSweet. It should be retested. Well, now that it is here on the market, what can we do to see that it does get investigated further?[22]

RECAP

TYPES OF SIGNPOSTS

Verbal transitions

Nonverbal transitions

Preview statements

Internal previews

Final summaries

Internal summaries

Supplementing Signposts with Presentation Aids

Transitions, summaries, and previews are the "glue" that holds a speech together. Such signposts can help you achieve a coherent flow of ideas and help your audience remember those ideas. Unfortunately, however, you cannot guarantee your audience's attentiveness to your signposts. In Chapter 1 we discussed the concept of noise as it affects the public speaking process. It is possible for your listeners to be so distracted by internal or external noise that they fail to hear or process even your most carefully planned verbal signposts.

One way in which you can increase the likelihood of your listeners' attending to your signposting is to prepare and use presentation aids to supplement your signposts. For example, you could display on an overhead transparency a bulleted or numbered outline of your main ideas as you initially preview them in your introduction, and again as you summarize them in your conclusion. Some speakers like to use one transparency or PowerPoint slide for each main point. Transitions between points are emphasized as the speaker displays the next transparency or slide. In Chapter 14, we will discuss guidelines for developing and using such presentation aids. Especially if your speech is long or its organization complex, you can help your audience remember your organization if you provide visual support for your signposts.

SUMMARY

The process of organization is by nature audience-centered. Speeches are organized for audiences, with the speaker keeping in mind at all times the unique needs, interests, and expectations of the particular audience. Organize your speech in a logical way so that audience members can follow, understand, and remember your ideas.

First, consider how best to organize your main ideas. Five common patterns of organization include chronological, topical, spatial, cause–effect, and problem–solution. These patterns are sometimes combined, and yet other organizational patterns may be dictated by culture.

Main ideas are often subdivided. Organize subpoints so that audience members can readily grasp, understand, and remember them. The five patterns for organizing main ideas can apply to subpoints as well.

With points and subpoints organized, your next task is to integrate your supporting material into a speech. It may help to begin by putting all main points, subpoints, and supporting material on note cards and then arranging those cards in order. Once you have placed supporting material where it belongs in your plan, incorporate the supporting material smoothly into your speech. One strategy involves (1) stating the point, (2) citing the source, (3) presenting the supporting material, and (4) explaining how the supporting material substantiates or develops the point.

When you have more than one piece of supporting material for a main idea or subpoint, you can organize the supporting material according to one of the five common patterns, or according to such strategies as primacy, recency, specificity, complexity, or soft-to-hard.

Finally, various types of signposts can help you communicate your organization to your audience. Signposts include verbal and nonverbal transitions, previews, and summaries. Presentation aids increase the likelihood that your listeners will attend to your signposting.

Chapters 10 and 11 will cover the two remaining parts of the organizational task: preparing your introduction and conclusion, and outlining your speech.

being audience-centered

A Sharper Focus

CONSIDERING YOUR AUDIENCE

▶ Organize your ideas in logical patterns to ensure that audiences can follow, understand, and remember what you say.

▶ The principle of recency notes that audiences tend to remember best what they hear last.

▶ If your topic is controversial and you know or suspect that your audience will be skeptical or hostile toward your ideas, you may want to organize your main ideas according to the principle of primacy, or putting the most important or convincing idea first.

▶ If you speak to an audience that is already fairly aware of a problem, but uncertain how to solve it, you should probably discuss the problem first and then the solution(s).

▶ If your audience knows about an action or program that has been implemented, but does not know the reasons for its implementation, you might select a solution–problem pattern of organization.

▶ You may add, regroup, or eliminate main ideas or subpoints at any stage in the preparation process, as you consider the needs, interests, and expectations of your audience.

► Your listeners may not remember too many specific facts and statistics after a speech, but they should remember the important points. Connecting ideas and supporting material make it more likely that they will.

► The words "finally" and "in conclusion" give the audience members implicit permission to stop listening, and they often do.

► Audience-centered speakers need to remember that the members of their audiences, unlike readers, cannot go back to review a missed point. Previews help to ensure that audience members will first anticipate and later remember the important points of a speech.

► Just as anticipating an idea helps audience members remember it, so mentally answering a question helps them plant the answer firmly in their minds.

► Like previews, summaries provide additional exposure to a speaker's ideas and can help ensure that audience members will grasp and remember them.

► Internal summaries are often used after two or three points have been discussed, to keep those points fresh in the minds of the audience members as the speech progresses.

► One way in which you can increase the likelihood of your listeners' attending to your signposting is to prepare and use visual aids to supplement your signposts.

CONSIDERING AUDIENCE DIVERSITY

► Each culture teaches its members patterns of thought and organization that are considered appropriate for various occasions and audiences. For example, most North Americans prefer a direct, linear organizational pattern. Semitic, Asian, Romance, and Russian speakers are more likely to prefer a less-direct, less-linear organizational pattern. Romance and Russian cultures tend to begin with a basic principle and then use facts and illustrations to support the main idea.

CRITICAL-THINKING QUESTIONS

Here are some examples of central ideas and main ideas. Identify the organizational pattern used in each group of main ideas. If the pattern is topical, do you think the speaker also considered primacy, recency, or complexity? If so, identify which one.

1. PURPOSE STATEMENT: At the end of my speech, the audience will be able to list and explain the three factors to consider in buying or renting a home.

   CENTRAL IDEA: The prospective home buyer or renter should consider three factors in selecting a home.

   MAIN IDEAS:
      I. Interior decorating
     II. Layout
    III. Location

2. PURPOSE STATEMENT: At the end of my speech, the audience will be able to explain three theories about what happened to the dinosaurs.

CENTRAL IDEA:	There are at least three distinct theories about what happened to the dinosaurs.
MAIN IDEAS:	I. A large asteroid hit Earth.
	II. A gradual climate shift occurred.
	III. The level of oxygen in the atmosphere gradually changed.

3. PURPOSE STATEMENT: At the end of my speech, the audience will be able to explain why provision for the mentally ill is inadequate in the United States.

CENTRAL IDEA: The process of caring for the mentally ill has broken down in the United States.

MAIN IDEAS:
I. Fewer than half of the needed number of community-based "halfway houses" exist.

II. Funding is inadequate.

III. Involuntary commitment is rare.[23]

4. PURPOSE STATEMENT: At the end of my speech, the audience will be able to describe the layout and features of the new university multipurpose sports center.

CENTRAL IDEA: The new university multipurpose sports center will serve the activity needs of the students.

MAIN IDEAS:
I. The south wing will house an Olympic-size pool.

II. The center of the building will be a large coliseum.

III. The north wing will include handball and indoor tennis facilities as well as rooms for weight lifting and aerobic workouts.

ETHICAL QUESTIONS

1. On pages 182–183, we suggest that a speaker should provide the credentials of the authors of supporting material used in a speech. If a speaker is unable to discover an author's credentials, could the speaker omit the author's name altogether? If no, why not? If so, under what circumstances?

2. Several times in this chapter we discuss the principles of primacy and recency. If a speaker has a statistic that offers overwhelming evidence of the severity of a given problem, is it ethical for the speaker to save that statistic for last, or should the speaker reveal immediately to the audience how severe the problem really is? In other words, is there an ethical distinction between primacy and recency? Discuss your answer.

SUGGESTED ACTIVITIES

1. Read one of the speeches in Appendix C. Answer the following questions:

   a. According to what pattern are the main points organized?

b. Identify any subpoints of the main points, and describe how they are organized.

c. Look at the supporting materials. If two or more are used to support any one main point or subpoint, what strategy do you think the speaker used to organize them?

d. Is there a preview statement? If so, what is it?

e. Is there a final summary? If so, what is it?

f. Find at least one example of each of the following:

A transition word or phrase

An internal preview

An internal summary

2. Select three topics from the following list. For each topic, write a purpose statement, a central idea, and two to five main points. Identify the organizational strategy you would use to organize those main points.

Being an organ donor

The electoral college

Funding of health-care research

Great blues guitarists

High adventure in our national parks

History of motion pictures

History of the Panama Canal

How to create a water garden

Protecting endangered species

Responsible pet ownership

Solving the problem of world hunger

Three well-known fad diets

USING TECHNOLOGY AND MEDIA

1. Watch a single story on one of the television prime-time news magazine programs, such as *20/20* or *Dateline*. Take notes on the types of supporting materials offered during the segment. Then identify the strategy or strategies by which those supporting materials were organized.

2. If you have access to computer software with an outlining feature, use it to prepare an outline for the speech topic you chose for Suggested Activity 2. Then evaluate the software. Did it make outlining easier or harder for you than doing so on your own?

The average man thinks about what he has said;
the above average man about what he is going to say.

ANONYMOUS

10

Introducing and Concluding Your Speech

objectives

After studying this chapter you should be able to do the following:

1. Discuss why introductions and conclusions are important to the overall success of a speech.

2. Explain the five purposes of the introduction to a speech.

3. List and describe ten methods of introducing a speech.

4. Explain the four purposes of the conclusion to a speech.

5. List and describe four methods of concluding a speech.

The opening seconds of a television commercial are carefully crafted to get your attention. The closing seconds rename the product or service, summarize its virtues, and often suggest where you can purchase it. The person who designed that message knows something you should know, too: The introduction and conclusion of a message are vital to achieving your communication goal. Just as a trumpet fanfare signals the appearance of an important person, your speech introduction signals the arrival of your message to your listeners. And just as most fireworks displays end with a grand finale, your speech should end, not necessarily with fireworks, but with a conclusion worthy of your well-crafted message.

Although they make up only about 20 percent of the total speech you deliver, the introduction and conclusion provide audiences with important first and final impressions of speaker and speech. These elements are too important to the overall success of your speech to be left to chance or last-minute preparation.

Many speakers think the first task in preparing a speech is to start drafting your introduction. Actually, the introduction is more often the last part of the speech you develop. A key purpose of your introduction is to provide an overview of your message. How can you do that until you know what the message is going to be? In Chapter 9, we discussed patterns and strategies for organizing the body of your speech, and we explained how to use appropriate transitions, previews, and summaries. Those tasks should precede the crafting of both the introduction and conclusion to your speech. In this chapter we will further explore organization by discussing introductions and conclusions.

Purposes of Introductions

Within a few seconds of meeting a person, you form a first impression that is often quite lasting. So, too, do you form a first impression of a speaker and his or her message within the opening seconds of a speech. The introduction may convince you to listen carefully to a credible speaker presenting a well-prepared speech, or it may send the message that the speaker is ill prepared and the message not worth your time. In a ten-minute speech, the introduction will probably last no more than a minute and a half. To suggest that the introduction needs to be well planned is an understatement, considering how important and yet how brief it is.

As a speaker, your task is to ensure that your introduction convinces your audience to listen to you. Specifically, a good introduction must perform five important functions:

- Get the audience's attention.

- Introduce the subject.

- Give the audience a reason to listen.

- Establish your credibility.

- Preview your main ideas.

Let's examine each of these five functions in more detail.

Get the Audience's Attention

A key purpose of the introduction is to gain favorable attention for your speech. Because listeners form their first impressions of the speech quickly, if the introduction does not capture their attention and cast the speech in a favorable light, the rest of the speech may be wasted on them. The speaker who walks to the podium and drones, "Today I am going to talk to you about . . ." has probably lost most of the audience in those first few boring words. Some specific ways to gain the attention of audiences will be discussed later in this chapter.

Why do we emphasize *favorable* attention? For a very good reason. It is possible to gain an audience's attention but in so doing to alienate them or disgust them so that they become irritated instead of interested in what you have to say. For example, a student began a pro-life speech with a graphic description of the abortion process. She caught her audience's attention but made them so uncomfortable that they could hardly concentrate on the rest of her speech.

Another student gave a speech on the importance of donating blood. Without a word, he began by savagely slashing his wrists in front of his stunned audience. As blood spurted, audience members screamed, and one fainted. It was real blood, but not his. The speaker worked at a blood bank. Using the bank's blood, he had placed a device under each arm that allowed him to pump out the blood as if from his wrists. He certainly captured his audience's attention! But they never heard his message. The shock and disgust of seeing such a display made that impossible. He did not gain favorable attention.

The moral of our two tales: By all means, be creative in your speech introductions. But also use common sense in deciding how best to gain the favorable attention of your audience. Alienating them is even worse than boring them.

Introduce the Subject

Perhaps the most obvious purpose of an introduction is to introduce the subject of a speech. Within a few seconds after you begin your speech, the audience should have a pretty good idea what you are going to talk about. Do not get so carried away with jokes or illustrations that you forget this basic purpose. Few things will frustrate your audience more than having to wait until halfway through your speech to figure out what you are talking about! The best way to ensure that your introduction does indeed introduce the subject of your speech is to include a statement of your central idea in the introduction.

In the introduction to a speech on geriatric medicine, Kathryn left little room for doubt about the subject of her speech: After opening the speech with an anecdote about her grandfather's poor health care at the hands of a doctor who misdiagnosed his disease, Kathryn said that doctors

> *have simply not been provided with proper medical training in the care of the elderly.*[1]

In a speech on the unreliability of eyewitness testimony, Vincent offered this statement of his central idea near the end of his introduction:

> *. . . eyewitness testimony can be both dangerous and misleading.*[2]

In both cases, the speakers clearly stated their central ideas in their introductions.

Give the Audience a Reason to Listen

Even after you have captured the attention of your audience and introduced the topic, you have to give the audience some reason to want to listen to the rest of your speech. An unmotivated listener quickly tunes out. You can help establish listening motivation by showing the members of your audience how the topic affects them directly.

In Chapter 8 we presented seven criteria for determining the effectiveness of your supporting material. One of those criteria was *proximity,* the idea that the information affects your listeners directly. Just as proximity is important to supporting materials, it is also important to speech introductions. "This concerns me" is a powerful reason to listen. Notice how Cody involves his audience with the dangers of personal watercraft:

You may not own one and you may not know anyone who does, but an increasing tide of accidents means that every time you visit the beach, you may be taking your life into your own hands.[3]

Cody does an especially good job of acknowledging the diverse experiences and involvement of his listeners with personal watercraft. Acknowledging that few of them may own jet skis or even know someone who does, Cody communicates that the danger is nonetheless everyone's problem.

Bill also uses proximity to motivate his audience to listen, in his introduction to a speech on 911 reforms:

Since the average American will call 911 at least twice in [his or her] lifetime, this is one problem we can't afford to ignore.[4]

By using a statistic, Bill too brings the problem home to his listeners.

It does not matter so much *how* or *when* you demonstrate proximity. It is essential that you, like Cody and Bill, *do* at some point establish that your topic is of vital personal concern to your listeners.

Establish Your Credibility

Credibility is the attitude listeners hold toward a speaker. A credible speaker is one whom the audience judges to be a believable authority and a competent speaker. A credible speaker is also someone the audience believes in and can trust. Even though we will discuss credibility in greater detail in Chapter 17, we stress here that as you begin your speech, you should be mindful of your listeners' attitudes toward you. When thinking of your listeners, ask yourself, "Why should they listen to me? What is my background with respect to the topic? Am I personally committed to the issues about which I am going to speak?"

Many people have so much admiration for a political or religious figure, an athlete, or an entertainer that they sacrifice time, energy, and money to hear these celebrities speak. When Pope John Paul II travels abroad, people travel great distances and stand for hours in extreme heat or cold to celebrate Mass with him.

But most people cannot take their own credibility for granted when they speak. If you can establish your credibility early in a speech, it will help motivate your audience to listen. One way to build credibility in the introduction is to be well prepared and to appear confident. Speaking fluently while maintaining eye contact does much to convey a sense of confidence. If you seem to have confidence in yourself, your audience will have confidence in you.

credibility
The attitude listeners hold toward a speaker

Famous speakers can use their position to bolster their credibility with an audience. But even National Security Adviser Condoleezza Rice would be wise to present evidence to her audience that she is qualified to speak about this topic.

[Photo: Ron Edmonds/AP/Wide World Photos]

A second way to establish credibility is to tell the audience of your personal experience with your topic. Instead of considering you boastful, most audience members will listen to you with respect. In a speech to the U.S. Chamber of Commerce in which he outlined the agenda of the 107th Congress, Senator Trent Lott of Mississippi offered this insight into his advocacy of an education package:

> *I'm the son of a schoolteacher, a lady that taught for 19 years. I went to public schools all my life from the 1st grade all the way through law school, and so did my wife, and so did my children.*[5]

Learning that Senator Lott was personally invested in public education undoubtedly gave members of his audience additional respect for his point of view.

Preview Your Main Ideas

A final purpose of the introduction is to preview the main ideas of your speech. As you saw in Chapter 9, the preview statement usually comes near the end of the introduction, included in or immediately following a statement of the central idea. The preview statement allows your listeners to anticipate the main ideas of your speech, which in turn helps ensure that they will remember those ideas after the speech.

As also noted in Chapter 9, a preview statement is an organizational strategy called a *signpost*. Just as signs posted along a highway tell you what is coming up, a signpost in your speech tells the listeners what to expect by enumerating the ideas or points that you plan to present. If, for example, you were giving a speech about racial profiling, you might say,

> *To end these crimes against color, we must first paint an accurate picture of the problem, then explore the causes, and finally establish solutions that will erase the practice of racial profiling.*[6]

Identifying your main ideas helps organize the message and enhances listeners' learning.

The introduction to your speech, then, should get your audience's attention, introduce the subject, give the audience a reason to listen, establish your credibility, and preview your main ideas. All this—and brevity too—may seem impossible to achieve. But it isn't!

RECAP

PURPOSES OF YOUR INTRODUCTION

Purpose	Method
Get the audience's attention.	Use an illustration, a startling fact or statistic, quotation, humor, a question, a reference to a historical event, a reference to a recent event, a personal reference, a reference to the occasion, a reference to a preceding speech.
Introduce the subject.	Present your central idea to your audience.
Give the audience a reason to listen.	Tell your listeners how the topic directly affects them.
Establish your credibility.	Offer your credentials. Tell your listeners about your commitment to your topic.
Preview your main ideas.	Tell your audience what you are going to tell them.

Effective Introductions

With a little practice, you will be able to write satisfactory central ideas and preview statements. It may be more difficult to gain your audience's attention and give them a reason to listen to you. Fortunately, there are several effective methods for developing speech introductions. Not every method is appropriate for every speech, but chances are that you can discover among these alternatives at least one type of introduction to fit the topic and purpose of your speech, whatever they might be.

Specifically, we will discuss ten ways of introducing a speech:

- Illustrations or anecdotes
- Startling facts or statistics
- Quotations
- Humor
- Questions
- References to historical events
- References to recent events
- Personal references
- References to the occasion
- References to preceding speeches

Illustrations or Anecdotes

Not surprisingly, because it is the most inherently interesting type of supporting material, an illustration or **anecdote** can provide the basis for an effective speech introduction. In fact, if you have an especially compelling illustration that you had planned to use in the body of the speech, instead you might do well to use it in your introduction. A relevant and interesting anecdote will introduce your subject and almost invariably gain an audience's attention. And a personal illustration can help establish your credibility.

Indiana University President Myles Brand related this personal experience to open a speech entitled "Academics First":

> *Last May, I took part in a news conference on Indiana University's Indianapolis Campus. I entered a large conference room overflowing with reporters and photographers who were waiting to learn the results of our investigation into allegations made against Coach Bob Knight. . . . The event was televised on state and national news programs. It received extensive coverage on the front pages, sports pages, and editorial pages of newspapers across the nation.*

> *Of course, as you know, that's not the end of the story. This past September, we held another press conference. This time, I relieved Bob Knight of his coaching responsibilities. Again, the media coverage was voluminous.*

> *But then I had a parallel experience. In November, we held another news conference in the same room. We announced that IU had received the largest private gift in its history—$105 million from the Lilly Endowment. The grant the foundation has given us—which is the largest single gift ever made—will fund the Indiana Genomics Initiative . . .*

> *Our announcement of this remarkable grant received good notice locally, but it was treated as a one-day story. Conversely, the Bob Knight saga played out over weeks and months.*[7]

In addition to relating a personal anecdote, Brand's introduction was also audience-centered, as it was delivered to the National Press Club. His press-conference experiences must have effectively captured the attention of these listeners.

For topics that do not lend themselves to personal illustrations, illustrations drawn from secondary sources can also be used effectively. Former First Lady Barbara Bush opened her 1990 Wellesley College commencement address with this secondary illustration:

> *Wellesley, you see, is not just a place, but an idea, an experiment in excellence in which diversity is not just tolerated, but is embraced.*

> *The essence of this spirit was captured in a moving speech about tolerance given last year by the student body president of one of your sister colleges. She related the story by Robert Fulghum about a young pastor who, finding himself in charge of some very energetic children, hit upon a game called "Giants, Wizards, and Dwarfs." "You have to decide now," the pastor instructed the children, "Which you are . . . a giant, a wizard, or a dwarf?" At that, a small girl tugging on his pants leg asked, "But where do the mermaids stand?"*

> *The pastor told her there are no mermaids. "Oh yes there are," she said. "I am a mermaid."*

anecdote
An illustration or brief story

This little girl knew what she was and she was not about to give up on either her identity or the game. She intended to take her place wherever mermaids fit into the scheme of things.[8]

Barbara Bush's story both introduced the subject of her address and captured the attention of her audience.

Startling Facts or Statistics

A second method of introducing a speech is the use of a startling fact or statistic. Startling an audience with the extent of a situation or problem invariably catches its members' attention as well as motivates them to listen further and helps them remember afterward what you had to say.

Jeffrey Zelms's audience must have come quickly to attention when he combined startling statistics with an effective presentation aid to introduce a speech on the vital role of minerals in everyday life:

To make a point in what I hope will be a memorable and dramatic way, let me call on my friend (house electrician).

(Abruptly, room is plunged into darkness)

Please, don't be alarmed. (JZ shines flashlight on his face as mini-spotlight.) *This is only temporary, I assure you. At least, that's my fondest hope.*

Now that I have your attention, let me pose a question. Since we're all here to discuss minerals education, what role do you think minerals play in generating electricity?

(Turns on 20 percent of lights)

About 20 percent of the country's electricity comes from nuclear plants, fueled by the mineral uranium.

(Turns on 60 percent of lights)

Here's the big factor. Almost 60 percent of the country's electric power comes from plans fueled by coal.

(Turns on the remaining 20 percent of lights)

The last approximately 20 percent of electricity generation comes from natural gas, hydro and a collection of other sources such as solar, wind power, biomass, and so on.[9]

The statistics Zelms presents are convincing and attention-getting. In addition, his manipulation of the house lights to make his point undoubtedly helped capture the attention of his listeners and was likely remembered by them long afterward.

Quotations

Using an appropriate quotation to introduce a speech is a common practice. Often a past writer or speaker has expressed an opinion on your topic that is more authoritative, comprehensive, or memorable than what you can say. Terrika opened her speech on the importance of community with a quotation from poet Johari Kungufu:

> *Sisters, Men*
> *What are we doin?*
> *What about the babies, our children?*
> *When we was real we never had orphans or children in joints.*
> *Come spirits*
> *drive out the nonsense from our minds and the crap from our dreams*
> *make us remember what we need, that children are the next life.*
> *bring us back to the real*
> *bring us back to the real*

"The Real." Johari Kungufu, in her poem, specifically alludes to a time in African history when children were not confused about who they were.[10]

A different kind of quotation, this one from an expert, was chosen by another speaker to introduce the topic of the disappearance of childhood in America:

"As a distinctive childhood culture wastes away, we watch with fascination and dismay." This insight of Neil Postman, author of Disappearance of Childhood, *raised a poignant point. Childhood in America is vanishing.*[11]

Because the expert was not widely recognized, the speaker included a brief statement of his qualifications. This authority "said it in a nutshell"—expressed in concise language the central idea of the speech.

Although a quote can effectively introduce a speech, do not fall into the lazy habit of turning to a collection of quotations every time you need an introduction. There are so many other interesting, and sometimes better, ways to introduce a speech that quotes should be used only if they are extremely interesting, compelling, or very much to the point.

Like the methods of organization discussed in Chapter 9, the methods of introduction are not mutually exclusive. Very often, two or three are effectively combined in a single introduction. For example, Thad combined a quotation and an illustration for this effective introduction to a speech on the funeral industry:

"Dying is a very dull, dreary affair. And my advice to you is to have nothing whatsoever to do with it." These lingering words by British playwright Somerset Maugham were meant to draw a laugh. Yet the ironic truth to the statement has come to epitomize the grief of many, including Jan Berman of Martha's Vineyard. In a recent interview with National Public Radio, we learn that Ms. Berman desired to have a home funeral for her mother. She possessed a burial permit and was legally within her rights. But when a local funeral director found out, he lied to her, telling her that what she was doing was illegal.[12]

Humor

Humor, handled well, can be a wonderful attention-getter. It can help relax your audience and win their goodwill for the rest of the speech. Lockheed CEO Vance Coffman used a humorous acknowledgment of his host city to open this speech to the Space Foundation Hall of Fame:

I'm always delighted to come back to Colorado Springs, the city that inspired "America the Beautiful." By way of comparison, I work in a suburb of Washington, D.C., the city that inspired America's 120,000-page federal tax code. So it's good to get back to a place which invokes the spirit of the "real America."[13]

Another speaker used humor to express appreciation for being invited to speak to a group by beginning his speech with this story:

Three corporate executives were trying to define the word fame.

One said, "Fame is getting invited to the White House to see the President."

The second one said, "Fame is being invited to the White House and while you are visiting, the phone rings and he doesn't answer it."

The third executive said, "You're both wrong. Fame is being invited to the White House to visit with the President when his Hot Line rings. He answers it, listens a minute, and then says, 'Here, it's for you!'"

Being asked to speak today is like being in the White House and the call's for me.[14]

Humor need not always be the stuff of Donald O'Connor's classic "Make 'Em Laugh" routine or Three Stooges slapstick comedy. It does not even have to be a joke. It may take more subtle forms, such as irony or incredulity. When General Douglas MacArthur, an honor graduate of the U.S. Military Academy at West Point, returned to West Point in 1962 to receive the Sylvanus Thayer award for service to his nation, he delivered his now-famous "Farewell to the Cadets." He opened that speech with this humorous illustration:

As I was leaving the hotel this morning, a doorman asked me, "Where are you bound for, General?" And when I replied, "West Point," he remarked, "Beautiful place. Have you ever been there before?"[15]

MacArthur's brief illustration caught the audience's attention and made them laugh—in short, it was an effective way to open the speech.

If your audience is linguistically diverse or composed primarily of listeners whose first language is other than English, you may want to choose an introduction strategy other than humor. Because much humor is created by verbal plays on words, people who do not speak English as their native language may not perceive the humor in an anecdote or quip that you intended to be funny. And rarely does humor translate well. Former President Jimmy Carter recalls speaking at a university near Kyoto, Japan, and being startled by unexpectedly hearty laughter in response to a short humorous anecdote he related. When he later asked his interpreter how he had translated the story so successfully, the interpreter finally admitted sheepishly, "I told them, 'President Carter has just told a funny story. Everyone laugh.'"[16]

Just as certain audiences may preclude your use of a humorous introduction, so may certain subjects. It would hardly be appropriate to open a speech on world hunger, for example, with a funny story. Nor would it be appropriate to use humor in a talk on certain serious crimes. Used with discretion, however, humor can provide a lively, interesting, and appropriate introduction for many speeches.

Questions

When using a question to open a speech, you will generally use a **rhetorical question,** the kind you don't expect an answer to. Nevertheless, your listeners will probably try to answer mentally. Questions prompt the audience's mental participation in your introduction. Such participation is an excellent way to ensure their continuing attention to your speech.

Lisa opened her speech on geographic illiteracy with a series of questions:

Can you name the states that border the Pacific Ocean? What country lies between Panama and Nicaragua? Can you name the Great Lakes?[17]

And Richard opened his speech on teenage suicide with this simple question:

Have you ever been alone in the dark?[18]

To turn questions into an effective introduction, the speaker must do more than just think of good questions to ask. He or she must also deliver the questions effectively. Effective delivery includes pausing briefly after each question, so that audience members have time to try to formulate a mental answer. After all, the main advantage of questions as an introductory technique is to "hook" the audience by getting them to engage in a mental dialogue with you. The speaker who delivers questions most effectively is also one who may look down at notes while he or she asks the question, but who then reestablishes eye contact with listeners. As we will discuss in more detail in Chapter 13, eye contact signals that the communication channel is open. Establishing eye contact with your audience following a question provides additional motivation for them to think of an answer.

Although it does not happen frequently, an audience member may blurt out a vocal response to a question intended to be rhetorical. If you plan to open a speech with a rhetorical question, be aware of this remote possibility, and plan possible appropriate reactions. If the topic is light, a Jay Leno–style return quip may win over the audience and turn the interruption into an asset. If the topic is more serious or the interruption is inappropriate or contrary to what you expected, you might reply with something like "Perhaps most of the rest of you were thinking . . . ," or you might answer the question yourself.

Questions are commonly combined with another method of introduction. For example, Beth opened her speech on the inadequacies of the current U.S. driver's license renewal system with three brief startling facts followed by a question:

In 31 states a blind man can be licensed to drive. In 5 states, just send in your check and they will send back your renewed license, no questions asked.

In 1916 my grandfather got his license for the first time. No exam was required; no exam has been required since. Ever wonder why our highways seem a bit unsafe today?[19]

Either by themselves or in tandem with another method of introduction, questions can provide effective openings for speeches. Like quotations, however, questions can also be "crutches" for speakers who have not taken the time to explore other options. Unless you can think of a truly engaging question, work to develop one of the other introduction strategies.

rhetorical question
A question intended to provoke thought, rather than a vocal answer

References to Historical Events

What American is not familiar with the opening line of Lincoln's classic Gettysburg Address: "Four score and seven years ago, our fathers brought forth on this continent a new nation, conceived in liberty, and dedicated to the proposition that all men are created equal"? Note that this opening sentence refers to the historical context of the speech. You, too, may find a way to begin a speech by making a reference to a historic event.

Every day is the anniversary of something. Perhaps you could begin a speech by drawing a relationship between a historic event that happened on this day and your speech objective. How do you discover anniversaries of historic events? You could consult Jane M. Hatch's *The American Book of Days;* this resource lists key events for every day of the year and also provides details of what occurred.[20] Another source, *Anniversaries and Holidays,* by Ruth W. Gregory, identifies and describes key holidays.[21] Finally, many newspapers have a section that identifies key events that occurred on "this day in history." If, for example, you know you are going to be speaking on April 6, you could consult a copy of a newspaper from April 6 of last year to discover the key commemorative events for that day.

We are not recommending that you arbitrarily flip through one of these sources to crank up your speech; your reference to a historic event should be linked clearly to the purpose of your speech. Note how Boeing vice president and comptroller Laurette Koellner opened her remarks on career management to the Amelia Earhart Society in Long Beach, California:

> *It is a great pleasure to address the Long Beach Chapter of the Amelia Earhart Society, and to honor people who—like the great Amelia—have exceeded expectations.*

> *Amelia Earhart had a brilliant career. She was the first to cross the Atlantic twice in an airplane and the second person ever to fly solo across the Atlantic. Like Amelia, each of us is responsible for managing his or her own career. We all have teammates, and we may have mentors. But, at the end of the day, planning and managing a career is the ultimate solo flight—for each of us.[22]*

References to Recent Events

If your topic is timely, a reference to a recent event can be a good way to open your speech. An opening taken from a recent news story can take the form of an illustration, a startling statistic, or even a quotation, gaining the additional advantages discussed under each of those methods of introduction. Moreover, referring to a recent event increases your credibility by showing that you are knowledgeable about current affairs.

"Recent" does not necessarily mean a story that broke just last week or even last month. An occurrence within the past year or so can be considered recent. Even a particularly significant event that is slightly older can qualify. Rebekah opened her speech, "Cherish Diversity," with a reference to just such an event:

> *The world has heard about Matthew Shepard, a young college student in Wyoming who was brutally murdered, allegedly because of his homosexuality. Brutally beaten by two high school drop-outs and left for dead overnight, he was found eighteen hours after the vicious attack, by two bicyclists who believed him to be a scarecrow.[23]*

Personal References

A reference to yourself can take several forms. You might reveal your reason for interest in the topic, as did Senator Trent Lott when he provided insight into his advocacy of public education in the speech introduction cited earlier in this chapter. You might express appreciation at having been asked to speak, as did Madeleine Albright when she delivered her first address as U.S. Secretary of State at Rice University in Houston, Texas, in February 1997:

> . . . thank you for the introduction and for the Texas hospitality.
>
> This is my first official trip as Secretary of State; and I can't imagine a better destination or more distinguished company.[24]

Or you might share a personal experience, such as this one offered by Vice President of the United States and Harvard alumnus Al Gore, at the opening of his address to the 1994 Harvard graduating class:

> Throughout our four years at Harvard the nation's spirits sank. The race riot in Watts was fresh in our minds when we registered as freshmen. Though our hopes were briefly raised by the passage of civil-rights legislation and the promise of a war on poverty, the war in Vietnam grew steadily more ominous and consumed the resources that were needed to make good on the extravagant promises for dramatic progress here at home. . . . All of this cast a shadow over each of our personal futures.[25]

Although personal references take a variety of forms, what they do best, in all circumstances, is to establish a bond between you and your audience.

References to the Occasion

References to the occasion are often made at weddings, birthday parties, dedication ceremonies, and other such events. It is customary to make a personal reference as well, placing oneself in the occasion. For example, when a neighborhood elementary school celebrates its twenty-fifth anniversary, its first principal might open her remarks this way:

> It is a special joy for me to be here this afternoon to help celebrate the twenty-fifth anniversary of Crockett Elementary School. How well I remember the excitement and anticipation of that opening day so many years ago. How well I remember the children who came to school that first day. Some of them are now your parents. It was a good beginning to a successful twenty-five years.

The reference to the occasion can also be combined with other methods of introduction, such as an illustration or a rhetorical question.

References to Preceding Speeches

If your speech is one of several being presented on the same occasion, such as a speech class, a symposium, or a lecture series, you will usually not know until shortly before your own speech what other speakers will say. Few experiences will make your

Address: http://www.ablongman.com/beebe

▼ | **Using the Web to Find an Attention-Catching Introduction**

Here are some sites that can help you in your search for the perfect, attention-catching introduction. As you consider whether you will use the information to catch your listener's attention consider the following:

1. Does the information relate to my purpose?

2. Will it be of interest to my audience?

3. Is the question or illustration in good taste?

QUOTATIONS

     Quotations about creative thinking and living.

                     http://www.bemorecreative.com

     An index of humorous and unusual quotations.

                http://www.yahoo.com/text/Reference/Quotations/Humorous/

     Bible quotations.

                 http://goon.stg.brown.edu/bible_browser/pbeasy.shtml

STATISTICS

     The Gallup Organization's Website.

                     http://www.gallup.com

     The Website of the U.S. Bureau of the Census.

                   http://www.census.gov

STORIES FROM LITERATURE

     Classic stories from literature, indexed by author.

                   http://www.literature.org

For further help in developing both introductions and conclusions, refer to the Allyn and Bacon Website:

                http://www.longman.com/pubspeak/organize/begend.html

stomach sink faster than hearing a speaker just ahead of you speak on your topic. Worse still, that speaker may even use some of the same supporting materials you had planned to use. When this happens, you must decide on the spot whether referring to one of these previous speeches will be better than using the introduction you originally prepared. It may be wise to refer to a preceding speech when another speaker has spoken on a topic so related to your own that you can draw an analogy. In a sense, your introduction becomes a transition from that earlier speech to yours. Here is an example of an introduction delivered by a fast-thinking student speaker under those circumstances:

When Juli talked to us about her experiences as a lifeguard, she stressed that the job was not as glamorous as many of us imagine. Today I want to tell you about another job that appears to be more glamorous than it is—a job that I have held for two years. I am a bartender at the Rathskeller.[26]

In summary, as you plan your introduction, remember that any combination of the methods just discussed is possible. With a little practice, you may find yourself choosing from several good possibilities as you prepare your introduction.

Purposes of Conclusions

Your introduction creates an important first impression; your conclusion leaves an equally important final impression. Long after you finish speaking, your audience is likely to remember the effect, if not the content, of your closing remarks.

Unfortunately, many speakers pay less attention to their conclusions than to any other part of their speeches. They believe that if they can get through the first 90 percent of a speech, they can think of some way to conclude it. Perhaps you have had the experience of listening to a speaker who failed to plan a conclusion. Awkward final seconds of stumbling for words may be followed by hesitant applause from an audience that is not even sure the speech is over. It is hardly the best way to leave people who came to listen to you.

An effective conclusion will serve four purposes:

- Summarize the speech.

- Reemphasize the main idea in a memorable way.

- Motivate the audience to respond.

- Provide closure.

Just as you learned ways to introduce a speech, you can learn how to conclude one. We will begin by considering the purposes of conclusions and will go on to study methods that can help you achieve those purposes.

Summarize the Speech

A conclusion is a speaker's last chance to repeat his or her main ideas for the audience. John effectively summarized his speech on emissions tampering, casting the summary as an expression of his fears about the problem and the actions that could solve those fears:

I'm frightened. Frightened that nothing I could say would encourage the 25 percent of emissions-tampering Americans to change their ways and correct the factors that cause their autos to pollute disproportionately. Frightened that the American public will not respond to a crucial issue unless the harms are both immediate and observable. Frightened that the EPA will once again prove very sympathetic to industry. Three simple steps will alleviate my fear: inspection, reduction in lead content, and, most importantly, awareness.[27]

Most speakers summarize their speech in the first part of the conclusion or perhaps even as the transition between the body of the speech and its conclusion.

When Hillary Rodham Clinton addressed the New York Police Benevolent Association, she knew they had endorsed her rival for her senate seat. The conclusion of her speech was her last chance to win them over. What strategies might have helped her win their support?

[Photo: Ed Bailey/AP/Wide World Photos]

Reemphasize the Central Idea in a Memorable Way

Another purpose of a conclusion is to restate the central idea of the speech in a memorable way. The conclusions of a number of famous speeches are among the most memorable statements we have. For example, General Douglas MacArthur's farewell to the nation at the end of his career concluded with these memorable words:

"Old soldiers never die; they just fade away." And like the old soldier of that ballad, I now close my military career and just fade away—an old soldier who tried to do his duty as God gave him the light to see that duty. Good-bye.[28]

But memorable endings are not the exclusive property of great orators. With practice, most people can prepare similarly effective conclusions. Chapter 12 offers ideas for using language to make your statements more memorable. As a preliminary example of the memorable use of language, here is how Noelle concluded her speech on phony academic institutions on the Internet:

What we have learned from all this is that we, and only we, have the power to stop [fraudulent learning institutions]. So we don't get www.conned.[29]

This speaker's clever play on "dot.com" helped her audience remember her topic and central idea.

The end of your speech is your last chance to impress the central idea on your audience. Do it in such a way that they cannot help but remember it.

Motivate the Audience to Respond

One of your tasks in an effective introduction is to motivate your audience to listen to your speech. Motivation is also a necessary component of an effective conclusion—not motivation to listen, but motivation to respond to the speech in some way. If your speech is informative, you may want the audience to think about the topic or to research it further. If your speech is persuasive, you may want your audience to take some sort of appropriate action—write a letter, buy a product, make a telephone call, or get involved in a cause. In fact, an *action* step is essential to the persuasive organizational strategy called the motivated sequence, which we discuss in detail in Chapter 17.

In a speech on antibacterial products, Amanda motivated her audience to stop abusing such products:

> *So the next time you reach for antibacterial toothpaste, antibacterial soap, or an antibacterial towel, remember the bacteria living in there, just waiting to be mutated.*[30]

Another speaker ended a speech on colon cancer with this conclusion:

> *Let's join Katie Couric in the crusade to conquer this disease that so few of us like to talk about, but most definitely should.*[31]

In both of the preceding examples, the speakers draw on the principle of proximity, discussed earlier in this chapter, to motivate their audiences. If audience members feel that they are or could easily be personally involved or affected, they are more likely to respond to your message.

Provide Closure

Probably the most obvious purpose of a conclusion is to let the audience know that the speech has ended. Speeches have to "sound finished."

You can attain **closure** both verbally and nonverbally. Verbal techniques include using such transitions as "finally," "for my last point," and "in conclusion." As noted in Chapter 9, use care in signaling your conclusion. For one thing, such a cue gives an audience unspoken permission to tune out. Notice what students do when their professor signals the end of the class session. Books and notebooks slam shut, pens are stowed, and the class generally stops listening. A concluding transition needs to be followed quickly by the final statement of the speech. We will discuss another verbal technique for closure—referring to the introduction—later in this chapter.

You can also signal closure with nonverbal cues. You may want to pause between the body of your speech and its conclusion, slow your speaking rate, move out from behind a podium to make a final impassioned plea to your audience, or signal with falling vocal inflection that you are making your final statement.

PURPOSES OF YOUR SPEECH CONCLUSION

Purpose	Technique
Summarize your speech.	Tell the audience what you told them.
Reemphasize the central idea in a memorable way.	Use a well-worded closing phrase. Provide a final illustration, quotation, or personal reference.
Motivate the audience to respond.	Urge the audience to think about the topic or to research it further. Suggest appropriate action.
Provide closure.	Use verbal and nonverbal transitions. Refer to your introduction.

closure
The quality of a conclusion that makes a speech "sound finished"

Effective Conclusions

Effective conclusions may employ illustrations, quotations, personal references, or any of the other methods of introduction we have already discussed. In addition, there are at least three other distinct methods of conclusions. These include references to the introduction, inspirational appeals or challenges, and appeals to action.

Methods Also Used for Introductions

Any of the methods of introduction discussed earlier can also help you conclude your speech. Quotations, for example, are frequently used in conclusions, as in this speech on homeless gay and lesbian youth:

> *When Elie Wiesel, a Holocaust survivor, accepted a Congressional Medal of Honor in 1985, he said, "I learned the danger of indifference, the crime of indifference. The opposite of love is not hate, but indifference." Every human tragedy could have been prevented if enough people had dared to speak out against injustice.*[32]

References to the Introduction

In our discussion of closure, we mentioned referring to the introduction as a way to end a speech. Finishing a story, answering a rhetorical question, or reminding the audience of the startling fact or statistic you presented in the introduction are excellent ways to provide closure. Like bookends at either side of a group of books on your desk, a related introduction and conclusion provide unified support for the ideas in the middle.

Sonja's topic dealt with the health problems caused by the reprocessing of medical devices. She had opened her speech with an illustration of a 7-year-old Cub Scout named Timothy Anderson, who was killed when his heart was sliced by a reprocessed heart catheter. Her conclusion was this:

> *Because while we all want our health care to be affordable, we need to resist the push to do so at the expense of our health. After all, Timothy Anderson will never build the model '57 Chevy he was to receive on his eighth birthday.*[33]

John had begun his speech on the need for catastrophic health insurance by quoting Robert Browning:

> *Grow old along with me!*
> *The best is yet to be,*
> *The last of life, for which the first was made.*[34]

He concluded his speech by referring to that Browning quotation:

> *Robert Browning tells us the last of life is as precious as the first. While the future will always hold uncertainty, with catastrophic health insurance we can more fully prepare for whatever is yet to be.*[35]

Benjamin had introduced his speech by talking about the downfalls inevitably suffered by the heroes of Greek mythology. He drew an analogy between the risks they faced and the risks inherent in the use of antibiotics—the dangers of overuse. Here is how Benjamin ended his speech:

The demise of Medusa carries with it one final message. With her death, Perseus received two drops of blood. One drop had the power to kill and spread evil; the other, to heal and restore well-being. Similarly, antibiotics offer us two opposite paths. As we painfully take stock in our hubris, in assuming that we can control the transformation of nature, we may ponder these two paths. We can either let antibiotics do the work of our immune systems and proper farm management, which may return us to the times when deathly plagues spread across the world, or we can save these miracle drugs for the times when miracles are truly needed.[36]

Each of the three examples just given is quite different. In the first, the speech opened and closed with an illustration; in the second, both introduction and conclusion centered on a quotation; and in the third, beginning and ending relied on an analogy between mythology and modern medicine. In all three speeches, the conclusion alluded to the introduction to make the speech memorable, to motivate the audience to respond, and to provide closure.

Inspirational Appeals or Challenges

Another way to end your speech is to issue an inspirational appeal or challenge to your listeners, rousing them to a high emotional pitch at the conclusion of the speech. The conclusion becomes the climax. One famous example comes from the "I Have a Dream" speech of Martin Luther King, Jr.:

From every mountainside, let freedom ring, and when this happens . . . when we allow freedom to ring, when we let it ring from every village and every hamlet, from every state and every city, we will be able to speed up that day when all of God's children, black men and white men, Jews and Gentiles, Protestants and Catholics, will be able to join hands and sing in the words of the old Negro spiritual, "Free at last! Thank God Almighty, we are free at last!"[37]

That King's conclusion was both inspiring and memorable has been affirmed by the growing fame of that passage through the years since he delivered the speech.

More recently, on September 15, 2001, George W. Bush delivered his weekly radio address—an address that was suddenly anything but routine, following the catastrophic terrorist attacks of September 11. He concluded his talk with this inspirational appeal:

Great tragedy has come to us and we are meeting it with the best that is in our country, with courage and concern for others. Because this is America. This is who we are. This is what our enemies hate and have attacked. And this is why we will prevail.[38]

King's and Bush's inspiring conclusions reemphasized their central ideas in a memorable way, motivated their audiences to respond, and provided closure to their speeches.

Appeals to Action

As we noted earlier, persuasive speeches often include an appeal to action in their conclusions. Note Travis's call for action as he urged his audience to take steps to prevent sleep deprivation:

Before we are all, literally, dead on our feet, let's take the easiest solution step of all. Tonight, turn off your alarm, turn down your covers, and turn in for a good night's sleep.[39]

SUMMARY

It is important to begin and end your speech in a way that is memorable and that also provides the repetition audiences need. A good introduction gets the audience's attention, introduces your subject, gives the audience a reason to listen, establishes your credibility, and previews your main ideas.

Introducing your subject and previewing the body of your speech can be accomplished by including your central idea and preview statement in the introduction. You can gain favorable attention and provide a motivation for listening by using one or a combination of the following: illustrations, startling facts or statistics, quotations, humor, questions, references to historical events, references to recent events, personal references, references to the occasion, or references to preceding speeches, if there are any.

Concluding your speech is just as important as introducing it, for it is the conclusion that leaves the final impression. Specifically, a conclusion should summarize your speech, reemphasize your central idea in a memorable way, motivate the audience to respond, and provide closure.

Conclusions may take any one of the forms used for introductions. In addition, you can refer to the introduction, make inspirational appeals or challenges, or make appeals to action.

Once you have planned the introduction and the conclusion, you have completed the final organizational step of the speech-preparation process.

being audience-centered
A Sharper Focus

CONSIDERING YOUR AUDIENCE

▶ Introductions and conclusions provide audiences with important first and final impressions of speaker and speech.

▶ As a speaker, your task is to ensure that your introduction convinces your audience to listen to you.

▶ If a speech introduction does not capture listeners' attention and cast the speech in a favorable light, the rest of the speech may be wasted on them.

▶ Your introduction should gain *favorable* attention for your speech. It is possible to gain an audience's attention but in so doing to alienate the members or disgust them so that they become irritated instead of interested in what you have to say.

▶ Within a few seconds after you begin your speech, the audience should have a pretty good idea of what you are going to talk about.

▶ You can help establish listening motivation by demonstrating proximity: the idea that the information you have presented affects your listeners directly.

▶ A credible speaker is one whom the audience judges to be a believable authority and a competent speaker. If you can establish your credibility early in a speech, that helps motivate your audience to listen.

▶ If you communicate confidence in yourself through fluency and eye contact, your audience will have confidence in you.

▶ You can help establish credibility by telling your audience of your personal experience with your topic.

▶ Previewing your main ideas helps organize your message and enhances listeners' learning.

▶ A relevant and interesting anecdote introduces your subject and almost invariably gains your listeners' attention.

▶ Startling an audience with the extent of a situation or problem invariably catches the members' attention, as well as motivates them to listen further and helps them remember afterward what you had to say.

▶ Humor, handled well, can help relax your audience and win their goodwill for the rest of the speech.

▶ Rhetorical questions prompt the audience's mental participation in your introduction, "hooking" the listeners by getting them to engage in a mental dialogue with you.

▶ Although personal references can take a variety of forms, what they do best, in all circumstances, is to establish a bond between you and your audience.

▶ A speech conclusion leaves an important final impression. Long after you finish speaking, your audience is likely to remember the effect, if not the content, of your closing remarks.

▶ Your speech conclusion is your last chance to repeat your main ideas for your listeners.

▶ Your speech conclusion is also your last chance to impress your central idea on your audience.

▶ One of your tasks in an effective conclusion is to motivate your audience to respond to your speech in some way.

▶ The most obvious purpose of a conclusion is to let the audience know that the speech has ended.

▶ An inspirational appeal or challenge in a conclusion can rouse listeners to a high emotional pitch.

CONSIDERING AUDIENCE DIVERSITY

▶ To demonstrate proximity, you must acknowledge the diverse experiences and involvement of your listeners with your topic.

▶ If your audience is linguistically diverse or composed primarily of listeners whose first language is other than English, you may want to choose an introduction strategy other than humor. Because much humor is created verbally, it may not be readily understood and rarely translates well.

CRITICAL THINKING QUESTIONS

1. Nakai is planning to give his informative speech on Native American music, displaying and demonstrating the use of such instruments as the flute, the Taos drum, and the Yaqui rain stick. He asks you to suggest a good introduction for the speech. How do you think he might best introduce his speech?

2. Knowing that you have recently visited the Vietnam Veterans Memorial, your American history professor asks you to make a brief presentation to the class about the Wall: its history, its symbolic meaning, and its impact on the families, comrades, and friends of those memorialized there. Write both an introduction and a conclusion for this speech.

3. How could you establish a motivation for your classroom audience to listen to you on each of the following topics?

   Cholesterol

   Elvis Presley

   The history of greeting cards

   Ozone depletion

   Prison reform

   Speed traps

ETHICAL QUESTIONS

Marty and Shanna, who are in the same section of a public-speaking class, are discussing their upcoming speeches. Marty has discovered an illustration that she thinks will make an effective introduction. When she tells Shanna about it, Shanna is genuinely enthusiastic. In fact, she thinks it would make a great introduction for her own speech, which is on a different topic, but still relevant to Marty's illustration. When the students are assigned their speaking days, Shanna realizes that she will speak before Marty. She badly wants to use the introductory illustration that Marty has discovered. Can she ethically do so, if she cites in her speech the original source of the illustration?

SUGGESTED ACTIVITIES

1. Using one of the topics suggested in Critical Thinking Question 3, write a complete introduction and conclusion for a speech. Then write a brief paragraph in which you identify and explain the principles you followed in preparing your introduction and conclusion.

2. Examine the sample speeches in Appendix C. Identify the approach each speaker uses to begin and conclude the speech.

3. On the Web or in the library, find a collection of quotations, such as *Bartlett's Familiar Quotations*. Select an interesting quotation that could be used to begin a speech on each of the following topics:

The joys of raising children

The dangers of watching too much television

The reasons everyone should take a geography course

The value of an education

USING TECHNOLOGY AND MEDIA

Begin a word-processing file of possible introductions and conclusions. Over the next few weeks, as you hear or read compelling stories or illustrations, startling facts or statistics, or humorous anecdotes, enter them into this file, with source citations. Then, when it comes time to work on the introduction of an upcoming speech—or even to choose a topic—cruise this file for ideas. Keeping such a file is a strategy used by many people who speak frequently in public.

Every discourse ought to be a living creature;
having a body of its own and head and feet;
there should be a middle, a beginning, and end,
adapted to one another and to the whole.

PLATO

11

Outlining Your Speech

objectives

After studying this chapter you should be able
to do the following:

1. Describe the purposes of a preparation outline
   and a delivery outline.

2. Identify and explain guidelines for preparing a
   preparation outline and a delivery outline.

3. Demonstrate standard outline form.

4. Prepare a preparation outline and a delivery
   outline for a speech you are working on.

5. Deliver a speech from speaking notes.

A while ago, a family decided to spend a weekend near the Texas Gulf Coast. Soon after they left home on a hot, cloudless June morning, the air conditioning in their car broke down. By late afternoon, the car was *very* hot, the family was *very* tired, and the prospect of an air-conditioned motel room was *very* welcome. The husband was driving and the wife navigating as they approached their destination. Only a few more minutes, they thought, and they would relax in the cool quiet of their room. Imagine their frustration when, a half hour later, they were still searching for the motel. "Let *me* see the map," demanded the exasperated husband.

"Here, if you think you can do better," snapped the wife. "This map is useless!"

Trying to remain cool and collected (no easy task with the temperature approaching 100°F), the husband studied the map. Sure enough, it looked as though they should be at the motel by now. In sweaty desperation, he finally stopped to ask for directions.

"Oh, you should've turned right four blocks back," explained a store clerk. The wife had been right. The map *was* useless, because it had not shown the necessary turn in the road.

This actually happened—to our family! We experienced directly the frustration of having an inaccurate map. Just as we rely on maps to find our way on unfamiliar roads, so we rely on outlines to be "speech maps." In Chapter 9, you learned approaches to organizing your ideas and supporting materials. In Chapter 10 you learned how to introduce and conclude your speech effectively and memorably. Now, in this chapter, we will discuss how to map, or outline, the organization you have developed.

Actually, most speakers find that they need to prepare two types of outline: (1) a preparation outline and (2) a delivery outline. Let's examine the purposes and requirements of each of these outlines in turn.

Preparation Outline

Although few speeches are written in paragraph form, most speakers develop a detailed **preparation outline** that includes main ideas, subpoints, and supporting material. It may also include the specific purpose, introduction, blueprint, conclusion, and signposts.

Developing a Preparation Outline

To begin your outlining task, you might try a technique known as **mapping** or clustering. Write on a sheet of paper all the main ideas, subpoints, and supporting material for the speech. Then use geometric shapes and arrows to indicate the logical relationships among them, as shown in Figure 11.1.

Nationwide Insurance speechwriter Charles Parnell favors yet another technique for beginning an outline:

I often start by jotting down a few ideas on the (computer) screen, then move them around as necessary to build some sort of coherent pattern. I then fill in the details as they occur to me.

preparation outline
Detailed outline that includes main ideas, subpoints, and supporting material, and that may also include specific purpose, introduction, blueprint, internal previews and summaries, transitions, and conclusion

mapping
A visual representation of how all the main ideas, subpoints, and supporting material of a speech relate to the central idea and to one another

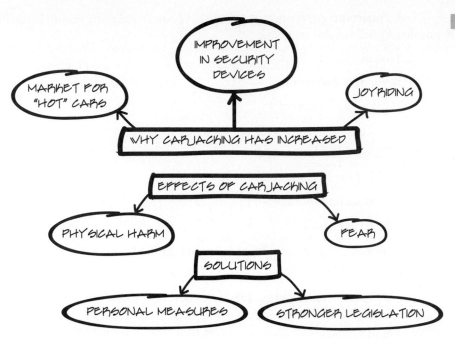

FIGURE 11.1

A map that shows the relationships among each of three main ideas and their subpoints. Main ideas are enclosed by rectangles; subpoints, by ovals. Supporting materials could be indicated by another shape and connected to the appropriate subpoints.

Source: Adapted from Michael Butterworth, "The Road to Security: How to Combat the Carjacking Crisis," in *Winning Orations 1993* (Mankato, MN: Interstate Oratorical Association, 1993) 23–25.

What that means is that you can really start anywhere and eventually come up with an entire speech, just as you can start with any piece of a puzzle and eventually put it together.[1]

Whatever technique you choose to begin your outline, your ultimate goal is to produce a plan that lets you judge the unity and coherence of your speech, to see how well the parts fit together and how smoothly the speech flows. Your finished preparation outline will help you make sure that all main ideas and subpoints are clearly and logically related and adequately supported.

The following suggestions will help you complete your preparation outline. However, keep in mind that different instructors may have different expectations for both outline content and format. Be sure to understand and follow your own instructor's guidelines.

WRITE YOUR PREPARATION OUTLINE IN COMPLETE SENTENCES, LIKE THOSE YOU WILL USE WHEN DELIVERING YOUR SPEECH. Unless you write complete sentences, you will have trouble judging the coherence of the speech. Moreover, complete sentences will help during your early rehearsals. If you write cryptic phrases, you may not remember what they mean.

USE STANDARD OUTLINE FORM. Although you did not have to use this form when you began to outline your ideas, you need to do so now. **Standard outline form** lets you see at a glance the exact relationships among various main ideas, subpoints, and supporting material in your speech. It is an important tool for evaluating your speech, as well as a requirement in many public-speaking courses. An instructor who requires speech outlines will generally expect standard outline form. To produce a correct outline, follow the instructions given here.

standard outline form
Conventional use of numbered and lettered headings and subheadings to indicate the relationships among parts of the speech

USE STANDARD OUTLINE NUMBERING.   Logical and fairly easy to learn, outline numbering follows this sequence:

   I. First main idea

      A. First subpoint of *I*

      B. Second subpoint of *I*

         1. First subpoint of *B*

         2. Second subpoint of *B*

            a. First subpoint of 2

            b. Second subpoint of 2

  II. Second main idea

It is unlikely that you will subdivide beyond the level of lowercase letters (*a*, *b*, etc.) in most speech outlines.

USE AT LEAST TWO SUBDIVISIONS, IF ANY, FOR EACH POINT.   Logic dictates that you cannot divide anything into one part. If, for example, you have only one piece of supporting material, incorporate it into the subpoint or main idea that it supports. If you have only one subpoint, incorporate it into the main idea above it. Although there is no firm limit to the number of subpoints you may have, if you have more than five, you may want to place some of them under another point. An audience will remember your ideas more easily if they are divided into blocks of no more than five.

INDENT MAIN IDEAS, POINTS, SUBPOINTS, AND SUPPORTING MATERIAL PROPERLY.   Main ideas, indicated by Roman numerals, are written closest to the left margin. Notice that the *periods* following the Roman numerals line up, so that the first *words* of the main ideas also line up.

    I. First main idea

   II. Second main idea

  III. Third main idea

Letters or numbers of subpoints and supporting materials begin directly underneath the first *word* of the point above.

   I. First main idea

      A. First subpoint of *I*

If a main idea or subpoint takes up more than one line, the second line begins under the first *word* of the preceding line:

I. Every speech has three parts.

   A. The first part, both in our discussion and in actual delivery, is the introduction.

The same rules of indentation apply at all levels of the outline.

RECAP

SUMMARY OF CORRECT OUTLINE FORM

Rule	Example
1. Use standard outline numbers and letters.	I. 　A. 　　1. 　　　a. 　　　　(1) 　　　　　(a)
2. Use at least two subpoints, if any, for each main idea.	I. 　A. 　B.
3. Properly indent main ideas, subpoints, and supporting material.	I. First main idea 　A. First subpoint of I 　　1. First subpoint of A 　　2. Second subpoint of A 　B. Second subpoint of I II. Second main idea

WRITE AND LABEL YOUR SPECIFIC PURPOSE AT THE TOP OF YOUR PREPARATION OUTLINE. Unless your instructor directs you to do otherwise, do not work the specific purpose into the outline itself. Instead, label it and place it at the top of the outline. Your specific purpose can serve as a yardstick by which to measure the relevance of each main idea, subpoint, and piece of supporting material. Everything in the speech should contribute to your purpose.

ADD THE BLUEPRINT, KEY SIGNPOSTS, AND AN INTRODUCTION AND CONCLUSION TO YOUR OUTLINE. Place the introduction after the specific purpose, the blueprint immediately following the introduction, the conclusion after the outline of the body of the speech, and other signposts within the outline. Follow your instructor's guidelines as to whether and how you should incorporate these elements into your numbering system.

Sample Preparation Outline

The sample outline that follows is for a ten-minute persuasive speech by student speaker Amanda Taylor.[2] Notice that in this example, the purpose, introduction, blueprint, signposts, and conclusion are separated from the numbered points in the body of the speech. Be sure to learn and follow your own instructor's specific requirements for how you should incorporate these elements.

Once you have completed your preparation outline, you can use it to help analyze and possibly revise the speech. The following questions can help you in this critical thinking task.

● *Does the speech as outlined fulfill the purpose you have specified?* If not, you need to revise the specific purpose or change the direction and content of the speech itself.

SAMPLE PREPARATION OUTLINE

Purpose: By the end of my speech, the audience will take steps to prevent drowsy driving.

Introduction: It was just after midnight, and Texas A&M student Brandon Kallmeyer was driving home after dropping off his girlfriend. After driving about 25 minutes, Brandon's pickup truck veered off the road and hit six college students walking to a fraternity party. Brandon was all right, but the six students were killed instantly. According to the *Houston Chronicle* of October 12, 1999, it was not alcohol which caused this—rather, drowsiness. Brandon fell asleep at the wheel. And unfortunately, this happens more often than we may think. The February 6, 2000, issue of the *Washington Post* explains that more than 100,0000 accidents occur every year due to drivers who fall asleep at the wheel. And of those, 10,000 end in fatalities.

Blueprint: During a personal interview on April 4, 2000, Roger Browers, the executive director of the North Central Florida Safety Council, explained that while the problem of people driving while drowsy is not a new one, it's not a diminishing one either. Therefore, it's important for us to examine this problem, and why it continues to escalate, in order to discover some steps we can take to help protect ourselves and the other driver.

I. Drowsy driving is a major problem on today's highways.

    A. People don't get enough sleep.

        1. Dr. Robert Stickgold, an expert on sleep at Harvard Medical School, stated in the March 2000 issue of *The Journal of Cognitive Neuroscience* that everyone needs approximately 8 hours of sleep a day to function effectively the next day. However the average American only receives around 6 hours of sleep, if even that.

        2. Not finding yourself tired on the job doesn't mean you're getting the right amount of sleep. Many times you won't realize you are tired while working due to the fact that your adrenaline may be reaching high levels because you are trying to reach a deadline.

Transition: Although our lack of zzz's may not have an impact in the workplace, it is causing a catastrophe on the highways.

    B. Sleepy drivers behave much as drunk drivers, but do not suffer the same social stigma.

        1. The *Toronto Star* of July 17, 1998, reports a survey by the American Automobile Association, or AAA, in which U.S. highway patrol officers each reported "stopping a motorist who appeared drunk only to find out that the driver was fatigued."

        2. The *St. Louis Post-Dispatch* of March 29, 2000, explains that sleeping does not have the same social stigma attached to drunk driving.

        3. According to the "2000 Sleep in America Poll," performed by the National Sleep Foundation, more than half of the over 1,000 adults responding to a telephone interview, reported driving while feeling drowsy in the past year—and a majority of those polled were outraged when feeling drowsy was compared to consuming alcohol.

Transition: Although the main cause of drowsy driving is not getting enough sleep the night before, there are several other factors that contribute to becoming tired on the road.

    C. There are additional reasons the problem of drowsy driving continues to escalate.

Writing the purpose statement at the top of the outline helps the speaker keep it foremost in mind.

As Amanda prepares her speech, she knows that she must first capture her audience's attention. She does so by relating an illustration, followed by startling statistics that demonstrate the magnitude of the problem. We discussed strategies for introductions in Chapter 10.

The blueprint comes at the end of Amanda's introduction. Here, the first sentence states the central idea (with the support of an authority). The second sentence previews the body of the speech.

The outline of the body of the speech begins here. The first main idea is indicated by the Roman numeral I. Subpoint A explores the first of three reasons drowsy driving is a major problem.

Subpoint 1 provides supporting material for A.

Subpoint 2 offers an explanation.

Amanda provides a transition to her second (B) subpoint.

Subpoint B explores a second reason drowsy driving is a problem.

Amanda offers expert testimony in support of subpoint B.

In subpoint 2, Amanda explains a further ramification of the problem.

Subpoint 3 provides statistical support for both the magnitude of the problem and the explanation Amanda provided in subpoint 2.

Amanda makes a smooth transition from subpoints A and B, to subpoint C.

Subpoint C states the third reason for the first main idea: that drowsy driving is a problem.

1. According to the Automobile Association Foundation's Website, last updated April 2, 2000, people are poor judges of their own sleepiness and cannot predict when they will actually fall asleep.

2. One of the biggest causes of becoming sleepy behind the wheel is alcohol consumption. The January 22, 2000, *St. Louis Post-Dispatch* released news of research performed by the Simmons Company, which found that consuming one alcoholic drink on 6 hours of sleep or less is equivalent to downing six shots before driving.

3. Cars are equipped with nice, cushy seats and carpeted floors and have temperature-regulated environments.

4. Most major roads have been engineered for comfort, removing the bumps, hills, and sharp turns.

5. "Highway hypnosis" is a huge factor in becoming drowsy while driving.

Each of subpoints 1–5 states an additional cause of drowsy driving.

Transition: Despite all the factors working against you when you get behind the wheel, there are steps that can be taken on both the national and personal level.

II. We can solve the problem of drowsy driving.

A. We can solve the problem on the national level.

1. The National Highway Traffic Safety Administration's Website, last updated April 17, 2000, states that rumble strips reduce crashes by 50 percent. But hardly any secondary roads have these strips. We need to lend our support to the Federal Highway Administration's efforts to add more rumble strips to roads. We can do this via their website at fhwa.dot.gov.

2. A new device called Autovue is being marketed. Autovue is a camera, which is mounted on the dashboard, windshield, or roof of your car, and which detects and emits a rumble-strip–like sound if a driver drifts out of a lane without the use of a turn signal.

Now Amanda provides a transition from her first main idea—the problem portion of her speech—to her second main idea—the solution(s). The second main idea of the speech is indicated by Roman numeral II.

Subpoint A suggests one level on which the problem can be solved.

Subpoint 1 describes one specific solution, supported by statistics.

Subpoint 2 describes a second national-level solution.

Transition: But while we wait for the rumble strips to be in place, and the Autovue to be installed on the dashboard, there are some steps we can take personally to help protect ourselves.

B. We can solve the problem of drowsy driving by taking a few personal precautions.

1. Try not to schedule your driving trips between midnight and 6 A.M., when most accidents happen.

2. If you must drive then, make sure you have someone sitting in the front seat with you.

3. Turn on the radio, chew gum, stretch your legs, slap your thighs, talk to yourself, sing, keep your eyes moving, and don't use cruise control.

4. Pull off at a safe place and take a short nap.

5. Get the recommended 7 to 8 hours of sleep a night.

Amanda provides a transition from subpoint A to subpoint B: from national solutions to personal ones.

Subpoint B suggests a second category of solutions to drowsy driving: personal precautions.

Subpoints 1–5 offer 5 different behaviors to prevent drowsy driving.

Conclusion: While this problem is as old as cars, it's not disappearing. And it won't disappear until we choose to do something about it. Today, we have gained a better understanding of the problem of falling asleep at the wheel, and why it continues to exist, while finally suggesting several initiatives to help end this epidemic. Six innocent college students were killed, all because someone didn't take the precautionary steps to avoid the tragedy. So next time you're on the road and you find yourself dozing off, pull over and take a nap, because those 30 minutes could save your life.

In her conclusion, Amanda summarizes her main ideas and refers back to the illustration with which she began her speech. Other methods of concluding a speech were discussed in Chapter 10.

Amanda provides closure by reiterating one of the simple personal solutions she had suggested and underscoring its potential significance.

- *Are the main ideas logical extensions (natural divisions, reasons, or steps) of the central idea?* If not, revise either the central idea or the main ideas. Like the first question, this one relates to the unity of the speech and is critical to making certain the speech "fits together" as a whole.

- *Do the signposts enhance the comfortable flow of each idea into the next?* If not, change or add previews, summaries, or transitions. If they are not adequate, the speech will lack coherence.

- *Does each subpoint provide support for the point under which it falls?* If not, then either move or delete the subpoint.

- *Is your outline form correct?* For a quick reference, check the earlier Recap box, "Summary of Correct Outline Form."

Having considered these five questions, you are ready to rehearse your speech, using the preparation outline as your first set of notes. See Chapter 13 for additional tips on effective rehearsal.

Delivery Outline

As you rehearse your speech, you will find that you need your preparation outline less and less. Both the structure and the content of your speech are pretty well set in your mind. At this point, you are ready to prepare a **delivery outline.**

Developing a Delivery Outline

A delivery outline, as the name implies, is meant to give you all you will need to present your speech in the way you have planned and rehearsed. However, it should not be so detailed that it encourages you to read it rather than speak to your audience. Here are a few tips:

- *Make the outline as brief as possible, and write in single words or short phrases rather than complete sentences.*

- *Include the introduction and conclusion in much shortened form.* You may feel more comfortable if you have the first and last sentences written in full in front of you. Writing out the first sentence eliminates any fear of a mental block at the outset of your speech. And writing a complete last sentence ensures a smooth ending to your speech and a good final impression.

- *Include supporting material and signposts.* Write out statistics, direct quotations, and key signposts. Writing key signposts in full ensures that you will not grope awkwardly for a way to move from one point to the next. In the sample delivery outline that follows, notice the statistics and sources written out in the introduction, and the transitions written out at key junctures—between IA and IB, IB and IC, IC and IIA, and IIA and IIB.

After you have rehearsed the speech several times, you will know where you are most likely to falter and can add or omit written transitions as needed.

- *Do not include your purpose statement in your delivery outline.*

- *Use standard outline form so that you can easily find the exact point or piece of supporting material you are seeking when you glance down at your notes.*

delivery outline
Condensed and abbreviated outline from which speaking notes are developed

TYPE	PURPOSE
Preparation outline	Allows speaker to examine speech for completeness, unity, coherence, and overall effectiveness. Serves as first rehearsal outline.
Delivery outline	Serves as basis for speaking notes.

Speaker's Homepage   **▬**   **X**

Address: http://www.ablongman.com/beebe

 Using Internet Resources to Improve Your Outlining Skill

Use the following sites to help you develop an outline for your next speech. Depending on your needs, one of these URLs should help you develop a clear, logical speech structure.

DEVELOPING AN OUTLINE

http://owl.english.purdue.edu/Handouts/general/gl_outlin.html

This site provides general guidance on how to develop an outline.

A SAMPLE OUTLINE

http://owl.english.purdue.edu/Handouts/general/gl_outlins.html

This site provides a detailed sample of an outline for a research paper; it can also help you develop a correct outline for your next speech.

ALTERNATIVE OUTLINE STRATEGIES AND STRUCTURES

http://www.ipl.org/teen/aplus/linksorganizing.htm#cubing

This site provides links to a variety of other sites that offer information about and examples of such outlining strategies as clustering, mapping, and cubing.

http://www.Richmond.edu/~writing/wweb/cluster.htm

Clustering is a technique that allows you to explore and connect many ideas as soon as they occur to you.

http://www.coun.uvic.ca/learn/program/hndouts/class1.html

Concept mapping, discussed on this site, can help you develop a strategy for classifying ideas.

http://www.richmond.edu/~writing/wweb/cubing.hml

Cubing is a technique that allows a writer or speaker to explore various aspects of a topic, rethinking the topic in a variety of ways.

Sample Delivery Outline

A delivery outline for Amanda's speech on drowsy driving is presented next. Note that the purpose is not included, and that the introduction and conclusion appear in shortened and bulleted form.

As you rehearse the speech, you will probably continue to revise the delivery outline. You may decide to cut further or revise signposts. Your outline should provide just enough information to ensure smooth delivery. It should not burden you with unnecessary notes or compel you to look down too often during the speech.

SAMPLE DELIVERY OUTLINE

Intro.:
- Texas A & M student Brandon Kallmeyer
- Driving 25 min.—truck veered off the road
- Hit 6 students walking to frat. party—killed instantly
- *Houston Chronicle*, October 12, 1999—not alcohol, drowsiness. Brandon fell asleep at the wheel.
- Happens more often than we may think. February 6, 2000, *Washington Post*: more than 100,0000 accidents every year due to drivers who fall asleep at the wheel. 10,000 end in fatalities.

Note both shortened version of, and use of bulleted phrases in, the introduction.

Central Idea/Preview Statement: During a personal interview on April 4, 2000, Roger Browers, executive director of the North Central Florida Safety Council, explained that problem, while not new, is not diminishing. Important:

1. To examine this problem and why it continues to escalate.
2. To discover some steps we can take to protect ourselves, other driver.

The preview is in list form to make it easy for the speaker to glance down and pick up major points to be previewed.

I. Drowsy driving—major problem

A. People don't get enough sleep.

1. Dr. Robert Stickgold, expert on sleep, Harvard Medical School, March 2000 issue of *The Journal of Cognitive Neuroscience:* everyone needs 8 hours of sleep; average only 6.
2. Adrenaline may mask on the job.

Both main ideas and subpoints are single words and short phrases. Note, though, that supporting material and sources are written out to ensure accuracy.

Trans.: Although our lack of zzz's may not have an impact in the workplace, it is causing a catastrophe on the highways.

B. Sleepy drivers like drunk drivers, but without stigma.

1. *Toronto Star,* July 17, 1998: AAA survey—U.S. highway patrol officers each reported "stopping a motorist who appeared drunk only to find out that the driver was fatigued."
2. *St. Louis Post-Dispatch,* March 29, 2000: sleeping ≠ social stigma of drunk driving.
3. "2000 Sleep in America Poll," National Sleep Foundation: more than ½ of over 1,000 adults reported driving while feeling drowsy in the past year—majority outraged when feeling drowsy was compared to consuming alcohol.

Transitions are labeled so that the speaker can find them quickly. The label itself is likely to be abbreviated, as it is here.

Note the use of the ≠ symbol. Such symbols, and numerals instead of written-out numbers, are among the kinds of shortcuts and abbreviations often used in delivery outlines.

Trans.: Although the main cause of drowsy driving is not getting enough sleep the night before, several other factors also contribute to becoming tired on the road.

Speaking Notes

Many speakers find paper difficult to handle quietly, so they transfer their delivery outlines to note cards. Note cards are small enough to hold in one hand, if necessary, and stiff enough not to rustle. Two or three note cards will give you enough space for a delivery outline; the exact number of cards you use will depend on the length of your speech. Type or print your outline neatly on one side, making sure that the letters and words are large enough to read easily. You may find it helpful to plan your note cards according to logical blocks of material, using one note card for the introduction,

---

    C. Addl. reasons

        1. Automobile Association Foundation's Website, last updated April 2, 2000: people poor judges of their own sleepiness; cannot predict when they will actually fall asleep.

        2. Alcohol consumption. January 22, 2000, *St. Louis Post-Dispatch* released research performed by Simmons—1 alcoholic drink on 6 hours of sleep or less = downing 6 shots before driving

        3. Cars comfortable

        4. Roads comfortable

        5. "Highway hypnosis"

Trans.: Despite all the factors working against you when you get behind the wheel, there are steps that can be taken on both the national and personal level.

II. Solutions

    A. National

        1. National Highway Traffic Safety Administration's Website, last updated April 17, 2000: rumble strips reduce crashes by 50 percent. Support: fhwa.dot.gov.

        2. Autovue camera

Trans.: But while we wait for the rumble strips to be in place, and the Autovue to be installed on the dashboard, there are some steps we can take personally to help protect ourselves.

    B. Personal

        1. Don't drive 12–6 A.M.—most accidents occur

        2. Front-seat passenger

        3. Radio, gum, stretch, slap, talk, sing, eyes, no cruise control

        4. Nap

        5. 7–8 hours of sleep a night

Concl.: • Problem as old as cars, not disappearing—won't until we choose to do something about it

        • Today, have gained a better understanding of the problem and why it continues to exist, while suggesting several initiatives to help end this epidemic.

        • 6 innocent college students killed, all because someone didn't take precautionary steps

        • So next time you're on the road and you find yourself dozing off, pull over and take a nap, because those 30 minutes could save your life.

Like the introduction, the conclusion is written in abbreviated, bulleted form. The final sentence is written out to ensure a fluent finish.

Experienced college lecturers are experts at preparing delivery outlines. Before preparing your own outline, you might ask instructors in your other courses to show you the notes they use.

[Photo: Con/Alon Reinnger/Woodfin Camp & Associates]

one or two for the body, and one for the conclusion. At any rate, plan so that you do not have to shuffle note cards midsentence. Number the note cards to prevent a fiasco if your notes get out of order.

Instead of using an outline, you might use an alternative format for your speaking notes. For example, you could use a map, such as the one illustrated in Figure 11.1. Or you could use a combination of words, pictures, and symbols, as in the notes reproduced in Figure 11.2. Although you may not be able to decipher all of Mark Twain's speaking notes, what is important is that they made sense to *him*.

Whatever form your notes take, they should make sense to *you*.

FIGURE 11.2

Speaking notes used by Mark Twain for a lecture on *Roughing It*, delivered in Liverpool, England, in 1874.

Source: Milton Meltzer, *Mark Twain Himself* (New York: Wings Books, 1960) 121.

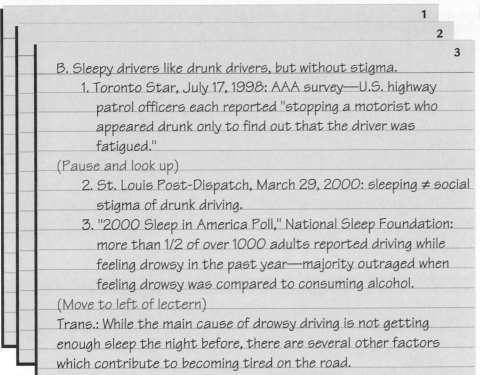

FIGURE 11.3

Your speaking notes can include delivery cues and reminders.

B. Sleepy drivers like drunk drivers, but without stigma.
    1. Toronto Star, July 17, 1998: AAA survey—U.S. highway patrol officers each reported "stopping a motorist who appeared drunk only to find out that the driver was fatigued."
(Pause and look up)
    2. St. Louis Post-Dispatch, March 29, 2000: sleeping ≠ social stigma of drunk driving.
    3. "2000 Sleep in America Poll," National Sleep Foundation: more than 1/2 of over 1000 adults reported driving while feeling drowsy in the past year—majority outraged when feeling drowsy was compared to consuming alcohol.
(Move to left of lectern)
Trans.: While the main cause of drowsy driving is not getting enough sleep the night before, there are several other factors which contribute to becoming tired on the road.

A final addition to your speaking notes will be delivery cues and reminders, such as "Louder," "Pause," or "Move in front of podium." (See Figure 11.3.) You could write your delivery cues in the margins by hand, or if the entire outline is handwritten, in ink of a different color. Several years ago, former President Gerald Ford accidentally read the delivery cue "Look into the right camera" during an address. Clearly differentiating delivery cues from speech content will help prevent such mistakes.

SUMMARY

Most public speakers prepare a preparation outline and a delivery outline. Each type has a different purpose and format.

A preparation outline includes your carefully organized main ideas, subpoints, and supporting material; it may also include your specific purpose, introduction, blueprint, internal previews and summaries, transitions, and conclusion. Write each of these elements in complete sentences and standard outline form. Use the preparation outline to begin rehearsing your speech.

After you have rehearsed several times from the preparation outline, prepare a delivery outline. This, with slight adjustments, becomes your final speaking notes. You need not include the purpose statement or central idea. Note all other ideas and materials only in as much detail as you will need when delivering the speech. You may eventually transfer the delivery outline to note cards and add delivery cues.

A Sharper Focus

CONSIDERING YOUR AUDIENCE

▶ An instructor who requires speech outlines will generally expect standard outline form.

▶ Because an audience will remember your ideas more easily if they are divided into blocks of no more than five, if you have more than five subpoints at any level of an outline, you may want to place some of them under another point.

▶ Your delivery outline should not be so detailed that it encourages you to read it rather than speak to your audience.

CONSIDERING AUDIENCE DIVERSITY

▶ Different instructors may have different expectations for outline content and format. Be sure to understand and follow your own instructor's guidelines.

CRITICAL THINKING QUESTIONS

1. The following delivery outline for the body of a speech contains a number of errors in standard outline form. Find five of those errors.

   Title: "The College Work-Study Program"

      I. Program Eligibility

         A. Four initial requirements for work-study students

            1. Have need for employment

            2. Good grades

            3. Be a full-time student

            4. Be a citizen or permanent resident of the United States

         B. Application

            1. Submit financial-aid form to Central State

     II. Job Assignments

         A. Jobs related to your major field of study

         B. Jobs using your special interests and skills

2. Myorka thinks it is silly to worry about using correct outline form for either her preparation or delivery outline. Do you agree with her? Give at least two reasons you do or do not.

3. Geoff plans to deliver his speech from some hastily scrawled notes on a sheet of notebook paper torn from his class notebook. What advice would you offer him for preparing more effective and efficient speaking notes?

ETHICAL QUESTIONS

1. Can a speaker legitimately claim that a speech is extemporaneous if he or she has constructed a detailed preparation outline? Explain your answer.

SUGGESTED ACTIVITIES

1. Select a speech from Appendix C. Prepare a delivery outline of that speech.

2. Discuss the pros and cons of having a speaker's outline in front of you while you are listening to the speech.

USING TECHNOLOGY AND MEDIA

1. Take notes as you listen to an audio or videotape of a speech. Then organize your notes into an outline that you think clearly and accurately reflects both the speaker's organization and the intended relationship among ideas and supporting materials.

2. If your word-processing program has an outlining function, experiment with it. Do you find it easier or more difficult to use than manually assigning Roman numerals, letters, and numbers?

A speech is poetry; cadence, rhythm, imagery, sweep!
A speech reminds us that words, like children, have the
power to make dance the dullest beanbag of a heart.

PEGGY NOONAN

12

Using Words Well: Speaker Language and Style

objectives

After studying this chapter you should be able to do the following:

1. Describe three differences between oral and written language styles.

2. List and explain four ways to use words effectively.

3. Explain how to adapt your language style to diverse listeners.

4. List and define three common figures of speech.

5. List and explain seven techniques for creating drama and cadence.

6. Offer tips for using language effectively in public speeches.

P eople lazily scanning the classified ads and headlines of their local newspapers must have rubbed their eyes in disbelief when they read the following:[1]

FORECLOSURE LISTINGS
Entire state of NJ available. Deal directly with owners. 5–8 months before auction. Call 201-286-1156.

BABYSITTER
Looking for infant to babysit in my home. Excellent references.

NEED Plain Clothes Security. Must have shoplifting experience. Apply between 8 A.M.–3 P.M. Mon.–Fri., at suite 207.

Unemployment Not Working, Critics Say

FAMILY CATCHES FIRE JUST IN TIME, CHIEF SAYS . . .

The Richard Harder family Sunday returned home from church just in time, Lindsey Fire Chief Tom Overmyer said. The family . . . got back from church about 11:15 A.M. to find their kitchen table on fire and . . .

STORE CLERK BETTER AFTER BEING SHOT

These ads and headlines from the "Headlines" files of comedian Jay Leno are, as he notes, funny "because they were never intended to be funny in the first place. That they're checked and rechecked by a proofreader makes them funnier still." Certainly they illustrate that using language accurately, clearly, and effectively can be a challenge, even for professional wordsmiths!

For public speakers, the task is doubly challenging. One must speak clearly and communicate ideas accurately. At the same time, it is important to present those ideas in such a way that your audience will listen to, remember, and perhaps act on what you have to say.

In this chapter we will focus on the power of language. We will suggest ways to communicate your ideas and feelings to others accurately and effectively. We will also discuss how the choice of words and word structures can help give your message a distinctive style. ▬

Oral versus Written Language Style

Your instructor has probably told you not to write your speech out word for word. The professor has said this because of the differences between speaking and writing. There are at least three major differences between oral and written language styles.

Oral Style Is More Personal

When speaking, you can look your listeners in the eye and talk to them directly. If you see that they don't like or don't understand what you are saying, you can adjust your statements and explanations to gain greater acceptance. In other words, you and your audience can interact, something a writer and reader cannot do. This interaction provides you, the public speaker, with personal contact and exchange of warmth with your audience, an experience not available to the writer working in seclusion.

That warmth and personal contact affect your speech and your verbal style. As a speaker, you are likely to use more pronouns (*I, you*) than you would in writing. You are also more likely to address specific audience members by name.

Oral Style Is Less Formal

Written communication often uses a rather formal language and structure. It should be noted that memorized speeches usually sound as if they were written because the words and phrases are longer, more complex, and more formal than those used by most speakers. Spoken communication, by contrast, is usually less formal, characterized by shorter words and phrases and less complex sentence structures. Speakers generally use many more contractions and colloquialisms than writers. Oral language is also much less varied than written language, with only fifty words accounting for almost 50 percent of what we say. Finally, spoken language is often less precise than written language. Speakers are more likely than writers to use somewhat vague quantifying terms, such as *many, much,* and *a lot*. The use of such terms may, in fact, be an asset to a speaker who wants to be thought of by his audience as "personal" and "connected." Walter Weintraub, a clinical professor of psychiatry at the University of Maryland Medical Center, once dubbed Bill Clinton a "mainstream" speaker, in part because of his "theatrical . . . use of such adverbial intensifiers as 'really,' 'very,' 'so,' and 'such.'"[2]

However, there are great variations within both oral and written styles. One speech may be quite personal and informal, whereas another may have characteristics more often associated with written style. For example, then President-elect George W. Bush used these simple words and short sentences in his December 13, 2000, election-victory speech:

> Republicans want the best for our nation. And so do Democrats. Our votes may differ, but not our hopes.[3]

Compare Bush's straightforward language and sentence structure with the more formal language and more complex sentence structures used by Al Gore to express a similar thought in his concession speech on that same evening:

While we yet hold and do not yield our opposing beliefs, there is a higher duty than the one we owe to political party. This is America, and we put country before party.[4]

Regardless of whether the communication is written or oral, the personality of the speaker or writer, the subject of the discourse, the audience, and the occasion all affect the style of the language used.

Oral Style Is More Repetitious

When you don't understand something you are reading in a book or an article, you can stop and reread a passage, look up unfamiliar words in the dictionary, or ask someone for help. When you're listening to a speech, those opportunities usually aren't available. For this reason, an oral style is and should be more repetitious.

When you study how to organize a speech, you learn to preview main ideas in your introduction, develop your ideas in the body of the speech, and summarize these same ideas in the conclusion. You build in repetition to make sure that your listener will grasp your message. Even during the process of developing an idea, it is sometimes necessary to state it first, restate it in a different way, provide an example, and finally, summarize it.

RECAP

ORAL VERSUS WRITTEN STYLE

ORAL STYLE	More personal, facilitating interaction between speaker and audience
	Less formal
	More repetitious
WRITTEN STYLE	Less personal, with no immediate interaction between writer and reader
	More formal
	Less repetitious

Using Words Effectively

As a speaker, your challenge is to use words well so that you can communicate your intended message. Ideally, language should be specific, concrete, simple, and correct. We shall discuss each of these factors.

Use Specific, Concrete Words

If you were to describe your pet snake to an audience, you would need to do more than say it is a serpent. Instead, you would want to use the most specific term possible, describing your snake as a ball python or, if you were speaking to an audience of scientists, perhaps as a *Python regius*. Specific words or terms such as *ball python* refer to individual members of a class of more general things such as *serpent* or *snake*.

Describing this object in general terms—as a stringed musical instrument—would hardly do it justice. Instead, what concrete details would you include in a verbal description to create an image of this object for your audience?

[Photo: Tom Main/Stone/Getty Images]

Specific words are often concrete words, which appeal to one of our five senses, whereas general words are often abstract words, which refer to ideas or qualities. A linguistic theory known as *general semantics* holds that the more concrete your words, the clearer your communication. Semanticists use a "ladder of abstraction" to illustrate how something can be described in either concrete or abstract language. Figure 12.1 shows an example. The words are most abstract at the top of the ladder and become more concrete as you move down the ladder.

Specific, concrete nouns create memorable images. At the September 14, 2001, Washington National Cathedral prayer service for victims of the September 11 terrorist attacks, George W. Bush said,

We have seen the images of fire and ashes and bent steel.[5]

The concrete nouns *fire, ashes,* and *steel* created much more specific images for Bush's listeners than would have abstract nouns such as *aftermath* or even *holocaust.*

Specific, concrete verbs can be especially effective. The late Representative Barbara Jordan of Texas, whose language skills one speechwriter describes as "legendary," recognized the power of concrete verbs.[6] For example, the first draft of a passage in her 1992 Democratic National Convention keynote stated,

The American dream is not dead. It is injured, it is sick, but it is not dead.

Jordan revised the line to read,

The American dream is not dead. It is gasping for breath, but it is not dead.

The concrete verb phrase "gasping for breath" brings alive the image Jordan intended to create.

When searching for a specific, concrete word, you may want to consult a **thesaurus.** But in searching for an alternative word, do not feel you have to choose the most obscure or unusual term to vary your description. Simple language can often evoke a vivid image for your listeners.

Abstract

Nature

Mammal

Dog

Pit Bull

Concrete

FIGURE 12.1

A "ladder of abstraction" is used by semanticists to show how a concept, idea, or thing can be described in either concrete or abstract terms.

thesaurus
An alphabetical list of words and synonyms

Use Simple Words

John F. Kennedy's inaugural address on January 20, 1961, was both eloquent and memorable. Although we will analyze some of the many stylistic features of that speech later in this chapter, perhaps its most significant attribute was its simplicity:

> *Theodore Sorensen, special counsel to the president and his principal speechwriter, has recorded that Kennedy specifically asked him to look into the "secret" of Lincoln's "Gettysburg Address," which he hoped to emulate. Sorensen reported that "Lincoln never used a two- or three-syllable word where a one-syllable word would do, and never used two or three words where one word would do." Thus, the guidelines for style emerged.[7]*

The best language is often the simplest. Your words should be immediately understandable to your listeners. Don't try to impress them with jargon and pompous language. Instead, as linguist Paul Roberts advises,

> *Decide what you want to say and say it as vigorously as possible . . . and in plain words.[8]*

In his essay "Politics and the English Language," George Orwell lists rules for clear writing, including this prescription for simplicity:

> *Never use a long word where a short one will do. If it is possible to cut a word out, always cut it out. Never use a foreign phrase, a scientific word, or a jargon word if you can think of an everyday English equivalent.[9]*

Tape-record your practice sessions. As you play the tape back, listen for chances to say what you want with simpler and fewer words. Used wisely, simple words communicate with great power and precision.

Use Words Correctly

> *I was listening to the car radio one day when a woman reading the news referred to someone as a* suede-o-intellectual. *I pondered through three traffic lights until I realized she wasn't talking about shoes, but a pseudointellectual.[10]*

A public speech is not the place to demonstrate your lack of familiarity with English vocabulary and grammar. In fact, your effectiveness with your audience depends in part on your ability to use the English language correctly. If you are unsure of the way to apply a grammatical rule, seek assistance from a good English usage handbook. If you are unsure of a word's meaning, use a dictionary.

Perhaps the greatest challenge to using words correctly is awareness of **connotations** as well as **denotations.** Language operates on two levels. The denotation of a word is its literal meaning, the definition you find in a dictionary. For example, the denotation of the word *notorious* is "famous." The connotation of a word is not usually found in a dictionary, but consists of the meaning we associate with the word, based on our past experiences. *Notorious* connotes fame for some dire deed. *Notorious* and *famous* are not really interchangeable. It is just as important to consider the connotations of the words you use, as it is to consider the denotations.

Pollster Frank Luntz demonstrated his awareness of the importance of connotations in his advice for politicians speaking to the American people:

connotation
The meaning we associate with a word, based on our past experience

denotation
The literal meaning of a word

Say you are cutting "bureaucrats," who have no friends, not "programs," which have lots. Repeat whenever you can that "it's time to put the government on a diet," and never say "orphanage."[11]

Luntz based his advice on responses from actual audiences. For example, test audiences agreed by a three-to-one margin that welfare children who have been abused would be better off in an orphanage. But when Luntz used the phrase "foster home" instead of "orphanage," the approval rating increased to five-to-one. Luntz's findings support the notion that a word may be denotatively correct but still not the right word for the speaker's purpose.

Sometimes connotations are private. For example, the word *table* is defined denotatively as a piece of furniture consisting of a smooth, flat slab affixed on legs. But when you think of the word *table*, you may think of the old oak table your grandparents used to have. *Table* may evoke for you an image of playing checkers with your grandmother. This is a private connotation of the word, a unique meaning based on your own past experiences. Private meanings are difficult to predict, but as a public speaker you should be aware of the possibility of audience members' private connotations. This awareness is particularly important when you are discussing highly emotional or controversial topics.

And finally, if your audience includes people for whom English is not their first language, to whom the nuances of connotation may not be readily apparent, it may be necessary to explain your intentions in more detail, rather than relying on word associations.

RECAP

USING WORDS EFFECTIVELY

To hold your audience's attention, keep your language concrete.

To keep your language simple, avoid a long word when a short one will do.

To use your language correctly, consider connotative as well as denotative meanings

---

Adapting Your Language Style to Diverse Listeners

To communicate successfully with the diverse group of listeners who comprise your audience, make sure your language is understandable, appropriate, and unbiased.

Use Language That Your Audience Can Understand

Even if you and all your public-speaking classmates speak English, you probably represent many varieties of the language. Perhaps some of your classmates speak in an **ethnic vernacular**, such as "Spanglish," the combination of English and Spanish often heard near the United States–Mexico border; Cajun, with its influx of French words, frequently spoken in Louisiana; or the African-American language variety sometimes known as "Ebonics." Some of you may reflect where you grew up by your **regionalisms**, words or phrases specific to one part of the country but rarely used in

ethnic vernacular
A variety of English that includes words and phrases used by a specific ethnic group

regionalism
A word or phrase used uniquely by English speakers in one part of the United States

quite the same way in other places. Others of you may frequently use **jargon**, the specialized language of your profession or hobby.

If you give a speech to others who share your ethnic, regional, or professional background, you can communicate successfully with them using these specialized varieties of English. However, if you give a speech to an audience as diverse as the members of your public-speaking class, where do you find a linguistic "common ground"?

The answer is to use **standard U.S. English**. Standard U.S. English is the language taught by schools and used in the media, business, and the government in the United States. "Standard" does not imply that standard U.S. English is inherently right and all other forms are wrong, only that it conforms to a standard that most speakers of U. S. English will readily understand—even though they may represent a variety of ethnic, regional, and professional backgrounds.

 ## Use Appropriate Language

Shortly after the September 11, 2001, terrorist attacks, U.S. Vice President Dick Cheney made remarks in which he referred to Pakistanis as "Paks." Although he was speaking admiringly of the Pakistani people, he was chided for his use of the term. The variation *Paki* is considered a slur, and *Pak* is only slightly less offensive. Columnist William Safire remarked, "Cheney probably picked up *Paks* in his Pentagon days, but innocent intent is an excuse only once; now he is sensitized, as are we all."[12]

A speaker whose language defames any subgroup—people of various ethnic, racial, and religious backgrounds or sexual orientation; women; people with disabilities—or whose language might be otherwise considered offensive or risqué runs a great risk of antagonizing audience members. In the case of people with disabilities, one recent study suggests that derogatory language used to describe this group adversely affects an audience's perceptions of the speaker's persuasiveness, competence, trustworthiness, and sociability.[13]

 ## Use Unbiased Language

Even speakers who would never dream of using overtly offensive language may find it difficult to avoid language that more subtly stereotypes or discriminates. Sexist language falls largely into this second category.

For example, not many years ago, a singular masculine pronoun (*he, him, his*) was the accepted way to refer to a person of unspecified sex:

Everyone should bring his *book to class tomorrow.*

This usage is now considered sexist and unacceptable. Instead, you may include both a masculine and a feminine pronoun:

Everyone should bring his or her *book to class tomorrow.*

Or you may reword the sentence so that it is plural and the pronounciation can be gender neutral:

All students should bring their *books to class tomorrow.*

Also now considered sexist is the use of a masculine noun to refer generically to all people. The editors of *The American Heritage Dictionary of the English Language,* Fourth Edition, consulted a usage panel of 200 writers and scholars on such questions

jargon
The specialized language of a profession

standard U.S. English
The English taught by schools and used in the media, business, and government in the United States

as whether the word *man* was acceptable as meaning "human" in some instances.[14] Only 58 percent of the women on the panel found such usage appropriate. Put another way, if you were speaking to an audience of these distinguished women, you would offend 42 percent of them by using a phrase such as "modern man." Although the word *man* is the primary offender, you should also monitor your use of such masculine nouns as *waiter*, *chairman*, *fireman*, and *Congressman*. Instead choose such gender-neutral alternatives as *server*, *chair*, *firefighter*, and *member of Congress*.

In addition to avoiding masculine nouns and pronouns to refer to all people, avoid sexist language that patronizes or stereotypes people:

Sexist	Unbiased
Barbara Bush, daughter of President George W. Bush and Laura, goes to Yale University.	Barbara Bush, daughter of President and Mrs. Bush, goes to Yale University.
	or
	Barbara Bush, daughter of George W. and Laura Bush, goes to Yale University.
The policeman is an underpaid professional who risks his life daily.	Police are underpaid professionals who risk their lives daily.
The male nurse took good care of his patients. (*Note:* The phrase "male nurse" implies that nursing is a typically female profession. The pronoun *his* clarifies the sex of the nurse.)	The nurse took good care of his patients.

As noted earlier, it is not always easy to avoid biased language. Even with good intentions and deliberate forethought, you can find yourself at times caught in a double bind. For example, suppose that Dr. Pierce is a young black female M.D. If you don't mention her age, race, and gender when you refer to her, you may reinforce your listeners' stereotypical image of a middle-aged white male physician. But if you *do* mention these factors, you may be suspected of implying that Dr. Pierce's achievement is unusual. There is no easy answer to this dilemma or others like it. You will have to consider your audience, purpose, and the occasion in deciding how best to identify Dr. Pierce.

As women and racial, ethnic, and other minorities have become increasingly visible in such professions as medicine, law, engineering, and politics, the public has grown to expect unbiased, inclusive language from news commentators, teachers, textbooks, and magazines—and from public speakers. Language that does not reflect these changes will disrupt your ability to communicate your message to your audience, which may well include members of the minority group to which you are referring.

 RECAP

ADAPTING YOUR LANGUAGE STYLE TO DIVERSE LISTENERS

To communicate successfully with diverse listeners, use language your audience can understand.

To avoid offending your audience, use appropriate language.

To communicate sensitivity to diverse subgroups, use unbiased language.

Crafting Memorable Word Structures

The President of the United States is scheduled to make an important speech in your hometown. You attend the speech and find his thirty-minute presentation both interesting and informative. In the evening, you turn on the news to see how the networks cover his address. All three major networks excerpt the same ten-second portion of his speech. Why? What makes certain portions of a speech quotable or memorable? Former presidential speechwriter Peggy Noonan has said,

> Great speeches have always had great soundbites . . . . They sum up a point, or make a point in language that is pithy or profound.[15]

In other words, memorable speeches are stylistically distinctive. They create arresting images. And they have what a marketing-communication specialist has termed "ear appeal":

> "Ear appeal" phrases can be like the haunting songs of a musical that the members of the audience find themselves humming on the way home. Even if people want to forget them, they can't.[16]

Earlier in this chapter, we discussed the importance of using words that are concrete, unbiased, vivid, simple, and correct. In this section, we turn our attention to groups of words, or word structures—phrases and sentences that create the drama, figurative images, and cadences needed to make a speech memorable by giving it both "eye and ear appeal."[17]

Creating Figurative Images

One way to make your message memorable is to use figures of speech to create arresting images. A **figure of speech** deviates from the ordinary, expected meanings of words, to make a description or comparison unique, vivid, and memorable. Common figures of speech include metaphors, similes, and personification.

METAPHORS AND SIMILES.   A **metaphor** is an implied comparison. In his presidential farewell address on January 18, 2001, Bill Clinton compared American diversity to a coat of many colors, admonishing his fellow citizens to

> Remember that America cannot lead in the world unless here at home we weave the threads of our coat of many colors into the fabric of one America.[18]

In addition to using related words to create the metaphor—*weave, threads, coat,* and *fabric*—Clinton gives Biblical authority to his comparison by alluding to the "coat of many colors" worn by Joseph in the Old Testament.

A **simile** is a less direct comparison that includes the word *like* or *as*. In his 2001 speech to the graduating class of Augsberg College in Minneapolis, NASA administrator Daniel Goldin told his audience that graduation is

> Like one of NASA's missions. Everyone experiences something different. And to be honest, we don't know exactly what is out there. That's precisely why we go.[19]

Speakers often turn to metaphor and simile in times that are especially momentous or overwhelming—times at which literal language seems insufficient. In the hours and

---

figure of speech
Language that deviates from the ordinary, expected meaning of words to make a description or comparison unique, vivid, and memorable

metaphor
An implied comparison between two things

simile
A direct comparison between two things that uses the word *like* or *as*

days after the September 11, 2001, terrorist attacks on the United States, various speakers described the World Trade Center towers collapse metaphorically as "one more circle of Dante's hell"; "nuclear winter"; and "the crater of a volcano."[20]

PERSONIFICATION. **Personification** is the attribution of human qualities to inanimate things or ideas. Franklin Roosevelt personified nature as a generous living provider in this line from his first inaugural address:

> *Nature still offers her bounty and human efforts have multiplied it. Plenty is at our doorstep.*[21]

Creating Drama

Another way in which you can make phrases and sentences memorable is to use the potential of such structures to create drama in your speech—to keep the audience in suspense or to catch them slightly off guard by saying something in a way that differs from the way they expected you to say it.

ONE SIMPLE BUT EFFECTIVE STRATEGY FOR CREATING DRAMA IS TO USE A SHORT SENTENCE TO EXPRESS A VITALLY IMPORTANT THOUGHT. We have already talked about the value of using short, simple words. Short, simple sentences can have much the same power. Columnist George F. Will recently pointed out that the most eloquent sentence in Lincoln's memorable second inaugural address is just four words long:[22]

> *And the war came.*

Other strategies for achieving drama in your speech include three stylistic devices: omission, inversion, and suspension.

WHEN YOU LEAVE OUT A WORD OR PHRASE THAT THE AUDIENCE EXPECTS TO HEAR, YOU ARE USING OMISSION. Telegrams often use an economy of words, because you are charged by the word, and the more you can leave out, the cheaper will be your cost. But, of course, the words you leave out must be understood by your listeners or readers. For example, a captain of a World War II Navy destroyer used omission to inform headquarters of his successful efforts at sighting and sinking an enemy submarine. He spared all details when he cabled back to headquarters: "Sighted sub—sank same." Using as few words as possible, he communicated his message in a memorable way. About 2,000 years earlier, another military commander informed his superiors in Rome of his conquest of Gaul with the economical message: "I came, I saw, I conquered." That commander was Julius Caesar.

THE TECHNIQUE OF REVERSING THE NORMAL WORD ORDER OF A PHRASE OR SENTENCE IS INVERSION. John F. Kennedy inverted the usual subject-verb-object sentence pattern to object-subject-verb in this brief declaration from his inaugural:

> *This much we pledge. . . .*[23]

Russian President Boris Yeltsin used a similarly inverted word order when he solemnly declared at the July 1998 entombment of the remains of Czar Nicholas II,

> *Guilty are those who committed this heinous crime. . . .*[24]

personification
The attribution of human qualities to inanimate things or ideas

omission
Leaving out a word or phrase the listener expects to hear

inversion
Reversing the normal word order of a phrase or sentence

SUSPENSION OCCURS WHEN YOU USE A KEY WORD OR PHRASE AT THE END OF A SENTENCE, RATHER THAN AT THE BEGINNING. When you read a mystery novel, you are held in suspense until you reach the end and learn "who done it." The stylistic technique of verbal **suspension** does something similar. When Al Gore conceded the 2000 presidential election in December of that year, he told his audience,

> *For the sake of our unity as a people and the strength of our democracy, I offer my concession.*[25]

Advertisers use the technique of suspension frequently. A few years ago, the Coca-Cola Company used suspension as the cornerstone of its worldwide advertising campaign. Rather than saying, "Coke goes better with everything," the copywriter decided to stylize the message by making *Coke* the last word in the sentence. The slogan became "Things go better with Coke." Again, the stylized version was more memorable because it used language in an unexpected way.

Creating Cadence

Even very small children can memorize nursery rhymes and commercial jingles with relative ease. As we grow older, we may make up rhythms and rhymes to help us remember such facts as "Thirty days hath September,/April, June, and November" and "Red sky at night/A sailor's delight." Why? Rhythms are memorable. The public speaker can take advantage of language rhythms, not by speaking in singsong patterns, but by using such stylistic devices as parallelism, antithesis, repetition, and alliteration.

PARALLELISM. **Parallelism** occurs when two or more clauses or sentences have the same grammatical pattern. When he delivered the Phi Beta Kappa oration at Harvard in 1837, Ralph Waldo Emerson cast these simple expressions in parallel structures:

> *We will walk on our feet; we will work with our own hands; we will speak our own minds.*[26]

Speaking directly to U.S. military personnel during his announcement of the October 8, 2001, start of bombing in Afghanistan, George W. Bush declared,

> *Your mission is defined, your objectives are clear, your goal is just.*[27]

Bush's use of three parallel subject-verb-predicate adjective structures adds memorable rhythm to his declaration.

ANTITHESIS. The word **antithesis** means "opposition." In language style, antithesis is a sentence having a parallel structure, but with the two parts contrasting each other in meaning. Speakers have long realized the dramatic potential of antithesis. In Franklin Roosevelt's first inaugural address, he declared,

> *Our true destiny is not to be ministered unto but to minister to ourselves and to our fellow men.*[28]

Both in meaning and in structure, his words foreshadowed the more famous remark of John F. Kennedy nearly thirty years later:

> *Ask not what your country can do for you; ask what you can do for your country.*[29]

suspension
Withholding a key word or phrase until the end of a sentence

parallelism
Using the same grammatical pattern for two or more clauses or sentences

antithesis
A two-part parallel structure in which the second part contrasts in meaning with the first

We will examine Kennedy's statement in greater detail later in this chapter.

More recently, British Prime Minister Tony Blair employed antithesis to note that he could not recall a situation prior to the September 11, 2001, terrorist attacks that had so quickly commanded a coalition of support,

> *not just from those countries involved in military action, but from many others in all parts of the world.*[30]

Antithesis is not restricted to politicians. When William Faulkner accepted the Nobel Prize for literature in 1950, he spoke the now famous antithetical phrase,

> *I believe that man will not merely endure: he will prevail.*[31]

An antithetical statement is a good way to end a speech. The cadence it creates will make the statement memorable.

REPETITION. **Repetition** of a key word or phrase gives rhythm, power, and memorability to your message. At the climax of Patrick Henry's "Liberty or Death" speech in 1775 was this passionate use of repetition:

> *The war is inevitable—and let it come! I repeat it, sir, let it come!*[32]

Twentieth-century speakers also recognize the power of repetition as a memorable stylistic device. In a speech honoring the Tuskegee Airmen and addressing issues of race in the modern U.S. military, former Deputy Secretary of Defense Rudy de Leon claimed that recruitment of minorities is only one part of the task facing the military:

> Our job is not finished *if we fail to recognize that each generation has its own unique problems and perceptions when it comes to race and ethnicity.*
>
> *We can ensure our rules and regulations are clear and fair.*
>
> But our job is not finished *if people believe that those rules and regulations are not being enforced fairly.*
>
> Our job is not finished *if the rules and regulations work for those in uniform, but they do not reach people in our civilian workforce. [emphasis added]*[33]

The repeated mantra, "our job is not finished" rings in one's mind long after hearing or reading the passage.

ALLITERATION. **Alliteration** is the repetition of a consonant sound (usually an initial consonant) several times in a phrase, clause, or sentence. Alliteration adds cadence to a thought. Two mid-twentieth-century orators who favored alliteration were Franklin Roosevelt and Winston Churchill. Roosevelt called for "discipline and direction" in his first inaugural address;[34] little more than a week later, in his first fireside chat, he urged weary listeners to have "confidence and courage."[35] Churchill, rousing English people to resist the Nazi onslaught in 1940, used the alliterative phrase "disaster and disappointment."[36] Addressing the Congress of the United States a year later, he praised "virility, valour and civic virtue."[37] More recently, during the 2000 presidential campaign, Dick Cheney, then candidate for vice president, claimed that his running mate George W. Bush leads by "conviction, not calculation."[38] Used sparingly, alliteration can add cadence to your rhetoric.

repetition
Emphasizing a key word or phrase by using it more than once

alliteration
The repetition of a consonant sound (usually the first consonant) several times in a phrase, clause, or sentence

RECAP   CRAFTING MEMORABLE WORD STRUCTURES

Word Structures with Figurative Imagery

METAPHOR	Make an implied comparison.
SIMILE	Compare by using the word like or as.
PERSONIFICATION	Attribute human qualities to inanimate things or ideas.

Word Structures with Drama

SHORT SENTENCE	Strike hard on an important idea by stating it in a short sentence.
OMISSION	Boil an idea down to its essence by leaving out understood words.
INVERSION	Reverse the expected order of words and phrases.
SUSPENSION	Place a key word at the end of a phrase or sentence.

Word Structures with Cadence

PARALLELISM	Use the same pattern to begin several sentences or phrases.
ANTITHESIS	In parallel structures, oppose one part of a sentence to another.
REPETITION	Repeat a key word or phrase several times for emphasis.
ALLITERATION	Use the same initial consonant sound several times in a phrase or sentence.

Analyzing a Memorable Word Structure

We'd like to illustrate all seven techniques for creating drama and cadence with one final example.[39] If you asked almost anyone for the most quoted line from John F. Kennedy's speeches, that quote would probably be "Ask not what your country can do for you; ask what you can do for your country," from his inaugural address. Besides expressing a noble thought, a prime reason this line is so quotable is that it uses all seven stylistic techniques.

"Ask not . . ." is an example of omission. The subject, *you*, is not stated. "Ask not" is also an example of inversion. In casual everyday conversation, we would usually say "do not ask" rather than "ask not." The inversion makes the opening powerful and attention-grabbing.

The sentence also employs the technique of suspension. The key message of the phrase is suspended or delayed until the end of the sentence: "ask what you can do for your country." If the sentence structure had been reversed, the impact would not have been as dramatic. Consider: "Ask what you can do for your country rather than what your country can do for you."

Kennedy uses parallelism and antithesis. The sentence is a parallel construction of two clauses, one in opposition to the other.

He also uses the technique of repetition. He uses a form of the word *you* four times in a sentence of seventeen words. In fact, he uses only eight different words in his seventeen-word sentence. Just one word in the entire sentence, *not*, occurs only once.

Address:　　http://www.ablongman.com/beebe

▼　　**Using Internet Resources to Polish Your Spoken Prose**

Consider the following Websites to help you find the words you need for your speech:

TO FIND THE MEANING OF A WORD

Oxford English Dictionary online:

http://dictionary.oed.com/entrance.dtl

The American Heritage Dictionary online:

http://www.bartleby.com/61/

Merriam-Webster's Collegiate Dictionary and Thesaurus, language dictionaries, specialty dictionaries, and other language tools:

http://www.yourdictionary.com/

Links to a variety of dictionaries, glossaries, and other reference tools:

http://www.abacon.com/pubspeak/organize/dict.html

TO FIND JUST THE RIGHT WORD

Roget's Thesaurus online:

http://www.bartleby.com/62/

TO FIND A RHYMING WORD

You need not necessarily pepper your speech with as many alliterations and rhymes as Jesse Jackson often does, but when you need to find just the right word to make your point with a rhyme, consider this source:

http://www.cs.cmu.edu/~dougb/rhyme.html

You just type in a word and search to see if there is a word that rhymes with it.

TO HELP WITH GRAMMAR AND STYLE

http://andromeda.rutgers.edu/~jlynch/Writing

http://www.bartleby.com/usage/

Definitions and examples from speeches of rhythm, parallel sentence structures, alliteration, rhyme, metaphorical language, overstatement, understatement, and concrete images:

http://www.ablongman.com/pubspeak/organize/style.html

A memorable speech can be a motivating force for the audience.

[Photo courtesy of AP/Wide World Photos]

Finally, Kennedy adds alliteration to the sentence with the words *ask, can,* and *country.* The alliterative *k* sound is repeated at more or less even intervals.

Although the passage we have analyzed does not include any figurative images, the speech from which it comes does have some memorable figurative language, most notably metaphors such as "chains of poverty," "beachhead of cooperation," and "jungle of suspicion." Kennedy used figurative imagery, drama, and cadence to give his inaugural address "eye and ear appeal" and make it memorable—not just to those who heard it initially, but also to those of us who hear, read, and study it more than forty years later.

Tips for Using Language Effectively

Having reviewed ways to add style and interest to the language of your speech, we must now consider how best to put those techniques into practice.

- Even though we have made great claims for the value of style, do not overdo it. Including too much highly stylized language can put the focus on your language rather than on your content. Use distinctive stylistic devices sparingly.

- Save your use of stylistic devices for times during your speech when you want your audience to remember your key ideas or when you wish to capture their attention. Some kitchen mixers have a "burst of power" switch to help churn through difficult mixing chores with extra force. Think of the stylistic devices we have reviewed as opportunities to provide a burst of power to your thoughts and ideas. Use them in your opening sentences, statements of key ideas, and conclusion.

- Short words are more forceful than long ones. Think of those monosyllabic commands—Sit! March! Stop! When a technical term is too unusual or cumbersome, find a way to describe the concept with another word, or use a simile or a metaphor. To talk about the process of floccinaucinihilipilification (the action or habit of estimating something as worthless) may make an interesting speech, but your audience will probably not remember the word itself.

- Use stylistic devices to economize. When sentences become too long or complex, see if you can recast them with antithesis or suspension. Also remember the possibility of omission.

SUMMARY

Carefully select and use words to give your ideas maximum impact. First, understand the differences between the way people talk and the way they write. In general, oral style is more personal, less formal, and more repetitious than is written style.

Words should be specific, concrete, and simple, and used correctly. Understand the connotations of words, as well as their denotations.

It is also important to adapt your language style to diverse listeners. Use language your listeners can understand, use appropriate language to avoid offending them, and use unbiased language to communicate sensitivity to subgroups.

You can create arresting images through such figures of speech as metaphors, similes, and personification. You can create drama and cadence with word structures such as short sentences, omission, inversion, suspension, parallelism, antithesis, repetition, and alliteration.

Effective speakers take great care in wording their speeches. Time invested in using words and word structures well can help you gain and maintain the attention of your audience, and can help your audience understand your message and remember what you say.

being audience-centered
A Sharper Focus

CONSIDERING YOUR AUDIENCE

▶ It is important for a public speaker to present ideas in such a way that the audience will listen to, remember, and perhaps act on what the speaker has to say.

▶ The personal contact and exchange of warmth between speaker and audience affect the verbal style of a speech.

▶ Speakers build in repetition to ensure that listeners will grasp the message.

▶ Specific, concrete, simple language can evoke clear images for listeners.

▶ Your effectiveness with your audience depends in part on your ability to use the English language correctly.

▶ As a public speaker you should be aware of the possibility of audience members' private connotations.

▶ Carefully crafted phrases and sentences can create the drama, figurative images, and cadences needed to give a speech both "eye and ear appeal" to an audience.

▶ Save your use of stylistic devices for times during your speech when you want your audience to remember your key ideas or when you wish to capture listeners' attention.

▶ If your audience includes people who speak English as a second language, to whom the nuances of connotation may not be readily apparent, it may be necessary to explain your intentions in more detail, rather than relying on word associations.

▶ To communicate successfully with diverse listeners, use language your audience can understand.

▶ To avoid offending your diverse audience, use appropriate language.

CRITICAL THINKING QUESTIONS

1. Toni practices her speech for you and asks for advice on polishing the speech, including polishing the style of her language. Offer Toni at least three general suggestions for using language effectively.

2. Not long ago, a reader wrote in a letter to "Dear Abby":

   . . . a woman does not have a maiden name until she takes a married name. What she has is a surname. *"Maiden" refers to a former name that was given up in favor of her husband's name. Women who retain their own names (or their surnames) after marriage do not have a maiden name.*

   This may sound picky to some, but for women (and their husbands) who choose this option, the term maiden name *is offensive.*[40]

   Analyze the reader's point in light of the discussion of sexist language in this chapter. Do you agree or disagree that the term *maiden name* is sexist? Why or why not?

3. The following are five memorable metaphors from historical speeches:[41]

   I have but one lamp by which my feet are guided, and that is the lamp of experience.

   an iron curtain

   snake pit of racial hatred

   Speak softly and carry a big stick.

   You shall not crucify mankind upon a cross of gold.

   First, explain what each metaphor means. Now express the same idea in ordinary language. What do you gain or lose by doing so?

ETHICAL QUESTIONS

1. A high school salutatorian, who had been raped when she was a 14-year-old sophomore, wanted to mention the experience in her salutatory speech, thanking the people who had helped her, and assuring her classmates that they could overcome even the most devastating experiences in life.[42] The principal, however, edited her speech, changing the word *rape* to the phrase "a terrible thing." The student claimed she needed to use the concrete word to emphasize con-

fronting such experiences head-on. The principal said he was simply suggesting ways to make the language of the speech more appropriate. Discuss the ethical implications of this debate over language style. Did the student have the right to call the attack "rape"? Or was the principal correct in censoring the term, out of consideration for the occasion and audience?

SUGGESTED ACTIVITIES

1. One of the challenges in coining metaphors and similes is to avoid clichés. For example, we all know such simile clichés as "hungry as a bear," "smooth as glass," and "pretty as a picture." But similes can be quite effective as attention-getting devices if they deviate from the expected. Invent at least three new endings for each of the following similes:

   Hungry as _____

   Smooth as _____

   Pretty as _____

   Mean as _____

   Smart as _____

2. Consult *Roget's Thesaurus*, or the thesaurus on your word-processing computer program, and find a more concrete or vivid word to express each of the following:

Clumsy	Increase
Cold	Little
Cry	Love
Error	Restore
Frightened	Rich
Full	Smooth
Great	Surprise

3. Find examples of omission, inversion, suspension, parallelism, antithesis, repetition, and alliteration in one or more of the speeches in Appendix C.

USING TECHNOLOGY AND MEDIA

1. Readability indexes such as the Fog Index can help you determine how easily your writing can be understood. The number of sentences per paragraph, words per sentence, and characters per word are all factors that affect readability. Some word-processing programs can evaluate readability. If your word-processing program offers this feature, write out the introduction or conclusion, or a main idea with subpoints and supporting materials, for your next speech. Run a readability test to determine how easily understandable your style is.

Speak the speech, I pray you,
as I pronounced it to you,
trippingly on the tongue.

WILLIAM SHAKESPEARE

Delivering Your Speech

objectives

After studying this chapter you should be able to do the following:

1. Identify three reasons delivery is important to a public speaker.

2. Identify and describe four types of delivery.

3. Identify and illustrate physical characteristics of effective delivery.

4. Describe the steps to follow when you rehearse your speech.

5. List four suggestions for enhancing the final delivery of your speech.

W hat's more important: what you say or how you say it? Delivery has long been considered an important part of public speaking. But is the delivery of your speech more important than the content of your message? Since ancient Greece, people have argued about the role delivery plays in public speaking.

More than 2,300 years ago, some thinkers held that delivery was not an "elevated" topic of study. In his classic treatise *The Rhetoric,* written in 333 B.C., Aristotle claimed that "the battle should be fought out on the facts of the case alone; and therefore everything outside the direct proof is really superfluous." Writing in the first century, Quintilian, Roman rhetorician and author of the first book on speech training, acknowledged the importance of delivery when he said that the beginning speaker should strive for an "extempore" or conversational delivery style. His countryman, the great orator Cicero, claimed that without effective delivery, "a speaker of the highest mental capacity can be held in no esteem, whereas one of moderate abilities, with this qualification, may surpass even those of the highest talent." Sixteen centuries later, the elocution movement carried the emphasis on delivery to an extreme. For elocutionists, speech training consisted largely of techniques and exercises for improving posture, movement, and vocal quality.

Today speech communication teachers believe that both content and delivery contribute to speaking effectiveness. A recent survey suggested that "developing effective delivery" is a primary goal of most speech teachers.[1] Considerable research supports the claim that delivery plays an important role in influencing how audiences react to a speaker and his or her message. It is your audience who will determine whether you are successful. Delivery counts.

Although some courses on public speaking are offered in various countries throughout the world, most of the formal instruction on how to deliver a speech is found in the United States. Our advice about speech delivery, therefore, is closely related to the discipline of communication here in the United States. It's not possible for us to provide a comprehensive compendium of each cultural expectation you may face as you give speeches in a variety of educational and professional settings, but throughout this chapter we will try to sample conventions and preferences of other cultures as we discuss the topics related to delivery. ▬

The Power of Speech Delivery

T he way you hold your notes, your gestures and stance, and your impatient adjustment of your glasses all contribute to the overall effect of your speech. **Nonverbal communication** is communication other than written or spoken language that creates meaning for someone. Nonverbal factors such as your eye contact, posture, vocal quality, and facial expression play a major role in the communication process. As much as 65 percent of the social meaning of messages is based on nonverbal expression.[2] Why does your delivery hold such power in affecting how your audience will receive your message? One reason is that listeners expect a good speaker to provide good delivery. Your unspoken message is also how you express your feelings and emotions to an audience. And ultimately, an audience believes what it *sees* more than what you *say.*

nonverbal communication
Communication other than written or spoken language that creates meaning

Listeners Expect Effective Delivery

In a public-speaking situation, nonverbal elements have an important influence on the audience's perceptions about a speaker's effectiveness. Communication researcher Judee Burgoon and her colleagues have developed a theory called **nonverbal-expectancy theory**. The essence of the theory is this: People have certain expectations as to how you should communicate.[3] If you don't live up to those expectations, your listeners will feel that you have violated their expectations. The theory predicts that if a listener expects you to have effective delivery, and your delivery is poor, you will lose credibility. There is evidence that although many speakers do not deliver speeches effectively, your audience expects a good speech to be well-delivered.

As we have also emphasized, audience members with different cultural backgrounds will hold different assumptions about how a speech should be presented. In our discussion of delivery, we note how the cultural and ethnic background of your audience affects the delivery style your listeners prefer.

What do most people consider effective delivery today? Effective speech delivery for most North American listeners has been described as "platform conversation." When you speak to an audience, strive for a natural, conversational tone. More than 100 years ago, speakers were taught to deliver more formal orations than the style of speaking most people prefer today. When you look at old newsreels of speakers during the early part of the twentieth century, their gestures and movement looked stilted and unnatural, because they were taught to use dramatic, planned gestures. Effective delivery today includes having good eye contact with your listeners. It also includes using appropriate gestures, just as you do in your interpersonal conversations with your friends (but, of course, avoiding distracting mannerisms such as jingling change in your pockets or unconsciously playing with your hair). Effective delivery also means your voice has a natural varied inflection (rather than a droning monotone) and an intensity that communicates you're interested in your listeners.

Of course, different audiences prefer different styles of delivery; there is not one "ideal" style of delivery or set of prescribed gestures that is appropriate for all audiences. If you are speaking to an audience of a thousand people, using a microphone to reach the back of the auditorium, your listeners may expect a more formal delivery style. Your public-speaking class members would probably find it odd if you spoke to them using a formal oratorical style that resembles the way a politician would have addressed a political rally in 1910.

Listeners Make Emotional Connections with the Speaker Through Delivery

Nonverbal behavior is particularly important in communicating feelings, emotions, attitudes, likes, and dislikes to an audience. One researcher found that we communication as little as 7 percent of the emotional impact of a message by the words we use.[4] About 38 percent hinges on such qualities of voice as inflection, intensity, or loudness, and 55 percent hinges on our facial expressions. Generalizing from these findings, we may say that we communicate approximately 93 percent of emotional meaning nonverbally. Although some scholars question whether these findings can be applied to all communication settings, the research does suggest that the manner of delivery provides important information about the speaker's feelings and emotions. Audience expectations can help you match the amount of emotional expression you exhibit to your listeners.

nonverbal-expectancy theory
A communication theory that suggests people have expectations as to how communication should be expressed. If expectations are violated, listeners will feel less favorable toward the communicator of the message

In addition, your delivery will affect your listeners' emotional responses to you. A recent study found that when a speaker's delivery was effective, the audience felt greater pleasure and had a more positive emotional response than when the same speaker had poor delivery.[5] In addition to these stronger emotional responses, listeners seemed to understand speakers better and believe them more when their delivery was good. Clearly, if you want your audience to respond positively to both you and your message, it pays to polish your delivery.

Listeners Believe What They See

"I'm very glad to speak with you tonight," drones the speaker in a monotone, eyes glued to his notes. His audience probably does not believe him. When our nonverbal delivery contradicts what we say, people generally believe the nonverbal message. In this case, the speaker is communicating that he's *not* glad to be talking to this audience.

We usually believe nonverbal messages because they are more difficult to fake. Although we can monitor certain parts of our nonverbal behavior, it is difficult to control all of it consciously. Research suggests that a person trying to deceive someone may speak in a higher vocal pitch, at a slower rate, and with more pronunciation mistakes than normal.[6] Blushing, sweating, and changed breathing patterns also often belie our stated meaning. As the saying goes, "What you do speaks so loud, I can't hear what you say."

 Methods of Delivery

The style of delivery you choose will influence your nonverbal behaviors. There are four basic methods of delivery from which a speaker can choose: manuscript speaking, memorized speaking, impromptu speaking, and extemporaneous speaking. Let's consider each in some detail.

Manuscript Speaking

You have a speech to present and are afraid you will forget what you have prepared to say. So you write your speech and then read it to your audience.

Speech teachers frown on this approach, particularly for public-speaking students. Reading is usually a poor way to deliver a speech. Although it may provide some assurance of not forgetting the speech, **manuscript speaking** is rarely done well enough to be interesting. You have probably attended a lecture that was read and wondered, "Why doesn't he just make a copy of the speech for everyone in the audience rather than reading it to us?"

However, some speeches should be read. One advantage of reading from a manuscript is that you can choose words very carefully when dealing with a sensitive and critical issue. The president of the United States, for example, often finds it useful to have his remarks carefully scripted. There are times, however, when it is impossible to have a manuscript speech at hand. Minutes following the September 11, 2001, attacks on the World Trade Center and the Pentagon, George W. Bush offered unscripted comments to reporters, in which he promised to hunt down "those folks who committed this act."

manuscript speaking
Reading a speech from a written text

Three days later, he spoke more eloquently from a manuscript at the Washington National Cathedral, where he said, "We are here in the middle hour of our grief. So many have suffered so great a loss, and today we express our nation's sorrow."[7] His prepared comments helped comfort an emotionally bruised nation.

When possible, during times of crisis, statements to the press by government or business leaders should be carefully crafted rather than tossed off casually. An inaccurate or misspoken statement could have serious consequences.

Roger Ailes, a media consultant to Republican presidents and governors, suggests that if you do have to read from a manuscript, to ensure maximum eye contact, you should type your speech in short, easy-to-scan phrases on the upper two thirds of the paper so that you do not have to look too far down into your notes.[8] Make eye contact at the ends of sentences. He also recommends that you should not read a speech too quickly. Use your index finger to keep your place in the manuscript so you don't lose your place.

The key to giving an effective manuscript speech is to sound as though you were *not* giving a manuscript speech. Speak with vocal variation—vary the rhythm, inflection, and pace of your delivery. Be familiar enough with your manuscript that you can make as much eye contact with your audience as possible. Use gestures and movement to add interest and emphasis to your message.

Memorized Speaking

"All right," you think, "since reading a speech is hard to pull off, I'll write my speech out word for word and then memorize it." You're pretty sure that no one will be able to tell, because you won't be using notes. **Memorizing** your speech also has the advantage of allowing you to have maximum eye contact with the audience. But most memorized speeches *sound* stiff, stilted, and overrehearsed. The inherent differences between speaking and writing are evident in a memorized speech, just as they can be heard in a manuscript speech. You also run the risk of forgetting parts of your speech and awkwardly searching for words in front of your audience. You also won't be able to make on-the-spot adaptations to your listeners if your speech is memorized. For these reasons, speech teachers do not encourage their students to memorize speeches for class presentation.

If you are accepting an award, introducing a speaker, making announcements, or delivering other brief remarks, however, a memorized delivery style is sometimes acceptable. But as with manuscript speaking, you must take care to make your presentation sound lively and interesting.

Impromptu Speaking

You have undoubtedly already delivered many **impromptu** presentations. Your response to a question posed by a teacher in class, or an unrehearsed rebuttal to a comment made by a colleague during a meeting, are examples of impromptu presentations. The impromptu method is often described as "thinking on your feet" or "speaking off the cuff." The advantage of impromptu speaking is that you can speak informally, maintaining direct eye contact with the audience. But unless a speaker is extremely talented or has learned and practiced the techniques of impromptu speaking, the speech itself will be unimpressive. An impromptu speech usually lacks logical organization and thorough research. There are times, of course, when you may be

memorized speaking
Delivering a speech word-for-word from memory without using notes

impromptu speaking
Delivering a speech without advance preparation

called on to speak without advance knowledge of the invitation or when something goes awry in your efforts to deliver your planned message. This was the case when former President Clinton was delivering his first State of the Union address in 1993 and the teleprompter scrolled the wrong text of his speech for seven minutes. What did he do as millions of people watched on television? He kept going. Drawing on his years of speaking experience, he continued to speak; no one watching knew about the error until afterward.

Clinton's efforts were somewhat more successful than was the performance given some years earlier by a friend of your authors, who is a Fellow at Cambridge University in England. Given the responsibility of conferring degrees on the graduates of his college, he had carefully memorized his Latin text, but found to his horror that his mind went blank when the moment arrived. Sheepishly, he admits, "I got through it by mumbling some bits of Latin I could remember, but I think I said something like 'Blessed be the fruit of thy womb.'"

What is the lesson from these examples? If you know you will be giving a speech, prepare and rehearse it. Don't just make mental notes or assume that you will find the words when you need it. It was Mark Twain who said, "A good impromptu speech takes about three weeks to prepare."

Reverend Jesse Jackson is known for his skill as an impromptu speaker. It's been reported that he got a *D* in his preaching class because he refused to write his sermons out word for word as his professor requested. He was able to deliver impromptu orations that skillfully and powerfully moved listeners to respond to his message. When he was to follow Jackson's charismatically delivered speech, Martin Luther King, Jr., once allegedly developed a sudden case of laryngitis.[9] The Reverend Jackson certainly has speaking talent, but he also uses principles and skills that you can use to enhance your impromptu speaking ability. For the times when you may be called on to deliver an improvised or impromptu speech, the following guidelines can help ease you through it.

- *Consider your audience.* Just as you have learned to do in other speaking situations, when you are called on for impromptu remarks, think first of your audience. Who are the members of your audience? What are their common characteristics and interests? What do they know about your topic? What do they expect you to say? What is the occasion of your speech? A quick mental check of these questions will help ensure that even impromptu remarks are audience-centered.

- *Be brief.* When you are asked to deliver an off-the-cuff speech, your audience knows the circumstances and will not expect or even want a lengthy discourse. One to three minutes is a realistic time frame for most impromptu situations. Some spur-of-the-moment remarks, such as press statements, may be even shorter.

- *Organize!* Even off-the-cuff remarks need not falter or ramble. Effective impromptu speakers still organize their ideas into an introduction, body, and conclusion. Consider organizing your points using a simple organizational strategy such as chronological order or a topical pattern. A variation on the chronological pattern is to use the past, present, future model of addressing an issue. This pattern is well known to students who compete in impromptu speaking contests. The speaker organizes the impromptu speech by discussing (1) what has happened in the past, (2) what is happening now, and (3) what may happen in the future.

- *Speak honestly, but with reserve, from personal experience and knowledge.* Because there is no opportunity to conduct any kind of research before delivering an impromptu speech, you will have to speak from your own experience and knowledge. Remember, audiences almost always respond favorably to personal illustrations, so use any appropriate and relevant ones that come to mind. Of course, the more knowledge you have about the subject to be discussed, the easier it will be to speak about it off the cuff. But do *not* make up information or provide facts or figures about which you are not certain. An honest "I don't know" or a very brief statement is more appropriate.

- *Be cautious.* No matter how much knowledge you have, if your subject is at all sensitive or your information is classified, be careful when discussing it during your impromptu speech. If asked about a controversial topic, give an honest but non-committal answer. You can always elaborate later, but you can never take back something rash you have already said. It is better to be cautious than sorry!

Research shows that an effective, emotional delivery can often send a stronger message than the speaker's words alone could send. This speaker is emotionally adamant that his problems must be addressed.

[© Syracuse Newspapers/Michelle Gabel/The Image Works]

Extemporaneous Speaking

If you are not reading from a manuscript, reciting from memory, or speaking impromptu, what's left? **Extemporaneous speaking** is the approach most communication teachers recommend for most situations. When delivering a speech extemporaneously, you speak from a written or memorized general outline, but you do not have the exact wording in front of you or in memory. You have rehearsed the speech so that you know key ideas and their organization, but not to the degree that the speech sounds memorized. An extemporaneous style is conversational; it gives your audience the impression that the speech is being created as they listen to it, and to some extent it is. Audiences prefer to hear something live rather than something canned. Even though you can't tell the difference between a taped or live performance when it is broadcast on TV, you would probably prefer seeing it live. Added interest and excitement is associated with seeing something happening now. An extemporaneous speech sounds live rather than as though it were prepared yesterday or weeks ago. The extemporaneous method reflects the advantages of a well-organized speech delivered in an interesting and vivid manner.

You develop an extemporaneous style by first rehearsing your speech, using many notes or perhaps looking at your full-content outline. As you continue to rehearse, try to rely less on your notes, but don't try to memorize your message word for word. After going over your speech a few times, you find that you have internalized the overall structure of the speech, although the exact way you express your ideas may vary. You rely less on your notes and focus more on adapting your message to your listeners. The final draft of your speaking notes may be an abbreviated outline or a few key words and essential facts or statistics that you want to remember.

extemporaneous speaking
Speaking from a written or memorized speech outline without having memorized the exact wording of the speech

RECAP: METHODS OF DELIVERY

MANUSCRIPT	Reading your speech from a prepared text
MEMORIZED	Giving a speech from memory without using notes
IMPROMPTU	Delivering a speech without preparing in advance
EXTEMPORANEOUS	Knowing the major ideas, which have been outlined; the exact wording has not been memorized

Characteristics of Effective Delivery

You have learned the importance of effective delivery and have identified four methods of delivery. You now know that for most speaking situations, you should strive for a conversational style. But you still may have a number of specific questions about enhancing the effectiveness of your delivery. Typical concerns include "What do I do with my hands?" "Is it all right to move around while I speak?" "How can I make my voice sound interesting?" Although these concerns may seem overwhelming, presenting a well-prepared and well-rehearsed speech is the best antidote to jitters about delivery. Practice and focus on communicating your message to your audience are vital for effective communication and great for your confidence. To help answer specific questions about presenting a speech, we consider seven major categories of nonverbal behavior that affect delivery: eye contact, gestures, movement, posture, facial expression, vocal delivery, and personal appearance.

Eye Contact

Of all the delivery features discussed in this chapter, the most important one in a public-speaking situation for North Americans is eye contact. Eye contact with your audience opens communication, makes you more believable, and keeps your audience interested. Each of these functions contributes to the success of your delivery. Eye contact also provides you with feedback about how your speech is coming across.

Making eye contact with your listeners clearly shows that you are ready to talk to them. Most people start a conversation by looking at the person they are going to talk to. The same process occurs in public speaking.

Once you've started talking, continued eye contact lets you know how your audience is responding to your speech. You don't need to look at your listeners continuously. As the need arises, you should certainly look at your notes, but also look at your listeners frequently, just to see what they're doing.

Most listeners will think you are capable and trustworthy if you look them in the eye. Several studies document a relationship between eye contact and increased speaker credibility.[10] Speakers with less than 50 percent eye contact are considered unfriendly, uninformed, inexperienced, and even dishonest by their listeners.

Another study showed that those audience members who had more than 50 percent eye contact with their speaker performed better in postspeech tests than did those who had less than 50 percent eye contact.[11] However, not all people from all cultures prefer the same amount of direct eye contact when listening to someone talk. In interpersonal contexts, people from Asian cultures, for example, prefer less direct eye contact when communicating with others.

Most audiences in the United States prefer that you establish eye contact with them even before you open your speech with your attention-catching introduction. When it's your time to speak, walk to the lectern (or the front of the audience if you're not using a lectern), pause briefly, and look at your audience before you say anything. Eye contact nonverbally sends the message, "I am interested in you; tune me in; I have something I want to share with you." You should have your opening sentence well enough in mind that you can deliver it without looking at your notes or away from your listeners.

Establish eye contact with the entire audience, not just with the front row or only one or two people. Look to the back and front and from side to side of your audience, selecting an individual to focus on and then moving on to someone else. You need not rhythmically move your head back and forth like a lighthouse beacon. It's best not to establish a predictable pattern for your eye contact. Look at individuals, establishing person-to-person contact with them—not so long that it will make a listener feel uncomfortable, but long enough to establish the feeling that you are talking directly to that individual. *Don't* look over your listeners' heads; establish eye-to-eye contact.

RECAP | **BENEFITS OF EYE CONTACT**

Lets your audience know you are interested in them and that you want to talk to them

Permits you to monitor audience reaction to your message in order to determine whether your audience is responding to you

Establishes your credibility

Helps your audience maintain interest and remember more of your message

 Gestures

The next time you have a conversation with someone, notice how both of you use your hands and bodies to communicate. Important points are emphasized with gestures. You also gesture to indicate places, to enumerate items, and to describe objects. Gestures have the same functions for public speakers. Yet many people who gesture easily and appropriately in the course of everyday conversations aren't sure what to do with their hands when they find themselves in front of an audience.

There is evidence that gestures vary from culture to culture. When he was mayor of New York City during the 1930s and 1940s, Fiorello La Guardia, fluent in Yiddish and Italian as well as English, would speak the language appropriate for each audience. One researcher studied old newsreels of the mayor and discovered that with the sound turned off viewers could still identify the language spoken by the mayor. How? When speaking English, he used minimal gestures. When speaking Italian, he used broad, sweeping gestures. And when speaking Yiddish, he used short and choppy hand movements.

Cultural expectations can help you make decisions about your approach to using gestures. Listeners from Japan and China, for example, prefer a quieter, less flamboyant use of gestures. When one of your authors spoke in England, several listeners noted the use of "typical American gestures and movement." British listeners seem to prefer that the speaker stay behind a lectern and use relatively few gestures. Other Europeans agree they can spot an American speaker because Americans typically are more animated in their use of gestures, movement, and facial expressions than are European speakers.

Public-speaking teachers often observe several unusual, inappropriate, and unnatural gestures among their students. Common problems include keeping your hands behind your back in a "parade rest" pose. We are not suggesting that you never put your hands behind your back, only that standing at parade rest during an entire speech looks awkward and unnatural and may distract your audience.

Another common position is standing with one hand on the hip in a "broken wing" pose. Worse than the "broken wing" is both hands resting on the hips in a "double broken wing." The speaker looks as though he or she might burst into a rendition of "I'm a Little Teapot." Again, we are not suggesting that you should never place your hands on your hips, only that to hold that one pose throughout a speech looks unnatural and will keep you from using other gestures.

Few poses are more awkward-looking than when a speaker clutches one arm, as if grazed by a bullet. The audience half expects the speaker to call out reassuringly, "Don't worry, Ma; it's only a flesh wound." Similarly, keeping your hands in your pockets can make you look as if you were afraid to let go of your change or your keys.

Some students clasp their hands and let them drop in front of them in a distracting "fig leaf clutch." Gestures can distract your audience in various other ways as well. Grasping the lectern until your knuckles turn white or just letting your hands flop around without purpose or control does little to help you communicate your message.

FUNCTIONS OF GESTURES. If you don't know what to do with your hands, think about the message you want to communicate. As in ordinary conversation, your hands should simply help emphasize or reinforce your verbal message. Specifically, note the following ways in which your gestures can lend strength to what you have to say: (1) repeating, (2) contradicting, (3) substituting, (4) complementing, (5) emphasizing, and (6) regulating.

- **Repeating.** Gestures can help you repeat your verbal message. For example, you can say, "I have three major points to talk about today," while holding up three fingers. Or you can describe an object as 12 inches long while holding your hands about a foot apart. Repeating what you say through nonverbal means can reinforce your message.

- **Contradicting.** Because your audience will sooner believe what you communicate nonverbally than verbally, monitor your gestures to make sure that you are not contradicting what you say. It is difficult to convey an image of control and confidence by using flailing gestures and awkward poses. You don't want to display behavior that will conflict with your intended image or message, nor do you want to appear stiff and self-conscious. So the crucial thing to keep in mind while monitoring your own behavior is to *stay relaxed*.

- **Substituting.** Not only can your behavior reinforce or contradict what you say, but your gestures can also substitute for your message. Without uttering a word, you can hold up the palm of your hand to calm a noisy crowd. Flashing two fingers to form a *V* for victory or raising a clenched fist are other common examples of how gestures can substitute for a verbal message.

● **Complementing.**   Gestures can also add further meaning to your verbal message. A politician who declines to comment on a reporter's question while holding up her hands to augment her verbal refusal, uses her gesture to complement or provide further meaning to her verbal message.

● **Emphasizing.**   You can give emphasis to what you say by using an appropriate gesture. A shaking fist or a slicing gesture with one or both hands helps emphasize a message. So does pounding your fist into the palm of your hand. Other gestures can be less dramatic but still lend emphasis to what you say. You should try to allow your gestures to arise from the content of your speech and your emotions.

● **Regulating.**   Gestures can also regulate the exchange between you and your audience. If you want the audience to respond to a question, you can extend both palms to invite a response. During a question-and-answer session, your gestures can signal when you want to talk and when you want to invite others to do so.

USING GESTURES EFFECTIVELY   Turn-of-the-century elocutionists taught their students how to gesture to communicate specific emotions or messages. Today teachers of speech act differently. Rather than prescribe gestures for specific situations, they feel it is more useful to offer suitable criteria (standards) by which to judge effective gestures, regardless of what is being said. Here are some guidelines to consider when working on your delivery.

● *Stay natural.* Gestures should be *relaxed,* not tense or rigid. Your gestures should flow with your message. Avoid sawing or slashing through the air with your hands unless you are trying to emphasize a particularly dramatic point. The pounding fist or raised forefinger in hectoring style will not necessarily enhance the quality of your performance.

● *Be definite.* Gestures should appear *definite* rather than as accidental brief jerks of your hands or arms. If you want to gesture, go ahead and gesture. Avoid minor hand movements that will be masked by the lectern.

● *Use gestures that are consistent with your message.* Gestures should be *appropriate* for the verbal content of your speech. If you are excited, gesture more vigorously. But remember that prerehearsed gestures that do not naturally arise from what you are trying to say are likely to appear awkward and stilted.

● *Vary your gestures.* Strive for *variety* and versatility in your use of gesture. Try not to use just one hand or one all-purpose gesture. Gestures can be used for a variety of purposes, such as enumerating, pointing, describing, and symbolizing an idea or concept (such as clasping your hands together to suggest agreement or a coming-together process).

● *Don't overdo it.* Gestures should be *unobtrusive;* your audience should focus not on the beauty or appropriateness of your gestures but on your message. Your purpose is to communicate a message to your audience, not to perform for your listeners in such a way that your delivery receives more attention than your message.

- *Coordinate gestures with what you say.* Gestures should be *well timed* to coincide with your verbal message. When you announce that you have three major points, your gesture of enumeration should occur simultaneously with your utterance of the word *three*. It would be poor timing to announce that you have three points, pause for a second or two, and then hold up three fingers.

- *Make your gestures appropriate to your audience and situation. Gestures must be adapted to the audience.* In more formal speaking situations, particularly when speaking to a large audience, bolder, more sweeping, and more dramatic gestures are appropriate. A small audience in a less formal setting calls for less formal gestures.

In summary, keep one important principle in mind: Use gestures that work best for you. Don't try to be someone that you are not. Jesse Jackson's style may work for him, but you are not Jesse Jackson. Your gestures should fit your personality. It may be better to use no gestures—just comfortably put your hands at your side—rather than to use awkward, distracting gestures or to try to counterfeit someone else's gestures. Your nonverbal delivery should flow from *your* message.

RECAP **EFFECTIVE GESTURES**

The Most Effective Gestures Are . . .

Natural and relaxed	Unobtrusive
Definite	Coordinated with what you say
Consistent with your message	Appropriate to your audience and situation
Varied	

Movement

Should you walk around during your speech, or should you stay in one place? If there is a lectern, should you stand behind it, or would it be acceptable to stand in front of it or to the side? Is it all right to sit down while you speak? Can you move among the audience, as Oprah Winfrey does on her TV talk show? You may well find yourself pondering one or more of these questions while preparing for your speeches. The following discussion may help you answer them.

Elizabeth Dole made headlines at the 1996 Republican National Convention not just because of what she said, but because of how she said it. When she delivered a speech in tribute to her husband, presidential nominee Senator Robert Dole, she walked among her audience on the floor of the convention hall. As she mentioned a person who had influenced Senator Dole's life, she walked over to that person and used him or her as a living visual aid. Her speech was effective because there was a purpose for her movement—it wasn't just random pacing through the audience.

You may want to move purposefully about while delivering your speech, but take care that your movement does not detract from your message. If the audience focuses on your movement rather than on what you are saying, it is better to stand still. No movement is better than distracting movement. In short, your movement should be consistent with the verbal content of your message. It should make sense rather than appear as aimless wandering.

As you consider incorporating movement into your speech, also be mindful of physical barriers that exist between you and your audience. Barriers such as a lectern, rows of chairs, a chalkboard, an overhead projector, or other audiovisual aids may act as obstacles between you and your audience. If physical barriers make you feel too far removed from your audience, move closer. Several studies suggest that in North America the most effective classroom teachers stand closer to their students.[12] They move out from behind their desks so they can have more eye contact with their students. Apparently this physical proximity enhances learning by increasing students' motivation to learn and also by creating a positive emotional response from students.[13]

You may also signal the beginning of a new idea or major point in your speech with movement. As you move into a transition statement or change from a serious subject to a more humorous one, movement can be a good way to signal that your approach to the speaking situation is changing.

Your use of movement during your speech should make sense to your listeners. Avoid random pacing and overly dramatic gestures. Temper our advice about proximity and other delivery variables by adapting to the cultural expectations of your audience.

Posture

Although few formal studies of posture in relation to public speaking have been conducted, there is evidence that the way you carry your body communicates significant information. One study even suggests that your stance can reflect on your credibility as a speaker.[14] Slouching across the lectern, for example, does not project an image of vitality and interest in your audience.

Whereas your face and voice play the major role in communicating a specific emotion, your posture communicates the *intensity* of that emotion. If you are happy, your face and voice reflect your happiness; your posture communicates the intensity of your joy.

Since the days of the elocutionists, few speech teachers or public-speaking texts have advocated specific postures for public speakers. Today we believe that the specific stance you adopt should come about naturally, as a result of what you have to say, the environment, and the formality or informality of the occasion. For example, during a very informal presentation it may be perfectly appropriate as well as comfortable and natural to sit on the edge of a desk. Most speech teachers, however, do not encourage students to sit while delivering classroom speeches. In general, avoid slouched shoulders, shifting from foot to foot, or drooping your head. Your posture should not call attention to itself. Instead, it should reflect your interest in the speaking event and your attention to the task at hand.

Facial Expression

Media experts today doubt that Abraham Lincoln would have survived as a politician in our appearance-conscious age of telegenic politicians. His facial expression, according to those who saw him, seemed wooden and unvaried.

Your face plays a key role in expressing your thoughts, and especially your emotions and attitudes.[15] Your audience sees your face before they hear what you are going to say. Thus, you have an opportunity to set the emotional tone for your message before you start speaking. We are not advocating that you adopt a phony smile that looks insincere and plastered on your face, but a pleasant facial expression helps establish a positive emotional climate. Your facial expression should naturally vary to be consistent with your message. Present somber news with a more serious expression. To communicate interest in your listeners, keep your expression alert and friendly.

Although we are technically capable of producing thousands of different facial expressions, we most often express only six primary emotions: happiness, anger, surprise, sadness, disgust, and fear. But when we speak to others, our faces are a blend of expressions rather than communicators of a single emotion. According to cross-cultural studies by social psychologist Paul Ekman, the facial expressions of these emotions are virtually universal, so even a culturally diverse audience will be able to read your emotional expressions clearly. When you rehearse your speech, consider standing in front of a mirror or, better yet, videotape yourself practicing your speech. Note whether you are allowing your face to help communicate the emotional tone of your thoughts.

Vocal Delivery

Have you ever listened to a DJ on the radio and imagined what he or she looked like, only later to see a picture and have your image of the announcer drastically altered? Vocal clues play an important part in creating the impression we have of a speaker. Based on vocal clues alone, you make inferences about a person's age, status, occupation, ethnic origin, income, and a variety of other matters. As a public speaker, your voice is one of your most important delivery tools in conveying your ideas to your audience. Your credibility as a speaker and your ability to communicate your ideas clearly to your listeners will in large part depend on your vocal delivery.

Vocal delivery includes pitch, rate, volume, pronunciation, articulation, pauses, and general variation of the voice. A speaker has at least two key vocal obligations to an audience: Speak to be understood, and speak with vocal variety to maintain interest.

SPEAKING TO BE UNDERSTOOD   To be understood, you need to consider four aspects of vocal delivery: volume, articulation, dialect, and pronunciation.

- Volume.   The fundamental purpose of your vocal delivery is to speak loudly enough so that your audience can hear you. The **volume** of your speech is determined by the amount of air you project through your larynx, or voice box. More air equals more volume of sound. Your diaphragm, a muscle in your upper abdomen, helps control sound volume by increasing air flow from your lungs through your voice box. If you put your hands on your diaphragm and say, "Ho-ho-ho," you will feel the muscles contracting and the air being forced out of your lungs. Breathing from your diaphragm rather than increasing air flow through your lungs alone can increase the volume of sound as well as enhance the quality of your voice.

- Articulation.   The process of producing speech sounds clearly and distinctly is **articulation.** In addition to speaking loudly enough, say your words so that your audience can understand them. Without distinct enunciation or articulation of the sounds that make up words, your listeners may not understand you or may fault you for simply not knowing how to speak clearly and fluently. Here are some commonly misarticulated words:[16]

volume
The softness or loudness of a speaker's voice

articulation
The process of producing speech sounds clearly and distinctly

Dint	*instead of*	didn't
Lemme	*instead of*	let me
Mornin	*instead of*	morning
Seeya	*instead of*	see you
Soun	*instead of*	sound
Wanna	*instead of*	want to
Wep	*instead of*	wept
Whadayado	*instead of*	what do you do

Many errors in articulation result from a simple flaw: laziness. It takes effort to articulate speech sounds clearly. We often get in a hurry to express our idea, or we just get into the habit of mumbling, slurring, and abbreviating. Such speech flaws may not keep your audience from understanding you, but poor enunciation does reflect on your credibility as a speaker.

The best way to improve your articulation of sounds is first to identify words or phrases that you have a tendency to slur or chop. Once you have identified them, practice saying the words correctly. Make sure you can hear the difference between the improper and proper pronunciation. A speech teacher can help you check your articulation.

● **Dialect.**　Most newscasters in North America use what is called standard American pronunciation and do not typically have a strong dialect. A **dialect** is a consistent style of pronouncing words that is common to an ethnic group or a geographic region such as the South, New England, or upper Midwest. In the southern part of the United States, people prolong some vowel sounds when they speak. And in the northern Midwest, the word "about" sometimes sounds a bit like "aboat." It took a bit of adjustment for many U.S. citizens to get used to President John Kennedy's Bostonian pronunciation of Cuba as "Cuber" or Harvard as "Haaavahd." Lyndon Johnson's Texas twang was a sharp contrast to America's ears in comparison to Kennedy's New England sound. And George W. Bush's Texas lilt also contrasts with the slight southern drawl of his predecessor, Bill Clinton.

Are dialects detrimental to effective communication with an audience? Although a speaker's dialect may pigeonhole that person as being from a certain part of the country, it won't necessarily result in audience loss of comprehension of the information unless the dialect is so pronounced that the listener can't understand what is being said. Research does suggest, however, that listeners tend to prefer a dialect similar to their own pronunciation style.[17] Many well-known and effective speakers have a pronounced dialect; Jesse Jackson, Bill Clinton, Jesse Helms, Billy Graham, and Garrison Keillor are all known for their rhetorical skill and also have some degree of a regional dialect. We don't recommend that you eliminate a mild dialect; but if your word pronunciation is significantly distracting to your listeners, consider modifying your dialect.

Radically changing a dialect is difficult and time consuming. The four elements of a dialect include intonation pattern, vowel production, consonant production, and speaking rate. A typical North American intonation pattern is predominantly a rising and falling pattern. The pattern looks something like this:

"Good ^morn ing.　How ^are you?"

Intonation patterns of other languages, such as Hindi, may remain on almost the exact same pitch level; native North American ears find the monotone pitch distracting.

dialect
A consistent style of pronouncing words that is common to an ethnic group or geographic region

A second element in any dialect is the way vowel sounds are produced. Many people who speak English as a second language often clip or shorten the vowel sounds, which can make comprehension more challenging. Stretching or elongating vowels within words can be a useful skill for such speakers to develop. If this is a vocal skill you need to cultivate, consider taping your speech and then compare it with the standard American pronunciation you hear on TV or radio.

Consonants in language, the third element in vocal dialects, vary depending on which language you are speaking. It is sometimes difficult to produce clear consonants that are not overdone. Consonants that are so soft as to be almost unheard may produce a long blur or unintelligible sound rather than a crisply articulated sound.

A fourth and final element in vocal dialect is the speaking rate. People for whom English is not their first language sometimes speak at too fast a rate in the hope this will create the impression of being very familiar with English. Slowing the rate just a bit often enhances comprehension for native English speakers listening to someone less familiar with English pronunciation. A rate that is too fast also contributes to problems with clipped vowels, soft or absent consonants, and an intonation pattern that is on one pitch level rather than comfortably varied.

● Pronunciation.   Whereas articulation is concerned with the production of sounds, **pronunciation** concerns the sounds that form words in standard English. Mispronouncing words can also detract from a speaker's credibility. Often, however, we are not aware that we are not using standard pronunciation unless someone points it out.

Some speakers reverse a speech sound by saying "aks" instead of "ask." Some allow an *r* sound to intrude into some words, saying "warsh" instead of "wash," or leaving out sounds in the middle of a word by saying "actchally" instead of "actually" or "Febuary" instead of "February." Some speakers also accent syllables in nonstandard ways; they say "po′ lice" instead of "police" or "um′ brella" rather than "umbrella."

If English is not your native language, you may have to spend extra time working on your pronunciation and articulation. Here are two useful tips to help you. First, make an effort to prolong your vowel sounds. Speeeeak tooooo prooooolooooong eeeeeeach vooooooowel sooooooound yooooooooou maaaaaaaake. Second, to reduce choppy-sounding word pronunciation, blend the end of one word into the beginning of the next. Make your speech flow from one word to the next, instead of separating it into individual, bite-size chunks of sound.[18]

SPEAKING WITH VARIETY   To speak with variety is to vary your pitch, rate, and pauses. It is primarily through the quality of our voices, as well as our facial expressions, that we communicate whether we are happy, sad, bored, or excited. If your vocal clues suggest that you are bored with your topic, your audience will probably be bored also. Appropriate variation in vocal pitch and rate as well as appropriate use of pauses can add zest to your speech and help maintain audience attention.

● Pitch.   Vocal **pitch** is how high or low your voice sounds. You can sing because you can change the pitch of your voice to produce a melody. Lack of variation in pitch has been consistently identified as one of the most distracting characteristics of ineffective speakers. A monotone is boring.

Everyone has a habitual pitch. This is the range of your voice during normal conversation. Some people have a habitually high pitch, whereas others have a low pitch. The pitch of your voice is determined by how fast the folds in your vocal cords vibrate.

pronunciation
The ability to use the proper sounds to form words clearly and accurately

pitch
How high or low your voice sounds

The faster the vibration, the higher the pitch. Male vocal folds open and close approximately 100 to 150 times each second; female vocal folds vibrate about 200 times per second, thus giving them a higher vocal pitch.

Your voice has **inflection** when you raise or lower the pitch as you pronounce words or sounds. Your inflection helps determine the meaning of your utterances. A surprised "ah!" sounds different from a disappointed "ah" or "ah?" Your vocal inflection is thus an important indicator of your emotions and gives clues as to how to interpret your speech.

In some cultures, vocal inflection plays a major role in helping people interpret the meaning of words. For example, Thai, Vietnamese, and Mandarin Chinese languages purposely use such inflections as monotone, low, falling, high, and rising.[19] If you are a native speaker of a language in which pitch influences meaning, be mindful that listeners do not expect this in many Western languages, although all languages rely on inflection to provide nuances of meaning.

The best public speakers vary their inflection considerably. We're not suggesting that you need to imitate a top-forty radio disk jockey when you speak. But variation in your vocal inflection and overall pitch helps you communicate the subtlety of your ideas.

Record your speech as you rehearse, and evaluate your use of pitch and inflection critically. If you are not satisfied with your inflection, consider practicing your speech with exaggerated variations in vocal pitch. Although you would not deliver your speech this way, it may help you explore the expressive options available to you.

- **Rate.** How fast do you talk? Most speakers average between 120 and 180 words per minute. There is no "best" speaking rate. Great speakers use no standard rate of speech that can account for their speaking skill. Daniel Webster purportedly spoke at about 90 words per minute, Franklin Roosevelt 110, President Kennedy a quick-paced 180. Martin Luther King, Jr., started his "I Have a Dream" speech at 92 words a minute and was speaking at 145 during his conclusion.[20] The best rate depends on two factors: your speaking style and the content of your message.

A common fault of many beginning speakers is to deliver a speech too quickly. One symptom of speech anxiety is that you tend to rush through your speech to get it over with. Relying on feedback from others can help you determine whether your rate is too rapid. Tape-recording your message and listening critically to your speaking rate can help you assess whether you are speaking at the proper speed. Fewer speakers have the problem of speaking too slowly, but a turtle-paced speech will almost certainly make it more difficult for your audience to maintain interest. Remember, your listeners can grasp information much faster than you can speak it.

You need not deliver your entire speech at the same pace. It is normal to speak more rapidly when talking about something that excites you. You slow your speaking rate to emphasize key points or ideas. Speaking rate is another tool you can use to add variety and interest to your vocal delivery. The pace of your delivery, however, should make sense in terms of the ideas you are sharing with your listeners.

- *Pauses.* It was Mark Twain who said, "The right word may be effective, but no word was ever as effective as a rightly timed pause." An appropriate pause can often do more to accent your message than any other vocal characteristic. President Kennedy's famous line, "Ask not what your country can do for you; ask what you can do for your country," was effective not only because of its language but also because it was delivered with a pause dividing the two thoughts. Try delivering that line without the pause; it just doesn't have the same power without it.

inflection
The variation of the pitch of your voice

Effective use of pauses, also known as *effective timing*, can greatly enhance the impact of your message. Whether you are trying to tell a joke, a serious tale, or a dramatic story, your use of a pause can determine the effectiveness of your anecdote. Jay Leno, David Letterman, and Chris Rock are masters at timing a punch line. Radio commentator Paul Harvey is known for his flair for vocal delivery. His dramatic pauses serve as meaningful punctuation in his talks.

Beware of the vocalized pause. Many beginning public speakers are uncomfortable with silence and so, rather than pausing where it seems natural and normal, they vocalize sounds such as "umm," "er," "you know," and "ah." We think you will agree that "Ask not ah what your er country can do ah for you; ask you know what you umm can do er for your uh country" just doesn't have the same impact as the unadorned original statement.

One research study counted how frequently certain people use "uhs."[21] Science professors in this study said "uh" about 1.4 times a minute; humanities professors timed in at 4.8 times a minute—almost 3.5 times more. Another psychologist counted the "ums" per minute of well-known speakers. "Wheel of Fortune" host Pat Sajak won the count with almost 10 "ums" per minute; David Letterman was a close second with 8.1. Former President Bill Clinton had only .79 vocalized pauses per minute. Former Vice President of the United States Dan Quayle had only .1. As a public speaker, you don't want to be the "winner" of this contest by having the most "uhs" and "ums" when you speak. Vocalized pauses will annoy your audience and detract from you credibility; eliminate them.

Silence can be an effective tool in emphasizing a particular word or sentence. A well-timed pause coupled with eye contact can powerfully accent your thought. Asking a rhetorical question of your audience such as "How many of you would like to improve your communication skills?" will be more effective if you pause after asking the question rather than rushing into the next thought. Silence is a way of saying to your audience: Think about this for a moment: Pianist Arthur Schnabel said this about silence and music: "The notes I handle not better than many pianists. But the pauses between the notes, ah, that is where the art resides."[22] In speech, too, an effective use of a pause can add emphasis and interest.

lavaliere microphone
A microphone that can be clipped to an article of clothing or worn on a string around your neck

boom microphone
A microphone that is suspended from a bar and moved to follow the speaker; often used in movies and TV

stationary microphone
A microphone attached to a podium or at the end of a rod that is usually located within 12 inches of a speaker's mouth

USING A MICROPHONE "Testing. Testing. One . . . two . . . three. Is this on?" These are not effective, attention-catching opening remarks. Yet countless public speakers have found themselves trying to begin their speech, only to be upstaged by an uncooperative public address system. No matter how polished your gestures or well intoned your vocal cues, if you are inaudible or use a microphone awkwardly, your speech will not have the desired effect.

There are three kinds of microphones, only one of which demands much technique. The **lavaliere microphone** is the clip-on type often used by newspeople and interviewees. Worn on the front of a shirt or dress, it requires no particular care other than not thumping it or accidentally knocking it off. The **boom microphone** is used by makers of movies and TV shows. It hangs over the heads of the speakers and is remote-controlled, so the speaker need not be particularly concerned with it. The third kind of microphone, and the most common, is the **stationary microphone.** This is the type that is most often attached to a lectern, sitting on a desk, or standing on the floor. Generally, the stationary microphones used today are multidirectional. You do not have to remain frozen in front of a stationary mike while delivering your speech. However, you do need to take some other precautions when using one.

First, if you have a fully stationary microphone, rather than one that converts to a hand mike, you will have to remain behind the microphone, with your mouth about the same distance from the mike at all times to avoid distracting fluctuations in the volume of sound. You can turn your head from side to side and use gestures, but you will have to limit other movements.

Second, microphones amplify sloppy habits of pronunciation and enunciation. Therefore, you need to speak clearly and crisply when using a mike.

Third, if you must test a microphone, count or ask the audience whether they can hear you. Blowing on a microphone produces an irritating noise! Do not tap, pound, or shuffle anything near the microphone. These noises, too, will be heard by the audience loudly and clearly. If your notes are on cards, quietly slide them aside as you progress through your speech. Notes on paper are more difficult to handle quietly, but do so with as little shuffling as you can manage.

Finally, when you are delivering your speech, speak directly into the microphone, making sure that your words are appropriately amplified. Some speakers, because they have a microphone in front of them, lower their volume and become inaudible.

Under ideal circumstances, you will be able to practice with the type of microphone you will use before you speak. If you have the chance, figure out where to stand for the best sound quality and how sensitive the mike is to extraneous noise. Practice will accustom you to any voice distortion or echo that might occur so that these sound qualities do not surprise you during your speech.

RECAP | **CHARACTERISTICS OF GOOD VOCAL DELIVERY**

Good Speakers	**Poor Speakers**
Have adequate volume	Speak too softly to be heard
Articulate speech sounds clearly and distinctly	Slur speech sounds
Pronounce words accurately	Mispronounce words
Have varied pitch	Have a monotonous pitch
Vary speaking rate	Consistently speak too fast or too slow
Pause to emphasize ideas	Rarely pause or pause too long

Personal Appearance

Most people have certain expectations about the way a speaker should look. One of your audience analysis tasks is to identify what those audience expectations are. This can be trickier than it might at first seem. John T. Molloy has written two books, *Dress for Success* and *Dress for Success for Women,* in an effort to identify what the well-dressed businessperson should wear. But as some of his own research points out, appropriate wardrobe varies, depending on climate, custom, culture, and audience expectations. It may be improper to wear blue jeans to a business meeting, but it would be just as inappropriate to wear a business suit to a rodeo or grade school picnic.

There is considerable evidence that your personal appearance affects how your audience will respond to you and your message, particularly during the opening moments of your presentation. If you violate their expectations about appearance, you will be less successful in achieving your purpose.

Styles and audience expectations change and are sometimes unpredictable. Therefore, a general rule of thumb to follow is this: When in doubt about what to wear, select something conservative. Also take your cue from your audience. You need not always mirror their appearance, but if you know that the males in your audience wear suits and ties and the females wear dresses, you would be wise to avoid dressing more casually.

Audience Diversity and Delivery

Most of the suggestions we have offered in this chapter assume that your listeners will be expecting a typical North American approach to delivery. However, these assumptions are based on research responses from U.S. college students who are mostly white and college-aged, so our suggestions are not applicable to every audience. As we have stressed throughout the book, you need to adapt your presentation to the expectations of your listeners, especially those from different cultural backgrounds. Consider the following suggestions to help you develop strategies for adapting both your verbal and nonverbal messages for a culturally diverse audience.

AVOID AN ETHNOCENTRIC MIND SET. As you learned in Chapter 5, **ethnocentrism** is an attitude that your own cultural approaches are superior to those from other cultures. When considering how to adapt your delivery style to your audience, try to view different approaches and preferences not as right or wrong but merely as different from your own.

CONSIDER USING A LESS DRAMATIC DELIVERY STYLE FOR PREDOMINANTLY HIGH-CONTEXT LISTENERS. As you recall from Chapter 5, a high-context culture places considerable emphasis on unspoken messages. Therefore, for a high-context audience, you need not be overly expressive. For example, for many Japanese people, a delivery style that included exuberant gestures, overly dramatic facial expressions, and frequent movements might seem overdone. A more subtle, less demonstrative approach would create less "noise" and be more effective.

IF YOU KNOW YOU WILL BE SPEAKING TO A GROUP OF PEOPLE FROM A CULTURAL BACKGROUND DIFFERENT FROM YOUR OWN, TRY TO OBSERVE OTHER SPEAKERS PRESENTING TO THAT AUDIENCE. Talk with people you may know who are familiar with the cultural expectations. Ask specific questions. When speaking in Poland, one of your authors expected the speech to start promptly at 11 A.M. as announced in the program and on posters. By 11:10 it was clear the speech would not begin on time. In Poland, it turns out, all students know about the "academic quarter." This means that most lectures and speeches begin at least 15 minutes, or a quarter hour, after the announced starting time. If your author had asked another professor about the audience's expectations, he would have known this custom in advance. As you observe or talk with speakers who have addressed your target audience, ask the following questions:

What are audience expectations about where I should stand while speaking?

Do listeners like direct eye contact?

Physical ability is just one of the diversity factors that can impact a speaker's delivery style.

[B. Daemmrich/The Image Works]

ethnocentrism
The attitude that one's own culture is superior to others

Address: http://www.ablongman.com/beebe

▼   Evaluating Speaker Delivery

It's one thing to read about speech delivery, but it's quite another to actually see and hear speakers deliver a message. If you have the proper software (like RealAudio, which you can download from the Internet at **<http://www.real.com/>** or RealVideo, which you can access through Timecase at **<http://www.timecast.com/sites/index.html>**), you can hear and sometimes see former and current presidents present political speeches. At some sites you can watch well-known individuals give a presentation; other sites just permit you to listen to a speech.

C-SPAN ON-LINE (REALAUDIO)

This site will let you listen to congressional and other political speeches.

<http://www.broadcast.com/television/>

HISTORY CHANNEL ARCHIVE OF SPEECHES

Each day a famous speech is presented. There is also a RealAudio archive of famous speeches.

<http://www.historychannel.com/speeches/index.html/>

MSU VINCENT VOICE LIBRARY

This site will permit you to hear recordings of U.S. presidents and other famous people in history.

<http://www.mus.edu/vincent/>

WEBCORP HISTORICAL SPEECHES ARCHIVE

You can hear speeches from the 1930s and after. You can also see video presentations from around the time of the Nixon Watergate scandal.

<http://www.webcorp.com/sounds/>

THE CMU PRONOUNCING DICTIONARY

This Website, which can help you with your pronunciation, was developed at Carnegie Mellon University. It uses phonetic markings to help you pronounce words properly.

<http://www.speech.cs.cmu.edu/cgi-bin/cmudict/>

When will the audience expect me to start and stop my talk?

Will listeners find movement and gestures distracting or welcome?

MONITOR YOUR LEVEL OF IMMEDIACY WITH YOUR AUDIENCE. Speaker **immediacy** involves how close you are to your listeners, the amount of eye contact you display, and whether you speak from behind or in front of a lectern. This is the immediacy principle: We move closer to things we like; and we move away from things we don't like.[23] North Americans seem to prefer immediacy behaviors from teachers. Some cultures may expect less immediacy; the key is not to violate what listeners expect.[24] When speaking in Japan, for example, we've been told that Japanese audiences don't expect speakers to move from behind a lectern and stand very close to listeners. Even in small seminars, Japanese speakers and teachers typically stay behind the lectern.

MONITOR YOUR EXPRESSION OF EMOTION. Not all cultures interpret and express emotions the same way. People from the Middle East and the Mediterranean are typically more expressive and animated in their conversation than are Europeans.[25] As we noted in Chapter 5, people from a high-context culture—a culture in which nonverbal messages are exceptionally important (such as Japanese or Chinese culture)—place greater emphasis on your delivery of a message than do people from a low-context culture (such as North Americans).[26] No, simply because you may be speaking to a low-context culture—a culture that places a high value on verbal messages—you do not have license to ignore how you deliver a message. Delivery is *always* important. But audience members from a high-context culture will rely heavily on your unspoken message to help them interpret what you are saying.

KNOW THE CODE. Communication occurs when both speaker and listener share the same code system—both verbal and nonverbal. One of your authors became very embarrassed after speaking to a Caribbean audience because he used a circled thumb and finger gesture to signal "OK" to compliment a student. Later he discovered that this was an obscene gesture—like extending a middle finger to a North American audience. Even subtle nonverbal messages communicate feelings, attitudes, and cues about the nature of the relationship between you and your audience, so it is important to avoid gestures or expressions that would offend your listeners.

Although we cannot provide a comprehensive description of each cultural expectation you may face in every educational and professional setting, we can remind you to keep cultural expectations in mind when you rehearse and deliver a speech. We are not suggesting that you totally abandon your own cultural expectations about speech delivery. Rather, we urge you to become sensitive and responsive to cultural differences. There is no universal dictionary of nonverbal meaning, so spend some time asking people who are from the same culture as your prospective audience about what gestures and expressions your audience will appreciate.

Rehearsing Your Speech: Some Final Tips

Just knowing some of the effective characteristics of speech delivery will not make you a better speaker unless you can put these principles into practice. Effective public speaking is a skill that takes practice. Practicing takes the form of rehearsing. As indicated in Figure 13.1, rehearsing your speech helps you prepare to deliver your speech to an audience. The following suggestions can help you make the most of your rehearsal time.

Do you want to make a good grade on your next speech? Research suggests that one of the best predictors of an effective speech is the amount of time you spend preparing and rehearsing your speech; instructors gave higher speech grades to students who spent more time rehearsing their speech; and gave lower speech grades to students who spent less time preparing and rehearsing.[27]

- Finish drafting your speech outline at least two days before your speech performance. The more time you have to work on putting it all together, the better.

- Before you prepare the speaking notes to take with you in front of your audience, rehearse your speech aloud to help determine where you will need notes to prompt yourself.

- Revise your speech as necessary to keep it within the time limits set by your instructor or whoever invited you to speak.

- Prepare your speaking notes. Use whatever system works best for you. Some speakers use pictorial symbols to remind them of a story or an idea. Others use complete sentences or just words or phrases in an outline pattern to prompt them. Most teachers advocate note cards for speaking notes.

- Rehearse your speech standing up so that you can get a feel for your use of gestures as well as your vocal delivery. Do not try to memorize your speech or choreograph specific gestures. As you rehearse, you may want to modify your speaking notes to reflect appropriate changes.

- If you can, present your speech to someone else so you can practice establishing eye contact. Seek feedback from your captive audience about both your delivery and your speech content.

- If possible, tape-record or videotape your speech during the rehearsal stage so that you can observe your vocal and physical mannerisms and make necessary changes. If you don't have a video camera, you may find it useful to practice before a mirror so you can observe your body language—it's low-tech, but it still works.

- Rehearse using all your presentation aids. As we discuss in the next chapter, don't wait until the last minute to plan, prepare, and rehearse with flipcharts, slides, overhead transparencies, or other aids that you will need to manipulate as you speak.

- Your final rehearsals should re-create, as much as possible, the speaking situation you will face. If you will be speaking in a large classroom, find a large classroom in which to rehearse your speech. If your audience will be informally seated in chairs in a semicircle, then this should be the context in which you rehearse your speech. The more realistic the rehearsal, the more confidence you will gain.

- Practice good delivery skills while rehearsing. Remember this maxim: Practice *makes* perfect if practice *is* perfect.

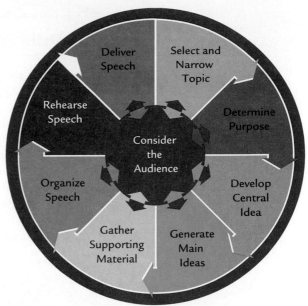

FIGURE 13.1

Rehearsing your speech delivery will help you present your speech with confidence.

Delivering Your Speech

The day arrives and you are ready. Using information about your audience as an anchor, you have developed a speech with an interesting topic and a fine-tuned purpose. Your central idea is clearly identified. You have gathered interesting and relevant supporting material (examples, illustrations, statistics) and organized it well. Your speech has an appropriate introduction, a logically arranged body, and a clear conclusion that nicely summarizes your key theme. You have rehearsed your speech several times; it is not memorized, but you are comfortable with the way you express the major ideas. Your last task is calmly and confidently to communicate with your audience. You are ready to deliver your speech.

As you approach the time for presenting your speech to your audience, consider the following suggestions to help you prepare for your successful performance (see Figure 13.2).

- At the risk of sounding like your mother, we suggest you get plenty of rest before your speech. Last-minute, late-night final preparations can take the edge off your performance. Many professional public speakers also advocate that you watch what you eat before you speak; a heavy meal or too much caffeine can have a negative effect on your performance.

- Review the suggestions in Chapter 2 for becoming a confident speaker. It is normal to have prespeech jitters. But if you have developed a well-organized, audience-centered message on a topic of genuine interest to you, you're doing all the right things to make your speech a success. Remember some of the other tips for developing confidence. Re-create the speech environment when you rehearse. Use deep breathing techniques to help you relax. Also make sure you are especially familiar with your introduction and conclusion. Act calm to feel calm.

- Arrive early for your speaking engagement. If your room is in an unfamiliar location, give yourself plenty of time to find it. As we suggested in Chapter 5, you may want to rearrange the furniture or make other changes in the speaking environment. If you are using audiovisual equipment, check to see that it is working properly and set up your graphic support material carefully. You might even project a slide or two to make sure they are in the tray right side up. Relax before you deliver your message; budget your time so you do not spend your moments before you speak hurriedly looking for a parking place or frantically trying to attend to last-minute details.

- Visualize success. Picture yourself delivering your speech in an effective way. Also, remind yourself of the effort you have spent preparing for your speech. A final mental rehearsal can boost your confidence and help ensure success.

Even though we have identified many time-tested methods for enhancing your speech delivery, keep in mind that speech delivery is an art rather than a science. The manner of your delivery should reflect your personality and individual style.

FIGURE **13.2**

You need to be audience-centered during the final step of the speechmaking process—delivering the speech.

Adapting Your Speech Delivery for Television

You may not plan to be a newscaster or politician whose messages are routinely broadcast to your community or nation on radio or TV, but you may have an opportunity to be interviewed for a news story or find that a speech you deliver is also going to be videotaped. And with the advent of satellite video teleconferences and the increasing use of video software on the Internet, it is becoming increasingly common to have your messages electronically televised to an audience that is not physically present. Should you use a different style of speaking when speaking to the media? When your message is telecast to others, use the principles and skills we've discussed already and keep the following additional specific guidelines in mind:

CONSIDER TONING DOWN GESTURES.   Most newscasters use head nods and facial expressions rather than gestures to help emphasize their points. Keep your hands still, and don't fidget with pens, hair, or clothing. Also, keep your hands away from your face. When you watch someone on TV, it's more like having an interpersonal conversation than hearing a formal speech. Of course, if your primary audience is the live audience when you present your speech, that should be the key audience to which you adapt your style of speaking. But if the target audience is watching on monitors elsewhere, tone down the gestures a bit.

DRESS FOR TV SUCCESS.   White clothing sometimes creates a glare on TV. Men not wearing a jacket may want to wear a light blue rather than a white dress shirt, and women should consider nonwhite clothing. You may also want to avoid black or dark gray—these colors can look too somber. Also avoid large patterns, jangling or shiny jewelry, and overly frilly or complicated necklines. Solid colors look best. The camera can add five to ten pounds to your appearance. No, you don't need to go on a crash diet before a TV appearance, but do wear clothes that make you look and feel your best.

MONITOR YOUR FACIAL EXPRESSIONS.   Also, be aware that TV amplifies facial expressions. Your listeners are seeing your expression up close rather than from a distance, as they would in a live public-speaking context. Therefore, if you have a tendency to use exaggerated or exceptionally dramatic expressions, realize that they will be seen from the camera's perspective rather than from an audience perspective. Smile appropriately, but make sure you're not smiling at inappropriate times. If you are asked a serious question and the camera cuts to you with a big grin on your face, it will appear that you are insensitive to the question.

KEEP YOUR TARGET AUDIENCE IN MIND.   If your message will be broadcast to many people, remind yourself whom you are trying to reach. If you're giving a persuasive presentation, realize that you do not necessarily want to persuade everyone who sees you in "TV land."

KEEP IT SHORT.   If you are giving a political speech or a presentation that you hope will be picked up by the media, realize that you will only be given a few seconds of air time for a news broadcast. Editors look for sound bites.

CHOOSE YOUR WORDS WITH CARE AND STYLE.   The sound bites that often get quoted or broadcast are those phrases that are particularly attention catching or that communicate the essence of your message in a memorable way. Review the strategies for creating drama (omission, inversion, suspension) or creating cadence (parallelism, antithesis, repetition, alliteration) that we presented in Chapter 12. When we recently served as consultants to a political candidate, we were asked to review a draft of her speech declaring her candidacy for the U.S. House of Representatives. The speech was good but had no obvious attention-catching, stylized phrases that would lend themselves to good quotes for the media. We suggested she add some repetition, alliteration, and parallelism. Sure enough, the phrases quoted in the media were those she had taken special care to stylize.

BECOME FAMILIAR WITH THE TECHNOLOGY BEFORE YOU SPEAK.   If you are being taped or broadcast in a studio, be sure to arrive in plenty of time so that you won't have to rush around making last-minute adjustments to your microphone.

Summary

In this chapter, we discussed the importance of effective speech delivery and identified suggestions for enhancing your delivery. The way you deliver your speech is the primary way in which you communicate your thoughts and emotions to an audience. Audiences will believe what they see more readily than what they hear.

Of the four methods of delivery—manuscript, memorized, impromptu, and extemporaneous—the extemporaneous method is most desirable in most situations. Speak from an outline without memorizing the exact words.

We have offered several suggestions for enhancing your delivery. Your gestures and movements should appear natural and relaxed, definite, consistent with your message, varied, unobtrusive, and coordinated with what you say. They should also be appropriate to your audience and situation. Eye contact is the single most important delivery variable: Looking at your audience helps control communication, establishes your credibility, maintains audience interest, and provides feedback about how your speech is coming across. Your facial expressions and vocal cues are the primary ways in which you communicate your feelings and emotions to an audience. How loudly you speak, how clearly you articulate, and how correctly you pronounce the words you use determine how well your audience will understand your thoughts; your vocal pitch, rate, and use of pauses help provide variation to add interest to your talk.

The chapter concluded with several final suggestions for rehearsing and delivering your speech. We suggested that you leave at least two days to focus on your speech delivery and develop your speaking notes. As much as possible, re-create the speech environment when you rehearse. You will be rewarded with a smoother delivery style and more confidence when you deliver your message.

being audience-centered

A Sharper Focus

CONSIDERING YOUR AUDIENCE

▶   Most audiences expect you to present a well-delivered speech, and it's important not to violate their expectations.

▶ Select your delivery style (manuscript, memorized, impromptu, or extemporaneous) to best connect with your audience as well as to achieve your speaking goal.

▶ Your use of gestures can provide cues to your audience as to whether you wish them to respond or ask questions about your message; an open-palm gesture, for example, often suggests you are open for questions or audience interaction.

▶ Speech gestures should not call attention to themselves; audience members should focus on your message rather than the beauty of your gestures.

▶ Rehearse your speech while keeping your audience in mind; imagine that your speaking audience is in front of you as you practice presenting your message.

▶ When presenting a message that will be televised or broadcast to a large audience, consider who constitutes your target audience—the people you most want to influence.

CONSIDERING AUDIENCE DIVERSITY

▶ Use of gestures while speaking varies from culture to culture; for example, listeners from Japan and China usually prefer quieter, less flamboyant gestures.

▶ How close you should stand to listeners depends on cultural expectations of audience members.

▶ If English is not your native language, you may have to spend extra time working on your pronunciation and articulation. Two helpful tips to consider: Prolong your vowel sounds and reduce choppy word pronunciation by blending the end of one word into the beginning of the next word.

▶ In languages such as Thai, Vietnamese, and Mandarin Chinese, vocal inflection plays a major role in affecting how to interpret the meaning of words.

▶ Avoid an ethnocentric mind-set when speaking to people from another culture; don't assume that they prefer the same type of delivery style you do.

▶ In general, consider using a less dramatic delivery style for predominantly high-context listeners; high-context listeners are those who place considerable emphasis on the nonverbal message and other elements of the speaking environment.

▶ If you know that you will be speaking to a group of people from a cultural background different from your own, try to observe other speakers presenting to that audience.

▶ Monitor your level of immediacy (physical closeness, use of lectern) with your audience.

▶ Monitor your expression of emotion; not all cultures interpret and express emotion the same way. People from high-context cultures will likely place greater emphasis on your delivery of a message than will people from low-contact cultures (such as North Americans).

CRITICAL THINKING QUESTIONS

1. Roger was so nervous about his first speech that he practiced his speech on the evolution of the television sitcom again and again. He could have given the

speech in his sleep. He had some great examples; his instructor had praised his outline; but as he gave his speech, he saw his classmates tuning out. What might he have done wrong, and how could he have rescued his speech?

2. Monique has difficulty knowing what to do with her hands when she speaks. Because she is self-conscious about her gestures, she often just puts her hands behind her back. What advice would you give Monique to help her use gestures more effectively?

3. Professor Murray speaks slowly and with a monotone; consequently, many of her students do not like to listen to her music history lectures. What can she do to give her voice some variety?

ETHICAL QUESTIONS

1. Most politicians at the state or national level hire image consultants to help them project the most positive impression of their skills and abilities. Is it ethical to use such consultants, especially if the sole objective is to manipulate constituents into thinking the speaker is more credible than he or she really is?

2. What can listeners do to be less distracted by the delivery and emotional elements of a speaker's message and focus more on the substance or content of the message?

SUGGESTED ACTIVITIES

1. Attend a political campaign speech. Pay particular attention to the politican's delivery. Provide a written critique of the speaker's use of posture, gesture, eye contact, vocal clues, and appearance. If you were a campaign consultant, what advice would you give this politician?

2. While you are rehearsing your next class speech, experiment with using a new delivery style. If you seldom, if ever, use gestures, practice using more gestures than normal. Make a conscious effort to change your vocal delivery style; if you normally have little vocal variation, try delivering your speech with considerable variation or changes in pitch, rate, volume, and intensity. After your experiment with a new delivery style, write a brief report describing what the advantages or disadvantages of the different delivery strategies were.

3. Survey your classmates on what they consider to be the ideal characteristics of effective delivery. Also ask them to describe their cultural and ethnic background. Note whether there are any differences in delivery expectations based on the cultural and ethnic makeup of your audience.

4. Instead of delivering your message to your public-speaking class, imagine that you were going to give a speech to an audience with a different background. Perhaps your mythical audience could be a different age, from a culture different from your own, or of a different mix of ethnic backgrounds. How would you go about determining the audience's expectations for delivery? What conscious decisions would you make about your speech delivery when presenting to this imaginary audience?

5. Audience-centered speakers adapt not only their delivery but also their dress and appearance to avoid creating "noise" and make the best impression on an audience. How would you adapt your dress and appearance when speaking to the following audiences?

Speaking to a local service group such as Rotary, Lions Club, or Kiwanis Club

Making an afternoon presentation at a college dormitory

Giving a talk about tips for being a good public speaker at your mother's business-executive colleagues

Presenting a review of the latest music video at the campus Music Video Club

Receiving an award from the local police department

Speaking at your place of worship

Speaking in your public-speaking class

USING TECHNOLOGY AND MEDIA

1. Videotape one of your speeches, either when you present it in front of your class or during your rehearsal. Critique your tape, focusing on your delivery. Write a 200- to 400-word analysis of your delivery strengths and weaknesses based on the principles and suggestions presented in the chapter.

2. Use a tape recorder to record your speech as you rehearse. Note whether your vocal rate, pitch, quality, and intensity communicate the emotions and feelings you wish to express to your listeners. Also note whether your pronunciation and articulation of words is clear and appropriate.

3. Watch a video or a film featuring public speakers from a culture different from your own. Note differences and similarities in the use of gestures and other nonverbal delivery cues.

4. Listen to well-known TV or radio broadcasters, such as Paul Harvey, Dan Rather, Diane Sawyer, Tom Brokaw, Peter Jennings, and Jane Pauley, noting how they pronounce words. If you are watching the announcer on TV, observe his or her eye contact and facial expression as well. Note whether the nonverbal message is consistent with the verbal message.

"On the Balcony," Oil on canvas. Peter Blake, Tate Gallery London/Art Resource, New York

T he soul never thinks without a picture.

ARISTOTLE

14

Using Presentation Aids

objectives

After studying this chapter you should be able
to do the following:

1. Discuss five ways in which presentation aids
help communicate ideas to an audience.

2. Describe the use of three-dimensional
presentation aids.

3. Identify ways of producing and using two-
dimensional presentation aids.

4. Discuss the uses of audiovisual aids.

5. Identify guidelines for developing presentation
aids.

6. Identify guidelines for using presentation aids.

Frazier walked to the front of the class and dramatically pulled a 2-foot papier-mâché model of a cockroach out of a sack. He attached a string to the "bug" and suspended it from the ceiling. Then he began his speech about how to rid a home of pests. The trouble was, no one listened to Frazier's message. His audience was obsessed with the creature dangling in midair.

The intention was good, but the execution was bad. Frazier had failed to use presentation aids effectively. Presentation aids—especially visual aids—are powerful tools. They can help communicate your ideas with greater clarity and impact than can words alone, but they can also overwhelm your speech. For maximum effectiveness, follow the guidelines described in this chapter.

A **presentation aid** is any object that calls on sight to help your audience understand your point. Charts, photographs, posters, drawings, graphs, slides, movies, and videos are just some of the types of presentation aids that we will discuss. Some of these, such as movies and videos, call on sound as well as sight to help you make your point.

When you are first required to give a speech using presentation aids, you may scratch your head, wondering, "How can I use presentation aids in an informative or persuasive speech? Those kinds of speeches don't lend themselves to visual images." As it happens, almost any speech can benefit from presentation aids. An assignment that requires you to use presentation aids is not as different from other types of speeches as you might at first think. Your general objective is still to inform, persuade, or entertain. The key difference is that you will use supporting material that can be seen, rather than only heard by an audience.

In this chapter, we look at presentation aids as an important communication tool and also examine several kinds. Toward the end of the chapter, we suggest guidelines for using presentation aids in your speeches.

The Value of Presentation Aids

Presentation aids are invaluable to you as an audience-centered speaker. They help your audience *understand* and *remember* your message, communicate your *organization* of ideas, gain and maintain *attention,* and illustrate a *sequence* of events or procedures.[1]

PRESENTATION AIDS ENHANCE UNDERSTANDING. Of your five senses, you learn more from sight than from all the others combined. In fact, it has been estimated that more than 80 percent of all information comes to you through sight.[2] To many people, seeing is believing. We are a visually oriented society. For example, most of us learn the news by seeing it presented on TV. Because your audience is accustomed to visual reinforcement, it is wise to consider how you can increase their understanding of your speech by using presentation aids. For example, in 1997 Defense Secretary William Cohen held up a five-pound bag of sugar during a television interview to illustrate how much of the deadly pathogen anthrax would be needed to kill half the population of Washington, D.C. His simple presentation aid was photographed and published in vir-

presentation aid
Any tangible object or supporting sound—including drawings, charts, graphs, images (video or photography), music—that helps communicate an idea to an audience

tually every newspaper in the country; it clearly helped him drive home his point about the frightening power of anthrax. As the old cliché has it, a picture (or in this case, a bag of sugar) is indeed worth a thousand words.

PRESENTATION AIDS ENHANCE MEMORY. Not only will your audience improve their understanding of your speech, but they will also better remember what you say as a result of visual reinforcement.[3] It is well known that you remember most what you understand best. Researchers estimate that you remember 10 percent of what you read, 20 percent of what you hear, 30 percent of what you see, and 50 percent of what you simultaneously hear and see. In your speech about the languages spoken in Africa, your audience is more likely to remember Arabic, Swahili, and Hausa if you display the words visually, rather than just say them.

PRESENTATION AIDS HELP LISTENERS ORGANIZE IDEAS. Most listeners need help understanding the structure of your speech. Even if you clearly lay out your major points, use effective internal summaries, and make clear transition statements, your listeners will welcome additional help. Listing major ideas on a chart, a poster, or an overhead transparency can add clarity to your talk and help your audience grasp your main ideas. Visually presenting your major ideas during your introduction, for example, can help your audience follow them as you bring them into the body of your speech. You can display key ideas during your conclusion to help summarize your message succinctly.

PRESENTATION AIDS HELP GAIN AND MAINTAIN ATTENTION. Keshia began her speech about poverty in America by showing a photo of the face of an undernourished child. She immediately had the attention of her audience. Chuck began his speech with the flash of his camera to introduce his photography lecture. He certainly alerted his audience at that point. Midway through her speech about the lyrics in rap music, Tomoko not only spoke the words but also displayed a giant poster of the song lyrics so that her audience could read the words and sing along. Presentation aids not only grab the attention of your listeners but also keep their interest when words alone might not.

PRESENTATION AIDS HELP ILLUSTRATE A SEQUENCE OF EVENTS OR PROCEDURES. If your purpose is to inform an audience about a process—how to do something or how something functions—you can do this best through actual demonstrations or with a series of visuals. Whether your objective is instructing people to make a soufflé or to build a greenhouse, demonstrating the step-by-step procedures helps your audience understand the processes.[4] If you wish to explain how hydroelectric power is generated, a series of diagrams can help your listeners understand and visualize the process.

When demonstrating how to make something, such as your prize-winning cinnamon rolls, you can have each step of the process prepared ahead of time and show your audience how you go through the steps of preparing your rolls. You could have the dough already mixed and ready to demonstrate how you sprinkle on the cinnamon. A climax to your speech could be to unveil a finished pan of rolls still warm from the oven. If time does not permit you to demonstrate how to prepare your rolls, you could have at hand a series of diagrams and photographs to illustrate each step of the procedure.

1. They help your audience understand your message.

2. They help your audience remember your message.

3. They communicate the organization of your message.

4. They gain and maintain audience attention.

5. They illustrate a sequence of events or procedures.

Types of Presentation Aids

The first question many students ask when they learn they are required to use presentation aids is "What type of presentation aid should I use?" We will discuss various kinds, grouped into three classifications: three-dimensional, two-dimensional, and audiovisual.

Three-Dimensional Presentation Aids

Although a real object can often be a very effective presentational aid, only an experienced animal handler should attempt to bring a live animal into a speaking situation.

[© Syracuse Newspapers/Tim Reese/The Image Works]

OBJECTS   You have played the trombone since you were in fifth grade, so now you decide to give an informative speech about the history and function of this instrument. Your trombone is an obvious presentation aid, which you could show to your audience as you talk about how it works. Perhaps you might play a few measures to demonstrate its sound and your talent.

Or you are an art major and have just finished a watercolor painting. Why not bring your picture to class to illustrate your talk about watercolor techniques?

Objects add interest because they are tangible. They can be touched, smelled, heard, and even tasted, as well as seen. Objects are real, and audiences like the real thing.

If you use an object to illustrate an idea, make sure that it can be handled with ease. If an object is too large, it can be unwieldy and difficult to show to your audience. Tiny objects can only be seen close up. It will be impossible for your listeners to see the detail on your antique thimble, the intricate needlework on your cross-stitch sampler, or the attention to detail in your miniature log cabin. Other objects can be dangerous to handle. One speaker, for example, attempted a demonstration of how to string an archery bow. He made his audience extremely uncomfortable when his almost-strung bow flew over the heads of his listeners. He certainly got their attention, but he lost his credibility.

model
A small object that represents a larger object

MODELS   If it is not possible to bring to the classroom the object you would like to show your audience, consider showing them a **model.** You cannot bring a World War II fighter plane to class, so buy or build a scale model instead. To illustrate her lecture about human anatomy, one student brought a plastic model of a skeleton. An actual human skeleton would have been difficult to get and carry to class. Make sure, however, that any model you use is large enough to be seen by all members of your audience. When Brad brought his collection of miniature hand-carved guitars to illustrate his talk on rock music, his too-small visuals didn't add to the message; they detracted from it.

Most colleges and universities do not allow firearms on campus. A drawing that shows the features of a gun is much safer than a real gun as a presentation aid. If you need to show the movable parts of a gun, perhaps a papier-mâché, plastic, or wood model would serve.

PEOPLE   In addition to inanimate objects, people can serve as presentation aids for a speech. Delia wanted to show some of her own dress designs, so she asked several women to model her clothes during her speech. Paul wanted to illustrate several wrestling holds, so he used a friend to help demonstrate how he won the district wrestling championship. Amelia, a choreographer for the Ballet Folklorico Mexicano, wanted to illustrate an intricate Latin folk dance, so she arranged to have one of the troupe's dancers attend her speech to demonstrate the dance.

Using people to illustrate your message can be tricky, however. It is usually unwise to ask for spur-of-the-moment volunteers for help while you are delivering your speech. Instead, choose a trusted friend or colleague before your presentation so that you can fully inform him or her about what needs to be done. Rehearse your speech using your living presentation aid.

Also, it is distracting to have your support person stand beside you doing nothing. If you don't need the person to demonstrate something during your opening remarks, wait and introduce the person to your audience when needed.

Generally, *you* can serve as a presentation aid to demonstrate or illustrate major points. If you are talking about tennis, you might bring your favorite racquet to class so that you can illustrate your superb backhand or simply show novices the proper way to hold this device. If you are a nurse or an emergency room technician giving a talk about medical procedures, by all means wear your uniform to establish your credibility.

Finally, do not allow your assistants to run away with the show. For example, don't let your dance student perform the *pas de bourre* longer than necessary to illustrate your technique. Nor should you permit your models to prance about too provocatively while displaying your dress designs. And don't allow your buddy to throw you when you demonstrate the wrestling hold that made you champ. Remember, your presentation aids are always subordinate to your speech. You must remain in control.

Two-Dimensional Presentation Aids

Although tangible, three-dimensional objects, models, and people can be used to illustrate a talk, the most common presentation aids are two-dimensional: drawings, photographs, maps, graphs, charts, slides, flipcharts, overhead transparencies, and the chalkboard. Today, you can use computer software to generate many of these forms, as we will discuss a little later in the chapter.

DRAWINGS   A drawing is a popular and often-used presentation aid because it is easy and inexpensive to make. Drawings can be tailored to your specific needs. To illustrate the functions of the human brain, for example, one student traced an outline of the brain and labeled it with large block letters to indicate where brain functions are located. Another student wanted to show the different sizes and shapes of leaves for trees in the area, so she drew enlarged pictures of the leaves, using appropriate shades of green.

You don't have to be a master artist to develop effective drawings. As a rule, large and simple line drawings are more effective for stage presentations than are detailed images. If you have absolutely no faith in your artistic skill, you can probably find a

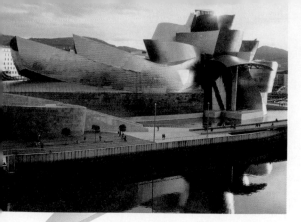

Photos make excellent presentational aids if they are effectively displayed. A speech about the Guggenheim Art Museum in Spain would not be complete without an effective visual image.

[Peter Menzel/Stock Boston]

FIGURE **14.1**

If you were to use it for a speech, this remarkable photograph would have to be enlarged so that the back row of your audience could distinguish clearly between the katydid and the rosebud.

[Photo: Frank Oberle/Stone/Getty Images]

friend or relative who can help you prepare a useful drawing, or you may be able to use computer software to generate simple line drawings or icons.

To see how simple drawings can help clarify ideas, you may want to take another look at the sample speech in Chapter 2 on pages 36–37, which incorporated visual aids.

PHOTOGRAPHS   Photographs can be used to show objects or places that cannot be illustrated with drawings or that an audience cannot view directly. The problems with photos, however, is that they are usually too small to be seen clearly from a distance. If your listeners occupy only two or three rows, it might be possible to hold a photograph close enough for them to see a key feature of the picture. The details will not be visible, however, beyond the first row. Passing a photograph among your listeners is not a good idea either; it creates competition for your audience's attention.

The only sure way to use a printed photograph as a presentation aid for a large audience is to enlarge it (see Figure 14.1). Some photo shops will produce poster-size color laser photocopies at a modest cost. You can also take a picture of your photograph with slide film and project the image onto a large screen with a slide projector. Or, using a scanner or digital camera, you can incorporate your image into a computer program such as PowerPoint and project your image using a TV monitor or video projection system. Later in the chapter we will discuss using computer images in your speeches.

SLIDES   Slides can help illustrate your talk if you have access to a screen and a slide projector. However, because of the increased use of computer-graphics programs such as PowerPoint, fewer speakers are illustrating their talks with slides. Slides can be made of charts and graphs that you develop on a computer. A photograph of your recent vacation might be too small to be seen, but a slide can be projected so that all can see the picture clearly. Automatic programming and remote-control features on many modern projectors help you change from one slide to the next without relying on anyone else for help. And audiences generally enjoy illustrated talks, which have an inherent attention factor that a speaker can use to advantage.

Working with slides can also present problems. Projector bulbs can burn out, and slides can jam in the projector. Moreover, with the lights out, you are less able to receive nonverbal feedback, and you cannot maintain eye contact with your audience.

Giving a slide lecture, therefore, requires considerable preparation. First, be sure the slides are right side up and in the order in which you want to show them during your speech. Second, know in which direction the slide carousel moves as it feeds the projector so that you will know how to load it. Third, know how to operate the programming feature or the remote-control switch so that you can move back and forth among your slides, if you wish.

MAPS   Most maps are designed to be read from a distance of no more than 2 feet. As with photographs, the details on most maps won't be visible to your audience. You could use a large map, however, to show general features of an area. Or you can use a magnified version of your map. Certain copiers can enlarge images as much as 200 percent. It is possible, using a color laser copier, to enlarge a standard map of Europe enough for listeners in the last row to see the general features of the continent. Using a dark marker, one speaker highlighted the borders on a map of Europe to indicate the countries she had visited the previous summer (see Figure 14.2). She used a red marker to show the general path of her journey.

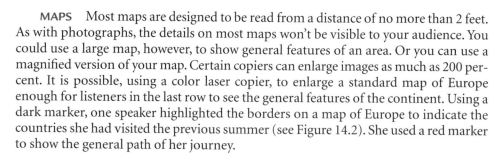

FIGURE 14.2

A map can be an effective visual aid, especially if the speaker personalizes it by highlighting the relevant information.

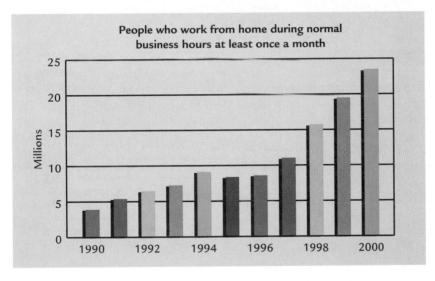

People who work from home during normal business hours at least once a month

FIGURE 14.3

Bar graphs can help summarize statistical information clearly so that the information is immediately visible to your audience.

Source: Joanne H. Pratt Associates.

GRAPHS A **graph** is a pictorial representation of statistical data in an easy-to-understand format. Because statistics are abstract summaries of many examples, most listeners find graphs an effective way to make the data more concrete. Graphs are particularly effective in showing overall trends and relationships among data. The four most common types of graphs are bar graphs, pie graphs, line graphs, and picture graphs. Many of today's computer presentation programs can easily convert statistics into visual form.

● Bar Graphs   A **bar graph** consists of flat areas—bars—of various lengths to represent information. The bar graph in Figure 14.3 clearly shows the number of people who work from home. This graph makes the information clear and immediately visible to the listeners. By comparison, words and numbers are more difficult to assimilate, especially in something as ephemeral as a speech.

graph
A pictorial representation of statistical data, often shows the relationship between sets of data

bar graph
A graph that consists of bars of various lengths to represent information

FIGURE 14.4

A pie graph shows general distribution of data.

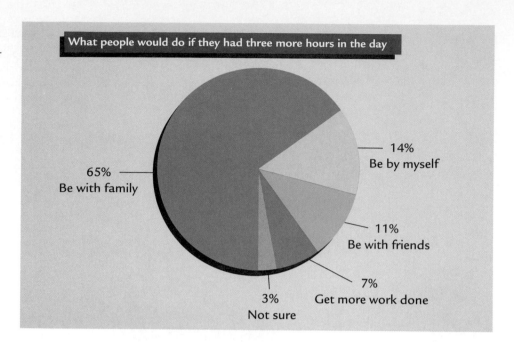

What people would do if they had three more hours in the day

14%
Be by myself

65%
Be with family

11%
Be with friends

7%
Get more work done

3%
Not sure

FIGURE 14.5

Line graphs show relationships between two or more variables.

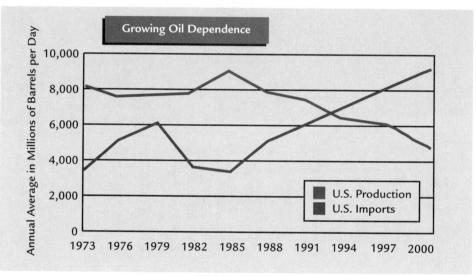

Growing Oil Dependence

Annual Average in Millions of Barrels per Day

U.S. Production
U.S. Imports

1973 1976 1979 1982 1985 1988 1991 1994 1997 2000

pie graph
A circular graph that shows the distribution of data in proportion to other data

line graph
A graph that shows relationships between two or more variables

picture graph
A graph that uses images or pictures to symbolize the data that appear on the graph

● Pie Graphs   A **pie graph** shows the general distribution of data. The pie graph in Figure 14.4 shows what people would do if they had three extra hours of free time. Pie graphs are especially useful in helping your listeners to see quickly how data are distributed in a given category or area.

● Line Graphs   **Line graphs** show relationships between two or more variables. Like bar graphs, line graphs plot a course through statistical data to show overall trends (Figure 14.5). A line graph can cover a greater span of time or numbers than a bar graph without looking cluttered or confusing.

As with other types of presentation aids, a simple line graph communicates better than a cluttered one.

FIGURE **14.6**

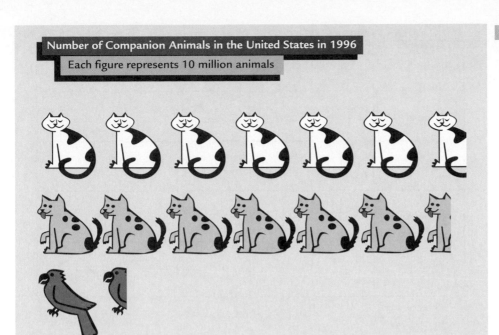

● **Picture Graphs**   In place of either a line or a bar, you can use pictures to supplement the data you are summarizing (Figure 14.6). **Picture graphs** look somewhat less formal and less intimidating than other kinds of graphs. One of the advantages of picture graphs is that they need few words or labels, which makes them easier for your audience to read.

CHARTS   **Charts** summarize and present a great deal of information in a small amount of space (Figure 14.7). They have several advantages. They are easy to use, reuse, and enlarge. They can also be displayed in a variety of ways. You can use a flipchart, a poster, or an overhead projector, which you can use to show a giant image of your chart on a screen. As with all other presentation aids, charts must be simple. Do not try to put too much information on one chart.

The key to developing effective charts is to prepare very carefully the lettering of the words and phrases you use. If the chart contains too much information, audience members may feel it is too complicated to understand, and ignore it. If your chart looks at all cramped or crowded, divide the information into several charts and display each as needed. Print your letters instead of writing them in longhand. In fact, given the availability of computers, a hand-lettered chart may seem unprofessional. Consider using a computer that has the software capability to prepare large charts or graphs. Make sure your letters are large enough to be seen clearly in the back row. Use simple words or phrases, and eliminate unnecessary words.

FLIPCHARTS   Flipcharts are often used in business presentations and training sessions, although the use of computer graphics has reduced their use in corporate presentations. They consist of a large pad of paper resting on an easel. You can either prepare your visuals on the paper before your speech or draw on the paper while speaking. Flipcharts are easy to use. During your presentation, you need only flip the page to reveal your next visual. Flipcharts are best used when you have brief information to display or when you want to summarize comments from audience members during a presentation.

picture graph
A graph that uses images or pictures to symbolize the data that appears on the graph

chart
A display of information in the form of words, numbers, or images, to communicate with an audience

FIGURE 14.7

Charts summarize and present a great deal of information in a small amount of space.

Team	W	L	Percent	GB	Streak
Toronto	84	69	.583	—	Won 2
Baltimore	78	64	.549	5	Lost 2
Milwaukee	77	65	.542	6	Won 2
New York	69	74	.483	14	Lost 1

Most experienced flipchart users recommend that you use lined paper to keep your words and drawings neat and well organized. Another suggestion is to make penciled-in speaking notes on the chart that only you can see. Brief notes on a flipchart are less cumbersome than using note cards or carrying a clipboard with notes. If you do use notes, however, be sure that they are few and brief; using too many notes will tempt you to read rather than have eye contact with your audience.

CHALKBOARDS AND WHITEBOARDS A fixture in classrooms for centuries, a chalkboard is often used to offer visual support for spoken words. Replacing chalkboards in both education and business settings are whiteboards; these more contemporary boards serve the same function as a chalkboard but instead of a black or green slate, the speaker writes on a whiteboard with a marker rather than a piece of chalk. Chalkboards and whiteboards have several advantages: They are low cost; simple to use; and low tech, so you don't need to worry about extension cords or special training.

Although you can find a chalkboard or whiteboard in most classrooms and boardrooms, many public-speaking teachers discourage overuse of them. Why? When you write on the board, you have your back to your audience; you do not have eye contact! Some speakers try to avoid that problem by having their visual on the board before their speech starts. But then listeners often look at the visual rather than listening to the introductory remarks. Moreover, chalkboards and whiteboards are probably the least novel presentation aids, so they are not particularly effective at getting or holding audience attention.

Use a board only for brief phrases or for very simple line diagrams that can be drawn in just a few seconds. It is usually better to prepare a chart, graph, or drawing on a poster or an overhead transparency than to use a chalkboard or whiteboard.

OVERHEAD TRANSPARENCIES As a student, you may be familiar with what an overhead projector looks like, but you may have had little experience using one yourself. This instrument projects an image drawn on clear sheets of plastic, called *transparencies,* onto a screen so that the image can be seen by a large group.

Overhead projectors are popular because they have several advantages. They allow you to maintain eye contact with your audience, yet still see your visual. Unlike other projectors, the overhead doesn't require that you turn off the lights in the room to see the projected image. You may wish to dim the lights a bit, but most images can be seen clearly in normal room light. Overhead projectors also permit you to prepare your transparency ahead of time and to mark on it during your presentation. If you do write during your speech, limit your markings to a few short words or to underlining key phrases.

Consider the following suggestions when using an overhead projector.

- If possible, practice with the overhead projector in the room in which you will be delivering your speech. That way you can be certain that the projector is the proper distance from the screen and that your image will be large enough to be seen.

- When you are not showing a visual, turn the overhead projector off so it does not detract from your speech.

- Do not put too much information on one transparency. Use no more than seven lines on one sheet. Do not use a full page of typewritten material in an overhead projection.

- Align the projector so that the head beams the image directly onto the screen. If the image is too low, it will get projected up and suffer distortion from a keystone effect (see Figure 14.8), which makes the image seem larger at the top and smaller at the bottom. Besides making sure the projector is properly aligned, you can tilt the projector screen forward if it is mounted high on a wall.

- When you use an overhead projector, you may need to increase the volume of your voice. The fan's motor, which keeps the high-intensity projector bulb cool, can be noisy.

- When developing your transparency, consider using a large type size. Using an 18-point, 24-point, or even larger **font** will make your words easier to read. Because most students develop written materials using a computer, it is very easy simply to increase the size of the type, even if it means putting your information on more than one transparency. Bigger *is* better.

FIGURE 14.8

Note the difference between an overhead projector image that produces a keystone effect and an image made by a projector that is properly adjusted.

font
The size and style of typewritten information

- Reveal one line of text at a time by blocking out the text below it with a sheet of paper. This helps hold the audience's interest.

- If possible, leave the bottom fourth of your transparency blank. Images projected low on the screen often are not visible to audience members in the back.

- Consider using the overhead projector without a transparency as a spotlight to highlight something you have written on a poster or chalkboard. With a large audience, an accent light can add emphasis to other visuals.

- Consider using color. Colored acetate sheets are available from most bookstores. You can also use different-colored markers to highlight key points.

- For ease of handling, place the transparency in a cardboard frame, available wherever acetate sheets are sold. A frame lessens the likelihood that the transparencies will stick together or become torn along the edges.

COMPUTER-GENERATED PRESENTATION AIDS Richard had worked hard on his presentation to the finance committee. He had prepared impressive-looking overhead transparencies, distributed a handout of his key conclusions, and had rehearsed his speech so that he had a well-polished delivery. But as he sat down after concluding his speech, certain he had dazzled his listeners, his colleague seated next to him poked him and said, "Why didn't you use PowerPoint slides?" Using computer-generated graphics with such popular software as PowerPoint has become an expectation of many audiences, especially in corporate America. **Computer-generated graphics** include the development and display of images, words, charts, and graphs designed and presented with the help of a computer and special computer software. Although computer-generated graphics can be overused and, like any presentation aid, if used improperly can distract from your message, they nonetheless open up professional-looking possibilities for illustrating your speech.

Technology can provide useful tools for speakers. But a glitzy software presentation cannot take the place of a carefully crafted speech.

[Syracuse Newspapers/ © Carl J. Single/The Image Works]

computer-generated graphics Images, charts, graphs, and words that are developed by using a computer program to present a high-quality graphic presentation of information

Using a presentation program such as PowerPoint, you can design and create complete presentation aids on your personal computer. You can then use the computer again to display the presentation to your audience by connecting your computer to a special large-screen projector or a liquid crystal display (LCD) panel that fits on top of an overhead projector. You can run the program manually using a mouse (some computers are even equipped with a wireless mouse) or the keyboard to advance the images as you speak, or you can set the program to run automatically. Even if you don't have access to a computer to use for your in-class presentation, you can create the graphic images using a computer at a commercial copy center or campus computer lab and then transfer the images to slides or overhead transparencies. Or you can print the images on paper and develop dazzling posters to display on an easel.

The various presentation software packages are designed to let you easily include a variety of aids in your presentation. For instance, you can develop a key word or phrase outline to emphasize your main points as you speak. You can also incorporate into the presentation graphs, charts, or drawings that you can create on the computer, using presentation software to display statistical information or illustrate particular points. You can also use a scanner to transfer any photograph or drawing into digital format, which you can then incorporate as a visual image in your presentation. If you have the necessary equipment, the presentation software can even incorporate video or audio clips. As with any presentation aid, the images or clips that you choose to display must help develop your central idea; otherwise do not include them.

There is an art to developing effective computer-generated graphics. But you don't have to be a professional artist to craft professional-looking images—that's the advantage of using them; virtually anyone can. In addition to learning the mechanics of the software program, keep the following tips in mind when designing computer graphics.[5]

KEEP SIGHTS AND SOUNDS SIMPLE In most aspects of communication, simple is better. Just because you can use fancy fonts and can add several images that would clutter your visual, we have a suggestion for you: Don't. Keep in mind what we've stressed throughout this chapter: Presentation aids *support* your message; they are not your message.

Most graphics software let you add sound effects to highlight your message. But just because you can add a zooming racecar to zip across the computer screen, or have words appear on your screen with typewriter sound as each letter pops in place, such sounds can detract from your speech. Competing cute sounds often lose their novelty after the first slide or two and can become irritating. We suggest that *you* be the soundtrack, not your computer.

REPEAT VISUAL ELEMENTS TO UNIFY YOUR PRESENTATION Use a common visual element, such as a bullet or visual symbol, at the beginning of each word or phrase on a list. Use common color schemes and spacing to give your visuals coherence. Also, avoid mixing and matching different fonts. You get a professional, polished look when you use a similar visual style for each of your images.

Both color and black-and-white images are available as **clip art.** Clip art consists of pictures and images that are either in "hard copy" or stored as images in a computer file. You can then incorporate these images into your visuals. Using clip art (as shown in Figure 14.9) can give your visuals and graphics a professional touch even if you did not excel in art class. Repeating the visual image can provide a consistent look and feel to your presentation.

clip art
Images or pictures that are stored in a computer file or exist in printed form, and that can be used to illustrate an idea

FIGURE **14.9**

Clip art can be used to illustrate visuals.

FIGURE **14.10**

Typefaces grouped by font type

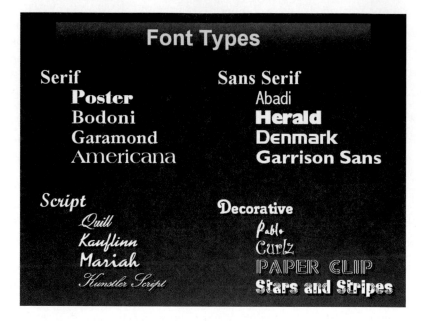

CHOOSE A TYPEFACE WITH CARE You'll be able to choose from among dozens of typefaces and fonts. Make an informed choice rather than just using a font because it strikes your fancy at the moment. One of the most readable fonts is Courier New, for example. Graphic designers divide typefaces into four different font types: serif, sans serif, script, and decorative. You'll see each of these illustrated in Figure 14.10. Serif fonts, like the ones you are reading in this book, are easier to read for longer passages because the little lines at the top and bottom of the letters (called *serifs*) help guide the eye from one letter to the next. Sans serif fonts (*sans* means without) do not have the extra lines. Script fonts are designed to look like handwriting; although interesting and dramatic, use them sparingly because they are harder to read. And use decorative fonts only when you want to communicate a certain special tone or mood. Regardless of which font style or typeface you use, don't use more than one or two typefaces on a single visual; if you do use two, designers suggest they should be from different font types.

MAKE INFORMED DECISIONS ABOUT USING COLOR   Color communicates. Red and orange are warm colors and communicate excitement and interest (which is why most fast-food restaurants use red, yellow, and orange in their color schemes; they literally want to make you hungry and catch your attention). Cooler colors such as green and blue have a more calming effect on viewers. Warm colors tend to come forward and jump out at the viewer, whereas cooler colors recede into the background. What are the implications of the power of color to communicate? Consider using warm colors for positive messages (for example, "Profits are up") and cooler colors for more negative messages ("We're losing money").

Designers caution against using certain color combinations. For example, if some audience members are color-blind, they won't be able to distinguish between red and green. Again, don't get carried away using color. To unify your presentation, use the same background color on all visuals and no more than two colors for words. Using a dark background with lighter-colored words can have a pleasing effect and can be easy to see.

ALLOW PLENTY OF TIME TO PREPARE YOUR PRESENTATION AIDS   Prepare your presentation aids well in advance of your speaking date so that you can make them as attractive and polished-looking as possible. Avoid late-night, last-minute presentation-aid construction. A sloppy, amateurish presentation aid will convey the impression that you are not a credible speaker, even if you have spent many hours preparing the verbal part of your speech. If you haven't used computer-generated graphics before, don't expect to whip out the software manual and produce professional-looking images the night before your presentation. Focus your final hours on rehearsing, not on learning a computer program.

Audiovisual Aids

Perhaps the most exciting presentation aids are those that join sound to sight in communicating ideas. You are probably familiar with all of these: movies, videotapes, CD-ROM, and digital video disks (DVDs), as well as audio aids such as tapes and compact discs. Now you can consider these familiar media in a new context. Instead of being passively entertained or instructed by them, you may use them actively to support your ideas.

VIDEOTAPES AND MOVIES   With the easy availability of video-cassette recorders (VCRs) and cameras, more public speakers are using videotapes to help communicate their ideas by showing brief scenes from a rented movie, an excerpt from a training video, or a video that you made yourself. High-quality VCRs permit stop-action freeze-frame viewing, and some have a slow-motion function. You can also play and replay a scene several times if you want your audience to watch subtle movement or action.

A 25-inch screen is generally visible to an audience of twenty-five or thirty people. For larger audiences, you will need several TV monitors or a large projection TV system. As noted earlier, you can use a large-screen video projector to display your video. Or, if it is available, you could use a liquid crystal display (LCD) panel connected to an overhead projector to project your image. Before you decide to use a videotape, however, think about whether it will really enhance your speech. Although movies can dramatically capture and hold your audience's attention, they are not really designed as supporting material for a speech. Usually, they are conceived as self-contained packages, and unless you show only short excerpts, they can quickly overwhelm your speech. Of course, if you are a skilled moviemaker, you will probably have enough control over your medium to tame it and make it serve your purpose. Be sure to rehearse with the equipment until you can handle it smoothly.

CD-ROM   One technology finding its way into classrooms, corporate meetings, training sessions, and lecture halls is the **CD-ROM.** These compact disks can include words, images, and audio or video clips. The files on CD-ROMS are read in the CD drives in a personal computer and can be displayed in combination with a large-screen video projector or an LCD panel connected to an overhead projector. All the information can be retrieved instantly because it is stored digitally; one disk can contain hundreds of images, sound bites, or an entire encyclopedia. While giving a lecture about Elizabeth Cady Stanton, you could click the computer mouse a couple of times to project her picture or hear an actress read one of her speeches. Or, if you want your audience to hear the dramatic opening four notes of Beethoven's *Fifth Symphony,* you can click the mouse to retrieve his famous dit, dit, dit, daaaaah while simultaneously showing Beethoven's music manuscript in his own handwriting. CD-ROM's key advantage is the ease and speed with which a speaker can retrieve audio or visual information.

DIGITAL VIDEO DISKS (DVDs)   A **digital video disk** (DVD) looks and operates like a CD-ROM except that a DVD contains much more information than is typically stored on a CD-ROM; for example, a DVD can hold an entire movie. A DVD produces exceptional sound and picture quality. DVD players can be connected directly to a TV set, similar to a video cassette recorder, or they may be connected to a computer. Many computers come equipped with DVD capabilities. Because you can stop and start a DVD at a precise place, you can be more confident that your movie or video will start exactly where you want it to start when you are ready to show it to an audience.

AUDIO AIDS   Tapes or audio compact disks (CDs) can complement a visual display—you might play a few measures of Bach's *Toccata and Fugue in D Minor* on tape, CD, or portable electronic keyboard to illustrate a point. While showing slides of her recent Caribbean vacation, a student used a recording of steel drum music as a soft introductory background for her talk. Another student interviewed students on campus about local parking problems. Rather than reading quotes from irate drivers who couldn't find a place to park, he played a few excerpts of taped interviews.

Probably the easiest and least expensive audio aid to use is a tape recorder that uses cassettes. It is small enough to handle easily, can be held up to a microphone to amplify the sound to a large audience, and can be cued to start exactly where you want it to. Mini CD recorders can record either voices or music; their small size makes them easy to handle, and the digital quality produces crystal-clear sound.

A compact disk has excellent fidelity, and it can be cued to start at a certain passage. Some CD players need a separate amplifier and speakers to take full advantage of the improved sound quality. But an average-size "boom box" will do the job nicely unless you have a very large audience. A CD burner permits you to record selected tracks of music either from another CD or from music you legally download from the Internet.

As with movies and videos, use audio aids sparingly. You do not want your speech's electronic soundtrack to interfere with your message.

CD-ROM
An electronic file of images, words, and sounds that is filed on a compact disk

Digital video disk (DVD)
Similar to a CD-ROM, except that it can store much more information (such as an entire feature-length movie) and play back the information with clarity and fidelity

Guidelines for Developing Presentation Aids

The following guidelines offer commonsense and research-based strategies that can help you prepare effective presentation aids for your speeches.

Make Them Easy to See

Without a doubt, the most violated principle of using presentation aids in public speaking is "Make it big!" Countless speeches have been accompanied by writing on a chart or graph too small to read, an overhead projector image not large enough to be legible, or a graph on a flipchart that simply can't be deciphered from the back row. If the only principle you carry away from this chapter is to make your presentation aid large enough to be seen by all in your audience, you will have gained more skill than a majority of speakers who use presentation aids in speeches. *Write big!*

Keep Them Simple

Simple presentation aids usually communicate best. Some students think that the visuals accompanying a speech must be as complicated as a Broadway production, complete with lights and costumes. Resist trying to make your visuals complicated. Indeed, *any* complexity is too much. Words should be limited to key words or phrases. Lengthy dissertations on poster board or an overhead usually do more harm than good. Don't cram too much information on one chart or overhead. If you have a great deal of information, it is better to use two or three simple charts or overhead transparencies than to attempt to put all your words on one visual.

Here's an outline of a speech to inform that uses simple visual aids (which could be displayed on charts or computer-generated graphics) to clearly communicate the ideas the speaker wishes to convey.[6]

TOPIC:	Standard editorial symbols
GENERAL PURPOSE:	To inform
SPECIFIC PURPOSE:	At the end of my speech, the audience should be able to use and interpret ten standard symbols for editorial changes in written material.

I. The following seven editorial symbols are commonly used to change written text.

    A. Use the "pigtail" symbol to delete a letter, a word, or a phrase.

    B. Use a caret (it looks like a housetop) to insert a space or letter or new text, or use it to insert punctuation.

    C. Use what look like two sideways parentheses to remove unwanted space.

D. Use this squiggle line to transpose letters, words, or phrases.

 E. Draw three lines under letters to capitalize them.

 F. Draw a slash through letters to change them to lower case.

 G. Write the word "stet" to undo previous editing marks.

II. Three editorial symbols are used to rearrange the format of text.

 A. Use brackets to add or remove indents or to correct the alignment of text.

 B. Use backward bracket marks around text that you want centered on the page.

 C. Use a symbol that looks like a backward "p" to mark the beginning of new paragraphs.

After the speech, the speaker could give each audience member a simple one-page handout summarizing these editorial markings.

Select the Right Presentation Aids

Because there are so many choices, you may wonder, "How do I decide which presentation aid to use?" Here are some suggestions.

- *Consider your audience.* Factors such as audience size dictate the size of the visual you select. If you have a large audience, do not choose a presentation aid unless everyone can see it clearly. The age, interests, and attitudes of your audience also affect your selection of audiovisual support.

- *Think of your speech objective.* Don't select a presentation aid until you have decided on the purpose of your speech.

- *Take into account your own skill and experience.* Use only equipment with which you are comfortable or have had practical experience.

- *Know the room in which you will speak.* If the room has large windows with no shades and no other way to dim the lights, do not consider using visuals that require a darkened room.

Do Not Use Dangerous or Illegal Presentation Aids

Earlier, we described a speech in which the speaker accidentally caused an archery bow to shoot over the heads of his startled audience. Not only did he lose

Speaker's Homepage　　　　　　　　　　　　　　　　　　　　　－　　　Ｘ

Address:　　http://www.ablongman.com/beebe

　Using the Internet as a Source for Visuals for Your Speeches

Whether it's Mona Lisa's beguiling smile, Grant Wood's famous "American Gothic" image of the farm couple standing in front of their home, or some other famous painting, you now have the resources of the world's art museums at your fingertips. With the click of a mouse, you can explore the art treasures of Russia's Hermitage or Paris' famous Louvre. Art treasures are only a fraction of the images you can retrieve from the Internet; you can download visual images from a variety of sources throughout the world.

TRY THIS: Here's a sampling of links from the Allyn and Bacon Website on public speaking and other sites that you can explore as a source of visuals for your speech. Download an image from one of the following sites for use as a visual aid in your presentation. Make sure you don't use it just because it is eye catching. Ask yourself, "Does it help communicate the key ideas of the speech?" If your answer is no, then don't use it in your speech.

ART LINKS

http://www.artcyclopedia.com

TIME LIFE PHOTO SITE:

http://www.pathfinder.com/photo/index.html

AMERICAN MEMORY COLLECTION FROM THE LIBRARY OF CONGRESS

http://www.lcweb2.loc.gov/ammem/collections/finder.html

YAHOO! SEARCH PAGE FOR ART GALLERIES:

http://dir.yahoo.com/Arts/Museums_Galleries_and_Centers/

HOTBOT

http://www.hotbot.com/

LYCOS PICTURES AND SOUNDS

http://www.lycos.com/lycosmedia.html

WORLD WIDE WEB VIRTUAL LIBRARY FOR AUDIO

http://www.comlab.ox.ac.uk/archive/audio.html

credibility because he was not able to string the bow successfully, but he also endangered his audience by turning his presentation aid into a flying missile. Dangerous or illegal presentation aids may either shock your audience or physically endanger them. These types of aids will also detract from your message. They are never worth the risk of a ruined speech or an injured audience member.

If your speech seems to call for a dangerous or illegal object or substance, substitute a model, picture, chart, or other representational device.

Guidelines for Using Presentation Aids

Now that we have offered strategies for developing effective presentation aids, here are some tips to help you use them for maximum audience impact.

Rehearse with Your Presentation Aids

Jane nervously approached her speech teacher ten minutes before class. She wondered whether class could start immediately, because her presentation aid was melting. She had planned to explain how to get various stains out of clothing, and her first demonstration would show how to remove chewing gum. But she had forgotten the gum, so she had to ask for a volunteer from the audience to spit out his gum so she could use it in her demonstration. The ice she had brought to rub on the sticky gum had by this time melted. All she could do was dribble some lukewarm water on the gummed-up cloth in a valiant but unsuccessful effort to demonstrate her cleaning method. It didn't work. To make matters worse, when she tried to set her poster in the chalkboard tray, it kept falling to the floor. She was left embarrassed and on the edge of tears. It was obvious that she had not rehearsed with her presentation aids.

Unlike Jane, Marti knew she had an important presentation the next day, and was well prepared. Because she was going to use PowerPoint computer graphics in her presentation, she carefully developed each visual to coordinate with her talk. She rehearsed her speech in the same room in which she would be speaking; she also practiced her presentation using the same computer that she would use for her speech. She competently sailed through her presentation without a hitch. Although the unexpected can always happen, Marti's thorough preparation and rehearsal boosted both her confidence and her credibility with her listeners.

Your appearance before your audience should not be the first time you deliver your speech while holding up your chart, turning on the overhead projector, operating the slide projector, or using the flipchart. Practice with your presentation aids until you feel at ease with them.

Have Eye Contact with Your Audience, Not with Your Presentation Aids

You may be tempted to talk to your presentation aid rather than to your audience. Your focus, however, should remain on your audience. Of course, you will need to glance at your visual to make sure that it isn't upside down or that it is the proper visual. But do not face it while giving your talk. Keep looking your audience in the eye.

Explain Your Presentation Aids

Some speakers believe that they need not explain a presentation aid. They think it's enough just to show it to their audience. Resist this approach. When you exhibit your chart showing the overall decline in the stock market, tell your audience what point you are trying to make. Visual support performs the same function as verbal support. It helps you communicate an idea. Make sure that your audience knows what that idea is. Don't just unceremoniously announce, "Here are the recent statistics on birth rates in the United States" and hold up your visual without further explanation. Tell them how to interpret the data. Always set your visuals in a verbal context.

Do Not Pass Objects Among Members of Your Audience

You realize that your marble collection will be too small to see, so you decide to pass some of your most stunning marbles around while you talk. Bad idea. While you are excitedly describing some of your cat's-eye marbles, you have provided a distraction for your audience. People will be more interested in seeing and touching your marbles than in hearing you talk about them.

What can you do if your object is too small to see without passing it around? If no other speaker follows your speech, you can invite audience members to come up and see your object when your speech is over. If your audience is only two or three rows deep, you can even hold up the object and move in close to the audience to show it while you maintain control.

Use Animals with Caution

Most actors are unwilling to work with animals—and for good reason. At best, they may steal the show. And most often, they are unpredictable. You may *think* you have the smartest, best-trained dog in the world, but you really do not know how your dog will react to a strange environment and an unfamiliar audience. The risk of having an animal detract from your speech may be too great to make planning a speech around one worthwhile.

A zealous student at a midwestern university a few years ago decided to give a speech on cattle. What better presentation aid, he thought, than a cow? He brought the cow to campus and led her up several flights of stairs to his classroom. The speech in fact went well. But the student had neglected to consider one significant problem: Cows will go up stairs but not down them.

Another student had a handsome, well-trained German shepherd guard dog. The class was enjoying his speech and his demonstrations of the dog's prowess until the professor from the next classroom poked his head in the door to ask for some chalk. The dog lunged, snarling and with teeth bared, at the unsuspecting professor. Fortunately, he missed—but the speech was concluded prematurely.

These and other examples emphasize our point: Use animals with care, if at all.

Use Handouts Effectively

Many speech instructors feel you should not distribute handouts during a speech. Handing out papers during your presentation will only distract your audience.

However, many audiences in business and other types of organizations expect a summary of your key ideas in written form. If you do find it necessary to use written material to reinforce your presentation, keep the following suggestions in mind.

- Don't distribute your handout during the presentation unless your listeners must refer to the material while you're talking about it. Do not distribute handouts that have only a marginal relevance to your verbal message. They will defeat your purpose.

- If you do need to distribute a handout and you see that your listeners are giving the written material more attention than they are giving you, tell them where in the handout you want them to focus. For example, you could say, "I see that many of you are interested in the second and third pages of the report. I'll discuss those items in just a few moments. I'd like to talk about a few examples before we get to page 2."

- After distributing your handouts, tell audience members to keep the material face down until you're ready to talk about the material; this will help listeners not be tempted to peek at your handout instead of keeping their focus on you and your message.

- Make sure you clearly number the pages on your handout material. This will make it easy for you to quickly direct audience members to specific pages in your handouts.

- To make sure your listeners know what page of your handouts you want them to focus on, prepare overhead transparencies of each page of your handout. You'll be able to display the specific page you're talking about. Even if the words are too small for audience members to read, they will be able to glance up and see what page you're on if they miss your verbal description of where you are in the material. With a transparency you can also quickly point to the paragraph or chart on the page you want them to focus on. It's not a good idea, however, to economize by *only* displaying material designed to be used as handouts on an overhead projector and not providing handouts. The print will undoubtedly be too small to be seen clearly.

- If your listeners do not need the information during your presentation, tell them that you will distribute a summary of the key ideas at the end of your talk. Your handout might refer to the specific action you want your audience to take, as well as summarize the key information you have discussed.

Time Your Visuals to Control Your Audience's Attention

A skillful speaker knows when to show a supporting visual and when to put it away. For example, it's not wise to begin your speech with all your charts, graphs, and drawings in full view unless you are going to refer to them in your opening remarks. Time the display of your visuals to coincide with your discussion of the information contained in them.

Jessica was extremely proud of the huge replica of the human mouth that she had constructed to illustrate her talk on the proper way to brush one's teeth. It stood over 2 feet tall and was painted pink and white. It was a true work of art. As she began her speech, she set her mouth model in full view of the audience. She opened her speech with a brief history of dentistry in America. But her listeners never heard a word.

Instead, they were fascinated by the model. Jessica would have done better to cover her presentation with a cloth and then dramatically reveal it when she wanted to illustrate proper tooth brushing.

Here are a few more suggestions for timing your presentation aids.

- Remove your presentation aid when you move to your next point, unless the information it contains will also help you communicate your next idea.

- Have your overhead transparency already in place on the projector. When you are ready to show your visual, simply turn on the projector to reveal your drawing. Change to a new visual as you make your next point. Turn the projector off when you are finished with your visual support.

- Consider asking someone beforehand to help you hold your presentation aid, turn the pages of your flipchart, or change the slides on the projector. Make sure you rehearse with your assistant so that all goes smoothly during your presentation.

Use Technology Effectively

You may be tempted to use some of the new technologies we have described because of their novelty rather than because of their value in helping you communicate your message. Most of them, however, are expensive. And some novice speakers are tempted to overuse presentation aids simply because they can quickly produce eye-catching visuals. Resist this temptation. Also consider that many classrooms and lecture rooms are not equipped with the necessary hardware. And realize that to project images from large-screen projectors or LCD panels, you may have to dim the lights or turn the overhead lights completely off. As we have noted, when you use audiovisual equipment that requires a dark room, you lose vital visual contact with your listeners.

Despite these drawbacks, CD-ROMs, DVDs, and computer-generated graphics are destined to play a growing role in public speaking. If your college or university is equipped for them, be sure to observe the basic cautions we have offered for other, less-glitzy visual aids. Keep your visuals simple. Make sure the words or images are large enough to be seen by your listeners. Integrate the words and images into your talk. Time your visuals to coincide with information you are presenting. And don't forget to rehearse with these visuals. It is especially important to learn in advance of your speech how to operate the hardware efficiently.

Remember Murphy's Law

According to Murphy's Law, if something can go wrong, it will. When you use presentation aids, you increase the chances that problems or snags will develop when you present your speech. The chart may fall off the easel, you may not find any chalk, the bulb in the overhead projector may burn out. We are not saying that you should be a pessimist, just that you should have backup supplies and a backup plan in case your best-laid plans go awry.

If something doesn't go as you planned, do your best to keep your speech on track. If the chart falls over, simply pick it up and keep talking; don't offer lengthy apologies. If you can't find the chalk you will need and it is your turn to speak, quietly ask a friend to go on a chalk hunt in another room. A thorough rehearsal, a double-check of your equipment, and extra supplies such as extension cords, projector bulbs, or masking tape can help repeal Murphy's Law.

RECAP | **CHECKLIST FOR PRESENTATION AIDS**

When Developing Presentation Aids

Are your presentation aids easy to see?

Are they simple and uncluttered?

Do they suit your audience, speech objectives, and speech environment?

Are they attractive and carefully prepared?

Are your presentation aids legal and nonthreatening to your audience?

When Using Your Presentation Aids During Your Speech

Have you rehearsed with your presentation aids?

Do you look at your audience when you talk, rather than at your presentation aids?

Do you explain your presentation aids, rather than just show them?

Can you avoid having to pass around your presentation aids?

Have you used well-timed handouts?

Do your presentation aids keep your audience's attention focused on your speech?

Can you operate the hardware you have chosen, and do you have backup supplies?

SUMMARY

Presentation aids are tools to help you communicate your ideas more dramatically than can words alone. There are different types of presentation aids, and general guidelines can help you use them effectively.

Presentation aids help influence your listeners' understanding and recollection of your ideas. They also help you communicate the organization of your ideas, gain and maintain the audience's attention, and illustrate a sequence of events or procedures.

Three-dimensional presentation aids include objects, models, and people. Two-dimensional presentation aids include drawings, photographs, slides, maps, graphs, charts, flipcharts, projected transparencies, and the chalkboard. Software graphics packages can be used to produce many of these options inexpensively and efficiently. Audiovisual aids include movies and videotapes. Audio aids such as tapes and compact disks can also be used to help communicate ideas to your listeners.

When you prepare your presentation aids, make sure your visuals are large enough to be seen clearly by all of your listeners. Adapt your presentation aids to your audience, the speaking environment, and the objectives of your speech. Prepare your visuals well in advance, and make sure they are not illegal or dangerous to use.

As you present your speech, remember these suggestions: Be sure to look at your audience, not your presentation aid; talk about your visual, don't just show it; avoid passing objects among your audience; use handouts to reinforce the main points in your speech; time your visuals carefully; and be sure to have backup supplies and a contingency plan.

A Sharper Focus

CONSIDERING YOUR AUDIENCE

▶ Use presentation aids to support your speech if they will help your listeners understand, remember, or attend to your message. Also use presentation aids if they help you organize your message or illustrate a sequence of events or procedures for your listeners.

▶ Determine the type of presentation aid (three-dimensional, two-dimensional, or audio) that best helps you communicate your message to your audience.

▶ Revealing one line of text at a time when you are projecting a list of items on an overhead projector helps maintain audience interest.

▶ When using computer-generated graphics (such as PowerPoint), don't let the technology overwhelm your audience: Use simple, brief lines of text and images.

▶ When preparing any presentation aid, keep several audience-centered guidelines in mind. For example, the audience should be the primary factor you consider when determining whether a presentation aid would enhance your presentation. And make presentation aids easy to see and simple.

▶ Maintain eye contact with your audience, not with your presentation aid.

▶ As a general rule, don't pass objects among your audience members while you speak.

CONSIDERING AUDIENCE DIVERSITY

▶ People from high-context cultures are more likely to focus on the pictures and images in your presentation aids. People from low-context cultures may be especially interested in words and text included on your visuals.

▶ Always consider the culturally preferred use of presentation aids when you deliver a speech. If you are uncertain what the expectations of your audience members are about your use of presentation aids; ask someone for advice who is familiar with the cultural expectations of your listeners.

▶ When you are speaking to members of a culture for which language may be a barrier, consider using images or pictures to help them remember your ideas.

▶ If you are using an interpreter because of language differences, give a copy of your presentational aids to your interpreter before you speak so that he or she can easily translate your message to your audience.

CRITICAL THINKING QUESTIONS

1. Nikki plans to give a talk to the Rotary Club in an effort to encourage the club members to support a local bond issue for a new library. She wants to make sure they understand how cramped and inadequate the current library is. What type of visual support could she use to make her point?

2. Professor Chou uses only the chalkboard to illustrate her anthropology lectures. Occasionally she writes a word or two on the board. What other types of visual or auditory aids could Professor Chou use to help in teaching her lessons?

3. Mayor Bryan is going to address the board of directors of a large microchip firm, hoping to lure them to his community. He plans to use handouts, several charts, a short video clip, and an overhead projector to show several transparencies. What advice would you give the mayor to make sure his presentation is effective?

ETHICAL QUESTIONS

1. Masha found the perfect pie chart in *USA Today* to illustrate her talk on U.S. census figures for population trends. If she tells her audience that the source of her visual is *USA Today,* does she also need to cite the U.S. Bureau of the Census?

2. Ceally wants to educate his college classmates about the increased use of profanity in contemporary music. He would like to play sound clips of some of the most offensive lyrics to illustrate his point. Would you advise Ceally to play these songs, even though doing so might offend several members of the audience?

3. Derrick is planning to give a speech about emergency first aid. His brother is a paramedic and licensed nurse. Is it ethical for Derrick to wear his brother's paramedic uniform without telling his listeners that the outfit belongs to his brother?

SUGGESTED ACTIVITIES

1. Use either computer software (such as PowerPoint) or poster board, markers, and a ruler to design presentation aids for a speech using the following information:

   a. In 1994 12% of disposable personal income was used toward paying down consumer debt; in 2001 14.5% of disposable personal income was used toward paying down consumer debt.

   In 1980 consumers spent 12% of their income for luxury items, 42% for everyday items, and 46% for replacement of products; in 2000 consumers spent 20% for luxury items, 24% for everyday items, and 56% for replacement products.

   Consumer spending trends:

1995	$5 trillion
1997	$5.5 trillion
1999	$6 trillion
2001	$7 trillion

   b. A speech about how third-party candidates have fared in presidential elections. Note the following statistics:

Year	Candidate	Highest Rating in Polls	Percentage of Popular Vote
1948	Henry Wallace	2%	2.4%
1968	George Wallace	20%	13.5%

1980	John Anderson	13%	6.6%
1992	Ross Perot	39%	19.0%
2000	Ralph Nader	4%	2.7%

c. A speech on career counseling. During the speech, statistics are quoted from *Parents* magazine, in which a woman undergoing career counseling is asked to lay out her ideal plan of time allotment. She hopes to spend 35 percent of her time at a part-time job, 10 percent doing housework, 20 percent in activities with her children, 12 percent cooking, 7 percent socializing, 6 percent watching TV, and 10 percent reading and working on hobbies.

d. A speech on the importance of calcium in the diet. *Good Housekeeping* reports on the calcium contents of certain common foods: 1 cup of 2 percent milk has 352 mg, 1 cup of lowfat yogurt has 294 mg, 1 ounce of cheddar cheese has 213 mg, 1 cup of ice cream has 194 mg, and 1 cup of broccoli has 136 mg.

2. As you look for photographs and other images and artwork to illustrate your message, make sure your representation of people in your pictures reflects appropriate ethnic and cultural diversity. If a large segment of your audience is of one particular demographic type (age, culture, gender, ethnicity), make especially sure that you have visual images that reflect the makeup of your audience.

3. If your audience is from a predominantly different culture or ethnic background from yourself, use that difference in selecting a topic and using supporting material. For example, you could easily talk about differences in the way holidays are celebrated, as well as differences in food, dress, nonverbal messages, and other cultural and ethnic traditions. Draw on stories, songs, and family anecdotes to illustrate your major points. Use the differences between you and your listeners to add interest to your message.

USING TECHNOLOGY AND MEDIA

1. If your school has a media resources center, make an appointment to visit it and review the electronic audio and video equipment that is available for your use. While you will undoubtedly be familiar with such AV (audiovisual) equipment as overhead projectors and videotape machines, ask about the availability of newer technology such as CD-ROMs, DVDs, personal computers for generating and displaying graphics, and liquid crystal display panels.

2. Review recent issues of magazines or journals that advertise the latest presentation technology. Journals such as *Training* or *Training and Development,* published by the American Society for Training and Development, are good magazines to peruse. Note the new technology that is being advertised, and be prepared to discuss how the new AV resources could enhance speech presentations.

3. Watch a national or local broadcast of the evening news and pay particular attention to visuals and graphics used to help communicate the news stories. Evaluate the effectiveness of the news program's use of visuals, using the criteria discussed in this chapter.

Not only is there an art in knowing a thing,
but also a certain art in teaching it.

CICERO

15

Speaking to Inform

objectives

After studying this chapter you should be able
to do the following:

1. Identify four goals of speaking to inform.

2. Describe five different types of informative
   speeches.

3. Effectively and appropriately use four strategies
   to enhance audience understanding.

4. Effectively and appropriately use three strategies
   to enhance audience interest.

5. Effectively and appropriately use four strategies
   to enhance audience recall of information
   presented in an informative speech.

As you participate in your company's management training class, the group facilitator turns to you and asks you to summarize your team's discussion about the importance of leadership.

Your sociology professor has required each student to give an oral report describing the latest findings from the U.S. census.

At the conclusion of your weekly staff meeting, your boss turns to you to give a brief report summarizing the new product you and your team are developing.

In each of these situations, your task is to give information to someone. Whether you are having spontaneous conversation or delivering a rehearsed speech, you will often find that your speaking purpose is to inform, or teach someone something you know. A recent survey of both speech teachers and students who had taken a speech course found that the single most important skill taught in a public-speaking class is how to give an informative speech.[1]

A **speech to inform** shares information with others to enhance their knowledge or understanding of the information, concepts, and ideas you present. When you inform someone, you assume the role of a teacher by defining, illustrating, clarifying, or elaborating on a topic.

Conveying information to others is a useful skill in most walks of life. You may find that informing others will be an important part of your job. As a regional manager of a national corporation, you may have to report sales figures every fiscal quarter; as an accountant, you may have to teach your administrative assistant how to organize your files. Other activities, such as teaching a Chinese cooking class or chairing monthly meetings of the Baker Street Irregulars, can also require you to provide information.

In this chapter, we will suggest ways to build on your experience and enhance your skill in informing others. We will discuss goals of informative speaking, examine different types of informative tasks, and discuss specific ways to inform others. Finally, we will present some general principles for making your informative presentations memorable.

Goals of Informative Speaking

Speaking to inform others can be a challenging task. As a student, you have first-hand experience that just because a teacher presents information, you don't always soak up knowledge like a sponge. Informing or teaching others is a challenge because of a simple fact: Presenting information does not mean that communication has occurred. Communication happens when the listeners make sense of the information.

When trying to help listeners make sense out of information, speakers often have one or more of the following goals in mind: to enhance understanding, to gain and maintain interest, or to ensure that listeners can remember what was said. Let's explore each of these three important informative-speaking goals.

speech to inform
sharing information with others to enhance their knowledge for and understanding about something. To inform is to teach others new information, ideas, concepts, principles, or processes

Speaking to Enhance Understanding

Understanding occurs when the listener accurately interprets your intended meaning of a message. Given the fragile nature of meaning, words and nonverbal expressions are often misunderstood by others. When your goal is to speak to enhance understanding, the words you select to improve understanding may actually hinder accurate meaning. Someone once noted that the 500 most common words in English vocabulary have over 14,000 different dictionary definitions! And these dictionary definitions do not include the personal or private meanings for words we use. Given the potential for misunderstanding, it's amazing we connect meaning as well as we do.

When your speaking goal is to enhance understanding, you must first make sure you are using words that your listeners will interpret in the same way as you do. How do you do this? Be audience-centered. If you are using words that require unique background or knowledge your listeners don't have, meaning communicated between you and your audience will be muddled. The stories you tell, the examples you use, and the statistics you cite will only make sense to the listener if he or she has a common understanding for the words you speak. Otherwise, the job would be like trying to write a term paper on a computer with software designed to keep track of your checkbook rather than to write sentences. Without a common framework, your message won't make sense.

Speaking to Maintain Interest

You may have carefully selected words, examples, and illustrations that your listeners understand, but if your listeners are bored and not focusing on your message, you won't achieve your informative-speaking goal. People may be interested in you and your topic for a variety of reasons. They often listen to what affects them directly, adds to their knowledge, satisfies their curiosity, or entertains them. These reasons are not

This whitewater tour guide knows he will have the interest of his listeners; they need to learn to handle a raft before they run the rapids. But other speakers may need to focus carefully on what they could do to maintain their listeners' interest.

[Richard Pasley/Stock Boston]

mutually exclusive. For example, if you were talking to a group of businesspeople about the latest changes in local tax policies, you would be discussing something that directly affects them, adds to their knowledge, and satisfies their curiosity. But your listeners' primary interest would be in how taxes would affect them. By contrast, if you were giving a lecture on fifteenth-century Benin sculpture to a middle-class audience at the YMCA, your listeners would be interested because your talk would add to their knowledge, satisfy their curiosity, and entertain them. Such a talk can also affect your listeners directly by making them more interesting to others. The commonality in both these speaking situations is the focus on listeners' interests and needs. If your audience members feel they will benefit from your speech in some way, your speech will interest them. And an interesting speech commands attention as well as respect.

Speaking to Be Remembered

You may remember from Chapter 4 that one day after hearing a presentation, most audience members will remember only about half of what was told to them. And they will recall only about 25 percent two weeks later. Your job as an informative speaker is to improve on those statistics. Just because listeners do not typically remember what a speaker says, it does not mean that *your* listeners are doomed to a similar fate.

Throughout this book we've offered strategies and suggestions to help listeners, remember information. Being organized, being appropriately redundant by using internal summaries and a final summary, as well as relating the message to listeners' interests, are all useful methods of helping your audience increase their retention of the message you've worked so hard to develop. Later in the chapter we'll offer additional suggestions for increasing audience recall of messages.

Types of Informative Speeches

Informative speeches can be classified according to the subject areas they cover. Classifying your speech can help you decide how to organize the information you want to present. As you will see in the following discussion, the demands of your purpose often dictate a structure for your speech. As you look at these suggestions about structure, however, remember that good organization is only one factor in your audience's ability to process your message. In the next section, we will discuss additional strategies for ensuring that your listeners will *understand* the information in your speech.

Speeches about Objects

A speech about an object might be about anything tangible—anything you can see or touch. You may or may not show the actual object to your audience while you are talking about it. (Chapter 14 suggests ways to use objects as presentation aids to illustrate your ideas.)

Objects that could form the basis of an interesting speech might include these:

A collection of yours (rocks, compact disks, antiques, baseball cards, and so on)

Sports cars

Cellos

Personal digital assistants (PDAs)

8-mm video cameras

WW II Memorial

Toys

Antique fiestaware

The time limit for your speech will determine the amount of detail you can share with your listeners. Even in a 30- to 45-minute presentation, you cannot talk about every aspect of any of the objects listed. So you will need to focus on a specific purpose. Here's a sample outline for a speech about an object:

TOPIC:	Dead Sea Scrolls
GENERAL PURPOSE:	To inform
SPECIFIC PURPOSE:	At the end of my speech, my audience should be able to describe how the Dead Sea Scrolls were found, why they are important to society, and the key content of the ancient manuscripts.

I. How the Dead Sea Scrolls were found

    A. The scrolls were found in caves near the Dead Sea.

    B. The scrolls were first discovered by a shepherd in 1947.

    C. In the late 1940s and early 1950s archeologists and Bedouins found 10 caves that contained Dead Sea Scrolls.

II. Why the Dead Sea Scrolls are important to society

    A. The Dead Sea Scrolls are the oldest known manuscripts of any books of the Bible.

    B. The Dead Sea Scrolls give us a look at Jewish life in Palestine over 2000 years ago.

III. The primary content of the Dead Sea Scrolls

    A. The Dead Sea Scrolls include all the books of the Old Testament except Esther.

    B. The Dead Sea Scrolls include fragments of the Septuagint, the earliest Greek translation of the Old Testament.

    C. The Dead Sea Scrolls include a collection of hymns used by the inhabitants of the Qumran Valley.

Speeches about objects may be organized topically, chronologically, or spatially. The speech about the Dead Sea Scrolls is organized topically. It could, however, be revised chronologically. The first major idea could discuss Jewish life in Palestine 2000 years ago. The second point could present information about how the scrolls were found in the 1940s and 1950s. The final major idea could discuss the construction of the museum in Jerusalem that houses the famous scrolls. Or the speech could be organized spatially, describing the physical layout of the caves in which the scrolls were found.

If a how-to discussion becomes the central focus of a speech, it then becomes a speech about a procedure.

Speeches about Procedures

A speech about a procedure discusses how something works (for example, the human circulatory system), or describes a process that produces a particular outcome (such as how grapes become wine). At the close of such a speech, your audience should be able to describe, understand, or perform the procedure you have described. Here are some examples of procedures that could make effective informative presentations:

How state laws are made

How the U.S. patent system works

How a rotary engine works

How to refinish furniture

How to select an inexpensive stereo system

How to plant an organic garden

How to use the Internet

Notice that all these examples start with the word *how*. A speech about a procedure usually focuses on how a process is completed or how something can be accomplished. Speeches about procedures are often presented in workshops or other training situations in which people learn skills.

Anita, describing how to develop a new training curriculum in teamwork skills, used an organizational strategy that grouped some of her steps together like this:

I. Conduct a needs assessment of your department.

    A. Identify the method of assessing department needs.

        1. Consider using questionnaires.

        2. Consider using interviews.

        3. Consider using focus groups.

    B. Implement the needs assessment.

II. Identify the topics that should be presented in the training.

    A. Specify topics that all members of the department need.

    B. Specify topics that only some members of the department need.

III. Write training objectives.

    A. Write objectives that are measurable.

    B. Write objectives that are specific.

    C. Write objectives that are attainable.

IV. Develop lesson plans for the training.

    A. Identify the training methods you will use.

    B. Identify the materials you will need.

Her audience will remember the four general steps much more easily than they could have hoped to recall if each aspect of the curriculum-development process were listed as a separate step.

Many speeches about procedures include visual aids (see Chapter 14). Whether you are teaching people how to hang wallpaper or how to give a speech, showing them how to do something is almost always more effective than just telling them how to do it.

Speeches about People

A biographical speech could be about someone famous or about someone you know personally. Most of us enjoy hearing about the lives of real people, whether famous or not, living or dead, who had some special quality about them. The key to presenting an effective biographical speech is to be selective. Don't try to cover every detail of your subject's life. Relate the key elements in the person's career, personality, or other significant life features so that you are building to a particular point rather than just reciting facts about an individual. Perhaps your grandfather was known for his generosity, for example. Mention some notable examples of his philanthropy. If you are talking about a well-known personality, pick information or a period that is not widely known, such as the person's childhood or private hobby.

One speaker gave a memorable speech about his neighbor:

To enter Hazel's house is to enter a combination greenhouse and zoo. Plants are everywhere; it looks and feels like a tropical jungle. Her home is always warm and humid. Her dog Peppy, her cat Bones, a bird named Elmer, and a fish called Frank can be seen through the philodendron, ferns, and pansies. While Hazel loves her plants and animals, she loves people even more. Her finest hours are spent serving coffee to her friends and neighbors, playing Uno with family until late in the evening, and just visiting about the good old days. Hazel is one of a kind.

Note how the speech captures Hazel's personality and charm. Speeches about people should give your listeners the feeling that the person is a unique, authentic individual.

One way to talk about a person's life is in chronological order—birth, school, career, marriage, achievements, death. However, if you are interested in presenting a specific theme, such as "Winston Churchill, master of English prose," you may decide instead to organize those key experiences topically. First you would discuss Churchill's achievements as a brilliant orator whose words defied Germany in 1940, and then trace the origins of his skill to his work as a cub reporter in South Africa during the Boer War of 1899 to 1902.

Speeches about Events

Where were you on September 11, 2001—the unforgettable day planes slammed into the twin towers of the World Trade Center and the Pentagon? Chances are that you clearly remember where you were and what you were doing on that and other similarly fateful days. Major events punctuate our lives and mark the passage of time.

A major event can form the basis of a fascinating informative speech. You can choose to talk about an event that you have either witnessed or researched. Your goal is to describe the event in concrete, tangible terms and to bring the experience to life for your audience. Were you living in Miami when Hurricane Andrew struck? Have you witnessed the inauguration of a president, governor, or senator? Have you experienced the ravages of a flood or earthquake? Have you seen how a tornado can rip through a small town like it did in Beebe, Arkansas, or Moore, Oklahoma, in 1999? Or you may want to re-create an event that your parents or grandparents lived through. What was it like to be in Pearl Harbor on December 7, 1941?

You may have heard a recording of the famous radio broadcast of the explosion and crash of the dirigible *Hindenburg*. The announcer's ability to describe both the scene and the incredible emotion of the moment has made that broadcast a classic. As that broadcaster was able to do, your purpose as an informative speaker describing an event is to make that event come alive for your listeners and to help them visualize the scene.

Most speeches built around an event follow a chronological arrangement. But a speech about an event might also describe the complex issues or causes behind the event and be organized topically. For example, if you were to talk about the Civil War, you might choose to focus on the three causes of the war:

I. Political

II. Economic

III. Social

Although these main points are topical, specific subpoints may be organized chronologically. However you choose to organize your speech about an event, your audience should be enthralled by your vivid description.

Speeches about Ideas

Speeches about ideas are usually more abstract than the other types of speeches. The following principles, concepts, and theories might be topics of idea speeches:

Principles of communication

Freedom of speech

Evolution

Theories of aging

Islam

Communal living

Trickle-down theory of economics

Most speeches about ideas are organized topically (by logical subdivisions of the central idea) or according to complexity (from simple ideas to more complex ones). The following example illustrates how one student organized an idea topic into an informative speech:

TOPIC:	Communication theory
GENERAL PURPOSE:	To inform
SPECIFIC PURPOSE:	At the end of my speech, the audience should be able to identify and describe three functions and three types of communication theory.

I. Communication theory has three important functions.

   A. Communication theory helps us explain how communication functions.

   B. Communication theory helps us make predictions about how people will communicate with others.

   C. Communication theory helps us be more in control of communication situations because we can explain and predict human-communication behavior.

II. There are several types of communication theory.

   A. Communication systems theory helps explain the transactive nature of communication.

   B. Rhetorical-communication theory helps us explain and predict how public speakers influence others.

   C. Functional group-communication theory identifies the important group-communication behaviors that can enhance group communication.

RECAP

TYPES OF INFORMATIVE SPEECHES

Speech Type	Description	Typical Organizational Patterns	Sample Topics
Objects	Present information about tangible things	Topical Spatial Chronological	The Rosetta Stone Museums International space station Voting machines
Procedures	Review how something works or describe a process	Chronological Topical Complexity	How to . . . Fix a carburetor Operate a nuclear-power plant Buy a quality used car Trap lobsters
People	Describe either famous people or personal acquaintances	Chronological Topical	Sojourner Truth Nelson Mandela Indira Gandhi Your granddad Your favorite teacher
Events	Describe an actual event that either has happened or will happen	Chronological Topical Complexity Spatial	The 2000 presidential election Inauguration Day Cinco de Mayo
Ideas	Present abstract information or principles, concepts, theories, or issues	Topical Complexity	Communism Success Buddhism Reincarnation

Strategies to Enhance Audience Understanding

The skill of teaching and enhancing understanding is obviously important to teachers, but it's also important to virtually any profession. Whether you're a college professor, chief executive officer of a Fortune 500® company, or a parent raising a family, you will be called on to teach and explain. At the heart of understanding someone is the ability to describe both old and new ideas to others. Just because an idea, term, or concept has been around for centuries doesn't mean that it will be easy to understand. A person hearing an old idea for the first time goes through the same process as if he or she were learning about the latest, cutting-edge idea. How do you enhance someone's knowledge or understanding? We suggest several powerful strategies.

Define Ideas clearly

With swift changes occurring in every area of life, new words and concepts appear almost daily. *Virtual reality, cyberspace, computer platform*, and *MP3* are just a few of the concepts that have recently come into use. Many word-processing software programs have a spell-checking feature built into the software. Note how often your computer may signal that a term is misspelled when the concept or term is so new that it was not included in the spell-check dictionary. As a public speaker, you are responsible for ensuring that your listeners understand the new words and concepts you discuss, particularly if the primary goal of your speech is to explain a new idea.

In Chapter 8, we discussed the use of definition as a type of supporting material. *Defining a term in words* can be particularly helpful in informative speeches, whether you quote words directly from a standard dictionary or use your own. In addition, you can use definitions by example and operational definitions.

A **definition by example** uses concrete examples to show the audience what the term or concept means. One student speaker, for example, defined the term *advertising* by pointing to the numerous advertisements for magazine subscriptions and credit card applications that were posted on the bulletin board at the front of the classroom. Another speaker who wanted to define *primitive antiques* displayed several examples of kitchen utensils and photographs of furniture to show her audience the defining characteristics of a primitive antique. In addition, she brought photographs of nonprimitive antiques and noted differences between the two classes of antiques to further clarify her definition. Using *negative examples* coupled with positive examples can be an effective strategy for teaching defining characteristics.

As we discussed in Chapter 8, an **operational definition** focuses on a particular procedure for observing or measuring the concept that is being defined. For example, if you are giving an informative speech about intelligence, you may choose to define intelligence by describing the procedures used in an IQ test and explaining how the test measures intelligence.

What is the best way to explain new ideas or concepts? It depends on the knowledge and experiences of your audience. If you are presenting completely new information to listeners, you may want to use simple, familiar examples. As a general rule, more sophisticated listeners will understand technical or operational definitions; less sophisticated listeners will appreciate clear, easy-to-understand definitions, coupled, if possible, with a vivid example.

definition by example
Uses concrete examples to show the audience what the term or concept means.

operational definition
Focuses on a particular procedure for observing or measuring the concept that is being defined

Use Principles and Techniques of Adult Learning

Most public-speaking audiences you face will consist of adults. A practical set of principles has been discovered to help adult learners learn. Perhaps you've heard of **pedagogy**, the art and science of teaching children to learn. The word *pedagogy* is based on the Greek words *paid,* which means "child," and *agogus,* which means "guide." Thus, pedagogy is the art and science of teaching children to learn. Adult learning is called **andragogy.**[2] *Andr* is the Greek word that means "adult." Andragogy is the art and science of teaching adults. Researchers and scholars have found andragogical approaches to learning best for adults. By adults we don't just mean people who are over 30; if you're a college student over the age of 18, you probably will fit the characteristics of an adult learner. What are andragogical or adult-learning principles? Here are some of the most important ones.

ADULTS LIKE TO BE GIVEN INFORMATION THEY CAN USE IMMEDIATELY. Most people who work in business have an in-basket on their desk to receive letters that must be read and work that must be done. Each of us also has a kind of mental in-basket, an agenda for what we want or need to accomplish. If you present adult listeners with information that they can apply immediately to their "in basket," they are more likely to focus and understand your message.

ADULT LEARNERS LIKE TO BE ACTIVELY INVOLVED IN THE LEARNING PROCESS. Rather than having your listeners passively sitting as you speak, consider asking them questions to think about or, in some cases, to respond to on the spot.

ADULT LEARNERS LIKE TO CONNECT THEIR LIFE EXPERIENCES WITH THE NEW INFORMATION THEY LEARN. Adult listeners are more likely to understand your message if you help them connect the new information with their past experiences. The primary way to do this is first to know the kinds of experiences that your listeners have had, then refer to those experiences as you present your ideas.

ADULT LEARNERS LIKE TO KNOW HOW THE NEW INFORMATION IS RELEVANT TO THEIR NEEDS AND THEIR BUSY LIVES. Most adults are busy. They have much to do; probably, if pressed, most will say their lives are too busy for their own good. So when speaking to an adult audience, realize that any information or ideas you share will more likely be heard and understood if you relate it to their chock-full-of-activity life. People working, going to school, raising families, and being involved in their community need to be shown how the ideas you share relate to their lives.

Clarify Complex Processes

If you are trying to tell your listeners about a complex process, you will need more than definitions to explain what you mean. Research suggests that you can demystify a complex process if you first provide a simple overview of the process with an analogy, model, picture, or vivid description.[3]

Before going into great detail, first give listeners the "big picture" or convey the gist of what the process is about.[4] *Analogies* (comparisons) are often a good way to do this.[5] For example, if you are describing how a personal computer works, you could say that it stores information like a filing cabinet or that computer software works like a piano

pedagogy
The art and science of teaching children to learn

andragogy
The art and science of teaching adults to learn

roll on an old-fashioned player piano. In addition to using an analogy, consider using a *model* or other visual aid to show relationships among the parts of a complex process, following the guidelines we presented in Chapter 14.

You can also *describe* the process, providing more detail than you do when you just define something. Descriptions answer questions about the who, what, where, why, and when of the process. Who is involved in the process? What is the process, idea, or event that you want to describe? Where and when does the process take place? Why does it occur, or why is it important to the audience? (Of course, not all of these questions apply to every description.)

Or, you could clarify the process with a *word picture*. As you learned in Chapter 8, word pictures are lively descriptions that help your listeners form a mental image by appealing to their senses of sight, taste, smell, sound, and touch. The following suggestions will help you construct effective word pictures.

- *Form a clear mental image of the person, place, or object before you try to describe it.*

- *Describe the appearance of the person, place, or object.* What would your listeners see if they were looking at it? Use lively language to describe the flaws and foibles, bumps, and beauties of the people, places, and things you want your audience to see. Make your description an invitation to the imagination—a stately pleasure dome into which your listeners can enter and view its treasures with you.

- *Describe what your listeners would hear.* Use colorful, onomatopoeic words, such as *buzz, snort, bum, crackle,* or *hiss.* These words are much more descriptive than the more general term *noise.* Imitate the sound you want your listeners to hear with their "mental ears." For example, instead of saying, "When I walked in the woods, I heard the sound of twigs breaking beneath my feet and wind moving the leaves above me in the trees," you might say, "As I walked in the woods, I heard the crackle of twigs underfoot and the rustle of leaves overhead."

- *Describe smells, if appropriate.* What fragrance or aroma do you want your audience to recall? Such diverse subjects as Thanksgiving, nighttime in the tropics, and the first day of school all lend themselves to olfactory imagery. No Thanksgiving would be complete without the rich aroma of roast turkey and the pungent, tangy odor of cranberries. A warm, humid evening in Miami smells of salt air and gardenia blossoms. And the first day of school evokes for many the scents of new shoe leather, unused crayons, and freshly painted classrooms. In each case, the associated smells greatly enhance the overall word picture.

- *Describe how an object feels when touched.* Use words that are as clear and vivid as possible. Rather than saying that something is rough or smooth, use a simile, such as "the rock was rough as sandpaper" or "the pebble was as smooth as a baby's skin." These descriptions appeal to both the visual and tactile senses.

- *Describe taste, one of the most powerful sensory cues, if appropriate.* Thinking about your grandmother may evoke for you memories of her rich homemade noodles; her sweet, fudgy, nut brownies; and her light, flaky, buttery pie crust. Descriptions of these taste sensations would be welcome to almost any audience, particularly your fellow college students subsisting mainly on dormitory food or their own cooking! More important, such description can help you paint an accurate, vivid image of your grandmother.

Address: http://www.ablongman.com/beebe

 Finding Late-Breaking News and Information for Your Speech

Some of the most interesting informative presentations include information about current events and late-breaking issues. Here are some Websites that will keep you wired to the latest information around the world.

EDITOR AND PUBLISHER

http://www.mediainfo.com/emedia/

This site provides links to media outlets all over the globe.

YAHOO! MEDIA AND NEWSPAPERS

http://dir.yahoo.com/News_and_Media/Newspapers/

This source connects you to several major daily newspapers.

BROADCAST.COM

http://www.broadcast.com

Using RealAudio, you can find out about key events that are happening live.

SITES AND SOUNDS FROM ABC

Up-to-the-minute news from the American Broadcasting Company can be found here.

http://www.abcnews.com

TOTAL NEWS

This Website has links for all the major news media, including CBS, USA Today, PR, CNN, MSNBC, and TIME Daily.

http://www.totalnews.com/

To help you develop ideas for an informative speech, go to the Allyn and Bacon Website on public speaking to use the 5w's *(who, what when, where, why)* to help you formulate an interesting informative speech topic.

http://www.ablongman.com/pubspeak/exercise/5wtopic.html/

- *Describe the emotion that a listener might feel if he or she were to experience the situation you relate.* If you experienced the situation, describe your own emotions. Use specific adjectives rather than general terms such as *happy* or *sad*. One speaker, talking about receiving her first speech assignment, described her reaction with these words: "My heart stopped. Panic began to rise up inside. Me? . . . For the next five days I lived in dreaded anticipation of the forthcoming event."[6]

Note how effectively her choices of such words and phrases as "my heart stopped," "panic," and "dreaded anticipation" describes her terror at the prospect of making a speech—much more so than if she had said simply, "I was scared."

The more vividly and accurately you can describe emotion, the more intimately involved in your description the audience will become.

Use Effective Visual Reinforcement

Research about learning styles suggests that many of your listeners are more likely to remember your ideas if you can reinforce them with presentation aids. As we noted in Chapter 14, pictures, graphs, posters, and computer-generated graphics can help you gain and maintain audience members' attention, as well as increase their retention. Today's audiences are exposed daily to a barrage of messages conveyed through highly visual electronic media—CD-ROM, the World Wide Web, and video. They have grown to depend on more than words alone to help them remember ideas and information. When you present summaries of data, a well-crafted line graph or colorful pie chart can quickly and memorably reinforce the words and numbers you cite.

Strategies to Enhance Audience Interest

Before you can inform someone, you must gain and maintain his or her interest. No matter how carefully crafted your definitions, skillfully delivered your description of a process, or visually reinforcing your presentation aid, if your listeners aren't paying attention you won't achieve your goal of informing them. Strategies for gaining and holding interest are vital in achieving your speaking goal.

In discussing how to develop attention-catching introductions in Chapter 10, we itemized several specific techniques for gaining your listeners' attention. The following strategies build on those techniques.

Establish a Motive for Your Audience to Listen to You

Most audiences will probably not be waiting breathlessly for you to talk to them. You will need to motivate them to listen to you.

Some situations have built-in motivations for listeners. A teacher can say, "There will be a test covering my lecture tomorrow. It will count toward 50 percent of your semester grade." Such threatening methods may not make the teacher popular, but they certainly will motivate the class to listen. Similarly, a boss might say, "Your ability to use these sales principles will determine whether you keep your job." As with the teacher, your boss's statement will probably motivate you to learn the company's sales principles. However, because you will rarely have the power to motivate your listeners with such strong-arm tactics, you will need to find more creative ways to get your audience to listen to you.

Don't assume that your listeners will be automatically interested in what you have to say. Pique their interest with a rhetorical question. Tell them a story. Tell them how the information you present will be of value to them. As the British writer G. K. Chesterton once said, "There is no such thing as an uninteresting topic; there are only uninterested people."[7]

Tell a Story

Good stories with interesting characters and riveting plots have fascinated listeners for millennia; the words "once upon a time . . ." have been a sure-fire attention getter since ancient times. A good story is inherently interesting.

The characteristics of a well-told tale are simple yet powerful. Stories are also a way of connecting your message to people from a variety of cultural backgrounds. Here we elaborate on some of the ideas about storytelling we introduced in Chapter 8. A good story includes conflict, incorporates action, creates suspense, and may also include humor.

- *A good story incorporates conflict.* Stories that pit one side against another, and descriptions of opposing ideas and forces in government, religion, or personal relationships foster attention. The Greeks learned long ago that the essential ingredient for a good play, be it comedy or tragedy, is conflict.

- *A good story includes action.* An audience is more likely to listen to an action-paced message than to one that listlessly lingers on an idea too long. Good stories have a beginning that sets the stage, a heart of the story that moves to a conclusion, and then an ending that ties up all the loose ends. The key to interest is a plot that moves along to hold interest.

- *A good story creates suspense.* TV dramas and soap operas long ago proved that the way to ensure high ratings is to tell a story with the outcome in doubt. Suspense is created when the characters in the story may do one of several things. A story that keeps people on the edge of their seats because they don't know what will happen next is another element in good storytelling.

- *A good story may incorporate humor.* A fisherman went into a sporting-goods store. The salesperson offered the man a wonderful lure for trout: It had beautiful colors, eight hooks, and looked just like a rare Buckner bug. Finally, the fisherman asked the salesperson, "Do fish really like this thing?"

  "I don't really know," admitted the salesperson, "I don't sell to fish."

  The speaker using this story could have simply said, "It's important to be audience-centered." Using a bit of humor makes the point while holding the listener's attention.

  Not all stories have to be funny. Stories may be sad or dramatic without humor. But adding humor at appropriate times usually helps maintain interest and attention.

Present Information that Relates to Your Listeners

Throughout this book, we have encouraged you to develop an audience-centered approach to public speaking. Being an audience-centered informative speaker means being aware of information that your audience can use. If, for example, you are going to teach your audience pointers about trash recycling, be sure to talk about specific recycling efforts on your campus or in your own community. Adapt your message to the people who will be in your audience.

Strategies to Enhance Audience Recall

Think of the best teacher you ever had. He or she was probably a good lecturer with a special talent for being not only clear and interesting but also memorable. The very fact that you can remember your teacher is a testament to his or her talent. Like teachers, some speakers are better than others at presenting information in a memorable way. In this final section, we review strategies that will help your audiences remember you and your message.

Build In Redundancy

It is seldom necessary for writers to repeat themselves. If readers don't quite understand a passage, they can go back and read it again. When you speak, however, it is useful to repeat key points. Audience members generally cannot stop you if a point in your speech is unclear or if their minds wander.

How do you make your message redundant without insulting your listeners' intelligence? We've already mentioned several techniques in this book. Permit us some redundancy here to make our point. A clear preview at the beginning of your talk as

Speakers, unlike writers whose audiences can go back to read the words again, have just one chance to get their message across. Therefore, speakers should seek ways to help listeners remember the message.

[© Daemmrich Photography]

well as a summary statement in your conclusion are the most straightforward ways to make sure listeners get your points. An internal summary, a short summary after key points during your speech, is another technique to help audiences remember key ideas. Using numeric signposts (the practice of numbering key ideas by saying, "My first point is. . . . My second point is. . . . And now here's my third point. . . .") is another way of making sure your audience can identify and remember key points. A reinforcing visual aid in which your key ideas are displayed on a PowerPoint slide or overhead transparency can also enhance recall. If you really want to ensure that listeners come away from your speech with essential information, consider preparing a handout or an outline of key ideas. But as we noted in the last chapter, when using a handout make sure the audience is focusing on you, not on your handout.

Pace Your Information Flow

Organize your speech so that you present an even flow of information, rather than bunch up a number of significant details around one point. If you present too much new information too quickly, you may overwhelm your audience. Their ability to understand may falter.

You should be especially sensitive to the flow of information if your topic is new or unfamiliar to your listeners. Make sure that your audience has time to process any new information you present. Use supporting materials both to help clarify new information and to slow down the pace of your presentation.

Again, do not try to see how much detail and content you can cram into a speech. Your job is to present information so that the audience can grasp it, not to show off how much you know.

Reinforce Key Ideas Verbally

You can reinforce an idea by using such phrases as "This is the most important point" or "Be sure to remember this next point; it's the most compelling one." Suppose you have four suggestions for helping your listeners avoid a serious sunburn, and your last suggestion is the most important. How can you make sure your audience knows that? Just tell them. "Of all the suggestions I've given you, this last tip is the most important one. Here it is: The higher the SPF level on your sunscreen, the better." Be careful not to overuse this technique. If you claim that every other point is a key point, soon your audience will not believe you.

Reinforce Key Ideas Nonverbally

You can also signal the importance of a point with nonverbal emphasis. Gestures serve the purpose of accenting or emphasizing key phrases, as italics do in written communication.

A well-placed pause can provide emphasis and reinforcement to set off a point. Pausing just before or just after making an important point will focus attention on your thought. Raising or lowering your voice can also reinforce a key idea.

Movement can help emphasize major ideas. Moving from behind the lectern to tell a personal anecdote can signal that something special and more intimate is about to be

BRAIN FINGERPRINTING

Informative Speech

By Chad Crowson, University of Texas at Austin

As the people of Council Bluffs, Iowa, went to bed on the night of July 22, 1977, everything seemed perfectly normal. And according to the *Omaha World Herald* on November 14, 2000, that's exactly why those same people were stunned the next morning, when they turned on the local news to find that one of their own was lying dead on the railroad tracks near Lake Manawa. After a short round of interrogations, police were quick to arrest Terry Harrington for the crime. Now, after 23 years of imprisonment, Terry is finally getting a chance to prove his original claim: that on that fateful night in 1977, he was with his friends at a concert 20 miles outside of town. Today, his hopes for exoneration hinge on a revolutionary new technology . . . the brain fingerprint.

According to Dr. Lawrence Farwell, the inventor of this mind-boggling technology, on BrainWaveScience.com, last updated March 8, 2001, the brain fingerprint is an astounding extension to our knowledge of how memory works. "The practical implication of brain fingerprinting is that serial killers go to prison, and innocent, falsely accused people have a chance to finally be freed." In order to understand this new, crime-fighting tool, we must, first, discuss what brain fingerprinting is and how it works; second, examine its effectiveness; and finally, explore what it holds in store for our future.

We've all heard about guilty people beating polygraphs, truth serums, and even hypnosis, but brain fingerprinting will put our minds at ease. *Law and Order,* no, not the TV show, the magazine for police management, reports in the June 1999 issue that "brain fingerprinting is based on the principle that the brain is central to all human activities. . . . if a subject has information pertaining to a crime, this information is permanently stored in the brain." With brain fingerprinting, this permanent record can be extracted to become the best source of evidence of a crime. The January 2001 issue of the *Journal of Forensic Sciences* explains the process. To set up the test, the suspect wears a headband equipped with sensors connected to an amplifier that feeds brain wave data into a computer. Then, the suspect is seated in front of a computer screen that flashes different visual stimuli. As the words and pictures are flashed upon the screen, the computer reads the suspect's electroencephalographs, or EEG, and records brain-wave patterns on a separate computer. The *Des Moines Register* notes on March 6, 2001, that the words and pictures will only remain for a fraction of a second. If the suspect recognizes it, a memory response will occur. For example, the *Times of London* points out on January 15, 2001, that "if a person is shown a series of random seven-digit numbers, and his or her phone number is buried among them, the phone number is the only one that will elicit the response." Thanks to this technology, then, we can measure whether or not a suspect has knowledge of a crime simply by including amongst the words and pictures things that only the perpetrator would know, such as the weapon used, or the particular set-up of the crime scene.

One hundred years ago, we marveled at the future possibilities of the newly discovered fingerprint. Twenty years ago, we wondered if DNA fingerprinting would ever work. Today, we're going to explore the mind-numbing effectiveness of the brain fingerprint. Now, the lie detector seldom has been accepted in court, because it measures physiological responses such as pulse, breathing rates, and sweating, which vary widely from person to person. But the *Independent of London* reports on January 12, 2001, that "brain fingerprinting looks for evidence of knowledge, not deception . . ." thereby avoiding physiological responses that can lead to inaccurate results. Based on more than 120 tests on FBI agents and tests for a U.S. intelligence agency, the U.S. Navy, and in real-life situations the *Village Voice* of February 27, 2001, notes that, "the process is 100 percent accurate."

Chad catches his listeners' attention with an interesting illustration.

Using contemporary research, Chad draws on an expert to define the key concept he will be discussing.

Note the clear preview of his three major ideas.

He develops his first point by using a variety of definitions and examples.

Chad now moves to his second point, which is to describe the effectiveness and reliability of brain fingerprints.

In brain fingerprinting, it seems that we have found our first form of reliable nonphysical evidence. But if you don't worry about ever being falsely accused, consider this. BrainWave-Science.com, last updated March 8, 2001, notes, "the total government budget devoted to crime has been estimated at $750 billion (a year). . . . Brain fingerprinting can solve these cases more quickly and accurately than has been possible before and thus . . . can save billions of dollars annually in the U.S. alone."

But before I go out of my mind and suggest that the government give all that money back to us in tax cuts, we must take a look at the concerns about the brain fingerprint and examine its future potential. While the brain fingerprint may raise Orwellian concerns, you, not Big Brother, must decide whether or not to take the test. Without such agreement, the test won't work and odds are, your alibi won't either. However, many worry that the brain fingerprint, much like the polygraph test, will never be accepted in court. Yet, the *Dallas Morning News* on February 11, 2001, points out that, to be admissible in court, scientific evidence must be not only relevant, but reliable. Because brain fingerprinting is completely computer controlled and no questions are asked or answered during the process, it is impossible for humans to bias the evidence or influence the person being tested. Dr. Farwell, himself, raises another concern, though: His machine cannot distinguish between knowledge obtained firsthand and knowledge learned elsewhere, like at trial or from the media. But *U.S. News and World Report* on January 15, 2001, states that you simply need to find details of the crime that weren't in court transcripts or publicized. The television news program *60 Minutes* explains in its December 10, 2000, broadcast that police knew the suspect in the Terry Harrington case escaped behind a building through waist-high weeds and grass. Then, that information was kept confidential and later used in the test on Harrington, who had no memory responses to the building or the weeds, thus making it impossible for him to be truly guilty.

Is your brain fried? Scrambled, perhaps? Well, rest assured that the concerns about brain fingerprinting are well under control and its future remains sunny side up. The *New York Times* reports on November 19, 2000, that brain fingerprinting "might bring a new level of legitimacy to extracting truth mechanically." The brain fingerprint may put to an end the legal wrangling associated with repressed memories. *U.S. News and World Report* states on March 26, 2001, that victims can bury any recollection of the traumatic events, making it impossible for them to help identify and testify against those accused. However, the knowledge of the event remains in their brain and often reappears later. The brain fingerprint can find that information in hidden recesses of the brain and put it to use long before the statute of limitations expires. And the brain fingerprint will also impact one of the biggest controversies in the legal system today: the reliability of children's testimony. Despite being viewed by legal scholars as easily coached witnesses, the testimony of children largely has been accepted in court. Consider the case of Gerald Amirault. The *Wall Street Journal* on May 12, 2000, describes that on an otherwise normal day in 1986, Gerald, his sister Cheryl, and their mother, Violet, were arrested and subsequently convicted of, "atrocious sexual crimes against children," the same children they nurtured every day at Fells Acres Day School in Massachusetts. Over the last 15 years, both his sister and mother have been exonerated, but Gerald Amirault still sits in a Massachusetts prison. Many, however, believe that all three convictions were based on false testimony of the children in the day care center, concocted by police and prosecutors. The brain fingerprint can help to ensure an honest and nonbiased recollection of events, enabling cases like this one to be more accurately resolved. Needless to say, fingerprinting has reached a new level.

After exploring what brain fingerprinting is and how it works, realizing its effectiveness, and discussing its future potential, we have developed a better understanding of a tool that promises to turn the criminal justice system on end. Terry Harrington continues his fight for freedom after 23 years of imprisonment. And, thanks to Dr. Farwell's brain-fingerprinting technology, he may finally get it. Little did he know when he started his fight that his ticket to freedom was right there, in the back of his mind.

He now moves to his third point, a point that he previewed in his introduction.

To establish his credibility, Chad draws on not only expert opinion but also magazine and TV programs with which his audience is familiar.

Here he uses rhetorical questions to maintain interest.

He concludes his speech, providing psychological closure by referring to the illustration he used to open his speech.

said. As we discussed in Chapter 13, your movement and gestures should be meaningful and natural, rather than seemingly arbitrary or forced. Your need to emphasize an idea can provide the motivation to make a meaningful movement.

To illustrate the principles and strategies of effectively informing others, we conclude this chapter with a sample speech. Note how Chad Crowson uses many of the approaches to crafting an informative speech that we've emphasized.

SUMMARY

To inform is to teach someone something you know. Public speakers use specific goals, principles, and strategies to inform others.

There are three goals of informative speeches—to enhance understanding, to maintain interest, and to be remembered. To achieve these goals, you have several different types of informative speeches you may deliver. Speeches about objects discuss tangible things. Speeches about procedures explain a process or describe how something works. Speeches about people can be about either the famous or the little known. Speeches about events describe major occurrences or personal experiences. Finally, speeches about ideas are often abstract and generally discuss principles, concepts, or theories.

To enhance your listeners' understanding of a message, (1) define ideas clearly, (2) clarify complex processes, (3) use principles and techniques of adult learning; use andragogical rather than pedagogical educational assumptions, (4) use definitions effectively, and (5) use effective visual reinforcement of your ideas when appropriate.

To gain and maintain interest in your informative talk, follow three important principles. First, establish a motive for your audience to listen to you. Next, tell a well-told story; a good story almost always works to keep listeners focused on you and your message. Finally, it is important to present information that relates to your listeners' interest; in essence, be audience-centered.

Help your listeners remember what you told them. Being redundant is one suggestion made that your English teacher told you to avoid; in oral communication, however, it is sometimes appropriate to foreshadow or restate the key ideas of your message. Pacing the flow of your information helps listeners recall your ideas. Reinforcing your ideas verbally and nonverbally can also help your audience members remember important points you make.

being audience-centered

A Sharper Focus

CONSIDERING YOUR AUDIENCE

▶ Reflect on your audience's background to help you decide whether you need to explicitly define terms you use in your speech.

▶ If you are presenting completely new information to listeners, use simple, familiar examples.

▶ If your audience consists of adult listeners, remember that adults like information that they can use immediately, like to be actively involved in the learning process, like to connect their life experience with the new information they learn, and like to know how the new information is relevant to their needs and busy lives.

▶ If you're describing a complex process to your listeners, use more than definitions to explain what you mean. Consider using analogies, word pictures, or visual aids to make your ideas clear.

▶ Most audiences will probably not be waiting breathlessly for you to talk to them. You will need to motivate them to listen to you. Think about what they are interested in and how they can apply the information you share.

▶ Being an audience-centered public speaker means being aware of information that your audience can use.

CONSIDERING AUDIENCE DIVERSITY

▶ A good story is a way to communicate ideas to people from various cultural backgrounds; many cultural groups, such as those from the Middle East, prefer stories and illustrations rather than detailed definitions and data.

▶ When speaking to a group that may have difficulty understanding your message because of language differences, it is important to build redundancy into your message. Use preview statements, internal summaries, and closing summaries to ensure that your audience captures your major points.

▶ Use visual images to reinforce your verbal message to people from a variety of cultural backgrounds; visual images can communicate clearly even when words are not clearly understood.

CRITICAL-THINKING QUESTIONS

1. You have been asked to speak to a kindergarten class about your chosen profession. Identify approaches to this task that would help make your message clear, interesting, and memorable to your audience.

2. Hillary Webster, M.D., will be addressing a medical convention of other physicians to discuss the recent weight-loss technique she has successfully used with her patients. What advice would you give to help her present an effective talk?

3. Ken's boss has given him the task of presenting a report to a group of potential investors about his company's recent productivity trends. The presentation includes many statistics. What suggestions would you offer to help Ken give an interesting and effective informative presentation?

ETHICAL QUESTIONS

1. Before giving a speech to your class in which you share personal information about a friend of yours, should you ask permission from your friend?

2. You are a chemistry major, and you are considering whether you should give a speech to your public-speaking class about how pipe bombs are made. Is this an appropriate topic for your audience?

3. In order to give your five-minute speech about nuclear energy, you are going to have to make the presentation very simple, even though the process you describe is complex. How can you avoid misrepresenting your topic? Should you let your audience know that you are oversimplifying the process?

SUGGESTED ACTIVITIES

1. From the following list of suggested topics for an informative speech, select five and develop a specific-purpose sentence for each. For one of those topics, identify two to four major ideas. Organize them topically, chronologically, or according to some other logical pattern of organization.

   How to get a better grade in public speaking

   The spread of terrorism in the Middle East

   How the U.S. Constitution was written

   A historical person I wish I could meet

   What makes a good teacher

   The best way to lose weight

   School violence

   Surrogate parenthood

   Safe-driving principles

   How the stock market works

   CB radios

2. Write a word picture—a vivid, colorful description that appeals to the senses—for one of the following scenes:

   A holiday when you were 6

   A visit to your grandparents' house

   Your first day at college

   Your most frightening experience

   Your most memorable birthday celebration

3. You've recently started to learn to play the cello. Your son's first-grade teacher has invited you to talk to your son's class about the cello. A local music club has also asked you to give a short talk about the joy and challenge of cello playing. How would you adapt your message to both groups? Consider such factors as length of your talk, ways of organizing your message, and, with the music-club group, principles and strategies for speaking to adult listeners.

4. If you are speaking to an audience in which many people speak English as a second language, which strategies for enhancing understanding, interest, and recall that we've presented in this chapter will be especially useful to you?

5. Describe the demographic and cultural characteristics of an audience to which you'd feel most comfortable presenting an informative talk. Identify the age, gender, ethnicity, cultural background, and other aspects of this "ideal audience." Even with these compatible listeners, what principles and strategies of informing them would you emphasize? Describe an audience composed of people who would significantly differ from your "comfort-zone" audience. How would you adapt your informative message to this different group of listeners?

USING TECHNOLOGY AND MEDIA

1. Use the key word thesaurus of an electronic database such as *Educational Resources Information Center* (ERIC) or the *Index to the Humanities* to help you select and explore a topic for an informative speech.

2. If your word-processing software includes an electronic dictionary, use it to define key terms and concepts in your informative speech. Use the thesaurus to help you make your language vivid.

3. You might find useful video or photo images to help you describe complex processes by consulting one of the many CD-ROM encyclopedias or searching the Internet. Although many electronic encyclopedias use fewer words to describe a process than print encyclopedias, they often include effective moving images or graphics. Use these for inspiration to develop your own visual aids.

. . . the power of speech, to stir men's blood.

WILLIAM SHAKESPEARE

16

Understanding Principles of Persuasive Speaking

objectives

After studying this chapter you should be able to do the following:

1. Define persuasion.

2. Describe cognitive dissonance.

3. Identify Maslow's five levels of needs, which explain how behavior is motivated.

4. Select and develop an appropriate topic for a persuasive speech.

5. Identify three principles of persuasive speaking.

It happens more than 600 times each day. It appears as commercials on TV and radio; as advertisements in magazines, newspapers, and billboards; and as fund-raising letters from politicians and charities. It also occurs when you are asked to give money to a worthy cause or to donate blood. "It" is persuasion. Efforts to persuade you occur at an average rate of once every two and a half minutes each day.[1] Because persuasion is such an ever-present part of your life, it is important for you to understand how it works. What are the principles of an activity that can shape your attitudes and behavior? What do car salespeople, advertising copywriters, and politicians know about how to change your thinking and behavior, that you don't?

In this chapter, we are going to discuss how persuasion works. Such information can help you sharpen your own persuasive skills and can also help you become a more informed receiver of the persuasive messages that come your way. In this chapter, we will define persuasion and discuss the psychological principles underlying all or most efforts at persuading others. We will also discuss some tips for choosing a persuasive speech topic and developing arguments for your speeches. In Chapter 17, we will examine some of the specific strategies for crafting a persuasive speech.

In Chapter 15, we discussed several strategies for informative speaking—the oral presentation of new information to listeners so that they will understand and remember what is communicated. The purposes of informing and persuading are interrelated. Why inform an audience? Why give new information to others? We often provide information to give listeners new insights that may affect their attitudes and behavior. Information alone has the potential to convince others, but if information is coupled with strategies to persuade, the chances of success increase. Persuasive speakers try to influence the listeners' points of view or behavior. If you want your listeners to respond to your persuasive appeal, you will need to think carefully about the way you structure your message to achieve your specific purpose.

Because of the interrelationship between persuasive speaking and informative speaking, you will build on the principles of informative speaking that you studied in Chapter 15. Your speech will still need to be well organized, with interesting supporting material, well-chosen language, smooth transitions, and fluent delivery. But now your speech purpose will target change or reinforcement of your audience's attitudes, beliefs, values, or behavior. As a persuasive speaker, you will need to develop arguments and evidence to support your speech's objective.

In this context, the word *argument* does not mean "quarrel" or "disagreement." Rather, it means "reason for believing something," and *evidence* is the proof that supports the reason. Arguments and evidence always go together, just as they do in a court of law.

Your credibility as a speaker is even more important when your objective is to persuade rather than inform listeners. Your audience is more likely to be persuaded if they believe, trust, and like you. To be fully persuasive, you will also need to appeal to your listeners' emotions as you try to change or reinforce their ideas and behavior. In short, the art of persuading others involves appeals to reason and emotion.

In persuasive speeches, the speaker asks the audience to make an explicit choice, rather than just informing them of the options. As a persuasive speaker, you will do more than teach; you will ask your listeners to respond to the information you share.

Audience analysis is crucial to achieving your goal. To advocate a particular view or position successfully, you must understand your listeners' attitudes, beliefs, values, and behavior. ▬

Persuasion Defined

Persuasion is the process of changing or reinforcing attitudes, beliefs, values, or behavior. Although knowing your listeners' attitudes, beliefs, and values can help you craft any message, these three variables—which we introduced in Chapter 5, when discussing psychological audience analysis—are especially important to consider when designing and delivering a persuasive message.

Stated more technically, our **attitudes** represent our likes and dislikes. An attitude is a learned predisposition to respond favorably or unfavorably toward something. In a persuasive speech, you might try to persuade your listeners to favor or oppose a new shopping mall, to like bats because of their ability to eat insects, or to dislike an increase in sales tax.

A persuasive speech could also change or reinforce a belief. A **belief** is what you understand to be true or false. If you believe in something, you are convinced it exists or is true. You have structured your sense of what is real and what is unreal to account for the existence of whatever you believe. If you believe in God, you have structured your sense of what is real and unreal to recognize the existence of God. Beliefs are typically based on past experiences. If you believe the sun will rise in the east again tomorrow, or that nuclear power is safe, you base these beliefs either on what you've directly experienced or on the experience of someone you find trustworthy. Beliefs are usually based on evidence, but we hold some beliefs based on faith—something we haven't directly observed but believe anyway.

A persuasive speech could also seek to change or reinforce a value. A **value** is an enduring conception of right or wrong, good or bad. If you value something, you classify it as good or desirable. If you do not value something, you think of it as bad or wrong. Values form the basis of your life goals and the motivating force behind your behavior. Most Americans value honesty, trustworthiness, freedom, loyalty, marriage, family, and money. Understanding what your listeners value can help you refine your analysis of them and adapt the content of your speech to those values.

Why is it useful to make distinctions among attitudes, beliefs, and values? Since the essence of persuasion is to change or reinforce these three qualities, it is very useful to know exactly which one you are targeting. Of the three qualities, audience values are the most stable. Most of us acquired our values when we were very young and have held on to them into adulthood. Our values, therefore, are generally deeply ingrained. It is not impossible to change the values of your listeners, but it is much more difficult than trying to change a belief or an attitude. Political and religious points of view, which are usually based on long-held values, are especially difficult to modify.

A belief is more susceptible to change than a value, but it is still difficult to alter. Beliefs are changed by evidence. You might have a difficult time, for example, trying to change someone's belief that the world is flat; you would need to show that existing evidence supports a different conclusion. Usually it takes a great deal of evidence to change a belief and alter the way your audience structures reality.

Attitudes (likes and dislikes) are easier to change than either beliefs or values. Today we may approve of the President of the United States; tomorrow we may disapprove because of a recent action he has taken. We may still *believe* that the country

persuasion
The process of changing or reinforcing a listener's attitudes, beliefs, values, or behavior

attitude
A learned predisposition to respond favorably or unfavorably toward something, a like or dislike of something

belief
The degree of confidence with which something is perceived as true or false

value
An enduring conception of right or wrong, good or bad

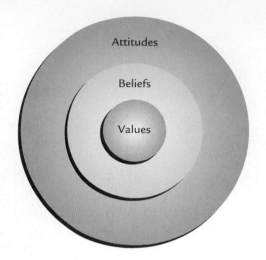

FIGURE **16.1**

Attitudes—our likes and dislikes—are more likely to change than are our beliefs or values. Our sense of what is right and wrong—our values—are least likely to change over time.

is financially stable, and we may still value a democratic form of government, but our *attitude* toward the President has changed because of his recent policy decision.

As Figure 16.1 shows, values are the most deeply ingrained; they change least frequently. That's why values are in the core of the model. Beliefs change, but not as much as attitudes. Trying to change an audience's attitudes is easier than attempting to change their values. We suggest that you think carefully about your purpose in making a persuasive speech. Know with certainty whether your objective is to change or reinforce an attitude, a belief, or a value. Then decide what you have to do to achieve your objective.

Speeches that focus on changing or reinforcing audience values emphasize how and why something is better than something else. Persuasive speeches that discuss abortion rights, animal rights, euthanasia, and embryo stem-cell research are examples of speech topics that typically touch on listeners' values.

Persuasive messages often attempt to do more than change or reinforce attitudes, beliefs, or values—they may attempt to change our behavior. To eat less, not to smoke tobacco, not to consume drugs, not to drink and drive, or to exercise more are typical goals of persuasive messages that we hear. It seems logical that knowing someone's attitudes, beliefs, and values will let us precisely predict how that person will behave. But we are complicated creatures and human behavior is not always neatly predicted. Sometimes our attitudes, beliefs, and values don't jibe with how we act. For example, you may know that if you're on a calorie-reducing diet, you should avoid that second helping of Dad's home-cooked meatloaf; but you cut off a slice, douse it with ketchup, and gobble it up anyway. Several factors motivate us to respond to persuasive messages: our actual and perceived needs, our tendency to avoid pain and seek pleasure, our emotional reactions and our compulsion to seek psychological balance and order in our lives. To further help you understand what motivates and persuades listeners, we'll examine factors of motivation in greater detail.

How to Motivate Listeners

It's late at night, and you're watching your favorite talk show before going to bed. The program is interrupted by a commercial extolling the virtues of ice cream. Suddenly, you remember that you have the flavor advertised, Royal Rocky Road. You apparently hadn't realized how hungry you were for ice cream until the ad reminded you of the lip-smacking goodness of the cool, creamy, smooth treat. Before you know it, you are at the freezer, doling out a couple of scoops of ice cream.

If the sponsor of that commercial knew how effective it had been, he or she would be overjoyed. The ad was persuasive and changed your behavior because the message was tailor-made for you. What principles explain why you were motivated to dig through the freezer at midnight for a carton of ice cream? At the heart of the persuasion process is the audience-centered process of motivating listeners to respond to your message. Persuasion works because listeners are motivated to respond to a message. An audience is more likely to be persuaded if you help members solve their problems or meet their needs. They can also be motivated if you convince them good things will happen to them if they follow your advice, or bad things will occur if they don't. Let's consider each of these strategies for motivating listeners in more detail.

Use Dissonance

Dissonance theory is based on the principle that people strive to solve problems and manage stress and tension in a way that is consistent with their attitudes, beliefs, and values.[2] According to the theory, when you are presented with information inconsistent with your current attitudes, beliefs, values, or behavior, you become aware that you have a problem; you experience a kind of discomfort called **cognitive dissonance**. The word *cognitive* has to do with our thoughts. *Dissonance* means "lack of harmony or agreement." When you think of a dissonant chord in music, you probably think of a series of sounds that are unpleasant or not in tune with the melody or other chords. Most people seek to avoid problems or feelings of dissonance. Cognitive dissonance, then, means that you are experiencing a way of thinking that is inconsistent and uncomfortable. If, for example, you smoke cigarettes and a speaker reminds you that smoking is unhealthy, this reminder creates dissonance. You can restore balance and solve the problem either by no longer smoking or by rejecting the message that smoking is harmful to you.

The need to restore balance is common. We have all experienced it at one time or another. If you are walking down a flight of stairs too fast and start to lose your balance, you will probably grab for the handrail so you won't fall. This is similar to the process that, according to dissonance theory, occurs psychologically when information you hear causes you discomfort.

Creating dissonance in a persuasive speech can be an effective way to change attitudes and behavior. The first tactic in such a speech is to identify an existing problem or need. For example, a speaker seeking to ban aerosol sprays could begin her speech by focusing on a need we all generally share, such as the need for a well-preserved environment. The speaker could then point out that the continued use of aerosol sprays depletes the ozone layer, which protects us from the sun's harmful rays. By doing so, the speaker is deliberately creating dissonance. She knows that people in her audience appreciate the convenience of aerosol sprays, so their attitudes about protecting the environment *conflict with* their feelings about getting housework done easily or styling their hair effectively. So her next move would aim at restoring the audience's sense of balance. She could claim that her solution—using nonaerosol sprays—can resolve the conflict. Using this strategy, the speaker may motivate the audience to change their behavior. The change itself is her objective.

Political candidates use a similar strategy. A mayoral candidate usually tries first to make his or her audience aware of problems in the community, then blames the current mayor for most of the problems. Once dissonance has been created, the candidate then suggests that these problems would be solved, or at least managed better, if he or she were to be elected as the city's next mayor. Using the principles of dissonance theory, the mayoral candidate first upsets the audience, then restores their balance and feeling of comfort by providing a solution to the city's problem: his or her selection as mayor.

Vonda Ramey, calling for more attention to children who cannot read, created dissonance in the minds of her listeners when she documented the widespread problem of illiteracy in her prize-winning oration "Can You Read This?"

Effective public-service messages often use cognitive dissonance to change people's behaviors. This technique is also often effective for public speakers.

[Rhoda Sidney/Stock Boston]

cognitive dissonance
The sense of disorganization that prompts a person to change when new information conflicts with previously organized thought patterns

Approximately two-thirds of U.S. colleges and universities have to provide remedial reading and writing courses for students. The University of California at Berkeley, which gets the top one-eighth of all high school students, has to put almost half of the freshmen in remedial composition classes.

Instructional materials used by the armed forces look like comic books, with pictures and simple language to help new recruits who have a problem reading. One manual has five pages of just pictures to show a soldier how to open the hood of a truck.[3]

Listeners are likely to experience some dissonance on learning how many people cannot read.

HOW LISTENERS COPE WITH DISSONANCE   Effective persuasion requires more than simply creating dissonance and then suggesting a solution to the problem. When your listeners confront dissonant information, a number of options are available to them besides following your suggestions. You need to be aware of other ways your audience may react before you can reduce their cognitive dissonance.[4]

- **Listeners may discredit the source.**   Instead of believing everything you say, your listeners could choose to discredit you. Suppose you drive a German-made BMW and you hear a speaker whose father owns a Chevrolet dealership advocate that all Americans should drive cars made in America. You could agree with him, or you could decide that the speaker is biased because of his father's occupation. Instead of selling your BMW and buying an American-made car, you could simply suspect the speaker's credibility and ignore the suggestion to buy American automobiles. When you seek to be a persuasive speaker, you need to ensure that your audience will perceive you as competent and trustworthy so that they will accept your message.

- **Listeners may reinterpret the message.**   A second way in which your listeners may overcome cognitive dissonance and restore balance is to hear what they want to hear. They may choose to focus on the parts of your message that are consistent with what they already believe and ignore the unfamiliar or controversial parts. Your job as an effective public speaker is to make your message as clear as possible so that your audience will not reinterpret your message. If you tell a customer looking at a new kind of computer that it takes ten steps to get into the word-processing program, but that the program is easy to use, the customer might focus on those first ten things and decide the computer is hard to use. Choose your words carefully, and use simple, vivid examples to keep listeners focused on what's most important.

- **Listeners may seek new information.**   Another way that listeners cope with cognitive dissonance when confronted with a distressing argument is to seek more information on the subject. Your audience members may look for additional information to negate your position and to refute your well-created arguments. As the owner of a minivan, you would experience dissonance if you hear a speaker describe the recent rash of safety problems with minivans. You might turn to your friend and whisper, "Is this true? Are minivans really dangerous? I've always heard they were safe." You would request new information to validate your ownership of a minivan. Similarly, when listeners hear a political speech that tries to change their view, they may seek new information to help justify their own stand on the issues.

- **Listeners may stop listening.** Some messages are so much at odds with listeners' attitudes, beliefs, and values that the audience may decide to stop listening. Most of us do not seek opportunities to hear or read messages that oppose our opinions. It is unlikely that a staunch Democrat would attend a fund-raiser for the state Republican party. The principle of selective exposure suggests that we tend to pay attention to messages that are consistent with our points of view and to avoid those that are not. When we do find ourselves trapped in a situation in which we are forced to hear a message that doesn't support our beliefs, we tend to tune the speaker out. We stop listening to avoid the dissonance. Being aware of the existing thoughts and feelings of the audience can help ensure that they won't tune you out.

- **Listeners may change their attitudes, beliefs, values, or behavior.** A fifth way an audience may respond to dissonant information is to do as the speaker wishes them to. As we have noted, if listeners change their attitudes, they can reduce the dissonance that they experience. You listen to a life-insurance salesperson tell you that when you die, your family will have no financial support. This creates dissonance; you think of your family as happy and secure. So you decide to take out a $100,000 policy to protect your family. This action restores your sense of balance. The salesperson has persuaded you successfully. The goals of advertising copywriters, salespeople, and political candidates are similar: They want you to experience dissonance so that you will change your attitudes, beliefs, values, or behavior.

Use Listener Needs

Need is one of the best motivators. The person who is looking at a new car because he or she needs one right now is more likely to buy one than the person who is just thinking about how nice it would be to drive the latest model. The more you understand what your listeners need, the greater the chances are that you can gain and hold their attention and ultimately get them to do what you want. The classic theory that outlines our basic needs was developed by Abraham Maslow.[5] Perhaps you've encountered this theory in a psychology class. Maslow suggests that there is a hierarchy of needs that motivates the behavior of all of us. Basic needs (such as food, water, and air) have to be satisfied before we can be motivated to respond to higher-level needs. Figure 16.2 illustrates Maslow's five levels of needs, with the most basic at the bottom. When attempting to persuade an audience, a public speaker tries to stimulate these needs in order to change or reinforce attitudes, beliefs, values, or behavior. Let's examine these needs in some detail.

Self-actualization needs

Self-esteem needs

Social needs

Safety needs

Physiological needs

FIGURE **16.2**

Maslow's hierarchy of needs.

PHYSIOLOGICAL NEEDS The most basic needs for all humans are physiological: air, water, and food. According to Maslow's theory, unless those needs are met, it will be difficult to motivate a listener to satisfy other needs. If your listeners are hot, tired, and thirsty, it will be more difficult to persuade them to vote for your candidate, buy your insurance policy, or sign your petition in support of local pet-leash laws. As a public speaker, you should be sensitive to the basic physiological needs of your audience so that your appeals to higher-level needs will be heard.

SAFETY NEEDS Once basic physiological needs are met, your listeners are concerned about their safety. We have a need to feel safe, secure, and protected, and we need to be able to predict that the need for safety of ourselves and our loved ones will be met. The classic sales presentation from insurance salespeople includes appeals to our need for safety and security. Many insurance sales efforts include photos of wrecked cars, anecdotes of people who were in ill health and could not pay their bills, or tales of the head of a household who passed away, leaving the basic needs of his or her family unmet. Appeals to use safety belts, stop smoking, start exercising, and use condoms all play to our need for safety and security.

In a speech titled "Emissions Tampering: Get the Lead Out," John appealed to his listeners' need for safety and security when he began his speech with these observations:

> A major American producer is currently dumping over 8,000 tons of lead into our air each year, which in turn adversely affects human health. The producers of this waste are tampering with pollution control devices in order to cut costs. This tampering escalates the amount of noxious gases you and I inhale by 300 to 800%. That producer is the American motorist.[6]

SOCIAL NEEDS We all need to feel loved and valued. We need contact and reassurance from others that they care about us. According to Maslow, these social needs translate into our need for a sense of belonging to a group (fraternity, religious organization, friends). Powerful persuasive appeals are based on our need for social contact. We are encouraged to buy a product or support a particular issue because others are buying the product or supporting the issue. The message is, to be liked and respected by others, we must buy the same things they do or support the same position they support.

SELF-ESTEEM NEEDS The need for self-esteem reflects our desire to think well of ourselves. Jesse Jackson is known for appealing often to the self-worth of his listeners by inviting them to chant, "I am somebody." This is a direct appeal to his listeners' need for self-esteem. Advertisers also appeal to our need for self-esteem when they encourage us to believe that we can be noticed by others or stand out in the crowd if we purchase their product. Commercials promoting luxury cars usually invite you to picture yourself in the driver's seat with a beautiful person next to you while you receive looks of envy from those you pass on the road. The powerful need for self-esteem fuels many persuasive messages.

SELF-ACTUALIZATION NEEDS At the top of Maslow's hierarchy is the need for **self-actualization.** This is the need to achieve our highest potential. For many years, the U.S. Army used the slogan "Be all that you can be" to tap into the need for self-actualization. Calls to be the best and the brightest are appeals to self-actualization. According to the assumption that our needs are organized into a hierarchy, the other four need levels must be satisfied before we can be motivated to achieve the ultimate in personal satisfaction.

self-actualization
The need to achieve our highest potential; to be " all that we can be"

Use Positive Motivation

A Depression-era politician claimed that a vote for him would result in a return to prosperity: "A chicken in every pot" was his positive motivational appeal. Positive motivational appeals are statements made by a speaker suggesting that good things will happen if the speaker's advice is heeded. A key to using positive motivational appeals effectively is to know what your listeners value. Knowing what audience members view as desirable, good, and virtuous can help you select the benefits of your persuasive proposal that best appeal to them.

What do most people value? A comfortable, prosperous life; stimulating, exciting activity; a sense of accomplishment; world, community, and personal peace; and happiness are some of the many things people value.

How can you use these values in a persuasive speech? When identifying reasons for your audience to think, feel, or behave as you want them to, review the values just listed to determine what benefits would accrue to your listeners. If, for example, you advocate that your listeners enroll in a sign-language course, what are the benefits to the audience? You could stress the sense of accomplishment, contribution to society, or increased opportunities for friendship that would develop if they learned this new skill. A speech advocating that recording companies print the lyrics of all songs on the label of the recording could appeal to family values.

Most salespeople know that it is not enough just to identify, in general terms, the features of their product. They must translate those features into an obvious benefit that enhances the customer's quality of life. It is not enough for the real-estate salesperson to say, "This floor is the new no-wax vinyl." It is more effective to add, "And this means that you will never have to get down on your hands and knees to scrub another floor." The car salesperson who recommends purchasing the extra maintenance agreement and says, "By purchasing this extra maintenance coverage, you will never have to worry about repair bills for as long as you own this car," also makes a positive feature a readily identifiable benefit for the listener. When using positive motivational appeals, be sure your listeners know how the benefits of your proposal can improve their quality of life or the lives of their loved ones.

Use Negative Motivation

"If you don't stop what you're doing, I'm going to tell Mom!" Whether that sibling realized it or not, he was using a persuasive technique called *fear appeal.* One of the oldest methods of trying to change someone's attitude or behavior, the use of a threat is also one of the most effective. In essence, the appeal to fear takes the form of an "if-then" statement. If you don't do *X,* then awful things will happen to you. A persuader builds an argument on the assertion that a need will not be met unless the desired behavior or attitude change occurs. The principal reason that appeals to fear continue to be made in persuasive messages is that they work. A variety of research studies support the following principles for using fear appeals.[7]

- *A strong threat to a loved one tends to be more successful than a fear appeal directed at the audience members themselves.* A speaker using this principle might say, "Unless you are able to get your children to wear safety belts, they could easily be injured or killed in an auto accident."

- *The more competent, trustworthy, or respected the speaker, the greater the likelihood that an appeal to fear will be successful.* A speaker with less credibility will be more successful with moderate threats. The U.S. surgeon general will be more successful in convincing people to use condoms to lessen the risk of AIDS than you will.

- *Fear appeals are more successful if you can convince your listeners that the threat is real and will probably occur unless they take the action you are advocating.* For example, you could dramatically announce, "Last year, thousands of smokers developed lung cancer and eventually died. Unless you stop smoking, there is a high probability that you could develop lung cancer, too."

- *In general, increasing the intensity of a fear appeal increases the chances that the fear appeal will be effective; this is especially true if the listener can take some action (the action the persuader is suggesting) to reduce the threat.*[8] In the past, some researchers and public-speaking textbooks reported that if a speaker creates an excessive amount of fear and anxiety in listeners, the listeners may find the appeal so strong and annoying that they stop listening. More comprehensive research, however, has concluded that there is a direct link between the intensity or strength of the fear appeal and the likelihood that audience members will be persuaded by the message. Fear appeals work. Strong fear appeals seem to work even better than mild ones assuming that evidence backs up the threat made by a credible speaker. The speaker who uses fear appeals has an ethical responsibility to be truthful and not exaggerate when trying to arouse listeners' fear.

The effectiveness of fear appeals is based on the theories of cognitive dissonance and Maslow's hierarchy of needs. The fear aroused creates dissonance, which can be reduced by following the recommendation of the persuader. Appeals to fear are also based on targeting an unmet need. Fear appeals depend on a convincing insistence that a need will go unmet unless a particular action or attitude change occurs.

RECAP

USING FEAR APPEALS TO PERSUADE

1. Fear appeals involving loved ones are often more effective than appeals involving audience members themselves.

2. The greater your credibility, the more likely your fear appeal will be effective.

3. You must convince your audience that the threat is real and could actually happen.

4. Strong fear appeals are more effective than mild fear appeals if there is evidence to support the threat made by the speaker.

Cognitive dissonance, needs, and appeals to the emotions, both positive and negative, can all persuade listeners to change their attitudes, beliefs, values, and behavior. Realize, however, that persuasion is not as simple as these approaches may lead you to believe. There is no precise formula for motivating and convincing an audience. Attitude change occurs differently in each individual; there are no magic words, phrases, or appeals. Persuasion is an art that draws on science. Cultivating a sensitivity to listeners' emotions and needs, and ethically using public-speaking strategies you have learned, will help you make your persuasive messages effective.

Theory	Description	Example
Cognitive Dissonance	Creating or stimulating discomfort by telling listeners about existing problems or information that is inconsistent with their currently held beliefs or known information.	Many high-school students today do not have computer-literacy skills. Without this knowledge, your students will not be competitive in today's job market. You should support the local school-bond proposal that would provide more money for computers in our school.
Hierarchy of Needs	People are motivated by unmet needs. The most basic are physiological, then safety needs, social needs, self-esteem needs, and finally self-actualization needs.	You could be the envy of people you know if you purchase this new, sleek sports car. You will be perceived as a person of high status in your community.
Positive Motivation	People will be more likely to pursue a particular course of thought or action if they are convinced that good things will happen to them if they support what the speaker advocates.	You should take a course in public speaking because it will increase your prospects of getting a good job. Effective communication skills are the most sought-after skills in today's workplace.
Negative Motivation	People seek to avoid pain and discomfort. They will be motivated to support what a speaker advocates if they are convinced that bad things will happen to them unless they do what the speaker suggests.	If you touch a letter or package mailed to you that looks suspicious because it is unusually lumpy, has no return address, is marked "personal" or "confidential," or is from someone you do not know, wash your hands after you touch the letter. Report the suspicious letter or package to the post office immediately. If you do not heed these suggestions, you increase the chances of being contaminated by a biological agent.

How to Develop Your Persuasive Speech

Now that you understand what persuasion is and how it works, let's turn our attention to the task of preparing a persuasive speech. The process of developing a persuasive speech follows the same audience-centered path you would take to develop any speech.

In the remaining portion of this chapter and the next, we will amplify our discussion of these essential steps, providing specific examples and strategies to help you prepare a persuasive message. In this chapter, we'll give you some tips for getting started with the speech-construction process. As illustrated by the center of our now-familiar model of the speechmaking process in Figure 16.3, you first consider your audience, especially when attempting to persuade listeners. We'll also provide additional guidance about developing a persuasive speech purpose as well as developing your central idea and generate major ideas for your speech. In the next chapter, we will provide additional practical strategies to help you enhance your credibility, use emotional persuasive appeals, and use evidence and reasoning as supportive material. We'll also present special strategies for organizing persuasive messages.

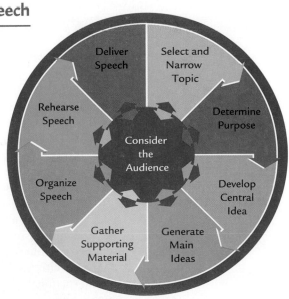

FIGURE **16.3**

Considering the audience is central to the speechmaking process.

Consider the Audience

Although being audience-centered is important in every speaking situation, it is vital when your objective is to persuade. It would be a challenge to persuade someone without knowing something about his or her interests, attitudes, beliefs, values, and behaviors. You may want to review the elements of audience analysis and adaptation that we presented in Chapter 5 to help you think more concretely about who your listeners are and why they should listen to you.

One essential aspect of being audience-centered that we've emphasized throughout the book is to be sensitive to the culturally diverse nature of most contemporary audiences. In our multicultural society, how persuasion works for one cultural group is different from how it works for others. Researchers have discovered no universal, cross-cultural approach to persuasion that is effective in each culture. North Americans, for example, tend to place considerable importance on direct observations and verifiable facts. Our court system places great stock in eyewitness testimony. People in some Chinese cultures, however, consider such evidence unreliable because they believe that what people observe is always influenced by personal motives. In some African cultures, personal testimony is also often suspect; it is reasoned that if you speak up to defend a person or friend, you have an ulterior motive and therefore the observation is discounted.[9] Although your audience may not always have listeners born and raised in Africa or China, given the growing diversity of Americans, that possibility is increasing. Or you may have listeners from other cultures with different perspectives. Our point: Don't design a persuasive message using strategies that would be effective only for you or those from your cultural background. The wise persuader consciously thinks about the persuasive strategies that will be effective for his or her listeners. An effective communicator is especially sensitive to cultural differences between him- or herself and the audience, while at the same time being cautious not to make stereotypical assumptions, based only on cultural factors, about an audience.

Select and Narrow Your Persuasive Topic

In your public-speaking class you may be given considerable latitude in selecting a topic. Deciding on a persuasive speech topic sometimes stumps beginning speakers. In Appendix B, we offer a few ideas to get you thinking about persuasive speech topics. But rather than just picking the first idea that pops into your mind, select a persuasive-speech topic that is important to you. What are you passionate about? What issues stir your heart and mind? You'll present a better speech if you've selected a topic you can speak about with sincere conviction. In addition to your interests, always reflect on your audience's passions and convictions. The ideal topic speaks to a need, concern, or issue of the audience as well as to your interests and zeal.

Controversial issues make excellent sources for persuasive topics. A controversial issue is a question about which people disagree. Here are several: Should the university increase tuition so that faculty members can have a salary increase? Should public schools distribute condoms to students? Should the government provide health insurance to all citizens? You need to be audience-centered—know the local, state, national, or international issues that interest your listeners. In addition, the best persuasive-speech topics focus on important rather than frivolous issues.

We recommend that you, as a student of public speaking, pay attention to the media and the Internet to help keep you current on the important issues of the day. If you're not already doing so, you should read at least one newspaper every day. Take a look at a national news magazine such as *Time, Newsweek,* or *U.S. News and World Report* to keep in touch with issues and topics of interest. The editorial page of the newspaper is also a good place to see what issues are of interest to people. Another interesting source of controversial issues is talk radio programs. Both national and local radio call-in programs may give you some ideas that are appropriate for a persuasive speech. You might also monitor chat rooms on the Internet or peruse the homepages of print and broadcast media for ideas. Even if you already have a clear idea of your speech topic, keeping up with the media and the Internet can give you additional ideas to help narrow your topic or find interesting and appropriate supporting material.

In addition to scanning Appendix B and looking for topics discussed in the media, use the brainstorming method we have presented in other chapters to identify your interests and convictions.

Determine Your Persuasive Purpose

When your goal is to persuade, you've already decided on your general purpose: You want the members of your audience to change or reinforce their attitudes, beliefs, value, or behavior. But you still must develop your specific purpose.

When you persuade others, you don't always have to strive for dramatic changes in the attitudes, beliefs, values, and behavior of your audience. Most people rarely make major life changes after hearing just one persuasive message. Your persuasive-speaking goal may be to move listeners *a bit closer* to your ultimate persuasive objective. If, for example, you are speaking to a group of retired people whom you know to be wary about increasing their taxes, yet whose support you'd like in the upcoming school-bond election to build a new high school, you're probably not going to convince them with a 10-minute speech, to support the bond. If, however, your goal were simply to help them see why a new high school would be advantageous to the community rather than to get their vote, your more realistic goal has a better chance of being achieved. Perhaps you or another supporter of the school bond could give another speech the following week in which you build on your message and explic-itly seek the retirees' vote for the bond. Sometimes it's useful to think of persuasion as a campaign in which you present several messages rather than pinning all your hopes on a single presentation. If your listeners are strongly against your ideas, just getting your listen-ers to listen may be quite an accomplishment. The more strongly your listeners hold a particular attitude, belief, value, or behavior pattern, the wiser it may be to have a more modest persuasive objective.

Patricia Ireland, speaker at an abortion rights rally, knows that it will be difficult to change the mind of someone who is totally against abortion. She might decide that a first step would be to persuade unreceptive members of her audience simply to listen to her message.

[Gary Wagner/Stock Boston]

Develop Your Central Idea and Main Ideas

The overall structure of your speech flows from your central idea and the main ideas that support your central idea. Your central idea, as you recall, is a one-sentence summary of your speech. When persuading others, most speakers find it useful to state their central idea in the form of a proposition. A **proposition** is a statement with which you want your audience to agree. In the following list, note how the propositions in actuality are the central idea of the speech:

All students should be required to take a foreign language.

Organic gardening is better for the environment than gardening with chemicals.

The United States should not provide economic aid to other countries.

There are three categories of propositions: fact, value, and policy. Determining which category your persuasive proposition fits into can not only help you clarify your central idea but can also give you an idea of how to select specific persuasive strategies that will help you achieve your specific purpose. Let's examine each type of proposition in more detail.

PROPOSITION OF FACT A **proposition of fact** focuses on whether something is true or false, on whether it did or did not happen. Al Gore received more votes nationwide than George W. Bush in the 2000 presidential election. The New York Yankees won the 2000 World Series. Texas is bigger than Poland. Each of these statements is a proposition of fact that can be verified simply by looking the answer up on the Internet. Other propositions of fact will take more time and skill—perhaps an entire persuasive speech—to prove. Here are examples of more controversial propositions of fact:

Talk radio is directly responsible for violence against U.S. government agencies.

When women joined the military, the quality of the military improved.

Children who were abused by their parents are more likely to abuse their own children.

U.S. foreign policy has increased the chance that the United States will experience more terrorist attacks.

The gasoline engine is the prime culprit in the deterioration of the ozone layer.

Global warming is not occurring in our atmosphere.

To prove each of these propositions, a speaker would need to provide specific supporting evidence. To persuade listeners to agree with a proposition of fact, the speaker must focus on changing or reinforcing their beliefs. A belief, as you recall, is the way in which a person structures reality to accept something as either true of false. Most persuasive speeches that focus on a proposition of fact begin by identifying one or more reasons that the proposition is true.

Tabitha's persuasive speech on the topic of fluorocarbons was based on a proposition of fact:

TOPIC:	Fluorocarbons from air-conditioning systems
GENERAL PURPOSE:	To persuade
PROPOSITION:	Fluorocarbons deplete Earth's ozone layer.

proposition
A statement that summarizes the ideas with which you want your audience to agree

proposition of fact
Focuses on whether something is true or false; on whether it did or did not happen

SPECIFIC PURPOSE: At the end of my speech, audience members should be able to state that fluorocarbons deplete the ozone layer and are therefore harmful to the environment.

MAIN IDEAS: I. Fluorocarbons are prevalent in old air-conditioning systems.

II. Fluorocarbons are a prime cause of ozone depletion.

A. Scientists have evidence that fluorocarbons deplete the ozone layer.

B. Congress has passed legislation limiting the use of fluorocarbons.

PROPOSITION OF VALUE   A **proposition of value** is a statement that calls for the listener to judge the worth or importance of something. Values, as you recall, are enduring concepts of good and bad, right and wrong. Value propositions are based on something being either good or bad, or on whether one thing or course of action is better than another thing or action. Note these examples:

It is wrong to turn away immigrants who want to come to the United States.

Democracy is a better form of government than Communism.

Speech communication is a better major than home economics.

A private-school education is more valuable than a public-school education.

Capital punishment is good for the country.

It is better for citizens to carry concealed weapons than to let criminals rule society.

Each of these propositions either directly states or implies that something is better than something else. Value propositions often directly compare two things and suggest that one of the options is better than the other.

Manny's speech was designed to convince his audience that contemporary rock music is better than classical music.

TOPIC: Rock music

GENERAL PURPOSE: To persuade

PROPOSITION: Rock music is better than classical music for three reasons.

SPECIFIC PURPOSE: After listening to my speech, the audience should listen to rock music more often than they listen to classical music.

MAIN IDEAS: I. More people listen to rock music than to classical music.

II. Rock music can increase worker productivity, whereas classical music is more likely to put people to sleep.

III. Rock music is more sophisticated than classical music.

proposition of value
Calls for the listener to judge the worth or importance of something

proposition of policy
Advocates a specific action—changing of policy, procedure, or behavior

PROPOSITION OF POLICY   The third type of proposition, a **proposition of policy,** advocates a specific action—changing a policy, procedure, or behavior. Note how all the following propositions of policy include the word "should"; this is a tip-off that the speaker is advocating a change in policy or procedure.

The Gifted and Talented Program in our school district should have a full-time coordinator.

Our community should set aside one day each month as "Community Cleanup Day."

Senior citizens should pay for more of their medical costs.

Each student at our school should receive a new personal computer.

In a speech based on a proposition of policy, Paul decided to convince his audience that academic tenure for college professors should be abolished. He organized his speech topically, identifying reasons academic tenure is no longer a sound policy for most colleges and universities. To support his proposition of policy, he used several propositions of fact. Note, too, that Paul's specific purpose involved specific action on the part of his audience.

TOPIC:	Academic tenure
GENERAL PURPOSE:	To persuade
PROPOSITION:	Our college, along with other colleges and universities, should abolish academic tenure.
SPECIFIC PURPOSE:	After listening to my speech, audience members should sign a petition calling for the abolition of academic tenure.
MAIN IDEAS:	I. Academic tenure is outdated.
	II. Academic tenure is abused.
	III. Academic tenure contributes to ineffective education.

Here's another example of a persuasive speech based on a proposition of policy. Again, note how the major ideas are propositions of fact used to support the proposition of policy.

TOPIC:	Computer education
GENERAL PURPOSE:	To persuade
PROPOSITION:	Every person in our society should know how to use a personal computer.
SPECIFIC PURPOSE:	After listening to my speech, all audience members who have not had a computer course should sign up for one.
MAIN IDEAS:	I. Most people who own a personal computer do not know how to use most of the features.
	II. Computer skills will help you with your academic studies.
	III. Computer skills will help you get a good job, regardless of your major or chosen profession.

Type	Definition	Examples
Proposition of fact	A statement that focuses on whether something is true or false.	The state legislature has raised tuition 10 percent during the last three years.
		There are more terrorist attacks in the world today than at any previous time in human history.
Proposition of value	A statement that either asserts something is better than something else or presumes what is right and what is wrong, or what is good and what is bad.	The electoral college is a better way to elect presidents than is direct popular vote.
		It is better to keep your financial records on a personal computer than to make the calculations by hand.
Proposition of policy	A statement that advocates a change in policy or procedures.	Our community should adopt a curfew for all citizens under eighteen.
		All handguns should be abolished.

Putting Persuasive Principles into Practice

We have identified some of the factors that can motivate an audience and have provided some clues for formulating a proposition for your speech. We conclude this chapter by discussing three general principles to help you link the theory of persuasion with the practice of persuasion.

- *Put your goal in terms that are consistent, rather than dissonant, with the attitudes, beliefs, values, and behavior of your audience.* You will be a more successful advocate if your audience thinks your proposition is compatible with their existing views. Again, we remind you to be audience-centered.

  One theory suggests that when listeners are confronted with a persuasive message, their responses can be classified into one of three categories: latitude of acceptance (they generally agree with the speaker), latitude of rejection (they disagree), and latitude of noncommitment (they're not sure how to respond).[10] As a persuasive speaker, it is in your interest to gain as much latitude of acceptance as you can while you are trying to change your audience's views. Your goal, of course, is to have your message fully accepted by your listeners. To do that, you will need to know where they stand on the issues before you craft your message so that you can adapt to their position.

- *Persuasion will be more likely to occur if the advantages of your proposition are greater than the disadvantages.* Whenever you make a decision to buy something, you do a brief cost–benefit analysis. You consider the cost of the item (a new computer at $1,500), and you also think of the benefits the purchase will bring (better grades, less time spent typing because editing is so easy). If the benefits of purchasing the new computer outweigh the costs, you decide to make the purchase.

  In a similar way, your job as a speaker is to convince your listeners that the benefits or advantages of adopting your point of view will outweigh whatever costs or disadvantages are associated with your proposal. Most salespeople are taught not to reveal what an item will cost until they are sure you understand the benefits of whatever they are selling. They want you to visualize owning and enjoying the product first. If you conclude that the benefits outweigh the costs, you will probably buy the product.

- *Persuasion will be more likely to occur if your proposal meets your listeners' needs.* We have already described Maslow's hierarchy of needs and how people are motivated to satisfy more basic needs first and then satisfy higher-level needs such as self-esteem and self-actualization. In the early stages of developing your persuasive message, identify how your proposal or viewpoint will satisfy the needs of your audience. What do your listeners need that they currently do not have? How can you adapt your message to tie into their unmet needs? Answering these questions can give you some useful and powerful strategies for developing your persuasive objective and speech.

The principles described in this chapter should give you some insight into the way persuasion works. Our overview of the approaches to persuasion should help you choose a persuasive topic and formulate a specific speech purpose. In Chapter 17, we will build on the principles reviewed here and suggest specific strategies for developing your persuasive message.

Summary

Various theories explain how persuasion works to change or reinforce attitudes, beliefs, and values, which are the determinants of behavior. You can build this theoretical knowledge into your speech preparation to deliver a persuasive message.

Persuasion is the process of changing or reinforcing attitudes, beliefs, values, or behavior. Attitudes are learned predispositions to respond favorably or unfavorably toward something. A belief is the way a person structures what is true and what is false. A value is a conception of right and wrong.

There are several ways to motivate listeners. These include the concept of cognitive dissonance, which holds that we all strive for balance or consistency in our thoughts. When a persuasive message invites us to change our attitudes, beliefs, values, or behavior, we respond by trying to maintain intellectual balance or cognitive consistency.

A second theory explains why we are motivated to respond to persuasion by proposing that we wish to satisfy our needs. Abraham Maslow identified a five-level hierarchy of needs: physiological, safety, social, self-esteem, and self-actualization.

Third, positive motivational appeals can help you develop a persuasive message by encouraging listeners to respond favorably to your message.

A fourth theoretical approach that helps us understand how persuasion works is the use of negative motivational appeals—notably, appeals to fear. Fear can motivate us to respond favorably to a persuasive suggestion. To avoid pain or discomfort, we may follow the recommendation of a persuasive speaker.

Preparing and presenting a persuasive speech requires the same approach as preparing any other kind of speech. A key first concern is to consider the audience. The next concern is an appropriate topic.

Finally, speakers can apply to choose broad principles of persuasion to prepare a persuasive speech.

Address: http://www.ablongman.com/beebe

▼ | **Finding Out About Congressional Legislation for Persuasive Speeches**

Y ou may find yourself giving a persuasive speech about issues pertaining to public policy and issues about which there is pertinent legislation in Congress. If so, the Internet can be a useful resource for finding out the latest information about existing and pending legislation.

CONGRESS TRACK

http://thomas.loc.gov/bss/d105/hot-subj.html/

The site will let you search for legislation by topic (listed in alphabetical order) and then identify legislation relevant to that topic. An "HR" prefix means that the legislation originated in the House of Representatives. An "S" means that it is a Senate bill.

You can find the entire text of the *Congressional Record,* speeches presented in Congress, by clicking on the "All Bill Summary and Status Information." If it has been discussed on the floor, then the entry will also be noted with the letters "CR," which stand for the *Congressional Record.*

YAHOO! DIRECTORY OF STATE AND LOCAL GOVERNMENTS

http://dir.yahoo.com/Government/States

WORLD-WIDE WEB VIRTUAL LIBRARY OF THE U.S. GOVERNMENT INFORMATION SOURCES

http://www.nttc.edu/gov_res.html/

STATE AND LOCAL GOVERNMENTS ON THE NET

http://www.piperinfo.com/state/states.html

An interesting site can help you find special-interest groups on the Web that can provide supporting arguments for positions you may advocate. The Idealist site address is <http://www.idealist.org>. Go to this site and find a group on the Internet whose interests parallel your own. Search for arguments and information that can help you develop your ideas for a persuasive speech. When using information from a special-interest group, remember that the information may be slanted or selected to support the group's position. Evaluate the arguments, evidence, and reasoning used to advance a cause or position.

A Sharper Focus

CONSIDERING YOUR AUDIENCE

▶ When persuading others, it is important that you understand your listeners' attitudes, beliefs, values, and behavior.

▶ To motive listeners to respond to your message, consider using one or more of the following strategies: Ethically use cognitive dissonance to your advantage, speak to listeners' needs, use positive motivational appeals, or use negative motivational appeals (such as fear appeals).

▶ Consider the interests and backgrounds of your listeners when selecting and narrowing your persuasive-speech topic.

▶ When crafting your central idea for your persuasive speech, develop a proposition of fact, value, or policy that is reasonable based on your audience's background and expectations.

CONSIDERING AUDIENCE DIVERSITY

▶ Persuasion is an art rather than an exact science; your audience's cultural background and expectations play a significant role in determining which persuasive strategies are effective and appropriate.

▶ Researchers have discovered no universal, cross-cultural approach to persuasion that is effective in every culture.

▶ North Americans place considerable importance on direct observation and verifiable facts. People from some Chinese and African cultures, however, may be more suspicious of eyewitness testimony.

▶ If you are speaking to a culturally diverse audience, don't design a persuasive message using strategies that would be effective only for you or those from your cultural background.

CRITICAL-THINKING QUESTIONS

1. Your local chamber of commerce has asked for your advice in developing a speakers' bureau that would address public-safety issues in your community. What suggestions would you offer to motivate citizens to behave in ways that would protect them from AIDS, traffic, and severe weather?

2. Martha has been asked to speak to the Association for the Preservation of the Environment. What are possible persuasive topics and propositions that would be appropriate for her audience?

3. If you were attempting to sell a new computer system to the administration of your school, what persuasive principles would you draw on to develop your message?

ETHICAL QUESTIONS

1. Zeta plans to give a persuasive speech to convince her classmates that term limits should be imposed for senators and members of Congress—even though she is personally against term limits. Is it ethical to develop a persuasive message based on a proposition with which you personally disagree?

2. Tom plans to begin his speech on driver safety using a graphic picture showing traffic-accident victims who were maimed and killed because they did not use safety belts. Is such graphic use of fear appeals ethical?

SUGGESTED ACTIVITIES

1. Collect four or five magazine advertisements for various products. Analyze the persuasive strategies in each ad. Look for applications of cognitive dissonance, Maslow's hierarchy of needs, positive appeals, or fear appeals. Which theory do you see being illustrated most often?

2. Write a short essay noting similarities and differences in preparing and presenting an informative speech and a persuasive speech.

3. Imagine that you've been asked to speak to the Federation of Chinese Students at your school about the advantages of becoming a communication studies major. Although there are many mass communication departments in China, there are few if any communication studies or speech communication departments; many students there are uncertain as to what communication students study. Describe what you would do to learn more about your listeners and how you would adapt your message to them.

4. Assume you live in a neighborhood that has strict rules about the external appearance of homes in the community. You and a group of your neighbors plan to speak before a meeting of community members, seeking their vote to let you and your neighbors paint your homes with colors appropriate to your culture rather than only white or beige, as prescribed in the community bylaws. In the audience are people from your own cultural background who support your position; there are also many who oppose your proposal. How would you determine who your target audience is? What persuasive strategies would be helpful in making your case to your target audience?

USING TECHNOLOGY AND MEDIA

1. Spend an evening watching TV, paying particular attention to the motivational appeals used in the commercials. Note whether the ad uses negative motivational strategies to convince you that you need the product. If you have a VCR, tape some of the commercials and bring them to class for discussion.

2. Listen to a tape recording of a motivational speaker attempting to help his or her listeners stop smoking, lose weight, or gain financial independence. Many are available at video stores for rent; others can be checked out of your school or public library. Analyze the persuasive strategies the speaker uses to achieve his or her goal.

3. If you have access to cable TV, watch a C-SPAN broadcast of a member of Congress attempting to argue for or against a particular proposition. Note whether it is a proposition of fact, value, or policy. Identify the persuasive strategies and organizational pattern the speaker uses.

S peech is power: Speech is to persuade,
to convert, to compel.

RALPH WALDO EMERSON

17

Using Persuasive Strategies

objectives

After studying this chapter you should be able
to do the following:

1. Identify strategies to improve your initial,
   derived, and terminal credibility.

2. Use principles of effective reasoning to develop
   a persuasive message.

3. Employ effective techniques of using emotional
   appeal in a persuasive speech.

4. Adapt your persuasive message to receptive,
   neutral, and unreceptive audiences.

5. Identify strategies for effectively organizing a
   persuasive speech.

The ancient Greek philosopher Aristotle defined *rhetoric* as the process of discovering the "available means of persuasion." What are these "available means" that can help you persuade an audience? In Chapter 16, we focused on the principles of persuasion to give you a general understanding of how persuasion works. In this chapter, we will discuss methods that can help you prepare your persuasive speech. Specifically, we will suggest how to gain credibility, develop well-reasoned arguments, and move your audience with emotion. We will also discuss how to adapt your specific message to your audience, and we will end with some suggestions for organizing your persuasive message.

Establishing Credibility

If you were going to buy a new car, to whom would you turn for advice? Perhaps you would ask a trusted family member, or you might seek advice from *Consumer Reports,* a monthly publication that reports studies of various products on the market, among them automobiles. In other words, you would probably turn to a source that you consider knowledgeable, competent, and trustworthy—a source you think is credible.

Credibility is the audience's perception of a speaker's competence, trustworthiness, and dynamism. As a public speaker, especially one who wishes to persuade an audience, you hope that your listeners will have a favorable attitude toward you. Current research points clearly to a relationship between credibility and speech effectiveness: The more believable you are to your listener, the more effective you will be as a persuasive communicator.

Aristotle used the term **ethos** to refer to a speaker's credibility. He thought that a public speaker should be ethical, possess good character, have common sense, and be concerned for the well-being of the audience. Quintilian, a Roman teacher of public speaking, felt that an effective public speaker also should be a person of good character. Quintilian's advice was that a speaker should be "a good man speaking well." The importance to a speaker of a positive public image has been recognized for centuries. But don't get the idea that credibility is something that a speaker literally possesses or lacks. Credibility is based on the listeners' mind-set regarding the speaker. Your listeners, not you, determine whether you have credibility or lack it.

Credibility is not just a single factor or a single view of you by your audience. It encompasses many factors and many views. Aristotle's speculations as to the factors that influence a speaker's ethical character have been generally supported by modern experimental studies.

One clear factor in credibility is **competence**—the speaker should be considered informed, skilled, or knowledgeable about the subject he or she is talking about. If a used-car salesman sings the virtues of a car on his lot, you want to know what qualifies him to give believable information about the car.

When you give a speech, you will be more persuasive if you convince your listeners that you are knowledgeable about your topic. If, for example, you say it would be a good idea for everyone to have a medical checkup each year, your listeners might mentally ask, "Why? What are your qualifications to make such a proposal?" But if you support your conclusion with medical statistics showing how having a physical exam each year dramatically leads to a prolonged life, you enhance the credibility of your sugges-

credibility
The audience's perception of a speaker's competence, trustworthiness, and dynamism

ethos
The term Aristotle used to refer to a speaker's character, credibility, and ethics

competence
The factor in a speaker's credibility that refers to his or her being perceived as informed, skilled, or knowledgeable

tion. Thus, one way to enhance your competence is to cite credible evidence to support your point.

A second major factor that influences your audience's response to you is **trustworthiness.** You trust people whom you believe to be honest. While delivering your speech, you have to convey to your audience your honesty and sincerity. Your audience will be looking for evidence that they can trust you, that you are believable.

Earning an audience's trust is not something that you can do simply by saying, "Trust me." Trust is earned by demonstrating that you have had experience dealing with the issues you talk about. Your listeners would be more likely to trust your advice about how to travel around Europe on $50 a day if you had been there, than they would if you took your information from a tour book you bought from the bargain table at the bookstore. Your trustworthiness may be suspect if you advocate something that will result in a direct benefit to you. That's why salespersons and politicians are often stereotyped as being untrustworthy; if you do what they say, they will clearly benefit from a sales commission if you buy a product, or gain power and position if you give your vote.

A third factor in credibility is the speaker's **dynamism** or energy. Dynamism is often projected through delivery. **Charisma** is a form of dynamism. A charismatic person possesses charm, talent, magnetism, and other qualities that make the person attractive and energetic. Many people considered Presidents Franklin Roosevelt and Ronald Reagan charismatic speakers.

Do you think Bill Moyers is a credible speaker? Why or why not?

[© Bob Daemmrich Photography]

Enhancing Your Credibility

Speakers build their credibility in three phases, the first of which is **initial credibility.** This is the impression of your credibility your listeners have even before you speak. Giving careful thought to your appearance and establishing eye contact before you begin your talk will enhance both your confidence and your credibility. It is also wise to prepare a brief description of your credentials and accomplishments so that the person who introduces you can use it in his or her introductory remarks. Even if you are not asked for a statement beforehand, be prepared with one.

Derived credibility is the perception of your credibility your audience forms as you present yourself and your message. Most of this book presents principles and skills that help establish your credibility as a speaker. Several specific research-supported skills for enhancing your credibility as you speak include establishing common ground with your audience, supporting your key arguments with evidence, and presenting a well-organized and well-delivered message.

You establish common ground by indicating in your opening remarks that you share the values and concerns of your audience. To begin to persuade an audience that they understand why the budget cuts they have enacted upset parents, politicians might speak of their own children. If you are a student persuading classmates to enroll in an economics class, you could stress that understanding economic issues will be useful for them as they face the process of interviewing for a career. Of course, you have an ethical responsibility to be truthful when announcing how you and your audience share common goals.

trustworthiness
The factor in a speaker's credibility that refers to his or her being perceived as believable and honest

dynamism
The factor in a speaker's credibility that refers to his or her being perceived as energetic

charisma
Characteristic of a talented, charming, attractive speaker

initial credibility
The impression of a speaker's credibility that listeners have before the speaker starts a speech

derived credibility
The perception of a speaker's competence, trustworthiness, and dynamism based on what the speaker says and does during a speech

Having evidence to support your persuasive conclusions strengthens your credibility. Margo was baffled as to why her plea for donations for the homeless fell flat. No one offered any financial support for her cause when she concluded her speech. Why? She offered no proof that there really were impoverished people in the community. If she had provided well-documented evidence that there was a problem and that the organization she supported could effectively solve the problem, she would have been more likely to have her position supported.

Presenting a well-organized message also enhances your credibility as a competent and rational advocate. Rambling, emotional requests rarely change or reinforce listeners' opinions or behavior. We will present specific organizational strategies for persuasive messages later in the chapter. Regardless of the organizational pattern you use, it is crucial to ensure that your message is logically structured with appropriate use of internal summaries, signposts, and enumeration of key ideas.

Your delivery also affects your derived credibility. For most North Americans, increased eye contact, varied vocal inflection, and appropriate attire has a positive influence on your ability to persuade listeners to respond to your message.[1] Why does delivery affect how persuasive you are? Researchers suggest that if your listeners expect you to be a good speaker and you aren't, they are less likely to do what you ask them to do.[2] So don't violate their expectations by presenting a poorly delivered speech. Effective delivery also enhances your ability to persuade, because it helps gain and maintain listener attention and affects whether listeners will like you.[3] If you can arouse listeners' attention and if they like you, you'll be more persuasive than if you don't gain their attention and they don't like you.

The last phase of credibility, called **terminal credibility** or final credibility, is the perception of your credibility your listeners have when you finish your speech. Again we emphasize the value of eye contact. Don't start leaving the lectern or the speaking area until you have finished your closing sentence. Even if there is no planned question-and-answer period following your speech, be ready to respond to questions from interested listeners.

RECAP

HOW TO ENHANCE YOUR CREDIBILITY

INITIAL CREDIBILITY: *Improving Your Image Before You Speak*

Give careful consideration to your appearance.

Establish eye contact with the audience before you begin speaking.

Prepare a brief description of your credentials and accomplishments that can be read to the audience.

DERIVED CREDIBILITY: *Improving Your Image During Your Speech*

Establish common ground with your audience.

Support your arguments with evidence.

Present a well-organized speech.

Present a well-delivered speech.

TERMINAL OR FINAL CREDIBILITY: *Developing a Lasting Positive Image*

End with eye contact.

Be prepared for questions.

terminal credibility
The final impression listeners have of a speaker's credibility after the speech has been concluded.

Using Logic and Evidence to Persuade

The reason we need to cut taxes is to improve the economy," claimed the politician on a Sunday-morning talk show. "The stock market has lost 300 points this month. People aren't buying things. A tax cut will put money in their pockets and give the economy a boost." In an effort to persuade reluctant members of her political party to support a tax cut, this politician was using a logical argument supported with evidence that stock prices were dropping. As we noted in Chapter 4 when we discussed how to be a critical listener, logic is a formal system of rules for making inferences. Because wise audience members will be listening, persuasive speakers need to give careful attention to the way they use logic to reach a conclusion. Aristotle called logic **logos**, which literally means "the word." Using words as well as statistical information to develop logical arguments can make your persuasive efforts more convincing. It can also clarify your own thinking and help make your points clear to your listeners. Logic is central to all persuasive speeches. In Chapter 4, we introduced a discussion of logic and evidence to help you become a critical listener or consumer of messages. We now amplify that discussion to help you use logical arguments and evidence to persuade others.

Aristotle also said that any persuasive speech has two parts: First, you state your case. Second, you prove your case. In essence, he was saying that you must present evidence and then use appropriate reasoning to lead your listeners to the conclusion you advocate. Reasoning is the process of drawing a conclusion from evidence. The Sunday-morning talk-show politician reached the conclusion that a tax cut was necessary because stock prices had tumbled and people weren't buying things. Evidence consists of the facts, examples, statistics, and expert opinions that you use to support the points you wish to make. When advancing an argument, it is your task to prove your point. Proof consists of the evidence plus the conclusion you draw from it. The evidence in the claim made by the politician is the lower stock-market value and fewer people buying things. The conclusion: We need a tax cut to stimulate the economy. Let's consider the two key elements of proof in greater detail. Specifically, we will look more closely at types of reasoning and provide ways to test the quality of evidence.

Understanding Types of Reasoning

Developing well-reasoned arguments for persuasive messages has been important since antiquity. If your arguments are structured in a rational way, you have a greater chance of persuading your listeners. There are three major ways to structure an argument to reach a logical conclusion: inductively, deductively, and causally.

INDUCTIVE REASONING Reasoning that arrives at a general conclusion from specific instances or examples is known as **inductive reasoning.** Using this classical approach, you reach a general conclusion based on specific examples, facts, statistics, and opinions. You may not know for a certainty that the specific instances mean the conclusion is true but, in all *probability*, the specific instances support the general conclusion. According to contemporary logicians, you reason inductively when you claim that an outcome is probably true because of specific evidence.

For example, if you were giving a speech attempting to convince your audience that foreign cars are unreliable, you might use inductive reasoning to make your point. You could announce that you recently bought a foreign car that gave you trouble. Your

logos
The term Greek philosopher Aristotle used to refer to logic—the formal system of using rules to reach a conclusion. Literally means "the word"

inductive reasoning
A process of reasoning using specific instances or examples to reach a general, probable conclusion

cousin also bought a foreign car that kept stalling on the freeway. Finally, your English professor told you her foreign car has broken down several times in the past few weeks. Based on these specific examples, you ask your audience to agree with your general conclusion: Foreign cars are unreliable.

Testing the Validity of Inductive Reasoning. As a persuasive speaker, your job is to construct a sound argument. That means basing your generalization on evidence. When you listen to a persuasive message, notice how the speaker tries to support his or her conclusion. To judge the validity of a **generalization** arrived at inductively, keep the following questions in mind.

- *Are There Enough Specific Instances to Support the Conclusion?* Are three examples of problems with foreign cars enough to prove your point that all foreign cars are unreliable? Of the several million foreign cars manufactured, three cars, especially if they are different makes, are not a large sample. If those examples were supported by additional statistical evidence that more than 50 percent of foreign-car owners complained of serious engine malfunctions, the evidence would be more convincing.

- *Are the Specific Instances Typical?* Are the three examples you cite representative of all foreign cars manufactured? How do you know? What are the data on the performance of foreign cars? Also, are you, your cousin, and your professor typical of most car owners? The three of you may be careless about routine maintenance of your autos.

- *Are the Instances Recent?* If the foreign cars you are using as examples of poor reliability are more than three years old, you cannot reasonably conclude that today's foreign cars are unreliable products. Age alone may explain the poor performance of your sample.

    The logic in this example, therefore, is not particularly sound. The speaker would need considerably more evidence to prove his or her point.

REASONING BY ANALOGY Reasoning by analogy is a special type of inductive reasoning. An **analogy** is a comparison. This form of reasoning compares one thing, person, or process with another, to predict how something will perform and respond. When you observe that two things have a number of characteristics in common and that a certain fact about one is likely to be true of the other, you have drawn an analogy, reasoning from one example to reach a conclusion about the other. If you try to convince an audience that mandatory safety-belt laws in Texas and Florida have reduced highway deaths and therefore should be instituted in Kansas, you are reasoning by analogy. You would also be reasoning by analogy if you claimed that capital punishment reduced crime in Brazil and therefore should be used in the United States as well. But as with reasoning by generalization, there are questions that you should ask to check the validity of your conclusions.

- *Do the Ways in Which the Two Things Are Alike Outweigh Those in Which They Are Different?* Can you compare the crime statistics of Brazil to those of the United States and claim to make a valid comparison? Are the data collected in the same way in both countries? Could other factors besides the safety-belt laws in Texas and Florida account for the lower automobile accident death rate? Maybe differences in the speed limit or the types of roads in those states can account for the difference.

generalization
An all-encompassing statement of truth

analogy
A special type of inductive reasoning in which you compare one thing, person, or process with another to predict how something will perform and respond

- *Is the Assertion True?* Is it really true that capital punishment has deterred crime in Brazil? Is it really true that mandatory safety-belt laws in Florida and Texas have reduced auto highway deaths? You will need to give reasons the comparison you are making is valid, and evidence that will prove your conclusion true.

DEDUCTIVE REASONING According to centuries-old perspectives, reasoning from a general statement or principle to reach a specific conclusion is called **deductive reasoning.** This is just the opposite of inductive reasoning. Contemporary logic specialists add that when the conclusion is *certain* rather than probable, you are reasoning deductively. The certainty of your conclusion is based on the validity or truth in the general statement that forms the basis of your argument. Deductive reasoning can be structured in the form of a syllogism. Let's define a syllogism and look at an example to illustrate how deductive reasoning is structured.

A **syllogism** is a way of organizing an argument. It has three elements: a major premise, a minor premise, and a conclusion. To reach a conclusion deductively, you start with a general statement that serves as the **major premise**. In a speech attempting to convince your audience that the communication professor teaching your public-speaking class is a top-notch teacher, you might use a deductive reasoning process. Your major premise is "All communication professors have excellent teaching skills." The certainty of your conclusion hinges on the soundness of your major premise. The **minor premise** is a more specific statement about an example that is linked to the major premise. Here's the minor premise in the argument you are advancing: "John Smith, our teacher, is a communication professor." The **conclusion** is based on the major premise and the more specific minor premise. In reasoning deductively, you need to ensure that both the major and minor premises are true and can be supported with evidence. The conclusion to our syllogism is, "John Smith has excellent teaching skills." The persuasive power of deductive reasoning derives from the fact that the conclusion cannot be questioned if the premises are accepted as true.

Here's another example you might hear in a speech. Ann was trying to convince the city council not to approve a building permit for Mega-Low-Mart, a large chain discount store that wants to move into her town. She believes the new store would threaten her downtown clothing-boutique business. Here's the deductive structure of the argument she advanced:

Major premise:	Every time a large discount store moves into a small community, the merchants in the downtown area lose business and the town loses tax revenue from downtown merchants.
Minor premise:	Mega-Low-Mart is a large discount store that wants to build a store in our town.
Conclusion:	If Mega-Low-Mart is permitted to open a store in our town, the merchants in the downtown area will lose business and the city will lose tax revenue.

The strength of her argument rests with the validity of her major premise. Her argument is sound if she can prove that moving large-chain discount stores into a town does, in fact, result in a loss of business and tax revenue for downtown merchants. (Also note her efforts to be audience-centered; Ann, addressing the city council, argues that

deductive reasoning
A process of reasoning from a general statement or principle to reach a specific, certain conclusion

syllogism
A three-part way of developing an argument; it has a major premise, and minor premise, and a conclusion

major premise
A general statement that is the first element of a syllogism

minor premise
A specific statement about an example that is linked to the major premise; it is the second element of a syllogism

conclusion
The logical outcome of an argument, which stems from the major premise and the minor premise

not only will she lose money but also that the city will lose tax revenue—something in which city council members are deeply interested.) In constructing arguments for your persuasive messages, assess the soundness of the major premise on which you build your argument. Likewise, when listening to a persuasive pitch from someone using a deductive argument, critically evaluate the accuracy of the major premise.

To test the truth of an argument organized deductively, consider the following questions.

- *Is the Major Premise (General Statement) True?* In our example about communication professors, is it really true that *all* communication professors have excellent teaching skills? What evidence do you have to support this statement? The power of deductive reasoning hinges in part on whether your generalization is true.

- *Is the Minor Premise (the Particular Statement) Also True?* If your minor premise is false, your syllogism can collapse right there. In our example, it is easy enough to verify that John Smith is a communication professor. But not all minor premises can be verified as easily. For example, it would be difficult to prove the minor premise in this example:

> All gods are immortal.
>
> Zeus is a god.
>
> Therefore, Zeus is immortal.

We can accept the major premise as true because immortality is part of the definition of *god*. But proving that Zeus is a god would be very difficult. In this case, the truth of the conclusion hinges on the truth of the minor premise.

CAUSAL REASONING   A third type of reasoning is called **causal reasoning.** When you reason by cause, you relate two or more events in such a way as to conclude that one or more of the events caused the others. For example, you might argue that having unprotected sex causes the spread of AIDS.

There are two ways to structure a causal argument. First, you can reason from cause to effect, moving from a known fact to a predicted result. You know, for example, that interest rates have increased in the past week. Therefore, you might argue that *because* the rates are increasing, the Dow Jones Industrial Average will decrease. In this case, you move from something that has occurred (rising interest rates) to something that has not yet occurred (decrease in the Dow). Weather forecasters use the same method of reasoning when they predict the weather. They base a conclusion about tomorrow's weather on what they know about today's meteorological conditions.

A second way to frame a causal argument is to reason backward, from known effect to unknown cause. You know, for example, that a major earthquake has occurred (known effect). To explain this event, you propose that the cause of the earthquake is a shift in the fault line (unknown cause). You cannot be sure of the cause, but you are certain of the effect. A candidate for President of the United States may claim that the cause of current high unemployment (known effect) is mismanagement by the present administration (unknown cause). He then constructs an argument to prove that his assertion is accurate. To prove his case, he needs to have evidence that the present administration mismanaged the economy. The key to developing strong causal arguments is in the use of evidence to link something known with something unknown. An understanding of the appropriate use of evidence can enhance inductive, deductive, and causal reasoning.

causal reasoning
A process of reasoning in which two or more events are related in such a way as to conclude that one or more of the events caused the others

Persuading the Diverse Audience

As we have stressed, effective strategies for developing your persuasive objective will vary depending on the background and cultural expectations of your listeners. Most of the logical, rational methods of reasoning discussed in the preceding sections evolved from Greek and Roman traditions of argument (see Appendix A). Rhetoricians from the United States typically use a straightforward factual-inductive method of supporting ideas and reaching conclusions.[4] First, they identify facts and directly link them to support a specific proposition or conclusion. For example, in a speech to prove that the government spends more money than it receives, the speaker could cite year-by-year statistics on income and expenditures to document the point. North Americans also like debates involving a direct clash of ideas and opinions. Our low-context culture encourages people to be more direct and forthright in dealing with issues and disagreement than do high-context cultures.

RECAP

COMPARING INDUCTIVE, DEDUCTIVE, AND CAUSAL REASONING

	Inductive Reasoning	Deductive Reasoning	Causal Reasoning
Reasoning begins	With specific examples	With a general statement	With something known
Reasoning ends	With a general conclusion	With a specific conclusion	With a speculation about something unknown occurring, based on what is known
Reasoning conclusion is	Probable or improbable	True or false	Likely or not likely
Reasoning is used	To reach a general conclusion or discover something new	To reach a specific conclusion by applying what is known	To link something known with something unknown
Example	When tougher drug laws went into effect in Kansas City and St. Louis, drug traffic was reduced. The United States should therefore institute tougher drug laws.	All bachelors are unmarried men. Frank is a bachelor. Therefore, Frank is an unmarried man.	Since the 70-mile-per-hour speed limit was reinstated, traffic deaths have increased. The increased highway speed has caused an increase in highway deaths.

Not all cultures assume a direct, linear, methodical approach to supporting ideas and proving a point.[5] People from high-context cultures, for example, may expect that participants will establish a personal relationship before debating issues. Some cultures use a deductive pattern of reasons, rather than an inductive pattern. They begin with a general premise and then link it to a specific situation when they attempt to persuade listeners. During several recent trips to Russia, your authors have noticed that to argue that Communism was ineffective, many Russians start with a general assumption: Communism didn't work. Then they use this assumption to explain specific current problems in areas such as transportation and education.

Middle Eastern cultures usually do not use standard inductive or deductive structures. They are more likely to use narrative methods to persuade an audience. They tell stories that evoke feelings and emotions, allowing their listeners to draw their own conclusions by inductive association.[6]

Although this text stresses the kind of inductive reasoning that will be persuasive to most North Americans, if your audience is from another cultural tradition, you may need to use alternative strategies.

Consider the following general principles to help you construct arguments that a culturally diverse audience will find persuasive.

EVIDENCE According to intercultural communication scholars Myron Lustig and Jolene Koester, "There are no universally accepted standards about what constitutes evidence."[7] They suggest that for some Muslim and Christian audiences, parables or stories are a dramatically effective way to make a point. A story is told and a principle is derived from the lesson of the story. For most North Americans and Europeans, a superior form of evidence is an observed fact. What may be convincing evidence to you may not be such an obvious piece of evidence for others. If you are uncertain as to whether your listeners will perceive your evidence as valid and reliable, you could test your evidence on a small group of people who will be in your audience before you address the entire group.

APPEALS TO ACTION In some high-context cultures such as in Japan and China, the conclusion to your message can be stated more indirectly. Rather than explicitly spell out the precise action, you can imply what you'd like your listeners to do. In a low-context culture such as the United States, listeners may generally expect you to be more direct in the action you'd like your audience members to take.

MESSAGE STRUCTURE North Americans often like a well-organized message with a clear, explicit link between the evidence used and the conclusion drawn. North Americans also are comfortable with a structure that focuses on a problem and then offers a solution, or a message in which the causes are identified and the effects are specified. Audiences in the Middle East, however, would expect less-formal structure and greater use of a narrative style of message development. In essence, narrative style is the use of stories and extended analogies, examples, and illustrations. The story is told, and the audience either infers the point or the speaker may conclude by making the point clear. *In some situations, it's better to get a message out of someone than to put a message into someone.* Being indirect or implicit may sometimes be the best persuasive strategy.

Not all audiences expect a speech to sound like an attorney making a legal case loaded with evidence. In fact, some lawyers decide, after "reading" their jury, that the best way to conclude their case is to tell a story rather than to provide a litany of the facts and evidence presented.

PERSUASIVE COMMUNICATION STYLE We've placed a considerable emphasis on logos by appropriately emphasizing logical structure and the use of evidence. But another cultural factor that influences how receptive listeners are to a message is the presentation style of the speech. A speaker's overall style includes the use of emotional appeals, delivery style, language choice, and rhythmic quality of the words and gestures used. Some Latin American listeners, for example, expect speakers to express more emotion and passion when speaking than North American listeners are accustomed to. If you focus only on analyzing and adapting to the use of logic and reasoning, without also considering the overall impression you make on your audience, you may win the arguments but still not achieve your overall goal. The best way to assess the preferred speaking style of an audience with which you're not familiar is to observe other successful speakers addressing the audience you will face. Or talk with audience members before you speak to identify expectations and communication-style preferences.

Supporting Your Reasoning with Evidence

You cannot simply state a conclusion without proving it with evidence. Evidence in persuasive speeches consists of facts, examples, statistics, and expert opinions.

In Chapter 8, we discussed the essential details of using these types of supporting material in speeches. When attempting to persuade listeners, it is useful to make sure that your evidence logically supports the inductive, deductive, or causal reasoning you are using to reach your conclusion.

When using facts to persuade, make sure your fact is really a fact. A **fact** is something that has been directly observed to be true or can be proved to be true. The shape of Earth, the number of women CEOs, the winner of the 1996 presidential election have all been directly observed or measured. Without direct observation or measurement, we can only make an inference. An **inference** is a conclusion based on available evidence, or partial information.

Examples are illustrations that are used to dramatize or clarify a fact. Only valid, true examples can be used to help prove a point. For example, one speaker, in an effort to document the increased violence in children's television programs, told her audience, "Last Saturday morning as I watched cartoons with my daughter, I was shocked by the countless times we saw examples of beatings and even the death of the cartoon characters in one half-hour program." The conclusion she wanted her audience to reach: Put an end to senseless violence in children's television programs.

A hypothetical example, one that is fabricated to illustrate a point, should not be used to reach a conclusion. It should be used only to clarify. David encouraged his listeners to join him in an effort to clean up the San Marcos River. He wanted to motivate his audience to help by asking them to "Imagine bringing your children to the river ten years from now. You see the river bottom littered with cans and bottles." His example, while effective in helping the audience to visualize what might happen in the future, does not prove that the river ecosystem will deteriorate. It only illustrates what might happen if action isn't taken.

Opinions can serve as evidence if they are made by an expert, someone who can add credibility to your conclusion. The best opinions are made by someone known to be unbiased, fair, and accurate. If the U.S. surgeon general has expressed an opinion regarding drug testing, his or her opinion would be helpful evidence. Even so, opinions are usually most persuasive if they are combined with other evidence, such as facts or statistics, that supports the expert's position.

A **statistic** is a number used to summarize several facts or samples. In an award-winning speech, Jeffrey Jamison used statistics effectively to document the serious problem of alkali batteries polluting the environment. He cited evidence from the *New York Times* that documents ". . . each year we are adding 150 tons of mercury, 130 tons of lead, and 170 tons of cadmium to the environment."[8] Without these statistics, Jeffrey's claim that alkali batteries are detrimental to the environment would not have been as potent. Again, you may want to review the discussion on the appropriate use of statistics in Chapter 8.

If you are using an inductive-reasoning strategy (from specific examples to a general conclusion), you need to make sure you have enough facts, examples, statistics, and

fact
Something that has been directly observed to be true or can be proved to be true

inference
A conclusion based on available evidence

example
An illustration used to dramatize or clarify a fact

opinion
Testimony or quotation that expresses attitudes, beliefs, or values of someone else

statistic
Numerical data that summarize facts and examples

credible opinions to support your conclusion. If you reason deductively (from a generalization to a specific conclusion), you need evidence to document the truth of your initial generalization. When developing an argument using causal reasoning, evidence is again vital when you attempt to establish that one or more events caused something to happen.

Avoiding Faulty Reasoning: Ethical Issues

We have emphasized the importance of developing sound, logical arguments supported with appropriate evidence. You have an ethical responsibility to use your skill in constructing well-supported arguments with logical reasoning and sound evidence. Not all people who try to persuade you will use sound arguments to get you to vote for them, buy their product, or donate money to their cause. Many persuaders use inappropriate techniques called fallacies. A **fallacy** is false reasoning that occurs when someone attempts to persuade without adequate evidence or with arguments that are irrelevant or inappropriate. You will be both a better and more ethical speaker and a better listener if you are aware of the following fallacies.

CAUSAL FALLACY   The Latin term for this fallacy is *post hoc, ergo propter hoc,* which translates as "after this; therefore, because of this." It refers to making a faulty causal connection. Simply because one event follows another does not mean that the two are related. If you declared that your school's football team won this time because you sang your school song before the game, you would be guilty of a **causal fallacy.** There are undoubtedly other factors that explain why your team won, such as good preparation or facing a weaker opposing team. For something to be a cause, it has to have the power to bring about a result. "That howling storm last night knocked down the tree in our backyard" is a more logical causal explanation.

Here are more examples of causal fallacies:

The increased earthquake and hurricane activity is caused by the increase in violence and war in our society.

As long as you wear this lucky rabbit's foot, you will never have an automobile accident.

The decline of morals in this country is caused by excessive government spending.

In each instance, there is not enough evidence to support the cause–effect conclusion.

BANDWAGON FALLACY   Someone who argues that "everybody thinks it's a good idea, so you should too" is using the **bandwagon fallacy.** Simply because someone says that "everyone" is "jumping on the bandwagon" or supporting a particular point of view does not make the point of view correct. Sometimes speakers use the bandwagon fallacy in a more subtle way in their efforts to persuade:

Everybody knows that talk radio is our primary link to a free and democratic society.

Most people agree that we spend too much time worrying about Medicare.

Everybody agrees with me that we need a change in Congress.

fallacy
False reasoning that occurs when someone attempts to persuade without adequate evidence or with arguments that are irrelevant or inappropriate

causal fallacy
Making a faulty cause-and-effect connection between two things or events

bandwagon fallacy
Reasoning that suggests that because everyone else believes something or is doing something, then it must be valid, accurate, or effective

Beware of sweeping statements that include you and others without offering any evidence that the speaker has solicited opinions.

EITHER–OR FALLACY   Someone who argues that there are only two approaches to a problem is trying to oversimplify the issues. "It's either vote for higher property taxes or close the library," asserts Daryl at a public hearing on tax increases. Such a statement ignores a variety of other solutions to a complex problem. The following are additional examples of inappropriate either–or simplistic reasoning:

Mothers should either stay home and spend less time at work, or we will have an increase in juvenile delinquency.

Either television violence is reduced, or we will have an increase in child and spouse abuse.

Either more people should start volunteering their time to work for their community, or your taxes will increase.

HASTY GENERALIZATION   A person who reaches a conclusion from too little evidence or nonexistent evidence is making a **hasty generalization.** For example, simply because one person became ill after eating the meat loaf in the cafeteria does not mean that everyone eating in the cafeteria will contract serious health problems because of food poisoning. Here are some additional hasty generalizations:

It's clear that our schools can't educate children well, because my niece went to school for six years and she still can't read at her grade level.

The city does a terrible job of taking care of the elderly, because my grandmother lives in a city-owned nursing home and the floors there are always filthy.

We don't need mandatory lawn-watering rules in our city, because the people I know do their best to conserve water.

ATTACKING THE PERSON   Also known as an **ad hominem** attack, Latin for "to the man," this involves attacking irrelevant personal characteristics about the person who is proposing an idea rather than attacking the idea itself. A statement such as "We know Janice's idea won't work because she has never had a good idea yet" does not really deal with the idea, which may be perfectly valid. Don't dismiss an idea solely because you have been turned against the person who presented it. Here are some more examples of ad hominem attacks:

Anyone who is a talk-radio host certainly has no idea how to develop a plan to reduce the deficit.

She was educated in a foreign country and could not possibly have good ideas for improving education in our community.

Tony is an awful musician and is not sensitive enough to chair such an important committee.

RED HERRING   The **red herring** fallacy takes place when someone attacks an issue by using irrelevant facts or arguments as distractions. This fallacy gets its name from an old trick of dragging a red herring across a trail to divert the dogs who may be following. Speakers use a red herring when they want to distract an audience from the real issues. For example, a politician who had been accused of taking bribes while in office

either–or fallacy
Oversimplifying an issue as having only one of two outcomes or choices (it's either this or that)

hasty generalization
Reaching a conclusion without adequate evidence to support the conclusion

ad hominem
Attacking irrelevant personal characteristics of the person who is proposing an idea, rather than attacking the idea itself

red herring
Using irrelevant facts of information to distract someone from the issue that needs to be discussed

calls a press conference. During the press conference, he talks about the evils of child pornography, rather than addressing the charge against him; he is using the red herring technique to divert attention from the real issue—did he or did he not take the bribe? An additional example of a fallacious argument using the red herring method comes from a speech against gun control: *The real problem is not eliminating handguns; the real problem is that pawnshops that sell guns are controlled by the Mafia.*

APPEAL TO MISPLACED AUTHORITY When ads use baseball catchers to endorse automobiles and TV heroes to sell political candidates or an airline or hotel, we are faced with the fallacious **appeal to misplaced authority.** Although we have great respect for these people in their own fields, they are no more expert than we are in the areas they are advertising. As both a public speaker and a listener, you must recognize what is valid expert testimony and what is not. For example, a physicist who speaks on the laws of nature or the structure of matter could reasonably be accepted as an expert. But if the physicist speaks on politics, the opinion expressed is not that of an expert and is no more significant than your own. The following examples are appeals to misplaced authority:

> Former Congressman Smith endorses the new art museum, so every business should get behind it, too.

> Our history professor recommended that we stay at the Frontier Place in Orlando, so it must be good.

> Katie Couric thinks this cookie recipe is the best, so you should try it too.

NON SEQUITUR If you argue that a new parking garage should not be built on campus because the grass has not been mowed on the football field for three weeks, you are guilty of a **non sequitur** (Latin for "it does not follow"). Grass growing on the football field has nothing to do with the parking problem. Your conclusion simply does not follow from your statement. The following are examples of non sequitur conclusions:

> We should not give students condoms, because TV has such a pervasive influence on our youth today.

> You should endorse me for Congress, because I have three children.

> We need more parking on our campus, because we are the national football champions.

> You should help pick up trash in our community, because our new cable-TV studio is now in operation.

Using Emotion to Persuade

Roger Ailes, political-communication consultant, has nominated several memorable moments as outstanding illustrations of speakers using emotional messages powerfully and effectively:[9]

> *Martin Luther King, announcing his vision of brotherhood and equality at the Lincoln Memorial in 1963, extolled, "I have a dream!"*

appeal to misplaced authority
Using the credibility of someone to endorse an idea or product without the person having appropriate credentials or expertise to provide such an endorsement

non sequitur
One idea or conclusion does not logically follow the previous idea or conclusion. Latin for "it does not follow"

General Douglas MacArthur, in announcing his retirement before a joint session of Congress, April 19, 1951, closed his speech with "Old soldiers never die; they just fade away. And like the old soldier of that ballad, I now close my military career and just fade away."

British Prime Minister Winston Churchill in his 1940 speech to the House of Commons in preparing his people for war intoned, "Let us therefore brace ourselves to our duties, and so bear ourselves that, if the British Empire and its Commonwealth last for a thousand years, men will still say, 'This was their finest hour.'"

Emotion is a powerful way to move an audience and support your persuasive purpose. Aristotle used the term **pathos** to refer to the use of appeals to emotion. An appeal to emotion can be an effective way to achieve a desired response from an audience. Whereas logical arguments may appeal to our reason, emotional arguments generally appeal to nonrational sentiments. Often we make decisions based not on logic, but on emotion.

Former U.S. Senator and Arkansas Governor Dale Bumpers made an emotional argument when defending his friend Bill Clinton during the Senate impeachment trial in 1999. He suggested that President Clinton had already suffered enough—conviction on perjury and obstruction of justice charges were not needed. In an emotional speech arguing that the Clinton family had been in prolonged emotional pain, Bumpers pleaded with choked voice, ". . . there is a human element in this case that has not been mentioned, and this is that the President and Hillary and Chelsea are human beings. . . . The relationship between husband and wife, father and child, has

pathos
Term Aristotle used to refer to appeals to human emotion

been incredibly strained, if not destroyed. There's been nothing but sleepless nights, mental agony, for this family for almost five years."[10] After days of viewing charts crammed with lists of logical arguments and evidence, many senators reported Bumpers' emotional arguments effective.

One theory suggests that emotional responses can be classified along three dimensions—pleasure, arousal, and dominance.[11] First, you respond with varying degrees of *pleasure or displeasure.* Pleasurable stimuli consist of such things as smiling, healthy babies, or daydreams about winning $1 million in a sweepstakes. Stimuli causing displeasure may be TV images of the beating of Rodney King by police or news stories of child abuse.

A second dimension of emotional responses exists on a continuum of *arousal–nonarousal.* You become aroused emotionally by such things as seeing a snake in your driveway, or you may be lulled into a state of nonarousal by a boring lecture.

The third dimension of emotional responses is one's feeling of *power or powerlessness* when confronted with some stimulus. When thinking about the destructive force of nuclear weapons or the omnipotence of God, you may feel insignificant and powerless. Or perhaps you feel a sense of power when you imagine yourself conducting a symphony or winning an election.

These three dimensions—pleasure, arousal, and power—are believed to form the bases of all our emotional responses. Theory predicts that if listeners feel pleasure and are also aroused by something, such as a political candidate or a product, they will tend to form a favorable view of the candidate or product. A listener's feeling of being powerful or powerless has to do with being in control and having permission to behave as he or she wishes. A listener who feels powerful is more likely to respond to the message.

As a public speaker trying to sway your listeners to your viewpoint, your job is to use emotional appeals to achieve your goal. If you wanted to persuade your listeners that capital punishment should be banned, you would try to arouse feelings of displeasure and turn them against capital punishment. Advertisers selling soft drinks typically strive to arouse feelings of pleasure when you think of their product. Smiling people, upbeat music, and good times are usually part of the formula for selling soda pop.

 ## Tips for Using Emotion to Persuade

Although the underlying theory of emotions may help you understand how emotions work, as a public speaker your key concern is "How can I ethically use emotional appeals to achieve my persuasive purpose?" Let's consider several methods.

USE CONCRETE EXAMPLES THAT HELP YOUR LISTENERS VISUALIZE WHAT YOU DESCRIBE   Using a concrete example of an emotionally moving scene can create a powerful response in your audience. Describing what it was like after a tornado destroyed the town of Saragosa, Texas, can evoke strong emotions in your listeners. The images used to evoke the emotions can also help communicate the power of nature and the value of taking proper precautions when a storm warning is sounded.

The town is no more. No homes in the western Texas town remain standing. The church where twenty-one people perished looks like a heap of twisted metal and mortar. A child's doll can be seen in the street. The owner, four-year-old Maria, will no longer play with her favorite toy; she was killed along with five of her playmates when the twister roared through the elementary school.

USE EMOTION-AROUSING WORDS   Words and phrases can trigger emotional responses in your listeners. *Mother, flag, freedom,* and *slavery* are among a large number of emotionally loaded words. Patriotic slogans, such as "Remember the Alamo" or "Remember Pearl Harbor," can produce strong emotional responses.

USE NONVERBAL BEHAVIOR TO COMMUNICATE YOUR EMOTIONAL RESPONSE
The great Roman orator Cicero believed that if you want your listeners to experience a certain emotion, you should first model that emotion for them. If you want an audience to feel anger at a particular law or event, you must display anger and indignation in your voice, movement, and gesture. As we have already noted, delivery plays the key role in communicating your emotional responses. If you want your audience to become excited about and interested in your message, you must communicate that excitement and interest through your delivery.

USE VISUAL IMAGES TO EVOKE EMOTIONS   In addition to nonverbal expressions, pictures or images of emotion-arousing scenes can amplify your speech. An image of a lonely homeowner looking out over his waterlogged house following the ravaging Houston, Texas, flood can communicate his sense of despair. A picture of children in war-torn Macedonia can communicate the devastating effects of violence with greater impact than can mere words alone. In contrast, a photo of a refugee mother and child reunited after an enforced separation can communicate the true meaning of joy. You can use similar images as visual aids to evoke your audience's emotions, both positive and negative. Remember, however, that when you use visual images, you have the same ethical responsibilities as you do when you use verbal forms of support: Make sure your image is from a credible source and that it has not been altered or taken out of context.

USE APPROPRIATE FEAR APPEALS   The threat that harm will come to your listeners unless they follow your advice is an appeal to fear. As discussed in Chapter 16, listeners can be motivated to change their behavior if appeals to fear are used appropriately. Research suggests that high fear arousal ("You will be killed in an auto accident unless you wear a safety belt") is more effective than moderate or low appeals, if you are a highly credible speaker.[12] However, you may be taking a risk in arousing too much anxiety in your listeners. They may find what you have to say so exaggerated that they stop listening to you. Hence, unless you are a highly credible speaker, moderate fear appeals directed toward your listeners or their loved ones seem to work best.

CONSIDER USING APPEALS TO SEVERAL EMOTIONS   Appealing to the fears and anxieties of your listeners is one of the most common types of emotional appeals used to persuade, but you could also elicit several other emotions to help achieve your persuasive goal.

● **Hope.**   Listeners could be motivated to respond to the prospect of a brighter tomorrow. When Franklin Roosevelt said, "The only thing we have to fear is fear itself," he was invoking hope for the future. Bill Clinton used this technique very effectively during his campaign by focusing on his roots in Hope, Arkansas.

● **Pride.**   "The pride is back" is a slogan used to sell cars. An appeal to pride can also be used to motivate listeners in a persuasive speech. The appeal to achieve a persuasive objective based on pride in oneself or one's country, state, or hometown can be very powerful.

- **Courage.**   Challenging your audience to take a bold stand or to step away from the crowd can emotionally charge your listeners to take action. Referring to courageous men and women as role models can help motivate your listeners to take similar actions. Patrick Henry's famous "Give me liberty, or give me death!" speech appealed to his audience to take a courageous stand on the issues before the people.

- **Reverence.**   The appeal to the sacred and the revered can be an effective way to motivate. Sacred traditions, revered institutions, or cherished and celebrated individuals can be used to help inspire your audience to change or reinforce attitudes, beliefs, values, or behavior. The late Mother Teresa, holy writings, and the Congress of the United States are examples of revered people or things that your listeners may perceive as sacred. As an audience-centered speaker, however, you need to remember that what may be sacred to one individual or audience may not be sacred to another.

TAP AUDIENCE MEMBERS' BELIEFS IN SHARED MYTHS   You may often hear people talking about a myth as something that is untrue. The Easter Bunny, the Tooth Fairy, and Santa Claus are often labeled myths. But in a rhetorical sense a **myth** is a belief held in common by a group of people and based on the values, cultural heritage, and faith. A myth may, in fact, be factual—or it may be based on partial truth that a group of people believes true. Myths are the "big stories" that give meaning and coherence to a group of people or culture. The myth of the "Old West" is that the pioneers of yesteryear were strong, adventurous people who sacrificed their lives in search of a better tomorrow. Our parents, grandparents, and great-grandparents belonged to "the greatest generation" because they overcame a devastating economic depression and were triumphant in two world wars. The myth of the 1950s is that of the *Leave It to Beaver* generation: U.S. families were prosperous and lived like Ward and June Cleaver and their sons Wally and "The Beaver," made famous by the TV program *Leave It to Beaver*. Religious myths are beliefs shared by a group of faithful disciples. So a myth does not mean "false," it refers to a belief that a group of people share and that provides emotional support for the way they view the world.

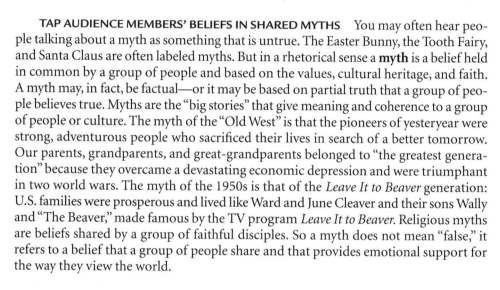

As a public speaker, you can draw on the myths you and your audience members believe to provide emotional and motivational support for your message. Referring to a shared myth is a way for you to identify with your listeners and help them see how your ideas support their ideas; it can help you identify with your audience and develop a common bond with its members. In trying to convince his listeners to vote, Ron argued, "We can't let down those who fought for our freedom. We must vote to honor those who died for the privilege of voting that we enjoy today." He was drawing on the powerful myth that people have died for our freedoms. To gain parent support for a new high school, Cynthia said, "Our parents and grandparents lived through the Great Depression and the world wars of the past century so that we can send our children to the best public schools in the world. Vote for the new high school." She was appealing to the myth that the previous generation sacrificed, so we also have a responsibility to sacrifice for our children. Again we reemphasize that *myth* does not mean "false" or "made up." People really did die for our freedom, and our parents and grandparents did live through the Depression and tragic world wars; a myth is powerful because the audience *believes* those events occurred. Myth becomes a powerful underlying story that evokes an emotional response to the message.

myth
From a rhetorical perspective, a myth is a shared belief based on the underlying values, cultural heritage, and faith of a group of people

Politicians use myth when they show pictures of themselves surrounded by their family. The underlying myth is "I cherish what you cherish—to live in a country that supports and nurtures the family values we hold dear." Appealing directly or indirectly to the commonly held myths of an audience is a powerful way to evoke emotional support for your message. But as with any form of support, especially emotional support, you have an ethical responsibility to use this strategy wisely and not to exploit your listeners.

Using Emotional Appeals: Ethical Issues

Regardless of which emotions you use to motivate your audience, you have an obligation to be ethical and forthright. Making false claims, misusing evidence to arouse emotions, or relying only on emotions without any evidence to support a conclusion violates ethical standards of effective public speaking.

A **demagogue** is a speaker who attempts to gain power or control over others by using impassioned emotional pleas and appealing to the prejudices of listeners. The word *demagogue* comes from the Greek term *demagogos,* meaning "popular leader." Speakers who become popular by substituting emotion and fallacies in place of well-supported reasoning are guilty of demagoguery. During the late 1940s and early 1950s, Wisconsin Senator Joseph McCarthy sought to convince the nation that closet Communists had infiltrated government, education, and the entertainment industry. This was at the height of the Cold War, and anything or anyone remotely connected to Communism elicited an immediate negative emotional response. For a time, McCarthy was successful in his effort to expose the unpatriotic Communists among us. His evidence, however, was scanty, and he relied primarily on scaring his listeners about the potential evil of alleged Communists. His trumped-up evidence and unethical use of fear appeals eventually undermined his credibility and earned him a reputation as a demagogue. You have an ethical responsibility not to misuse emotional appeals when persuading others.

Your credibility, reasoning, and emotional appeals are the chief ways to persuade an audience. Now you need to refine your technique. Your use of these persuasive strategies depends on the composition of your audience. As we have observed several times before, an early task in the public-speaking process is to analyze your audience. This is particularly important in persuasion. Audience members are not just sitting there waiting to respond to every suggestion a speaker makes.

RECAP   **TIPS FOR USING EMOTION TO PERSUADE**

Use concrete examples.

Use emotion-arousing words.

Use nonverbal behavior to communicate your emotional response.

Use visual images.

Use appropriate fear appeals.

Use appeals to a variety of emotions such as hope, pride, courage, or reverence.

Tap audience members' beliefs in shared myths.

demagogue
A speaker who gains control over others by using unethical emotional pleas and appeals to listeners' prejudices

Strategies for Adapting Ideas to People and People to Ideas

One definition of persuasive communication nicely summarizes the importance of adapting your message to your audience. "Rhetoric," suggests Donald C. Bryant, "is the process of adjusting ideas to people and people to ideas."[13] Your appeals to reason, emotion, and your own credibility are all dependent on the attitudes, beliefs, and values of your listeners.

Audience members may hold differing views of you and your subject. Your task is to find out if there is a prevailing viewpoint held by a majority of your listeners. If they are generally friendly toward you and your ideas, you need to design your speech differently from the way you would if your listeners were neutral, apathetic, or hostile. Research studies as well as seasoned public speakers can offer some useful suggestions to help you adapt your approach to your audience. We will discuss three general responses your audience may have to you: receptive, neutral, and unreceptive.

Persuading the Receptive Audience

It is always a pleasure when the audience you face already supports you and your message. In speaking to a receptive group, you can explore your ideas in greater depth than otherwise. Here are some suggestions that may help you make the most of your speaking opportunity.

IDENTIFY WITH YOUR AUDIENCE To establish common ground with her audience, Rita told her audience of fellow students, "Just like most of you, I struggle to pay my way through college. That's why I support expanding the campus work-study program." Like Rita, if you are a college student speaking to other college students with similar backgrounds and pressures, point to your similar backgrounds and struggles. Emphasize the similarities between you and your audience. What other common interests do you have? The introductory portion of your speech is a good place to mention your common interests and background.

CLEARLY STATE YOUR SPEAKING OBJECTIVE When speaking to a group of her campaign workers, mayoral candidate Maria Hernandez clearly stated early in her speech, "My reason for coming here today is to ask each of you to volunteer three hours a week to help me become the next mayor of our city." We have stressed several times how important it is to provide an overview of your major point or purpose. This is particularly so when speaking to a group who will support your point of view.[14]

TELL YOUR AUDIENCE EXACTLY WHAT YOU WANT THEM TO DO Besides telling your listeners what your speaking objective is, you can also tell them how you expect them to respond to your message. Be explicit in directing your listeners' behavior.

ASK LISTENERS FOR AN IMMEDIATE SHOW OF SUPPORT Asking for an immediate show of support helps to cement the positive response you have developed during your speech. For example, Christian evangelists usually speak to favorable audiences. Evangelist Billy Graham always asks those who support his Christian message to come forward at the end of his sermon.

USE EMOTIONAL APPEALS EFFECTIVELY   You can usually move a favorable audience to action with strong emotional appeals while also reminding them of the evidence that supports your conclusion. If the audience already supports your position, you need not spend a great deal of time on lengthy, detailed explanations or factual information. You can usually assume that your listeners are already in possession of much of that material.

MAKE IT EASY FOR YOUR LISTENERS TO ACT   Is it a good idea not only to tell your listeners precisely what you want them to do and ask for an immediate response, but it is also good to make sure that what you're asking them to do is clear and easy. If you're asking them to write or e-mail someone, hand out postcards already addressed to the recipient or distribute an e-mail address printed on a card for handy reference. If you want the recipient to call someone, make sure each person has the phone number—it's even better if you can give a toll-free number.

Persuading the Neutral Audience

Think how many lectures you go to with an attitude of indifference. Probably quite a few. Many audiences will fall somewhere between wildly enthusiastic and unreceptive; they will simply be neutral or indifferent. They may be neutral because they don't know much about your topic or because they just can't make up their minds whether to support your point of view. They may also be indifferent because they don't see how the topic or issue affects them. Regardless of the reason for your listeners' indifference, your challenge is to make them interested in your message. Let's look at some approaches to gaining their attention and keeping their interest.

This sales representative believes she is facing a receptive audience. How might her presentation be different in a more neutral or even hostile environment?

[Spencer Grant/PhotoEdit]

CAPTURE YOUR LISTENERS' ATTENTION EARLY IN YOUR SPEECH   "Bill Farmer died last year, but he's about to fulfill his lifelong dream of going into space."[15] In the sample speech about the high cost of funerals that concludes this chapter, Karmen Kirtley's provocative opening statement effectively captures the attention of her listeners.

REFER TO BELIEFS THAT MANY LISTENERS SHARE   When speaking to a neutral audience, identify common concerns and values that you plan to address. Martin Luther King's "I Have a Dream" speech (Appendix C) illustrates a reference to his listeners' common beliefs.

RELATE YOUR TOPIC NOT ONLY TO YOUR LISTENERS BUT ALSO TO THEIR FAMILIES, FRIENDS, AND LOVED ONES   You can capture the interest of your listeners by appealing to the needs of people they care about. Parents will be interested in ideas and policies that affect their children. People are generally interested in matters that may affect their friends, neighbors, and others with whom they identify, such as members of their own religion or economic or social class.

BE REALISTIC IN WHAT YOU CAN ACCOMPLISH   Don't overestimate the response you may receive from a neutral audience. People who start with an attitude of indifference are probably not going to become as enthusiastic as you are after hearing just one speech. Persuasion does not occur all at once or at a first hearing of arguments.

Persuading the Unreceptive Audience

One of the biggest challenges is to persuade audience members who are against you or your message. If they are hostile toward you personally, your job is to seek ways to enhance your acceptability and persuade them to listen to you. If they are unreceptive to your point of view, there are several approaches that you can use to help them listen to you.

DON'T IMMEDIATELY ANNOUNCE THAT YOU PLAN TO CHANGE THEIR MINDS
Paul wondered why his opening sales pitch ("Good morning. I plan to convince you to purchase this fine set of knives at a cost to you of only $250") was not greeted enthusiastically. If you immediately and bluntly tell your listeners that you plan to change their opinions, it can make them defensive. It is usually better to take a more subtle approach when announcing your persuasive intent.[16]

BEGIN YOUR SPEECH BY NOTING AREAS OF AGREEMENT BEFORE YOU DISCUSS AREAS OF DISAGREEMENT   In addressing the school board, one community member began his persuasive effort to convince board members they should not raise taxes by stating, "I think each of us here can agree with one common goal: We want the best education for our children." Once you help your audience understand that there are issues on which you agree (such as agreeing that the topic you will discuss is controversial), your listeners may be more attentive when you explain your position.

DON'T EXPECT A MAJOR SHIFT IN ATTITUDE FROM A HOSTILE AUDIENCE   Set a realistic limit on what you can achieve. A realistic goal might be to have your listeners hear you out and at least consider some of your points.

ACKNOWLEDGE THE OPPOSING POINTS OF VIEW THAT MEMBERS OF YOUR AUDIENCE MAY HOLD   Summarize the reasons individuals may oppose your point of view. Doing this communicates that you at least understand the issues.[17] Your listeners will be more likely to listen to you if they know that you understand their viewpoint. Of course, after you acknowledge the opposing point of view, you will need to cite evidence and use arguments to refute the opposition and support your conclusion. In speaking to a neighborhood group about the possibility of building a new airport near their homes, City Manager Anderson early in his talk acknowledged, "I am aware that a new airport brings unwanted changes to a neighborhood. Noise and increased traffic are not the type of challenges you want near your homes." He went on to identify the actions the city would take to minimize the problems a new airport would cause.

ESTABLISH YOUR CREDIBILITY   Being thought credible is always an important goal of a public speaker, and it is especially important when talking to an unreceptive audience. Let your audience know about the experience, interest, knowledge, and skill that give you special insight into the issues at hand.

CONSIDER MAKING UNDERSTANDING RATHER THAN ADVOCACY YOUR GOAL

Sometimes your audience disagrees with you because its members just don't understand your point. Or they may harbor a misconception of you and your message. For example, if your listeners think that AIDS is transferred though kissing or other casual contact rather than through unprotected sexual contact, you'll first have to acknowledge their beliefs and then construct a sound argument to show how inaccurate their assumptions are. To change such a misconception and enhance accurate understanding, experienced speakers use a four-part strategy.[18]

- *Summarize the common misconceptions about the issue or idea you are discussing.* "Many people think that AIDS can be transmitted through casual contact such as kissing or that it can easily be transmitted by your dentist or physician."

- *State why these misconceptions may seem reasonable.* Tell your listeners why it is logical for them to hold that view or identify "facts" they may have heard that would lead them to their current conclusion. "Since AIDS is such a highly contagious disease, it may seem reasonable to think it can be transmitted through such casual contact."

- *Dismiss the misconceptions and provide evidence to support your point.* Here you need sound and credible data to be persuasive. "In fact, countless medical studies have shown that it is virtually impossible to be infected with the AIDS virus unless you have unprotected sexual contact or use infected and unsterilized hypodermic needles from someone who has AIDS." In this instance, you would probably cite specific results from two or three studies to lend credibility to your claim.

- *State the accurate information that you want your audience to remember.* Reinforce the conclusion you want your listeners to draw from the information you presented, with a clear summary statement such as "According to recent research, the most common factor contributing to the spread of AIDS is unprotected sex. This is true for individuals of all sexes and sexual orientations."

Strategies for Organizing Persuasive Messages

Is there one best way to organize a persuasive speech? The answer is no. Specific approaches to organizing speeches depend on audience, message, and desired objective. But how you organize your speech does have a major effect on your listeners' response to your message.

Research suggests that there are some general principles to keep in mind when preparing your persuasive message.[19]

- *If you feel that your audience may be hostile to your point of view, advance your strongest arguments first.* If you save your best argument for last, your audience may have already stopped listening.

- *Do not bury key arguments and evidence in the middle of your message.* Information presented first and last is more likely to be remembered by your listeners. In speaking to his fraternity about the evils of drunk driving, Frank wisely began his speech with his most powerful evidence: The leading cause of death among college-age males is alcohol-related automobile accidents. He got their attention with his sobering fact.

- *If you want your listeners to take some action, it is best to tell them what you want them to do at the end of your speech.* If you call for action in the middle of your speech, it won't have the same power as including it in your conclusion.

- *When you think your listeners are well informed and are familiar with the disadvantages of your proposal, it is usually better to present both sides of an issue, rather than just the advantages of the position you advocate.* If you don't acknowledge arguments your listeners have heard, they will probably think about them anyway.

- *Make some reference to the counterarguments, and then refute them with evidence and logic.* It may be wise to compare the proposal you are making with an alternate proposal, perhaps one offered by someone else. By comparing and contrasting your solution with another recommendation, you can show how your proposal is better.

Even though we have discussed ways of organizing speeches in Chapter 9, there are special ways to organize persuasive speeches. Here we present four organizational patterns: problem–solution, refutation, cause and effect, and the motivated sequence.

Problem–Solution

The most basic organizational pattern for a persuasive speech is to make the audience aware of the problem, then present a solution that clearly solves it. Almost any problem can be phrased in terms of something you want more of or less of. The problem–solution pattern works best when a clearly evident problem can be documented and a solution can be proposed to deal with the evils of the well-documented problem.

If you are speaking to an apathetic audience or the listeners are not aware that a problem exists, a problem–solution pattern works nicely. Your challenge will be to provide ample evidence to document that your perception of the problem is accurate. You'll also need to convince your listeners that the solution you advocate is the most appropriate one to resolve the problem.

Many political candidates use a problem–solution approach. *Problem:* The government wastes your tax dollars. *Solution:* Vote for me and I'll see to it that government waste is eliminated. *Problem:* We need more and better jobs. *Solution:* Vote for me and I'll institute a program to put people back to work.

Note how the following arguments used in Jason Fruit's speech, "The Dangers of Electromagnetic Fields," first document a clear problem and then recommend strategies for managing the problem.

PROBLEM:

I. Power lines and power stations around the country emit radiation and are now being shown to increase the risk of cancer.

   A. Childhood leukemia rates are higher in children who live near large power lines.

   B. The International Cancer Research Institute in Lyon, France, published a report linking electromagnetic fields and childhood cancer.

SOLUTION:

    II. Steps can be taken to minimize our risk of health hazards caused by electromagnetic energy.

       A. The federal government should establish enforceable safety standards for exposure to electromagnetic energy.

       B. Contact your local power company to make sure its lines are operated safely.

       C. Stop using electric blankets.

       D. Use protective screens for computer-display terminals.

The problem–solution arrangement of ideas applies what we learned about cognitive dissonance in Chapter 16. Identify and document a concern that calls for change, and then suggest specific behaviors that can restore cognitive balance.

Refutation

Another way to persuade an audience to support your point of view is to prove that the arguments against your position are false, to refute them. To use refutation as a strategy for persuasion, you first identify objections to your position that your listeners may hold and then refute or overcome those objections with arguments and evidence. You would be most likely to use refutation as your organizational strategy when your position is being attacked. Or, if you know what your listeners' chief objections are to your persuasive proposal, you could organize your speech around the arguments your listeners hold.

As we noted earlier, research suggests that in most cases it is better to present both sides of an issue rather than just the advantages of the position you advocate. Even if you don't acknowledge arguments your listeners have heard, they will probably think about them anyway.

Suppose, for example, you plan to speak to a group of real-estate developers advocating a new zoning ordinance that would reduce the number of building permits granted in your community. Your listeners will undoubtedly have some concerns over how the ordinance will affect new housing starts and the overall economic forecast. You could organize your presentation to this group using those two obvious concerns as major issues to refute. Your major points could be as follows:

    I. The new zoning ordinance will not cause an overall decrease in the number of new homes built in our community.

    II. The new zoning ordinance will have a positive effect on the economic growth in our community.

After your persuasive presentation with a refutation strategy, if there is a question-and-answer forum, you should be prepared to answer questions. Credible evidence, facts, and data will be more effective than emotional arguments alone when you face an audience that you know is not in favor of your persuasive objective. In your postspeech session, you can use your refutation skills to maintain a favorable audience response to your message in the face of criticism or attacks on the soundness of your logic.

Cause and Effect

Like the problem–solution pattern to which it is closely related, the cause and effect approach was introduced in Chapter 9 as a useful organizational strategy. One way to use the cause–effect method is to begin with an effect or problem, and then identify the causes of the problem in an effort to convince your listeners that the problem is significant. A speech on the growing problem of gangs might focus on poverty, drugs, and a financially crippled school system.

You could also organize a message by noting the problem and then spelling out the effects the problem has. If you identify the problem as too many unsupervised teenagers roaming your community's streets after 11 P.M., you could organize a speech noting the effects this problem is having on your fellow citizens.

The goal of using cause-and-effect organization for a persuasive speech is to convince your listeners that one event caused another. As we noted earlier, you argue that something known caused something else to happen. For example, you may try to reason that students in your state have low standardized test scores because they had poor teachers. Of course, you must prove that there are no other factors responsible for the low test scores. It may not be the teachers who caused the low test scores; perhaps it was the lack of parent involvement, or one of a number of other factors.

The challenge in using a cause-and-effect organizational strategy is to *prove* that one event *caused* something else to occur. Simply because two events occurred at the same time does not prove that there is a cause-and-effect relationship. Earlier we noted the causal fallacy "after this; therefore, because of this" (also known by its Latin name, *post hoc, ergo propter hoc*). Here's an example of the challenge in documenting a cause-and-effect relationship: A study found that people who spend several hours daily on the Internet are also psychologically depressed; this does not necessarily *prove* that Internet use causes depression. Other factors could cause the depression—perhaps people who are depressed are more likely to use the Internet. Or psychologically depressed people may find general comfort and security in using technology.

Simply noting that one event happened and some other event or behavior may be related to the event does not prove cause and effect.

Here's an example of how a persuasive speech could be organized using a cause-and-effect strategy:

I. High uncertainty exists about whether interests rates will increase or decrease. *(cause)*

II. Money markets are unstable in Asia, Eastern Europe, and Latin America. *(cause)*

III. There has been a rise in unemployment. *(cause)*

IV. Because of the existing economic uncertainty, you should decrease the amount of money you have invested in stocks; if you don't, you will lose money. *(effect)*

The Motivated Sequence

The motivated sequence is a five-step organizational plan that has proved successful for several decades. Developed by Alan Monroe, this simple yet effective strategy for organizing speeches incorporates principles that have been confirmed by research and practical experience.[20] Based on the problem–solution pattern, it also uses the cognitive-dissonance approach, which we discussed in Chapter 16: First disturb your listeners, and then point them toward the specific change you want them to adopt. The five steps are attention, need, satisfaction, visualization, and action.

1. *Attention.* Your first goal is to get your listeners' attention. In Chapter 10, we discussed specific attention-catching methods of beginning a speech. Remember the particular benefits of using a personal or hypothetical example, a startling statement, an unusual statistic, a rhetorical question, or a well-worded analogy. The attention step is, in essence, the introduction to your speech.

Vic Vieth began his prize-winning speech titled "Prisoners of Conscience" with this dramatic, attention-catching description:

Tenzin Chodrak lived on nine ounces of grain a day as he was forced to work a rock-hard soil beneath a beating sun. In time, his hair fell out and his eyebrows fell off. Tortured by his hunger, he ate rats and worms and, eventually, his leather jacket.[21]

2. *Need.* After getting the attention of your audience, now establish why your topic, problem, or issue should concern your listeners. Arouse dissonance. Tell your audience why the current program, politician, or whatever you're attempting to change is not working. Convince them there is a need for a change. You must also convince your listeners that this need for a change affects them directly. During the need step, you should develop logical arguments backed by ample evidence to support your position.

To document the need for greater involvement in human rights issues around the world, Vic established the need for concern in his "Prisoners of Conscience" speech with the following:

There is no accurate estimation of the number of the world's prisoners of conscience. [Prisoners of conscience are people who have been jailed for beliefs and convictions that challenge their government.] Human rights organizations are overburdened and understaffed, and what estimates they do provide us are only the roundest of guesses. Still, Amnesty International says there are perhaps 10,000 in the former Soviet Union and 2,000 in Poland, 15,000 in Turkey, and 10,000 spread across Africa, 5,000 in South America, and some 100,000 are strung across Pakistan, Afghanistan, Iran, Iraq, South Korea, and the Philippines. In its most recent state of the world report, the United Nations conceded [that] our planet is still racked with "political liquidations, mass killings, and torture."[22]

3. *Satisfaction.* After you present the problem or need for concern, you next briefly identify how your plan will satisfy the need. What is your solution to the problem? At this point in the speech, you need not go into great detail. Present enough information so that your listeners have a general understanding of how the problem may be solved.

Vic established the satisfaction step in his speech when he noted, "First, we must recognize that human rights is a worthy objective.... Second, once we recognize human rights as a worthy objective, we can move to make it once again a part of our foreign policy."[23]

4. *Visualization.* Now you need to give your audience a sense of what it would be like if your solution were or were not adopted. You could take a *positive-visualization* approach: Paint a picture with words to communicate how wonderful the future will be if your solution is adopted. You could take a *negative-visualization* approach: Tell your listeners how awful things will be if your solution is not adopted. If they think things are bad now, just wait; things will get worse. Or you could present both a positive and a negative visualization of the future: The problem will be solved if your solution is adopted, and the world will be a much worse place if your solution is not adopted.

In moving to this step for his "Prisoners of Conscience" speech, Vic used a positive-visualization approach when he said, "If we can muster the moral decency to defend political freedom, we may one day achieve political freedom for everyone, everywhere."[24]

He could have had an even stronger visualization step by noting the specific benefits of supporting his solution. He could have helped his audience visualize the specific joy men and women will have once they are set free. Martin Luther King's moving "I Have a Dream" speech (Appendix C) provided strong positive visualization:

> *I have a dream that one day this nation will rise up and live out the true meaning of its creed, "We hold these truths to be self-evident, that all men are created equal."*

> *I have a dream that one day on the red hills of Georgia the sons of former slaves and the sons of former slaveowners will be able to sit down together at the table of brotherhood.*

> *I have a dream that one day even the state of Mississippi, a state sweltering with the heat of injustice, sweltering with the heat of oppression, will be transformed into an oasis of freedom and justice.*

> *I have a dream that my four little children will one day live in a nation where they will not be judged by the color of their skin but by the content of their character. I have a dream today.*

> *I have a dream that one day, down in Alabama, with its vicious racists, with its governor having his lips dripping with the words of interposition and nullification, one day right there in Alabama little black boys and black girls will be able to join hands with little white boys and white girls as sisters and brothers. I have a dream today.*

> *I have a dream that one day every valley shall be exalted, every hill and mountain shall be made low, the rough places will be made plane and the crooked places will be made straight, and the glory of the Lord shall be revealed, and all flesh shall see it together.*[25]

5. *Action.* This last step forms the basis of your conclusion. You tell your audience the specific action they can take to implement your solution. Identify exactly what you want your listeners to do. Give them simple, clear, easy-to-follow steps to achieve your goal. For example, you could give them a phone number to call for more information, provide an address so that they can write a letter of support, hand them a petition to sign at the end of your speech, or tell them for whom to vote. Outline the specific action you want them to take.

In the "Prisoners of Conscience" speech, Vic identified some specific actions his audience could take:

> *It's up to us to support the work of organizations such as America's Watch and Amnesty International, chapters of which are on almost every campus, and it's up to*

us to elect, this election year, a government which places high on its list of priorities the defense of human rights.[26]

You can modify the motivated sequence to suit the needs of your topic and audience. If, for example, you are speaking to a receptive audience, you do not have to spend a great deal of time on the need step. They already agree that the need is serious. They may, however, want to learn about some specific actions that they can take to implement a solution to the problem. Therefore, you would be wise to emphasize the satisfaction and action steps.

Conversely, if you are speaking to a hostile audience, you should spend considerable time on the need step. Convince your audience that the problem is significant and that they should be concerned about the problem. You would probably not propose a lengthy, detailed action.

If your audience is neutral or indifferent, spend time getting their attention and inviting their interest in the problem. The attention and need steps should be emphasized.

The motivated sequence is a guide, not an absolute formula. Use it and the other suggestions about speech organization to help you achieve your specific objective. Be audience-centered; adapt your message to your listeners.

Aristotle defined *rhetoric* as "the process of gathering the available means of persuasion." In this chapter, we have described some of the means available to you.

ORGANIZATIONAL PATTERNS FOR PERSUASIVE

Type	Definition	Example
Problem–solution	Present the problem; then present the solution	I. The national debt is too high. II. We need to raise taxes to lower the debt.
Refutation	Anticipate your listeners' key objections to your proposal and then address them.	I. Even though you may think we pay too much tax, we are really undertaxed. II. Even though you may think the national debt will not go down, tax revenue will lower the deficit.
Cause–effect	First present the cause of the problem; then note how the problem affects the listeners. Or identify a known effect; then document what causes the effect.	I. The high national debt is caused by too little tax revenue and too much government spending. II. The high national debt will increase both inflation and unemployment.
Motivated sequence	A five-step pattern of organizing a speech, consisting of these steps: attention, need, satisfaction, visualization, action.	I. *Attention:* Imagine a pile of $1000 bills 67 miles high. That's our national debt. II. *Need:* The increasing national debt will cause hardships for our children and grandchildren. III. *Satisfaction:* We need higher taxes to reduce our debt. IV. *Visualization:* Imagine our country in the year 2050; it could have low inflation and full employment or be stuck with a debt ten times our debt today. V. *Action:* If you want to lower the debt by increasing tax revenue, sign my petition that I will send to our senators.

Genetic Discrimination

By Stephen Zammit, Cornell University

Forty-five-year-old Gary Avery has a predisposition. You might say he was born that way. His tendency wasn't a factor at work, where he had a spotless employment record. But when health problems struck, Gary was forced to tell people at the office. His employer didn't understand. In fact, the company decided that Gary's tendencies meant he was practicing a risky lifestyle, and invited him to pay for the costly treatment himself. But as the *Los Angeles Times* of February 25, 2001, reveals, this is not your typical coming-out story. You see, Gary Avery is about as gay as the Reverend Jerry Falwell. Rather, Gary has carpal tunnel syndrome. His employer sought to evade insurance coverage by secretly testing his blood to prove Gary was predisposed from birth with the carpal tunnel gene. The secret was uncovered by his wife, Nurse Avery.

To catch attention, Steve starts his speech with an example that includes an element of suspense; the audience will want to listen to find out what Gary Avery's "predisposition" is.

Strange as it may seem, in a country that bans discrimination on the basis of race, religion, gender, and, increasingly, sexual orientation, discriminating on the basis of genes is not only legal, it's happening. *Scientific American* of January 2001 reports that in Massachusetts alone, 785 people have been denied insurance coverage or lost their jobs. And since human genome researcher Francis Collins adds, "All of us carry probably four or five really fouled-up genes," we are all at risk. Unless we want to live in a country where "everything our genes say can, and will, be used against us," genetic discrimination must be stopped. To see how, let's first uncover the abuses of genetic testing; next, see why reform is not imminent, and finally, suggest solutions, so as science delves ever deeper into the genetic code, no one will be delving into yours.

Here he presents the key idea he will later develop in more detail.

Delving into the problem reveals that it is two-fold: opportunity for abuse, and abuse. The February 26, 2001, *Washington Times* explains that science can already test DNA for a predisposition to *hundreds of diseases*. In the hands of a trained professional, the results can be medically invaluable. In the hands of insurance companies and the employers who retain them, the results can be like giving whiskey and car keys to teenage boys. The ability to predict which employees or policyholders might be the most expensive, is just too juicy.

Off the record, a year 2000 American Management Association survey found that 13% of employers confidentially admit to genetic testing. But the opportunity for greater abuse is underscored by a 2000 American Medical Association finding that 65.9% of companies draw fluids to test workers for illegal drug use. And with DNA in hand, the real abuse starts. There is no federal statistic for companies to report "people we've screwed over because of their genes." However, the March 5, 2001, *U.S. News & World Report* insists patient advocacy groups have compiled hundreds of cases. They range from a 30-year veteran shown the door after he was found predisposed for multiple sclerosis, to a mother whose first-grade son was denied coverage because of a potential developmental disorder.

Steve uses statistical evidence to prove the significance of the problem he is describing.

No wonder genetic counselor Karen Eant told the *Baltimore Sun* of February 25, 2001, when taking the new breast cancer test, "A lot of women won't even give me their real name." This legitimate fear leaves millions of Americans facing a ridiculous choice, between their health and their job. Faced with telling her employer, office clerk Terri Sergeant is glad she sought preventive care for her lung disease, even though the *Raleigh News and Observer* of October 22, 2000, reports, when she told her employer, she was fired. In the words of Dr. Philip Chance, a genetic test developer, the idea of these tests was "to help people who can seek preventive treatment. What is being done is a perversion.

A specific example humanizes the statistical information he's already presented.

Perverse stories like Terri Sergeant's and Gary Avery's have prompted every Western European country to ban genetic discrimination, but reform in the U.S. is not inevitable, due to insurance interests and legal limbo. In fairness, some defenders of the current system are thoughtful—others appear to be a little genetically slighted themselves.

For example, insurance industry spokesman Chip Kahn writes in the February 13, 2001, *USA Today* that since an authoritative Wake Forest study shows the insurance industry does not currently discriminate, any new legislation is, quote, "a solution in search of a problem." And sure enough, the 1999 study documents not one report of genetic discrimination in insurance . . . based on a survey of insurance company spokespersons.

But Columnist Andrew Sullivan is not an industry shill, and he writes in the August 6, 2000, *Seattle Post Intelligencer* that genetic discrimination is a rational extension of the principle behind insurance. This is absolutely true. But given that everyone has flawed DNA, it is fundamentally *IR-rational to single out those of us who are more likely to come down with expensive diseases* in the future. The *Bergen County Record* of February 13, 2001, adds, "It seems much more logical, and less expensive, to assume that everyone is predisposed to something and charge us all the same."

The law reflects that logic in only one branch of government. Before he left office, President Clinton signed an order banning genetic discrimination in the executive branch, which is great if you're planning to spend the rest of your life working for a federal agency. And while 24 states have taken action, the April 2001 *Harvard Business Review* argues these laws are a patchwork of loopholes and exemptions that do not offer the broad protection necessary. Legally, when it comes to our most sensitive genetic information, gene privacy expert Joanne Hustead, explains your "video rental records are more protected."

As it stands, our genes can, and are, being used against us. The best hope for our loved ones would be to have the Gary Avery advantage—a medical expert in the house. That's where we come in. We can use our newfound expertise to push for government oversight, industry responsibility, and personal awareness.

The passage of federal legislation will rely on a lawmaker who knows the toll of being born into a disadvantaged family: Senator Ted Kennedy. In fairness, Kennedy has a strong record of passing bipartisan health legislation. But in a March 21, 2001, telephone interview, Kennedy staffer David Bowen explained that most major issues promising easy solvency through legislation result in bad laws. Instead, Kennedy's Senate Health Committee would like a hearing on the issue. Just as Senate hearings shone sunlight on IRS abuses, and sparked reform, a similar parade of scientists, victims, and even the insurance industry would help Congress pass good legislation.

But without a good-faith commitment from the insurance industry, no reform can be perfect. The next time you pay an insurance bill, consider including a short note telling your company how you feel. While that may sound trite, Denver-based One Health Plan is the first in the nation to pay for genetic testing and implement barriers to prevent abuse. As medical director Dr. Steve Gorschow explained in an April 13, 2001, telephone interview, it was customer feedback that caused them to take a hard look at their policy.

Finally, we can spread the words of genetic counselor Vivian Weinblatt, quoted in the previously cited *U.S. News and World Report.* "Wait for the law to change before getting genetic tests, and make the same lifestyle changes as if the test was positive." For example, a person with a family history of breast cancer might forgo genetic testing and be vigilant about regular breast exams. If an employer does require blood samples, get a list of the tests to be run for your records. When Janice Avery raised this red flag, Gary Avery's company backed down.

Unfortunately, there are millions who don't have a registered nurse watching over them. They don't know about The Abuses of Genetic Testing, aren't aware that Change Isn't Imminent, and certainly don't know that Protection Is Within Reach. Even though Gary Avery's story has a happy ending, thousands like him are faced with an outrageous choice: risk your health or risk your job. Wouldn't it be nice if they didn't have to choose?

He establishes the credibility of his source by noting that the columnist he's quoting does not work for an insurance company.

After describing the problem, Steve now begins to describe a potential solution.

Note how he offers a specific, practical way of taking action.

Steve offers additional suggestions as a solution to the problem.

He concludes his speech by referring to his opening example and provides closure by offering a lingering rhetorical question.

SUMMARY

Means of persuasion are techniques that can help you convince your listeners to follow your recommendations. You can persuade with credibility, logic, and emotion.

Credibility is the view that a listener has of a speaker. The three factors of credibility are competence, trustworthiness, and dynamism. Specific strategies can enhance your credibility before, while, and after you speak.

Using effective logical arguments hinges on the proof you employ. Proof consists of evidence plus the reasoning that you use to draw conclusions from evidence. Three types of reasoning are inductive reasoning from specific instances or examples to reach a general, probable conclusion; deductive reasoning from a general statement to reach a specific, more certain conclusion; and causal reasoning, relating two or more events in such a way as to conclude that one or more of the events caused the others. You can use four types of evidence: facts, examples, opinions, and statistics. Avoid using fallacious arguments.

Emotion theory has identified three dimensions of emotional response to a message: pleasure–displeasure, arousal–nonarousal, and power–powerlessness. Specific suggestions for appealing to audience emotions include using examples; emotion-arousing words; nonverbal behavior; selected appeals to fear; and appeals to such emotions as hope, pride, courage, or the revered.

To persuade skillfully, you need to adapt your message to receptive, neutral, and unreceptive audiences.

Four patterns for organizing a persuasive speech are problem–solution, refutation, cause–effect, and the motivated sequence. The five steps of the motivated sequence are attention, need, satisfaction, visualization, and action. Adapt the motivated sequence to your specific audience and persuasive objective.

being audience-centered

A Sharper Focus

CONSIDERING YOUR AUDIENCE

▶ To arouse listeners' emotions, use concrete examples, emotion-arousing words, expressive delivery, and visual images that will help them visualize what you describe.

▶ To establish common ground and provide emotional support for your message, draw on common myths and stories that you and your audience members believe.

▶ To persuade the receptive audience, consider the following strategies: Identify with the audience. State your speaking objective. Tell them what you want the audience members to do. Ask for an immediate show of support. Use emotional appeals effectively. Make it easy for your listeners to act.

▶ To persuade the neutral audience, draw on these persuasive approaches: Capture your listeners' attention early in your speech by referring to beliefs that many listeners share. Relate your topic not only to your listeners but also to their families, friends, and loved ones. Be realistic in what you expect to accomplish.

▶ For an unreceptive audience, consider these persuasive strategies: Don't immediately announce that you plan to change your listeners' minds. Begin your speech by noting areas of agreement before you discuss areas of disagreement. Don't expect a major shift in attitude from a hostile audience. Acknowledge the opposing points of view that members of your audience may hold. Establish your credibility early in your message. Consider making understanding rather than advocacy your goal. Advance your strongest argument first.

▶ If you want your listeners to take some action following your speech, it is best to tell them what you want them to do during the conclusion of your speech.

▶ When your listeners are well informed and are familiar with the disadvantages of your proposal, present both sides of an issue, rather than just the advantages of your position.

▶ Refer to counterarguments your audience may already know, and then refute these counterarguments with evidence and logic.

▶ Adapt the motivated sequence (attention, need, satisfaction, visualization, and action) to your audience. For example, if your listeners are apathetic, emphasize the attention and need steps. Or, if you are speaking to a favorable audience, be sure to present a clear action to take.

CONSIDERING AUDIENCE DIVERSITY

▶ Keep the cultural expectations of your listeners in mind when using strategies to establish or maintain your credibility; credibility is in the mind of the beholder.

▶ For North Americans, research suggests that increased eye contact, varied vocal inflection, and appropriate attire have a positive influence on your ability to persuade listeners to respond to your message.

▶ Most North Americans prefer clearly structured arguments.

▶ Before debating issues, people from high-contact cultures often prefer to establish a personal relationship between speaker and listener.

▶ Middle Eastern cultures usually do not use standard inductive- or deductive-reasoning structures; they are more likely to use narrative (storytelling) strategies to evoke feelings and emotions, allowing their listeners to draw their own conclusions by inductive associations. In some high-context cultures such as Japan and China, the conclusion to a message is stated more indirectly. In a low-context culture such as the United States, listeners may generally expect you to be more direct in the action you'd like your audience members to take.

▶ North Americans usually prefer a well-organized message with a clear, explicit link between the evidence used and the conclusion drawn. Middle Eastern cultures often expect less-formal structure to arguments and persuasive appeals.

▶ Some Latin America listeners often expect speakers to express more emotion and passion when speaking than North American listeners are accustomed to.

CRITICAL THINKING QUESTIONS

1. Imagine that you are delivering your final speech of the semester in your public-speaking class. What specific strategies can you implement to enhance your initial, derived, and final credibility as a public speaker in the minds of your classmates?

2. Josh McCoy is speaking to his neighborhood homeowners' association, attempting to persuade his neighbors that a crime-watch program should be organized. What logical arguments and emotional strategies would help him ethically achieve his persuasive objective?

3. Janice Hakawa is pondering options for organizing her persuasive speech, which has the following purpose: "The audience should be able to support the establishment of a wellness program for our company." Using this purpose, draft the main ideas for a speech organized according to each of the following organizational patterns: problem–solution, refutation, cause–effect, the motivated sequence.

ETHICAL QUESTIONS

1. Karl has a strong belief that the tragedy of the Holocaust could occur again. He plans to show exceptionally graphic photographs of Holocaust victims during his speech to his public-speaking class. Is it ethical to show graphic emotion-arousing photos to a captive audience?

2. Tony was surfing the Internet and found just the statistics he needs for his persuasive speech. Yet he does not know the original source of the statistics—just the Internet address. Is that sufficient documentation for the statistics?

3. Martika wants to convince her classmates, a captive audience, that they should join her in a twenty-four-hour sit-in at the university president's office to protest the recent increase in tuition and fees. The president has made it clear that any attempt to occupy his office after normal university closing hours will result in arrests. Is it appropriate for Martika to use a classroom speech to encourage her classmates to participate in the sit-in?

SUGGESTED ACTIVITIES

1. Identify three nationally known credible speakers. Identify methods and strategies that the speakers use to establish their credibility in a speaking situation.

2. Develop strategies for presenting the same persuasive-speech objective to three different audiences: an unreceptive audience, a neutral audience, and a receptive audience. Note the different strategies that you used in attempting to adapt your message to different listeners.

3. Identify the faulty reasoning in the following arguments:

    We have to do something about the quality of life in our state. Either we should build more prisons or build more schools.

Everyone knows we need to spend more money on the environment.

As soon as the Republicans took control of Congress, the stock market in Mexico had trouble. The Republicans are to blame for the problems in Mexico.

It is obvious that anyone who switched from one political party to another party can have no credible options for balancing the federal budget.

4. Imagine that you want to convince the chamber of commerce in your town to give you and a group of students a grant to support a statewide career fair. You have evidence that career fairs in other communities bring in revenue for a variety of businesses and stores. Although you are armed with facts, figures, and statistics, you realize that the cultural background of several key members of the chamber would respond better to a more narrative persuasive approach. What would be some key narratives, stories, or extended examples that you could share to achieve your persuasive goal?

5. What steps of the motivated sequence would you emphasize for the following audiences?

You want to convince a group of North American businesspeople to invest in your company; they are skeptical.

You want to ask a local garden club composed of mostly retired elementary-school teachers to vote for you for city council.

You represent a neighborhood association who wants to convince members of a local church not to build a four-story parking garage on their property.

You want the Hispanic chamber of commerce to donate money to a student scholarship at your school.

6. Using the different audiences listed in the previous situation, what would be appropriate or inappropriate myths to use to support your persuasive goal?

USING TECHNOLOGY AND MEDIA

1. As you listen to TV or radio commercials, try to identify the steps of the motivated sequence. Note which of the five steps the commercials emphasize most or least.

2. Discuss the appropriateness of unsolicited telephone sales pitches. What are their advantages and disadvantages as a means of persuasion?

Historians agree that the greatest banquet speech in history was the one by the ancient Greek philosopher Socrates moments after he drank hemlock. "Gack," he said, falling face-first into his chicken. The other Greeks applauded like crazy.

DAVE BARRY

18

Special-Occasion Speaking

objectives

After studying this chapter you should be able to do the following:

1. Identify and explain the requirements for two types of speaking situations likely to arise in the workplace.

2. List and describe nine types of ceremonial speeches.

3. Explain the purpose and characteristics of an after-dinner speech.

here is money in public speaking. Many of the ex-presidents, generals, athletes, and entertainment personalities who speak professionally earn five- or even six-figures for a single talk. Former President Gerald Ford earns $60,000 a speech, and former President Bush $80,000. In the $100,000-plus range are former President Bill Clinton and former U.S. Senator John Glenn.[1]

Although most of us will never be rewarded with such lucrative contracts for our public-speaking efforts, it *is* likely that we will at some time be asked to make a business or professional presentation or to speak on some occasion that calls for celebration, commemoration, inspiration, or entertainment. Special occasions are important enough and frequent enough to merit study, regardless of the likelihood of resulting wealth or fame for the speaker.

In this chapter, we will discuss the various types of speeches that may be called for on special occasions, and examine the specific and unique audience expectations for each. First, we will discuss two speaking situations that are likely to occur in the workplace. We will then turn our attention to several types of ceremonial speeches and the after-dinner speech.

Public Speaking in the Workplace

Nearly every job requires some public-speaking skills. In many careers and professions, public speaking is a daily part of the job. Workplace audiences may range from a group of three managers to a huge auditorium filled with company employees. Presentations may take the form of routine meeting management, reports to company executives, training seminars within the company, or public-relations speeches to people outside the company. The occasions and opportunities are many, and chances are good that you will be asked or expected to do some on-the-job public speaking in the course of your career.

Reports

One of the most common types of on-the-job presentations is the **report.** You may be asked to report on how to increase sales in the next quarter or to present a market survey your division has conducted in the past several months. Whatever the specific objective of the report, the general purpose is to communicate information or policy, sometimes ending with a persuasive appeal to try some new course of action.

Most successful reports are structured in a manner similar to the following:

- When you are presenting your report, keep in mind that your audience is there to hear you address a particular need or problem. Begin by briefly acknowledging that situation.

- If you are reporting on a particular project or study, first discuss what your research group decided to do to explore the problem. Then explain how you gathered the information.

report
An oral presentation of information or policy made in and related to the workplace

- Finally, present the possible solutions you have come up with. For some reports, the most important part is this outline of new courses of action or changes in present policy. In addition, tell your audience what's in it for them—what benefits will accrue to them directly as a result of the new proposal. One business consultant suggests,

> *Tune your audience into radio station WIIFM—What's In It For Me. Tell your listeners where the benefits are for them, and they'll listen to everything you have to say.*[2]

In addition to listening to the presentation, audience members usually receive a hard copy or e-mail attachment of the report.

Public-Relations Speeches

People who work for professional associations, blood banks, utility companies, government agencies, universities, churches, or charitable institutions, as well as commercial enterprises, are often called on to speak to an audience about what their organization does or about a special project the organization has taken on. These speeches can be termed **public-relations speeches.** They are designed to inform the public and improve relations with them—either in general, or because a particular program or situation has raised some questions.

As in presenting reports, the public-relations speaker first discusses the need or problem that has prompted the speech. Then he or she goes on to explain how the company or organization is working to meet the need or solve the problem, or why it feels there is no problem.

It is important in public-relations speaking to anticipate criticism, whether it comes from the audience as a whole or from a minority contingent. The speaker may suggest and counter potential problems or objections, especially if past presentations have encountered some opposition to the policy or program. The speaker should emphasize the positive aspects of the policy or program and take care not to become unpleasantly defensive. He or she wants to leave the impression that the company or organization has carefully worked through potential pitfalls and drawbacks. It should be noted that not all public-relations speeches make policy recommendations. Many simply summarize information for those who need to know. For example, local developer Jack Brooks is very aware that many of those present at the city-council meeting are opposed to his developing an area of land within the popular Smythson Creek greenbelt. Rather than ignore the objections, he deliberately and carefully addresses them:

> *Many of you here tonight played in the Smythson Creek greenbelt as children. It was there that you learned to swim and that you hiked with your friends. I, too, share memories of those experiences.*
>
> *I want to assure you that my proposed development will actually help to preserve the greenbelt. We will dedicate in perpetuity an acre of unspoiled greenbelt for each acre we develop. Further, we will actively seek to preserve that unspoiled land by hiring an environmental specialist to oversee its protection.*
>
> *As things stand now, we risk losing the entire greenbelt to pollution and unmanaged use. I can promise a desirable residential development, plus the preservation of at least half the natural environment.*

public-relations speech
A speech designed to inform the public, to strengthen alliances with them, and possibly to recommend policy

Chapter 19 will address other workplace communication challenges, such as meeting management and various forums for group presentations.

Ceremonial Speaking

Ceremonial speeches make up a broad class of speeches delivered on many kinds of occasions. We will explore nine types of ceremonial speeches: introductions, toasts, award presentations, nominations, acceptances, keynote addresses, commencement addresses, commemorative addresses and tributes, and eulogies.

Introductions

Most of us have heard poor introductions. A nervous speaker making a **speech of introduction** stands up and mispronounces the main speaker's name. Or the introducer speaks for five or ten minutes him- or herself.

An introductory speech is much like an informative speech. The speaker delivering the introduction provides information about the main speaker to the audience. The ultimate purpose of an introduction, however, is to arouse interest in the speaker and his or her topic. When you are asked to give a speech of introduction for a featured speaker or an honored guest, your purposes are similar to those of a good opening to a speech: You need to get the attention of the audience, build the speaker's credibility, and introduce the speaker's general subject. You also need to make the speaker feel welcome while revealing some personal qualities to the audience so that they can feel they know the speaker more intimately. There are two cardinal rules of introductory speeches: be brief and be accurate.

- *Be brief.* The audience has come to hear the main speaker or honor the guest, not to listen to you.

- *Be accurate.* Nothing so disturbs a speaker as having to begin by correcting the introducer. If you are going to introduce someone at a meeting or dinner, ask that person to supply you with relevant biographical data beforehand. If someone else provides you with the speaker's background, make sure the information is accurate. Be certain that you know how to pronounce the speaker's name and any other names or terms you will need to use.

This short speech of introduction adheres to the two criteria we have just suggested: It's brief and it's accurate.

This evening, friends, we have the opportunity to hear one of the most innovative mayors in the history of our community. Mary Norris's experience in running her own real-estate business gave her an opportunity to pilot a new approach to attracting new businesses to our community, even before she was elected mayor in last year's landslide victory. She was recently recognized as the most successful mayor in our state by the Good Government League. Not only is she a skilled manager and spokesperson for our city, but she is also a warm and caring person. I am pleased to introduce my friend, Mary Norris.

Finally, keep the needs of your audience in mind at all times. If the person you are introducing truly needs no introduction to the group, do not give one! Just wel-

speech of introduction
A speech that provides information about another speaker

come the speaker and step aside. "Friends" (or "Ladies and gentlemen"), "please join me in welcoming our guest speaker for tonight, the former chairman of this club, Mr. Daniel Jones." Note that the President of the United States is always introduced simply "Ladies and gentlemen, the President of the United States."

Toasts

Most people are asked at some time or another to provide a **toast** for some momentous occasion—a wedding, a celebration of a child's birth, a reunion of friends, or a successful business venture. A toast is a brief salute to such an occasion, usually accompanied by a round of drinks and immediately followed by the raising or clinking together of glasses or goblets. The custom is said to have taken its name—*toast*—from the old custom of tossing a bit of bread or crouton into a beverage for flavoring.[3] "Drinking the toast" was somewhat like enjoying a dunked doughnut.

The modern toast is usually quite short—only a few sentences at most. Some toasts are very personal, as, for example, one given by a best man who is a close friend of both the bride and the groom. In contrast, a toast made by someone who does not know the primary celebrants as intimately may be more generic in nature. Here is an example of such a generic wedding toast:

> *When the roaring flames of your love have burned down to embers, may you find that you've married your best friend.*[4]

If you are asked to make an impromptu toast, let your audience and the occasion dictate what you say. Sincerity is more important than wit. At a dinner your authors attended in Moscow, Russia, a few years ago, all the guests were asked to stand at some point during the meal and offer a toast. Although this Russian custom took us by surprise, one friend of ours gave a heartfelt and well-received toast that went something like this:

> *We have spent the past week enjoying both the natural beauty and the man-made marvels of your country. We have visited the exquisite palaces of the czars and stood in amazement before some of the world's great art treasures. But we have also discovered that the most important national resource of Russia is the warmth of her people. Here's to new and lasting friendships.*

Our Russian hosts were most appreciative. The rest of us were impressed. Mary's toast was a resounding success because she spoke sincerely about her audience and the occasion.

Award Presentations

Presenting an award is somewhat like introducing a speaker or a guest: Remember that the audience did not come to hear you, but to see and hear the winner of the award. Nevertheless, delivering a **presentation speech** is an important responsibility, one that has several distinct components.

First, when presenting an award, you should refer to the occasion of the presentation. Awards are often given to mark the anniversary of a special event, the completion of a long-range task, the accomplishments of a lifetime, or high achievement in some field.

toast
A brief salute to a momentous occasion

presentation speech
A speech that accompanies an award

The best acceptance speeches are brief, sincere, and encouraging to others who may be working toward the same goals.

[Photo: Joseph Sohm/Stock Boston]

Next, you should talk about the history and significance of the award. This section of the speech may be fairly long if the audience knows little about the award; it will be brief if the audience is already familiar with the history and purpose of the award. Whatever the award, a discussion of its significance will add to its meaning for the person who receives it.

The final section of the award presentation will be naming the person to whom it has been given. The longest part of this segment is the description of the achievements that elicited the award. That description should be given in glowing terms. Hyperbole is appropriate here. If the name of the person getting the award has already been made public, you may refer to him or her by name throughout your description. If you are going to announce the individual's name for the first time, you will probably want to recite the achievements first and leave the person's name for last. Even though some members of the audience may recognize from your description the person about whom you are talking, you should still save the drama of the actual announcement until the last moment.

Nominations

Nomination speeches are similar to award presentations. They, too, involve noting the occasion and describing the purpose and significance of, in this case, the office to be filled. The person making the nomination should explain clearly why the nominee's skills, talents, and past achievements serve as qualifications for the position. And the actual nomination should come at the end of the speech. When Senate minority leader Everett Dirksen nominated Barry Goldwater for the Republican presidential candidacy in 1964, he emphasized those personal qualities of the admittedly controversial candidate that he thought would appeal to the audience:

nomination speech
A speech that officially recommends someone as a candidate for an office or position

> *Whether in commerce or finance, in business or industry, in private or public service, there is such a thing as Competence. What is it but the right vision, the right touch, in the right way, at the right time? What man could be a jet pilot without this touch? But Barry Goldwater has demonstrated it over and over in his every activity.*

As Chief of Staff of his state National Guard, he brought about its desegregation shortly after World War II and long before Civil Rights became a burning issue. He brought integration to his own retail enterprises. For his own employees he established the 5-day week and a health and life insurance plan. All this was done without fanfare or the marching of bands.[5]

And Dirksen ended his speech with the nomination itself:

I nominate my friend and colleague, Barry Goldwater of Arizona, to be the Republican candidate for President of the United States.

 Acceptances

For every award or nomination, there is usually at least a brief **acceptance speech.** Acceptance speeches have received something of a bad name because of the lengthy, emotional, rambling, and generally boring speeches delivered annually on prime-time TV by the winners of the film industry's Oscars. As the late humorist Erma Bombeck once wryly noted,

People exchange wedding vows in under thirty seconds. . . . You only get thirty seconds to come up with the final "Jeopardy" answer. My kids can demolish a pizza in thirty seconds.

So how long does it take to say, "Thank you?"[6]

The same audience who may resent a lengthy oration will readily appreciate a brief, heartfelt expression of thanks. In fact, brief acceptance speeches can actually be quite

acceptance speech
A speech of thanks for an award, nomination, or other honor

insightful, even inspiring, and leave the audience feeling no doubt that the right person won the award. Two months before he died in 1979, John Wayne accepted an honorary Oscar with these touching words:

> *Thank you, ladies and gentlemen. Your applause is just about the only medicine a fella would ever need. I'm mighty pleased I can amble here tonight. Oscar and I have something in common. Oscar first came on the Hollywood scene in 1928. So did I. We're both a little weatherbeaten, but we're still here and plan to be around a whole lot longer.[7]*

If you ever have to give an acceptance speech, it may be impromptu, because you may not know that you have won until the award is presented. A fairly simple formula should help you compose a good acceptance speech on the spur of the moment.

First, you should thank the person making the presentation and the organization that he or she represents. It is also gracious to thank a few people who have contributed greatly to your success—but not a long list of everyone you have ever known, down to the family dog.

Next, you should comment on the meaning or significance of the award to you. PLO leader Yasser Arafat interpreted his 1994 Nobel peace prize as a catalyst for continuing efforts toward peace in the Middle East:

> *I realize that this award, which is of ultimate significance and gesture, was not granted to me and to my two partners . . . to crown an endeavor that we have completed but rather to encourage us to continue a road which we have started, continue in wider steps and deeper consciousness in order to convert the option of peace—the peace of the brave—from mere theory to a practice in reality.[8]*

You may also wish to reflect on the larger significance of the award to the people and ideals it honors. In an eloquent acceptance speech, Elie Wiesel, Holocaust survivor, author, and lifelong advocate of human rights, began his acceptance speech for the 1986 Nobel peace prize with these words:

> *It is with a profound sense of humility that I accept the honor you have chosen to bestow upon me. I know your choice transcends me. This both frightens and pleases me.*
>
> *It frightens me because I wonder: Do I have the right to represent the multitudes who have perished? Do I have the right to accept this great honor on their behalf? I do not. That would be presumptuous. No one may speak for the dead, no one may interpret their mutilated dreams and visions.*
>
> *It pleases me because I may say that this honor belongs to all the survivors and their children, and through us, to the Jewish people with whose destiny I have always been identified.[9]*

Finally, try to find some meaning the award may have for your audience—people who respect your accomplishments and who may themselves aspire to similar achievements. In what has become one of the most often quoted acceptance speeches ever made, novelist William Faulkner dedicated his 1950 Nobel prize for literature to

> *the young men and women already dedicated to the same anguish and travail, among whom is already that one who will some day stand here where I am standing.[10]*

Keynote Addresses

A **keynote address** is usually presented at or near the beginning of a meeting or conference. The keynote emphasizes the importance of the topic or purpose of the meeting, motivates the audience to learn more or work harder, and sets the theme and tone for other speakers and events.

The hardest task the keynote speaker faces is being specific enough to arouse interest and inspire the audience. One way in which a keynote speaker can succeed in his or her task is to incorporate examples and illustrations to which the audience can relate. The late Texas congresswoman Barbara Jordan delivered two Democratic National Convention keynote addresses, one in 1976 and the other in 1992. Note how she used specific examples in this excerpt from the 1992 keynote:

The American dream . . . is slipping away from too many. It is slipping away from too many black and brown mothers and their children; from the homeless of every color and sex; from the immigrants living in communities without water and sewer systems. The American dream is slipping away from the workers whose jobs are no longer there because we are better at building war equipment that sits in warehouses than we are at building decent housing.[11]

Commencement Addresses

Cartoonist Garry Trudeau has said that commencement speeches "were invented largely in the belief that outgoing college students should never be released into the world until they have been properly sedated."[12] Unfortunately, most commencement speeches deserve Trudeau's assessment. They are often oblivious to the audience on an occasion that demands and deserves audience-centeredness. To be audience-centered, a commencement speaker must fulfill two important functions.

An audience-centered commencement speaker remembers that the occasion is the graduates' day. The speech should acknowledge their hard work and inspire them as they move to the next phase of their lives.
[Kenneth Lambert/AP/Wide World Photos]

keynote address
A speech that sets the theme and tone for a meeting or conference

commencement address
A speech delivered at a graduation or commencement ceremony

First, the commencement speaker should praise the graduating class. Because the audience includes the families and friends of the graduates, the commencement speaker can gain their goodwill (as well as that of the graduates themselves) by pointing up the significance of the graduates' accomplishments. Author Kurt Vonnegut congratulated the 1998 graduates of Rice University in the opening seconds of his commencement address:

> *God bless you and those who made it possible for you to study at this great American university. By becoming informed and reasonable and capable adults, you have made this a better world than it was before you got here.*[13]

A second function of an audience-centered commencement speaker is to turn graduates toward the future. A commencement address is not the proper forum in which to bemoan the world's inevitable destruction or the certain gloomy economic future of today's graduates. Rather, commencement speakers should offer bright, new goals and try to inspire the graduates to reach for them. NASA administrator Daniel S. Goldin told the 2001 graduates of Augsburg College in Minneapolis that

> *Overcoming the unexpected and discovering the unknown is what ignites our spirit. It is what life is all about.*[14]

Commencement speakers who want to be audience-centered can learn from Hewlett Packard CEO Carly S. Fiorina. In the spring of 2000 Fiorina consulted by e-mail with the Massachusetts Institute of Technology graduating class she was about to address. She discovered that students wanted a speech based on life experience, not theory, and advice on how to make the decisions needed to live life. And, Fiorina adds, "On one point there was complete unanimity: Please don't run over your time."[15]

Commemorative Addresses and Tributes

Commemorative addresses—those delivered during special ceremonies held to celebrate some past event—are often combined with tributes to the person or persons involved. For example, a speech given on the Fourth of July both commemorates the signing of the Declaration of Independence and pays tribute to those who signed it. Your town's sesquicentennial celebrates both the founding and the founders of the town. And if you were asked to speak at the reception for your grandparents' fiftieth wedding anniversary, you would probably relate the stories they've told you of their wedding day and then go on to praise their accomplishments during their fifty years together.

The speaker who commemorates or pays tribute is, in part, an informative speaker. He or she needs to present some facts about the event and/or people being celebrated. Then the speaker builds on those facts, urging the audience to let past accomplishments inspire them to achieve new goals. Speaking at Pointe du Hoc, France, during June 1994 ceremonies to commemorate the fifty-year anniversary of D-Day, Bill Clinton paid tribute to the assembled veterans:

commemorative address
A speech delivered during special ceremonies held in memory of some past event and/or the person or persons involved

> *We are the children of your sacrifice. We are the sons and daughters you saved from tyranny's reach. We grew up behind the shield of the strong alliances you forged in blood upon these beaches, on the shores of the Pacific and in the skies above us. We flourished in the nation you came home to build. The most difficult days of your lives bought us fifty years of freedom.*[16]

His tribute completed, Clinton added this challenge:

Let us carry on the work you began here. You completed your mission here, but the mission of freedom goes on; the battle continues.

Eulogies

Speeches of tribute delivered when someone has died are an especially difficult form of commemorative address. When you deliver a **eulogy,** you should mention—indeed, linger over—the unique achievements of the person to whom you are paying tribute and, of course, express a sense of loss. At the funeral of former First Lady Jacqueline Kennedy in 1994, Senator Edward Kennedy remembered his sister-in-law in this way:

> *She was a blessing to us and to the nation, and a lesson to the world on how to do things right, how to be a mother, how to appreciate history, how to be courageous.*
>
> *No one else looked like her, spoke like her, wrote like her, or was so original in the way she did things.*[17]

It is also proper in a eulogy to include personal, even tasteful humorous recollections of the person who has died. In his April 27, 1994, eulogy for former President Richard M. Nixon, Senator Robert Dole related this incident:

> *In her marvelous biography of her mother, Julie [Nixon Eisenhower] recalls an occasion where Pat Nixon expressed amazement at her husband's ability to persevere in the face of criticism. To which the President replied, "I just get up every morning to confound my enemies."*[18]

Eulogies are opportunities to pay tribute to the achievements of the dead and provide comfort for the living. It is always effective to remind listeners how fortunate they were to have shared in the joys and sorrows of the person they are mourning.

[Photo: Seth Resnick/Stock Boston]

eulogy
A speech of tribute to someone who has died

Finally, turn to the living, and encourage them to transcend their sorrow and sense of loss and feel instead gratitude that the dead person had once been alive among them. In eulogizing his sister, Diana, the Princess of Wales, Earl Spencer affirmed,

> *Today is our chance to say thank you for the way you brightened our lives, even though God granted you but half a life. We will all feel cheated, always, that you were taken from us so young, and yet we must learn to be grateful that you came along at all.*[19]

After-Dinner Speaking

If you are a human being or even a reasonably alert shrub, chances are that sooner or later a club or organization will ask you to give a speech. The United States is infested with clubs and organizations, constantly engaging in a variety of worthwhile group activities such as (1) eating lunch; (2) eating dinner; (3) eating breakfast; and of course (4) holding banquets. The result is that there is a constant demand for post-meal speakers, because otherwise all you'd hear would be the sounds of digestion.[20]

With typically irreverent wit, columnist Dave Barry thus begins his observations of the activity known as after-dinner speaking. Certainly he is right about one thing: the popularity of mealtime meetings and banquets with business and professional organizations and service clubs. And with such meetings inevitably comes the requirement for an **after-dinner speech.**

Interestingly, not only is the after-dinner speech not always after *dinner* (as Barry points out, the meal is just as likely to be breakfast or lunch), but it is also not always *after* anything. The after-dinner speech may also be delivered before the meal or even between courses. Former First Lady Barbara Bush preferred to schedule speeches first and dinner later during state dinners. In another variation, Librarian of Congress James Billington, at a dinner in honor of philosopher Alexis de Tocqueville, served up one speech between each course, "so that one had to earn the next course by listening to the speech preceding it."[21] Regardless of the variation, the after-dinner speech is something of an institution, and one with which a public speaker should be prepared to cope.

After-dinner speeches may present information or persuade, but their primary purpose is to entertain. The theme of the meeting may suggest or even dictate the speaker's central idea, but he or she will usually avoid "heavy" subjects, such as diseases or social ills. The best after-dinner speech is one that makes a thought-provoking point with humor. Mark Twain is said to have been "an after-dinner speaker of such repute that in his heyday no consequential banquet was complete without him."[22]

For most speakers, humor is the challenge of the after-dinner speech. Even the speaker who knows how to gather and organize information and deliver it effectively may be at a loss when it comes to techniques and strategies for creating humor. The Comedy Gym, in Austin, Texas, a school for aspiring stand-up comedians, advocates that one of the best ways to create humor is to start with what speakers know—"themselves, their lives, what makes *them* laugh."[23] Notice how student Chris O'Keefe uses a personal anecdote (and some well-timed props) to open his speech on reading Shakespeare:

> *At a certain point in my life, I came to the realization that I wanted to spend my life's effort to become a great playwright. (Looks at watch) It has been about an hour and a half now and the feeling is still going strong. As a matter of fact, I have*

after-dinner speech
An entertaining speech, usually delivered in conjunction with a mealtime meeting or banquet

already written my first play. (Pulls out play) *I wrote it out in the hall, or really wherever I could find a place to sit down.* (Pulls out toilet paper) *I hope that a hundred years from now people still admire, appreciate, and respect my work.*[24]

If you do not have an endless supply of original funny stories, you may be comforted to learn that sourcebooks of humor are available.

It is true that some people seem to be "naturally" funny. Nonverbal comic devices such as timing and facial expression are their usual style. If you are not a funny person—if, for example, you cannot get a laugh from even the funniest joke—you may choose to prepare and deliver an after-dinner speech that is lighthearted and clever rather than uproariously funny. Such a speech can still be a success.

SUMMARY

Chances are that at some time most of us will be called on to speak in a business or professional setting, or for some occasion that calls for celebration, commemoration, inspiration, or entertainment. These *special-occasion speeches* are critical-thinking activities that require the speaker to synthesize and apply his or her speaking skills to unique situations.

Public-speaking skills are used frequently in the workplace, from making report presentations, to representing your company or profession before the public. These two professional speaking challenges each have unique requirements.

Ceremonial speeches include introductions, toasts, award presentations, nominations, acceptances, keynote addresses, commencement addresses, commemorative addresses and tributes, and eulogies.

Finally, after-dinner speaking is an established institution that at its best makes a thought-provoking point with humor.

being audience-centered

A Sharper Focus

CONSIDERING YOUR AUDIENCE

▶ When presenting a business report, keep in mind that your audience is there to hear you address a particular need or problem.

▶ When you present solutions to the problem you have explored in a business report, tell the members of your audience what benefits will accrue to them directly as a result of the new proposal.

▶ When you are introducing a speaker, remember that the audience has come to hear the main speaker, not to listen to you. Be brief.

▶ If the person you are introducing truly needs no introduction to the group, do not give one.

▶ If you are asked to make an impromptu toast, let your audience and the occasion dictate what you say.

▶ As with introducing a speaker, when you present an award, remember that the audience did not come to hear you. Be brief.

▶ The same audience who may resent a lengthy oration will readily appreciate a brief, heartfelt expression of thanks for an award or nomination.

▶ A commencement is an occasion that demands and deserves audience-centeredness.

▶ When called on to deliver a eulogy, encourage your audience to transcend their sorrow and sense of loss and feel instead gratitude that the dead person had once been alive among them.

CONSIDERING AUDIENCE DIVERSITY

▶ Workplace audiences may range from a group of three managers to a huge auditorium filled with company employees.

▶ It is important in public-relations speaking to anticipate criticism, whether it comes from the audience as a whole or from a minority contingent.

CRITICAL THINKING QUESTIONS

1. Maya has to present her first report to her colleagues at work. You and she became friends when you took public speaking as college sophomores, and she has called to ask your advice in preparing for this oral presentation. Explain to Maya how she can apply to her report presentation some of the principles and skills the two of you learned in public-speaking class.

2. Pulitzer prize–winning poet Rita Dove is coming to campus for a series of readings and lectures. Because you are president of the English Club, you have been asked to introduce Dove for her opening reading. What will you do to ensure that you follow the two "cardinal rules" of introductory speeches?

ETHICAL QUESTIONS

1. You have been a member of the jury during a highly publicized and controversial murder trial in your community. After the verdict is delivered, you find yourself in great demand as a keynote speaker for meetings of local organizations. Several offer to pay you well. Is it ethical to "cash in" on your experiences in this way?

2. Even during times of intense personal crisis—for example, the death of a family member—the press relentlessly pursues celebrities to try to elicit impromptu statements. Is this an ethical practice? Does the public's right to know justify the invasion of privacy?

SUGGESTED ACTIVITIES

1. Attend a special-occasion speaking event, such as a school commencement, an award ceremony, or a luncheon for the retiring editor of your school newspaper. Write a critique of the speeches given, and evaluate the speeches based on the criteria presented in this chapter.

2. Pair up with another student in the class to discuss your common interests, vocational goals, and hobbies. Discover something your partner does well, and invent an award that you could give your colleague. Deliver a short presentation speech in which you bestow your award (for example, "Best Short Story Written in English Class" or "Best Piano Player in the Community"). The recipient of the award should then deliver a short acceptance speech.

3. Prepare and deliver to your classmates a toast of no more than four sentences for one of the following occasions:

   a. A party for your best friend's birthday

   b. A family celebration of the birth of a new child

   c. A dinner celebrating your brother's, sister's, or friend's new job

   d. The successful completion of your public-speaking class

USING TECHNOLOGY AND MEDIA

Videotape several of the acceptance speeches during some televised awards ceremony—the Oscars, the Tony Awards, the Country Music Awards, or the Peoples' Choice Awards, for example. Analyze the success of these speeches, based on the suggestions offered in this chapter.

Never doubt that a small group of thoughtful concerned citizens can change the world. Indeed, it's the only thing that ever has.

MARGARET MEAD

19

Speaking in Small Groups

objectives

After studying this chapter you should be able to do the following:

1. Define small-group communication.

2. Organize group problem solving, using the steps of reflective thinking.

3. Participate effectively in a small group as a member or leader.

4. Contribute effectively to a group meeting.

5. Develop a plan for coordinating a group project.

6. Present group conclusions in a symposium, forum, panel presentation, or written report.

It has been estimated that more than 11 million meetings are held every day in the United States. Groups are an integral part of our lives. Work groups, family groups, therapy groups, committees, and class-project groups are just a few of the groups in which we may participate at one time or another. Chances are that you have had considerable experience in communicating in small groups.

Why learn about group communication in a public-speaking class? Aristotle identified the link between public speaking and group discussion over two thousand years ago when he wrote, "Rhetoric is the counterpart of dialectic." By this he meant that our efforts to persuade are closely linked to our group efforts to search for truth.

In Aristotle's time, people gathered to discuss and decide public issues in a democratic manner. Today we still turn to a committee, jury, or task force to get facts and make recommendations. We still "search for truth" in groups. And, as in ancient Athens, once we believe we have found the truth, we still present the message to others in speeches and lectures.

This chapter concentrates on group problem solving and decision making for at least three main reasons.[1] First, you will spend a major part of your work time in small groups. Up to 15 percent of a typical organization's total personnel budget is spent on group work. Middle managers generally spend up to 35 percent of their time working in groups. Most senior managers work in groups up to 60 percent of their working day.[2] A second reason to learn about groups is that it can help reduce some of the uncertainty and anxiety you may have about group deliberations. If you know more about group processes, you can improve your skill at working in groups and therefore your enjoyment of it as well.

A third reason to learn about communicating effectively in groups is to capitalize on the advantages of working in groups while minimizing the disadvantages of collaborating with others. What are the advantages of working in groups compared with working alone? There are several:[3]

- Groups usually have more information available.

- Groups are often more creative; the very presence of others can spark innovation.

- When you work in groups, you're more likely to remember what you discussed, because you're actively rather than passively involved in processing information.

- Group participation usually results in group members being more satisfied with their results than if someone just told them what to do.

There are also disadvantages to working in groups:

- Group members may use excessive pressure to get others to conform to their point of view.

- One person may dominate the discussion.

- Group members may rely too much on others and may not do their part.

- Group work is more time consuming; many people consider this the biggest disadvantage.

There's value in knowing that working in groups has both virtues and challenges; you can actively work to foster the advantages of group work, as well as recognize and navigate around the disadvantages.

In this chapter, you will learn some key communication principles and skills to help you work as a productive member of a team. Specifically, you will discover what small group communication is, describe ways to improve group problem solving, recognize leadership skills, and become an effective group participant or group leader. You will also learn some tips for planning and executing a group project. By the end of the chapter, you will be able to use various formats for reporting group findings to others.

What is **small group communication?** It is interaction among three to around a dozen people who share a common purpose, feel a sense of belonging to the group, and influence one another. When groups are larger than twelve people, communication usually resembles public speaking more than group interaction.

Is there a difference between a group and a team? Yes. A **team** is a coordinated small group of people organized to work together, with clearly defined roles and responsibilities, explicitly stated rules for operation, and well defined goals.[4] A team is a special kind of group that, as our definition suggests, emphasizes coordinating activity with more clearly defined structure of who does what. All teams are groups, but not all groups are teams. Think of a sports team in which members play by rules, have assigned roles, and have a clear objective—to win the game. So, too, work teams have more well defined procedures for accomplishing the task. Teams are formed for a variety of reasons, such as to sell products, get a political candidate elected, or build an international space station.

Solving Problems in Groups and Teams

A central purpose of many groups and teams is solving problems. Problem solving is a means of finding ways of overcoming obstacles to achieve a desired goal. How can we raise money for the new library? What should be done to improve the local economy? How can we make higher education affordable for everyone in our state? Each of these questions implies that there is an obstacle (lack of money) blocking the achievement of a desired goal (new library, more local income, affordable education).

Imagine that you have been assigned to suggest ways to make a college education more affordable. The problem: The high cost of higher education keeps many people from their goal of attending college. How would you begin to organize a group to solve this problem? In 1910 John Dewey, a philosopher and educator, identified the way most individuals tackle a problem. He called his method of problem solving **reflective thinking.** His multistep method has been adapted by many groups as a way to organize the process of solving problems. Here are his suggestions: (1) Identify and define the problem, (2) analyze the problem, (3) generate possible solutions, (4) select the best solution, and (5) test and implement the solution. Although not every problem-solving discussion has to follow these steps, reflective thinking does provide a helpful blueprint that can relieve some of the uncertainty that exists when groups try to solve problems.

small group communication
Interaction among three to twelve people who share a common purpose, feel a sense of belonging to the group, and influence one another

team
A coordinated small group of people organized to work together, with clearly defined roles and responsibilities, explicit rules, and well-defined goals

reflective thinking
A method of structuring a problem-solving discussion that includes the following steps: (1) identify and define the problem, (2) analyze the problem, (3) generate possible solutions, (4) select the best solution, and (5) test and implement the solution

1. Identify and Define the Problem

Groups work best when they define their problem clearly and early in their problem-solving process. To reach a clear definition, the group should consider the following questions:

- What is the specific problem that concerns us?

- What terms, concepts, or ideas do we need to understand in order to solve the problem?

- Who is harmed by the problem?

- When do the harmful effects occur?

Policy questions can help define a problem and also identify the course of action that should be taken to solve it. As you recall from Chapter 16, policy questions begin with the words such as "What should be done about" or "What could be done to improve." Here are some examples:

- What should be done to improve security at U.S. airports?

- What should be done to improve the tax base in our state?

- What steps can be taken to improve the U.S. trade balance with other countries?

If your group were investigating the high cost of pursuing a college education, for example, after defining such key terms as "higher education" and "college" and gathering statistics about the magnitude of the problem, you could phrase your policy question this way: "What could be done to reduce the high student cost of attending college?"

2. Analyze the Problem

Ray Kroc, founder of McDonald's, said, "Nothing is particularly hard if you divide it into small jobs." Once the group understands the problem and has a well-worded question, the next step is to analyze the problem. **Analysis** is a process of examining the causes, effects, symptoms, history, and other background information that will help a group eventually reach a solution. When analyzing a problem, a group should consider the following questions:

- What is the history of the problem?

- How extensive is the problem?

- What are the causes, effects, and symptoms of the problem?

- Can the problem be subdivided for further definition and analysis?

- What methods do we already have for solving the problem, and what are their limitations?

- What new methods can we devise to solve the problem?

- What obstacles might keep us from reaching a solution?

analysis
To examine the causes, effects, and history of a problem to understand it better

To analyze the problem of the high cost of attending college, your discussion group will have to use the library or Internet to research the history of the problem and existing methods of solving it (see Chapter 7).

Included in the process of analyzing the problem is identifying **criteria**. Criteria are standards for identifying an acceptable solution. They help you recognize a good solution when you discover one; criteria also help the group stay focused on the group's goal. Typical criteria for an acceptable solution specify that the solution should be implemented on schedule, should be agreed to by all group members, should be achieved within a given budget, and should remove the obstacles causing the problem.

For example, the owner of a small hardware store called a meeting to deal with the problem of increased competition when a new, large hardware store that belonged to a national franchise opened in town. In analyzing this problem, two main criteria emerged: bringing old customers back into the store while still generating a profit, and turning things around within three months or the store would be out of business.

Only after the group members have identified and analyzed the problem are they ready to generate possible solutions.

[Myrleen Ferguson/PhotoEdit]

 ### 3. Generate Possible Solutions

When your discussion group has identified, defined, and analyzed the problem, you will be ready to generate possible solutions using group brainstorming (see Chapter 6). Use the following guidelines:

- *Set aside judgment and criticism.* Criticism and faultfinding stifle creativity. If group members find withholding judgment difficult, have the individual members write suggestions on paper first and then share the ideas with the group.

- *Think of as many possible solutions to the problem as you can.* All ideas are acceptable, even wild and crazy ones. Piggyback off one another's ideas. All members must come up with at least one idea.

- *Have a member of the group record all the ideas that are mentioned.* Use a flipchart or chalkboard, if possible, so that all ideas can be seen and responded to.

- *After a set time has elapsed, evaluate the ideas, using criteria the group has established.* Approach the solutions positively. Do not be quick to dismiss an idea, but do voice any concerns or questions you might have. The group can use brainstorming again later if it needs more creative ideas.

 ### 4. Select the Best Solution

Next, the group needs to select the solution that best meets the criteria and solves the problem. At this point, the group may need to modify its criteria or even its definition of the problem.

criteria
Standards for identifying an acceptable solution to a problem

After the group has narrowed the list of possible solutions, research suggests that the most effective groups carefully consider the pros and the cons of each proposed solution.[5] Groups that don't do this often make poor decisions because they haven't carefully evaluated the implications of their solution; they haven't looked before they leaped.

To help the group evaluate the solution, consider the following questions:

- Which of the suggested solutions deals best with the obstacles?

- Does the suggestion solve the problem in both the short and the long term?

- What are the advantages and disadvantages of the suggested solution?

- Does the solution meet the established criteria?

- Should the group revise its criteria?

- What is required to implement the solution?

- When can the group implement the solution?

- What result will indicate success?

To reach group agreement on a solution, some group members will need to abandon their attachment to their individual ideas for the overall good of the group. Experts who have studied how to achieve **consensus**—all members supporting the final decision—suggest that it helps to summarize frequently and keep the group oriented toward its goal. Emphasizing where group members agree, clarifying misunderstandings, writing down known facts for all members to see, and keeping the discussion focused on issues rather than emotions are also strategies that facilitate group consensus.[6]

5. Test and Implement the Solution

The group's work is not finished when it has identified a solution. "How can we put the solution into practice?" and "How can we evaluate the quality of the solution?" have yet to be addressed. The group may want to develop a step-by-step plan that describes the process for implementing the solution, a time frame for implementation, and a list of individuals who will be responsible for carrying out specific tasks.

RECAP

STEPS IN PROBLEM SOLVING: REFLECTIVE THINKING

1. Identify and clearly define the problem.

2. Analyze the problem and identify criteria.

3. Generate possible solutions.

4. Select the best solution.

5. Test and implement the solution.

consensus
All group members support and are committed to the decision of the group

Tips for Participating in Small Groups

To be an effective group participant, you have to understand how to manage the problem-solving process. But knowing the steps is not enough; you also need to prepare for meetings, evaluate evidence, effectively summarize the group's progress, listen courteously, and be sensitive to conflict.

Come Prepared for Group Discussions

To contribute to group meetings, you need to be informed about the issues. Prepare for group discussions by researching the issues. If the issue before your group is the use of asbestos in school buildings, for example, research the most recent scientific findings about the risks of this hazardous material. Chapter 7 described how to use the library and the resources of the Internet to gather information for your speeches. Use those research techniques to prepare for group deliberations as well. Bring your research notes to the group; don't just rely on your memory or your personal opinion to carry you through the discussion. Without research, you will not be able to analyze the problem adequately.

Do Not Suggest Solutions before Analyzing the Problem

Research suggests that you should analyze a problem thoroughly before trying to zero in on a solution.[7] Resist the temptation to settle quickly on one solution until your group has systematically examined the causes, effects, history, and symptoms of a problem.

Evaluate Evidence

One study found that a key difference between groups that make successful decisions and those that don't, lies in the ability of the group members to examine and evaluate evidence.[8] Ineffective groups are more likely to reach decisions quickly without considering the validity of evidence (or sometimes without any evidence at all). Such groups usually reach flawed conclusions.

Help Summarize the Group's Progress

Because it is easy for groups to get off the subject, group members need to summarize frequently what has been achieved and to point the group toward the goal or task at hand. One research study suggests that periodic overviews of the discussion's progress can help the group stay on target.[9] Ask questions about the discussion process rather than the topic under consideration: "Where are we now?" "Could someone summarize what we have accomplished?" and "Aren't we getting off the subject?"

Listen and Respond Courteously to Others

Chapter 4's suggestions for improving listening skills are useful when you work in groups, but understanding what others say is not enough. You also need to respect their points of view. Even if you disagree with someone's ideas, keep your emotions in check and respond courteously. Being closed-minded and defensive usually breeds group conflict.

Help Manage Conflict

In the course of exchanging ideas and opinions about controversial issues, disagreements are bound to occur.[10] You can help prevent conflicts from derailing the problem-solving process by doing the following:

- Keep the discussion focused on issues, not personalities.

- Rely on facts rather than on personal opinions for evidence.

- Seek ways to compromise; don't assume that there must be a winner and a loser.

- Try to clarify misunderstandings in meaning.

- Be descriptive rather than evaluative and judgmental.

- Keep emotions in check.

If you can apply these basic principles, you can help make your group an effective problem-solving team.

Using the Power of Technology in Small Groups

Instead of holding a face-to-face meeting, many organizations are turning to virtual meetings. E-mail, special software programs, web conferencing, and video conferences permit group members to work together when they cannot be physically present. Live and in-person meetings will certainly not become obsolete, but they take time to organize and attend. Using the power of technology, team leaders can distribute and receive feedback about ideas quickly, without having to call a meeting.

The term *group decision support systems* (GDSSs) describes a collection of software that helps make electronic meetings via e-mail function more effectively. Some software programs help group members brainstorm solutions and show the ideas generated to all team members on computer screens. Other programs help group members evaluate potential solutions by recording and averaging ratings and ranking solutions.

Another increasingly used method of holding meetings includes using video conferences to help people interact who are miles or even continents apart. Using closed-circuit TV, satellite-linked TV, or video cameras connected to personal computers via the Internet, more organizations are finding video meetings an effective way to interact. The obvious advantage to a video conference is that you can both see and hear the participants, rather than interacting only with words on a computer screen.

A growing body of research helps us use technology more effectively to hold electronically mediated meetings. Here's a summary of some of the latest research findings:[11]

- *Generating ideas.* Generating ideas using GDSSs often leads to an increase in the number of ideas generated when compared to face-to-face brainstorming.

- *Problem solving.* E-mail, video conferences, and other electronically mediated methods of holding a meeting seem to work best if the task is structured and follows a step-by-step process.

- *Managing relationships.* Some (but not all) group members find it more difficult to manage conflict and negotiate relationship issues using mediated methods rather than meeting in person to deal with relationship issues.

- *Critical thinking.* Some research suggests that using e-mail to send and receive messages may contribute to greater polarization of opinions; group members may take a more extreme position when putting information in writing than when communicating orally.

- *Technical support.* Electronic meetings will flow more smoothly if team members have the support of an expert to help handle the inevitable hardware and software glitches that sometimes occur when using new technology.

Leadership in Small Groups

To lead is to influence others. Some see a leader as one individual empowered to delegate work and direct the group. In reality, however, group leadership is often shared.

Leadership Responsibilities

Leaders are needed to help get tasks accomplished and maintain a healthy social climate for the group. Rarely does one person perform all these leadership responsibilities, even if a leader is formally appointed or elected. Most often a number of individual group members assume some specific leadership task, based on their personalities, skills, sensitivity, and the group's needs. If you determine that the group needs a clearer focus on the task or that maintenance roles are needed, be ready to influence the group appropriately to help get the job done in a positive, productive way. Figure 19.1 shows the specific roles for both *task* and *maintenance* functions.[12]

Leadership Styles

Leaders can be described by the types of behavior, or leadership styles, that they exhibit as they influence the group to help achieve its goal. When you are called on to lead, do you give orders and expect others to follow you? Or do you ask the group to vote on the course of action to follow? Or maybe you don't try to influence the group at all. Perhaps you prefer to hang back and let the group work out its own problems.

These strategies describe three general leadership styles: *authoritarian, democratic,* and *laissez-faire.*[13] Authoritarian leaders assume positions of superiority, giving orders and assuming control of the group's activity. Although authoritarian leaders can usually organize group activities with a high degree of efficiency and virtually eliminate uncertainty about who should do what, most problem-solving groups prefer democratic leaders.

FIGURE **19.1**

Leadership roles in groups and teams

LEADERSHIP ROLES IN GROUPS AND TEAMS

Leaders Help Get Tasks Accomplished

TASK LEADERSHIP ROLES

Agenda setter: helps establish the group's agenda

Secretary: takes notes during meetings and distributes handouts before and during the meeting

Initiator: proposes new ideas or approaches to group problem solving

Information seeker: asks for facts or other information that helps the group deal with the issues and may also ask for clarification of ideas or obscure facts

Opinion seeker: asks for clarification of the values and opinions expressed by group members

Information giver: provides facts, examples, statistics, and other evidence that help the group achieve its task

Opinion giver: offers opinions about the ideas under discussion

Elaborator: provides examples to show how ideas or suggestions would work

Evaluator: makes an effort to judge the evidence and the conclusion the group reaches

Energizer: tries to spur the group to further action and productivity

Leaders Help Maintain a Healthy Social Climate

GROUP MAINTENANCE LEADERSHIP ROLES

Encourager: offers praise, understanding, and acceptance of others' ideas

Harmonizer: mediates disagreements that occur between group members

Compromiser: attempts to resolve conflicts by trying to find an acceptable middle ground between disagreeing group members

Gatekeeper: encourages the participation of less talkative group members and tries to limit lengthy contributions of other group members

Having more faith in their groups than do authoritarian leaders, democratic leaders involve their groups in the decision-making process rather than dictating what should be done. Democratic leaders focus more on guiding discussion than on issuing commands.

Laissez-faire leaders allow a group complete freedom in all aspects of the decision-making process. They do little to help the group achieve its goal. This style of leadership

FIGURE **19.2**

Leadership Styles

LEADERSHIP STYLES

Authoritarian	**Democratic**	**Laissez Faire**
1. All determination of policy made by leader.	1. All policies are a matter of group discussion and decision, encouraged and assigned by the leader.	1. Complete freedom for group or individual decisions; minimum leader participation.
2. Techniques and activity steps dictated by the authority, one at a time; future steps are always largely uncertain.	2. Discussion period yields broad perspectives; general steps to group goal are sketched out; when technical advice is needed, leader suggests alternative procedures.	2. Leader supplies various materials, making it clear that he or she can supply information when asked, but taking no other part in the discussion.
3. Leader dictates specific work tasks and teams.	3. Members are free to work with anyone; group decides on division of tasks.	3. Complete nonparticipation of leader.
4. Leader tends to be personal in praise or criticism of each member; remains aloof from active group participation except when directing activities.	4. Leader is objective or fact-minded in praise and criticism, trying to be a regular group member in spirit without doing too much of the work.	4. Leader offers infrequent spontaneous comments on member activities and makes no attempt to appraise or control the course of events.

(or nonleadership) often leaves a group frustrated because it lacks guidance and has to struggle with organizing the work. Figure 19.2 compares the three styles.

What is the most effective leadership style? Research suggests that no single style is most effective in all group situations. Sometimes a group needs a strong authoritarian leader to make decisions quickly so that the group can achieve its goal. Although most groups prefer a democratic leadership style, leaders sometimes need to assert their authority to get the job done. The best leadership style depends on the nature of the group task, the power of the leader, and the relationship between the leader and his or her followers.

One contemporary approach to leadership is transformational leadership. Transformational leadership is not so much a particular style of leadership as it is a quality or characteristic of relating to others.[14] **Transformational leadership** is the process of influencing others by building a shared vision of the future, inspiring others to achieve, developing quality individual relationships with others, and helping people see how what they do is related to a larger framework or system. To be a transformational leader is not just to perform specific tasks or skills, but to have a philosophy of helping others see "the big picture" and inspiring them to make the vision of the future reality.[15] Transformational leaders are good communicators who support and encourage rather than demean or demand.

transformational leadership The process of influencing others by building a shared vision of the future, inspiring others to achieve, developing quality individual relationships with others, and helping people see how what they do is related to a larger framework or system

Managing Meetings

Even though millions of meetings take place each day, most people don't like them. President John Kennedy was quoted as saying, "Most committee meetings consist of twelve people to do the work of one." Others agree with humorist Dave Barry's analogy between a modern business meeting and a funeral, noting that in both "you have a gathering of people who are wearing uncomfortable clothing and would rather be somewhere else. The major difference is that most funerals have a definite purpose. Also, nothing is ever really buried in a meeting."[16]

What bothers meeting attendees most? Here's what one research team found bothers people the most about meetings: discussions that drift off the subject; lack of goals or agenda; inconclusive, disorganized, rambling meetings that start late; meetings that last too long; and meetings with no follow-up.[17]

If these are the key meeting problems, what are the solutions? The short answer to this question is a simple one: Don't do these things. You may, however, need more direction than that, so here are a few suggestions to help you manage group meetings with skill.

To be effective, a meeting should have a balance between two characteristics: structure and interaction. *Structure* involves such attributes as an organized agenda and a logical, rational approach to discussing the issues. A meeting with too much structure resembles a speech. When there is a minimum of interaction and only one or two people do all the talking, participants may wonder why there is a need for a meeting; the information could have been distributed by memo. *Interaction* includes the dynamic process of managing the talk and group discussion. A meeting with too much interaction and not enough structure rambles and digresses and has no clear purpose. The key to managing a meeting is to strike a proper balance between structure and interaction.

How to Give Meetings Structure

As a leader, the most powerful tool you have to give a meeting structure is an **agenda,** a brief list or description of what you will discuss, arranged in chronological order. Develop an agenda by determining your overall goal. Most meetings have one or more of the following goals: to share information, to discuss issues, to make decisions, and to solve problems.

Some experts suggest that if sharing information is one goal, it should be done early in the meeting, especially if the information is related to decisions and actions the group will take later in the meeting.[18] Often groups spend too much time on early agenda items and give less attention to those scheduled for late in the meeting (when most people want to leave). Therefore, do not schedule important items for the end of the meeting. Instead, cover vital issues early, and use the end of the meeting to determine what needs to happen at the next meeting, to summarize the action that needs to be taken, and to determine who will do what.

If you are a meeting leader, keep your eye on two things: the clock and the agenda. Think of your agenda as the map—where you want to go. Think of the clock as your gas gauge—the amount of fuel you have to get where you want to go. If you are running low on fuel (time), you will either need to budget more or recognize that you will not get where you want to go.

agenda
A written description of the items and issues that a group will discuss during a meeting

How to Foster Group Interaction

In addition to giving a meeting structure, leaders should ensure that a meeting is interactive. A meeting is not a speech during which the leader talks and the rest of the group listens. Draw out quiet members by calling them by name and asking for their opinions. You may need to ask more talkative members to hold their comments until all have contributed to the discussion. Another strategy for encouraging participation and keeping the discussion on track is periodically to summarize group members' contributions.

Even if you are not the designated leader or meeting facilitator, you can use strategies to enhance the quality of discussion. One research team made the following recommendations for meeting participants:[19]

- *Organize your contributions, and make one point at a time.* Rambling and disorganized comments increase the likelihood that the meeting will stray from the agenda.

- *Support your ideas with evidence.* Facts, statistics, and well-selected examples help keep the group focused on the task.

- *Listen actively and monitor your nonverbal messages.* Check your understanding of group-member comments by summarizing or paraphrasing, and watch your own body language.

Speaker's Homepage　　　　　　　　　　　　　　　　　　　　　－　Ｘ

Address:　　**http://www.ablongman.com/beebe**

▼ | **Using Parliamentary Procedure to Give Structure to Large Groups**

Some say chairing a large-group meeting is like herding cats. It's difficult. We have noted that effective meetings need a balance of two things: structure and interaction. When you try to lead a very large group, you need to reach for considerable structure to help you keep the group focused on its goals.

Parliamentary procedure is a system of rules and formal procedures to help keep a very large group organized. We emphasize that a small group does not need to use parliamentary procedure—it would be overkill. But if you have the opportunity and challenge to chair a large group or a formal meeting, knowing what motions need a two-thirds majority to be approved and what "call the question" means can be very valuable. The basic parliamentary procedure information that you need in order to organize a group may be found at this Website:

http://www.calweb.com/~laredo/cuesta5.htm

This site has an easy-to-navigate table of contents that makes it simple to find the parliamentary rules you need.

Here's another useful site that summarizes basic principles of parliamentary procedure:

http://www.acs.brockport.edu/~rduncan/parliament.html

As you have undoubtedly noticed, the skills of being a good meeting participant mirror the skills of being a good communicator when giving a speech. Presenting organized, thoughtful, audience-centered, well-supported, and well-presented ideas will enhance the overall quality of meeting deliberations.

Presenting Group Recommendations

After a group has reached a decision, solved a problem, or uncovered new information, the group often presents its findings to others. The audience-centered principles of presenting an effective speech apply to group members designing a group oral presentation. As our now-familiar model of being an audience-centered speaker suggests in Figure 19.3, the first and most important step is to analyze the audience that will be listening to the presentation. Who are the listeners? What do they need to know? What are their interests and backgrounds? Groups often make the mistake of trying to tell the audience too much. You need not summarize the process of every action and method the group used to reach its conclusion. Tell the listeners the essential information. Often the group can summarize the details in writing rather than verbalize them in an oral presentation.

As when developing an individual speech, make sure you have a clear purpose with a developed central idea and that you have clear major ideas to present. This is a group effort, so you need to make sure *each* group member can articulate the purpose of the oral presentation. Consider using the audience-centered model as a checklist to ensure that each group member knows what the narrowed topic is, the specific behavioral purpose ("At the end of this presentation, the audience should be able to . . ."), the central idea, main ideas, how the ideas are supported, and the overall outline for the presentation.

You have probably spent a good portion of your time in your group gathering information and evidence to reach your conclusion. Share with the audience the key forms of support. And don't forget to use examples, analogies, illustrations, and other forms of supporting material that will help maintain interest.

In organizing your group's oral presentation, review the methods of organizing a speech that we discussed in Chapter 9. If your group is presenting recommendations to solve a problem, you could use the steps in the reflective-thinking problem-solving process to organize the key pieces of your report.

Finally, make sure your group has rehearsed the presentation. As we discussed in Chapter 13, an impromptu presentation may sound conversational; but it can lack organizational structure if group members do not know what each other member will present. The first time you hear what your fellow group members are going to say should *not* be when your group is delivering the presentation to an audience.

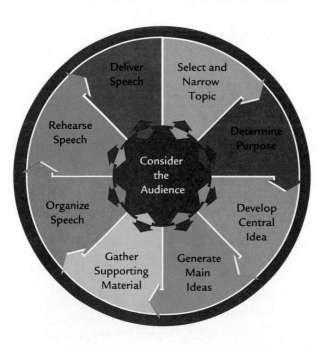

FIGURE **19.3**

Use the audience-centered model of public speaking as an agenda to help your group plan a group presentation.

Unless a format for your group presentation has been specified, your group will need to determine what type of presentation you will deliver. Three primary oral formats exist for sharing recommendations with an audience: symposium presentations, forum presentations, panel discussion. Finally, you will need to decide whether your group will prepare a written report. We will discuss these forms in the following sections.

Symposium Presentation

A **symposium** is a public discussion in which a series of short speeches is presented to an audience. The members of the group share the responsibility of presenting information to a larger group. Usually a moderator and the group members are seated in front of the audience, each prepared to deliver a brief report. Each speaker should know what the others will present so the same ground is not covered twice. At the end of the speeches, the moderator can summarize the key points that were presented. The audience can then participate in a question-and-answer session or a forum presentation.

Forum Presentation

A **forum presentation** consists of an audience directing questions and comments to a group, and group members responding with short impromptu speeches. In ancient Rome, the forum was a marketplace where citizens went to shop and discuss the hot issues of the day. It later became a public meeting place where political speeches were often delivered.

A forum often follows a more structured presentation, such as a symposium or a prepared speech by one group member. Forum presentations work best when all group members know the issues and are prepared to respond unhesitatingly to questioners.

Panel Discussion

A **panel discussion** is an informative group presentation. Individuals on the panel may use notes containing key facts or statistics, but they do not present formal speeches. Usually a panel discussion is organized and led by an appointed chairperson or moderator.

An effective moderator gets all the panelists to participate, summarizes their statements, and serves as a gatekeeper to make sure that no member of the panel dominates the discussion. Panel discussions are often followed by a question-and-answer period, or forum.

Written Report

Written reports summarize a group's key deliberations and final recommendations. Such reports often accompany a symposium, forum, or panel discussion.

The steps of reflective thinking can provide a way to organize a report. Begin by describing the group members; then present the definition of the problem the group

symposium
A public discussion in which a series of short speeches is presented to an audience

forum presentation
A question-and-answer session that usually follows a public discussion or symposium

panel discussion
A group discussion designed to inform an audience about issues or a problem or to make recommendations

discussed. Next, include the problem analysis, criteria that were established, possible solutions, the best solution, and suggestions for implementing the solution. For the sake of clarity, use headings and subheadings liberally throughout the report. The length of the report will vary with the significance of the problem and the length of time the group has spent together. Include a bibliography of the sources used to reach the group's conclusion.

Tips for Planning a Group Presentation

Working in groups takes a coordinated team effort. If you are used to developing reports and speeches on your own, it may be a challenge to work with others on a group assignment. Consider these suggestions to enhance teamwork:

- *Make sure each group member understands the task or assignment, and work together to identify a topic.* Take a few moments to verbalize the goals and objectives of the assignment. Don't immediately plunge in and try to start dividing up the work just so you can hurry off to your next class or responsibility.

- *If your group assignment is to solve a problem or to inform the audience about a specific issue, try brainstorming to develop a topic or problem question (see Chapter 6).* Then assess your audience's interests as well as group members' interests and talents to help you choose among your ideas.

The original Roman Forum was a lively marketplace, where acrobats as well as speakers commanded public attention.

[Photo: North Wind Pictures]

- *Give group members individual assignments.* After you decide on your group's presentation topic, divvy up the tasks involved in investigating the issues. Also devise a plan for keeping in touch with one another frequently to share information and ideas.

- *Develop a group outline and decide on an approach.* After group members have researched key issues, begin drafting an outline of your group presentation, following the steps of the reflective-thinking process we presented earlier in this chapter.

- *Decide on your presentation approach.* Determine whether you will use a symposium, forum, or panel presentation, or some combination of these approaches. Make decisions about who will present which portions of your outline and how to integrate them. Your presentation should have an introduction and a definite ending that reflect your group's work as an integrated problem-solving team.

- *Rehearse the presentation.* Just as you would for an individual speech, rehearse the presentation. If you are using visual aids, be sure to incorporate them in your rehearsal. Also, be sure to time your presentation when you rehearse.

- *Incorporate principles and skills of effective audience-centered public speaking when giving the group presentation.*

- *Armed with a well-planned outline, present your findings to your audience, incorporating the skills and principles of effective public speaking.* If you are using a symposium format, each group presentation is essentially a mini-speech. A panel or forum presentation is more extemporaneous and may even have an impromptu quality, but your delivery and comments should still be well organized. In addition, your visual aids should enhance your presentation by being clear and attractive.

Tips for Making a Group Presentation

The skills needed for giving a group presentation mirror those we've presented throughout the book. But because of the increased challenge of coordinating your communication efforts with other group or team members, keep the following tips in mind as you offer your conclusions or recommendations.

- *Clarify your purpose.* Just as when presenting a solo speech, it's important for listeners to know what your speaking goal is and to explain why you are presenting the information to them; it's also important for each group member to be reminded of what the overarching goal of the presentation is. It would be useful if the first speaker could ensure the audience has a good understanding of the group's purpose. If your group is responding to a specific discussion question, it may be useful to write the question or purpose of the presentation on a chalkboard, whiteboard, flipchart, or overhead transparence.

- *Use presentation aids effectively.* You can use presentation aids not only to clarify your purpose, but also to summarize key findings and recommendations. Visual aids can serve the important functions of helping to provide unity to your group presentation. If your group is using PowerPoint visuals, consider having each group member use the same template and font style to add to the coordinated look and feel of your presentation.

- *Assign someone to serve as coordinator or moderator.* As we've noted, groups need a balance between structure and interaction. Without adequate structure conversation can bounce from person to person without a clear focus. A moderator can help provide needed structure to a group presentation by introducing both the topic and group members. A moderator can also help keep track of time and ensure that one or more people don't dominate the discussion or speak too little.

- *Be ready to answer questions.* Communication, as we've emphasized, is more than just giving people information; it also includes responding to feedback and questions from listeners. Group presentations often include a question-and-answer session (forum) following the presentation. Besides being informed about your topic, it's a wise idea to have thoroughly read any written report the group has distributed.

     You may find some questioners who offer pointed or hostile questions. How do you handle those? First, keep your composure. Although easier said than done, remember that you don't want the emotional defensiveness of the moment to trigger you to say or do something you'll later regret. Second, you could try to rephrase a very negative question to defuse the sting embedded in it. For example, if someone asks you, "Why did you make such a mess of things by recommending a budget increase?" you could rephrase by saying, "The question was, Why did we recommend a controversial budget increase?" Finally, if someone asks a question that has just been asked and answered, or asks an irrelevant or poorly worded question, don't provide an instant critique of the questioner. Be polite, tactful, and gracious. Rather than self-righteously saying, "That's a dumb question" or "Someone just asked that," calmly provide a to-the-point answer and move on. If you don't understand a question, just ask for more clarification. Also, don't let a questioner start making a speech. If it looks like a questioner is using the question-and-answer period to give an oration, gently ask: "And what is your question?" or "How can we help you?" Such questions should result in a question that you can then address and return the communication process back to the control of the group rather than an overzealous audience member.

SUMMARY

Research has shown that effective group members prepare for meetings, evaluate evidence, summarize the group's progress, listen well, and help manage group conflict.

Leaders perform the useful functions of organizing the work, helping to achieve the task, and maintaining the social climate of the group. Leaders of small groups adopt one or more of three styles: authoritarian, democratic, or laissez-faire. The best style depends on the group task, the leader's authority, and the leader's relationship with other group members.

Meeting leaders are responsible for preparing and distributing an agenda, keeping the meeting on track, and making sure there is balanced participation by meeting members. Other group members make sure their contributions are well-organized, relevant, and understood by others. Listening and monitoring the nonverbal messages of others can also promote effectiveness.

A Sharper Focus

CONSIDERING YOUR AUDIENCE

▶ Consider using presentation aids when presenting your group recommendations to an audience; they help your group stay organized, and the audience will be more likely to understand your key ideas.

▶ There is no one best leadership style that works when leading groups and teams; the best leadership style depends on the goals of the group and the background of the group or team members. Adapt to the group.

▶ Transformational group leaders develop a personal relationship with group members and adapt their communication to establish genuine, sincere connection with group members.

▶ If the group seems to bounce from topic to topic, it needs more structure. If one person dominates the discussion, the group needs more interaction.

▶ The audience-centered principles of designing and presenting a speech also apply to a group when preparing recommendations to share with an audience.

CONSIDERING AUDIENCE DIVERSITY

▶ Be aware of cultural differences when communicating with others in a small group. For example, group members who come from a high-context culture will be especially aware of nonverbal messages and relationship cues. Low-context group members will more than likely be interested in focusing on solutions and completing the task.

▶ When presenting group recommendations to an audience, keep the cultural background of your listeners in mind, just as you would when delivering a speech to a culturally diverse audience.

CRITICAL THINKING QUESTIONS

1. Imagine that you are a member of a school board in a small, economically depressed community. The board is trying to decide whether to build new schools to relieve the severe student-overcrowding problem. To build new schools would result in a hefty, unpopular tax increase for community property owners. What procedures should the board use to systematically analyze the problem?

2. Ken is the manager of a shoe store. Each week he presides over a team meeting of all employees in the store. The employees are having difficulty reaching consensus about a new work schedule. What communication behaviors would help Ken facilitate consensus and manage group conflict?

3. Your group, which has attempted to suggest ways of reducing the high cost of attending college, is ready to make its report to the college president. What are some possible methods or group formats of sharing the group's findings with the administration?

ETHICAL QUESTIONS

1. Karen is working in a group with four other people. One group member, José, seems to have taken charge and is making assignments for other group members. Although José's leadership skills are helping to get a lot accomplished, Karen resents his overly zealous efforts to take charge. Should Karen keep quiet and just go along with José, or should she speak up and express her concerns about his actions?

2. Cheryl has found an article in the *National Review* that summarizes the problem and identifies several solutions for the group project she is working on. Should she urge the group to base its decisions on this one article, or should the group keep looking for more information?

3. Kim Lee is a member of the Right to Life Organization on campus. Her position in the club calls for her to do research for other club members about abortion issues. For her class group project, she has talked other group members into discussing the abortion issue. Afterward, she plans to distribute the research of other group members to members of her Right to Life Organization. Is it ethical for her to do so without telling them of her plan?

SUGGESTED ACTIVITIES

1. Identify groups to which you belong, and indicate how each group engages in small-group communication as defined in this chapter.

2. For each of the problems listed, cite possible criteria for a solution.

   Violence on TV

   Child abuse

   Increase in U.S. domestic terrorism

   Teenage smoking

   Health care for the poor

3. Compare the advantages and disadvantages of using the following methods for reporting group recommendations:

   Symposium presentation

   Forum presentation

   Panel discussion

   Written report

4. Select one of the following policy questions and, working with other group members, brainstorm possible solutions.

   What could be done to decrease illegal drug use in the United States?

   What strategies would improve communication between parents and teenagers?

   What strategies could lower the crime rate on your campus?

   What could be done to eliminate overcrowding in some of America's most popular national parks?

5. Your group is presenting its research findings to a class that includes people with culturally diverse backgrounds. Given the principles and strategies discussed throughout the book, what approaches should the group consider to ensure the class understands the message?

USING TECHNOLOGY AND MEDIA

1. While working on a group project, videotape one of your meetings. After the meeting, watch the video, noting your own use of group communication skills. Describe the various leadership roles that you assumed during the meeting. Describe how effectively your group developed and followed an agenda.

2. If you have access to the Internet and have participated in an interactive discussion with someone on a bulletin board or other electronic forum, describe the differences between electronically mediated discussions and live, face-to-face interaction with others. Note advantages and disadvantages of discussion in cyberspace compared with face-to-face discussion.

3. Based on the discussion about using technology for visual aids in Chapter 14, describe various types of media and electronic visual aids (for example, computer graphics, videos, CD-ROM) that you could use to present group recommendations to an audience. Discuss ways that your team could use these media effectively. For example, while one group member is giving an oral presentation, other group members might operate the VCR or overhead projector. Brainstorm other ways electronic resources might enhance a team presentation.

Epilogue

Now that you are about to complete your public-speaking course, you may barely be able to resist the temptation to pat yourself on the back. Before taking this course, you, like the survey population we mentioned in Chapter 2, may have feared public speaking more than death! But you have survived and perhaps even excelled. Now you can file away your notes and will never have to give another speech, right? Wrong!

There is indeed life after public-speaking class—a life that will demand frequent practice and sharpening of the skills to which you have been introduced in this course. Your classroom experience has taught you how to become a better public speaker. We hope that it has also taught you to become your own best critic—able to say, "I need more eye contact," or "I need a statistic to prove this point," or "I need a transition here." But one course cannot make you a polished speaker. Learning to speak in public is an ongoing process rather than a static goal.

In the years to come, both in college and beyond, you will use and continue to develop your public-speaking skills in many areas of your professional and personal life. In Chapter 2 of this text, we discussed some of the skills you would learn and practice as a public speaker: organization, audience analysis and adaptation, research, effective presentation, and critical listening. Certainly you will find yourself applying these skills to numerous situations—to speaking opportunities, of course, but also to other situations that require critical listening and analytic thinking. As you take other courses, apply for a job, prepare a report for your company, attend city council meetings, and go about your day-to-day personal business, you will find yourself using the skills you learned in your public-speaking class.

Of course, chances are that you will also find yourself in a number of actual public-speaking situations. Perhaps you will give few "laboratory" speeches like those you have given in your speech class. But you will undoubtedly deliver one or more of the types of special-occasion speeches that we discussed in Chapter 18. You will introduce a speaker, present or

Your completion of this course is the commencement of your continuing development as a public speaker.

[Photo: Charles Gupton/Stock Boston]

Address: http://www.ablongman.com/beebe

 Learning More About Communication

As you end your study of public speaking, you may want more information about the study of communication. Students who select communication studies or speech communication as a major or minor pursue a wide variety of careers and professions, including business, law, government, education, social services, and many others. As we mentioned in Chapter 1, communication skills are highly valued.

TRY THIS: To learn more about the study of communication, the following Web address of the World Communication Association offers a wealth of links to communication organizations, several departments of communication, communication journals and newsletters, and information about related areas of study. Click on "Useful Internet Resources for Communication Studies" at the following address:

http:ilc@.doshisha.ac.jp/users/kkitao/organi/wea

receive an award, deliver a speech to commemorate a person or an occasion, give a book review, or make a sales pitch. And you will look back to this course for guidance.

Realistically, you will not remember every detail of the course or of this text. But we hope that you will remember the bottom line: that to be effective, public speaking must be *audience-centered*. Every step of the public-speaking process, from selecting and narrowing the topic, to preparing the speech, to final delivery, must be approached with the audience in mind. If the audience does not understand your message or does not respond as you had hoped, your speech cannot be a success, regardless of the hours of research or rehearsal you may have dedicated to the task.

One final note about the audience-centered approach is in order here: Being audience-centered is not the same as being manipulative. As we discussed in Chapter 2, if you adapt to your audience to the extent that you abandon your own values and sense of truth, you have become an unethical speaker rather than an audience-centered one. An audience-centered speaker does not tell an audience only what its members want to hear.

One of the types of special-occasion speeches we discussed in Chapter 18 was the commencement address. Your completion of this course is also the commencement—the beginning—of your continuing development as a public speaker. The traditional theme of the commencement speaker is "Go forth. You have been prepared for the future." With what better thought can we leave you? Go forth. You have been prepared for the future.

Appendix A:
The Classical Tradition of Rhetoric

By Thomas R. Burkholder

Preparing and delivering a speech always seems to be a very personal task. You must research your own topic. You must analyze and attempt to adapt to the particular audience you will face. You must find a way to cope with your own nervousness. When you confront those problems, it is sometimes helpful to remember that countless others have done so before you. And for as long as people have been giving speeches, they have been looking for ways to make them better. In fact, the study of speeches and speechmaking, or the study of rhetoric, dates back to the earliest years of Western civilization, hundreds of years before the birth of Christ. So in a way, your own efforts are a continuation of that classical tradition.

Speechmaking is probably as old as language itself. And speech criticism is probably as old as listening! But perhaps the earliest recorded evidence of "rhetorical consciousness," the awareness of excellence in speechmaking, appears in the epic poetry of Homer, the ancient Greek poet. His *Iliad*, composed before 700 B.C., contains numerous well-organized speeches or orations. They appear in scenes depicting debates between humans and gods, in councils of military leaders, and so forth. And they demonstrate that the ancient Greeks had a clear sense of rhetorical excellence.

The Earliest Teachers of Rhetoric

We will probably never know who first offered advice to another person who was preparing to deliver an oration. But many ancient writers credit a teacher named Corax with the "invention" of rhetoric sometime around 476 B.C. Corax was a resident of the city of Syracuse on the island of Sicily. He developed a "doctrine of general probability," to be used by speakers in the courts. Imagine a small man being brought into court and accused of beating a much larger, stronger man. According to the doctrine of general probability, the small man should defend himself by saying something like "It is surely unlikely (not probable) that I would beat this man. After all, he is much larger and stronger than I. I would be crazy to risk making him angry by hitting him." But the larger man could resort to the same doctrine in response: "Of course people would think it unlikely that he would hit me. That is exactly why he felt safe in doing it!"

Another similar exchange was the basis of the most famous story about Corax and his student Tisias. Tisias refused to pay Corax for his lessons in rhetoric, so Corax sued him in court. Corax addressed the judges: "Tisias must pay me regardless of your decision. If he wins the case, that proves the lessons I taught him were valuable and I deserve payment. And if he loses, the court will force him to pay. So either way, he must pay." But Tisias responded, "I shall pay nothing. If I lose the case, that will prove the training I received from Corax was worthless and he does not deserve payment. But if I win the case, the court will decree that I owe him nothing. So either way, I shall not pay." The judges quickly tired of such banter and threw the case out of court with the admonition *Mali corvi malum ovum,*" or "A bad egg from a bad crow!" Legend has it that Tisias promptly left Syracuse and opened his own school of rhetoric in Greece.

Beginning of the Greek Tradition: The Sophists

Whether Tisias actually went to Greece is unknown. But by the middle of the fifth century B.C., schools of rhetoric flourished in the Greek city states. Citizens often spoke in the assemblies or legislatures, and because there were no lawyers, they presented their own cases in the courts. It was soon apparent that the most skilled speakers prevailed in the assembly and won in court. Speech teachers were in great demand. The Greeks called these teachers "Sophists," a term that literally means "wisdom bearer." The rhetorical training offered by these teachers varied greatly. Some, such as Antiphon (480–411 B.C.) and Lysias (459–380 B.C.), were actually logographers. They merely wrote speeches to be delivered by their clients and made no effort to provide training in rhetoric. Others, like Protagoras (481–411 B.C.) and Gorgias (485–380 B.C.), advertised themselves as teachers of eloquence, or the art of effective speaking.

Protagoras is often considered to be the originator of academic debating, because he required his students to argue opposing sides of issues. He believed that each side of important questions had merit, and that humans could never be certain of the "truth." Thus, he encouraged his students to build the strongest possible case for the side of the issue they were assigned to debate. Such training, he felt, would best prepare his students to conduct their affairs in the assembly and the courts. Gorgias was perhaps the first teacher of rhetoric to encourage careful use of language. He believed that speakers would be more persuasive if their speaking style was embellished. He encouraged the use of stylistic devices familiar to modern writers, such as assonance, alliteration, antithesis, and parallelism.

One of the most famous Sophists was Isocrates (436–338 B.C.). Unlike Protagoras and Gorgias, who taught only rhetoric, Isocrates claimed to train citizens to be statesmen. He made rhetoric the center of a more fully developed course of study designed to make his students wise as well as eloquent. Isocrates believed that three qualities were necessary for a person to be a great orator and statesman. First, that person must possess natural ability. Second, that ability must be developed and refined through practice and experience. Finally, to be a great orator and statesman, a person must be well educated, not just in rhetoric, but in philosophy as well. While no one can teach natural ability, Isocrates endeavored to provide his students with practice, experience, and philosophical education.

Although the Sophists attracted many students, and many Sophists became wealthy from their teaching efforts, they were not without their critics. Many felt that the training provided by the Sophists was worthless, if not dangerous. Teachers like Gorgias were accused of providing worthless training by emphasizing florid language with no regard for substance. Teachers like Protagoras were accused of training speakers to "make the worse case appear the better" by urging speakers to develop strong speeches on both sides of any issue. And Sophists in general were often criticized for failing to make their students better, more virtuous people. Without question, the most severe critic of the Sophists was the great Greek philosopher, Plato (427–347 B.C.).

Plato

Plato was the student of Socrates (469–399 B.C.), and he went on to become one of the most profound and influential thinkers in history. In 385 B.C., Plato founded the famous Academy in Athens. The Academy attracted the best and brightest students and teachers in all of Greece, and remained in operation for almost nine hundred years. Plato's writings were a major influence in the development of Western philosophy and culture. His *Republic* was a blueprint for the ideal political state ruled over by a philosopher-king. His other writings covered a wide variety of subjects, including psychology, logic, and rhetoric. Most of his writings were "dialogues," which resembled plays in which the characters discussed important issues. In many of Plato's dialogues, Socrates was the chief character.

In a typical dialogue, Plato had Socrates attempt to determine the truth relevant to the issue at hand by engaging other characters in a series of questions and answers. That approach is now frequently called the "Socratic method" or the "Platonic method." It illustrated the process of "dialectic," which Plato believed was the means of discovering truth. The dialogues were often named after the characters who opposed Socrates in the discussion. Two of the dialogues, *Gorgias* and *Phaedrus*, named after those Sophists, dealt explicitly with rhetoric.

Plato's dialogues are complicated and often difficult to understand fully. Scholars have debated their meaning for centuries. Some have argued that *Gorgias* and *Phaedrus* presented inconsistent and conflicting views of rhetoric; that Plato condemned rhetoric in *Gorgias* and then praised it in *Phaedrus*. In fact, when taken together, the two dialogues presented Plato's clear and coherent view of the nature and function of rhetoric.

In *Gorgias*, Plato, through the character of Socrates, condemned rhetoric *as practiced* by many Sophists of his day. He said that the rhetoric of the Sophists was merely a "knack" or a form of flattery, intended only to please the ears of listeners much like cookery pleases the palate. He condemned the Sophists for using florid language, pleasant to the ear, to "make the worse case appear the better." And he accused them of first claiming to impart wisdom and thus to make their students more just and virtuous, and then of failing to do so. But these charges were leveled at rhetoric as the Sophists practiced it, not at rhetoric itself.

In *Phaedrus*, once again through the character of Socrates, Plato praised rhetoric as it *ought to be practiced*. The Sophists focused their attention on speaking in assemblies and courts. But Plato saw the true rhetoric as a means of using language to influence the minds of listeners, wherever they might be. Going further, he saw rhetoric as a means of influencing the very souls of listeners, thus making them more virtuous. The difference between the Sophistic and Platonic ideas of rhetoric grew from Plato's understanding of "truth."

In Plato's view, truth, or knowledge, existed on several levels. The lowest, least reliable, yet most common level was called *doxa*. This sort of knowledge was the product of the human senses, of what people observed. It was least reliable because it was so easily corrupted; the senses were easily misled. Thus, Plato's condemnation of the rhetoric of the Sophists grew from its aim of pleasing (and often, he felt, misleading) the senses of listeners. On the other end of Plato's scale was *episteme,* or true knowledge. It was the product not of sensory observation, but rather of philosophical inquiry. For Plato, rhetoric as it ought to be practiced was grounded in *episteme.* Only this "true" rhetoric could be trusted to influence the souls of listeners.

The idea of rhetoric based on truth is appealing. But before we award too much praise to Plato, we must know also that he thought most people were not capable of achieving true knowledge. Only philosophers could attain true knowledge, and thus, in the ideal political state described in his *Republic,* only the philosopher-king was allowed to use rhetoric, for the good of the state. Such uses of rhetoric are frightening. Seen in that light, the Sophists' idea that both sides of important issues should be debated in public seems preferable indeed.

Aristotle

Plato's most famous student was Aristotle (384–322 B.C.). Of all ancient scholars, including Plato, no other was more influential than Aristotle. He wrote extensively on subjects as diverse as philosophy, drama, natural science, and rhetoric. Like his teacher, Aristotle had a profound effect on the development of Western culture.

Throughout his life, Aristotle was directly associated with the most brilliant and important people of his time. His father, Nicomachus, was physician in the court of Amyntas II, king of Macedon and father of Philip the Great. When Aristotle was seventeen, he was sent to Athens to study in the Academy. There he remained until Plato's death. In 343 B.C., he was summoned back to Macedon to become tutor to Philip's son, Alexander the Great. Aristotle returned to Athens in 335 B.C. and eventually founded his own school, the Lyceum. After the death of Alexander in 323 B.C., he came under suspicion in Athens because of his prior close association with Macedon. Aristotle fled to the city of Chalcis where he died the next year.

Aristotle's *Rhetoric* is the earliest systematic discussion of speechmaking of which we have record. It probably existed first as his own notes for lectures he gave to students in the Lyceum. Legend has it that his students edited and published those notes after Aristotle's death. His approach to rhetoric was influenced by the philosophy of Plato. But his practical suggestions for speakers demonstrate that Aristotle was influenced by the Sophists as well. In effect, he was able to transcend both Plato and the Sophists and form a distinctive theory of rhetoric. The impact of his work continues today. Indeed, much of what appears earlier in this textbook originated with Aristotle.

Like Plato, Aristotle believed in true or ultimate knowledge. Also like Plato, he believed that only through philosophical inquiry, which was beyond the ability of most people, could true knowledge be attained. But Plato viewed rhetoric as a means through which, for the good of the state, philosopher-kings might manipulate those incapable of gaining true knowledge. Aristotle took a very different position. He believed that even those who could not attain true knowledge could, nevertheless, be persuaded to the good. Thus, persuasion was an acceptable, although inferior, substitute for true knowledge. In Plato's ideal state, only the philosopher-king could employ rhetoric because in the hands of the unenlightened, rhetoric could do great harm. In contrast, Aristotle believed that rhetoric was a morally neutral art. He did not restrict the use of rhetoric to rulers alone because he believed that, in any dispute, good would prevail provided both sides were equally well prepared; that is, provided both sides were equally well trained in rhetoric.

Aristotle envisioned rhetoric as an art, as a system that could be taught. He defined rhetoric as "the faculty of discovering, in any given case, the available means of persuasion." These means of persuasion he classified into three types: *ethos,* or ethical appeals, based on the degree of credibility awarded to a speaker by listeners; *logos,* or logical appeals; and *pathos,* or appeals to listeners' emotions. The *Rhetoric* offered speakers extremely detailed suggestions for discovering, understanding, and implementing each means of persuasion.

Aristotle also classified the different situations, or "given cases," in which speeches might be given. Those were: deliberative, or legislative speaking; forensic, or speaking in the courts; and epideictic, or what he called the "ceremonial oratory of display." Today, we would call that last type "special-occasion" speaking. According to Aristotle, those types were determined by the role listeners must play in each case; by the sort of "decision" they must make after hearing a particular speech. In that regard, Aristotle, like this textbook, took an "audience-centered approach" to speechmaking.

In Aristotle's system of classification, those who hear deliberative speeches were asked to render a decision regarding the most expedient course for future action. Those who heard forensic speeches were asked to judge the justice or injustice of a person's past action. And those who heard epideictic speeches were asked to award either praise or blame to the subject (usually a person) of the speech, and to judge the orator's skill as well. The *Rhetoric* offered speakers detailed suggestions for demonstrating the expedience or inexpediency of proposed courses of action, the justice or injustice of a person's deeds, and those qualities worthy of praise or blame. Aristotle also allowed for considerable overlap between the three types, indicating that although one type would predominate, elements of all three might appear in a single speech.

His discussions of expediency, justice, and qualities worthy of praise or blame, made Aristotle's *Rhetoric* more than a simple "handbook" for speakers. Those discussions provided a philosophical or ethical foundation for speechmaking. But its practical suggestions made the *Rhetoric* an extremely useful manual for public speaking as well.

The Roman Tradition

The Greek tradition of rhetoric had its most immediate, and perhaps its greatest, influence in the Roman educational system. In the second century B.C., Rome's military might extended the Republic to the east. There, Romans became familiar with Greek culture and the Greek educational system. Much of what they discovered was incorporated into Roman society, and that included training in rhetoric. In fact, rhetorical training eventually became the center of Roman education.

The Roman education system was designed to prepare citizens to participate in the affairs of the state. Primarily, that meant citizens must be prepared to speak in the legislatures and the courts. Rhetorical instruction began in the Roman grammar schools. There, students engaged in a progressive series of written and spoken exercises called the *Progymnasmata.* The lessons built on each other, with each more difficult than the one that preceded it. Near the end of the program of instruction, students were assigned a thesis which required them to develop arguments on a given theme, such as whether it was more noble to be a soldier or a lawyer. The series of lessons culminated in exercises in which students were required to speak for and against an existing law.

With grammar-school instruction completed, most students moved on to schools of rhetoric. Instruction there was more broad in scope, but it continued to focus on preparing students to be productive citizens of Rome; that is, to be effective speakers. Students were required to learn a vast body of rhetorical theories and concepts based on centuries of oratorical study. They were taught that the art of rhetoric consisted of five separate arts: *invention,* which involved gathering and analyzing facts and physical evidence; *arrangement,* or organization; *style,* or the eloquent and effective use of language; *memory,* or recollection of the speech for presentation; and *delivery.* These five classical "canons" of rhetoric are familiar to today's students of public speaking. The exercises in which students in Roman times participated were of two types, *suasoria* and *controversia.* Suasoria were exercises in legislative speaking. Students debated hypothetical questions of public policy, laws, and so forth. *Controversia* were exercises in forensic or legal speaking. Students argued opposing sides of hypothetical court cases, much as present-day law students do in "moot court" contests.

Following their training in schools of rhetoric, Roman students were often apprenticed to practicing rhetoricians, such as legislators or lawyers. There the students were given opportunities to learn by observing other speakers in legislative and judicial situations. Thus, the entire Roman educational system was designed to prepare citizens to assume roles as orators in the society. Rome produced many scholars who contributed to the rhetorical tradition. Two of the most important were Cicero (106–43 B.C.) and Quintilian (A.D. 35–95).

Marcus Tullius Cicero was the child of an upper middle-class family from central Italy. Social custom dictated that he pursue his education in Rome, where he studied with the leading rhetoricians of his day. According to many, he became the greatest orator in all Rome. His most famous works on the theory and practice of rhetoric were *De Inventione,* written when he was approximately twenty years old; *De Oratore,* published in 55 B.C.; and *Brutus* and *Orator,* both written in approximately 46 B.C. Cicero's aim in these works was to gather, synthesize, and expand on the greatest teachings of previous Greek and Roman rhetoricians. He was appalled by the emphasis given to style and delivery in some schools of rhetoric, and felt the true orator should be a fully educated person. Cicero saw rhetoric as far more than courtroom pleading. Rather, he believed that the ideal orator was the learned philosopher-statesman, who used his talent for the good of the state. In his view, the true orator should be able to speak with eloquence and wisdom on any important subject.

Marcus Fabius Quintilianus was born in the part of the Roman Empire that is now Spain. Like Cicero, he was the product of a traditional Roman education. But unlike Cicero, Quintilian lived in a time when oratory began to be repressed. Tyrants ruled the Roman Empire; the legislative speaking, and even the legal speaking, which characterized Cicero's time, were greatly restricted. Despite that fact, or perhaps because of it, Quintilian's aim as a teacher of rhetoric was to educate the perfect orator. His most famous rhetorical treatise was *Institutio Oratoria,* which emphasized the moral and ethical uses of rhetoric. For Quintilian, the ideal orator was "a good man speaking well." Unfortunately, that dictum has been much abused by many modern rhetorical scholars, often to justify the study of the speaking and speeches of only highly successful political figures who were usually white and male. In fact, Quintilian urged those who would become great orators to pursue not only eloquence, but excellence in morality and ethical character as well—qualities that are certainly not limited to, or perhaps even characteristic of, successful politicians!

Conclusion

The rhetorical tradition that began with the ancient Greeks and Romans has been a significant influence in Western civilization. Their theories and guidelines for successful rhetorical practice have been analyzed, refined, and extended by countless scholars for thousands of years. This textbook is a part of that tradition. Many of the rhetorical principles and suggestions for effective speechmaking which appear in this book can be traced through the ages back to such classical rhetoricians as Isocrates, Plato, Aristotle, Cicero, and Quintilian. Throughout history, other rhetorical scholars have made important contributions as well. But as you work to prepare your own speeches, to be delivered in class or in other settings, it is interesting and perhaps even comforting to know that your efforts are a continuation of a classical tradition of rhetoric which is as old as Western culture.

RECAP — THE CLASSICAL TRADITION OF RHETORIC

Rhetoricians	Dates	Contributions
The First Teachers		
Corax and Tisias	476 B.C.	Doctrine of general probability
The Greek Tradition		
The Sophists		
Protagoras	481–411 B.C.	Originator of academic debate
Gorgias	485–380 B.C.	Effective language use
Isocrates	436–338 B.C.	The orator-statesman
Plato	427–347 B.C.	*Gorgias* and *Phaedrus;* philosopher-king as orator
Aristotle	384–322 B.C.	*Rhetoric;* philosophical and practical guide for orators; rhetoric as a teachable art
The Roman Tradition		
Cicero	106–43 B.C.	*De Inventione, De Oratore, Brutus,* and *Orator;* Rome's greatest orator; philosopher-statesman as the ideal orator
Quintilian	A.D. 35–95	*Institutio Oratoria;* eloquence combined with moral and ethical excellence; the good man speaking well

Aristotle, *Rhetoric and Poetics*. W. Rhys Roberts and Ingram Bywater, trans. New York: Modern Library, 1954.

Black, Edwin. "Plato's View of Rhetoric." *Quarterly Journal of Speech 44* (Dec. 1958): 361–74.

Clark, Donald Lemen. *Rhetoric in Greco–Roman Education*. New York: Columbia UP, 1957.

Guthrie, W. K. C. *The Sophists*. Cambridge, Eng.: Cambridge UP, 1971.

Hamilton, Edith, and Huntington Cairns, eds. *The Collected Dialogues of Plato*. Princeton: Princeton UP, 1961.

Kauffman, Charles. "The Axiological Foundations of Plato's Theory of Rhetoric." *Central States Speech Journal* 33 (Summer 1982): 353–66.

Kennedy, George. *The Art of Persuasion in Greece*. Princeton: Princeton UP, 1963.

Murphy, James J., ed. *A Synoptic History of Classical Rhetoric*. Davis, CA: Hermagoras P, 1983.

Murphy, James J., ed. *Quintilian on the Teaching of Speaking and Writing*. Translations from Books 1, 2, and 10 of *Institutio Oratoria*. Carbondale: Southern Illinois UP, 1987.

Watson, J. S., trans., *Cicero on Oratory and Orators*. Carbondale: Southern Illinois UP, 1970.

Appendix B:
Suggested Speech Topics

One of the more challenging tasks for beginning speakers is deciding what to talk about. We identified several suggestions in Chapter 6 to help you select and narrow your topic. Specifically, we suggested that you should

1. Consider the audience.

2. Consider the demands of the occasion.

3. Consider yourself.

   We also described several techniques to help you with your topic-selection hunt:

1. Brainstorm—free-associate topics until you have a long list before you start to critique your topics.

2. Listen to the media and read; keep current on the news of the day.

3. Scan lists and indexes.

4. Use Internet search engines.

   To help prime your creative pump, we have included the following list of topics.* As presented here, most of the topics are appropriate for an informative speech. Depending on your point of view, they could also be adapted for persuasive speech topics.

 ## Informative Speech Topics

Why go to graduate school?
The history and significance of the Panama Canal
What's happening in Afghanistan? (or another country?)
Why are so many dot.com companies going broke?
What exactly happened on Black Monday?
What's the current role of health education?
What's going on with nuclear energy?

---

*We thank Professor Russell Wittrup, Austin Community College, for sharing his speech-topic ideas with us.

What is the privacy act?

Is censorship going on in the United States?

What's involved in being an organ donor?

What are the standards used to get credit cards?

The history of the situation in Bosnia

The evolution of the musician as a popular hero

What are the facts on world hunger?

What are the facts on the homeless in the United States?

Who is a powerful contemporary writer?

What is subliminal advertising?

The social/economic problems in Mexico (or another country)

The history of the gay-rights movement

What the experts say about choosing a career

Present trends in animal conservation

What goes into making a compact disk?

What's the United States doing about littering?

How is technology affecting education?

Which diets really work?

What is socialized medicine?

What do primary elections tell us?

What are the goals of general education courses?

The facts on child abuse

What the experts say predicts a good marriage

New discoveries in health care

What's the current status on finances for U.S. education?

What's happening with solar energy?

The facts on religious cults

What's happening with the draft?

What are the rights of adopted children?

The facts about legalized prostitution

How happy are marriages without children?

What is involved in being a blood donor?

What has the 70-mph speed limit done for safety?

What's being done to save national parks?

Who gets guaranteed student loans and why?

What are new methods in waste disposal?

Why people become vegetarians

Tips on bicycle safety and protection

The implications of the Internet for education

What is the Electoral College?

Is there life on other planets?

What exactly are money-market funds?

What the experts say about crime prevention

The previous decade in the Middle East

How do we choose a president in the United States?

How does the stock market work?

What's being done to find a cure for AIDS?

What's being done to make reparations to Native Americans?

Rap music as cultural expression

Do we have any ecological crises?

What measures are in place to protect us from bioterrorism?

What are the job forecasts for the future?

What's the background to the problems in Ireland?

What's the media's role in shaping the news?

What's the New Age movement?

The latest in genetic engineering

Technology in the twenty-first century

The changing job market

What is "sexist" language?

New trends in advertising

What does "English as an official language" mean?

How are movie ratings determined?

What are the facts about legalized gambling?

Are there any new concepts in mass transportation?

What is the role of the ACLU?

The impact of the instant replay in sports

How are maps made?

What is the latest in stereophonic technology?

How is the rate of inflation determined?

How is a loudspeaker made?

The effect of telephone deregulation

The history of the _____ river

The history of the _____ building

What's the future for real estate?

The history of blue laws

How can you test yourself for blood-alcohol level?

What's being done about TV violence?

What can/cannot a chiropractor do for you?

What is the foreign exchange-student program?

What kinds of work do volunteers do?

Tips on fire prevention in dorms

The facts about diet pills

What happens in drug-therapy clinics?

The history of jazz (or select another type of music)

What is electroshock therapy?

The history of cable TV

How do unions work?

Living together

Success of designated-smoking-area laws

The history of cremation customs

How does cloning work?

What is stem-cell research?

What are the current child-custody laws?

Multiple births

The facts about teenage alcoholism

New breakthroughs for the handicapped

What is the Consumer Protection Agency?

How are scholarships awarded?

What is the "Sunset Law" for government agencies?

What is the impact of the new immigration laws?

What has been the impact of recycling centers?

Why the change in marriage and divorce rates?

Sexual harassment: what it is and how to deal with it if it happens to you

Is there a "glass ceiling" for working women?

Persuasive Speech Topics

We should reduce our fat intake.

We should reduce our body weight.

Spend more leisure time doing [something].

Volunteer for [something].

The electoral-college system for electing presidents should be changed.

Every U.S. citizen should spend two years in mandatory community service.

State drug laws should be changed.

The income-tax system should be changed.

All undergraduate courses should be graded on a pass/fail basis only.

Everyone should take a foreign language.

Everyone should read a weekly news magazine regularly.

Couples should (or should not) live together before marriage.

We devote too much attention to college athletics.

Don't (or do) invest in the stock market.

The United States should have a tougher trade policy.

All farmers should be given low-interest loans.

The government should provide health care for all.

Divorce laws should be changed.

Spend less time watching TV.

Casino gambling should (or should not) be legalized in this state.

Birth-control pills should (or should not) be dispensed by state-supported schools.

The federal court system needs to be changed.

A college education should be available to all citizens at no cost.

Teachers should be paid more.

Nuclear-power plants should (or should not) be phased out.

Developing alternative energy sources must become a national priority.

School choice should (or should not) be promoted.

Affirmative action is the best way to overcome discrimination.

What working mothers and fathers need from their employers.

Why a national health-care system will (or won't) work.

College students should (or shouldn't) be given the opportunity to pay off their tuition through public service.

The use of animals in research should be fully regulated.

It's time to put an end to violence on television.

All students should be required to take a public-speaking course.

The United States should (or should not) invest in the stock market to save Social Security.

Stem-cell research is a good [or bad] thing.

We should increase drilling for oil in national parks and forests.

The United States should (or should not) drastically change its foreign policy in response to the events of September 11, 2001.

Appendix C:
Speeches for Analysis and Discussion

 **I Have a Dream***

by Martin Luther King, Jr., Washington, D.C., August 28, 1963

I am happy to join with you today in what will go down in history as the greatest demonstration for freedom in the history of our nation.

Five score years ago, a great American, in whose symbolic shadow we stand today, signed the Emancipation Proclamation. This momentous decree came as a great beacon light of hope to millions of Negro slaves, who had been seared in the flames of withering injustice. It came as a joyous daybreak to end the long night of their captivity.

But one hundred years later, the Negro is still not free. One hundred years later, the life of the Negro is still sadly crippled by the manacles of segregation and the chains of discrimination. One hundred years later, the Negro lives on a lonely island of poverty in the midst of a vast ocean of material prosperity. One hundred years later, the Negro is still languished in the corners of American society and finds himself an exile in his own land. And so we've come here today to dramatize a shameful condition.

In a sense we've come to our nation's Capitol to cash a check. When the architects of our republic wrote the magnificent words of the Constitution and the Declaration of Independence, they were signing a promissory note to which every American was to fall heir. This note was a promise that all men—yes, black men as well as white men—would be guaranteed the inalienable rights of life, liberty, and the pursuit of happiness.

It is obvious today that America has defaulted on this promissory note insofar as her citizens of color are concerned. Instead of honoring this sacred obligation, America has given the Negro people a bad check—a check which has come back marked "insufficient funds."

But we refuse to believe that the bank of justice is bankrupt. We refuse to believe that there are insufficient funds in the great vaults of opportunity of this nation. And so we've come to cash this check—a check that will give us upon demand the riches of freedom and the security of justice.

We have also come to this hallowed spot to remind America of the fierce urgency of now. This is no time to engage in the luxury of cooling off or to take the tranquilizing drug of gradualism. Now is the time to make the real promises of democracy. Now is the time to rise from the dark and desolate valley of segregation to the sunlit path of racial justice. Now is the time to lift our nation from the quicksands of racial injustice to the solid rock of brotherhood. Now is the time to make justice a reality for all of God's children.

It would be fatal for the nation to overlook the urgency of the moment. This sweltering summer of the Negro's legitimate discontent will not pass until there is an invigorating autumn of freedom and equality. Nineteen sixty-three is not an end, but a beginning. Those who hope that the Negro needed to blow off steam and will now be content will have a rude awakening if the nation returns to business as usual. There will be neither rest nor tranquility in America until the Negro is granted his citizenship rights. The whirlwinds of revolt will continue to shake the foundations of our nation until the bright day of justice emerges.

But there is something that I must say to my people, who stand on the warm threshold which leads into the palace of justice. In the process of gaining our rightful place, we must not be guilty of wrongful deeds. Let us not seek to satisfy our thirst for freedom by drinking from the cup of bitterness and hatred.

We must forever conduct our struggle on the high plane of dignity and discipline. We must not allow our creative protest to degenerate into physical violence. Again and again we must rise to the majestic heights of meeting physical force with soul force.

The marvelous new militance which has engulfed the Negro community must not lead us to a distrust of all white people. For many of our white brothers, as evidenced by their presence here today, have come to realize that their destiny is tied up with our destiny. They have come to realize that their freedom is inextricably bound to our freedom. We cannot walk alone.

As we walk, we must make the pledge that we shall always march ahead. We cannot turn back. There are those who are asking the devotees of civil rights, "When will you be satisfied?" We can never be satisfied as long as the Negro is the victim of the unspeakable horrors of police brutality. We can never be satisfied as long as our bodies, heavy with the fatigue of travel, cannot gain lodging in the motels of the highways and hotels of the cities. We cannot be satisfied as long as the Negro's basic mobility is from a smaller ghetto to a larger one. We can never be satisfied as long as our children are stripped of their selfhood and robbed of their dignity by signs stating "For Whites Only." We cannot be satisfied as long as a Negro in Mississippi cannot vote and a Negro in New York believes he has nothing for which to vote. No, no, we are not satisfied, and we will not be satisfied until justice rolls down like waters, and righteousness like a mighty stream.

I am not unmindful that some of you have come here out of great trials and tribulations. Some of you have come fresh from narrow jail cells. Some of you have come from areas where your quest for freedom left you battered by the storms of persecution and staggered by the winds of police brutality. You have been the veterans of creative suffering. Continue to work with the faith that unearned suffering is redemptive.

Go back to Mississippi, go back to Alabama, go back to South Carolina, go back to Georgia, go back to Louisiana, go back to the slums and ghettos of our Northern cities, knowing that somehow this situation can and will be changed. Let us not wallow in the valley of despair.

I say to you today, my friends, so even though we face the difficulties of today and tomorrow, I still have a dream. It is a dream deeply rooted in the American dream.

I have a dream that one day this nation will rise up and live out the true meaning of its creed, "We hold these truths to be self-evident, that all men are created equal."

I have a dream that one day on the red hills of Georgia the sons of former slaves and the sons of former slaveowners will be able to sit down together at the table of brotherhood.

I have a dream that one day even the state of Mississippi, a state sweltering with the heat of injustice, sweltering with the heat of oppression, will be transformed into an oasis of freedom and justice.

I have a dream that my four little children will one day live in a nation where they will not be judged by the color of their skin but by the content of their character. I have a dream today.

I have a dream that one day, down in Alabama, with its vicious racists, with its governor having his lips dripping with the words of interposition and nullification, one day right there in Alabama little black boys and black girls will be able to join hands with little white boys and white girls as sisters and brothers. I have a dream today.

I have a dream that one day every valley shall be exalted, every hill and mountain shall be made low, the rough places will be made plane and the crooked places will be made straight, and the glory of the Lord shall be revealed, and all flesh shall see it together.

This is our hope. This is the faith that I go back to the South with. With this faith we will be able to hew out of the mountain of despair a stone of hope. With this faith we will be able to transform the jangling discords of our nation into a beautiful sym phony of brotherhood. With this faith we will be able to work together, to pray together, to struggle together, to go to jail together, to stand up for freedom together knowing that we will be free one day.

This will be the day—this will be the day when all of God's children will be able to sing with new meaning, "My country 'tis of thee, sweet land of liberty, of thee I sing. Land where my fathers died, land of the Pilgrims' pride, from every mountain-side, let freedom ring." And if America is to be a great nation, this must become true.

So let freedom ring from the prodigious hilltops of New Hampshire. Let freedom ring from the mighty mountains of New York. Let freedom ring from the heightening Alleghenies of Pennsylvania!

Let freedom ring from the snowcapped Rockies of Colorado! Let freedom ring from the curvaceous slopes of California!

But not only that. Let freedom ring from Stone Mountain of Georgia!

Let freedom ring from Lookout Mountain of Tennessee!

Let freedom ring from every hill and molehill of Mississippi. From every mountainside, let freedom ring.

And when this happens, when we allow freedom to ring—when we let it ring from every village and every hamlet, from every state and every city—we will be able to speed up that day when all of God's children, black men and white men, Jews and Gentiles, Protestants and Catholics, will be able to join hands and sing, in the words of the old Negro spiritual, "Free at last! Free at last! Thank God almighty, we are free at last!"

Making Democracy Work: Your Responsibility to Society

Cynthia Opheim, Professor and Chair, Department of Political Science, Southwest Texas State University

President Supple, Regent Flores, and members of the platform party, colleagues, friends and families of our graduates, my family, graduates. *Les felicito por este logro!* I congratulate you for this achievement! You've made it! After concentrated effort, sacrifice, and expense, you've accomplished a distinct achievement: a graduate education.

Let's take a moment to celebrate this achievement. Only 7.5 percent of the adult population in this country earn graduate degrees; only 6.5 percent of the adult population in Texas (only 4.5 in Arkansas, but who's comparing?). Today, the average difference in annual income between those with a Bachelors versus those with a Masters degree is almost $11,000.

Your educational accomplishments have officially placed you into a category that my colleagues, political scientists, refer to as "elites." (I prefer the term "meritocracy.")

While you enjoy your new status as the educated elite (or the meritocracy), you must know that it places new responsibilities on you. It is up to you, even more than others, to make our democracy work! I do feel a little guilty giving you this message; you've worked very hard for months and years and now I'm telling you that your responsibilities are greater than ever! "Give me a break," you say. Well, I can't; the stakes are too high.

Democracies are not automatically self-sustaining. Samuel Huntington, a prominent scholar, notes that there have been three great waves of democracy in the last 200 years, that is, three historical periods where democracies have emerged: a long slow wave from 1828 to 1926; a post-World War II wave, from 1945–1964; and the present wave beginning in 1976. The first two waves ended with a reverse wave of democratic breakdowns during which some of the new or reestablished democracies collapsed. Will the new century bring a third reverse wave? If so, how will the reversals occur? It has been said that "the death of democracy is not likely to be an assassination from ambush. It will be a slow extinction from apathy, indifference, and undernourishment."

This evening I'd like to lay out two strategies for making our democracy work, a basic recipe that you, as the most educated members of our society, should think about. The first is informed participation in public life. Participation in political or public life is the most basic corollary of democracy. I challenge you to organize a group, circulate a petition, attend a public hearing, run for the school board, volunteer in a hospital, email your congressional representative, speak out at a city council meeting, organize a meals-to-the-elderly program. As the most educated members of our society, you should play a leading role in civic life.

Notice, however, there is an additional responsibility attached to participating: staying informed. In one of my favorite quotes, Thomas Jefferson said, "Ignorant participation is not democratic." Staying informed should be easier for you than for many—you would not be sitting here if you didn't already know how to cultivate the discipline and love for learning you've had in graduate school. Continue these habits: read at least one or two articles from the international section of the newspaper; take the time to decipher both sides of an issue; listen (really listen) to someone whose point of view is different from your own (I tell my students, if you're a liberal, turn on Rush Limbaugh; if you're a conservative, listen to one of Jesse Jackson's speeches—tough challenges no doubt); try to think about the interest of the broader community. Apply the principles of informed democracy in your work and in your life; if you are a manager or administrator, be aggressive about seeking advice.

Above all, THINK about the responsibility you as elites have to make our democracy work. Prove Adolf Hitler wrong when he said, "What luck for rulers that men do not think."

The second strategy for making our democracy work is to carefully select and then respect our political leaders. It's this second part of the recipe that is the greatest challenge. Fewer people are voting; less than half of those eligible voted in the last presidential election. Yet our responsibility for selecting the right leaders is as crucial to the success of our democracy as participation in the process itself.

Your educational training has given you the capacity to analyze important public issues and tie those issues to candidates and public officials. Thus you have a special commitment to do so.

Once we select our leaders, it's crucial that we have at least some trust in them. This is the most difficult challenge of all in America. Americans have always distrusted power and those who hold power. In my political science classes I always tell my students that we have an antipolitical political tradition. We have always embraced a culture of individualism and dissent, never more so than today as the media lays bare the weaknesses and failures of our leaders.

The very procedures of open democratic decision-making encourage our suspicion of those who engage in it. Democracy is messy; it is not efficient. We often witness our leaders discussing, arguing, amending, compromising and it frustrates us. Most of us believe Mark Twain was right when he said there are two things you should never watch being made: "sausage and legislation."

But at some point we must trust our leaders. Why? Because it gives them greater flexibility to deal with difficult issues. It's important that they possess a reserve of mass confidence that allows them to call on citizens to make short-term sacrifices for long-term goals. School board members may ask permission from the public to borrow money through the sale of bonds to improve the schools. Congress may have to reduce funding for a popular program to direct funds to something more important. When trust is low, leaders are pressured to make short-sighted decisions at the expense of a healthy future.

Many of you, the meritocracy, have been and will be selected as leaders. To those of you selected, I ask that you always remember how crucial it is to maintain the trust of those you lead. There is likely to be intense scrutiny of you and your actions. Be aware that these days, you must not only act ethically, you must maintain the appearance of acting ethically. Always remember you build trust over time; you lose it quickly.

So tonight while we celebrate your achievement, and it is an extraordinary achievement, remember your special responsibility to our society. It is you I think of now when I read the comments Alexander Hamilton made about our new constitutional system in 1789. He's describing the great experiment in democracy that is America when he states that ". . . it is reserved to the people of this country, by their conduct and example, to decide the important question, whether societies of men are really capable or not of establishing good government from reflection and choice, or whether they are forever destined to depend on accident and force."

Be involved, stay informed, select your leaders carefully, nurture trust in your own leadership, and help make our great experiment a success!

Congratulations!

Have a happy and productive life.

Antibiotic-Resistant Bacteria

Sarah Root, Central Michigan University

Perhaps it was mother's intuition that sent Susan Canterbury into her 2-year-old son Dalton's room to wake him. He was lifeless, too weak to move. In the ambulance Dalton had a seizure. Tests at the hospital showed bacterial meningitis, and that the strain of pneumococcus infecting Dalton's brain was resistant to penicillin. After doctors administered significantly high doses of another powerful antibiotic, Dalton regained consciousness. An ophthalmologist later examined Dalton, and determined that due to the resistance of the meningitis, the optical portion of Dalton's brain had been damaged, and Dalton would be blind.

According to the May 10, 1999, edition of *U.S. News and World Report,* approximately 133 million antibiotics are prescribed by doctors annually, and roughly 190 million doses are administered in hospitals daily. This gross abuse of easily accessible antibiotics is leading to the emergence of antibiotic-resistant bacteria, aggressive bacteria that can no longer be eliminated or detained by conventional methods. The rapid increase in these drug-resistant bugs is leaving us without defense. To fully understand the hazards of antibiotic resistant bacteria, we must first examine the problem of these "superbugs." Then, we will discuss what is causing us to become powerless against them. Finally, we will look at the opportunities available to squash the impending danger.

The problem is multifaceted. First, there is the issue of communicability, and second, the problem of beefier bugs able to resist a multitude of treatments. Merely being around an individual carrying a drug-resistant bacterial strain can result in violent illness. The March 2000 issue of *The Cause* newsletter published by the Centers for Disease Control studied one child carrying a drug-resistant strain of otitis media, or middle ear infection, in an Ohio daycare center. Studies showed how this infection had spread to parents and staff in addition to causing recurring ear infections in 20% of children at the center. We can easily contract a resistant bug from someone that already has it, and now is the time when we are most at risk. The *USA Today* of June 1, 1999 states that crowded conditions promote the passage of bacteria from one person to another. The same article goes on to state, that bacterial meningitis, a disease causing fever, lethargy, nausea, and sometimes death, is on the rise among college students. Antibiotics are becoming increasingly useless against this epidemic.

Second, is the problem of beefier bugs. According to the March 15, 1999, edition of the *Financial Times,* resistance is now found in a multitude of dangerous bacteria. You see, if a pathogen becomes resistant to one type of antibiotic, its chances of forming immunity to all others are significantly higher. According to the April 30, 1999, edition of the *Omaha World Herald,* Dr. Dale Gerding, Chief of Medicine at the Chicago VA Health Care System, states that we are now critically close to having no treatment for several resistant organisms. Increased resistance is thought to have caused 350,000 cases of middle ear infections and 210 cases of bacterial meningitis per year in the United States. The *LA Times* of Sept. 20, l999, reports that a bug known as campylobacter, causing severe diarrhea, fever, vomiting and abdominal pains in approximately 4 million Americans per year has now become increasingly resistant to antibiotics. The result of this increased resistance? Potent new wonderbugs, able to resist anything in our arsenal.

Not so long ago, we wouldn't have been worried about finding a drug to treat Dalton's bacterial meningitis. However, now, by our own creation, many will suffer unnecessary pain and death due to these superbugs. We have caused this domino effect in two ways; first, through the overprescription of antibiotics, and second, through improper usage. First, according to Dr. Diane M. Dwyer's speech at the Feb. 25, 1999, Committee of Public Health in Maryland, overprescription is one of the major contributing factors leading to the spread of resistant infections.

As reported in the Antibiotic Resistance website, published by the Centers for Disease Control, last updated March 12, 2000, 44% of kids are prescribed antibiotics for colds, and 46% for upper respiratory infections. Both of these are caused by viruses, against which antibiotics are completely useless. The CDC estimates that approximately 50 million courses of antimicrobial agents are issued unnecessarily in the United States each year. Our doctors and hospitals are doling out a cure, and we blindly accept. You see, we have bacteria present in our bodies at all times in small doses. It's when these bacteria become resistant to antibiotics that any lowering of the immune system or exposure to outside bacteria can leave us with an illness that can't be cured. According to the *New Straits Times* of July 20, 1999, throwing antibiotics at bacteria that don't call for them expands on the opportunity for evolution of resistance.

Second, as published in the Sept. 22, 1999, edition of *The Plain Dealer,* Dr. Richard P. Wenzel, author of an article on the development of antibiotic-resistant bacteria, pinpoints contributory human failings, states, "patients' don't finish the course of treatment once they feel better. Failure to run the course of treatment allows bacteria that have evolved partial resistance to survive, rather than finishing them off."

We as consumers simply don't see a downside to using antibiotics, and when we are using them, we see no need to run the course of our prescription. In a recent survey conducted by Bernadette Albanese, pediatric infectious disease specialist and public advocate for Use Antibiotics Wisely, suburban physicians admit they are part of the problem, but state that the problem is confounded by an uneducated public. In a recent survey conducted by *Pediatrics,* 96% of doctors surveyed stated that parents had recently requested antibiotics for their children when they were not necessary.

When you or someone you love gets sick, the most natural solution is to go to the doctor and ask for a prescription. However, we have seen how take two pills and call me in the morning may actually amplify the problem. We need to uncover solutions that won't leave us vulnerable to the attack of these superbugs. The first solution is simply, education, and the second is the continuation and expansion of vaccine information.

People need to be made aware of not only how antibiotics can actually be harmful when overused, but also what illnesses warrant antibiotic use, versus those that don't. According to the Inside Baltimore Health website, last updated March 6, 2000, in the tradition of the Use Antibiotics Wisely programs, similar programs need to be established in our hospitals, offices, and schools, in order to educate parents and students before the problem worsens. For more information, the Antibiotic Resistance website through the CDC offers an order form for educational information on how to use antibiotics judiciously. In addition to education, we could help curb this problem of antibiotic-resistant bacteria with the continuation and expansion of vaccine information. Just as giving antibiotics to bacteria makes them resistant to the treatment, giving vaccines to us makes us resistant to the bacteria.

As stated in the June 7, 1999, edition of *U.S. News and World Retort,* health organizations are urging all college students to get the standard meningococcal vaccine, which could have prevented 75% of fatal meningitis cases observed during a five-year Johns Hopkins study. Currently, only parents of incoming freshmen receive vaccine information in only 80 colleges and universities. If this program were expanded nationwide and information sent to all incoming students, then vaccines would prove much more effective in reducing the chance of contracting a superbug. According to the previously cited *USA Today,* Evan Bozof, a junior at Georgia Southwestern University, died from bacterial meningitis only 26 days after his headache began. If Evan had gotten his vaccine, he would still be alive today. Spread the word, get the vaccine. I received my menimmune shot upon walking in my college health services and filling out a five-minute form. Finally if you or someone you love are feeling a little under the weather make sure it's an illness that can actually be helped by antibiotics before you ask your doctor for a prescription. If you do need antibiotics, the *New Straits Times* of July 23, 1999, warns, follow the instructions judiciously, taking all of the drug until it is gone—regardless of whether or not you feel better.

So today we have looked at the problem of antibiotic-resistant bacteria, discussed possible causes for the emergence of these superbugs, and uncovered solutions that, if enacted, could solve for these possibly fatal bacterium. In late March of last year a small miracle took place. Dalton Canterbury stood up and for the first time since he'd been home walked right up to his mother. One month later, Dalton had regained a great deal of his eyesight, although his unfortunate ordeal leaves him with continuing seizures, and vision and learning problems. Given the proper attention and respect, this problem of antibiotic-resistant bacteria will not reach us or those we love. All it takes is an understanding of the problem, and a little effort, and we will not fall victim to its danger.

Unsanitary Hotels

Kittie Grace, Hastings College

2,300,000 people in America sleep in a motel room each night. These people sleep in a bed that has been visited by thousands, brush their teeth in that same sink and even take a shower from the same tub, reports figures published in the January 13, 2000, *Denver Rocky Mountain News*. And recently, according to the August 8, 1999, *Hotel and Motel Management Journal* or *HMMJ,* in Atlantic City, NJ, two unsuspecting German tourists shared a motel room which had been cleaned that morning, but a foul smell permeated through the room. After the third complaint, housekeeping cleaned under the bed, finding the body of a dead man decomposing, all because housekeeping failed to clean under the bed, in the first place.

Fred Prassack, director of security and safety at the Peabody Orlando, lodging which is a mere four hours away, said of a similar incident in the February 7, 2000, *HMMJ,* "If the guestroom [appears] 'clean' [when a body is found] there's no reason it couldn't be available for rent later that day."

The information I'm about to present is so disturbing that you may subconsciously reject it. As Leon Festinger describes in his cognitive dissonance theory, when presented with information that challenges our current beliefs about reality we may discard the information or make changes in our views about a facet of an activity we love. To fully comprehend the problem of hotel and motel room hazards, we will first, identify them, second we will observe the causes, and finally, I mean finally, solve this problem for good.

Given the nature of this audience, the problem of unsanitary hotel rooms affects each of us almost every weekend. The July 7, 1999, *HMMJ,* a journal that you would think would cover up hotel mistakes, warns more than 40 million people get sick, and 80,000 die each year from hand- and air-borne bacteria found in motels. This is particularly relevant when one considers that in Florida, no records are kept on the number of people with contagious diseases outside of tuberculosis and AIDS, reports the officials from the Florida State Department of Health in a personal interview on April 14, 2000. Implying that it is unknown how many workers in the hotel room are contagious.

If these records aren't kept then the number of people who become sick by staying in a hotel room may be greater than we think.

With over 2 million people sleeping in a hotel each night, if the room is not cleaned appropriately you could become one of the 40-million-plus infected each year. In essence, we are playing Russian roulette with our health because we don't know if the room we are staying in is safe. In a research study conducted on 25 hotel and motel rooms from all over the country by *Prime Time Live,* every sampled blanket and bed-spread had deposits which when analyzed by a lab turned out to be semen and urine. This can be explained by the simple fact that economically, blankets can't be washed after every stay according to the January 10, 2000, *HMMJ.*

Unclean linen is a particular problem because we regenerate our entire skin more than once a month, notes the April 27, 1999, *Gazette,* implying that if sheets aren't changed, and rooms aren't cleaned, including under the bed, hundreds of thousands of cells remain when we check out. This becomes a biological banquet for bugs and bacteria that cause us physical harm. Jan Chung is one woman who received a rash from a $180-a-night hotel room in New York due to unclean sheets.

Becoming infested with crabs is another risk unwashed hotel sheets pose, warns the New York University Medical Center. In the previously noted study, mold was also found on all bathroom floors, and high levels of bacteria were detected in 21 of the 25 rooms. Chuck Gerba, a microbiologist at the University of Arizona, conducted a similar study and found fecal contamination and *E. coli* on the hotel room phones and TV remotes. Dr. Gerba believed the culprit was a dirty rag, spreading germs instead of picking them up. Ice and coffee makers are also problem spots for motels, reports the September 6, 1999, *HMMJ,* because when not cleaned bacteria grows inside and infects you with the first cup or cube.

If you believe the problem is trivial, consider the fact that in 1998, Best Western was investigated by an independent inspection agency, Pricewaterhouse Coopers. The company found that the cleanliness of the rooms was atrocious and stated that by this year, 308 hotels will close their doors due to failed inspections. Other hotels have received health citations as well, states the *HMMJ,* July 19, 1999, including Howard Johnson, Wyndham, and the Hilton, which is the hotel chain the tournament hotel, DoubleTree, is affiliated with. We have identified this shocking problem; now we need to see why we are paying to suffer and sleep in other people's filth.

The causes are two-fold: hotel workers, and in-house hotel inspections. The July 2, 1999, *Detroit News* says that sometimes managers want rooms to be made up quickly, sometimes in 8 minutes or less if two cleaners work as a team. Jim McManemon, Vice President of the Ritz Carlton Hotel, states that "cleanliness" depends on the expertise of the people who are working and it is difficult to maintain capable employees. Which leads to an annual turnover rate for most hotels of 52% notes the March 24, 1999, *Atlanta Journal Constitution.* This means each year a hotel has to retrain its employees, making certification training essential. Therefore, there is little expertise in the cleaning industry, allowing hazards to ensue.

The second cause is in house hotel inspections. Motels and hotels are individually owned and operated, and therefore cannot be regulated by national inspections, reports employees from Econo Lodge, Super 8, and Best Western on September 12, 1999. Still, all three employers were quick to note that they were checked out twice a year by their own corporate chain inspectors. In other words the inspections were all done in-house. This causes another related problem. Because independent inspections are not conducted on all motels, there is no way to derive a direct link between unsanitary hotels and health hazards.

Essentially, the cause of this problem is circular. In-house inspections are used to deal with the problem. The problem isn't documented because in-house inspections don't require a formal report. Without a formal report, we will never know how bad the problem is. Until the problem can be documented, in-house inspections will continue. In-house inspections do work if the motel or hotel is a member of an independent regulatory agency such as the American Automobile Association or AAA because they conduct surprise inspections, reports the official AAA Web page last updated March 24, 2000. The ones we have to worry about are those who don't have independent inspectors because they are notified when they have to clean up their act.

The *Hotel and Motel Management Journal* even realizes how abhorrent our hotel room hazards are, and the causes of our hotel colds are clear; now we can look at a simple solution: quit forensics. But because no one, including me, is likely to carry out this solution, we can look at more pragmatic solutions on the governmental, industrial, and the personal levels.

On the governmental level, the state Department of Health should be the agency to oversee all inspections of hotels and motels that don't have independent inspectors. Because this independent agency inspects all state hospitals, hospices, health clinics, and assisted living homes, the agency can do the same for all motels and hotels, states the official Florida Department of Health web page, last updated April 12, 2000.

On the industrial level, owners need to make sure their employees are certified cleaning professionals, but how? Outside consultants, or sanitation experts, must be used to instruct workers regarding proper cleaning procedures. Jim Abrams, executive V.P. of the California Hotel and Motel Association says that certification training is crucial to keep housekeepers aware of correct cleaning procedures, which include addressing usually neglected trouble spots such as bacteria-filled ice and coffee machines. The Econo Lodge is one hotel implementing this type of training, states the August 2, 1999, *St. Petersburg Time.* Tim Shy, V.P. of the Econo Lodge says, "the Mr. Clean Housekeeping program has trained the staff to the point of certification. Guest complaints are now down 38%."

Realistically, the government may not effectively inspect every hotel and managers may not clean up their act, but there are still steps we can take to protect ourselves. Perhaps the easiest solution is to become a AAA member. For $49 a year, among other items, you will receive this book which lists every hotel that has had a AAA inspection. Additionally, if you find unsanitary conditions in your hotel, ask to stay in a different room. Wash your hands as much as possible to protect you from most germs, says Dr. John Jernigan of Emory University. Also, we can make our own lightweight travel kit equipped with pillowcases, sheets, and a sanitizer. The 1999 *Adams Report* states that sanitizers, like Lysol or anti-bacterial spray kills 99.9 percent of common germs in seconds. If you still know that you have experienced hazardous hotel conditions take photographs of the room and contact local health authorities, reports the *Nolo's 2000 on-line Legal Encyclopedia.*

We have now uncovered the secrets of hazardous hotel rooms, examined the causes, and became reassured by solutions. The German couple's experience was not isolated. In 1994 the same scenario occurred, only this time, a five-foot-tall woman was found decomposing under a Miami Beach hotel bed. Because we know how to protect ourselves we should never fall victim to a hair-raising experience such as this. We should take the steps to protect ourselves, relax in the clean room, and sleep tight instead of letting the bedbugs bite.

The Cost of Our Conscience: Changing Patent Laws for Overpriced Prescription Drugs

James M. Ficaro, University of Texas at Austin

Stephanie Ray and Justine Namuli have a lot in common. Both are nine years old, both enjoy playing house, chasing young boys around their neighborhood, and both are infected with HIV, the virus that causes AIDS. But that is where the similarities end, because Stephanie lives in Phoenix, Arizona, where she will receive regular treatment and medicine and is expected to live into late adulthood. Justine lives in Kamapala, Uganda, where she will not receive such treatment and will not live past the age of twenty-seven. What a difference 9,000 miles can make.

The *World Health Organization* March 2001 fact sheet reports that "every year 12.7 million people living outside the United States, die of infectious diseases." The *Strait Times of Singapore* of March 3, 2001, notes that "this is due, in large part, to unnecessarily overpriced prescription drugs." While a problem that exists worlds away may seem to have little effect on us, the *Baltimore Sun* of March 4, 2001, explains that the U.S. National Security Council has recently announced that infectious diseases in foreign nations pose a threat to U.S. national security because they can lead to revolutionary war and ethnic wars, genocide, and even political destabilization. So, to better understand how we can make prescription drugs more available to those who need them most, we must first examine why our help is warranted, second understand why these drugs are so expensive, and finally offer a new plan to help prevent this epidemic from continuing.

The issue of prescription drugs was one that was expressly addressed during the U.S. 2000 presidential election. And while this problem does exist domestically, the U.S. situation pales in comparison to the one overseas. The March 24, 2001, *Boston Globe* reports that "malaria kills one million people a year, tuberculosis kills two million a year and cholera kills nearly three million a year; yet virtually none of these deaths occur within U.S. borders." *CNN Online* of March 9, 2001, explains that while "treatments exist for the 25 million infected with this trio of diseases, less than one half of one percent can actually afford them." Moreover, *Time* magazine of February 12, 2001, notes, "of the 36 million people in the world infected with AIDS, 99% of them live in developing nations, which simply cannot afford treatment."

Americans are at risk too. Epidemics simply don't stop at borders or bodies of water, many of these near-eradicated illnesses can quickly re-enter America because more and more immigrants are entering the United States with infectious diseases. The *Columbus Dispatch* of January 27, 2001, reports that "over 40% of all new tuberculosis cases are found in foreign residents." Just last year in Virginia, a tuberculosis outbreak infected 78 people and was traced back to a Russian emigrant who was working at a Burger King. Dr. Lee Reichmann, a tuberculosis expert, told *60 Minutes* on July 23, 2000, that "a new tuberculosis drug has not been created in nearly 25 years and if an epidemic were to start in the U.S. there would not be enough drugs to stop it."

Fortunately, this problem is easily traced to the pharmaceutical industry; a business where morals are skewed by the bottom line. This is apparent through their abuse of the U.S. patent system and price inflation.

Under normal conditions, a patent for a new drug lasts only ten years. During that time no other company may produce that drug. After ten years, however, the patent expires and other companies are allowed to produce generic versions of the name brand drug. But there are some ways around the patent system and name-brand pharmaceutical companies are taking advantage of them in order to prolong their patents. The *Minneapolis Star-Tribune* of February 12, 2001, reports that many pharmaceutical companies actually pay generic companies to not produce a generic brand of their drug after the patent has expired. Federal Trade Commission is currently investigating a domestic case that alleges that pharmaceutical giant Eli Lilly paid rival Mylon Laboratories $147 million not to produce a generic form of Prozac when its patent expires at the end of this year. Also, another scheme that many pharmaceutical companies employ is to alter their drug in some way so that its effect is the same, yet the drug is different enough to warrant a new patent. The *Glasgow Herald* of August 11, 2000, notes, "even changing the color of a pill can allow a drug to be re-patented," assuring another ten years of profit for the pharmaceutical industry.

The pharmaceutical industry is also guilty of price inflation. Many drug companies contend that they must charge these high prices in order to keep up the high rate of research and development that they perform. But these concerns are grossly exaggerated. The *Boston Globe* of March 1, 2001, reports that the U.S. federal government through the National Institute of Health (NIH) pays for one half of all basic research and development performed by the private sector. The industry only has to pay $25 billion a year, pocket change for a group of companies that last year grossed over $106 billion in profits alone. The *Wall Street Journal* of March 7, 2001, goes even further explaining, "pharmaceutical companies could reduce prices by as much as 50% and still earn massive profits." Besides, this practice could represent potential violations of U.S. anti-trust legislation. After all, *Forbes* magazine of March 5, 2001, reminds us that a federal judge in California found Microsoft guilty in a class action lawsuit of "knowingly overcharging their consumers for their product." And that was computer software; the pharmaceutical companies are letting millions of people die in their quest for the almighty dollar.

While definitely a daunting task, this problem is not an insurmountable one; there are some things that can be done but the government as well as us, needs to get involved.

First, the government should enact an emergency patent relief law, which would temporarily circumvent patent rights in times of emergency. Doing so will allow other drug companies to produce generic versions of life-saving drugs that could cost as much as a third less, notes the *Milwaukee Journal Sentinel* of March 7, 2001. Already, explains the *New York Times* of April 20, 2001, the South African government has recently enacted an emergency patent relief law, which allowed them to produce cheaper versions of crucial drugs. Forty pharmaceutical companies filed suit to invalidate the law, but recently dropped the case, acknowledging the enforceability of the legislation. The United States must now take the lead and set a global precedent.

Second, as an incentive to any company that sells its drugs overseas at cost or donates them, the U.S. government should offer a corporate tax subsidy. While it is sad that such a wealthy industry requires such motivation to do the right thing the U.S. government must use whatever means necessary to remedy this problem. The *New York Times* of January 20, 2001, reports that the "U.S. government budgets $1.5 billion to fight AIDS and other infectious diseases worldwide." By using a portion of this money to cover these corporate tax breaks, the U.S. government will be able to solve this problem at its core; by allowing the necessary drugs to be distributed to those [who] need them most.

Finally, we must understand that worldwide epidemics are not solved in a matter of ten minutes and that individual solutions are hard to come by, yet as college students, faculty, and concerned citizens, there are some things we can do. First, we must follow the example of students from Yale University. The *Montreal Gazette* of March 24, 2001, reports that after several students discovered that the university owned a patent for a crucial ingredient in anti-AIDS medication, campus-wide protests and class boycotts occurred. The result: Yale University has now relaxed its patent. Many universities have such patents since most of the research for these advanced drugs is conducted at universities. To find out what drug patents your college or university may own just swing by your biochemistry department; the information is readily available. Finally, as the world's second largest generation in history, one which will soon be in charge of companies just like Eli Lilly, we must continue to practice some sort of corporate responsibility; that we understand they want to make money . . . but at what cost to our conscience.

Even though this problem resides in a world many of us can hardly begin to comprehend, it makes the effort no less necessary. By examining the need for a new plan of action, understanding where the obstacles lie, and finally exploring new solutions we were able to understand that this problem can and needs to be solved. In order to completely understand the experiences faced by Justine Namuli, consider the self-exam offered by the *Arizona Republic* of July 6, 2000. "Close your eyes and picture the United States with 70% of all adults ill from a deadly disease . . . then pretend you can't afford the cure."

 ## Schadenfreude

by Karon Bowers, Bradley University

It was a whirlwind romance of chicken McNuggets, sweaty smooches, and fumbling passes. It was my junior year. I was a cheerleader dating the football team captain. It was my birthday—Thursday, 10:30 A.M., right after third period typing, in the locker bay. It happened to be the celebration of our one-month anniversary. But Captain Cool decided to dump me for a really ugly freshman cheerleader, Thelma Valentine. I hated her. According to "Dear Diary" entry number 430, October 1, 1986: "Weren't you the one that tried to hurt me with goodbye? Did you think I'd crumble? Did you think I'd lay down and die? Oh no. Not I. I will survive. Hey. Hey."* After wishing for every possible disaster, from car crashes to a burning case of any venereal disease, I resigned myself to accepting fate and cheering on everyone—but him: "Go team go! Go all the way! Except for Shawn, I hope you die today!" My dreams came true. He broke his arm. Yes! Life was beautiful! There was to be no date! I was overcome by inner pleasure over his misfortune. What was I experiencing? The knowledge that I was Elizabeth Montgomery's bewitched TV child Tabitha. Okay, maybe not, but it was schadenfreude. Not Frugen Glazen or Farfigneuten, but Schadenfreude, that little twinge of pleasure we all feel when fate deals a bad hand—to someone else.

In order to understand this phenomenon, we must, first, learn how to spell it; second, examine what schadenfreude is; third, focus on why it exists; and finally, explore some ways we can learn to deal with schadenfreude.

Now first, schadenfreude—S-C-H-A-D-E-N-F-R-E-U-D-E—schadenfreude.

Second, what does this word mean? *Schadenfreude* is a German word with *schaden* meaning "damage" and *freude* meaning "joy." This is not to be confused with Sigmund Freud(e), who studied a different kind of joy all together.

*"I Will Survive" Words and music by Frederick J. Perren and Dino Fekaris. Copyright © 1978 Universal-Polygram International Publishing, Inc. on behalf of itself and Perren-Vibes Music, Inc. (ASCAP) International copyright secured. All rights reserved.

Schadenfreudites live by the philosophy, "It's not enough that I succeed. Others must fail." You know, it's that feeling you get when you see someone getting a ticket on the side of the road. You're not thinking, "Oh gosh buddy, tough break." You're thinking, "Ha Ha, you got a ticket, not me."

In *Newsweek* of November 2, 1987, Michael O'Neill explains that schadenfreude is our way of asserting superiority over others and thus feeling better about ourselves. But have you ever been sitting there, mocking the fuchsia and pea green lavender fashion fiasco on the guy next to you, only to turn around and find your best friend laughing at your Farrah Fawcett, dippity-dooed, Aquanet hair-sprayed bouffant, velour v-neck, Hushpuppy sweater, and dirt-brown, wedged Bass loafers? I have. It's not funny.

Well, now that we know how to spell *schadenfreude* and what it is, we need to understand why it exists. One reason we experience schadenfreude is that we are, by nature, competitive. "Oh no, Karon, say it isn't so! Say that I have been doing this activity all of my life just for the camaraderie." Yeah, right, and Debbie did Dallas just for artistic integrity! The February 1991 edition of *Gentleman's Quarterly*—I read it for the Obsession ads—explains that schadenfreude breeds in environments where success and failure are measured. Take for example the Olympic finals of women's figure skating. You know, when I saw Kristi Yamaguchi fall, I thought, "Oh, Kristi. You sold the gold. It's Debi Thomas revisited." But then I sat and watched as every other skater fell on her sequined, cheesy, tutu pitooter, and I thought, "Hey, Kristi, way to go for the gold. You hexed 'em!" Schadenfreude. Now that's some ancient secret, huh? For many of us though, success is not always winning the big prize. It's just getting closer to it than our rivals do, which often pits us in a battle of one-upmanship. "You think you had it rough? My dad grounded me for three weeks!" "Well, my dad locked me in the garage for three days!" "Well, my dad used to stab me!" "Oh yeah? How hard and how many times?"

Another reason we experience schadenfreude is that we are all afraid of failing. In her book, *The Impostor Phenomenon,* Dr. Pauline Rose Clance explains that the fear of failure invades our lives. So when we have an opportunity to laugh at someone else, it gives us a sense of reprieve. The clown slipping on a banana peel allows us to laugh freely because we realize that he is in no real danger. The mime slipping on a banana peel and snapping his spine in two assures us that there is justice in the world. However, if you see an old woman on a walker ambling down the street, and suddenly she slips on a banana peel and her life alert button is nowhere to be found . . . yeah, well, maybe it's not that healthy. The point is, as long as it's not our butts getting busted, it's funny. These feelings are very natural. It's only when individuals allow themselves to become victims of schadenfreude that they tend to believe that they are supreme beings, that no one and nothing can touch them. Witness Leona Helmsley. Witness Leona Helmsley going off to jail. Witness Leona Helmsley being dragged around prison hooked to the belt loops of Carol, being traded for a carton of Newport Kings. In reality, these individuals merely avoid any real world situation that would put them at risk, limiting their ability to learn and grow.

So far we've examined what schadenfreude is and why it exists, and now it's time to learn how we can deal with it.

First, we need to learn to question our own behavior and actions rather than laughing at others' shortcomings. As Molly Douglas explains in her book, *Teen Girl Talk: A Guide to Beauty, Fashion, and Health,* "Unfortunately, today's society implies that only the beautiful succeed. Dismiss this theory now! It's rubbish! And as for others, remember it is important to have inner beauty." Well, Douglas goes on to state, "Your first period can be worrisome, but it shouldn't be." Liar! By focusing on improving our own behavior and actions rather than laughing at others' shortcomings, we can not only sincerely feel better about ourselves, but also be more likable, have friends, get picked first in kickball, get those nice, cute bunny Valentines instead of the hippo-rhino-snake-buzzard-circling-over-a-dead-carcass-on-a-highway variety which you used to give to all those schadenfreudites in the fourth grade.

Second, we need to realize that failures are as important as successes. As Michael O'Neill explains in his article, "Let's Hear It for the Losers," "Losing is a primal element of progress." You lose only to gain more later. This is also known as the Oprah Winfrey diet plan.

Finally, if you continue to feel little twinges of schadenfreude, remember the immortal words of Dire Straits: "Sometimes you're the windshield. Sometimes you're the bug." Sometimes you feel like a nut. Sometimes you don't . . . because schadenfreude is a question of perspective.

Well, after understanding what schadenfreude is, why it exists, and how we can learn to deal with it, it is clear that schadenfreude will continue to be a part of the human psyche. It's only after we understand the schadenfreude beast that we can tame it.

So, what happened when my latest beau dumped me? It was our fourth anniversary. It was the day before our wedding. It was while I was getting my new Toni perm. I said, "Stop right there. I gotta know right now. Do you love me? Will you love me forever?" Witness "Dear Diary" entry number 2786, March 27, 1992. "Dear Diary: I gave him Thelma's number. They deserve each other."

Notes

CHAPTER 1

1. Louis Nizer, Reflections Without Mirrors, quoted in Jack Valenti, *Speak Up with Confidence: How to Prepare, Learn, and Deliver Effective Speeches* (New York: Morrow, 1982) 34.
2. James C. Humes, *The Sir Winston Method: Five Secrets of Speaking the Language of Leadership* (New York: Morrow, 1991) 13–14.
3. As quoted in Brent Filson, *Executive Speeches: Tips on How to Write and Deliver Speeches from 51 CEOs* (New York: Wiley, 1994) 1.
4. Dee-Ann Durbin, "Study: Plenty of Jobs for Graduates in 2000," *Austin American-Statesman* 5 Dec. 1999: A28.
5. Dan B. Curtis, Jerry L. Winsor, and Ronald D. Stephens, "National Preferences in Business and Communication Education," *Communication Education* 38 (Jan. 1989) 6–14. See also Iain Hay, "Justifying and Applying Oral Presentations in Geographical Education," *Journal of Geography in Higher Education* 18. 1 (1994): 44–45.
6. John F. Kennedy, Inaugural Address of 1961 (Washington, DC: National Archives and Records Administration, 1987) 6.
7. Melinda Henneberger, "In Speech Process Reversal, Gore Wrote, Aides Whittled," *The New York Times* 18 Aug. 2000: A1.
8. Frank Bruni, "Bush Returns to Yale, But Welcome Is Not All Warm," *The New York Times* 22 May 2001: A10.
9. L. M. Boyd, syndicated column, *Austin American-Statesman* 8 Aug. 2000: E3.
10. Herman Cohen, *The History of Speech Communication: The Emergence of a Discipline: 1914–1945* (Annandale, VA: Speech Communication Association, 1994) 2.
11. Mark Twain, *The Adventures of Tom Sawyer,* 1876, ed. Stephen Railton and the U of Virginia Library, 2000, 4 July 2001 <http://etext.virginia.edu/railton/about/srchmtf.html>.
12. George W. Bush, Address to the nation on 11 Sept. 2001, in *The New York Times* 22 Sept. 2001: A4.
13. Adetokunbo F. Knowles-Borishade, "Paradigm for Classical African Orature," *Diversity in Public Communication: A Reader,* Christine Kelly et al. ed. (Dubuque, IA: Kendall-Hunt, 1995) 100.
14. Patricia A. Sullivan, "Signification and African-American Rhetoric: A Case Study of Jesse Jackson's 'Common Ground and Common Sense' Speech," *Communication Quarterly* 41.1 (1993): 1–15.
15. George W. Bush, Address to a joint session of Congress on 20 Sept. 2001, 21 Sept. 2001 <http://dailynews.yahoo.com/h/ap/2000920/us/bush_text.html>.

CHAPTER 2

1. Survey conducted by R. H. Bruskin and Associates, *Spectra* 9 (Dec. 1973): 4.
2. Steven Booth Butterfield, "Instructional Interventions for Situational Anxiety and Avoidance," *Communication Education* 37 (1988): 214–23.
3. Joe Ayres and Theodore S. Hopf, "The Long-Term Effect of Visualization in the Classroom: A Brief Research Report," *Communication Education* 39 (1990): 75–78.
4. Maili Porhola, "Orientation Styles in a Public-Speaking Context," paper presented at the national Communication Association Convention, Seattle, Washington, Nov. 2000; Ralph R. Behnke and Michael J. Beatty, "A Cognitive-Physiological Model of Speech Anxiety," *Communication Monographs* 48 (1981): 158–163.
5. Amy M. Bippus and John A. Daly, "What Do People Think Causes Stage Fright?" Naïve Attributions About the Reasons for Public-Speaking Anxiety," *Communication Education* 48 (1999): 63–72.
6. Ralph R. Behnke and Chris R. Sawyer, "Milestones of Anticipatory Public-Speaking Anxiety," *Communication Education* 48 (Apr. 1999): 165–72; Chris R. Sawyer and Ralph R. Behnke, "State Anxiety Patterns for Public Speaking and the Behavior Inhibition System," *Communication Reports* 12 (Winter 1999): 33–41.
7. Leon Fletcher, *How to Design & Deliver Speeches* (New York: Longman, 2001) 3.
8. Peter D. MacIntyre and J. Renee MacDonald, "Public-Speaking Anxiety: Perceived Competence and Audience Congeniality," *Communication Education* 47 (Oct. 1998):359–65.
9. Joe Ayers and Theodore S. Hopf, "Visualization: A Means of Reducing Speech Anxiety," *Communication Education* 34 (1985): 318–23.
10. Joe Ayres and Brian L. Heuett, "An Examination of the Impact of Performance Visualization," *Communication Research Reports* 16 (1999): 29–39.
11. MacIntyre and MacDonald, "Public-Speaking Anxiety" R. B. Rubin, A. M. Rubin, and F. F. Jordan, "Effects of Instruction on Communication Apprehension and Communication Competence," *Communication Education* 46 (1997): 104–14.
12. Peter D. MacIntyre and J. Renee MacDonald, "Public-Speaking Anxiety" Peter D. MacIntyre and K. A. Thivierge, "The Effects of Audience Pleasantness, Audience Familiarity, and Speaking Contexts on Public-Speaking Anxiety and Willingness to Speak," *Communication Quarterly* 43 (1995): 456–66; Peter D. MacIntyre, K. A. Thivierge, and J. Renee MacDonald, "The Effects of Audience Interest, Responsiveness, and Evaluation on Public-Speaking Anxiety and Related Variables," *Communication Research Reports* 14 (1997): 157–68.
13. Ralph R. Behnke and Chris R. Sawyer, "Public Speaking Procrastination as a Correlate of Public-Speaking Communication Apprehension and Self-Perceived Public-Speaking Competence," *Communication Research Reports* 16 (1999): 40–47.

14. The late Waldo Braden, long-time professor of speech communication at Louisiana State U, presented a memorable speech at the 1982 Florida Speech Communication Association in which he emphasized "The audience writes the speech" to indicate the importance and centrality of being an audience-centered speaker.

15. Clifford Stoll, as cited by Kevin A. Miller, "Capture: The Essential Survival Skill for Leaders Buckling Under Information Overload," *Leadership* (Spring 102): 85.

16. Greg Winter, "The Chips are Down: Frito-Lay Cuts Costs with Smaller Servings," *Austin-American Statesman* 2 Jan. 2001: A6.

17. We thank Barbara Patton of Southwest Texas State U for sharing her speech outline with us.

18. Sample speech written by Christopher D. Therit, Millersville U, Department of Communication and Theatre, Millersville, Pennsylvania.

CHAPTER 3

1. Bill Carter and Felicity Barringer, "Patriotic Time, Dissent Is Muted," *The New York Times* 28 Sept. 2001: B8.

2. National Communication Association, "NCA Credo for Communication Ethics," 1999, 27 June 2001 <http://www.natcom.org/conferences/Ethics/ethicsconfcredo99.htm>.

3. Samuel Walker, *Hate Speech* (Lincoln: University of Nebraska Press, 1994) 162.

4. "Libel and Slander," *The Ethical Spectacle* 1 June 1997 <http://www.spectacle.org/freespch/musm/libel.html>.

5. "Three Decades Later, Free Speech Vets Return to UC Berkeley," *Sacramento Bee* 3 Dec. 1994: A1.

6. James S. Tyre, "Legal Definition of Obscenity; Pornography," 1 June 1997 <http://internet.ggu.edu/university_library/reg/_legal_obscene.html>.

7. "Supreme Court Rules: Cyberspace Will be Free! ACLU Hails Victory in Internet Censorship Challenge," *American Civil Liberties Union Freedom Network* 26 June 1997, 1 June 1998 <http://www.aclu.org/news/no62697a.html>.

8. Sue Anne Pressley, "Oprah Winfrey Wins Case Filed by Cattlemen," *Washington Post* 27 Feb. 1998, 1 June 1998 <http://www.washingtonpost.com/wp-srv/WPlate/1998-02/27/1001-022798-idx.html>.

9. Carter and Barringer, A1.

10. Walker, *Hate Speech,* 2.

11. Edwin R. Bayley, *Joe McCarthy and the Press* (Madison: Wisconsin U Press, 1981) 29.

12. Tom Wicker, "Improving the Debates," *The New York Times* 21 June 1991 A16.

13. Bill Bradley, "Race and the American City," address delivered in the U.S. Senate, 26 Mar. 1992, reprinted in *Representative American Speeches, 1991–92,* ed. Owen Peterson (New York: Wilson, 1992) 139.

14. Peg Tyre, "Improving on History," *Newsweek* 2 July 2001: 34.

15. Tyre, "Improving on History" 34.

16. *Publication Manual of the American Psychological Association,* 4th ed. (Washington, DC: American Psychological Association, 1994) 294.

17. New York City Department of Health, "Facts About Mold" Mar. 2001, 27 June 2001 <http://www.ci.nyc.ny.us/html/doh/html/ei/eimold.html>.

18. Harold Barrett, *Rhetoric and Civility: Human Development, Narcissism, and the Good Audience* (Albany: SUNY, 1991) 154.

19. Kenneth L. Woodward, "Heard Any Good Sermons Lately?" *Newsweek* 4 Mar. 1996: 51.

20. Patricia Sullivan, "Signification and African-American Rhetoric: A Case Study of Jesse Jackson's 'Common Ground and Common Sense' Speech," *Communication Quarterly* 41.1 (1993): 11.

21. Richard M. Weaver, "A Responsible Rhetoric," delivered at Purdue University, 29 Mar. 1955, ed. Thomas Clark and Richard Johannesen for *The Intercollegiate Review* (Winter 1976–77): 82.

22. Waldo W. Braden, *Abraham Lincoln, Public Speaker* (Baton Rouge: Louisiana State U P, 1988) 90.

23. Bob Dart, "How a Team of Writers Crafted the Bush Speech," *The Austin American-Statesman* 22 Sept. 2001: A6.

24. Adam Nagourney, "Speakers Being Given Absolute Freedom to Stick to the Script," *The New York Times* 3 Aug. 2000): A21.

CHAPTER 4

1. Study conducted by Paul Cameron, as cited in Ronald B. Adler and Neil Town, *Looking Out/Looking In: Interpersonal Communications* (New York: Holt, Rinehart and Winston, 1981) 218.

2. L. Boyd, *Austin-American Statesman* 7 Dec. 1995: E7.

3. John T. Masterson, Steven A. Beebe, and Norman H. Watson, *Invitation to Effective Speech Communication* (Glenview, IL: Scott, Foresman, 1989) 4.

4. Ralph G. Nichols and Leonard A. Stevens, "Six Bad Listening Habits," in *Are You Listening?* (New York: McGraw-Hill, 1957).

5. M. Fitch-Hauser, D. A. Barker, and A. Hughes, "Receiver Apprehension and Listening Comprehension: A Linear or Curvilinear Relationship?" *Southern Communication Journal* (1988): 62–71.

6. Fitch-Hauser, Barker, and Hughes, "Receiver Apprehension and Listening Comprehension."

7. Albert Mehrabian, *Nonverbal Communication* (Hawthorne, NY: Aldine, 1972).

8. Paul Ekman and Wallace Friesen, "Head and Body Cues in the Judgement of Emotion: A Reformulation," *Perceptual and Motor Skills* 25 (1967): 711–24.

9. Nichols and Stevens, "Six Bad Listening Habits."

10. Paul Rankin, "Listening Ability: Its Importance, Measurement and Development," *Chicago Schools Journal* 12 (Jan. 1930): 177–79.

11. John N. Gardner and A. Jerome Jewler. *Your College Experiences: Strategies for Success,* 2nd ed. (Belmont, CA: Wadsworth, 1995) 104.

12. Mike Allen, Sandra Berkowitz, Steve Hunt, and Allan Louden, "A Meta-Analysis of the Impact of Forensics and Communication Education on Critical Thinking," *Communication Education* 48 (Jan. 1999): 18–30.

13. Cited by Marie Hochmuth, ed., A *History and Criticism of American Public Address,* vol. 3 (New York: Longmans, Green, 1955) 4; and James R. Andrews, *The Practice of Rhetorical Criticism* (New York: Macmilllan, 1983) 3–4.

14. Andrews, *The Practice of Rhetorical Criticism.*

15. John T. Masterson, Steven A. Beebe, and Norman H. Watson, *Invitation to Effective Speech Communication* (Glenview, IL.: Scott, Foresman, 1989) 5.

CHAPTER 5

1. For an excellent review of gender and persuasability research see Daniel J. O'Keefe, *Persuasion: Theory and Research* (Newbury Park, CA: Sage, 1990) 176–77. Also see James B. Stiff, *Persuasive Communication* (New York: The Guilford Press, 1994) 133–36.

2. O'Keefe, *Persuasion.*

3. O'Keefe, *Persuasion.*

4. Gregory Herek, "Study Offers 'Snapshot' of Sacramento-Area Lesbian, Gay, and Bisexual Community," 23 July 2001 <http://psy-web.ucdavis.edu/rainbow/html/sacramento_study.html>.

5. For an excellent literature review about sexual orientation and communication, see T. P. Mottet, "The Role of Sexual Orientation in Predicting Outcome Value and Anticipated Communication Behaviors," *Communication Quarterly* 48 (2000): 233–239.

6. The research summarized here is based on pioneering work by Geert Hofstede, *Culture's Consequences: International Differences in Work-Related Values* (Beverly Hills, CA: Sage, 1984). Also see Edward T. Hall, *Beyond Culture* (New York: Doubleday, 1976).

7. Genaro C. Armas, "Foreign-Born Population in U.S. Tops 28.3 Million," *Austin-American Statesman* 3 Jan. 2001: 2A.

8. Todd S. Purdum, "California Census Confirms Whites Are in Minority," *The New York Times* 30 Mar. 2001: 1A.

9. Eric Schmitt, "Whites in Minority in Largest Cities, the Census Shows," *The New York Times* 30 Apr. 2001: A1.

10. Genaro C. Armas, "Early Census Results Show an Increase in County's Diversity," *Austin-American Statesman* 9 Mar. 2001: A7.

11. Armas, "Early Census Results."

12. David W. Kale, "Ethics in Intercultural Communication," in *Intercultural Communication: A Reader*, 6th ed., ed. Larry A. Samovar and Richard E. Porter (Belmont, CA: Wadsworth, 1991) 423; also see discussion in Myron W. Lustig and Jolene Koester, *Intercultural Competence: Interpersonal Communication Across Cultures* (New York: HarperCollins, 1996) 347.

13. Larry A. Samovar and Richard E. Porter, *Communication Between Cultures* (Stamford, CT: Wadsworth and Thomson Learning, 2001) 29.

14. Henry Sweets, "Mark Twain in India," *The Fence Painter: Bulletin of the Mark Twain Boyhood Home Associates* 26 (Winter 1996): 1.

15. For an excellent discussion of how to adapt to specific audience situations, see Jo Sprague and Douglas Stuart, *The Speaker's Handbook* (Fort Worth: Harcourt, Brace, Jovanovich, 1992) 345.

16. Lieberman, *Public Speaking in the Multicultural Environment*. (Boston: Allyn and Bacon, 2000). Also see Edward T. Hall, *The Silent Language* (Greenwich, CT: Fawcett, 1959); and Edward T. Hall, *The Hidden Dimension* (Garden City, NY: Doubleday, 1966).

● CHAPTER 6

1. L. M. Boyd, syndicated column.

2. Bruce Gronbeck, from his presidential address, delivered at the annual conference of the Speech Communication Association, ts., November 1994.

3. Henry H. Sweets III, "Mark Twain's Lecturing Career Continuation—Part II," *The Fence Painter* (Winter 2000–2001).

4. Monique Russo, "The 'Starving Disease' or Anorexia Nervosa," student speech, University of Miami, 1984.

5. Jennifer Travis, "The World Through a Child's Eyes," in *Winning Orations 1994* (Mankato, MN: Interstate Oratorical Association, 1994) 103.

6. Brian Sosnowchik, "The Cries of American Ailments," in *Winning Orations 2000* (Mankato, MN: Interstate Oratorical Association, 2000) 114.

7. Judith Humphrey, "Taking the Stage: How Women Can Achieve a Leadership Presence," *Vital Speeches of the Day* 1 May 2001: 437.

8. Adapted from Erin Gallagher, "Upholstered Furniture Fires: Sitting in the *Uneasy* Chair," in *Winning Orations 2000* (Mankato, MN: Interstate Oratorical Association, 2000) 99–101.

9. Adapted from Nicole Tremel, "The New Wasteland: Computers," in *Winning Orations 2000* (Mankato, MN: Interstate Oratorical Association, 2000).

10. Erin Kane, "Alternative Defense," in *Winning Orations 1995* (Mankato, MN: Interstate Oratorical Association, 1995) 82.

● CHAPTER 7

1. Richard J. Smith and Mark Gibbs, *Navigating the Internet* (Indianapolis: Same Publishing, 1994) 2.

2. The authors are indebted to Terrence A. Doyle's *Quick Guide to the Internet for Speech Communication* (Boston: Allyn and Bacon, 1998), from which much of the information in this section, including the advanced search activity and the Website annotations, is taken or adapted.

3. Elizabeth Kirk, "Practical Steps in Evaluating Internet Resources," 7 May 2001, 22 May 2001 <http://milton.mse.jhu.edu:8001/research/education/practical.html>.

4. James A. W. Heffernan et al., *Writing: A College Handbook*, 5th ed. (New York: Norton, 2001) 53–54.

5. Paul Gorski, "A Multicultural Model for Evaluating Educational Web Sites," Dec. 1999, 22 May 2001 <http://curry.edschool.virginia.edu/go/multicultural/ net/comps/model.html>.

6. Matthew Mirapaul, "Making Federal Web Sites Friendly to Disabled Users," *The New York Times* 11 June 2001: B2.

7. The World's Easiest Quiz? Joke-of-the-Day.com. (25 Feb. 1998): http://www.joke-of-the-day.com Copyright 1997/1998 JOKE-OF-THE-DAY.com/TWT. All rights reserved. Permission is granted to reprint or distribute Joke-of-the-Day's jokes as long as this full copyright notice is included, including the subscription information. To get a joke every day, e-mail us at <Subscribe@joke-of-the-day.com>.

● CHAPTER 8

1. Bettijane Levine, "Fighting the Giant," *Los Angeles Times* 10 Aug. 1994: E-1.

2. Eric Quinones, "It Was a Dark and Stormy Sales Pitch, and Maybe It Worked," *The New York Times* 1 Aug. 1999: BU4.

3. Tami Longaberger, "Diversity: It's Right, It's Here, Embrace It," *Vital Speeches of the Day* 15 Nov. 2000: 91.

4. George W. Bush, address to a joint session of Congress on 20 Sept. 2001 (21 Sept. 2001): <http://dailynews.yahoo.com/h/ap/20010920/us/bush_text.html>.

5. Glen Martin, "Tragic Trilogy," in *Winning Orations 1994* (Mankato, MN: Interstate Oratorical Association, 1994) 74.

6. Carrie A. Lydon, "Higher Exploitation: Universities Profiting from Sweatshop Labor," in *Winning Orations 2000* (Mankato, MN: Interstate Oratorical Association, 2000) 34.

7. Professor Frazer White, University of Miami.

8. Patricia Lopez, "Hear Today—Gone Tomorrow," in *Winning Orations 1999* (Mankato, MN: Interstate Oratorical Association, 1999) 56.

9. Tammy Frisby, "Floss or Die," in *Winning Orations 1998* (Mankato, MN: Interstate Oratorical Association, 1998) 68.

10. Nathaniel Grow, untitled speech, in *Winning Orations 2000* (Mankato, MN: Interstate Oratorical Association, 2000) 96.

11. Shannon Burger, "Will It Hurt?" in *Winning Orations 1994* (Mankato, MN: Interstate Oratorical Association, 1994) 89.

12. "Emotional Abuse," *Austin American-Statesman* 14 Jan. 1988: E2.

13. Barbara Bush, "Choices and Change" (1 June 1990), in Halford Ross Ryan, ed., *Contemporary American Public Discourse* (Prospect Heights, IL: Waveland Press, 1992) 382.

14. Percy Bysshe Shelly, "Ode to the West Wind."

15. Sonya Dehn, "A Silent Thief," in *Winning Orations 1995* (Mankato, MN: Interstate Oratorical Association 1995) 96.

16. Elizabeth Cady Stanton, address to the first women's rights convention (1848), in Houston Peterson, ed., *A Treasury of the World's Great Speeches* (New York: Simon & Schuster, 1965) 388–92.

17. Eric B. Wolff, title unknown, in *Winning Orations 1994* (Mankato, MN: Interstate Oratorical Association, 1994) 67.

18. Richard D. Propes, "Alone in the Dark," in *Winning Orations 1985* (Mankato, MN: Interstate Oratorical Association) 23.

19. Ajay Krishnan, "Is Mr. Goodwrench Really Mr. Rip Off?" in *Winning Orations 1998* (Mankato, MN: Interstate Oratorical Association, 1998) 120.

20. "Sorry, You've Got the Wrong Number," *The New York Times* 26 May 2001: A17.

21. Joseph D. Stephens, "Corporate Sponsored Day Care," in *Winning Orations 1985* (Mankato, MN: Interstate Oratorical Association, 1985) 83.

22. George W. Bush, address to a joint session of Congress on 27 Feb. 2001, in *Congressional Quarterly Weekly* 3 Mar. 2001: 497.

23. Sandra Mims Rowe, "Leading the Way Out of the Credibility Crisis," delivered to the American Society of Newspaper Editors annual convention, 1 Apr. 1998, in Calvin M. Logue and Jean DeHart, eds., *Representative American Speeches 1998–1999* (New York: Wilson, 2000) 176.

24. Kate Schlemmer, "ABC and Decay," in *Winning Orations 1995* (Mankato, MN: Interstate Oratorical Association, 1995) 29.

25. Dena Craig, "Clearing the Air About Cigars," in *Winning Orations 1998* (Mankato, MN: Interstate Oratorical Association, 1998) 13.

26. Rajiv Khanna, "Distortion of History," in *Winning Orations 2000* (Mankato, MN: Interstate Oratorical Association, 2000) 47.

27. Vanessa Harikul, "Prescription for Disaster," in *Winning Orations 2000* (Mankato, MN: Interstate Oratorical Association, 2000) 11.

28. Evelyn Breznik, "Our Nation's Shame: The Injustice of Idle Rape Kits," in *Winning Orations 2000* (Mankato, MN: Interstate Oratorical Association, 2000) 70.

29. Stephanie Aduloju, "Whitewashed," in *Winning Orations 2000* (Mankato, MN: Interstate Oratorical Association, 2000) 83.

30. Robert Rager, "Amusement Park Safety," in *Winning Orations 1985* (Mankato, MN: Interstate Oratorical Association, 1985) 38.

31. April Kinney, untitled speech, in *Winning Orations 2000* (Mankato, MN: Interstate Oratorical Association, 2000) 134.

32. Rager, "Amusement Park Safety" 38.

33. Rager, "Amusement Park Safety" 38.

34. Joseph K. Ott, "America's Internal Cold War," in *Winning Orations 1985* (Mankato, MN: Interstate Oratorical Association, 1985) 45.

35. Ott, "America's Internal Cold War" 45.

36. Nichole Olson, "Flying the Safer Skies," in *Winning Orations 2000* (Mankato, MN: Interstate Oratorical Association, 2000) 122.

CHAPTER 9

1. Adapted from Bill Gallagher, "E-911: A 'Call' for Reform," in *Winning Orations 1999* (Mankato, MN: Interstate Oratorical Association, 1999) 113–15.

2. Information in this example comes from National Institutes of Health, "Stem Cells: A Primer," May 2000 (19 July 2001): <http://www.nih.gov/news/stemcell/primer.htm>.

3. Adapted from John Kuehn, title unknown, *Winning Orations 1994* (Mankato, MN: Interstate Oratorical Association, 1994) 83–85.

4. Adapted from Vonda Ramey, "Can You Read This?" in *Winning Orations 1985* (Mankato, MN: Interstate Oratorical Association, 1985) 32–35.

5. Adapted from Laurel Johnson, "Where There's a Will There's a Way," in *Winning Orations 1986* (Mankato, MN: Interstate Oratorical Association, 1986) 59–62.

6. Adapted from Amy Stewart, title unknown, in *Winning Orations 1994* (Mankato, MN: Interstate Oratorical Association, 1994) 47–49.

7. The following information is adapted from Devorah A. Lieberman, *Public Speaking in the Multicultural Environment* (Englewood Cliffs, NJ: Prentice Hall, 1994).

8. Ben Sutherland, "Terminator 101: Media Literacy in the Information Age," in *Winning Orations 1995* (Mankato, MN: Interstate Oratorical Association, 1995) 33.

9. Loren Schwarzwalter, "An Answer for America's Future," in *Winning Orations 1987* (Mankato, MN: Interstate Oratorical Association, 1987) 86–87.

10. Mindy Moschel, "Something to Chew On," in *Winning Orations 2000* (Mankato, MN: Interstate Oratorical Association, 2000) 147.

11. Carrie A. Lydon, "Higher Exploitation: Universities Profiting from Sweatshop Labor," in *Winning Orations 2000* (Mankato, MN: Interstate Oratorical Association, 2000) 35.

12. Nichole Olson, "Flying the Safer Skies," in *Winning Orations 2000* (Mankato, MN: Interstate Oratorical Association, 2000) 122.

13. Rebecca Schwartz, "Personal Watercraft Safety," in *Winning Orations 1998* (Mankato, MN: Interstate Oratorical Association, 1998) 61.

14. Melody Hopkins, "Collegiate Athletes: A Contradiction in Terms," in *Winning Orations 1986* (Mankato, MN: Interstate Oratorical Association, 1986) 111.

15. Linh Thu Q. Do, "Children of the Diet Culture," in *Winning Orations 1999* (Mankato, MN: Interstate Oratorical Association, 1999) 122.

16. Arwen Williams, Organic Farming: Why Our Pesticide Paranoia Is Starving the World," in *Winning Orations 2000* (Mankato, MN: Interstate Oratorical Association, 2000) 145.

17. Molly A. Lovell, "Hotel Security: The Hidden Crisis," in *Winning Orations 1994* (Mankato, MN: Interstate Oratorical Association, 1994) 18.

18. Neela Latey, "U.S. Customs Procedures: Danger to Americans' Health and Society," in *Winning Orations 1986* (Mankato, MN: Interstate Oratorical Association, 1986) 22.

19. Susan Stevens, "Teacher Shortage," in *Winning Orations 1986* (Mankato, MN: Interstate Oratorical Association, 1986) 27.

20. Green, "Radon in Our Homes" 5.

21. Ben Crosby, "The New College Disease," in *Winning Orations 2000* (Mankato, MN: Interstate Oratorical Association, 2000) 133.

22. Lori Van Overbeke, "NutraSweet," in *Winning Orations 1986* (Mankato, MN: Interstate Oratorical Association, 1986) 58.

23. Adapted from Heath Honaker, "A New Brand of Homeless," in *Winning Orations 1986* (Mankato, MN: Interstate Oratorical Association, 1986) 108–11.

CHAPTER 10

1. Kathryn Kasdorf, untitled speech, in *Winning Orations 1985* (Mankato, MN: Interstate Oratorical Association, 1985) 16.

2. Vincent Stephens, "In the Eye of the Witness," in *Winning Orations 1995* (Mankato, MN: Interstate Oratorical Association, 1995) 50.

3. Cody Nesbitt, untitled speech, in *Winning Orations 2000* (Mankato, MN: Interstate Oratorical Association, 2000) 4.

4. Bill Gallagher, "E-911: A 'Call' for Reform," in *Winning Orations 1999* (Mankato, MN: Interstate Oratorical Association, 1999) 113.

5. Trent Lott, speech presented to the U.S. Chamber of Commerce, 14 Jan. 2001, in *Congressional Quarterly Weekly* 27 Jan. 2001: 241.

6. Jennifer Sweeney, "Racial Profiling," in *Winning Orations 2000* (Mankato, MN: Interstate Oratorical Association, 2000) 1.

7. Myles Brandy, "Academics First: Reforming Intercollegiate Athletics," *Vital Speeches of the Day* 1 Apr. 2001: 367.

8. Barbara Bush, "Choices and Change," *Vital Speeches of the Day* 1 July 1990: 549.

9. Jeffrey Zelms, "'The Survivor' Is a Sham: Mining and Minerals Are Real," *Vital Speeches of the Day* 15 Oct. 2000: 18–19.

10. Terrika Scott, "Curing Crisis with Community," in *Winning Orations 1995* (Mankato, MN: Interstate Oratorical Association, 1985) 11.

11. Theresa Clinkenbeard, "The Loss of Childhood," in *Winning Orations 1984* (Mankato, MN: Interstate Oratorical Association, 1987) 4.

12. Thad Noyes, "Dishonest Death Care," in *Winning Orations 1999* (Mankato, MN: Interstate Oratorical Association, 1999) 73.

13. Vance Coffman, "The Risk of Playing It Safe: The Importance of Research and Development," *Vital Speeches of the Day* 1 May 2001: 428.

14. Joe Griffith, *Speaker's Library of Business Stories, Anecdotes, and Humor* (Englewood Cliffs, NJ: Prentice Hall, 1990) 335.

15. Douglas MacArthur, "Farewell to the Cadets," address delivered at West Point, 12 May 1962. Reprinted in Richard L. Johannesen, R. R. Allen, and Wil A. Linkugel, eds., *Contemporary American Speeches*, 7th ed. (Dubuque, IA: Kendall/Hunt, 1992) 393.

16. "Insert Funny Story Here," *Austin American-Statesman* 7 Apr. 2001: A14.

17. Lisa M. Kralik, "Geographical Illiteracy," in *Winning Orations 1987* (Mankato, MN: Interstate Oratorical Association, 1987) 76.

18. Richard Propes, "Alone in the Dark," in *Winning Orations 1985* (Mankato, MN: Interstate Oratorical Association, 1985) 22.

19. Beth Moberg, "Licensed to Kill," in *Winning Orations 1985* (Mankato, MN: Interstate Oratorical Association, 1985) 89.

20. Jane M. Hatch, *The American Book of Days* (New York: Wilson, 1978).

21. Ruth W. Gregory, *Anniversaries and Holidays* (Chicago: American Library Association, 1975).
22. Laurette Koellner, "Managing Your Career: The Ultimate Solo Flight," *Vital Speeches of the Day* 15 Jan. 2001: 213.
23. Rebekah Olson, "Cherish Diversity," in *Winning Orations 1999* (Mankato, MN: Interstate Oratorical Association, 1999) 142.
24. Madeline Albright, "Building a Bipartisan Foreign Policy," address delivered at Rice University, 7 Feb. 1997. 24 June 1998 <http://riceinfo.rice.edu/projects/reno/speeches/19970207 _Albright_Baker. html>.
25. Al Gore, "The Cynics Are Wrong," address delivered at Harvard U, 9 June 1994. Abridged and reprinted in *Harvard Magazine* (July–Aug. 1994): 28.
26. Student speech, University of Miami, 1981.
27. John Ryan, "Emissions Tampering: Get the Lead Out," in *Winning Orations 1985* (Mankato, MN: Interstate Oratorical Association, 1985) 63.
28. MacArthur, "Farewell to the Cadets" 396.
29. Noelle Stephens, "the WWW.CON of Higher Education," in *Winning Orations 1999* (Mankato, MN: Interstate Oratorical Association, 1999) 12.
30. Amanda Taylor, "Antibacterial Products: The Dirty Truth," in *Winning Orations 1999* (Mankato, MN: Interstate Oratorical Association, 1999) 15.
31. David Naze, "Colon Cancer: The Insidious Disease," in *Winning Orations 1999* (Mankato, MN: Interstate Oratorical Association, 1999) 32.
32. Daniel Roth, "Homeless Gay and Lesbian Youth: Confronting an Unseen Problem," in *Winning Orations 2000* (Mankato, MN: Interstate Oratorical Association, 2000) 110.
33. Sonja Ralston, "Medical Reprocessing," in *Winning Orations 2000* (Mankato, MN: Interstate Oratorical Association, 2000) 131.
34. Robert Browning, "Rabbi Ben Ezra," *Dramatis Personae* (1864), quoted by John Mietus, Jr., "The Best Is Yet to Be," in *Winning Orations 1987* (Mankato, MN: Interstate Oratorical Association, 1987) 54.
35. Mietus, "The Best Is Yet to Be" 57.
36. Benjamin P. Berlinger, "Health and the Hubris of Human Nature: The Tragic Myth of Antibiotics," in *Winning Orations 1987* (Mankato, MN: Interstate Oratorical Association, 1987) 35.
37. Martin Luther King, Jr., "I Have a Dream," in Richard L. Johannesen, R. R. Allen, and Wil A. Linkugel, eds., *Contemporary American Speeches*, 7th ed. (Dubuque, IA: Kendall/Hunt, 1992) 369.
38. George W. Bush, weekly radio address delivered on 15 Sept. 2001. Reprinted in *The New York Times* 16 Sept. 2001: A5.
39. Travis Kirchhefer, "The Deprived," in *Winning Orations 2000* (Mankato, MN: Interstate Oratorical Association, 2000) 151.

● CHAPTER 11

1. Charles Parnell, "Speechwriting: The Profession and the Practice," *Vital Speeches of the Day* 15 Jan. 1990: 56.
2. Both sample outlines in this chapter are adapted from Amanda Taylor, "Drowsy Driving: A Deadly Epidemic," in *Winning Orations 2000* (Mankato, MN: Interstate Oratorical Association, 2000) 12–15.

● CHAPTER 12

1. Advertisements and headlines compiled by Jay Leno, *Headlines* (New York: Wing Books, 1992).
2. "President's Body Language Loud and Clear," *The Sun* (Baltimore) 10 Aug. 1994: 1D.
3. George W. Bush, Presidential victory speech, delivered at Austin, Texas, 13 Dec. 2000, 14 Dec. 2000: <http://dailynews.yahoo.com/h/ap/20001214/el/recount_bush_ text_1.html>.
4. Al Gore, "The Common Good of All Americans" (presidential election-concession speech), *Vital Speeches of the Day* 1 Jan. 2001: 163.
5. George W. Bush, remarks delivered on 14 Sept. 2001, at the Washington National Cathedral prayer service for victims of the September 11, 2001, terrorist attacks. Reprinted in *The New York Times* 15 Sept. 2001: A6.
6. Max Woodfin, "Three Among Many Lives Jordan Touched," *Austin American-Statesman* 20 Jan. 1996: A13.
7. National Archives and Records Administration, *Kennedy's Inaugural Address of 1961* (1987) 1.
8. Paul Roberts, "How to Say Nothing in Five Hundred Words," in William H. Roberts and Gregoire Turgeson, eds., *About Language* (Boston: Houghton Mifflin, 1986) 28.
9. George Orwell, "Politics and the English Language," reprinted in William H. Roberts and Gregoire Turgeson, eds., *About Language* (Boston: Houghton Mifflin, 1986) 282.
10. Erma Bombeck, "Missing Grammar Genes Is, Like, the Problem," *Austin American-Statesman* 3 Mar. 1992.
11. Ann Devroy, "House Republicans Get Talking Points: GOP Pollster's Memo Offers Advice on How to Win with Words," *Washington Post* 2 Feb. 1995: A9.
12. William Safire, "Words at War," *The New York Times Magazine* 30 Sept. 2001: Section 6.
13. John S. Seiter, Jarrod Larsen, and Jacey Skinner, "'Handicapped' or 'Handicappable?': The Effects of Language About Persons with Disabilities on Perceptions of Source Credibility and Persuasiveness," *Communication Reports* 11:1(1998): 21–31.
14. Edward Rothstein, "Is a Word's Definition in the Mind of the User?" *The New York Times* 25 Nov. 2000: A21.
15. Peggy Noonan, *What I Saw at the Revolution* (New York: Random House, 1990) 71.
16. Michael M. Klepper, *I'd Rather Die Than Give a Speech* (New York: Carol Publishing Group, 1994) 45.
17. We acknowledge the following source for several examples used in our discussion of language style: William Jordan, "Rhetorical Style," *Oral Communication Handbook* (Warrensburg, MO: Central Missouri State U, 1971–1972) 32–34.
18. Bill Clinton, "Farewell Address," *Vital Speeches of the Day* 1 Feb. 2001: 229.
19. "At College Graduations, Wit and Wisdom for the Price of Airfare," *The New York Times* 28 May 2001: A10.
20. Michiko Kakutani, "Struggling to Find Words for a Horror Beyond Words," *The New York Times* 13 Sept. 2001: E1.
21. National Archives and Records Administration, *Franklin Roosevelt's Inaugural Address of 1933* (1988) 22.
22. George F. Will, "'Let Us . . .'? No, Give It a Rest," *Newsweek* 22 Jan. 2001: 64.
23. John F. Kennedy, inaugural address (20 Jan. 1961), in Bower Aly and Lucille F. Aly, eds., *Speeches in English* (New York: Random House, 1968) 272
24. Boris Yeltsin, quoted in Charles W. Holmes, "Finale for a 'Century of Blood,'" *Austin American-Statesman* 18 July 1998: A1.
25. Gore, "The Common Good" 162.
26. Ralph Waldo Emerson, "The American Scholar," delivered 31 Aug. 1837, in Glenn R. Capp., ed., *Famous Speeches in American History* (Indianapolis: Bobbs-Merrill, 1963) 84.
27. George W. Bush, announcement on 7 Oct. 2001, of United States military strike in Afghanistan. Reprinted in *The New York Times* 8 Oct. 2001: B6.
28. National Archives and Records Administration, *Franklin D. Roosevelt's Inaugural Address of 1933* (1988) 13–14.
29. John F. Kennedy, inaugural address 275.
30. Tony Blair, address on 7 Oct. 2001, to the British people about Britain's role in the attacks on Afghanistan. Reprinted in *The New York Times* 8 Oct. 2001: B6.
31. William Faulkner, acceptance of the Nobel prize for literature, delivered 10 Dec. 1950, in Peterson, *A Treasury of the World's Great Speeches* 814–15.
32. Patrick Henry, "Liberty or Death," delivered 23 Mar. 1775, in Glenn

R. Capp, ed., *Famous Speeches in American History* (Indianapolis: Bobbs-Merrill, 1963) 22.

33. Rudy deLeon, "The Tuskegee Airmen," *Vital Speeches of the Day* 1 Nov. 2000: 43.

34. National Archives and Records Administration, *Franklin Roosevelt's Inaugural Address of 1933* 22.

35. Franklin D. Roosevelt, first fireside chat on 12 Mar. 1933, in Peterson, *Treasury* 751–54.

36. Winston Churchill, "finest hour" address, delivered 18 June 1940, in Peterson, *Treasury* 754–60.

37. Winston Churchill, address to the Congress of the United States, delivered on 26 Dec. 1941, in Bower Aly and Lucille F. Aly, eds., *Speeches in English* (New York: Random House, 1968) 233.

38. Dick Cheney, acceptance speech for the republican vice-presidential nomination, delivered 2 Aug. 2000, *The New York Times* 3 Aug. 2000: A24.

39. Adapted from Jordan, *Oral Communication Handbook* 34.

40. "Dear Abby," *San Marcos Daily Record* 5 Jan. 1993: 7.

41. Activity developed by Loren Reid, *Speaking Well* (New York: McGraw-Hill, 1982) 96.

42. "Reference to Rape Edited from Graduation Speech," *The Kansas City Star* 5 June 1995: B3.

CHAPTER 13

1. James W. Gibson, John A. Kline, and Charles R. Gruner, "A Reexamination of the First Course in Speech at U.S. Colleges and Universities," *Speech Teacher* 23 (September 1974): 206–14.

2. Ray Birdwhistle, *Kinesics and Context* (Philadelphia: U of Pennsylvania, 1970).

3. Judee K. Burgoon and Beth A. Le Poire, "Nonverbal Cues and Interpersonal Judgments: Participant and Observer Perceptions of Intimacy, Dominance, Composure, and Formality," *Communication Monographs* 66 (1999): 105–124; Beth A. Le Poire and Stephen M. Yoshimura, "The Effects of Expectancies and Actual Communication on Nonverbal Adaptation and Communication Outcomes: A Test of Interaction Adaptation Theory," *Communication Monographs* 66 (1999): 1–30.

4. Albert Mehrabian, *Nonverbal Communication* (Hawthorne, NY: Aldine, 1972).

5. Steven A. Beebe and Thompson Biggers, "The Effect of Speaker Delivery upon Listener Emotional Response," paper presented at the International Communication Association meeting, May 1989.

6. Paul Ekman, Wallace V. Friesen, and K. R. Schere, "Body Movement and Voice Pitch in Deception Interaction," *Semiotica* 16 (1976): 23–27; Mark Knapp, R. P. Hart, and H. S. Dennis, "An Exploration of Deception as a Communication Construct," *Human Communication Research* 1 (1974): 15–29.

7. Adam Clymer, "Defining a Leader First by His Words," *The New York Times* 16 Sept. 2001: 12 (Section 4).

8. Roger Ailes, *You Are the Message* (New York: Doubleday, 1989) 37–38.

9. David Gates, "Prince of the Podium," *Newsweek* June 14, 1996: 82.

10. Steven A. Beebe, "Eye Contact: A Nonverbal Determinant of Speaker Credibility," *Speech Teacher* 23 (Jan. 1974): 21–25; Steven A. Beebe, "Effects of Eye Contact, Posture and Vocal Inflection upon Credibility and Comprehension," *Australian Scan Journal of Nonverbal Communication* 7–8 (1979–1980): 57–70; Martin Cobin, "Response to Eye Contact," *Quarterly Journal of Speech* 48 (1963): 415–19.

11. Beebe, "Eye Contact" 21–25.

12. James C. McCroskey, Virginia P. Richmond, Aino Sallinen, Joan M. Fayer, and Robert A. Barraclough, "A Cross-Cultural and Multi-Behavioral Analysis of the Relationship Between Nonverbal Immediacy and Teacher Evaluation," *Communication Education* 44 (1995): 281–90.

13. Timothy P. Mottet and Steven A. Beebe, "Relationships Between Teacher Nonverbal Immediacy, Student Emotional Response, and Perceived Student Learning," *Communication Research Reports* (in press).

14. Michael J. Beatty, "Some Effects of Posture on Speaker Credibility," library paper, Central Missouri State U, 1973.

15. Paul Ekman, Wallace V. Friesen, and S. S. Tomkins, "Facial Affect Scoring Technique: A First Validity Study," *Semiotica* 3 (1971).

16. Adapted from Lester Schilling, *Voice and Diction for the Speech Arts* (San Marcos: Southwest Texas State U, 1979).

17. Mary M. Gill, "Accent and Stereotypes: Their Effect on Perceptions of Teachers and Lecture Comprehension," *Journal of Applied Communication* 22 (1994): 348–61.

18. These suggestions were made by Jo Sprague and Douglas Stuart, *The Speaker's Handbook* (Fort Worth, TX: Harcourt Brace Jovanovich, 1992) 331, and were based on research by Patricia A. Porter, Margaret Grant, and Mary Draper, *Communicating Effectively in English: Oral Communication for Non-Native Speakers* (Belmont, CA: Wadsworth, 1985).

19. James W. Neuliep, *Intercultural Communication: A Contextual Approach* (Boston: Houghton Mifflin, 2000) 247.

20. Stephen Lucas, *The Art of Public Speaking* (New York: Random House, 1986) 231.

21. Research cited by Leo Fletcher, *How to Design & Deliver Speeches* (New York: Addison Wesley Longman, 2001) 73.

22. "Comment," *The New Yorker* 1 Mar. 1993.

23. For an excellent review of the effects of immediacy in the classroom, see Albert Mehrabian *Silent Messages* (Belmont, CA: Wadsworth, 1981).

24. James C. McCroskey, Aino Sallinen, Joan M. Fayer, Virginia P. Richmond, and Robert A. Barraclough, "Nonverbal Immediacy and Cognitive Learning: A Cross-Cultural Investigation," *Communication Education* 45 (1996): 200–11.

25. Larry A. Samovar and Richard E. Porter *Communication Between Cultures* (Stamford, CT: Thomson Learning, 2001) 166.

26. William B. Gudykunst, *Bridging Differences: Effective Intergroup Communication* (Thousand Oaks, CA: Sage, 1998) 12.

27. Kent E. Menzel and Lori J. Carrell, "The Relationship Between Preparation and Performance in Public Speaking," *Communication Education* 43 (194): 17–26.

CHAPTER 14

1. Emil Bohn and David Jabusch, "The Effect of Four Methods of Instruction on the Use of Visual Aids in Speeches," *The Western Journal of Speech Communication* 46 (Summer 1982): 253–65.

2. J. S. Wilentz. *The Senses of Man* (New York: Crowell, 1968).

3. Michael E. Patterson, Donald F. Dansereau, and Dianna Newbern, "Effects of Communication Aids and Strategies on Cooperative Teaching," *Journal of Educational Psychology* 84 (1992): 453–61.

4. Richard E. Mayer and Valerie K. Sims, "For Whom Is a Picture Worth a Thousand Words? Extensions of a Dual-Coding Theory of Multimedia Learning," *Journal of Educational Psychology* 86 (1994): 389–401.

5. We acknowledge Dan Cavanaugh's excellent supplement *Preparing Visual Aids for Presentation* (Boston: Allyn and Bacon/Longman, 2001) as a source for many of our tips and suggestions.

6. We thank Stan Crowley, a student at Southwest Texas State U, for his permission to use his speech outline.

CHAPTER 15

1. John R. Johnson and Nancy Szczupakiewicz, "The Public Speaking Course: Is It Preparing Students with Work-Related Public Speaking Skills?" *Communication Education 36* (April 1987): 131–37.

2. Malcolm Knowles, *Self-Directed Learning* (Chicago: Follett, 1975).

3. Katherine E. Rowan, "A New Pedagogy for Explanatory Public Speaking: Why Arrangement Should Not Substitute for Invention," *Communication Education* 44 (1995): 236–50.

4. Rowan, "A New Pedagogy for Explanatory Public Speaking."

5. Michael A. Boerger and Tracy B. Henley, "The Use of Analogy in Giving Instructions," *Psychological Record* 49 (1999): 193–209.

6. Marcie Groover, "Learning to Communicate: The Importance of Speech Education in Public Schools," in *Winning Orations 1984* (Mankato, MN: Interstate Oratorical Association, 1984) 7.

7. As cited by Eleanor Doan, *The New Speaker's Sourcebook.* (Grand Rapids, MI: Zondervan, 1968).

8. Chad Crowson "Brain Fingerprints," in *Winning Orations 2000* (Northfield, MN: Interstate Oratorical Association, 2000).

● CHAPTER 16

1. Alvin Toffler, *Future Shock* (New York: Bantam Books, 1970) 3.

2. Leon Festinger, *A Theory of Cognitive Dissonance* (Evanston, IL: Row, Peterson, 1957).

3. Vonda Ramey, "Can You Read This?" in *Winning Orations, 1985* (Mankato, MN: Interstate Oratorical Association, 1985) 36.

4. For additional discussion, see Wayne C. Minnick, *The Art of Persuasion* (Boston: Houghton Mifflin, 1967).

5. Abraham H. Maslow, "A Theory of Human Motivation," in *Motivation and Personality* (New York: Harper & Row, 1954), chap. 5.

6. John Ryan, "Emissions Tampering: Get the Lead Out," in *Winning Orations 1985* (Mankato, MN: Interstate Oratorical Association, 1985) 50.

7. For a discussion of fear appeal research, see Irving L. Janis and Seymour Feshback, "Effects of Fear Arousing Communications," *Journal of Abnormal and Social Psychology* 48 (Jan. 1953): 78–92; Frederick A. Powell and Gerald R. Miller, "Social Approval and Disapproval Cues in Anxiety-Arousing Situations," *Speech Monographs* 34 (June 1967): 152–59; and Kenneth L. Higbee, "Fifteen Years of Fear Arousal: Research on Threat Appeals, 1953–68," *Psychological Bulletin* 72 (Dec. 1969): 426–44.

8. Paul A. Mongeau, "Another Look at Fear-Arousing Persuasive Appeals," in Mike Allen and Raymond W. Preiss, eds., *Persuasion: Advances Through Meta-Analysis* (Creskill, NJ: Hampton Press, 1998) 65.

9. See discussion in Myron W. Lustig and Jolene Koester, *Intercultural Competence: Interpersonal Communication Across Cultures* (New York: HarperCollins, 1996) 347; Larry A. Samovar and Richard E. Porter, *Communication Between Cultures* (Stamford, CT: Wadsworth and Thomson Learning, 2001) 29.

10. C. W. Sherif, M. Sherif, and R. E. Nebergall, *Attitudes and Attitude Change: The Social Judgment-Involvement Approach* (Philadelphia: Saunders, 1965).

● CHAPTER 17

1. For an excellent meta-analysis of forty-nine studies examining the influence of delivery variables and persuasion, see Chris Segrin, "The Effects of Nonverbal Behavior on Outcomes of Compliance Gaining Attempts," *Communication Studies* 44 (1993): 169–87.

2. Judee K. Burgoon, T. Birk, and M. Pfau, "Nonverbal Behaviors, Persuasion, and Credibility," *Human Communication Research* 17 (1990): 140–69.

3. Segrin, "The Effects of Nonverbal Behavior on Outcomes of Compliance Gaining Attempts."

4. For an excellent discussion of the influence of culture on public speaking, see Devorah A. Lieberman, *Public Speaking in the Multicultural Environment* (Englewood Cliffs, NJ: Prentice Hall, 1994) 10.

5. Devorah Lieberman and G. Fisher, "International Negotiation," in Larry A. Samovar and Richard. E. Porter, eds., *Intercultural Communication: A Reader* (Belmont, CA: Wadsworth, 1991) 193–200.

6. Lieberman and Fisher, "International Negotiation."

7. Myron W. Lustig and Jolene Koester, *Intercultural Competence: Interpersonal Communication Across Cultures* (New York: HarperCollins, 1996) 223.

8. Jeffrey E. Jamison, "Alkali Batteries: Powering Electronics and Polluting the Environment," in *Winning Orations 1991* (Mankato, MN: Interstate Oratorical Association, 1991) 43.

9. Roger Ailes, *You Are the Message* (New York: Doubleday, 1989).

10. "Weight of History Is 'On All of Us,' Senate Is Told by One of Its Own," *New York Times* 22 Jan. 1999: A17.

11. Albert Mehrabian and J. A. Russell, *An Approach to Environmental Psychology* (Cambridge: MIT Press, 1974); T. Biggers and B. Pryor, "Attitude Change as a Function of Emotion Eliciting Qualities," *Personality and Social Psychology Bulletin* 8 (1982): 94–99; Steven A. Beebe and T. Biggers, "Emotion-Eliciting Qualities of Speech Delivery and Their Effect on Credibility and Comprehension," paper presented at the annual meeting of the International Communication Association, New Orleans, May 1989.

12. See Irving Janis and S. Feshback, "Effects of Fear-Arousing Communication," *Journal of Abnormal and Social Psychology* 48 (1953): 78–92; Fredric A. Powell, "The Effects of Anxiety-Arousing Message When Related to Personal, Familial, and Impersonal Referents," *Speech Monographs* 32 (1965): 102–6.

13. Donald C. Bryant, "Rhetoric: Its Functions and Its Scope," *Quarterly Journal of Speech* 39 (Dec. 1953): 26.

14. William L. Benoit, "Forewarning and Persuasion," in Mike Allen and Raymond W. Preiss, eds., *Persuasion: Advances Through Meta-Analysis* (Cresskill, NJ: Hampton Press, 1998) 139–54.

15. Karmen Kirtley, "Grave Matter: The High Cost of Living," in *Winning Orations 1997* (Mankato, MN: Interstate Oratorial Association, 1997).

16. William L. Benoit, "Forewarning and Persuasion."

17. Mike Allen, "Comparing the Persuasive Effectiveness One- and Two-Sided Message," in Mike Allen and Raymond W. Preiss, eds., *Persuasion: Advances Through Meta-Analysis* (Cresskill, NJ: Hampton Press, 1998) 87–98.

18. Rowan, "A New Pedagogy for Explanatory Public Speaking."

19. Carl I. Hovland, Arthur A. Lunsdaine, and Fred D. Sheffield, "The Effects of Presenting 'One Side' versus 'Both Sides' in Changing Opinions on a Controversial Subject," in *Experiments on Mass Communication* (Princeton: Princeton U, 1949). Also see Arthur Lunsdaine and Irving Janis, "Resistance to 'Counter-Propaganda' Produced by a One-Sided versus a Two-Sided 'Propaganda' Presentation," *Public Opinion Quarterly* (1953): 311–18.

20. Douglas Ehninger, Bruce E. Gronbeck, Ray E. McKerrow, and Alan H. Monroe, *Principles and Types of Speech Communication* (Glenview, IL: Scott, Foresman 1986) 15.

21. Vic Vieth, "Prisoners of Conscience," in *Winning Orations 1984* (Mankato, MN: Interstate Oratorical Association, 1984) 46.

22. Vieth, "Prisoners of Conscience" 47.

23. Vieth, "Prisoners of Conscience" 47.

24. Vieth, "Prisoners of Conscience" 49.

25. Martin Luther King, Jr., "I Have a Dream" (28 Aug. 1963), in Houston Peterson, ed., *A Treasury of the World's Great Speeches* (New York: Simon & Schuster, 1965) 835–39.

26. Vieth, "Prisoners of Conscience" 49.

● CHAPTER 18

1. CBS News, "Eye on Politics," 15 Feb. 2001, 7 June 2001 <http://www.cbsnews.com/now/story/O,1597,272386-412.00.shtml.>

2. Roger E. Flax, "A Manner of Speaking," *Ambassador* (May–June 1991): 37.

3. *Slainte! Toasts, Blessings, and Sayings,* Mar. 1998, (29 June 1998): <http://zinnia.umfacad.maine.edu/~donaghue/toasts.html>.

4. Jeff Brooks, toast available *Wedding Toasts,* Mar. 1998, 29 June 1998 <http://zinnia.umfacad.maine.edu/~donaghue/toasts07.html>.

5. Everett M. Dirksen, "Nominating Speech for Barry Goldwater" (15 July 1964), in James R. Andrews and David Zarefsky, eds., *Contemporary American Voices* (New York: Simon & Schuster, 1965) 815.

6. Erma Bombeck, "Abbreviated Thank-you's Allow Us More Time to Study Danson's Head," *Austin American-Statesman* 22 June 1993: F3.

7. Cindy Pearlman, "Oscar Speeches: Statues in Their Hands, Feet in Their Mouths," *Austin American-Statesman* 24 Mar. 1997: E8.

8. "Arafat Calls for Speedier Peace in Nobel Speech," Reuter News Agency 10 Dec. 1994.

9. Elie Wiesel, "Acceptance of the 1986 Nobel Peace Prize," *The New York Times* 11 Dec. 1986: A8.

10. William Faulkner, acceptance of the Nobel prize for literature (10 Dec. 10 1950), in Houston Petersen, ed., *A Treasury of the World's Great Speeches* (New York: Simon & Schuster, 1965) 815.

11. Barbara Jordan, "Change: From What to What?" *Vital Speeches of the Day* 15 Aug. 1992: 651.

12. Abel, David, "Commencement Addresses Leave Audiences Lost," *The Boston Globe* 5 June 2000: B4.

13. Kurt Vonnegut, "Title: I have no name for it, and hope nobody else comes up with one," delivered at Rice U commencement 9 May 1998. 29 June 1998: <http://www.ruf.rice.edu/~presiden/Speakers/Commence98.html>

14. "At College Graduations, Wit and Wisdom for the Price of Airfare," *The New York Times* 28 May 2001: A10.

15. Abel, "Commencement Addresses Leave Audiences Lost," B4.

16. Bill Clinton, speech at Pointe du Hoc, France (June 1994), as quoted in David Shribman, "President, a Child of World War II, Thanks a Generation," *Boston Globe* 7 June 1994: 1.

17. Edward Kennedy, eulogy for Jacqueline Kennedy Onassis (May 1994), as quoted in "The Texts of Personal Tributes and Poems at the Services for Mrs. Onassis," *The New York Times* 24 May 1994: A10.

18. Robert Dole, "Eulogy for Former President Richard M. Nixon," *Vital Speeches of the Day* 1 June 1994: 483.

19. Earl Spencer, eulogy for Diana, Princess of Wales, September 1997. Available *Britannia* 29 June 1998 <http://www.britannia.com/diana/article4.html>.

20. Dave Barry, "Speak! Speak!" *Austin American-Statesman* 2 June 1991: C4.

21. Sarah Booth Conroy, "State Dinners Offer Speech as First Course," *Austin American-Statesman* 10 November 1989.

22. Fatout, Paul, *Mark Twain on the Lecture Circuit* (Bloomington: Indiana U 1960) 7.

23. Debi Martin, "Laugh Lines," *Austin American-Statesman* 20 May 1988: D1.

24. Chris O'Keefe, untitled speech, in John K. Boaz and James Brey, eds., *1987 Championship Debates and Speeches* (Speech Communication Association and American Forensic Association, 1987) 99.

● CHAPTER 19

1. Group communication principles presented in this chapter are adapted from Steven A. Beebe and John T. Masterson, *Communicating in Small Groups. Principles and Practices,* 7th ed. (Boston: Allyn and Bacon, 2003).

2. Roger K. Mosvick and Robert B. Nelson, *We've Got to Start Meeting Like This! A Guide to Successful Business Meeting Management* (Glenview, IL: Scott, Foresman, 1987) 3.

3. This discussion is based on Beebe and Masterson, *Communicating in Small Groups* chap. 1.

4. Our definition of a team is based on a discussion in Beebe and Masterson, *Communicating in Small Groups*; and in Steven A. Beebe, Susan J. Beebe, and Diana K. Ivy, *Communication Principles for a Lifetime* (Boston: Allyn and Bacon, 2001) 240–41.

5. R. Y. Hirokawa and A. J. Salazar, "Task-Group Communication and Decision-Making Performance," in L. Frey ed., *The Handbook of*

Group Communication Theory and Research (Thousand Oaks, CA: Sage, 1999) 167–91; D. Gouran and R. Y. Hirokawa, "Functional Theory and Communication in Decision-Making and Problem-Solving Groups: An Expanded View," in R. Y. Hirokawa and M. S. Poole, eds., *Communication and Group Decision Making* (Thousand Oaks, CA: Sage, 1996) 55–80.

6. C. A. VanLear and E. A. Mabry, "Testing Contrasting Interaction Models for Discriminating Between Consensual and Dissentient Decision-Making Groups," *Small Group Research* 30 (1999): 29–58; also see T. J. Saine and D. G. Bock, "A Comparison of the Distributional and Sequential Structures of Interaction in High and Low Consensus Groups," *Central States Speech Journal* 24 (1973): 125–39.

7. Randy Y. Hirokawa and Roger Pace, "A Descriptive Investigation of the Possible Communication-Based Reasons for Effective and Ineffective Group Decision Making," *Communication Monographs* 50 (Dec. 1983): 363–79.

8. Randy Y. Hirokawa, "Group Communication and Problem-Solving Effectiveness: An Investigation of Group Phases," *Human Communication Research* 9 (Summer 1983): 291–305.

9. Dennis S. Gouran, "Variables Related to Consensus in Group Discussion of Question of Policy," *Speech Monographs* 36 (Aug. 1969): 385–91.

10. For a summary of research about conflict management in small groups, see S. M. Farmer and J. Roth, "Conflict-Handling Behavior in Work Groups: Effects of Group Structure, Decision Processes, and Time," *Small Group Research* 29 (1998): 669–713; also see Beebe and Masterson, *Communicating in Small Groups*.

11. For an excellent review of communication technology and group communication, see C. R. Scott, "Communication Technology and Group Communications," in L. Frey, ed., *The Handbook of Group Communication Theory and Research* (Thousand Oaks, CA: Sage, 1999) 432–72; also see C. R. Scott, L. Quinn, C. E. Timmerman, and D. M. Garrett, "Ironic Uses of Group Communication Technology: Evidence from Meeting Transcripts and Interviews with Group Decision Support System Uses," *Communication Quarterly* 46 (1998): 353–74; K. J. Chun and H. K. Park, "Examining the Conflicting Results of GDSS Research," *Information & Management* 33 (1998): 313–25.

12. Kenneth D. Benne and Paul Sheats, "Functional Roles of Groups Members," *Journal of Social Issues* 4 (Spring 1948): 41–49.

13. Ralph White and Ronald Lippitt, "Leader Behavior and Member Reaction in Three 'Social Climates,' " in Darwin Cartwright and Alvin Zander, eds., *Group Dynamics*, 3rd ed. (New York: Harper & Row, 1968) 319.

14. Peter M. Senge, "Leading Learning Organizations," in Richard Beckhard et al., eds., *The Leader of the Future* (San Francisco: Jossey-Bass, 1996); Bernard M. Bass and M. J. Avolio, "Transformational Leadership and Organizational Culture," *International Journal of Public Administration* 17 (1994): 541–54; Lynn Little, "Transformational Leadership," *Academic Leadership* 15 (Nov. 1999): 4–5.

15. Francis J. Yammarino and Alan J. Dubinsky, "Transformational Leadership Theory: Using Levels of Analysis to Determine Boundary Conditions," *Personnel Psychology* 47 (1994): 787–809.

16. Dave Barry, *Dave Barry's Guide to Life* (New York: Wing Books, 1991) 311.

17. Mosvick and Nelson, *We've Got to Start Meeting Like This!*

18. Thomas A. Kayser, *Mining Group Gold* (El Segundo, CA: Serif Publishing, 1990) 42.

19. Mosvick and Nelson, *We've Got to Start Meeting Like This!*

Index